GRAND SLAM
GOLF

COURSES OF THE MASTERS, THE U.S. OPEN, THE BRITISH OPEN, THE PGA CHAMPIONSHIP

GRAND SLAM
GOLF

A GOLF MAGAZINE BOOK BY
GEORGE PEPER

COURSE PHOTOGRAPHS BY
MIKE KLEMME

PAINTINGS BY
ELIZABETH PEPER

HARRY N. ABRAMS, INC., PUBLISHERS, NEW YORK

CONTENTS

Editor: Margaret L. Kaplan • Designers: Bob McKee and Beth Tondreau • Photo Editor: John K. Crowley

Library of Congress Cataloging-in-Publication Data
Peper, George. Grand slam golf: Courses of the Masters, the U.S. Open, the British Open,
the PGA Championship / by George Peper; course photographs by Mike Klemme; course paintings by Elizabeth Peper.
p. cm. "A Golf magazine book." Includes bibliographical references (p.) and index. ISBN 0-8109-3359-4
1. Golf courses—Guide-books. 2. Golf—Tournaments—Statistics.
I. Klemme, Mike. II. Peper, Elizabeth. III. Title.
GV975.P464 1991
796.352'06'8—dc20   91-7650
                                                      CIP

HALF TITLE: *The 11th hole at the Oak Tree Golf Club.* TITLE: *During the first round of the 1990 British Open,
played on the Old Course at St. Andrews, Scotland, Nick Faldo ends with a lengthy pitch-and-run that drops for an
eagle two and a round of 67. Photos © Phil Sheldon.* CONTENTS: *The 16th hole at the Oakland Hills Country Club.*

THE GRAND SLAM

It was O.B. Keeler, close friend and biographer of Bobby Jones, who added "Grand Slam" to the lexicon of golf. Keeler borrowed the term from contract bridge to describe Jones's singular feat of winning four national championships—the U.S. Amateur, the U.S. Open, the British Amateur, and the British Open—all in the same year.

That year was 1930, but so awesome was Jones's achievement that even as it was unfolding—and for many months thereafter—no one could summon the words to describe it. According to Charles Price, "Jones had broken the game's sound barrier, flown into its ionosphere, touched its fourth dimension. He had gone so far into golf-space that only afterward did the public feel that what he had done needed a vernacular handle."

In fact, it was not until years later that the magnitude of the Grand Slam was placed in proper perspective when, in 1950, the Associated Press voted Jones's feat "the supreme athletic achievement of this century." Ironically, by that time the very notion of a golf Grand Slam had blurred beyond recognition. A major reason was that Jones had retired a few weeks after his triumphant season, and the world of golf had no other player nearly his equal. For almost a decade Bobby Jones had dominated the game more certainly than any game had ever been dominated. And, incredibly, he had done so as an amateur. Never again would an amateur golfer be the man to beat in a National Open.

With Jones in retirement, the Open was wide open, and the Amateur became a free-for-all. Furthermore, in 1931 the USGA introduced sectional qualifying for the Amateur, simultaneously broadening the field of entrants and honing the on-site survivors via twenty regional hurdles. The new system bred a crop of fresh faces every year, all but prohibiting the ascension of a second Jones.

The loss of Bobby Jones robbed the Amateur Championship of much of its prestige. Jones had been its lightning rod, the man who attracted the fans and the headlines. After his retirement he attended the championships only as an interested observer, but his mere presence in the gallery drew more attention than the matches themselves.

At about the same time, the Depression started to take its toll. Country clubs shut down by the hundreds, and gentlemen golfers in the mold of Bobby Jones either gave up the game in order to find honest work, or became "businessmen golfers," better known as pros. Big-time amateur golf would never be as big again.

These three interrelated phenomena—Joneslessness, economic disquietude, and the decline of top-level amateur golf—produced aftershocks in the British national championships as well. The British Amateur, least prestigious of the four titles, became virtually a nonevent for Americans, while progressively fewer of our top pros boarded the transatlantic steamers for the Open.

Those who did had little success. During the golden decade between 1924 and 1933, Americans had won nine of ten British Opens. Between 1934 and 1960—a span of twenty-seven years—America produced only two victories, one by Sam Snead (1946) and one by Ben Hogan (1953). The British Open slid into the doldrums.

But then, one man suddenly revived it and simultaneously revived the concept of a Grand Slam. When in 1960 the game's most electrifying player, Arnold Palmer, won both the Masters and the U.S. Open, he booked a flight to St. Andrews, Scotland, reasoning that if he could somehow add the British Open title and then win the PGA Championship at home, he would have a sort of modern Grand Slam.

Palmer's quest came to an end on the final hole of the Old Course, where Kel Nagle beat him by a single stroke. But the next year, at Royal Birkdale, he won it, and he repeated at Troon in 1962. By that time he had singlehandedly renewed interest among the leading American professionals in the world's oldest championship. During the same period he had helped to elevate the prestige of the Masters, his four victories in 1958, 1960, 1962, and 1964 adding new luster to the tournament founded by Bobby Jones.

Arnie was the darling of the media, especially television, and as he made known his quest for more victories in the Masters, the two national Opens, and, most of all, his burning desire to win at least one PGA Championship, he reintroduced the concept of four elite events to a new and burgeoning generation of American golfers.

As the Palmer era came to a close, a new majors monomaniac took the stage in the form of Jack Nicklaus. Early in his career, Nicklaus embraced the quest with confident vigor, openly stating that his single goal was to win as many major championships as possible. Between 1962 and 1986 he won more than anyone in history—an all-time record six Masters, an all-time record five PGA's, a record-equalling four U.S. Opens, and three British Opens. Nicklaus's career total of eighteen major championship victories, like Jones's one-year "impregnable quadrilateral," may be approached, but will never be equalled.

The Grand Slam invented by Palmer thus was patented by Nicklaus. Today, "winning the Grand Slam" refers not only to the Jonesian feat of annexing all four in one year, but more loosely to the notion of amassing the four titles in the course of one's career. Only four players have done it—Gene Sarazen, Ben Hogan, Gary Player, and Jack Nicklaus—and nine others have come within one event: Sam Snead never won the U.S. Open; Tommy Armour, Jim Barnes, Walter Hagen, and Lee Trevino missed out on the Masters; Arnold Palmer and Tom Watson lack only the PGA Championship; and Byron Nelson and Raymond Floyd never won the British Open.

No one has won all four of the modern major championships in a single year, and it's extremely unlikely that anyone ever will. Hogan did come close, winning the Masters, U.S. Open, and British Open in 1953, a schedule conflict depriving him of the chance to complete the slam. In 1972, Nicklaus duplicated Palmer's 1960 feat, taking the first two legs before falling a stroke short at the British Open, and several players have won two titles in a single year, most recently Nick Faldo in 1990.

Today, sixty years after the winning of the Grand Slam and thirty years after its reincarnation, approximately thirty courses continue to host the four championships. The Masters is of course played annually at the Augusta National Golf Club in Augusta, Georgia; the U.S. Open pays regular visits to a handful of venerable venues; the British Open rotates among a collection of links courses on the Scottish and English coasts; and the PGA of America moves its Championship around the United States to a roster of testing sites, some old and some new. Each of these courses is among the finest in the world, yet no two are remotely alike. Collectively, as of this writing, these thirty courses have hosted precisely 200 major championships. This book is a tour of those courses and those events, a celebration of the people, places and events of the modern Grand Slam.

ATLANTA ATHLETIC CLUB

DULUTH, GEORGIA
U.S. Open: 1976
PGA Championship: 1981

Golf was the farthest thing from the minds of the sixty-five Atlanta businessmen who assembled in 1898 and formed a club "to promote health by exercise and to encourage manly sports and social relations among its members."

The game, after all, was barely ten years old in the States, and most of its practitioners were tweedy northerners. Within another decade, however, this Atlanta Athletic Club would not only discover golf, it would captivate and cultivate the greatest player America had ever seen, Bobby Jones.

In 1908, when the AAC's swimmers, boxers, baseball, and basketball players decided they wanted to try golf, they hired Tom Bendelow to design a course on a parcel of land five miles outside the city. In this area, called East Lake, one of the club's members, Colonel Robert P. Jones, had taken a summer home for himself, his wife, and their 6-year-old son.

In the same year, the club imported a Carnoustie Scotsman named Stewart Maiden as professional, an occurence which Bobby Jones referred to in his biography, *Down the Fairway*, as the greatest break of his life:

The splay-footed 6-year-old who became the dominant championship golfer of his era, Bobby Jones. Photo: United States Golf Association

It wasn't long before I was following him about the East Lake course and watching him . . . and after tagging along four or five holes I would leave the match and go back to our house . . . and get a cap full of old balls and my mashie and putter and go out to the thirteenth green and pitch them all on and

putt them all out, over and over again. It was pretty good practice, I suppose.

He watched and learned and mimicked Maiden's swing, a swing whose languid grace belied its massive power. That summer, at age 6, Jones won his first trophy, a tiny silver-plated cup three inches high, after beating a few of the neighborhood kids in an impromptu six-hole competition at East Lake. One of those kids was a 9-year-old lass named Alexa Stirling, who would go on to win three consecutive U.S. Women's Amateur Championships, also using Stewart Maiden's swing.

Jones was so thrilled, he slept with the little cup that night. That tiny trophy was the first of over a hundred victories for the most productive amateur golfer the game has ever seen. Three years later Jones won the junior championship of the AAC, defeating an opponent seven years older than he. And five years after that, at age 14, Bobby began his unparalleled career in the major national championships, traveling north to Merion in Pennsylvania for the 1916 U.S. Amateur, where he led the first round of qualifying and reached the third round of match play before bowing to the defending champion, Bob Gardner.

It was seven years before Jones won his first title, the 1923 U.S. Open at Inwood, but from that year through the conclusion of his brief career, he utterly dominated the major events. In twenty-one

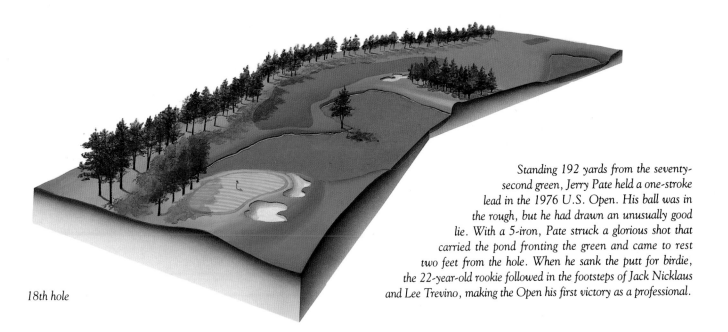

18th hole

Standing 192 yards from the seventy-second green, Jerry Pate held a one-stroke lead in the 1976 U.S. Open. His ball was in the rough, but he had drawn an unusually good lie. With a 5-iron, Pate struck a glorious shot that carried the pond fronting the green and came to rest two feet from the hole. When he sank the putt for birdie, the 22-year-old rookie followed in the footsteps of Jack Nicklaus and Lee Trevino, making the Open his first victory as a professional.

appearances in the National Opens and Amateurs of America and Great Britain, he won thirteen titles and finished second five times. For eight seasons he dominated the U.S. Open as no one ever has, winning four times, finishing second twice, and losing twice more in playoffs. He retired in 1930 after his crowning conquest—victories in the U.S. Amateur, U.S. Open, British Amateur, and British Open in a single year—a Grand Slam which, more than sixty years later, remains the most extraordinary achievement the game has ever witnessed.

Throughout his career Jones's home club remained the AAC. His victory in the 1925 U.S. Amateur at Oakmont came over a fellow Atlanta Athletic Club member, Watts Gunn, marking the only time in Open history that two members of the same club had met in the final match. Even after he founded the Augusta National Golf Club and began hosting the Masters, Jones retained an active role at the Athletic Club, serving a term as president and sitting on the board of directors for nineteen years.

In November of 1971 the vice president of the USGA received a letter from Jones, then a frail man of 69 in the final stages of a severely crippling spinal disease called syringomyelia. The letter was written on behalf of the AAC, and it read, in part:

> Although you will understand that I am not likely to take much part in a golf tournament in 1975, our membership is most eager to be awarded the privilege of being awarded the USGA Open Championship for that year; and I should be most happy if my old club should become the host for my favorite golf tournament.

Thirty-one days later, on December 18, 1971, Bob Jones died.

There was never any doubt that his wish would be granted. From the beginning, however, there were questions about the course.

This was not East Lake. In 1968 the membership had voted 900 to 551 to sell the old course in order to pay for construction of a new

facility on 614 acres near the Chattahoochee River in Duluth, just northeast of Atlanta. The new course—actually courses—included twenty-seven holes by Robert Trent Jones, designed in 1967, plus nine more designed by Joe Finger in 1970. Finger's nine became the outward half of the Open course with one of the Trent Jones nines the inward side. This course is known as the Highlands, the other eighteen as Riverbend.

"It is a good course but not a great course," said then-USGA Executive Director P.J. Boatwright, Jr., in announcing that the Open would move to Atlanta in 1976, a year later than Jones had requested. "It could become great with some changes," he added.

Most of the members were pleased to have the extra year to get their act together, and the club's first move was to invite architects George and Tom Fazio to instill some greatness in the Highlands layout.

It was a Jekyll and Hyde course that the Fazios faced, with Finger's front nine long and open, Trent Jones's back shorter and heavily wooded. The uncle/nephew team made big changes, remodeling every bunker on the course and plotting more than twice as much sand on the front nine as the back. The fairway bunkers were moved farther from the tees, to catch the pros' longer drives, greenside bunkers were tucked closer to greens, and all were deepened.

Fifteen new tees were built and six greens were made smaller. The Fazios also changed the pars of three holes, transforming the 11th from a benign downhill par five to one of the most difficult—and controversial—par fours in the history of the Open, lengthening the 12th from a long four to an easily reachable five, and converting the 18th from a layup par five for the members into an heroic par four with a 200-yard all-or-nothing approach.

The redesigned Highlands did not rank in USGA-defined greatness with classic Open sites such as Oakmont and Pebble Beach, but the Fazios can be credited with having taken an uneven, rather charmless layout and fashioning a balanced test of shotmaking.

The strength of the Highlands course is in its stern and varied par fours. There are a dozen of them, six on each nine, and within each sextet two holes dogleg from left to right, two move from right to left, and two play dead straight. The six longest average over 460 yards, the six shortest average barely 400, and they range from the tightly testing 10th at 374 to the monster that immediately follows it at 470.

A limber back is needed from the very start, for the first three holes weigh in at 456, 458, and 469 yards. All three play to closely bunkered greens, and the 3rd hole has an out-of-bounds fence running down its entire right side.

The 4th hole serves notice that the par threes are just as hard as the fours. At 210 yards, it is one of the shortest of AAC's "short" holes, all four of which play across water. When the pin is up front, anyone who goes for it had better use plenty of club and plenty of courage; otherwise the ball will find water either on the fly or in the more agonizing way, by carrying into the far bank and then trickling down the slope.

The two par-five holes are the breathers. Indeed, they may be easier places to score four than many of the par fours. Number 5 is comfortably within reach of any long hitter who can avoid sand on the teeshot and carry more sand on the approach.

The most intimidating drive on the front nine comes at the 8th, a dogleg left over a pond to a bunker-strewn landing area. The player may bite off as much sand and water as he dares, leaving a mid to short iron to the elevated green.

The tree-lined tautness of the back nine is heralded with the teeshot at 10. Most players show respect here and hit an iron through the chute of pines. But the approach is equally demanding since this green is only 3,000 square feet—smaller than some Atlanta swimming pools.

When they unveiled the 11th, it was the longest par four in U.S. Open history—480 yards. An acute dogleg left, the second shot must be played with a long iron or wood from a downhill lie to a shallow, bunker-guarded green that was originally designed to accept pitch shots, not 1-irons. At one stretch in the Open, fifteen consecutive players failed to get home in two. Not surprisingly, it was the source of widespread discontent. For the PGA Championship, five years later, the hole was shortened ten yards and the Fazios moved the green to the right, thereby lessening the angle of the dogleg, the severity of the challenge, and the stridence of the carping.

Reasonable birdie opportunities occur at 12, 13, and 14, a par five and two comparatively short fours, but the 15th hole signals the start of one of the sternest final stretches anywhere. The toughest of the par threes, 15 plays over the left edge of a pond to an L-shaped green that is bisected by a hogback. It is followed by a rightward doglegging par four with a semiblind uphill second shot to a two-tiered amphitheater green.

The 17th looks as if it was transplanted from the number 3 course at Medinah, where three of the short holes play over Lake Kadijah in much the same way as this slightly downhill 213-yarder. The green is wide but not deep, so accurate club selection is as important as a controlled swing.

And the best is saved for last, a brute of a dogleg left with a pond that runs down the last 200 yards of the left side, then pokes its nose in front of the green. A lone bunker guards the inside knee of the dogleg, and it is over that bunker that the ideal teeshot should be directed. Just beyond the bunker is a swale. If the drive doesn't carry to the bottom of that swale, the second shot over the pond will have to be played with a long iron or wood from a downhill lie—a tough assignment, no matter who is addressing the ball. In the tradition of the grand finales at Pebble Beach, Doral, TPC Sawgrass, and Harbour Town, this is a hole built to produce agony and ecstasy.

Jerry Pate found both. In the first round of the 1976 Open, Pate's approach shot came to rest on the bank just inches from the far side of the pond. As he approached his ball he heard a mixture of laughter and groans from the gallery. A frog had hopped onto his ball and caused it to roll down into the water. Pate bogeyed the hole and finished at one over par 71.

Three days later Pate returned to that hole with a one-stroke lead, and he played one of the most glorious shots in the history of the Open. In between those two moments, that 1976 Open—the first East Coast Open played south of Washington, D.C.—had a few ups and downs of its own.

This was the Open which undoubtedly marked the nadir of several years of deteriorating relations between the touring professionals and the officials of the USGA. As they had at Oakmont, Winged Foot, and Medinah the three previous years, the pros complained. They complained about the design of the course and the redesign. They complained about the enormous length of the course and this year they even complained about the enormous length of their own irons shots.

It seems that the club had ordered new mowing equipment, and the mowers had been shipped with 18-inch wheels instead of 17-inch. That translated to fairways that were mowed to 3/4-inch height instead of 1/2-inch, resulting in shots the pros call "flyers" because they lack the requisite backspin and fly almost like knuckleballs, usually sailing well beyond their intended targets.

"I hit a 9-iron 155 yards and a wedge 135 yards," said Hale Irwin. "I can't do it, but I did it today." David Graham, who shot 78, mounted a blistering attack on USGA Assistant Director Frank Hannigan, to which the puckish Hannigan replied, "Things could be worse, David. You could be working for a living."

While the pros all had trouble, one amateur did not. Slender, self-effacing Mike Reid, three weeks past graduation from Brigham Young University, led the field by three strokes on a 67. He is the

OPPOSITE: *15th hole*

18th hole

last amateur to lead any round of an Open. Although he was to disappear quickly, on rounds of 81-80-72, Reid went on to become one of the most consistent performers on the PGA Tour in the 1980s.

In round two the mowers were lowered and things settled down as John Mahaffey moved into the lead at 139, a stroke ahead of Al Geiberger, Rod Funseth, Ben Crenshaw, and Jerry Pate. Mahaffey claimed his 68 could have been a 63 but for poor putting, the same malady that had cost him the Open a year earlier at Medinah, where he had lost in a playoff to Lou Graham.

In the rain-interrupted third round Mahaffey managed another 68 and increased his lead to two over Pate, three over Geiberger, and four over a charging Tom Weiskopf who had played his last nine holes in thirty-two strokes, including a near-ace at the 15th.

It was those four who battled it out the final day. With three holes left, Mahaffey, at three under par, held a one-stroke edge over Pate, two over Weiskopf and three over Geiberger. When Mahaffey hooked his teeshot at the 16th, however, it led to a bogey that brought him into a tie with Pate. Up ahead, Geiberger sank a 20-footer for birdie at 17, so he and Weiskopf stood on the final tee, each a stroke back of the co-leaders.

Mahaffey's teeshot to 17 squirted way to the right. Although on the green he was sixty feet from the flag, Pate hit his ball onto the back fringe, twenty-five feet from the hole. Both players struck their approach putts too strongly—Mahaffey ten feet past the hole, Pate five—but John missed his par putt, Jerry made his, and thereby the

22-year-old rookie who had never won a professional event took the Open lead for the first time.

Weiskopf and Geiberger both had caught the rough with their final teeshots, both had layed up short of the pond, both had pitched on, and both had holed gut-wrenching, par-saving putts to stay a stroke behind Pate.

Then both Pate and Mahaffey struck their drives into that same gnarly Bermuda grass rough. Mahaffey had the longer shot, and by far the more difficult lie. But there was no laying up. He lashed at it with his 4-wood, but the moment he struck it he knew his hopes were dead. Into the pond it splashed, and for the second straight year he had narrowly lost the Open.

When Pate reached his ball he was pleasantly surprised. It was sitting cleanly atop the grass. With 192 yards to the flag and the pin set in the lower front portion of the green just a few feet from the lake, Pate selected a 5-iron and hit a high majestic shot that covered the flag all the way. It stabbed the green four feet from the hole and rolled to a stop two feet away. With the birdie, the Open was his by two strokes on a score of three under par 277.

Pate, the 1974 U.S. Amateur Champion, was the youngest player on the Tour at the time, and by making the Open his first professional victory he joined an elite twosome—Jack Nicklaus and Lee Trevino. He seemed destined to forge a career similar to theirs, but neck and back injuries plagued his lyrical swing. Although he won another seven tournaments in the half dozen years following the Open, by 1983 he had virtually disappeared. Today he designs courses and is a commentator for ABC television.

Whereas at age 22 Jerry Pate had won two national titles, at the same age Larry Nelson had played golf for less than one year. A Vietnam veteran, Nelson was working as a draftsman in an aircraft plant in northern Georgia in 1969 when his wife gave him a set of golf clubs for Christmas. Three months later he joined nearby Pine Tree Golf Club and played his first eighteen holes on the 7004-yard course in ninety-five strokes, the highest score he was ever to shoot. Less than a year later, he shot a 69 on the same course. Two years after that—barely three years after taking up the game—he entered the PGA Tour qualifying tournament and won his card. Although he had played just one seventy-two-hole event, he learned the ways of the pro circuit quickly and since 1975 has consistently been one of the top money winners on the Tour, amassing ten victories—including two PGAs and a U.S. Open—in the process.

Nelson, a soft-spoken Georgia gentleman in the tradition of Bobby Jones, was a man who went about his business with no fanfare. But a few months before the 1981 PGA he had scored an uncharacteristically theatrical win in the Greensboro Open, holing-out a bunker shot for victory on the final green. At the AAC, he needed no such heroics. After opening with an even-par 70 he strung together a pair of 66's and took a four-stroke lead over Fuzzy Zoeller, five over Tom Kite and Andy North.

On Sunday, no one got within arm's length of Nelson. When at the 13th hole he hit an 8-iron five feet from the flag and made birdie—his fourth birdie in four days on that hole—he took a five-stroke lead. Zoeller picked up one more stroke over the last five holes, but with a final round score of 71 Nelson quietly won by four and set the competitive course record at 273.

That record will never be broken, because today's Highlands course is a good deal different. In 1988, Arnold Palmer and Ed Seay did substantial work to the course, making changes—mostly softening—on about two thirds of the 18 holes.

Inside the AAC clubhouse, however, the past lives on. Photos of Nelson and of Pate adorn the walls of the corridors. There is also a photo of the club's first athletic director, John Heisman, who later became Georgia Tech's first football coach and the man for whom the Heisman Trophy is named. And in a room on the second floor of the clubhouse the club's most illustrious members—Alexa Stirling, Watts Gunn, and others—are remembered, along with the roster of equally prominent club professionals: two-time Open Champion Alex Smith; Stewart Maiden and his brother Jimmy; 1909 Open Champion George Sargent and his son Harold, each a past president of the PGA of America.

Adjoining that room is another room, this one packed with dozens of trophies, medals, clubs, balls, photographs, and clippings. All of this memorabilia—including a tiny silverplated cup—pertains to the same club member, the hero of the Atlanta Athletic Club and the inspiration to golfers everywhere, Bobby Jones.

Tour rookie Jerry Pate outgunned several veterans for his first victory, the 1976 U. S. Open. Photo: © Leonard Kamsler

U.S. Open: June 17-20, 1976

Jerry Pate	71	69	69	68	277	1
Tom Weiskopf	73	70	68	68	279	T2
Al Geiberger	70	69	71	69	279	T2
John Mahaffey	70	68	69	73	280	T4
Butch Baird	71	71	71	67	280	T4
Hubert Green	72	70	71	69	282	6
Tom Watson	74	72	68	70	284	7
Lyn Lott	71	71	70	73	285	T8
Ben Crenshaw	72	68	72	73	285	T8
Johnny Miller	74	72	69	71	286	10

PGA Championship: August 6-9, 1981

Larry Nelson	70	66	66	71	273	1
Fuzzy Zoeller	70	68	68	71	277	2
Dan Pohl	69	67	73	69	278	3
Bob Gilder	74	69	70	66	279	T4
Keith Fergus	71	71	69	68	279	T4
Bruce Lietzke	70	70	71	68	279	T4
Jack Nicklaus	71	68	71	69	279	T4
Isao Aoki	75	68	66	70	279	T4
Greg Norman	73	67	68	71	279	T4
Tom Kite	71	67	69	72	279	T4

Scorecard

HOLE	YARDS	PAR
1	456	4
2	458	4
3	469	4
4	210	3
5	546	5
6	445	4
7	185	3
8	422	4
9	419	4
OUT	3610	35
10	374	4
11	470	4
12	510	5
13	390	4
14	415	4
15	215	3
16	410	4
17	213	3
18	463	4
IN	3460	35
TOTAL	7070	70

The Masters
AUGUSTA NATIONAL GOLF CLUB

AUGUSTA, GEORGIA
The Masters

On November 18, 1930, six weeks after he had completed the Grand Slam, Bobby Jones sent a letter to the USGA formally announcing his retirement from championship golf. He retired, at age 28, because he was exhausted by the unremitting pressure of competition, because he had accomplished every goal he had set for himself, and because he wanted to pursue a dream.

Seven months later, that dream began to take shape when Jones and a group of investors purchased 365 acres of land near Augusta, Georgia, and in January of 1933 it became a reality when the Augusta National—Bobby Jones's dream course and dream club—opened for play.

Fruitlands was the name of the property. It had been a nursery owned and operated by a Belgian family headed by Prosper Julius Alphonse Berckmans. A dazzling assortment of trees, flowers, and shrubs flourished on the property. Azaleas were everywhere, along with dogwood, redbud, daffodils, camellias, jasmine, woodbine, and a dozen others, enough species to name each of the eighteen holes after a different tree or plant. Atop the highest hill on the property a long driveway, lined with a double row of sixty-two magnolia trees, led to the Berckmans's stately plantation home.

Jones fell in love with the place the minute he laid eyes on it. In his autobiography, *Golf Is My Game*, he wrote:

> When I walked out on the grass terrace under the big trees behind the house and looked down over the property, the experience was unforgettable. It seemed that this land had been lying here for years waiting for someone to lay a golf course upon it. Indeed, it even looked as though it already were a golf course.

But Jones, although the finest player the game had ever seen, knew little about the mechanics of golf architecture. By his own admission, "No man learns to design a golf course simply by playing golf, no matter how well." He needed help. What's more, this was the Depression era, a time when golf clubs and courses were not being built, but were being closed down by the dozen. And whereas Jones had an engineering degree from Georgia Tech, a bachelor's degree in English from Harvard, and a law degree from Emory, he knew little about real estate financing. He needed help there too.

Fortunately, he was a wise judge of people, and he enlisted the partnership of two extraordinarily talented men—Alister Mackenzie and Clifford Roberts. Roberts, a tall, bespectacled Wall Street banker with Augusta connections, had befriended Jones during the 1920s. It was he who first alerted Jones to the Fruitlands property and he who secured the option to buy it for $70,000, about $200 an acre. Roberts then convinced several of his wealthy New York and Georgia friends to underwrite the project. Once the Augusta National was formed, Jones became its President and Roberts its Chairman, and for four decades the two of them ran the club with consummate skill.

Although Donald Ross was the preeminent architect of the era, there was never any question that the designer of the Augusta National would be Mackenzie. Jones had met him thanks to Johnny Goodman, the Nebraska farmboy who had shocked the world by upsetting Jones in the first round of the 1929 U.S. Amateur at Pebble Beach. With several free days on his hands, Jones had stuck around the Monterey Peninsula, and he played Mackenzie's recently opened jewel, Cypress Point. He engaged in lengthy walks and talks with the designer, and by week's end he was convinced that Mackenzie should be the sculptor of his dream course.

After all, Mackenzie, although a Yorkshireman, was of Scottish ancestry (which he played up by frequently wearing kilts), and the paradisiacal playing field in Jones's mind had a distinctly Scottish flavor, with broad, rolling fairways, large, undulating greens, and a minimum of rough and bunkers. Bobby's favorite championship site was St. Andrews, a place possessed of strategy and mystery, and he hoped to translate the charms of the Old Course to his new course. In his own words, he wanted a course that would "give pleasure to the greatest possible number of players, without respect to their capabilities." This was exactly in sync with Mackenzie's philosophy, to build courses for "the most enjoyment for the greatest number."

Mackenzie did the routing of the Augusta National, but during the construction process Jones made numerous refinements to the fairways and greens by playing hundreds of experimental drives and approaches and carefully noting where each ball landed and bounced. Mackenzie made his last site inspection in the summer of 1932, when the design was complete but had not been grassed, and declared, "Augusta National represented my best opportunity and, I believe, my finest achievement." Sadly, he never saw the finished course. After a trip to Scotland in 1933 he returned to his California home seriously ill, and died in January of 1934.

Shortly after the Augusta National opened, one of the members suggested that the club play host to a future U.S. Open. Jones and Roberts rejected this notion for a number of reasons, not the least of which was the fact that the Open was played in June, and that was too late and too hot a time to visit the Deep South. But Roberts recognized an opportunity, and proposed that the club instead invent an event of its own. He suggested calling it the "Masters Tournament."

Jones loved the idea but hated the name, deeming it presumptuous, so in March of 1934 the first "Augusta National Invitation Tournament" was held. (It was also the last Augusta National Invitation Tournament. The press, led by Jones's good friend and fellow club member Grantland Rice, got wind of the name "Masters," and newspaper reports quickly carried that name.)

The field included past U.S. Open and Amateur Champions and British Open and Amateur Champions as well as members of the U.S. Walker Cup and Ryder Cup teams—all the friends Jones had made during his years of competition.

As President of the club and the official host, Jones himself played, unsheathing his game to the public for the first time since his retirement. But his prolonged absence from competition was apparent. Although he began with three pars and a birdie, his opening round was a 76, and he followed that with a 74 and two 72s, fin-

Alister Mackenzie plotted the Augusta National, but Bobby Jones "tested" the emerging course, hitting countless experimental shots such as this drive to the 8th fairway. Photo: Frank Christian Studio, Augusta, Georgia

ishing in a tie for thirteenth, ten strokes behind the winning score of Horton Smith. That would be his best finish in twelve appearances. In 1940 he withdrew after two rounds with what was diagnosed as bursitis. Years later it became apparent that his condition was more serious. Eventually, the ailment was identified as syringomyelia, a crippling spinal disease. Soon Jones was walking with a cane, then wearing a leg brace, then confined to a wheelchair. The last Masters he attended was in 1968, and in December of 1971 he died.

He left behind a tournament that will live forever. Golf writer Charles Price, a confidant of Jones and the definitive authority on the history of the Augusta National, is fond of pointing out that The Masters is not the championship of anything. Not a country or state, not an association, not even the club championship of the Augusta National Golf Club. Yet it is without question a major championship.

How and why is that? There is no simple answer, no single moment when The Masters became a major. It occurred gradually as an amalgam of many people and events. Certainly, from the very beginning the tournament had three important advantages: the aegis of Bobby Jones, the loyalty of the players—who gladly came out of respect and friendship for Jones—and the sportswriters, who annually made the stop at Augusta on their northward trek at the end of baseball's spring training.

The tournament surely earned its name in year two when one of the game's unquestioned masters, Gene Sarazen, finished on top, thanks to a masterpiece 4-wood in the final round. Three strokes behind Craig Wood with four holes to play, Sarazen made up all three with one swing when his second shot at the par-five 15th sailed 220 yards across the fronting pond, onto the green, and into the hole for a double eagle. It spurred him to tie Wood, whom he beat in a 36-hole playoff the next day.

Under Cliff Roberts's meticulous guidance, The Masters soon became known as the best-run tournament in the world, as the chairman introduced myriad innovations that made the week in Augusta an eagerly anticipated rite of spring for gallery, press, and competitors. Multiple leaderboards, special roped-off vantage points for spectators, uniformed marshalls, free pairing sheets and parking spaces, and reasonably priced refreshments all became trademarks of The Masters, as did the tradition of presenting each champion a green coat, token of honorary membership in the club.

During the first two decades of The Masters, its prestige grew simply from the caliber of players who won it. In addition to Sarazen, the early champions included Byron Nelson, Ralph Guldahl, Jimmy Demaret, Sam Snead, and Ben Hogan. When in 1953 Hogan won his second Masters and then added victories in the U.S. and British Opens, his feat was hailed as a triple crown and he was given a tickertape parade through New York City.

Still, in those days the British Open itself was in the doldrums and no Americans considered it—or The Masters—on a par with the U.S. Open. In truth, if one moment pushed both The Masters and the modern British Open over the edge into majordom, it was in 1960, when Arnold Palmer invented the modern Grand Slam.

Palmer had won his second Masters that year, birdieing the 71st and 72nd holes on national television to nip Ken Venturi by a stroke. Then he had blitzed through the last eighteen at Cherry Hills in sixty-five strokes to edge Jack Nicklaus and Ben Hogan in the U.S. Open. In an airplane on his way to Scotland three weeks later, he reasoned that if he could add victories at the British Open at St. Andrews and then the PGA Championship at Firestone, he'd have the four most prestigious prizes in the game.

Palmer won neither of those events, but his audacious quest stamped the notion of a big four indelibly on the consciousness of the golf world.

The last—and perhaps most important—ingredient in the elevation of The Masters has been the golf course itself. During the past half century or so, the Augusta National has undergone numerous changes, some of them major, others mere tweaks, but fundamentally it has remained the test that Jones and Mackenzie intended, a superbly strategic design and perhaps the finest thinking man's golf course this side of St. Andrews.

On the scorecard, its two nines seem in perfect balance, each a par 36 with two fives, two threes, and five fours. The front measures 3465 yards, the back 3440. But scorecards can be misleading. There are no water hazards in play on the first nine holes; on the second nine, ponds and streams menace the soul and backswing on five holes. Still, the outward half, while less spectacular, is no less stern.

When a wind blows out of the northwest, the hardest hole on the course is number 1. A dogleg of 400 yards, it begins with a teeshot across a swooping valley to the brow of a hill, then angles rightward toward a slightly elevated green. There are fewer than fifty bunkers on the Augusta National, because Mackenzie knew how to get maximum intimidation from minimal sand. Number 1 has only two bunkers, but each is placed with consummate cunning. The first, on the right side of the driving zone, forces all but the strongest hitters to play safely to its left. But such caution will leave a more difficult approach because the other bunker, at greenside, blocks an approach from anywhere left of center-fairway. The green sits on the highest point of the course and is full of subtle breaks, but in the final round of the 1968 Masters it was no problem for Roberto De Vicenzo, who knocked a 9-iron into the hole for an eagle 2. But an afternoon that started in joy ended in grief when De Vicenzo, after tieing Bob Goalby for 72 holes, discovered that he had signed an incorrect scorecard and was forced to settle for second place.

Bob Jones didn't care much for par fives where, in his words, "you don't start playing golf until the third shot," so the long holes on the Augusta National aren't actually that long. Number 2, a steeply downhill 555 yards, presents an excellent birdie chance, particularly for the player who can carry his drive to the point where

1st hole

the hole begins its sharpest descent, and thereby gain a big bounce forward. Players have been known to hit as little as a 9-iron into this green, though long irons and 4-woods are the rule. Champions don't win on this hole, but they do occasionally use it to scare the rest of the field, as Seve Ballesteros did in 1983, when he began his final round birdie-eagle-par-birdie, his three on number 2 coming after he knocked a 4-wood fifteen feet from the hole. His fast start vaulted him into a lead he never lost.

Jones and Mackenzie tried to invest each hole with several lines of attack, permitting the player to choose among conservative, mildly aggressive, and audacious routes. At the 360-yard 3rd hole, for example, the pros play from the tee with anything from a 3-iron to a driver. The shorter club will take the left-hand bunkers out of play by staying shy of them, while the driver has the chance of clearing them—or finding bigger trouble in the grassy mounds to the left or the trees to the right. The small green sits on top of a steep mound, and it also offers a choice, especially if the pin is on the shallower left side. One may go for it, hoping to clear the mound

yet hold the green, or play safely to the right. Correct club selection and precise execution are critical here.

Every hole on the course has been eagled in Masters play at least once except for number 4, which has never been aced. Masters lore holds that on this hole Jones and Mackenzie attempted to simulate the 11th at St. Andrews, deemed by many to be the finest one-shotter in the game. The broad, swooping green and bunker placement have some similarity, but this 205-yard hole is thirty yards longer than its model.

The tee of the 5th is at the westernmost part of the course. Few Masters spectators venture that far, and like most of the outward nine, the hole never appears on television. This is a pity, because the 435-yard par four is one of the best tests on the course. The teeshot is half blind to a fairway that falls from right to left en route to a surging two-tiered green modeled after the green of the Road Hole (number 17) at St. Andrews. One year Sam Snead stood at the front of this green facing a fifty-foot birdie putt up the slope to the second tier. He stroked it smoothly—a bit too smoothly—and

as it reached the crest of the slope it stopped and rolled all the way back to his feet. Then the Slammer stroked it again—this time into the hole for a par.

Another fiendishly sloped green stares sixty feet up at its assailants on the 6th tee, a picturesque 180-yard par three. In 1954, amateur Billy Joe Patton put his name in The Masters record book when he aced the hole during the final round. Patton actually led that tournament for most of the week and was on his way to making history until his agonizing trip through the back nine. On the two inward par fives he used a catastrophic thirteen strokes and finished one stroke out of a Snead-Hogan playoff won by Sam.

Number 7 is something of a misfit. On a course known for its spacious fairways, this hole is tightly lined with trees. On a course that rewards length, the heart of this teeshot landing area may be reached comfortably with an iron. On a course with fewer bunkers than virtually any great course in the world, this green is ringed by sand. And on a course known for its broad, rolling greens, this putting surface is barely fifteen paces from front to back. Number 7 is an exceptional hole, but it's also an exception. During the first four Masters it measured a bunker-free 340 yards, an attempt to simulate the drivable 18th hole at the Old Course. That didn't work in Georgia, and in 1938, at the suggestion of Horton Smith, the green was moved to a perch twenty-three feet above the fairway. Now, when a player stands over his approach shot, he sees no putting surface, very little flagstick, and lots of sand in the three deep bunkers

OPPOSITE: *2nd hole*. ABOVE: *5th hole*. BELOW: *7th hole*

9th hole

that front the green. This is one green where a lofted approach is not only advisable, but mandatory.

The 8th hole, another Jonesian par four-and-a-half, is a reminder of the incalculable advantage that longer hitters have on this course. A massive bunker on the right side of the fairway gives pause to any player who cannot carry the ball 240 yards, while power players may look beyond it and aspire to an eagle putt on the green 535 yards up a steep hill. In the final round of the 1986 Masters, before Jack Nicklaus took control, two of the leaders were Tom Kite and Seve Ballesteros. Paired together, they both eagled this hole from off the green, Kite wedging in from eighty yards, Ballesteros pitching in from fifty yards.

The 9th is a par four of 435 yards that runs roughly parallel to number 1, the teeshot falling into the bottom of the valley, the approach playing straight uphill to a green tilting severely from back to front. It was here in 1986 that Nicklaus began his most famous charge. He was six strokes behind Greg Norman when he knocked in an eleven-foot birdie that launched him into the most fabled back nine in Masters history and his record sixth title at age 46.

Interestingly, for the inaugural Masters the current first nine holes were played as the second nine, and vice versa. Although Mackenzie had called for the course to be played as it is today, Jones made a last-minute switch prior to opening day. But after the inau-

gural tournament, the nines were reversed to their present status.

In time, Jones came to realize the power of the inward nine. "The finishes of The Masters Tournament have almost always been dramatic and exciting," he said. "It is my conviction that this has been the case because of the make-or-break quality of the second nine. This nine can provide excruciating torture for the front-runner trying to hang on. Yet it can yield a very low score to the player making a closing rush."

It begins at the top of a hill near the clubhouse with the longest par four on the course. At 485 yards, number 10 is actually longer than the par-five 13th hole. But it sweeps downward while banking gracefully left through a corridor of pines and camellias. Those who are sufficiently daring to gun their drives along the left tree line will be rewarded with several yards of extra roll. The large green was the scene of two dramatic putts during the 1980s, the first of them by Ben Crenshaw, who began his surge to the 1984 title by slipping in a sixty-footer for birdie. The other was much shorter, a distance of barely two feet, and it was missed by Scott Hoch in a sudden-death playoff for the 1989 title. Had he sunk it, he would have been the champion. Instead, he allowed Nick Faldo to survive, and Faldo beat him on the next green.

Indeed, number 11 is Nick Faldo's hole. In 1990 he joined Jack Nicklaus as the only men to win consecutive Masters when he again won in sudden death, again at the 11th hole. A year earlier, he had sunk a dramatic twenty-foot birdie putt. In 1990, he got some help from Raymond Floyd, who pulled his approach shot into the pond that hugs this green.

In fact, four of the five Masters sudden-death playoffs have ended on this 455-yard par four. In 1979 Fuzzy Zoeller hit an 8-iron to fifteen feet and sank the putt to beat Tom Watson and unfortunate Ed Sneed, who had allowed the other two into a playoff when he had bogeyed each of the last three holes of regulation play. And in 1987, 11 was the scene of one of the most dramatic shots in major championship history, when Larry Mize chipped into the hole from a position in no-man's-land, 140 feet to the right of the hole, to steal the title from Greg Norman. It was the second such lightning bolt Norman had been forced to absorb in consecutive majors. At Inverness the previous August, Bob Tway had blasted out of a bunker and into the hole to wrench the PGA from Norman's grasp.

In addition to the pond, two bunkers lurk at the back of the green where Rae's Creek also begins its menacing path. Ben Hogan had such respect for these combined threats that he gave the entire green a wide berth. "If you ever see me on this green with my second shot," he once said, "you'll know I missed the shot."

In a 1957 article for *Sports Illustrated*, Herbert Warren Wind coined the term Amen Corner to describe the area composed of the second half of the 11th hole, the short 12th, and the first half of the 13th, borrowing the name from an old jazz recording, "Shouting at the Amen Corner." His expression caught on, perhaps because, as Dave Marr once suggested, "If you get through these three holes in even par, you believe a bit more in God."

Jack Nicklaus calls number 12 "the toughest tournament hole in golf." Gary Player calls it "the toughest par three in the world."

Who knows what Tom Weiskopf calls it—in 1982 he took a 13 on it, the highest single-hole score in Masters history.

It is only 155 yards long, but this is 155 yards of compressed architectural guile, an ingenious combination of perils seen and unseen. There is Rae's Creek, lapping across the entire width of the green; there is a broad bunker in front and two more beyond; and between them is the shallowest—and fastest—putting surface on the course. The 12th green is shaped like a footprint, and at its instep, just beyond the front bunker, it is only twenty-four feet deep. But the most intimidating factor is the invisible demon, the wind. Although the tee and green here are shielded, the shot to the hole passes through 100 yards of air space where it is buffeted by northwest breezes swirling down the fairway of the next hole. Accurate club selection requires a combination of experience, skill, patience, and guts.

One year, Bob Rosburg thought he had the gusts deciphered when he pulled a 5-iron from his bag. But as he made impact the air went still, and Rosburg's ball sailed forty yards over the green and into the property of the adjacent Augusta Country Club. Moments later he hit a second ball—with the same 5-iron—and it stopped fifteen feet from the hole.

In 1962, Arnold Palmer was leading the tournament when in the final round his teeshot embedded in the sandy upslope beyond the green. When he asked for free relief, he was told he'd have to play the ball as it lay. Palmer disagreed but played the ball out, making a 5. Then he dropped a second ball into a clean lie and played it out as well, making a 3. At the 14th tee Bobby Jones approached Arnie and told him he had made the correct interpretation—his ball had not been in a hazard and therefore he had been entitled to relief.

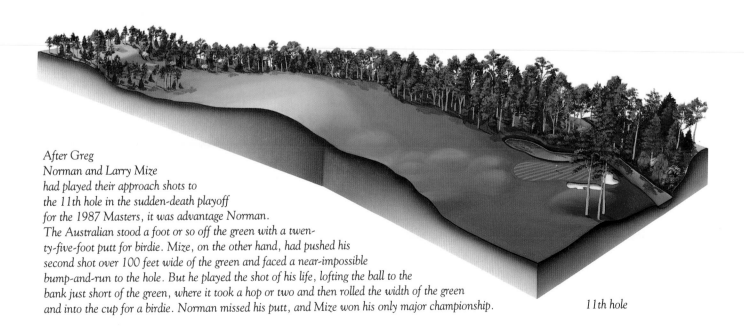

After Greg
Norman and Larry Mize
had played their approach shots to
the 11th hole in the sudden-death playoff
for the 1987 Masters, it was advantage Norman.
The Australian stood a foot or so off the green with a twenty-five-foot putt for birdie. Mize, on the other hand, had pushed his
second shot over 100 feet wide of the green and faced a near-impossible
bump-and-run to the hole. But he played the shot of his life, lofting the ball to the
bank just short of the green, where it took a hop or two and then rolled the width of the green
and into the cup for a birdie. Norman missed his putt, and Mize won his only major championship.

11th hole

Masters tradition calls for the previous year's winner to help the new Champion into his coat, but when Nick Faldo defended successfully in 1990, Masters Chairman Hord Hardin did the honors. Photo: © Leonard Kamsler

Background: Augusta, Hole 11

ABOVE: *12th hole*. BELOW: *13th hole*. OPPOSITE: *14th hole*

From that point Palmer went on to win the third of his four titles.

This is also the only temperature-controlled green in the world. Since the Augusta National closes down completely from May to November, the course is kept in immaculate condition. In the early '80s, the club converted all eighteen of its greens from Bermuda grass to a faster bent grass surface, and shortly thereafter it became apparent that number 12 needed special help in recovering from frosts. So a network of pipes was installed beneath the surface. Now, during the cold months, a pump behind the green circulates warm water through the pipes, and the surface is kept at a constant temperature of 70 degrees.

Claude Harmon, Bill Hyndman, and Curtis Strange have aced this hole in Masters competition, and with Harmon's shot goes a classic Ben Hogan tale. Hitting first, Harmon made his stroke of perfection and got not a word of reaction from the steely Hogan, who then played a shot within a few feet of the hole and made his putt for a birdie. As the two headed for the 12th tee, the Hawk finally spoke.

"You know, Claude," he said, "that's the first 2 I've ever made on that hole."

The 13th hole, a majestic par five that is probably the most famous hole on the course, and certainly the most photographed, was designed by Mackenzie at almost the moment he first laid eyes on the property. At the lowest point of the property, it parallels the path of a little creek, winding around a right-to-left corner 465 yards where the creek crosses in front of a billowing green.

Big hitters once again have an advantage, assuming they can play a high draw around the towering pines trees that line the left side of the hole. Such a shot will roll with the contour of the fairway and leave a mid or long iron to the green. Weaker teeshots, and anything to the right of center, will invariably mean a lay up short of the creek. "Twenty years ago, I could cut the corner by hitting a 3-wood over those trees," says Nicklaus, adding that "twenty years ago, the trees were a good deal shorter."

The hole, named Azalea for the dazzlingly colorful shrubs that border the creek, has been the scene of much theater. Byron Nelson sank a fifty-foot eagle chip here to vault toward his first victory in 1937, and two years later Ralph Guldahl knocked a 3-wood six inches from this pin en route to his win, but this is also where Billy Joe Patton came to grief when his second shot fell into the fronting creek, and Curtis Strange still agonizes over the 4-wood shot he hit into the creek while leading the final round in 1985.

Number 14, a par four of 405 yards, is the only hole from 11 to 16 that is not menaced by water. But this large and diabolically contoured two-tier green is a hazard in itself. There is no easy pin position, and the putt from the front edge up the four-foot rise to the

back is probably the hardest read-and-stroke on the course. In fact, on his way to the 1975 title, Jack Nicklaus knocked that putt *off* the green. Ken Venturi three-putted this hole each of the three Sundays he was in contention for the title.

The 15th, where Gene Sarazen struck his shot heard 'round the world, plays 500 yards, the last 250 of them sharply downhill to a broad, shallow green fronted by a pond. Behind the green is more water. A good drive here leaves an opportunity and a decision— whether to gun for the green, usually with anything from a 4-iron to a 3-wood, or to lay up and hope for a pitch-and-putt birdie. Nicklaus made his big move here in 1986, striking a 4-iron to fifteen feet and then making the eagle.

The hole on the Augusta National that Jack Nicklaus owns is number 16. Originally a short, undramatic par three, it was reworked in 1947 by Robert Trent Jones and now plays 170 yards across a long pond to another fiendish target. Hitting the green here is not enough. One must hit the correct sector of the green, or else be ready to three-putt. A ridge, nearly two feet high, climbs diagonally across from right-front to back-left, slicing the kidney-shaped surface into two peanut-shaped tiers. The teeshot is made more fretful by the presence of three bunkers, to the left, right-front, and right-rear, the last of them being the most fearsome on the course.

Nicklaus nearly holed his 6-iron teeshot here on Sunday in 1986, and in 1975 this was the site of the most dramatic putt of his career,

LEFT: *On Sunday in 1986, 46-year-old Jack Nicklaus sank this birdie putt at number 10 to launch a back-nine score of 30 that propelled him into his record sixth green coat. Photo: © Frank Christian Studio, Augusta, Georgia.* BELOW: *16th hole*

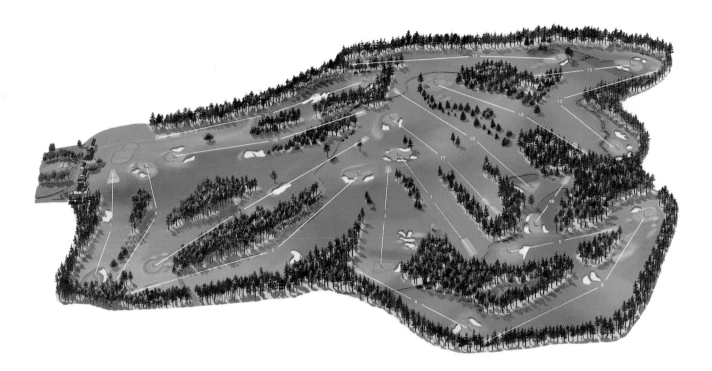

a slope-climbing forty-footer that jumped him out of a three-way tie with Tom Weiskopf and Johnny Miller and into green coat number five. In the eleven Masters between 1977 and 1987 he played the hole forty-one times without a bogey, registering thirty pars and eleven birdies.

This was also the last birdie in regulation play in each of Nick Faldo's back-to-back victories. In both 1989 and 1990 he capped his back-nine charge here by sinking a lengthy, twisting, downhill putt for a deuce.

On the other hand, Ben Hogan bogeyed 16 in each of his 18-hole playoffs, losing to Byron Nelson in 1942 and Sam Snead in 1954, each by a stroke, and Nelson had some misfortune of his own here. In 1957 he struck a teeshot so straight that it hit the flag—and caromed back into the pond.

Number 17 does not seem too difficult on the card. It is only 400 yards long, there is no water, and the large green is accessible. But two trees pinch the drive, one of them called the Eisenhower Tree. The former President, a club member and close friend of Jones, had a penchant for hitting it. Assuming its limbs can be avoided, the assignment on the approach is once again to find the pin, or an area of the green that will allow a reasonable putt at it. Indeed, this sometimes means firing *away* from the pin. As Byron Nelson once observed, "At Augusta, it's often better to be 20 feet to one side of the cup than six feet to the other side."

Eleven holes on the course are doglegs, but only two—the first and the last—move from left to right. Those who are unable to fade the ball at 18 will risk finding one of two steep-faced bunkers at the corner of the turn. Alternatively, the choice is to lay up short of the sand, leaving a much longer approach, uphill all the way to a long, narrow green. In 1988, Sandy Lyle took this cautious approach but overcooked his 1-iron and found one of the bunkers anyway. From

there he played the best shot of his life, a majestic 7-iron that stopped ten feet in back of the hole. He sank the birdie putt to beat Mark Calcavecchia by a stroke. Gary Player and Arnold Palmer have also birdied 18 to win, as has Art Wall, who won in 1959 on the heels of birdies on five of the last six holes. For theatrics, however, it's hard to beat the otherwise unassuming Doug Ford, who capped his 1957 victory by exploding out of the left-hand bunker and into the hole for a birdie.

The Masters remains strictly an invitational event, not just for competitors but for spectators as well. Daily tickets may be purchased for the practice days and the traditional Par-3 Contest on Wednesday, but once play begins, access is limited to the players and their immediate families, officials, press, and a few thousand lucky "patrons." These are the folks who years ago began coming to the tournament and wisely have retained their privileges. Any patron who fails to renew his option and does not have an excellent excuse is summarily debadged, and the first person on the waiting list—cut off years ago and still numbering about 5,000—gets the nod.

Even more exclusive than the patrons' roster or the competitors' invitation list is the membership of the club itself. As one reporter wrote, "The Augusta National is a golf club that looks as if it dropped out of heaven, and it's just as hard to get into." However, history was made in September of 1990 when the club accepted its first black member, following a controversy over discrimination at the PGA Championship site that year, Shoal Creek, a club that had been founded by Augusta National member Hall Thompson.

The current Augusta National membership numbers just over 300, most of them from outside the Augusta area. The current Chairman is Jackson Stephens. And the President—in Perpetuity—is Bobby Jones.

March 22-25, 1934

Horton Smith	70	72	70	72	284	1
Craig Wood	71	74	69	61	285	2
Billy Burke	72	71	70	73	286	T3
Paul Runyan	74	71	70	71	286	T3
Ed Dudley	74	69	71	74	288	5
Willie MacFarlane	74	73	70	74	291	6
Harold McSpaden	77	74	72	69	292	T7
Al Espinosa	75	70	75	72	292	T7
Jimmy Hines	70	74	74	74	292	T7
Macdonald Smith	74	70	74	74	292	T7

April 4-8, 1935

Gene Sarazen	68	71	73	70	282		
						144	1
Craig Wood	69	72	68	73	282		
						149	2
Olin Dutra	70	70	70	74	284		3
Henry Picard	67	68	76	75	286		4
Denny Shute	73	71	70	73	287		5
Lawson Little, Jr.	74	72	70	72	288		6
Paul Runyan	70	72	75	72	289		7
Vic Ghezzi	73	71	73	73	290		8
Jimmy Hines	70	70	77	74	291		T9
Byron Nelson	71	74	72	74	291		T9
B. Cruickshank	76	70	73	72	291		T9
Joe Turnesa	73	71	74	73	291		T9

April 2-6, 1936

Horton Smith	74	71	68	72	285	1
Harry Cooper	70	69	71	76	286	2
Gene Sarazen	78	67	72	70	287	3
B. Cruickshank	75	69	74	72	290	T4
Paul Runyan	76	69	70	75	290	T4
Ray Mangrum	76	73	68	76	293	T6
Ed Dudley	75	75	70	73	293	T6
Ky Laffoon	75	70	75	73	293	T6
John Dawson	77	70	70	77	294	T9
Henry Picard	75	72	74	73	294	T9

April 1-4, 1937

Byron Nelson	66	72	75	70	283	1
Ralph Guldahl	69	72	69	76	285	2
Ed Dudley	70	71	71	74	286	3
Harry Cooper	73	69	71	74	287	4
Ky Laffoon	73	70	74	73	290	5
Jimmy Thomson	71	73	74	73	291	6
Al Watrous	74	72	71	75	292	7
Tommy Armour	73	75	73	72	293	T8
Vic Ghezzi	72	72	72	77	293	T8
Jimmy Hines	77	72	68	77	294	T10
Leonard Dodson	71	75	71	77	294	T10

April 1-4, 1938

Henry Picard	71	72	72	70	285	1
Ralph Guldahl	73	70	73	71	287	T2
Harry Cooper	69	77	71	71	287	T2
Paul Runyan	71	73	74	70	288	4
Byron Nelson	73	74	70	73	290	5
Ed Dudley	70	69	77	75	291	T6
Felix Serafin	72	71	78	70	291	T6
Dick Metz	70	77	74	71	292	T8
Jimmy Thomson	74	70	76	72	292	T8
Jimmy Hines	75	71	75	72	293	T9
Vic Ghezzi	75	74	70	74	293	T9
Lawson Little, Jr.	72	75	74	72	293	T9

March 30 - April 2, 1939

Ralph Guldahl	72	68	70	69	279	1
Sam Snead	70	70	72	68	280	2
Billy Burke	69	72	71	70	282	T3
Lawson Little, Jr.	72	72	68	70	282	T3
Gene Sarazen	73	66	72	72	283	5
Craig Wood	72	73	71	68	284	6
Byron Nelson	71	69	72	75	287	7
Henry Picard	71	71	76	71	289	8
Ben Hogan	75	71	72	72	290	9
Toney Penna	72	75	72	72	291	T10
Ed Dudley	75	75	69	72	291	T10

April 4-7, 1940

Jimmy Demaret	67	72	70	71	280	1
Lloyd Mangrum	64	75	71	74	284	2
Byron Nelson	69	72	74	70	285	3
Ed Dudley	73	72	71	71	287	T4
Harry Cooper	69	75	73	70	287	T4
Willie Goggin	71	72	73	71	287	T4
Henry Picard	71	71	71	75	288	T7
Craig Wood	70	75	67	76	288	T7
Sam Snead	71	72	69	76	288	T7
Toney Penna	73	73	72	72	290	T10
Ben Hogan	73	74	69	74	290	T10

April 3-6, 1941

Craig Wood	66	71	71	72	280	1
Byron Nelson	71	69	73	70	283	2
Sam Byrd	73	70	68	74	285	3
Ben Hogan	71	72	75	68	286	4
Ed Dudley	73	72	75	68	288	5
Sam Snead	73	75	72	69	289	T6
Vic Ghezzi	77	71	71	70	289	T6
Lawson Little, Jr.	71	70	74	75	290	8
Lloyd Mangrum	71	72	72	76	291	T9
Harold McSpaden	75	74	72	70	291	T9
Willie Goggin	71	72	72	76	291	T9

April 9-13, 1942

Byron Nelson	68	67	72	73	280		
						69	1
Ben Hogan	73	70	67	70	280		
						70	2
Paul Runyan	67	73	72	71	283		3
Sam Byrd	68	68	75	74	285		4
Horton Smith	67	73	74	74	287		5
Jimmy Demaret	70	70	75	75	290		6
E.J. Harrison	74	70	71	77	292		T7
Lawson Little, Jr.	71	74	72	75	292		T7
Sam Snead	78	69	72	73	292		T7
Gene Kunes	74	74	74	71	293		T10
Chick Harbert	73	73	72	75	293		T10

April 4-7, 1946

Herman Keiser	69	68	71	74	282	1
Ben Hogan	74	70	69	70	283	2
Bob Hamilton	75	69	71	72	287	3
Ky Laffoon	74	73	70	72	289	T4
Jimmy Demaret	75	70	71	73	289	T4
Jim Ferrier	74	72	68	75	289	T4
Sam Snead	74	75	70	71	290	T7
Clayton Heafner	74	69	71	76	290	T7
Byron Nelson	72	73	71	74	290	T7
Chick Harbert	69	75	76	70	290	T7

April 3-6, 1947

Jimmy Demaret	69	71	70	71	281	1
Byron Nelson	69	72	72	70	283	T2
Frank Stranahan	73	72	70	67	283	T2
Ben Hogan	75	68	71	70	284	T4
Harold McSpaden	74	69	70	71	284	T4
Henry Picard	73	70	72	71	286	T6
Jim Ferrier	70	71	73	72	286	T6
Ed Oliver, Jr.	70	72	74	71	287	T8
Chandler Harper	77	72	68	70	287	T8
Lloyd Mangrum	76	73	68	70	287	T8
Toney Penna	71	70	75	71	287	T8
Dick Metz	72	72	72	71	287	T8

Pro Shop

April 8-11, 1948

Claude Harmon	70	70	69	70	279	1
Cary Middlecoff	74	71	69	70	284	2
Chick Harbert	71	70	70	76	287	3
Jim Ferrier	71	71	75	71	288	T4
Lloyd Mangrum	69	73	75	71	288	T4
Ed Furgol	70	72	73	74	289	T6
Ben Hogan	70	71	77	71	289	T6
Byron Nelson	71	73	72	74	290	T8
Harry Todd	72	67	80	71	290	T8
Herman Keiser	70	72	76	73	291	T10
Bobby Locke	71	71	74	75	291	T10
Dick Metz	71	72	75	73	291	T10

April 7-10, 1949

Sam Snead	73	75	67	67	282	1
Johnny Bulla	74	73	69	69	285	T2
Lloyd Mangrum	69	74	72	70	285	T2
Johnny Palmer	73	71	70	72	286	T4
Jim Turnesa	73	72	71	70	286	T4
Lew Worsham, Jr.	76	75	70	68	289	6
Joe Kirkwood, Jr.	73	72	70	75	290	7
Jimmy Demaret	76	72	73	71	292	T8
Clayton Heafner	71	74	72	75	292	T8
Byron Nelson	75	70	74	73	292	T8

April 6-9, 1950

Jimmy Demaret	70	72	72	69	283	1
Jim Ferrier	70	67	73	75	285	2
Sam Snead	71	74	70	72	287	3
Ben Hogan	73	68	71	76	288	T4
Byron Nelson	75	70	69	74	288	T4
Lloyd Mangrum	76	74	73	68	291	6
Clayton Heafner	74	77	69	72	292	T7
Cary Middlecoff	75	76	68	73	292	T7
Lawson Little, Jr.	70	73	75	75	293	9
Fred Haas, Jr.	74	76	73	71	294	T10
Gene Sarazen	80	70	72	72	294	T10

April 5-8, 1951

Ben Hogan	70	72	70	68	280	1
Skee Riegel	73	68	70	71	282	2
Lloyd Mangrum	69	74	70	73	286	T3
Lew Worsham, Jr.	71	71	72	72	286	T3
Dave Douglas	74	69	72	73	288	5
Lawson Little, Jr.	72	73	72	72	289	6
Jim Ferrier	74	70	74	72	290	7
Johnny Bulla	71	72	73	75	291	T8
Byron Nelson	71	73	73	74	291	T8
Sam Snead	69	74	68	80	291	T8

April 3-6, 1952

Sam Snead	70	67	77	72	286	1
Jack Burke, Jr.	76	67	78	69	290	2
Al Besselink	70	76	71	74	291	T3
Tommy Bolt	71	71	75	74	291	T3
Jim Ferrier	72	70	77	72	291	T3
Lloyd Mangrum	71	74	75	72	292	6
Julius Boros	73	73	76	71	293	T7
Fred Hawkins	71	73	78	71	293	T7
Ben Hogan	70	70	74	79	293	T7
Lew Worsham, Jr.	71	75	73	74	293	T7

April 9-12, 1953

Ben Hogan	70	69	66	69	274	1
Ed Oliver, Jr.	69	73	67	70	279	2
Lloyd Mangrum	74	68	71	69	282	3
Bob Hamilton	71	69	70	73	283	4
Tommy Bolt	71	75	68	71	285	T5
Chick Harbert	68	73	70	74	285	T5
Ted Kroll	71	70	73	72	286	7
Jack Burke, Jr.	78	69	69	71	287	8
Al Besselink	69	75	70	74	288	9
Julius Boros	73	71	75	70	289	T10
Chandler Harper	74	72	69	74	289	T10
Fred Hawkins	75	70	74	70	289	T10

April 8-12, 1954

Sam Snead	74	73	70	72	289		
						70	1
Ben Hogan	72	73	69	75	289		
						71	2
Billy Joe Patton	70	74	75	71	290		3
E.J. Harrison	70	79	74	68	291		T4
Lloyd Mangrum	71	75	76	69	291		T4
Jerry Barber	74	76	71	71	292		T6
Jack Burke, Jr.	71	77	73	71	292		T6
Bob Rosburg	73	73	76	70	292		T6
Al Besselink	74	74	74	72	294		T9
Cary Middlecoff	73	76	70	75	294		T9

April 7-10, 1955

Cary Middlecoff	72	65	72	70	279	1
Ben Hogan	73	68	72	73	286	2
Sam Snead	72	71	74	70	287	3
Bob Rosburg	72	72	72	73	289	T4
Mike Souchak	71	74	72	72	289	T4
Julius Boros	71	75	72	71	289	T4
Lloyd Mangrum	74	73	72	72	291	7
E. Harvie Ward, Jr.	77	69	75	71	292	T8
Stan Leonard	77	73	69	74	292	T8
Dick Mayer	78	72	72	71	293	T9
Byron Nelson	72	75	74	72	293	T9
Arnold Palmer	76	76	72	69	293	T9

April 5-8, 1956

Jack Burke, Jr.	72	71	75	71	289	1
Ken Venturi	66	69	75	80	290	2
Cary Middlecoff	67	72	75	77	291	3
Lloyd Mangrum	72	74	72	74	292	T4
Sam Snead	73	76	72	71	292	T4
Jerry Barber	71	72	76	75	294	T6
Doug Ford	70	72	75	77	294	T6
Shelley Mayfield	68	74	80	74	296	T8
Tommy Bolt	68	74	78	76	296	T8
Ben Hogan	69	78	74	75	296	T8

April 4-7, 1957

Doug Ford	72	73	72	66	283	1
Sam Snead	72	68	74	72	286	2
Jimmy Demaret	72	70	75	70	287	3
E. Harvie Ward, Jr.	73	71	71	73	288	4
Peter Thomson	72	73	73	71	289	5
Ed Furgol	73	71	72	74	290	6
Jack Burke, Jr.	71	72	74	74	291	T7
Dow Finsterwald	74	74	73	70	291	T7
Arnold Palmer	73	73	69	76	291	T7
Jay Hebert	74	72	76	70	292	10

April 3-6, 1958

Arnold Palmer	70	73	68	73	284	1
Doug Ford	74	71	70	70	285	T2
Fred Hawkins	71	75	68	71	285	T2
Stan Leonard	72	70	73	71	286	T4
Ken Venturi	68	72	74	72	286	T4
Cary Middlecoff	70	73	69	75	287	T6
Art Wall	71	72	70	74	287	T6
Billy Joe Patton	72	69	73	74	288	8
Claude Harmon	71	76	72	70	289	T9
Jay Hebert	72	73	73	71	289	T9
Billy Maxwell	71	70	72	76	289	T9
Al Mengert	73	71	69	76	289	T9

April 2-5, 1959

Art Wall, Jr.	73	74	71	66	284	1
Cary Middlecoff	74	71	68	72	285	2
Arnold Palmer	71	70	71	74	286	3
Dick Mayer	73	75	71	68	287	T4
Stan Leonard	69	74	69	75	287	T4
Charles R. Coe	74	74	67	73	288	6
Fred Hawkins	77	71	68	73	289	7
Julius Boros	75	69	74	72	290	T8
Jay Hebert	72	73	72	73	290	T8
Gene Littler	72	75	72	71	290	T8
Billy Maxwell	73	71	72	74	290	T8
Billy Joe Patton	75	70	71	74	290	T8
Gary Player	73	75	71	71	290	T8

April 7-10, 1960

Arnold Palmer	67	73	72	70	282	1
Ken Venturi	73	69	71	70	283	2
Dow Finsterwald	71	70	72	71	284	3
Billy Casper	71	71	71	74	287	4
Julius Boros	72	71	70	75	288	5
Walter Burkemo	72	69	75	73	289	T6
Ben Hogan	73	68	72	76	289	T6
Gary Player	72	71	72	74	289	T6
Lionel Hebert	74	70	73	73	290	T9
Stan Leonard	72	72	72	74	290	T9

April 6-10, 1961

Gary Player	69	68	69	74	280	1
Charles R. Coe	72	71	69	69	281	T2
Arnold Palmer	68	69	73	71	281	T2
Tommy Bolt	72	71	74	68	285	T4
Don January	74	68	72	71	285	T4
Paul Harney	71	73	68	74	286	6
Jack Burke, Jr.	76	70	68	73	287	T7
Billy Casper	72	77	69	69	287	T7
Bill Collins	74	72	67	74	287	T7
Jack Nicklaus	70	75	70	72	287	T7

April 5-9, 1962

Arnold Palmer	70	66	69	75	280		
						68	1
Gary Player	67	71	71	71	280		
						71	T2
Dow Finsterwald	74	68	65	73	280		
						77	T2
Gene Littler	71	68	71	72	282		4
Mike Souchak	70	72	74	71	287		T5
Jimmy Demaret	73	73	71	70	287		T5
Jerry Barber	72	72	69	74	287		T5
Bill Maxwell	71	73	72	71	287		T5
Ken Venturi	75	70	71	72	288		T9
Charles R. Coe	72	74	71	71	288		T9

April 4-7, 1963

Jack Nicklaus	74	66	74	72	286	1
Tony Lema	74	69	74	70	287	2
Julius Boros	76	69	71	72	288	T3
Sam Snead	70	73	74	71	288	T3
Dow Finsterwald	74	73	73	69	289	T5
Ed Furgol	70	71	74	74	289	T5
Gary Player	71	74	74	70	289	T5
Bo Winninger	69	72	77	72	290	8
Don January	73	75	72	71	291	T9
Arnold Palmer	74	73	73	71	291	T9

April 9-12, 1964

Arnold Palmer	69	68	69	70	276	1
Dave Marr	70	73	69	70	282	T2
Jack Nicklaus	71	73	71	67	282	T2
Bruce Devlin	72	72	67	73	284	4
Billy Casper	76	72	69	69	286	T5
Jim Ferrier	71	73	69	73	286	T5
Paul Harney	73	72	71	70	286	T5
Gary Player	69	72	72	73	286	T5
Dow Finsterwald	71	72	75	69	287	T9
Ben Hogan	73	75	67	72	287	T9
Tony Lema	75	68	74	70	287	T9
Mike Souchak	73	74	70	70	287	T9

April 8-11, 1965

Jack Nicklaus	67	71	64	69	271	1
Arnold Palmer	70	68	72	70	280	T2
Gary Player	65	73	69	73	280	T2
Mason Rudolph	70	75	66	72	283	4
Dan Sikes	67	72	71	75	285	5
Gene Littler	71	74	67	74	286	T6
Ramon Sota	71	73	70	72	286	T6
Frank Beard	68	77	72	70	287	T8
Tommy Bolt	69	78	69	71	287	T8
George Knudson	72	73	69	74	288	10

April 7-11, 1966

Jack Nicklaus	68	76	72	72	288		
						70	1
Tommy Jacobs	75	71	70	72	288		
						72	T2
Gay Brewer, Jr.	74	72	72	70	288		
						78	T2
Arnold Palmer	74	70	74	72	290		T4
Doug Sanders	74	70	75	71	290		T4
Don January	71	73	73	75	292		T6
George Knudson	73	76	72	71	292		T6
Raymond Floyd	72	73	74	74	293		T8
Paul Harney	75	68	76	74	293		T8
Billy Casper	71	75	76	72	294		T10
Jay Hebert	72	74	73	75	294		T10
Bob Rosburg	73	71	76	74	294		T10

April 6-9, 1967

Gay Brewer, Jr.	73	68	72	67	280	1
Bobby Nichols	72	69	70	70	281	2
Bert Yancey	67	73	71	73	284	3
Arnold Palmer	73	73	70	69	285	4
Julius Boros	71	70	70	75	286	5
Paul Harney	73	71	74	69	287	T6
Gary Player	75	69	72	71	287	T6
Tommy Aaron	75	68	74	71	288	T8
Lionel Hebert	77	71	67	73	288	T8
R. De Vicenzo	73	72	74	71	290	T10
Bruce Devlin	74	70	75	71	290	T10
Ben Hogan	74	73	66	77	290	T10
Mason Rudolph	72	76	72	70	290	T10
Sam Snead	72	76	71	71	290	T10

April 11-14, 1968

Bob Goalby	70	70	71	66	277	1
R. De Vicenzo	69	73	70	66	278	2
Bert Yancey	71	71	72	65	279	3
Bruce Devlin	69	73	69	69	280	4
Frank Beard	75	65	71	70	281	T5
Jack Nicklaus	69	71	74	67	281	T5
Tommy Aaron	69	72	72	69	282	T7
Raymond Floyd	71	71	69	71	282	T7
Lionel Hebert	72	71	71	68	282	T7
Jerry Pittman	70	73	70	69	282	T7
Gary Player	72	67	71	72	282	T7

April 10-13, 1969

George Archer	67	73	69	72	281	1
Billy Casper	66	71	71	74	282	T2
George Knudson	70	73	69	70	282	T2
Tom Weiskopf	71	71	69	71	282	T2
Charles Coody	74	68	69	72	283	T5
Don January	74	73	70	66	283	T5
Miller Barber	71	71	68	74	284	7
Tommy Aaron	71	71	73	70	285	T8
Lionel Hebert	69	73	70	73	285	T8
Gene Littler	69	75	70	71	285	T8

April 9-13, 1970

Billy Casper	72	68	68	71	279		
						69	1
Gene Littler	69	70	70	70	279		
						74	2
Gary Player	74	68	68	70	280		3
Bert Yancey	69	70	72	70	281		4
Tommy Aaron	68	74	69	72	283		T5
Dave Hill	73	70	70	70	283		T5
Dave Stockton	72	72	69	70	283		T5
Jack Nicklaus	71	75	69	69	284		8
Frank Beard	71	76	68	70	285		9
Bob Lunn	70	70	75	72	287		T10
Chi Chi Rodriguez	70	76	73	68	287		T10

April 8-11, 1971

Charles Coody	66	73	70	70	279	1
Johnny Miller	72	73	68	68	281	T2
Jack Nicklaus	70	71	68	72	281	T2
Don January	69	69	73	72	283	T4
Gene Littler	72	69	73	69	283	T4
Gary Player	72	72	71	69	284	T6
Ken Still	72	71	72	69	284	T6
Tom Weiskopf	71	69	72	72	284	T6
Frank Beard	74	73	69	70	286	T9
R. De Vicenzo	76	69	72	69	286	T9
Dave Stockton	72	73	69	72	286	T9

April 6-9, 1972

Jack Nicklaus	68	71	73	74	286	1
Bruce Crampton	72	75	69	73	289	T2
Bobby Mitchell	73	72	71	73	289	T2
Tom Weiskopf	74	71	70	74	289	T2
Homero Blancas	76	71	69	74	290	T5
Bruce Devlin	74	75	70	71	290	T5
Jerry Heard	73	71	72	74	290	T5
Jim Jamieson	72	70	71	77	290	T5
Jerry McGee	73	74	71	72	290	T5
Gary Player	73	75	72	71	291	T10
Dave Stockton	76	70	74	71	291	T10

April 5-9, 1973

Tommy Aaron	68	73	74	68	283	1
J.C. Snead	70	71	73	70	284	2
Jim Jamieson	73	71	70	71	285	T3
Jack Nicklaus	69	77	73	66	285	T3
Peter Oosterhuis	73	70	68	74	285	T3
Bob Goalby	73	70	71	74	288	T6
Johnny Miller	75	69	71	73	288	T6
Bruce Devlin	73	72	72	72	289	T8
Masashi Ozaki	69	74	73	73	289	T8
Gay Brewer, Jr.	75	66	74	76	291	T10
G. Dickinson	74	70	72	75	291	T10
Don January	75	71	75	70	291	T10
Chi Chi Rodriguez	72	70	73	76	291	T10

April 11-14, 1974

Gary Player	71	71	66	70	278	1
Dave Stockton	71	66	70	73	280	T2
Tom Weiskopf	71	69	70	70	280	T2
Jim Colbert	67	72	69	73	281	T4
Hale Irwin	68	70	72	71	281	T4
Jack Nicklaus	69	71	72	69	281	T4
Bobby Nichols	73	68	68	73	282	T7
Phil Rodgers	72	69	68	73	282	T7
M. Bembridge	73	74	72	64	283	T9
Hubert Green	68	70	74	71	283	T9

April 10-13, 1975

Jack Nicklaus	68	67	73	68	276	1
Johnny Miller	75	71	65	65	277	T2
Tom Weiskopf	69	72	66	70	277	T2
Hale Irwin	73	74	71	64	282	T4
Bobby Nichols	67	74	72	69	282	T4
Billy Casper	70	70	73	70	283	6
Dave Hill	75	71	70	68	284	7
Hubert Green	74	71	70	70	285	T8
Tom Watson	70	70	72	73	285	T8
Tom Kite	72	74	71	69	286	T10
J.C. Snead	69	72	75	70	286	T10
Lee Trevino	71	70	74	71	286	T10

April 8-11, 1976

Raymond Floyd	65	66	70	70	271	1
Ben Crenshaw	70	70	72	67	279	2
Jack Nicklaus	67	69	73	73	282	T3
Larry Ziegler	67	71	72	72	282	T3
Charles Coody	72	69	70	74	285	T5
Hale Irwin	71	77	67	70	285	T5
Tom Kite	73	67	72	73	285	T5
Billy Casper	71	76	71	69	287	8
Roger Maltbie	72	75	70	71	288	T9
Graham Marsh	73	68	75	72	288	T9
Tom Weiskopf	73	71	70	74	288	T9

Azaleas

April 7-10, 1977

Tom Watson	70	69	70	67	276	1
Jack Nicklaus	72	70	70	66	278	2
Tom Kite	70	73	70	67	280	T3
Rik Massengale	70	73	67	70	280	T3
Hale Irwin	70	74	70	68	282	5
David Graham	75	67	73	69	284	T6
Lou Graham	75	71	69	69	284	T6
Ben Crenshaw	71	69	69	76	285	T8
Raymond Floyd	71	72	71	71	285	T8
Hubert Green	67	74	72	72	285	T8
Don January	69	76	69	71	285	T8
Gene Littler	71	72	73	69	285	T8
John Schlee	75	73	69	68	285	T8

April 6-9, 1978

Gary Player	72	72	69	64	277	1
Rod Funseth	73	66	70	69	278	T2
Hubert Green	72	69	65	72	278	T2
Tom Watson	73	68	68	69	278	T2
Wally Armstrong	72	70	70	68	280	T5
Bill Kratzert	70	74	67	69	280	T5
Jack Nicklaus	72	73	69	67	281	7
Hale Irwin	73	67	71	71	282	8
Joe Inman	69	73	72	69	283	T9
David Graham	75	69	67	72	283	T9

April 12-15, 1979

Fuzzy Zoeller	70	71	69	70	280	
					4-3	1
Ed Sneed	68	67	69	76	280	
					4-4	T2
Tom Watson	68	71	70	71	280	
					4-4	T2
Jack Nicklaus	69	71	72	69	281	4
Tom Kite	71	72	68	72	283	5
Bruce Lietzke	67	75	68	74	284	6
Lanny Wadkins	73	69	70	73	285	T7
L. Thompson	68	70	73	74	285	T7
Craig Stadler	69	66	74	76	285	T7
Hubert Green	74	69	72	71	286	T10
Gene Littler	74	71	69	72	286	T10

April 10-13, 1980

Seve Ballesteros	66	69	68	72	275	1
Gibby Gilbert	70	74	68	67	279	T2
Jack Newton	68	74	69	68	279	T2
Hubert Green	68	74	71	67	280	4
David Graham	66	73	72	70	281	5
Gary Player	71	71	71	70	283	T6
Ben Crenshaw	76	70	68	69	283	T6
Ed Fiori	71	70	69	73	283	T6
Tom Kite	69	71	74	69	283	T6
Larry Nelson	69	72	73	69	283	T6
Jerry Pate	72	68	76	67	283	T6

April 9-12, 1981

Tom Watson	71	68	70	71	280	1
Johnny Miller	69	72	73	68	282	T2
Jack Nicklaus	70	65	75	72	282	T2
Greg Norman	69	70	72	72	283	4
Tom Kite	74	72	70	68	284	T5
Jerry Pate	71	72	71	70	284	T5
David Graham	70	70	74	71	285	7
Ben Crenshaw	71	72	70	73	286	T8
Raymond Floyd	75	71	71	69	286	T8
John Mahaffey	72	71	69	74	286	T8

April 8-11, 1982

Craig Stadler	75	69	67	73	284	
					4	1
Dan Pohl	75	75	67	67	284	
					5	2
Seve Ballesteros	73	73	68	71	285	T3
Jerry Pate	74	73	67	71	285	T3
Tom Kite	76	69	73	69	287	T5
Tom Watson	77	69	70	71	287	T5
Larry Nelson	79	71	70	69	289	T7
Curtis Strange	74	70	73	72	289	T7
Raymond Floyd	74	72	69	74	289	T7
Andy Bean	75	72	73	70	290	T10
Mark Hayes	74	73	73	70	290	T10
Fuzzy Zoeller	72	76	70	72	290	T10
Tom Weiskopf	75	72	68	75	290	T10

April 7-11, 1983

Seve Ballesteros	68	70	73	69	289	1
Ben Crenshaw	76	70	70	68	284	T2
Tom Kite	70	72	73	69	284	T2
Raymond Floyd	67	72	71	75	285	T4
Tom Watson	70	71	71	73	285	T4
Hale Irwin	72	73	72	69	286	T6
Craig Stadler	69	72	69	76	286	T6
Gil Morgan	67	70	76	74	287	T8
Dan Pohl	74	72	70	71	287	T8
Lanny Wadkins	73	70	73	71	287	T8

Clubhouse

April 12-15, 1984

Ben Crenshaw	67	72	70	68	277	1
Tom Watson	74	67	69	69	279	2
David Edwards	71	70	72	67	280	T3
Gil Morgan	73	71	69	67	280	T3
Larry Nelson	76	69	66	70	281	5
Ronnie Black	71	74	69	68	282	T6
David Graham	69	70	70	73	282	T6
Tom Kite	70	68	69	75	282	T6
Mark Lye	69	66	73	74	282	T6
Fred Couples	71	73	67	72	283	10

April 11-14, 1985

Bernhard Langer	72	74	68	68	282	1
Seve Ballesteros	72	71	71	70	284	T2
Raymond Floyd	70	73	69	72	284	T2
Curtis Strange	80	65	68	71	284	T2
Jay Haas	73	73	72	67	285	5
Gary Hallberg	68	73	75	70	286	T6
Bruce Lietzke	72	71	73	70	286	T6
Jack Nicklaus	71	74	72	69	286	T6
Craig Stadler	73	67	76	70	286	T6
Fred Couples	75	73	69	70	287	T10
David Graham	74	71	71	71	287	T10
Lee Trevino	70	73	72	72	287	T10
Tom Watson	69	71	75	72	287	T10

April 10-13, 1986

Jack Nicklaus	74	71	69	65	279	1
Tom Kite	70	74	68	68	280	T2
Greg Norman	70	72	68	70	280	T2
Seve Ballesteros	71	68	72	70	281	4
Nick Price	79	69	63	71	282	5
Tom Watson	70	74	68	71	283	T6
Jay Haas	76	69	71	67	283	T6
Payne Stewart	75	71	69	69	284	T8
Bob Tway	70	73	71	70	284	T8
Tommy Nakajima	70	71	71	72	284	T8

April 9-12, 1987

Larry Mize	70	72	72	71	285	
					4-3	1
Greg Norman	73	74	66	72	285	
					4-X	T2
Seve Ballesteros	73	71	70	71	285	
					5-X	T2
Ben Crenshaw	75	70	67	74	286	T4
Roger Maltbie	76	66	70	74	286	T4
Jodie Mudd	74	72	71	69	286	T4
Jay Haas	72	72	72	73	289	T7
Bernhard Langer	71	72	70	76	289	T7
Jack Nicklaus	74	71	73	70	289	T7
Tom Watson	71	72	74	72	289	T7
D.A. Weibring	72	75	71	71	289	T7

April 7-10, 1988

Sandy Lyle	71	67	72	71	281	1
Mark Calcavecchia	71	69	72	70	282	2
Craig Stadler	76	69	70	68	283	3
Ben Crenshaw	72	73	67	72	284	4
Fred Couples	75	68	71	71	285	T5
Greg Norman	77	73	71	64	285	T5
Don Pooley	71	72	72	70	285	T5
David Frost	73	74	71	68	286	8
Bernhard Langer	71	72	71	73	287	T9
Tom Watson	72	71	73	71	287	T9

April 6-9, 1989

Nick Faldo	68	73	77	65	283	
					5-3	1
Scott Hoch	69	74	72	69	283	
					5-X	2
Ben Crenshaw	71	72	70	71	284	T3
Greg Norman	74	75	68	67	284	T3
Seve Ballesteros	71	72	73	69	285	5
Mike Reid	72	71	71	72	286	6
Jodie Mudd	73	76	72	66	287	7
Chip Beck	74	76	70	68	288	T8
J.-M. Olazabal	77	73	70	68	288	T8
Jeff Sluman	74	72	74	68	288	T8

April 5-8, 1990

Nick Faldo	71	72	66	69	278	
					4-4	1
Raymond Floyd	70	68	68	72	278	
					4-X	2
John Huston	66	74	68	75	283	T3
Lanny Wadkins	72	73	70	68	283	T3
Fred Couples	74	68	72	69	284	5
Jack Nicklaus	72	70	69	74	285	6
Seve Ballesteros	74	73	68	71	286	T7
Bill Britton	68	74	71	73	286	T7
Bernhard Langer	70	73	69	74	286	T7
Scott Simpson	74	71	68	73	286	T7
Curtis Strange	70	73	71	72	286	T7
Tom Watson	77	71	67	71	286	T7

April 11-14, 1991

Ian Woosnam	72	66	67	72	277	1
J. M. Olazabal	68	71	69	70	278	2
Lanny Wadkins	67	71	70	71	279	T3
Tom Watson	68	68	70	73	279	T3
Ben Crenshaw	70	73	68	68	279	T3
Steve Pate	72	73	69	65	279	T3
Jodie Mudd	70	70	71	69	280	T7
Andrew Magee	70	72	68	70	280	T7
Ian Baker-Finch	71	70	69	70	280	T7
Tommy Nakajima	74	71	67	69	281	T10
Hale Irwin	70	70	75	66	281	T10

BALTUSROL GOLF CLUB

SPRINGFIELD, NEW JERSEY
U.S. Open: 1903, 1915, 1936, 1954, 1967, 1980, 1993

It is the only golf club named after a murder.

Baltus Roll was a farmer who owned a small patch of land outside the town of Springfield, New Jersey. A strange fellow, he had the habit of paying his bills with gold and silver coins which he carried in his stockings. This led the townfolk to speculate about what other riches he might have stashed at his home.

On the evening of Washington's Birthday, 1831, two men went up to Roll's farmhouse, knocked the door down, dragged him out, tied him and beat him, and left him face down in a puddle of icy water. They then ransacked the house, finding nothing. Roll's wife, who had fled into the woods, ran to a neighbor's house, and the neighbor returned to find Baltus Roll dead.

Shortly thereafter the police arrested Peter B. Davis, a local innkeeper, and Lycidias Baldwin, a derelict, and charged them with the murder. Davis was tried in nearby Newark and acquitted on a technicality but incarcerated instead on three counts of forgery. Baldwin fled to Morristown, where he killed himself in a room above a tavern.

Sixty-four years after the killers came Keller. A wealthy New Yorker and publisher of the New York Social Register, Louis Keller owned 100 acres in Springfield. In 1895, sensing that golf was beginning to catch on with the upper crust, he bought 500 more acres, hired Englishman David Hunter to design a nine-hole course, and started a golf club.

3rd hole

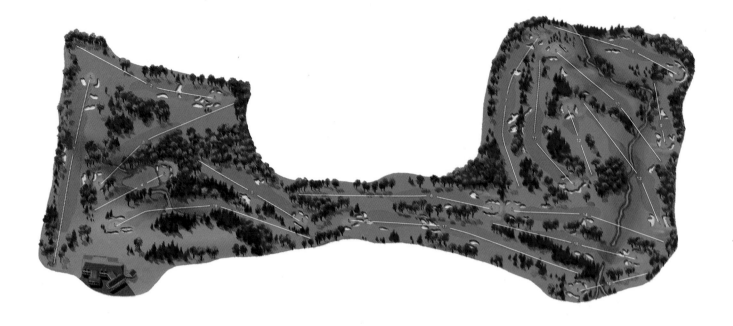

The layout measured 2372 yards and only two of the holes were longer than 300 yards, but the 9th was an incongruous par five of 517 yards. Apparently, after plotting the first eight holes, Mr. Hunter found himself well removed from the clubhouse.

When Keller learned that his course was situated at the scene of what the New York papers had called "the crime of the century," he christened the property "Baltusrol," compressing the victim's name while eschewing an opportunity for the golfingly homonymous "Balldoesroll."

In any case, by 1898 Keller had a full 18 holes and a full membership of socialites happily paying their annual dues of $10. Two years later Baltusrol held the first of its thirteen national championships, the 1901 U.S. Women's Amateur. It was won, for the first of two consecutive times, by Genevieve Hecker, who prevailed in the final match, 5 and 3, while decked out in a sailor hat, a starched collar, and a blouse with sleeves the size of watermelons.

Far less flamboyant was the winner of the next championship at Baltusrol, the first of the club's six U.S. Opens. Willie Anderson was a mysterious and laconic Scotsman who had emigrated from North Berwick in 1898 to become Baltusrol's first professional. Although the son of a pro, he had, by all accounts, played no golf in Scotland. But once in America, he mastered the game quickly and won the 1901 U.S. Open at Myopia Hunt Club in Boston.

At Baltusrol, two years later, his 72-hole score of 307 was twenty-four strokes lower than at Myopia, largely because of the introduction of the Haskell wound ball. Back then, they played the Open in two 36-hole days. At the halfway point Anderson, at 147, led by five strokes on the strength of his opening 73, then a course record. On day two, however, he slipped, recording a quintuple-bogey eight on one of the par threes (surely the only time in history that an Open Champion has won with an 8 on a par three) and

was caught by David Brown. In the 18-hole playoff next day, neither man distinguished himself, Anderson's 82 edging Brown's 84.

Anderson thus became the first player to win the U.S. Open twice. His victory at Baltusrol was also the first of three straight Open wins, an unparalleled achievement. With the third of those, he became the first man to win four Opens, a feat that has never been bettered, but has been matched by Messrs. Jones, Hogan, and Nicklaus.

On March 27, 1909, disaster struck the club when the original clubhouse burned to the ground. According to legend, this was a particularly unsettling event for at least one member, a philandering husband who arrived at his Manhattan home early on the morning of the 28th and told his wife that he had spent the night at Baltusrol. Without saying a word, the Mrs. handed him the morning paper, the front page of which carried a story on the fire.

The current clubhouse, a sprawling English manor, was constructed the same year at a cost estimated at $100,000. In 1989 a *GOLF Magazine* poll ranked that clubhouse as the second finest in the world, exceeded only by the Royal & Ancient Golf Club of St. Andrews. Indeed, so attractive was Baltusrol's physical plant that, during the late 1980s, rumors circulated that the club had captured the fancy of the acquisitive Japanese, their alleged interest spurred in part by the fact that in 1980 Isao Aoki had nearly won the Open here. Although club officials deny that a formal offer was ever made, one rumor held that each vested Baltusrol member stood to receive one million dollars. In any case, the suitors apparently were rebuffed in the early stages of courtship.

The arrival of the 1915 Open brought both the arrival and departure of Jerry Travers. Travers was unquestionably the most feared amateur of his era, a four-time U.S. Amateur Champion who was a terror at match play. But no one gave him much of a chance to win an Open, because at stroke play his game was suspect. The book on Travers said he was a fine putter and scrambler, but he had to be; his teeshots were erratic.

At Baltusrol, however, Travers confounded his critics. As he reached the halfway point of the final round he knew that if he could play the last nine holes in one under par, he would win. It was thus match play vs. Old Man Par. At the 10th, the driver got him in trouble—a slice out of bounds, followed by a hook into the rough on his next shot. In those days, the stroke-and-distance penalty didn't exist, and he managed to make four. At 11, he topped his drive but again saved par, this time with a thirty-five-foot putt. Then Travers settled down, got his requisite birdie at the 15th, and finished with three rock-solid pars. His score of 297 brought a one-stroke victory over Tom McNamara. Shortly thereafter, at the age of 28, Travers retired and became a cotton broker on Wall Street, thus setting a precedent for the next—and last—of the great amateurs, Bobby Jones.

Anderson and Travers won their Opens on a course that no longer exists. In 1920 the original 6189-yard par 74 layout was scrapped and two years later it was replaced by thirty-six holes, now known as the Upper and Lower Courses, both designed by a local genius named Albert W. Tillinghast.

Tillinghast, who lived in Harrington Park, New Jersey, and commuted by chauffeured limousine to his Manhattan office, was a golf architect and much more. The only son of a wealthy Philadelphia couple, he turned to architecture at age 32 after dabbling in a half dozen other pursuits. A visit to St. Andrews had turned him on to the game, and he became a good enough player to compete in several U.S. Amateurs, not to mention earning a twenty-fifth-place finish in the 1910 Open. He was equally adept at cricket, billiards, polo, and bridge. Tillinghast was also a writer of fiction and humor, credited with having added the word "birdie" to the golf lexicon; an advocate of public golf and one of the founding fathers of the PGA of America; an accomplished photographer; and a theater lover who was an angel for several Broadway plays.

Above all, however, Tillie the Terror knew how to design golf courses, including both layouts at Winged Foot, the San Francisco Golf Club, Ridgewood, and Quaker Ridge, all top-100 courses. At Baltusrol, he used the original land plus 172 newly purchased acres and designed not one but two completely new courses.

The Upper clings to the steep incline of one of the Watchung Mountains, and is thus characterized by sidehill lies, woodsy vistas, and fiercely fast, sloping greens. It is an enjoyable course for the members, but is not regarded as a full-blooded test of today's pros.

Nonetheless, it was the scene of one of the more dramatic—and probably the most controversial—Open victories in history. In 1936, Tony Manero, a driving range pro and the son of a Yonkers

When Tony Manero, an obscure driving-range pro, hit this opening teeshot in the final round of the 1936 Open, no one expected him to win. But his course-record 67 gave him a two-stroke victory over hapless Harry Cooper. Photo: UPI/Bettmann

grocer, had gotten into the Open by winning a three-hole playoff for the last qualifying place in his district. But at Baltusrol he was inspired, and in the final round, according to *Golfing Magazine*, "the trance that makes champions engulfed him and he won in a coma of furious and precise clouting and nerveless putting," shooting a 67 that took him from four strokes behind to a two-stroke victory over the luckless Harry Cooper.

Cooper, a perennial bridesmaid and likely the best golfer in history never to win a major championship, had played superb golf for three rounds. At the fifty-second hole, he had exploded from a bunker into the hole for a birdie, then sunk a 45-foot putt for another birdie at the fifty-third. His 211 total was a new three-round record, and fate appeared to be with him this time.

Cooper's final eighteen was also solid enough until the stretch run when he bogeyed three of the last five holes. Still, his score of 284 was a new Open record, and he seemed safe enough. He was in the clubhouse receiving congratulations when the word came in—Manero had played the front nine in 33 and then had birdied 12 and 13. Five under for the day, he had made up six strokes. If he could play par golf over the last few holes, he would win.

This is where the controversy came in. Manero's companion that day was Gene Sarazen, the wily campaigner who had already won himself a Grand Slam and much more. Throughout the final hour of play, Sarazen calmed his friend with encouraging words. But several reporters claimed that Sarazen had also given Manero advice on club selection, a clear violation of the Rules. After Manero finished at 282, the press raised a formal complaint. The USGA met behind closed doors for over an hour, then announced that Manero's victory would stand.

Two footnotes accompany this Open. First, during the week of the Championship the USGA met with the leading golf ball makers and decided that it would be inadvisable to attempt to build any greater distance into the golf ball. Note the word "inadvisable." This was in the days before the USGA had established strict limits on the performance of balls. Second, this was the site of Ben Hogan's first Open appearance (he missed the cut); in 1967 it would become the site of his last appearance as well.

Baltusrol's Lower Course, site of the 1954, 1967, and 1980 Opens, is a flatter, more open design that lacks the bucolic charm of the Upper. Stark and stern, its difficulty comes from its length (a par 70 of 7076 yards), its 126 cunningly placed bunkers, and its testing par fours. The 1954 Champion, Ed Furgol, likened the course to Augusta National "only 60 percent tighter off the tees."

Those hard par fours begin right at the 1st hole, a par five that Robert Trent Jones converted to a four as part of a strengthening job prior to the 1954 Open. Two fairway bunkers—one on each side of the fairway—narrow the teeshot landing area, with out of bounds farther to the left, a creek farther to the right. Still, this is not a drive that should be smoothed into position, since the hole is 465 yards long.

Sam Snead's opening teeshot in 1954 hit the OB fence and came to rest right next to it; undaunted, the Slammer turned an 8-iron upside down and slapped a left-handed shot 160 yards. But surely no one had more trouble getting off this tee than Seve Ballesteros. In the 1980 Open, the reigning British Open Champion arrived seven minutes late for his Thursday tee time and was disqualified. He exploded in anger at officials but then accepted his fate. When asked later that year what effect the incident had had on him, he smiled and said, "I got a contract from Rolex."

In the 1967 Open, Deane Beman had a more auspicious start. Playing in just his second tournament as a professional, Beman holed-out a 230-yard 4-wood for eagle. That week he played number one in just twelve strokes, adding two birdies and a par. Four under on this hole, he was eight over on the rest of the course and eventually tied for sixth place.

There's more out of bounds to the left of the 2nd hole, with the teeshot tightened by cross bunkers at the 260 mark, forcing the pros to lay up with long irons or fairway woods, then pitch to a bunker-flanked green that tilts from right to left. Number 3 plays from one chute of trees to another chute of trees, doglegging left and downhill to a humpbacked green. The small creek several yards in front of the green does not concern the pros as much as the large bunker beyond it.

The most photographed hole at Baltusrol is undeniably the 4th, and anyone who judges the course from such photos is getting a false picture, as this 194-yard par three is totally out of character with the rest of the property. In contrast to the wide-open bigness of the Lower Course, this has a rather sylvan feeling, playing over a pond—the only substantial body of water on the course—to a green nestled in a stand of trees. It is not the original hole designed by Tillinghast but part of the redesign done by Robert Trent Jones. He added fifty yards to the length of the hole while also enlarging the green to accept a longer shot.

Jones was roundly criticized for making the hole too severe, but he effectively silenced his detractors the first time he played the hole. In a group with 1954 Open Chairman C.P. Burgess and club pro Johnny Farrell, Jones stepped up and struck his teeshot into the hole for an ace. "Gentlemen, the defense rests," he said. "I think the hole is eminently fair."

The hole has continued to summon the sublime and the ridiculous. In the 1980 Open, Tom Watson hit an 8-iron that struck the green two inches in back of the hole and then sucked back in for an ace. On the other hand, one member is said to have thrown his entire bag of clubs into the pond. His name—perhaps appropriate—was Henry Topping.

The hardest hole in the past three Opens has been number 6, a par four of 470 yards where accuracy and length are equally vital. Its

OPPOSITE: *4th hole*

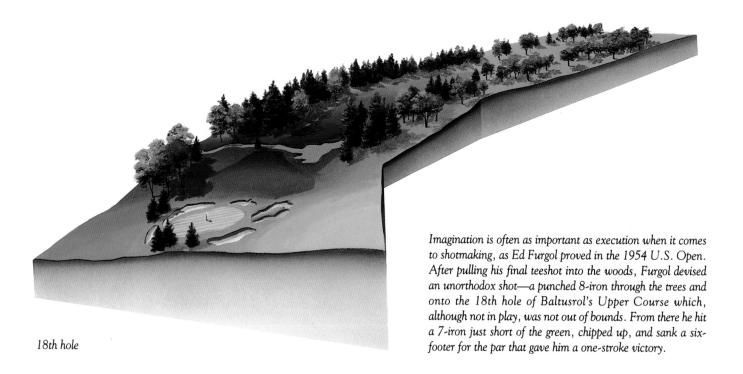

18th hole

Imagination is often as important as execution when it comes to shotmaking, as Ed Furgol proved in the 1954 U.S. Open. After pulling his final teeshot into the woods, Furgol devised an unorthodox shot—a punched 8-iron through the trees and onto the 18th hole of Baltusrol's Upper Course which, although not in play, was not out of bounds. From there he hit a 7-iron just short of the green, chipped up, and sank a six-footer for the par that gave him a one-stroke victory.

undulating fairway is lined with bunkers and trees, and although the green is large, like most greens on this course it is closely bunkered. Besides, it must be approached with a long iron and wood, often from some sort of uphill, downhill, or sidehill lie.

Anyone who can hurdle 6 with a par has another tall assignment at the 7th, another members' par five that Trent Jones transformed into a 470-yard four. It doglegs right, and the dogleg is cuttable but for the presence of two big bunkers smack in the gambler's line. The green is the widest on the course, but not very deep, and behind it is an out of bounds fence. This was a pivotal hole in the Palmer-Nicklaus battle for the 1967 Open, Nicklaus sinking a twenty-two-foot putt as Palmer missed from close range.

The pros play almost nothing but par fours until they get to the 16th hole—twelve of the first fifteen holes are two-shotters. But Baltusrol's finish is "odd"—a three followed by back-to-back fives. The 16th green on the original course was surrounded by water; today it is almost completely ringed with sand. The longest of four long par threes, it plays 216 yards from a slightly elevated tee. This is the green that is closest to the mountain slope, and it is probably the most treacherous to putt. In 1954 Gene Littler failed to note the influence of the mountain, and thereby missed a crucial three-footer in his stretch battle for the title.

The 17th is a 623-yard examination in patience, power, and positioning. The drive must carry 230 yards just to reach the fairway. From there, the second must be played across the Sahara Desert, a mass of sand that crosses the fairway at about the 400-yard mark. After that it's uphill to a plateau green with seven more bunkers guarding front and left. In all there are fourteen bunkers on the hole.

In the 1926 U.S. Amateur—the only Amateur from 1924 to 1928 that Bobby Jones did *not* win, Jones came to this hole battling with George Von Elm in the morning half of the final match. After Jones made his putt for par here the crowd stampeded to the 18th tee, unsettling Von Elm, who faced a three-footer for a halve. Recognizing the situation, Jones conceded the putt to his opponent. Ironically, in the afternoon round it was on 17 that Jones lost the title to Von Elm, 2 and 1.

It is a testimony to Jones's power that, in 1926, when the 18th hole measured 526 yards, he regularly reached the green in two with a 2-iron approach. Today, the hole is only a few yards longer, yet even with our vastly improved clubs and balls few players go for this green with an iron. A creek running down the left side and then cutting across the fairway discourages all but the foolhardy from trying to cut yardage off this right-to-left dogleg. But a teeshot too far to the right will take the green out of reach. In any case, the assignment will be to carry a nest of bunkers to a relatively shallow plateau green. When Tillinghast designed this hole, only two superb shots could reach it, and that remains the case today.

When the pros arrived for the '54 Open, they found a course of 7060 yards, making it the longest par 70 in Open history. And the course took its toll. A 69 by Billy Joe Patton, the irrepressible amateur who had come within a stroke of stealing that year's Masters from Hogan and Snead, was the only score under par in the first round. Patton then ballooned to 76 the next day, relinquishing the top spot to Gene Littler, the reigning Amateur Champion, a 23-year-old who had turned pro only a few months earlier. Littler, at 139, led the defending Open Champion Ben Hogan by two. But the next day both champions collapsed, as Patton had, with 76s, leaving the lead to Ed Furgol, a 37-year-old club pro from St. Louis whose left arm was permanently bent at a 70-degree angle, the result of a childhood accident that had never mended properly.

Sinking a 50-foot putt for birdie on the 54th hole, Furgol had taken a one-stroke lead over Dick Mayer, three over Littler. In the final round Furgol played flawlessly from tee to green but putted miserably, missing eight birdie opportunities of fifteen feet or less. Both Mayer and Littler gained ground, and the tournament wasn't settled until 18. Mayer, tied with Furgol and playing just ahead of him, sliced his last teeshot into pine trees, had to play a second drive, and finished with a double-bogey 7 for 286. Furgol thus needed only to avert a similar disaster. But his own teeshot looked just as bad as Mayer's, a pull hook that dived into the left woods that separate the Lower Course from the Upper.

He had a swing but no opening to the fairway—at least not to the fairway of the hole he was playing. But he did have a play up the 18th hole of the Upper Course—in fact, he remembered Hogan doing the same thing after a poor drive in an earlier round—so that is the way he went. "Taking an 8-iron for the most critical shot of my career," he wrote later, "I cut the ball through the opening with a silent prayer." From there he hit a 7-iron just short of the green, chipped to six feet, and made the putt for a par five.

Furgol didn't know it then, but he needed that putt. Just behind him, Littler had pulled to within a stroke. Moments later, Littler stood over a nine-foot birdie putt to tie, but he missed it and Ed Furgol, in the tradition of Jerry Travers and Tony Manero, became the dark-horse Champion.

The '54 Open was also marked by two "firsts," both of them signs of the increased popularity of the game. It was the first time that an Open was televised nationally, by NBC TV. And it was the first time that the Open fairways were cordoned off. Ten miles of rope and 2,000 stakes were used to separate the gallery from the players. Architect Jones had suggested the idea, as much to protect his

course as to protect the players. Today, it is standard operating procedure at all professional events.

The last two Opens at Baltusrol have not gone to dark horses; they have been won by the Golden Bear. In 1967, Jack Nicklaus set a new 72-hole Open record of 275; then, in 1980, he lowered that mark to 272. Among the U.S. Open sites, no course holds sweeter memories for Nicklaus than Baltusrol.

It was at Baltusrol in 1967 that Lee Trevino burst onto the scene, finishing fifth. This was also the year that Marty Fleckman, an amateur from the University of Houston, led the first and third rounds before collapsing with an 80.

But the big story was the two players just in back of Fleckman after fifty-four holes—Arnold Palmer and Nicklaus. This Open arguably marks the changing of the guard from Palmer to Nicklaus. This was a rivalry that had burned hot ever since Oakmont in 1962, where Jack had won his first Open in a playoff over Arnold. Prior to Oakmont, Palmer had won five major championships, Nicklaus none. In the years since Oakmont, the score had been Nicklaus six, Palmer three. After Baltusrol, Palmer would never win another major, while Nicklaus would take another dozen, for a record total of eighteen.

Paired together in the third round, the two superstars went at each other as if in match play, yet neither played well. Through the first sixteen holes there was not a birdie between them. At one point Nicklaus said, "Let's stop playing each other and play the

The changing of the guard, 1967. Arnold Palmer could only stand and watch as Jack Nicklaus stormed to a new U.S. Open record of 275. Photo: Marvin E. Newman for Sports Illustrated © Time Inc.

course." Finally Jack sank a twelve-footer for a four at 17, then both players made four at the last. With 18 to go they were tied, one back of Fleckman.

On Sunday Nicklaus birdied five holes on the front nine for a 31, shot 65, and beat Arnold by four. Coming to the 18th the only question was whether he could make the birdie 4 he needed to break Ben Hogan's 72-hole record. Nicklaus later recalled the moment. "I was scared," he said. "My teeshot was off to the right in the rough. I was forced to play short of the water on my second and now only a miracle would give me a birdie. I decided on a hard 1-iron and hit the best long iron I've ever hit to the front right side of the green twenty-two feet from the hole."

From there Nicklaus took out the putter he had borrowed from Deane Beman earlier in the week, a bull's-eye model with a white-painted face which he had nicknamed White Fang, and rolled the ball dead into the cup for the record 275.

Thirteen years later, an article in the 1980 U.S. Open program was entitled "Jack Will Be Back." It was a bold prediction, for Nicklaus was at a crossroads. Since 1975 he had won only one major championship, the '78 British Open at St. Andrews. More important, at the end of 1979 he had slipped to seventy-first place on the PGA Tour money list. Prior to that he had never finished lower than fourth.

But Baltusrol inspired him. In the opening round he came to 18 as he had in the last round of 1967, in need of a birdie to better an Open record, this time the 18-hole mark of 63. At the time, *GOLF Magazine* was offering a $50,000 bonus to anyone who could better either the one- or four-day record in any of the four majors. Nicklaus, after three splendid shots, had left himself a four-footer for a 62. He was well aware of the bonus, and by his own admission he "chickened out" on the putt, blocking the ball to the right. Still, his 63—along with one by Tom Weiskopf—led the tournament.

His main challenger turned out to be not Weiskopf, his longtime friend and rival, but Isao Aoki of Japan. Using only fifty putts over the first thirty-six holes, Aoki shot 136, two in back of Nicklaus, who added a 71 to his opening round. Nicklaus's 134 was also an Open record. On Saturday a third straight round of 68 moved Aoki into a tie with Nicklaus, so on Sunday it became a matter of head-to-head match play.

After eight holes Jack was one ahead. Then Aoki bogeyed 9 and the lead was two. That was the way it remained. Each time Aoki seemed to make a move, Nicklaus was there to answer him, most

18th hole

dramatically at the 17th hole, where, after Aoki knocked his third shot to within five feet for a certain birdie, Nicklaus rammed home a twenty-footer for a four of his own. As it hit the hole, Jack raised his putter in the air, did a little dance, and screwed his face into a grin of pure joy, a picture that became the cover photo for a half dozen books and magazines.

At 18, both players broke the 72-hole record, Aoki stunning the huge—and hugely partisan—gallery with a pitch shot that nearly went into the hole for an eagle. Nicklaus, putting first, rolled in his birdie for the winning 272, three better than the mark he had set here in 1967. He thus won not only the tournament, but the GOLF

Magazine bonus that had eluded him in round one. After accepting the cheers of the crowd, Nicklaus raised his arms to call for quiet. Aoki still had a four-footer to stroke, and Jack knew that if Isao could make it, he too would be awarded the $50,000 bonus. Aoki knocked the ball dead center.

The Japanese was pleased with his finest finish ever in a major championship, but no one was happier than Nicklaus. On the enormous 18th hole scoreboard, the scorekeeper had spelled out a message that said it all: "Jack Is Back."

He will undoubtedly be back again when Baltusrol hosts a record seventh Open in 1993.

U.S. Open: June 26-27, 1903

Willie Anderson	149	76	82	307 83	1
David Brown	156	75	76	307 84	2
Stewart Gardner	154	82	79	315	3
Alex Smith	154	81	81	316	4
Donald Ross	158	78	82	318	5
Jack Campbell	159	83	77	319	6
L. Auchterlonie	154	84	83	321	7
Findlay Douglas	156	82	84	322	8
John Hobens	157	82	84	323	T9
Willie Smith	161	83	79	323	T9
Alex Ross	165	78	80	323	T9

U.S. Open: June 15-18, 1915

Jerry Travers	148	73	76	297	1
Tom McNamara	149	74	75	298	2
R. MacDonald	149	73	78	300	3
Jim Barnes	146	76	79	301	T4
Louis Tellier	146	76	79	301	T4
Mike Brady	147	75	80	302	6
George Low	152	76	75	303	7
Fred McLeod	150	76	79	305	T8
Jock Hutchison	153	76	76	305	T8
George Sargent	152	79	75	306	T10
Jack Park	154	75	77	306	T10
Emmett French	156	75	75	306	T10
Gilbert Nicholls	159	73	74	306	T10
Tom Kerrigan	153	76	77	306	T10
Alex Campbell	151	74	81	306	T10
Wilfrid Reid	155	75	76	306	T10
Walter Hagen	151	76	79	306	T10

U.S. Open: June 10-12, 1936

Tony Manero	73	69	73	67	282	1
Harry Cooper	71	70	70	73	284	2
Clarence Clark	69	75	71	72	287	3
Macdonald Smith	73	73	72	70	288	4
Henry Picard	70	71	74	74	289	T5
Wiffy Cox	74	74	69	72	289	T5
Ky Laffoon	71	74	70	74	289	T5
Ralph Guldahl	73	70	73	74	290	T8
Paul Runyan	69	75	73	73	290	T8
Denny Shute	72	69	73	77	291	10

Waterfall

U.S. Open: June 17-19, 1954

Ed Furgol	71	70	71	72	284	1
Gene Littler	70	69	76	70	285	2
Dick Mayer	72	71	70	73	286	T3
Lloyd Mangrum	72	71	72	71	286	T3
Bobby Locke	74	70	74	70	288	5
Tommy Bolt	72	72	73	72	289	T6
Ben Hogan	71	70	76	72	289	T6
Shelley Mayfield	73	75	72	69	289	T6
Freddie Haas	73	73	71	72	289	T6
Billie Joe Patton	69	76	71	73	289	T6

U.S. Open: June 15-18, 1967

Jack Nicklaus	71	67.	72	65	275	1
Arnold Palmer	69	68	73	69	279	2
Don January	69	72	70	70	281	3
Billy Casper	69	70	71	72	282	4
Lee Trevino	72	70	71	70	283	5
Deane Beman	69	71	71	73	284	T6
Bob Goalby	72	71	70	71	284	T6
G. Dickinson	70	73	68	73	284	T6
Dave Marr	70	74	70	71	285	T9
Kel Nagle	70	72	72	71	285	T9
Art Wall	69	73	72	71	285	T9

U.S. Open: June 12-15, 1980

Jack Nicklaus	63	71	70	68	272	1
Isao Aoki	68	68	68	70	274	2
Tom Watson	71	68	67	70	276	T3
Keith Fergus	66	70	70	70	276	T3
Lon Hinkle	66	70	69	71	276	T3
Mark Hayes	66	71	69	74	280	T6
Mike Reid	69	67	75	69	280	T6
Mike Morley	73	68	69	72	282	T8
Hale Irwin	70	70	73	69	282	T8
Andy North	68	75	72	67	282	T8
Ed Sneed	72	70	70	70	282	T8

Scorecard

HOLE	YARDS	PAR
1	465	4
2	377	4
3	438	4
4	194	3
5	388	4
6	470	4
7	470	4
8	374	4
9	205	3
OUT	3381	34
10	454	4
11	428	4
12	193	3
13	393	4
14	409	4
15	430	4
16	216	3
17	630	5
18	542	5
IN	3695	36
TOTAL	7076	70

GOLF *Magazine* Rankings:
25th in the World
16th in the U.S.A.

PGA
U.S. Open

BELLERIVE COUNTRY CLUB

ST. LOUIS, MISSOURI
U.S. Open: 1965
PGA Championship: 1992

She was just a kid, but she was big for her age.

When the 1965 U.S. Open came to Bellerive Country Club, it was the youngest course ever to host the Championship, having been opened only five years before. At 7191 yards, Bellerive was also the longest test the Open had ever seen.

She was tough, too, and built to please a tough man—Hord Hardin. Yes, the same Hord Hardin who recently retired as Chairman of the Augusta National Golf Club, site of The Masters. A St. Louis banker, Hardin was hardly the master of Bellerive, but he was the golf chairman, a former club president, and a pretty fair player—good enough to have been the club champion twenty-two times through the course of five decades. He had also reached the semifinals of the Western Amateur when it had been held at Bellerive in 1949.

But that was the old Bellerive course. Designed in 1908 by Robert Foulis of St. Andrews, a disciple of Old Tom Morris and brother of British Open Champion James Foulis, the original eighteen holes had been fine for the generation of members who founded the club then known as the St. Louis Field Club. But Hardin was among a large group of members who had come to believe that the old Belle was past her prime. Besides, the St. Louis population had begun to shift westward and the Foulis course was to the north of the city, a lengthy trip for most of the members. When in the mid '50s the club agreed to purchase 353 acres of rolling farmland twenty-two miles west of the city, Hardin was put in charge of selecting an architect.

Displaying the same iron will he would bring to power a quarter century later at Augusta, Hardin went directly to the best man in the business—Robert Trent Jones—and pinned him to a deal.

"Trent came and inspected the property, then he told us he'd do the course and that his fee would be 10 percent of the total cost of the design and construction," Hardin recalls. "I told him that was ridiculous, since it only encouraged him to push up the cost of the job. Instead, I offered him a flat fee, and he took it."

The late '50s and early '60s were the height of the Trent Jones era of golf architecture, and Bellerive became one of his period pieces. Jones's trademarks were airport runway tees, broad fairways tightened by grasping, inkspot bunkers, and greens the size of polo fields. Bellerive has all of these, along with a few thousand trees—many of them uprooted from the old course and replanted on the new—plus a meandering creek that comes menacingly into play on nearly half the holes.

And then there is the wind, the southwest wind that invariably whistles off the Missouri River and into the faces of Bellerive's assailants as they play down the last few holes. The par-three 16th, for instance, a hole of 218 yards, can call for anything from a 7-iron, downwind, to a driver, into the teeth.

All but one of the par fours on the course is over 400 yards, and the first three of them—holes 1, 2, and 5—average nearly 440 yards. The toughest of that trio is the 5th, a 453-yarder whose narrow fairway is bordered by out of bounds on the left and a pond on the right. The fairway also tilts slightly toward the pond. This is followed by a par three of 198 yards to a 140-foot-long green that snakes along the edge of a pond. Three bunkers line the back of the green, making club selection difficult, even when the wind is not blowing.

In the 1965 Open no one reached either of the par fives—the 8th or the 17th—in two shots. For the 1992 PGA Championship there will be a third par five, and that one also promises to be untouchable. The 4th hole, formerly a 470-yard par four, has been stretched to 556 yards by Trent Jones, who returned in 1988 to give the course a modified facelift. Now, anyone who wants to reach this hole in two will have to hit a second shot that is both long and high, as this green, like so many at Bellerive, is elevated and guarded by flanking front bunkers.

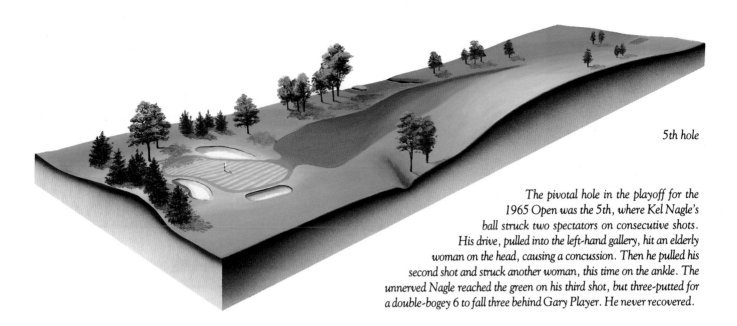

5th hole

The 8th doglegs 581 yards with a ditch cordoning the entire right side of the fairway. The wide green is bisected by a humpback, so the pitch shot had better find the correct side. For the Bellerive members, the 10th hole is longer than either 4 or 8, a brutish 576 yards, but for the pros this thickly wooded dogleg left is converted to a 470-yard par four where the second shot must be played over a creek to a shallow green that is hard to hold, having been designed to be attacked with a wedge, not a long iron. When Jones completed this hole, he declared it the hardest on the course.

The 373-yard 11th provides a brief breather, but then it's back to work at the 12th, another 460-yarder. It doglegs slightly left from an elevated tee where trees encroach from both sides. Bunkers dot the inside angle of the dogleg, and the lengthy second is played to a terraced green set into a hillside.

The hard push home begins at 14, where the green is 14,000 square feet—about thrice the size of an average green. It's an easy enough target to hit, but equally easy to three-putt if the approach shot doesn't finish within shouting distance of the flag. The long 15th, a par four of 456 yards, is guarded on the left by tall trees and on the right by bunkers and out of bounds. The second shot will be blind to all but the longest hitters, as this green sits on a plateau at the far side of a dip in the fairway.

In a major championship, any player who makes his par three at the 16th will gain ground on the field. And number 17, a whopping 614 yards, is unreachable when the tee is all the way back, a "hit-me-if-you-dare" hole when the tee is up, making it about 570 yards. But at any length the last 100 yards are over a lake.

The final hole has little romance or drama in its design; like the rest of the course, it's simply no-nonsense tough. A 454-yard dogleg left with out of bounds to the right, it plays to a large terraced green flanked by two cavernous bunkers.

When it opened on Memorial Day, 1960, Bellerive was a full-blooded examination in golf, capable of testing both the shotmaking and patience of the game's best players. And with the bicentennial of the city of St. Louis approaching in 1965, visions of a U.S. Open danced in the members' heads.

Once again, the club turned to Hardin, then a member of the USGA's Executive Committee (later to become the Association's President). He appealed to the USGA's sense of history and made an effective case. Indeed, he was able to shake up the Open schedule a bit. "The USGA had promised to take the championship to San Francisco in '65," Hardin recalls, "but we talked to the people at Olympic and they agreed to wait a year."

As the Open approached, some observers claimed that Bellerive should have been the course to wait a year, or maybe more. Some of the areas were raw, many of the transplanted trees were still saplings, and one fairway was lined with rows of grass that had not yet knitted together. Today, the USGA would never risk its biggest show on such speculative terrain.

The other topic on Open eve was the perennial question of who was favored to win. Virtually everyone envisioned a long hitter taming this long course—a Nicklaus, a Palmer, or perhaps a Souchak. Everyone, that is, except Gary Player. The peripatetic South African had a vision of his own.

Back then, the top players took the Open more seriously than they do today, to the extent that they arrived several days ahead to learn the nuances of the course. In '65, Player and Nicklaus came to Bellerive on the Wednesday before the week of the Open and played careful practice rounds, taking a half hour or so on each hole to learn the contours of the fairway, the vagaries of the wind, the consistency of the sand, the subtle slopes of the green. Nicklaus left after three days, but Player stayed until the Open began, playing the

OVERLEAF: *17th hole*

13th hole

course each day, then analyzing his rounds each night. When Nicklaus returned, he noticed a new Player, as he recalled it in his biography, *The Greatest Game of All:*

> I could see that his game was tuned to a very fine pitch. When he's swinging well, Gary doesn't have that lashing-down move at the start of his downswing that causes him to lose his balance at the finish. Then he's hitting the ball too hard for Gary Player. At Bellerive he was taking his hands back into a high position and starting them down smoothly. What is more, he wasn't trying to draw the ball; he was trying to hit it straight, which is the way Gary should play.

During those extra days Gary had not only improved his swing, he had had a mystical revelation. It seems there was a board near the Bellerive clubhouse on which were listed the names of all the past Open Champions. The last entry on the list was "Ken Venturi—1964." Player claims that once, while passing that board, he had a vision. "I saw—I mean I really *saw*—my own name under Venturi's. There it was in gold lettering just like his: '1965—Gary Player.'"

Those were the days when Player existed on a diet of wheat germ, raisins, bananas, nuts, honey, and intense exercise, and when he wore only one color—black—claiming it brought him extra

energy. In fact, he wore the same black polo shirt each day at Bellerive, washing it in his hotel room each night. He also played with black-shafted clubs, part of an endorsement of fiberglass shafts (although some have claimed that Gary's shafts were actually painted steel). Most important, however, these were the days when no one in the world, with the exception of Nicklaus, brought to a major tournament the combined talent, determination, and guts of Gary Player.

He opened with a 70, two strokes in back of 44-year-old Australian Kel Nagle, who would prove to be the only other man with a chance to win this championship. Palmer and Nicklaus, the two favorites, never even threatened. Arnie, who confessed to being baffled by the course, shot a pair of 76s and missed the cut for the first time in any event in four years. Jack had a 78 and never recovered.

A second 70 on Friday put Player one ahead of Nagle and Mason Rudolph. That left two rounds to go—and for the first time in U.S. Open history, that meant two days.

The experience a year earlier, with Ken Venturi barely staggering home in 100-degree heat at Congressional, had convinced the USGA that the 36-hole final day had become more of a test of endurance than of skill. It was also a relief for the USGA, which had found the task of moving seventy or so players through two rounds of golf a logistical nightmare, particularly in years when the weather was uncooperative. But the main reason may have been television. NBC had come to St. Louis with dozens of cameras and a crew of seventy-five because this would be the first Open to be telecast in color. The new format allowed them to present shows on both Saturday and Sunday—and that meant more income for the USGA. Bellerive was arguably the beginning of the big-money era for the not-for-profit USGA. Today the Association has expanded its staff and services many times over and has relocated from a modest townhouse in New York City to impressive headquarters on several hundred acres in Far Hills, New Jersey, thanks in large part to its lucrative contracts with the TV networks. The current deal with ABC is worth several million dollars per year and constitutes the lion's share of the USGA's income.

Player slipped a stroke over par on Saturday but managed to stretch his lead to two strokes over Nagle and now Frank Beard. On Sunday, Nagle got back within a stroke with four holes to go but then came a cropper at 15, catching a bunker on his teeshot and then three-putting for a double-bogey 6. "I've blown it," he said, and it seemed as if he had. With three holes to go Player had a three-stroke lead.

But then it was Gary's turn to crack. At the par-three 16th he skied his teeshot and it pelted down into the bunker at the right-front of the green. From a semiburied lie he managed to get the ball within fifteen feet, but then three-putted. Meanwhile Nagle, playing one hole ahead of him, was sinking a putt for birdie 4 at the 17th. Suddenly, they were tied, and that's how the seventy-two holes ended. Nagle shot 69, Player 71, for 282.

The playoff was unremarkable except for its early turning point, at the 5th hole. With Player one up, Nagle took a big swing at his drive and pulled it into the gallery, where it struck an elderly woman

in the forehead, knocking her temporarily unconscious. Visibly shaken and still in the rough, Nagle again pulled the ball on his second shot and, incredibly, hit another woman, this time in the ankle. He played the rest of the hole in a half daze, reaching the green in three and taking three putts for a nightmarish double-bogey 6. Player's lead was three strokes and that became his margin of victory—71 to 74.

Player thus became the first foreign winner of the Open since Englishman Ted Ray at Inverness in 1920. With this, his first U.S. Open victory, he joined Gene Sarazen, Ben Hogan, and Jack Nicklaus as the only players to win all four of the modern Grand Slam events, his three earlier victories being the 1958 PGA at Southern Hills, the 1959 British Open at Muirfield, and the 1961 Masters.

At the awards ceremony he announced that he was donating his entire $25,000 first prize to charity, $20,000 back to the USGA for junior golf and $5,000 to cancer research in memory of his mother, who had died of cancer. Then he went home and named his 125-acre timber farm near Johannesburg—he named it Bellerive.

In the past quarter century Player's timber farm has grown and matured, and so has its namesake. The Bellerive that hosts the 1992 PGA Championship will be a course of close to 7300 yards, playing to a par of 71. Trent Jones and Roger Rulewich have redesigned fifty of the eighty-two bunkers, replacing the cut lips with mounds and moguls, and have also created new greens at the 3rd, 12th, 13th, and 17th holes. Mother Nature has done some work too. All of those seedlings and saplings from 1965 are fully mature trees. Together with the water hazards, the bunkers, and the out-of-bounds markers, they will make Bellerive a stern test of accuracy as well as strength.

Superstitious Gary Player wore the same black polo shirt five days in a row en route to victory in the 1965 Open. Photo: AP/Wide World Photos

U.S. Open: June 17–21, 1965   *Scorecard*

Gary Player	70	70	71	71	282	
					71	1
Kel Nagle	68	73	72	69	282	
					74	2
Frank Beard	74	69	70	71	284	3
Julius Boros	72	75	70	70	287	T4
Al Geiberger	70	76	70	71	287	T4
Bruce Devlin	72	73	72	71	288	T6
Raymond Floyd	72	72	76	68	288	T6
Tony Lema	72	74	73	70	289	T8
Gene Littler	73	71	73	72	289	T8
Dudley Wysong	72	75	70	72	289	T8

HOLE	YARDS	PAR
1	434	4
2	437	4
3	170	3
4	556	5
5	453	4
6	198	3
7	401	4
8	581	5
9	426	4
OUT	3656	36
10	470	4
11	373	4
12	457	4
13	180	3
14	411	4
15	456	4
16	222	3
17	614	5
18	454	4
IN	3637	35
TOTAL	7293	71

British Open

CARNOUSTIE

CARNOUSTIE, SCOTLAND
British Open: 1931, 1937, 1953, 1968, 1975

One by one they came. On steamships from the North Sea, first to the East—to Boston and New York and Philadelphia—then to Atlanta and Chicago and Detroit and the West. Wearing old brown shoes and floppy tweed caps, their wind-reddened faces etched with determination, they came to teach golf to America. To teach the game, and to play it, to fashion our equipment, to design our courses, and to maintain them.

By 1925, 300 such men had come and assumed positions as golf professionals at the best clubs in the United States. All had come from the same tiny town on Scotland's Firth of Tay—Carnoustie.

The nickname "Auld Gray Toon" has been given to nearby St. Andrews, eleven miles across the bay, but Carnoustie, always in the golfing shadow of St. Andrews, seems older and grayer. Whereas St. Andrews, by the turn of the twentieth century, was already a busy center of learning, religion, and seaside recreation, the more remote Carnoustie remained a drab little community of millworkers, blacksmiths, and artisans, a place where, according to Henry Longhurst, the big event of the week was the arrival of the local fish train.

It is therefore arguable that the dour citizens of this village on the Angus Coast were even more hopelessly "given up" to the game than were their more celebrated neighbors in Fife. After all, since the sixteenth century Carnoustie has been a hotbed of golf—and nothing else.

Ben Hogan didn't have good things to say about the Carnoustie course, but he recalls the 1953 British Open as his most satisfying victory. Photo: AP/Wide World Photos

Until well into this century the Carnoustie course was comparatively unheralded and untested except by the residents of Carnoustie. But that all changed in 1931 when the British Open came here for the first time.

What the contestants encountered was a long, hard course—at 7200 yards unquestionably the longest and perhaps the hardest in Open history. It was a course on which no one had ever broken 70, and after four days of assault by 109 of the world's best players, it remained that way.

Fittingly, this first Open at Carnoustie was won by a Scotsman who had emigrated to America to become a golf professional. Tommy Armour, a native of Edinburgh, was said to talk, write, teach, and play the game better than anyone except the incomparable Bobby Jones. When he arrived in Carnoustie, he had already won several titles, including the 1927 U.S. Open and the 1930 PGA. But this was the victory he would cherish most.

After three rounds Armour trailed Argentina's José Jurado by three strokes, but in strong shifting winds Armour completed the tournament with a gritty 71. Macdonald Smith, one of the local boys who had gone to America, needed to finish in par 3-4-5 to win, but instead made 5-6-5 and finished three back, and the dark horse Jurado came to the final hole thinking he needed a 5 to tie. He made it, only to discover that his information had been wrong—he had needed a 4.

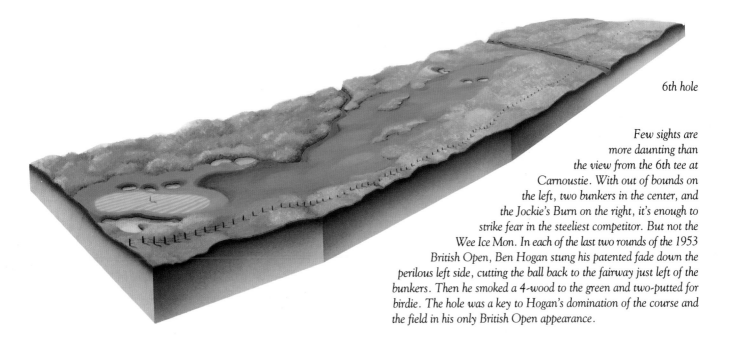

6th hole

*Few sights are
more daunting than
the view from the 6th tee at
Carnoustie. With out of bounds on
the left, two bunkers in the center, and
the Jockie's Burn on the right, it's enough to
strike fear in the steeliest competitor. But not the
Wee Ice Mon. In each of the last two rounds of the 1953
British Open, Ben Hogan stung his patented fade down the
perilous left side, cutting the ball back to the fairway just left of the
bunkers. Then he smoked a 4-wood to the green and two-putted for
birdie. The hole was a key to Hogan's domination of the course and
the field in his only British Open appearance.*

The diminutive, feisty Armour became the prototype for the four players who were to follow him as conquerors of Carnoustie; all of them were men of small stature and immense will. Perhaps the most impressive of this quartet was Henry Cotton, who in 1937 triumphed over not only the best players in Britain and Europe but the entire U.S. Ryder Cup Team, not to mention Mother Nature. In *GOLF Magazine*, Al Laney, the stylish *New York Tribune* reporter, vividly recalled the final day:

Before dawn there came a storm of rain, a steady downpour, relentless, unyielding and driven from the sea with sweeping force by a blustery wind, cold and drenching. Before noon the low-lying first green was under, play had to be stopped while it was cleared, and there was a real possibility that the whole course would become unplayable. A more melancholy golfing scene I have never witnessed, but conditions grew so much worse by afternoon that one began to remember the morning as not so bad.

Cotton fought grimly and methodically, matching his compact three-quarter swing against the elements and the course. With a virtually flawless 71—the same score Armour had closed with six years earlier—he won by two strokes. "Like Hogan he gave an impression of coldness," wrote Laney "but there was also the feeling as with Hogan that the ball had been given no option, and that there was nothing he could not achieve." It was the second of three Open Championships for the best British golfer of the mid-century. Cotton died in 1987 not long after he had been knighted by the Queen.

In 1953 Ben Hogan came to Carnoustie, a man with a mission. He had been to Britain only once before, with the 1949 Ryder Cup Team, but that was shortly after the bus accident that nearly killed him, so he was unable to play. This time he meant business. Earlier in the year Hogan had won the Masters and U.S. Open. A win at Carnoustie would give him a triple crown, the greatest feat since Jones won the Grand Slam in 1930.

With typical perspicacity Hogan arrived ten days before the championship and set about deciphering the course. He did not simply play it, he walked it—backwards—striding from green back to fairway, fairway to tee, to determine the best spots in which to position his approaches and drives. In his rounds he often hit two or three drives to different areas of the fairways, researching various angles of attack.

Hogan didn't think much of Carnoustie. He said the greens were "like putty" and offered to import a lawn mower from Texas, and he mocked the methods of the Scottish greenkeepers. "They just go out and seed a tee on level ground and then seed the green the same

In 1937, stylish Henry Cotton beat the entire U.S. Ryder Cup Team as well as Mother Nature in winning the second of his three Opens. At left is Charles Whitcombe, who finished fourth.

The grandstands are empty and it's a rainy Monday, but none of that bothers Tom Watson in 1975 as he two-putts the 18th hole to win the first of his five British Opens, in a playoff over Jack Newton. Photo: AP/Wide World Photos

way. In between they mow the grass for a fairway," he said. But by tournament time Hogan knew Carnoustie's bumps and rolls as intimately as any of the local caddies. By tournament time, he had also made a change in his swing, adapting to the bone-hard fairways that jarred his wrists at impact by switching to more of a picking technique that the Scots use.

The result is that he played perhaps the best golf of his life, beginning with a 73 and then improving with each round on scores of 71-70-68, the final round a course record that gave him a four-stroke victory. He later called this his most satisfying victory. "Certainly others were pleasurable," he said, "but none of them gave me the feeling, the desire to perform, that gripped me in Scotland."

Hogan became only the third player in history to win the U.S. and British Opens in the same year (the others were Jones and Sarazen) and the first to combine the two national championships with a win in The Masters. On his return to the States, Hogan was given a ticker tape parade in New York City.

The victory also put Hogan in Sarazen's company as the only players to win all four of the Grand Slam events. They were later joined by the next man to triumph at Carnoustie, Gary Player.

It was a struggle all the way for the tenacious little South African, who began the final day two strokes in back of Billy Casper, one behind Bob Charles, and one ahead of Jack Nicklaus. Not one of the four was able to equal par over the last eighteen, as a knifing

east wind made the 7252-yard course play both long and tight. Both Nicklaus and Player later declared Carnoustie the toughest course in the world.

Casper, who had led the championship by four strokes at the halfway mark, lost his game on the front nine and Player took the lead with Charles and Nicklaus a stroke behind. It was still anyone's title when, at the par-five 14th Player hit the shot that won the championship, a 3-wood approach that came to rest less than a yard from the flag for a tap-in eagle that gave him a two-stroke lead that became his margin of victory. Nicklaus and Charles tied for second.

In all, Nicklaus has finished second in the British Open an astonishing seven times, most dramatically at Turnberry in 1977 where he dueled head to head over the final 36 holes with Tom Watson as Watson seized the second of his five Open victories.

Watson's first had come two years earlier, at Carnoustie. It didn't come easily, despite the fact that the usual Carnoustie winds were comparatively quiet all week and the course had been softened by rain. What happened was that a number of strong players played strongly. After three rounds, twenty men were under par, and at least a dozen of them had a chance to win. A course record 66 had put South Africa's Bobby Cole at 204, twelve under par and one stroke ahead of young Australian Jack Newton. Johnny Miller was another stroke behind, with Watson a stroke in back of him. A large group of players at six under included the redoubtable Nicklaus.

With one hole to go, it was still a wide-open Open. Watson,

Newton, Miller, Nicklaus, and Cole all had chances, with 279 the score needed to reach a playoff. Nicklaus came first; needing a birdie, he could do no better than par. Watson also needed a birdie, and with a brave 25-footer, he got it, taking the lead in the clubhouse. Then came Miller, needing only a par to join Watson. But he found sand off the tee and made bogey. Finally there were Cole and Newton, the former needing a birdie to tie Watson, the latter a birdie to win. Both of them made pars, so it was Newton and Watson who faced off for 18 holes the next morning.

The playoff was also nip and tuck. Through thirteen holes they were all even. Then Watson played the pivotal shot of the day, a chip-in eagle from just short of the par-five 14th, only moments after Newton had laid his own shot dead to the hole for a birdie. But Watson gave the stroke back at the short 16th (if 235 yards may be said to be short), a hole that had given him fits all week. Both players made routine pars at 17, and both hit fine drives at the final hole. The critical difference was in their approach shots as Newton pulled his into the bunker and Watson found the green, thirty feet away. Newton blasted to ten feet, Watson two-putted and then stood to the side as Newton's last chance slid by the left side.

Historians will look back on this victory as the coming of age of Tom Watson. Although unquestionably a talented player, he had been labeled a choker largely because of his final-round collapses in the two previous U.S. Opens at Winged Foot and Medinah. The press stories said his swing—and his nerves—didn't hold up under pressure. But at Carnoustie Tom Watson won the battle with himself and began a remarkable run of form that would take him to four more British Opens, two Masters, and a U.S. Open within the following eight years. Thereafter he seemed to lose some of his putting touch and some of his fire. Since 1984, he has won only once.

For Newton, the ensuing years brought modest success and then tragedy. He went on to play the U.S. circuit and won the 1978 Buick Open before toppling to 173rd on the money list in 1981. Then in 1983 he suffered a freak accident, walking into the whirring propeller of a private airplane at the Sydney Airport. He lost his right arm. Today he is a TV commentator and golf writer in Australia.

The Watson-Newton playoff was the last 18-hole playoff in British Open history. The championship now uses a unique system involving stroke play over either four or five holes, depending upon the configuration of the hosting course. If the playoff ends in a tie, it's sudden death from there forward. A different four holes are chosen for each venue—usually those running most closely to the clubhouse. At Carnoustie the playoff holes likely would be number 1 plus the last three. But at Carnoustie, any four holes would do nicely. All 18 are good, all 18 are tough.

"It is a giant of a course," wrote Patric Dickinson, "and like a

1st hole

giant it can flick you to perdition with its little finger. But on the whole it is a friendly giant who prefers not to show his strength but to defeat you by wiles which one would, rather, attribute to a midget—by cunning changes of direction, by narrowing, subtle ditches, and by the winding of the Barry Burn."

It was designed in 1839 by the man generally considered to be the first professional golfer, Allan Robertson of St. Andrews, who plotted ten holes along the flat stretch of sandy subsoil beside the Firth of Tay. Robertson's longtime rival, Old Tom Morris, redesigned the course in 1867 and added the eight holes that brought it up to the number that St. Andrews had made standard. In 1926 James Braid added a few new tees, greens, and bunkers, and five years later, after the steel shaft had made some of those bunkers obsolete, a Dundee accountant named James Wright did another redesign and removed several of them. According to Wright, "Too many bunkers on a course are a misery to mediocre players, no inconvenience to good players, and a financial burden."

The fairways of Carnoustie are humpy but not bumpy, the greens are contoured but not sloped. It is fair and honest golf, with no crazy bounces, few blind shots. No more than two consecutive holes play in the same direction, thus making the journey interesting no matter from which direction the wind may blow. And weaving through it all, adding an element that is virtually absent from the other rota courses, is the steep-sided Barry Burn. In play on the 10th, 17th and 18th holes, and in mind on a couple of others, it can range in width from two to twenty-five feet. Its tributary, Jockie's Burn, menaces four holes on the front.

Carnoustie has what is arguably the strongest collection of par fours in the British Isles. There are twelve of them, ranging from 372 to 464 yards, five of 450 yards or longer. Moving left, right, and straight, some with the wind, others against, some lined with out of bounds, others with water or woods or gorse. No two of them are remotely similar.

First-tee jitters can be fatal, with Jockie's Burn crossing the fairway a few yards in front of the blocks, ready to catch a topped drive. But the opening hole is a relatively benign par four over a rise to a green set in a little valley all its own. In the opening round of the '53 Open, Hogan hit a 2-iron into the wind for his approach; downwind the next day, he got home with a wedge.

Number 2 is a marvelous left-to-right dogleg that is as beautiful an example of linksland golf as one can find. It snakes naturally along the base of a sandhill which runs down its right side and finishes at a two-tiered green nestled in a mini-amphitheater. A round pot bunker sits smack in the middle of the driving area, causing a fair amount of controversy. Horton Smith once smacked a beautiful teeshot here.

"Ye're in the boonker," his caddie said.

"Why, I don't think so," said Smith. "I never hit a better drive in my life."

"Nivertheless, ye're in the boonker," was the reply.

Great short par fours started in Scotland, and the third at Carnoustie is one of them. Although only 336 yards, it demands constant care, first with an iron teeshot to avoid a mini-forest called a sea woods. From there it's a ticklish wedge to a small green perched just on the other side of Jockie's Burn.

The course takes on a heath-and-heather look at the 4th and 5th, the latter hole doglegging gracefully to the right with Jockie's Burn crossing the fairway at the 270-yard mark. The two-tiered green, shared with number 14, may be the stiffest putting assignment on the course. The pivotal shot in Ben Hogan's final round came at the sloping green of the 5th, a left-to-right dogleg where, from a ticklish lie on the edge of a bunker, he chipped the ball fifty feet into the hole for a birdie.

Hogan followed with another birdie at the 6th, one of the more psychologically daunting par fives in the game. The teeshot must avoid Jockie's Burn on the right, a pair of bunkers in the center, and out of bounds on the left. Into the wind, that can be a tall order. The second shot is complicated by the burn, which juts halfway across the fairway at just about the point where a good second shot would land.

Jack Nicklaus has less than happy memories of number 6. In the final round of the 1968 Open he hooked his teeshot out of bounds. It cost him two shots, and that was the margin by which he failed to catch Gary Player. Twenty years later, when asked if he could pick one "mulligan" from his career—one shot on which he would like to have a second chance—Nicklaus unhesitatingly chose that teeshot at number 6.

Out of bounds continues to haunt the left side of holes 7, 8, and 9, the last of these also lined on the left by a deep, dark forest of evergreens that looks as if it has been transplanted from Banff or Pinehurst.

Each of Carnoustie's holes has a name as well as a number, and the award for most exotic name goes to the 10th, South America. According to legend, a young Carnoustie resident, David Nicoll, had intended to emigrate to South America to seek his fortune. However, the night before his departure his friends threw a high-octane farewell party for him and Nicoll overindulged. He ended up asleep in a spinney near the 10th tee, and never did make his journey.

The hole seems out of character, not only with Carnoustie but with links courses everywhere. The fairway is absent of bumps and rolls, there are trees and bushes down the left side, a stream (the Barry Burn) running in front of the green, and more trees—tall ones—just to the right of the putting surface. Into a stiff wind, no one tries to reach this 414-yard par four in two. Downwind, the teeshot may pitch into the steep face of any of five bunkers—four to the right side of the fairway, one to the left.

The 11th and 12th holes are comparative breathers, a straightforward par four followed by a heather-and-gorse-lined par five of 482 yards where accuracy is more important than power. They are followed by a short par three that plays hardest when it plays short-est, downwind. Stopping the ball on the surface of this bunker-sur-rounded green can be very difficult in a strong following breeze.

The true strength of Carnoustie is in its finishing stretch of five holes. Into a prevailing wind, it features one par three that could be a par four, one par four that could be a par five, and one par five that could be a par six. This is by general agreement the most fearsome finish in golf.

That par five is the 14th. At 482 yards it is about the same length as the 12th hole, but it never plays that way. Downwind, or in no wind, it can be easily reachable, as Gary Player and Tom Watson both proved with their final-round eagles en route to victory. It is a dogleg left, with the tee fronted by heather and gorse and no fair-way in sight. One bunker sits on the right side of the landing area, three lurk on the left, and to the left of them is out of bounds. The second shot of 200 yards must carry over a pair of cavernous bunkers that loom on a ridge in the center of the fairway. Despite the name of these twin bunkers—Spectacles—the approach is completely blind.

Number 15, a par four of 430 yards, doglegs left through a valley of terrain that banks contrarily from left to right, thus calling for a very carefully controlled teeshot. A series of bumps and ridges fronts the generous, low-lying green.

How hard is number 16? Ask Tom Watson. In five attempts in 1975—the four rounds of the Open plus the playoff—Watson failed to make par here. "The closest I came was lipping out a 40-footer," he said. From the championship tees, it plays 250 yards to a green that is shaped like an overturned cereal bowl, tossing errant shots right and left into bunkers. In the windy final round of the 1968 Open, the entire field teed off with drivers and only Jack Nicklaus reached the pin. Perhaps no par three anywhere is more demand-ing of length with accuracy.

Enjoy the 17th hole the first time you play it; after that you'll be terrified. Barely visible except for its bridges, the Barry Burn snakes across this fairway three times, the last time at the 260-yard mark, with the result that you can find water with a hook, a slice, or a straight shot. And just to complicate matters, a bunker sits in the center of the fairway at about 220 yards. The overall impression is that of a mine field. In 1968, Nicklaus solved this puzzle by rearing back and hitting a colossal drive that flew over all the trouble and came to rest 350 yards away.

A similar challenge awaits at the final tee, where the burn some-

13th hole

12th hole

how manages to present itself first on the left and then the right side of the fairway. It runs down that right side and then crosses one last fiendish time, just in front of the green, where it is also at its greatest width, twenty-five feet. The left side of the fairway offers little solace, only an out-of-bounds fence.

Originally a par four, the 18th played as a par five in 1937 and also in 1953, when Frank Stranahan, the muscular amateur from Toledo, eagled it twice on the final day to finish second to Henry Cotton. It remained a par five in 1953 and 1968 before reverting to a four in 1975, a par four that requires two shots of surpassing accuracy as well as length. This is unquestionably the toughest finishing hole on any British championship course. Into a wind, it may be the toughest finishing hole in the world.

Just behind this monumental test of golf sits an architectural embarrassment. The Carnoustie clubhouse looks like an abandoned 1950s elementary school. But it does remind us that this remains a simple, unpretentious town with a public course, a public treasure, that anyone can enjoy.

It is a subject of international regret that Carnoustie has not hosted an Open since 1975. Originally, poor course condition had something to do with this, but today the agronomy and maintenance are improved, so the main impediment is the lack of sufficient hotel accommodations in the area. However, the Dundee area, ten miles away, is expanding and among all knowledgeable golfers there is hope for a return. For, as the late Pat Ward-Thomas, golf correspondent for *The Guardian* once wrote, "Rarely can it be said of any course that it has no weaknesses. But it can be said of Carnoustie."

An early photo of the 18th hole. A par four in the 1931 Open, it played as a five in 1937, 1953, and 1968 before reverting to a four in 1975.
Photo: © Nick Birch

British Open: June 3-5, 1931

Tommy Armour	73	75	77	71	296	1
Jose Jurado	76	71	73	77	297	2
Percy Alliss	74	78	73	73	298	T3
Gene Sarazen	74	76	75	73	298	T3
Macdonald Smith	75	77	71	76	299	T5
Johnny Farrell	72	77	75	75	299	T5
M. Churio	76	75	78	71	300	T7
W.H. Davies	76	78	71	75	300	T7
Arthur Lacey	74	80	74	73	301	9
Henry Cotton	72	75	79	76	302	10

British Open: July 7-9, 1937

Henry Cotton	74	72	73	71	290	1
Reg Whitcombe	72	70	74	76	292	2
Charles Lacey	76	75	70	72	293	3
C. Whitcombe	73	71	74	76	294	4
Byron Nelson	75	76	71	74	296	5
Ed Dudley	70	74	78	75	297	6
W. Laidlaw	77	72	73	76	298	T7
Alf Padgham	72	74	76	76	298	T7
Arthur Lacey	75	73	75	75	298	T7
Horton Smith	77	71	79	72	299	10

British Open: July 9-11, 1953

Ben Hogan	73	71	70	68	282	1
Frank Stranahan	70	74	73	69	286	T2
Dai Rees	72	70	73	71	286	T2
Peter Thomson	72	72	71	71	286	T2
Antonio Cerda	75	71	69	71	286	T2
R. De Vicenzo	72	71	71	73	287	6
Sam King	74	73	72	71	290	7
Bobby Locke	72	73	74	72	291	8
Peter Alliss	75	72	74	71	292	T9
Eric Brown	71	71	75	72	292	T9

British Open: July 11-14, 1968

Gary Player	74	71	71	73	289	1
Jack Nicklaus	76	69	73	73	291	T2
Bob Charles	72	72	71	76	291	T2
Billy Casper	72	68	74	78	292	4
Neil Coles	75	76	71	73	295	T5
Gay Brewer	74	73	72	76	295	T5
Al Balding	74	76	74	72	296	7
R. De Vicenzo	77	72	74	74	297	T8
Bruce Devlin	77	73	72	75	297	T8
Arnold Palmer	77	71	72	77	297	T8

British Open: July 9-12, 1975

Tom Watson	71	67	69	72	279	
					71	1
Jack Newton	69	71	65	74	279	
					72	2
Bobby Cole	72	66	66	76	280	T3
Jack Nicklaus	69	71	68	72	280	T3
Johnny Miller	71	69	66	74	280	T3
Graham Marsh	72	67	71	71	281	6
Peter Oosterhuis	68	70	71	73	282	T7
Neil Coles	72	69	67	74	282	T7
Hale Irwin	69	70	69	75	283	9
George Burns	71	73	69	71	284	T10
John Mahaffey	71	68	69	76	284	T10

Scorecard

HOLE	YARDS	PAR
1	406	4
2	464	4
3	345	4
4	381	4
5	391	4
6	575	5
7	395	4
8	172	3
9	475	4
OUT	3604	36
10	455	4
11	370	4
12	482	5
13	167	3
14	482	5
15	463	4
16	248	3
17	432	4
18	440	4
IN	3539	36
TOTAL	7143	72

GOLF *Magazine* Rankings:
23rd in the World
7th in the U.K.

CHERRY HILLS COUNTRY CLUB

DENVER, COLORADO
U.S. Open: 1938, 1960, 1978
PGA Championship: 1941, 1985

Assemble a dozen golf historians and ask each one to name the greatest U.S. Open in history, and you can bet on this—at least half of them will choose 1960 at Cherry Hills.

There has never been a tournament quite like it. It was the last Open Ben Hogan threatened to win, the first Open Jack Nicklaus threatened to win, and the only Open Arnold Palmer not only threatened to win, but did. In style.

Twenty-nine years old at the time, Palmer had won the Masters two months earlier, birdieing the 17th and 18th holes to edge Ken Venturi by a stroke. He was the favorite when he shouldered his way

1st hole

onto Cherry Hills's first tee in round one. But his opening drive brought trouble—a pushed shot into a ditch that resulted in a double-bogey 6.

From that point forward, Palmer was playing catch-up. A 72 left him four in back of Mike Souchak. After the second round, he was eight behind as Souchak, with a 67-135, broke the 36-hole Open record by three strokes; and after the morning round on Saturday, Palmer was still seven back.

Still, he hadn't counted himself out. At lunch with a few friends, Palmer said, "I wonder what would happen if I shot a 65?"

"Nothing," said Bob Drum, golf writer for the *Pittsburgh Press*, "you're out of it."

"The hell I am," Palmer said. "A 65 would give me 280 and that's the kind of score that wins Open Championships."

"Sure," said Drum wryly, "and if you go out and drive the first green, you might make a hole in one."

Palmer climbed onto the tee of that 346-yard hole like a prize-fighter entering a ring, then lashed a drive that bounced through the collar of rough and hopped onto the putting surface, twenty feet from the hole. Moments later he two-putted for a birdie that launched the most famous come-from-behind charge in a career full of famous come-from-behind charges. Palmer birdied six of the first seven holes, shot 30 on the front nine, 35 on the back, and hit his target—65-280—victory.

He had two very important pursuers—Hogan and Nicklaus. With six holes to go, Nicklaus had held a one-stroke lead, but at age 20 he lacked the intrepid putting he was later to patent. Three-

putts from short range at both 13 and 14 took him out of the fray.

After the round, Nicklaus's pairing partner observed, "I played 36 holes today with a kid who should have won this thing by 10 strokes." That pairing partner was Hogan, who didn't play too badly himself. In a one-day display of tee-to-green shotmaking that was extraordinary even by his standards, Hogan hit the first thiry-four greens he approached; it was the thirty-fifth that did him in.

Hogan was tied with Palmer as he stood on the 17th fairway. He had less than 100 yards for this third shot to the par five, with the pin cut close to the front of the green, just a few yards from the edge of the stream that encircles the green. He had two options—either pitch the ball safely to the middle of the green, thereby assuring a two-putt par but a less-than-likely birdie; or play the aggressive shot, a more precise pitch that would flirt with the water in order to finish close to the flag.

He knew that a good shot would not be good enough. Palmer, playing directly behind him, would certainly gun for a birdie. Hogan would have to do the same. When he lofted the ball into the soft breeze it looked perfect, and the crowd began to roar in anticipation. But their cheers suddenly turned to gasps and then to an eerie hush as the ball landed a foot short of the green and fell backward into the moat. Hogan waded into the water, his right trouser leg rolled up to the knee. He was able to blast the ball to the green, but two-putted for a bogey that sent him to the final hole one stroke behind Palmer. Apparently unsettled by his disaster, Hogan drove into the lake at 18 and finished in a tie for ninth place, four strokes behind Palmer.

The victory at Cherry Hills was the beginning not only of Palmer's superstardom but of big-time golf as we know it, and the birth of the familiar equation Palmer + Eisenhower + television = golf explosion. During the 1960s millions of Americans took up the game and dozens of commercial sponsors jumped on the pro golf bandwagon as Arnold, Jack, Gary Player, and a legion of lesser lights reaped the rewards. In 1960, the entire PGA Tour purse was $1.3 million. Today, most single tournaments are worth more, and the total Tour tops $20 million, with the PGA Senior Tour (for pros 50 and older) playing for more than $10 million.

Also that week, the notion of the modern Grand Slam was born. On an airplane from Denver to New York, Palmer sat with his friend Drum and began musing on his accomplishments. "You know, there will never be another Grand Slam the way Bobby Jones did it," he said, "but what if a guy were to win The Masters, U.S. Open, British Open, and PGA Championship in the same year? That would be a Grand Slam." Drum began writing about the Grand Slam in his stories for the *Pittsburgh Press*, and the rest is history. Palmer went to St. Andrews that year and nearly won the British Open, then returned and won it in both 1961 and 1962. His victories and continued pursuit of the tournament brought the British Open back from nearly two decades in the doldrums, and today it is regarded by many as the world's ultimate championship.

Cherry Hills thus holds an important place, not only in the history of the U.S. Open but in the fabric of professional golf. But there is more to the history of Cherry Hills than 1960. This is a course that has produced dramatic golf for over a half century, through two other Opens and two PGA Championships.

Charges such as Palmer's are not uncommon on this course designed in 1922 by William Flynn, where almost half of the par fours are reachable with a wedge, and where the mile-high Denver air means the ball flies about 10 percent farther than at sea level. The front nine, nearly 500 yards shorter than the back, is particularly vulnerable, beginning with that site of Palmer's tragedy and triumph, number 1.

Up until 1960 it was 346 yards, but after Palmer subdued it in the final round, the Cherry Hills elders got upset and decided to toughen it. Which architect did they call on for the redesign? Palmer. He and partner Ed Seay created a new tee that added fifty-three yards to the hole. In the next major championship—the 1978 Open—it played as a mid-length—and dull—par four. The PGA of America restored it to its 1960 length for the 1985 championship, but surprisingly almost no one tried for the green, many of the competitors laying up with as little as a 4-iron.

The pond that comes into play at 17 and 18 also threatens at the left side of the 2nd green, a 420-yard par four that calls for two well-placed shots. In 1960 Palmer holed a thirty-foot chip shot here for his second birdie, then made it three in a row when he wedged it stiff at the 3rd, another par four that is drivable—just 328 yards—but well protected by a quartet of greenside bunkers. Placement is

also important at the 4th, a dogleg left of 431 yards with trees down both sides of the fairway. Palmer made it four in a row here on a twenty-footer.

Ironically, he did not birdie number 5, the only par five on the front nine. It is a 543-yard dogleg right to a plateau green that is reachable with two strong shots. Lee Trevino eagled this hole to take the lead in the final round of the '85 PGA.

The course begins to toughen at the 8th hole, a par three of 234 yards with a bunker at the left front of the green, mounds to the right. It is followed by the longest and toughest par four on the front. Number 9 is an uphill dogleg right whose fairway banks right, toward a grove of evergreens. The relatively flat green is the largest on the course.

The difficult 9th is an augur of things to come on the inward half. Number 10, a 437-yard par four, tumbles downhill along roughly a parallel line to 9. Andy North, the man who won the 1978 U.S. Open here, got no help from this hole—he bogeyed it four straight days.

The last of Arnold Palmer's final-round birdies in 1960 came at the 11th, and it remains a birdie hole. Although 577 yards, it is relatively trouble free and the green is within reach of the longest hitters. In the third round of the 1978 Open Jack Nicklaus was in contention when he hit two drivers back-to-back here on Saturday, the second one finishing six feet from the pin; he made the putt for an eagle. Shortly thereafter, however, he visited a portable toilet, and the stop apparently upset his rhythm. At the 13th hole he hit one of the worst shots of his life, a heavy wedge that landed thirty yards short of the green and fell into a fronting creek. He took a triple-bogey 7—six of those shots from within 100 yards of the hole. After that he was never a factor in the tournament. The 13th hole had also been bad luck for Jack eighteen years earlier. He was holding a one-stroke lead in the 1960 Open, and this time he hit a lovely wedge twelve feet from the hole; then he three-putted.

Ben Hogan picked the 14th hole as one of the finest par fours in America. It doglegs left, but anyone who plans to play a hook had better be confident of his technique; there is out of bounds to the right and Little Dry Creek (which isn't dry) running down the left side. The long downhill second shot must avoid sand on the right and the creek left and beyond. This hole has played well over par in each of the five major championships held here.

Herb Graffis, the two-fisted editor of *Golfing Magazine*, called the final four holes at Cherry Hills "four horrible hussies who revel in luring noble men to destruction."

Number 15, a 215-yard par three, presents a similar problem to the approach at the previous hole, a downhill shot to a green with bunkers left and right and Little Dry Creek gurgling left and behind. Andy North nearly lost it all here in the last round of the 1978 Open after he caught sand on his teeshot, failed to get out on his next, and took a double-bogey 5 that reduced his three-stroke lead to one.

How tough is the 16th hole? It is the site of the highest single-

7th hole

hole score in the history of the Open, recorded by a man named Ray Ainsley in 1938. Ainsley had been four off the lead after round one and was on his way to a similar score in the second when disaster struck. After a good drive on this par-four dogleg right, he hit his 5-iron approach shot into the creek, which in those days ran around the left edge of the green. When he reached the area a little boy came up and said, "Mister, your ball went into the creek so I took it out." Ainsley told the boy to put it back, and he did. Ainsley then took out his pitching wedge and began chopping at the ball.

"He was whacking at that thing like a meat chopper," said his fellow competitor, Bob McKinney. "There was a big old fat guy, maybe 250 pounds, who was keeping count of the strokes, yelling them out like a referee at a boxing match—five!—six!—seven!—eight! Then he started laughing so hard he couldn't keep the count and I took over. Finally Ray popped one out." At that point a little girl in the gallery is said to have turned to her mother and said, "Mommy, he's stopped hitting it so it must be dead." Ainsley then three-putted for his inglorious record score: 19.

Although only 555 yards, Cherry Hills' 17th hole invariably

taxes the pros for an average score in excess of par. The teeshot must be threaded between two long, deep, high stands of trees. A strong, straight drive will offer the chance of going for the green. In a practice round (and in a strong following wind) Jack Nicklaus once reached it with a 7-iron. But this is a small target, set on an island—a target that is not designed to be approached with 4-woods, Denver air or not. Of course, a cautious lay-up on the second shot often leaves the kind of decision that faced the unfortunate Ben Hogan in 1960. In the 1985 PGA Lee Trevino's four scores reflected the fascination of this hole: 3-4-5-6. On Thursday, his poorly hit second shot skipped across the water and led to an eagle; on Sunday, his bogey cost him the title.

Architect Flynn defied dictum by plotting two back-to-back par fives as his last two holes. The pros play number 18 as a par four, but their scores would suggest it's closer to a par four and a half. Some fifty years ago, the Golf Course Superintendents Association of America chose this as America's Best Hole. In *Sports Illustrated* Ben

OVERLEAF: *17th hole*

Hogan called it one of the hardest fours in America. Others have called 18 a variety of things, printable and otherwise.

No par four looks longer on the scorecard (it's 491 yards) or from the tee (the last 100 or so are straight up one of the few hills on Cherry Hills). The teeshot must be played over a lake, and it's one of those "I dare you" shots. The more you bite off, the shorter your second shot. Out of bounds and dense rough flank the right side, and the small plateau green is fronted by sand.

All sorts of strange things happened here in 1960. Doug Sanders came to this tee with a chance to take the first-round lead when, in the middle of his backswing, a fish leaped out of the lake and splashed down so loudly that he flinched his shot into the water and took a double bogey. He said later that the fish "sounded like someone unloading a truck of empty beer cans." Mike Souchak could have put the tournament out of reach here, but in the third round he hit his teeshot out of bounds after he heard a spectator crank up a movie camera during his backswing. Souchak took a double bogey and gave Arnold Palmer just enough room for hope. And the terrible-tempered Tommy Bolt, after hitting two teeshots into the lake, finally got one over and then hurled his driver into the drink. A youngster ran and fished it out. Then, chased by Bolt's caddie, he absconded over a fence, to the amusement of the gallery.

In 1978 Andy North sank a mammoth birdie putt here to take the 54-hole lead, but it was the short one he faced for bogey a day later that everyone remembers. North had battled the golf Hall of Fame all week, and in the end the top ten positions included Jack Nicklaus, Gary Player, Tom Watson, Johnny Miller, Tom Weiskopf, and Hale Irwin. But his closest pursuers, J.C. Snead and Dave Stockton, were in the clubhouse at two under when North, four under, teed up on 18. After pushing his teeshot into the rough,

pulling his second into more rough, hitting a fat wedge into the front bunker and exploding out, North found himself staring at a four-footer to win the Open. A stiff wind was blowing into his face as he crouched over the ball and extended his arms well down the rusted shaft of his old Cash-In putter. So strong was the wind that he stepped away from the putt twice, then finally settled in and rolled the ball into the middle of the cup.

North used that putt to tie an Open record set by Billy Casper at Olympic in 1966. His 114 putts were the fewest ever over four rounds. It was only the second victory of North's career and, strangely, he would win only one more time—another U.S. Open—seven years later at Oakland Hills.

The 1978 Open is significant for at least one other statistic. In round one, a young man named Bob Impaglia was assessed two strokes for slow play, the first such penalty in the history of professional golf.

Forty years earlier, Cherry Hills was the site of the first Open west of the Mississippi. It was also the site of Ralph Guldahl's second straight Open victory. A stolid, uncharismatic 26-year-old out of Dallas, Guldahl is best remembered for his habit of combing his tousled black hair between shots. Like North, he birdied 18 in his third round, sinking a fifty-foot chip shot, but like Palmer he had a stiff assignment going into the final 18. He was four strokes in back of leader Dick Metz. But by the 5th hole of the afternoon round, they were even. Metz, who stumbled all day, posted a 79 as Guldahl shot 69 and won by an astounding six strokes, the Open's largest victory margin in seventeen years. Guldahl thus joined Willie Anderson, Johnny McDermott, and Bobby Jones as the only back-to-back Open Champions (since joined by Ben Hogan and Curtis Strange). At the time Guldahl, according to *Golfing Magazine*, was

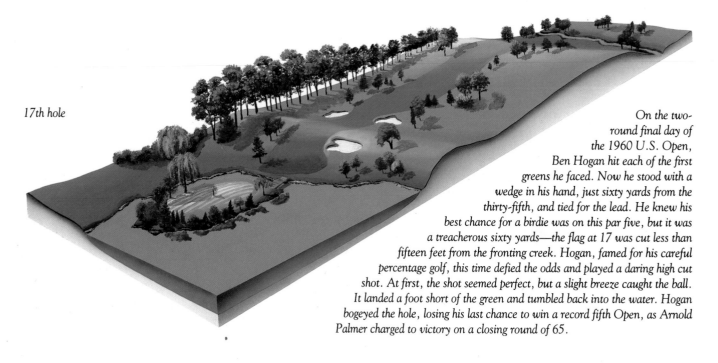

17th hole

On the two-round final day of the 1960 U.S. Open, Ben Hogan hit each of the first greens he faced. Now he stood with a wedge in his hand, just sixty yards from the thirty-fifth, and tied for the lead. He knew his best chance for a birdie was on this par five, but it was a treacherous sixty yards—the flag at 17 was cut less than fifteen feet from the fronting creek. Hogan, famed for his careful percentage golf, this time defied the odds and played a daring high cut shot. At first, the shot seemed perfect, but a slight breeze caught the ball. It landed a foot short of the green and tumbled back into the water. Hogan bogeyed the hole, losing his last chance to win a record fifth Open, as Arnold Palmer charged to victory on a closing round of 65.

regarded in some circles as "the greatest golfer the game has ever seen . . . a better putter than Vardon and a longer driver, better than Jones at approaches of any length, better than Hagen at recoveries." He won The Masters and two other events in 1939, but then mysteriously lost his game. After 1940, he never won again.

When the pros next came to Cherry Hills, for the 1941 PGA, the strong favorites were Byron Nelson, the defending champion, and Sam Snead, the defending runner-up. Sam lost in the early going but Lord Byron progressed, with victories over Gene Sarazen and Ben Hogan, to the finals, where he met Vic Ghezzi, an obscure pro from New Jersey. After twenty-seven holes of the 36-hole match Nelson was three up, but then Ghezzi birdied the first three holes of the back nine to pull even. From there on the match see-sawed back and forth—Nelson went up, then Ghezzi, then Nelson pulled even on 17 after nearly holing his wedged third shot for an eagle. At 18, Ghezzi had a chance to win with a two-putt par. Instead, he made a three-putt bogey.

They halved the first playoff hole, and then on the second hole, it was settled, but in a strange way. For years the actual truth of what happened on that thirty-eighth green remained a mystery, neither competitor willing to talk about it, until Nelson agreed to speak in a 1988 interview with GOLF Magazine:

Vic and I had both chipped up to almost exactly forty-two inches from the cup, and I was ruled away. Those were the days of the stymie, and balls weren't marked. As I took my stance, my shoe nudged Ghezzi's ball. I looked up at him and said something like, "Well, that's the match." He said he didn't want to win that way because no damage had been done. PGA officials came over and told Vic it was a penalty, that he had to take it. He insisted he didn't want to win that way. This all took a long time—ten minutes or so—and they finally ruled I should putt. By this time I was confused by all kinds of thoughts. One of them was that if I won now, people would say, "he won but he didn't win." I did NOT miss the putt intentionally, but all the confusion in my mind didn't help me make it. The ball lipped out; Vic made his and that was that.

In 1960 and 1978 Palmer and North emerged from final round free-for-alls in which any of several players might have won, but in 1985 the PGA Championship came down to another one-on-one battle, between two of the game's finest shotmakers, Lee Trevino and Hubert Green.

Trevino, who had won the PGA a year earlier at Shoal Creek, was trying to become the first man to win two in a row since Denny Shute in 1936-37. After two rounds he was well on his way, taking the lead at 134. Putting like a demon, he had used just fifty-five strokes in the first thirty-six holes. Two back were Green and Doug Tewell, who in round one had needed a par on 18 to tie the all-time

Having stepped away from it twice, Andy North coaxes in the three-footer for bogey that won him the first of two U.S. Opens. Photo: Tony Triolo for Sports Illustrated © Time Inc.

PGA 18-hole record. Instead he had bogeyed for a course record 64. In round three strong winds whipped across the course and only Green could better par. His 70 staked him to a three-stroke lead.

Trevino made up ground fast on Sunday, and when both he and Hubert hit their approach shots inside two feet at 9, they went three up on the field. With four holes to go, they remained even; then Lee's wand lost its magic. He three-putted from 12 feet as Hubert two-putted from 50. They halved 16 and then Lee pushed his teeshot at 17 into trouble on the right. Feeling he had to make birdie, he tried to play his second shot out of rough and through trees. But the gamble failed and his ball remained in the rough. From there he was unable to hold his third shot on the green. With a bogey he lost another stroke to Green's routine par.

When Lee reached the 18th in two and Hubert bunkered his second, it looked as if Trevino had an outside chance of catching up. But almost nonchalantly, Hubert stepped into the bunker, exploded his ball, and hit the pin, the ball coming to rest one foot away. He won by two strokes.

Critics say that Cherry Hills, even at 7100 yards or more, is too short to hold another major championship, that the mile-high air that in 1985 allowed some pros to average more than 300 yards on their teeshots is too much of a factor. These pundits may be right with regard to the Open. But the PGA of America, which is committed to moving its championship around the country, knows that in the northwestern states there is no venue that offers the same mixture of facilities, accommodation, rich history, and challenging golf as Cherry Hills. The PGA will likely return at least once more.

18th hole

U.S. Open: *June 9-11, 1938*

Ralph Guldahl	74	70	71	69	284	1
Dick Metz	73	68	70	79	290	2
Harry Cooper	76	69	76	71	292	T3
Toney Penna	78	72	74	68	292	T3
Byron Nelson	77	71	74	72	294	T5
Emery Zimmerman	72	71	73	78	294	T5
Frank Moore	79	73	72	71	295	T7
Henry Picard	70	70	77	78	295	T7
Paul Runyan	78	71	72	74	295	T7
Gene Sarazen	74	74	75	73	296	10

PGA Championship: *July 7-13, 1941*

Vic Ghezzi def. Byron Nelson, 38 holes

U.S. Open: *June 16-18, 1960*

Arnold Palmer	72	71	72	65	280	1
Jack Nicklaus	71	71	69	71	282	2
Dutch Harrison	74	70	70	69	283	T3
Julius Boros	73	69	68	73	283	T3
Mike Souchak	68	67	73	75	283	T3
Ted Kroll	72	69	75	67	283	T3
Jack Fleck	70	70	72	71	283	T3
Dow Finsterwald	71	69	70	73	283	T3
Ben Hogan	75	67	69	73	284	T9
Jerry Barber	69	71	70	74	284	T9
Don Cherry	70	71	71	72	284	T9

U.S. Open: *June 15-18, 1978*

Andy North	70	70	71	74	285	1
J.C. Snead	70	72	72	72	286	T2
Dave Stockton	71	73	70	72	286	T2
Hale Irwin	69	74	75	70	288	T4
Tom Weiskopf	77	73	70	68	288	T4
Andy Bean	72	72	71	74	289	T6
Billy Kratzert	72	74	70	73	289	T6
Johnny Miller	78	69	68	74	289	T6
Jack Nicklaus	73	69	74	73	289	T6
Gary Player	71	71	70	77	289	T6
Tom Watson	74	75	70	70	289	T6

PGA Championship: *August 8-11, 1985*

Hubert Green	67	69	70	72	278	1
Lee Trevino	66	68	75	71	280	2
Andy Bean	71	70	72	68	281	T3
Tze-Chung Chen	69	76	71	65	281	T3
Nick Price	73	73	65	71	282	5
Tom Watson	67	70	74	72	283	T6
Corey Pavin	66	75	73	69	283	T6
Fred Couples	70	65	76	72	283	T6
Buddy Gardner	73	73	70	67	283	T6
Lanny Wadkins	70	69	73	72	284	T10
Peter Jacobsen	66	71	75	72	284	T10

Scorecard

HOLE	YARDS	PAR
1	346	4
2	421	4
3	328	4
4	431	4
5	543	5
6	171	3
7	405	4
8	234	3
9	438	4
OUT	3317	35
10	437	4
11	577	5
12	207	3
13	387	4
14	470	4
15	215	3
16	433	4
17	555	5
18	491	4
IN	3772	36
TOTAL	7089	71

GOLF *Magazine* Rankings:
66th in the World
17th in the U.S.A.

CONGRESSIONAL COUNTRY CLUB

BETHESDA, MARYLAND
U.S. Open: 1964
PGA Championship: 1976

Few competitors in any sport have known either the agony or the ecstasy of Ken Venturi. Agony, when in 1956, with a four-stroke lead and a chance to become the only amateur golfer ever to win The Masters, he collapsed with an 80 in the final round and let Jackie Burke sneak in the back door. And ecstasy, eight years later when, after a protracted slump had left him on the doorstep of despair, he summoned 36 holes of courageous golf on a sweltering Saturday in June to become the U.S. Open Champion.

On the eve of that 1964 Open at Congressional Country Club, virtually no one was picking Venturi. In a poll of 150 sportswriters, sixty-five picked Jack Nicklaus to win, twenty-five chose Arnold Palmer, and only two named Venturi. Winless in four years due to a series of injuries, the one-time Golden Boy from San Francisco had plummeted to near-obscurity. In 1963 he had made only $3,848, cashing checks in just eight of the twenty-seven tournaments he had entered. He had not even qualified for an Open in three years.

"I was so discouraged I was tempted to give up the game," he said later. "I got to a point where I was ashamed to show up at a golf course. I was afraid to shoot a good round because I knew a bad round was sure to follow. I was really at rock bottom."

But late in 1963 he began to feel well for the first time. Then, shortly before the Open, he finished third in the Thunderbird Classic and sixth at the Buick Open—not fantastic, yet better than he had done in two seasons, an indication that both his ability and his confidence had returned.

A few weeks before the Open Venturi got a letter from a priest, Father Francis Murphy, in Burlingame, California, the parish near his home. In effect, it told him to keep his composure, not to let anything get him too up or too down, and to ask God to let him do the best he could. Venturi said those words ran through his mind as he teed off at Congressional.

His opening round of 72 left him four back of Palmer, the only man in the field to break 70 on the 7153-yard course, the longest par 70 in Open history. The next day Palmer added a 69 but lost his lead as Tommy Jacobs tied the 18-hole U.S. Open record with a 64.

"My whole game simply came together," said Jacobs. "It was like picking up a bridge hand and seeing thirteen spades." Jacobs took the halfway lead at 136 with Palmer one back; then it was four more strokes to third-place Bill Collins and one more to Venturi, six behind.

The last two rounds were played on one of the hottest, most humid days in the hot, humid history of the Open. It was 100 degrees in the shade, and in one part of the course an official held a thermometer that read 115.

But Venturi's game in the morning round was even hotter. Flying his irons straight at the flag and sinking every makable putt, he reached the turn in thirty strokes. His rhythmical nine holes—3-3-4—3-3-4—3-3-4—tied an Open record, and when Jacobs played the same stretch in 36, they were suddenly tied for the lead.

Eventually the heat began to tell on Venturi. At the 16th tee he turned to his playing companion, Ray Floyd, and said, "I don't know if I can make it in." He did, but three-putted both the 17th and 18th for a 66 that left him two back of Jacobs, two ahead of Palmer.

As Venturi rode the golf cart that took him from the 18th tee to the locker room for the forty-five-minute break between rounds, his face was pale, his eyes were glazed, and it seemed questionable whether he had another swing, let alone another round, left in him. In the locker room a Congressional member, Dr. John Everett, examined him and advised him not to go out, but there was never a question in Venturi's mind. So Everett gave him a few salt tablets and some iced tea and recommended he lie down for a half hour.

Among the spectators who awaited Venturi's arrival on the first tee that afternoon there was sort of an Indianapolis 500 race-goer's apprehension, the feeling that a man was going to crash and burn on the track. But miraculously, Venturi's golf was unaffected as he strode up and down the steaming hills. As Tommy Jacobs went four over in the first nine holes, Venturi held at even par to take a two-stroke lead. Palmer and everyone else was now out of it, and when Jacobs bogeyed 10, it was Venturi's tournament to win or lose.

Steeling himself with more salt tablets and iced tea from Dr.

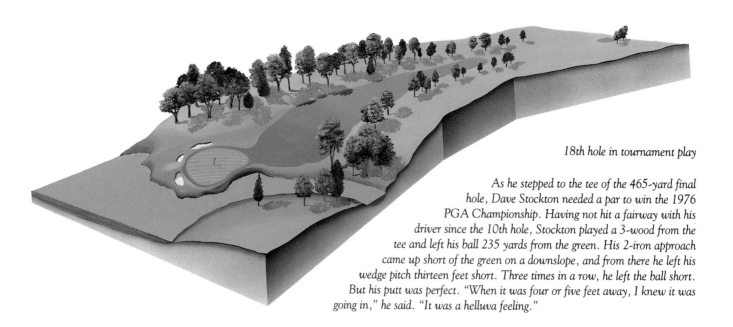

18th hole in tournament play

As he stepped to the tee of the 465-yard final hole, Dave Stockton needed a par to win the 1976 PGA Championship. Having not hit a fairway with his driver since the 10th hole, Stockton played a 3-wood from the tee and left his ball 235 yards from the green. His 2-iron approach came up short of the green on a downslope, and from there he left his wedge pitch thirteen feet short. Three times in a row, he left the ball short. But his putt was perfect. "When it was four or five feet away, I knew it was going in," he said. "It was a helluva feeling."

Everett, Venturi added three more pars at 10 through 12. When a twenty-foot putt dropped into the hole for a birdie at 13, Venturi closed his eyes and looked toward the heavens—a four-stroke lead.

But there were five hot, difficult holes to go, and Venturi was not getting any stronger. Seeing USGA official Joe Dey, he said, "You can slap me with a two-stroke penalty for slow play, but I am going to slow down a bit." There came no penalty, only three pars and a bogey, and on 18 the words from Dey, "Hold your head up, Ken. You're the champion now." Tramping shakily down the final hill at 18, he removed his cap for the first time all day as the tumultuous applause rang in his ears. In the words of Herbert Warren Wind, "His face was taut with fatigue and strain, and yet curiously radiant with pride and happiness."

When his final putt fell into the hole for a score of 278, the second lowest total in the history of the championship to that point, Venturi dropped his putter. As tears filled his eyes he said, "My God, I've won the Open."

Venturi's struggle caused the USGA to abandon the 36-hole final day and extend the tournament to four days, with a conclusion on Sunday, a move that, not coincidentally, resulted in much greater television revenue.

Television also had a hand in the machinations of the next championship at Congressional, the 1976 PGA. When weekend rain forced a postponement of the conclusion until Monday it also moved the PGA of America to make the quick decision that, in the event of a playoff, the championship would be decided not over eighteen holes but in sudden death, a break with a policy that had stood ever since the PGA had gone to stroke play in 1958. They needn't have bothered, for Dave Stockton settled matters with a dramatic thirteen-foot putt on the 72nd hole.

The course played differently than it had in 1964 because of the wet conditions and because a dozen years add height to most things that grow. The Open had been played just a couple of seasons after Robert Trent Jones had revamped Congressional, creating a championship course from parts of the original layout by Devereux Emmet as well as nine holes that Jones himself had added in 1957. It was still a young course then, but not in '76. Said Jack Nicklaus, "In 1964 they had little pines dotting the rough. Now those pines are high and as wide as a tent."

Long-hitting Tom Weiskopf led the first round on a 65 that included four deuces, one of them a 169-yard 6-iron that went into the cup at the 6th for an eagle. Gil Morgan and Tom Kite were a stroke back. On Friday Weiskopf faltered as Morgan added a 68 to take a four-stroke lead over Kite. His 134 total tied the 36-hole PGA record.

At this point, Stockton trailed by eight strokes. But if one word describes the game of Dave Stockton, it's scrappy. Never a stylist and hardly a long hitter, Stockton made his name and his money by his ability to scramble out of any sort of trouble and by putting like an angel. And although he ranked fifty-first on the Tour money list when the PGA began, he had several victories, including the 1970 PGA, to his credit. He knew how to win. In round three he posted a 69 to tie four other players at 211. In front of him were Don January at 210; Morgan, who had slipped with a 75 to join Nicklaus at 209; and a new leader, Charles Coody, at 207.

On Monday's final round, all of those players and more had a chance to win. Coody lost his lead early with a bogey at 1 and a double bogey at 3 as Morgan and Nicklaus went to the front. Then, in varying degrees they all stumbled with bogeys and double bogeys of their own. Meanwhile Stockton was mounting a charge. A thirty-five-foot birdie putt at the 7th put him one back of then-leader January, and when January, playing in front of him, birdied the 8th, Stockton sank another thirty-five-footer to keep pace.

Then he got his break. At the 10th January took a double bogey and moments later Stockton birdied 11 to take a two-stroke lead. But he gave it back with bogeys on 13 and 14. And suddenly, not only January but Ray Floyd, who had birdied 15 and 16, was within a stroke of him. Stockton managed pars at 15 and 16, then made an up-and-down from a bunker at 17. Coming to the final hole, he needed a par to win, a bogey to go into sudden death. For most of the way—a weak teeshot, a weak second shot, a weak pitch—it looked like a bogey, but Stockton's forte came to the fore. Faced with a mid-length putt for victory, he stroked it into the heart.

The original course at Congressional was designed during the Roaring Twenties after two Indiana Congressmen decided to create a place where members of Congress could play golf and entertain friends. President Calvin Coolidge officially opened the club in 1924, and among the early members were John D. Rockefeller, Vincent Astor, Charlie Chaplin, Harvey Firestone, Bernard Baruch, Hiram Walker, and William Randolph Hearst. Through the years, the list of honorary members has included Presidents Coolidge, Hoover, Harding, Taft, Nixon, and Ford. During World War II the club took on a strange new role, serving as a site for secret training of troops by the OSS, forerunner of the CIA.

Vice President Dan Quayle, a low-handicap golfer, is a current Congressional member, and he has often lamented the fact that the U.S. Open has been absent from Congressional for over a quarter century. "This is the nation's capital, and the national championship should come to the nation's capital," he has said.

If and when the Open does return to Congressional, it will be played on a markedly different course from the one the players saw in 1964. In the late 1980s, after the Kemper Open, which had been played here for several years, left for the new TPC at Avenel, Rees Jones, son of Robert Trent Jones, was invited to inspect the course with an eye toward resurfacing his father's greens for better turf grass. (Washington D.C. lies in a transitional area as far as grass for putting greens is concerned; too far north for Bermuda grass, too far south for bent.) But after Jones offered some constructive criticisms on the course layout, the members reasoned that if they were going to lose their course for a year of facelifting, it might as well be a thorough job. What resulted was a major reworking of virtually every hole on the course. Not only was every green rebuilt, many of the fairways were resculpted for better definition and visibility from the tee. Mounds and valleys were created to direct shots, and dozens of bunkers and grassy hollows were added to catch them.

"I tried to preserve the course's redeeming characteristics while eliminating its unfair demands," says Jones, although he also stiffened many of its challenges, particularly on the approach shots, where he pulled bunkers and grassy hollows tight to the greens and

Exhausted but elated, Ken Venturi makes the final putt to win the 1964 Open. Photo: AP/Wide World Photos

9th hole

set several greens on diagonals to their fairways so that a pin position on the front left might now call for a 5-iron while one in the back right could be a 3 or even a 2. The redesign is a course without the hard edges and blindness of its progenitor. A kinder, gentler Congressional, it wants its attacker to play well—and if he doesn't, it holds little mercy.

The biggest changes may have come in the short holes. On Trent Jones's course, three of them played uphill; on Rees Jones's remake, two play downhill and the other two, although slightly uphill, appear level from the tee. One of those is the 2nd, where the tee was both elevated and lengthened and the green was lowered and surrounded by six bunkers.

The lengthy 3rd hole was dotted with grassy hollows to the right of the teeshot landing area as well as an enfilade of three bunkers, each one encroaching a bit more on the fairway, each one a bit tougher to escape. Those who choose to go after a pin on the right of the green will now have to deal with a grass bunker and two pot bunkers.

The teeshot at number 4 used to be blind, but no more, thanks to some shaving of the fairway. This remains, however, a difficult dogleg par four, the site of Tommy Jacobs's disastrous double bogey

in the final round of the Open. The 5th is a sweeping dogleg that climbs a hill into which Jones the younger has built three bunkers. On the right, a series of grassy mounds and hollows tells the assailant that his hole turns left. Three more bunkers hug the contours of the new green.

The first appearance of water is at the 6th, a members' par five that is traditionally converted to a four for championship play. Jack Nicklaus double bogeyed this hole in 1976 when his approach bounced off the side of the green and into the hazard that guards the front and right edges. Tied for the lead at the time, he never recovered. Today, that approach is complicated by two new bunkers to the left side of the green, which now has three tiers.

A dramatic change took place at the 7th, a par three which was so severely uphill, the surface of the green was not visible from the tee. Rees Jones raised the tee and lowered the green, bringing it—and four new bunkers—into full view.

Prior to its redesign, the 9th at Congressional was one of the more controversial holes in Open history, a 607-yard downhill par five with a ravine just in front of its small green, making a go for

OPPOSITE: *18th hole*

the green ill advised in two shots and problematical even in three. Jones widened the landing area for the second shot, eliminated much of the left-to-right pitch, and mounded the right side to create a generous valley. He also completely revamped the greensite, adding bunkers and grassy hollows on the face of the slope to stop short shots from rolling down to the bottom of the hill. Even his father approved of this change.

The 10th, another members' five that plays as a four for the pros, remains a difficult par with a green guarded by water on the right, except that now the green is even closer to the water, and three new bunkers penalize those who give it too wide a berth to the left.

Number 11, one of the few holes that move from right to left, now has a regraded fairway that also slopes that way, making a relatively easy par four a bit easier. The 12th is another dramatically changed par three. An elevated tee and a greatly enlarged green with four distinct levels combine to excuse a slightly errant teeshot while rewarding only an accurate one.

The 13th, where Venturi made his final birdie in 1964, is a 469-yard par four that presents a downhill lie for the approach to an elevated green. The new green is less elevated than the old, but this is still a tough place to make a three.

Several new bunkers help define the 14th hole, a 451-yard par four where the second shot must be played across a deep hollow. It was here in 1964 that a temperature of 115 was recorded. As Venturi tramped through that hollow in the final round, he thought for a moment that he had stopped breathing. It was the site of his only bogey on the back nine.

At the final par five, number 15, Jones elevated the tee to make the landing area visible, but also brought into view a quartet of bunkers in the landing area and placed more sand and grass bunkers around the green area to give pause to long hitters hoping to cover the 583 yards in two shots.

The 16th hole, which played as the 17th in both of the championships, plays downhill 441 yards to a valley. Previously, big drives resulted in downhill lies for the approach, but now the fairway is terraced and dotted with hollows. Five bunkers and more of Jones's signature knolls and hollows surround the green.

Number 17, the former 18th hole, was left intact, its broad fairway tumbling down to a peninsula green with water on the left and bunkers to the right and rear, but those bunkers now hug the green more tightly than before. Should championship golf return to Congressional, this will probably be the 18th hole once again, because the final hole on the members' course is a 179-yard par three. Jones added a new tee to the right side of this one-shotter, making it appear to be more surrounded by water than it was formerly. He also lowered the green substantially so that the water is not simply in mind, it is in play. In a championship, this hole would undoubtedly play as the 10th, the 10th as the 11th, the 11th as the 12th, etc., with the conclusion of the course at the members' 17th.

The redesigned Congressional opened in the spring of 1990. Some of its members feel that, from the championship tees, it's easier than the old course, others swear it's harder. Nearly all would love to see the pros decide the question in another Open or PGA.

U.S. Open: June 18-20, 1964

Ken Venturi	72	60	66	70	278	1
Tommy Jacobs	72	64	70	76	282	2
Bob Charles	72	72	71	68	283	3
Billy Casper	71	64	69	71	285	4
Gay Brewer	76	69	73	68	286	T5
Arnold Palmer	68	69	75	74	286	T5
Bill Collins	70	71	74	72	287	7
Dow Finsterwald	73	72	71	72	288	8
Bob Rosburg	73	73	70	73	289	T9
Johnny Pott	71	73	73	72	289	T9

PGA Championship: August 12-15, 1976

Dave Stockton	70	72	69	70	281	1
Ray Floyd	72	68	71	71	282	T2
Don January	70	69	71	72	282	T2
Jerry Pate	69	73	72	69	283	T4
John Schlee	72	71	70	70	283	T4
Jack Nicklaus	71	69	69	74	283	T4
David Graham	70	71	70	72	283	T4
Ben Crenshaw	71	69	74	70	284	T8
Tom Weiskopf	65	74	73	72	284	T8
Jerry McGee	68	72	72	72	284	T8
Charles Coody	68	72	67	77	284	T8

Pro Shop

Scorecard

HOLE	YARDS	PAR
1	402	4
2	235	3
3	455	4
4	427	4
5	407	4
6	544	5
7	174	3
8	362	4
9	607	5
OUT	3613	36
10	507	5
11	400	4
12	187	3
13	469	4
14	451	4
15	583	5
16	441	4
17	440	4
18	179	3
IN	3657	36
TOTAL	7270	72

THE COUNTRY CLUB

BROOKLINE, MASSACHUSETTS
U.S Open: 1913, 1963, 1988

In the spring of 1893, Mr. Arthur Hunnewell of Wellesley, Massachusetts, swung his hickory-shafted mashie and struck a gutta-percha ball ninety yards down a crude fairway and straight into an equally crude cup. Thus began golf at The Country Club.

Several of Hunnewell's fellow club members (nongolfers all) witnessed this inaugural stroke of genius—and they were not impressed. According to golf historian Herbert Warren Wind, "As they saw it, Mr. Hunnewell had done no more than he had set out to do. As a matter of fact, the archers, riders, and marksmen were rather let down when Hunnewell and other golfers failed to supply further holes in one, and went away very skeptical about the future of so imperfect a game." After all, their club—The Country Club—had been founded a decade earlier for tennis, lawn bowling, dining, and "to have race meetings occasionally and music in the afternoon." Not for golf.

Besides, this game had come from France. Although golf had been played for a few years by some transplanted Scotsmen settled

David and the Goliaths. America's first golf hero, 19-year-old Francis Ouimet, accepts congratulations from the two British titans, Harry Vardon and Ted Ray.

around New York City, none of the Bostonians was aware of that. As far as they knew, golf had come to America via Florence Boit, a young woman from Pau who had brought her clubs with her when she visited her aunt and uncle, the aforementioned Arthur Hunnewell, in the summer of 1892.

Since there were no courses, Florence played to flowerpots on the Hunnewell estate. This strange behavior captured the attention of one of the neighbors, Mr. Laurence Curtis, who wrote a letter to The Country Club board of governors and asked if golf could be introduced. They gave the request a cautious okay and granted Curtis and two other members permission to build a course, with the stipulation that it not cost more than $50.

Six holes were designed, and within a short time these expanded to nine and then eighteen. The Country Club's first full course was reasonably long by turn-of-the-century standards—5200 yards—but it continued to compete for attention and space with other club activities, sharing its acreage with a steeple-chase course, a pigeon-shooting area, and a polo field. Hoof prints on fairways and stray balls on bridle paths led to spirited confrontations between equestrians and golfers.

Indeed, for a time golfers at The Country Club were viewed as "disturbers of the very ethics on which this club was founded," according to the recollection of G. Herbert Windelar, one of the first players. "Golfers were voted, I think, by a majority of the members as a nuisance, and were looked upon somewhat as the untouchables are in India."

But gradually, inexorably, the game prevailed. In 1894 Brookline became one of the five charter members of the United States Golf Association, and today, nearly a century after that first stroke by Mr. Hunnewell, this bastion of Boston Brahminism boasts three nines—the Clyde, the Primrose, and the Squirrel—and remains one of the most prestigious playgrounds in America. The Country Club was the first club to host two Walker Cup matches (1932 and 1973), has been the site of twelve national championships, and is the only club in America to have hosted six different USGA competitions.

Three U.S. Opens have been played here, and the first of them changed the face of American golf when a bespectacled 20-year-old lad who lived across the street from the club beat two titans from Great Britain and single-handedly launched golf onto the front page and into the public consciousness.

Francis Ouimet had spent his formative years as a caddie, watching the best players at The Country Club, then scampering across to a neighborhood cow pasture to imitate their swings on a makeshift three-hole course that he and his brother had devised.

But he had never watched the likes of Harry Vardon, the winner of five British Opens, or Ted Ray, the longest hitter of his time. In September of 1913 Vardon led one group of Open qualifiers with a 36-hole score of 151 and Ray led the others with 148. But Ouimet held his own with a 152, then continued to stay on the heels of the two British masters, posting rounds of 77 and 74 to stay within four strokes of co-leaders Vardon and Wilfrid Reid and two behind Ray. In round three, another 74 left him in a tie with Vardon and Ray, with eighteen to go. Walter Hagen, playing in his first Open, also made a strong bid; he was tied for the lead with five holes to play. But at the 14th, when he tried to approach the green with a wood from a slippery lie, he topped the ball, and the result was a triple-bogey 7. Hagen finished three strokes out of the playoff.

Ouimet, who had shot 43 on the front nine of the final, calculated with six holes to go that he would need two birdies at the par threes and pars at the four par fours to tie. At the short 13th he missed the green with his teeshot, but chipped in for his 2. He stayed on schedule with pars at both 14 and 15 but could manage only a par at the short 16th, so with two to go he needed a par and a birdie. His 3 came at the difficult 17th, where he rattled home a twenty-footer. On 18, after missing the green with his approach, Ouimet bravely sank a par putt of five feet.

The next day his steady golf outlasted the two Brits as Ouimet's 72 took the title by five strokes from Vardon, six from Ray. Vardon was only a stroke behind as they came to the 17th, but there he found a bunker with his teeshot and bogeyed as Ouimet again made birdie, and at that point the championship was decided.

His victory, the first by an amateur in the Open, proved that in the quarter century since golf had taken hold in the States, the home-grown talent had become a match for the best in the world. The soft-spoken Ouimet thus became the first American golf hero. He never turned professional, but went on to become one of the game's best amateurs and best-loved people. Years later he was named the first American captain of the Royal & Ancient Golf Club of St. Andrews, Scotland.

It was exactly a half century before the USGA, following its pen-chant for tradition and anniversaries, brought the Open back to The Country Club. But it was not mere nostalgia that prompted the return. Dick Wilson of the firm of Toomey & Flynn had added a third nine to the property, and the USGA had taken parts of that nine, in combination with the original 18, to form a testing composite course.

But the main challenge of the 1963 Open came from Mother Nature in the form of a howling, near-gale-force wind that wrought havoc with the entire field. Jack Nicklaus, the defending champion, missed the cut, and in the final round Sam Snead posted an inglorious 83 (but not as inglorious as the 91 by Tommy Aaron). The low total that year was 293—the highest score in any Open since 1935—and once again it was shared by three players.

Julius Boros, Jackie Cupit, and Arnold Palmer were the trio at the top. Cupit had blown his chance to win it in regulation when at the 17th hole he drove into rough, needed three strokes to reach the green and three more to get down for a 6. Palmer also three-putted 17, missing a two-footer. A day later they could look back regretfully on those errors, as the 43-year-old Boros dominated the playoff, shooting a 70 that was good enough for a three-stroke victory over Cupit, six over Palmer.

The Open did not return for a quarter century, and before it did

Julius Boros, age 43, subdued Arnold Palmer, Jackie Cupit, Mother Nature, and the Old Lady on Clyde Street to win the 1963 Open. Photo: AP/Wide World Photos

2nd hole

the course known as "The Old Lady on Clyde Street" underwent a facelift at the gentle hands of Rees Jones. Strictly speaking, his work was not a redesign in the way of his famous father's work at Oakland Hills et al. It was a restoration, a return to the style and feel of the original course. Using old photographs as his guide, Rees recontoured the landing areas, reshaped many bunkers and eliminated others, and added chocolate drop mounds in appropriate areas. Several tees were rebuilt, and a number of fairways were torn up, reseeded, and narrowed. He also tore up the 1st, 4th, and 17th greens and remodeled them, meticulously matching the subsoil mixture to that of the existing greens to insure a uniformity of firmness and speed.

Jones's work was unanimously lauded by officials and players. Greg Norman called the composite layout the best U.S. Open course he had ever seen, and his colleagues echoed their approval. The Old Lady was herself again, more enticing than ever and dressed to kill a new generation of suitors.

When Sunday of the 1988 Open concluded, two of the game's best players stood atop the field. On the 75th anniversary of the Ouimet-Vardon-Ray playoff, another Anglo-American confrontation took shape, as Nick Faldo squared off against Curtis Strange.

Faldo was then the British Open Champion, but for the first day

or so at Brookline he had played second fiddle to another British titleholder, the reigning Masters Champ, Sandy Lyle. An opening 68 had given Lyle a share of the lead, and when he turned the front nine in 32 on Friday, Grand Slam talk began. But at that point his driver became balky, and Lyle started to slide. He finished the Open in a tie for twenty-fifth, and it signaled the beginning of his virtual disappearance as a factor in international golf.

Meanwhile, the 1987 U.S. Open Champion, Scott Simpson, took the halfway lead at 135 with the 1987 Masters Champion, Larry Mize, one behind. Strange shared third with Bob Gilder at 137 while Faldo, Paul Azinger, and Fred Couples lurked a stroke further back with the tumbling Lyle. Twenty-four hours later, it was Strange in the lead by one over Faldo, Gilder, and Simpson.

Faldo, who had made eighteen straight pars in the final round of his victory at Muirfield, began Sunday in the same way, matching the card at each of the first fourteen holes. Then he birdied 15 to go into a tie with Strange, with whom he was paired. But the tie lasted only until Faldo bunkered his teeshot at the par-three 16th and made bogey as Strange holed from twenty-five feet for par. With two holes to go, Strange had a one-stroke lead, but at 17, the hole that had tripped up Harry Vardon, Jackie Cupit, and Arnold Palmer, Curtis Strange also stubbed his toe. After hitting his

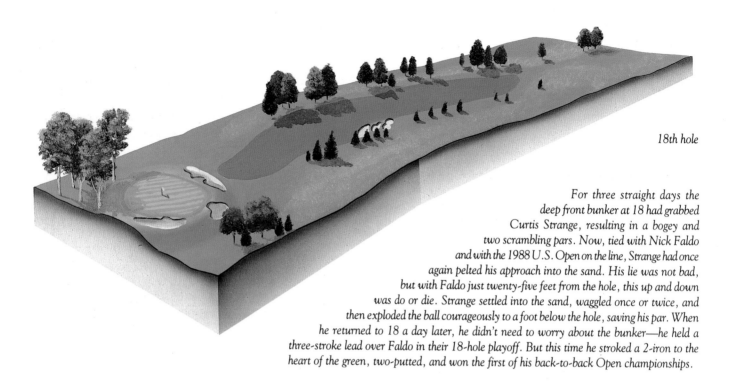

18th hole

For three straight days the deep front bunker at 18 had grabbed Curtis Strange, resulting in a bogey and two scrambling pars. Now, tied with Nick Faldo and with the 1988 U.S. Open on the line, Strange had once again pelted his approach into the sand. His lie was not bad, but with Faldo just twenty-five feet from the hole, this up and down was do or die. Strange settled into the sand, waggled once or twice, and then exploded the ball courageously to a foot below the hole, saving his par. When he returned to 18 a day later, he didn't need to worry about the bunker—he held a three-stroke lead over Faldo in their 18-hole playoff. But this time he stroked a 2-iron to the heart of the green, two-putted, and won the first of his back-to-back Open championships.

approach shot fifteen feet from the hole, Strange misjudged the speed of his first putt and knocked it six feet past the hole. When the comebacker failed to fall, he and Faldo went to the 72nd hole all even.

There, after a good drive, Strange did exactly the same thing he'd done in each of the first three rounds—he plunked his approach into the broad, deep bunker that fronts the green. His lie was good, but the pressure was enormous. "I went in there thinking this was just for a $5 Nassau, not to get into a U.S. Open playoff," said Strange. He exploded to a foot below the hole and got his par. When Faldo two-putted from twenty-five feet, the game was on for Monday.

In the playoff Strange got first blood when Faldo bogeyed the 3rd hole, and Curtis was never behind all day. The key hole was the 433-yard 13th, where Strange sank a twenty-nine-foot birdie putt as Faldo three-putted from fifty feet. That stretched Curtis's margin from one stroke to three, a lead he carried to 18. This time Curtis hit the final green and two-putted for his par as Faldo bogeyed. The final scores were Strange 71, Faldo 75.

For Strange, it was not only the fulfillment of a dream, it was the fulfillment of a mission dedicated to his father, a golf professional who had started him in the game before dying of cancer at age 38 when Curtis was only 14. And it was also the fulfillment of a career that had always brimmed with potential but had lacked the big victories that separate superior players from the rest. Spurred by his Open victory, Strange went on to win four events on the U.S. Tour, including the lucrative Nabisco Championships. He became the PGA Tour Player of the Year and set a new single-season money-winning record of $1,147,644. A year later he won a second-straight

U.S. Open at Oak Hill, solidifying his position as one of the pre-eminent players of the modern era.

Peter Jacobsen owns the course record at The Country Club, a 64 in the final round of the 1988 Open, and his scoring attests to the notion that low numbers are built on the front nine. Jacobsen began his Sunday round with a string of seven straight 3s en route to an outward half of 30.

Although this nine is 470 yards shorter than the back, it begins with a brutish 452-yard dogleg. A long, drawn drive will leave a mid or long iron to this green surrounded by bunkers. The first par three occurs early, at the 185-yard 2nd, where the pros hit anything from a 3- to 5-iron to the slightly elevated green. Then it's back to a long four at the 3rd, where outcroppings of rock add definition and interest to the 448-yard journey. Jones expanded the green here, but his generosity also brought the pond that lies beyond it more into play.

At the 338-yard 4th, the green is invisible from the tee, but that doesn't stop the game's longest hitters from trying to find it with their drives. Jones's new green is half the size of the former target, and is flanked with bunkers and backed with chocolate-drop mounds. On this hole, power will yield eagles and birdies only if it is accompanied by precision. A gentle fade is needed at the 5th hole, which doglegs 439 yards from left to right, but if that fade grows into a slice, the second shot will have to be played from dense trees and over a nest of greenside bunkers.

One of the shortest fours in championship golf is number 6, just 312 yards. But the landing area here is tightened by rough and a half dozen bunkers. Smart golfers, regardless of their strength, lay up with irons here.

The 201-yard teeshot at number 7 may be the most testing iron shot on the front half, since the green is one of the narrowest on the course. It also slopes sharply away, calling for a Jack Nicklaus long iron, a high shot that lands softly. A line of trees down the left cautions players to favor the right side, but Rees Jones complicated that assignment when he added three fairway bunkers in the right side of the landing area. The right is also the place to miss this green, as a bunker hugs the opposite side and to the left of that bunker is a steep slope down to a pond.

The teeshot at number 9 must thread through a valley between two rock ledges. A very big drive will carry the grassy hill at the halfway mark, leaving a good opportunity to get home in two on this 510-yard par five. Weaker hitters will have to contend with a stream that crosses the fairway about 100 yards short of the green. And all comers will have to deal with the cluster of greenside bunkers.

Ben Crenshaw, one of The Country Club's biggest boosters, calls holes 10, 11, and 12 "The Wall," a trio of testing par fours that must be vaulted by anyone hoping to conquer the inward nine. Number 10 favors power hitters who can carry the large mound at the end of the driving area. Those who do will have as little as a wedge into this 439-yard par four, but those who don't (and that includes most mortals) may have up to 200 yards left to this green guarded in front by two bunkers.

Rees Jones calls number 11 "one of the best holes in golf, even though it's not a hole." In actuality, this 453-yard monster is a combination of two holes—a par four and a par three—from the Primrose Nine. It calls for a right-to-left teeshot followed by a long iron down a slight hill and over water fronting the green. Arnold Palmer has nasty memories of this hole. He scored triple bogey/ bogey/triple bogey here in his last three rounds of the 1963 Open, including the playoff.

Number 12 is one of the hardest par fours in the world. Even the longest hitters will face a stiff assignment, a steep uphill shot to a fairway that is nearly blind and doglegs sharply left just before reaching a green ringed by five bunkers. In the 1988 Open this was the toughest hole of the week, taxing the competitors for an average of 4.42 strokes.

3rd hole

Clubhouse

The Country Club is not an especially pretty or charming course, but hole number 13 is an exception. From an elevated tee the player sees not only the tumbling fairway but a broad pond to the right of it. A careful teeshot will leave a downhill approach to a beautifully bunkered green surrounded by tall trees. Number 14, a 527-yard par five, is reachable in two if the teeshot is a power fade that rides the left-to-right fairway. The green is elevated, but there is an opening between the flanking bunkers, enough room to thread a long, rolling approach. In round one of the 1988 Open Curtis Strange got home in two here and made an eagle, one of six made on this hole during that Open.

The 15th is 434 yards on the card, but playing from an elevated tee it is a bit shorter. A good drive here will favor the left side since this broad fairway sweeps from left to right. Number 16 calls for a precise shot of 185 yards, particularly when shooting for a pin in the right-front where a large bunker looms. Other bunkers hug the left and right of this green, but they are sanctuaries compared to the road and out of bounds beyond.

Most of the drama in the Opens at The Country Club has unfolded at number 17. It was here that Vardon lost in 1913, here that Palmer and Cupit lost in 1963, and here that Strange gave away his lead in the final round of 1988. On paper, it does not seem to be a forbidding hole, a 381-yard par four, but thick rough encroaches on the left side where two bunkers lurk as well, and the long, slender, contoured green is guarded by a half dozen bunkers right and left and grassy chocolate drops to the rear. It's tougher than it looks.

Number 18 offers no such subtlety. It is merely a stiff par four, bending quietly right to left around three bunkers restored by Jones. The approach is to an elevated bowl-shaped green fronted by one massive bunker and three smaller ones. The back of the green is shaded by venerable elm trees, and just beyond them is the rambling colonial clubhouse which has stood, along with the challenge of The Country Club, for more than ninety years.

U.S. Open: September 16-19, 1913

Francis Ouimet	77	74	74	79	304		
					72	1
Harry Vardon	75	72	78	79	304		
					77	T2
Edward Ray	79	70	76	79	304		
					78	T2
Walter Hagen	73	78	76	80	307	T4
Jim Barnes	74	76	78	79	307	T4
Macdonald Smith	71	79	80	77	307	T4
Louis Tellier	76	76	79	76	307	T4
John McDermott	74	79	77	78	308	8
Herbert Strong	75	74	82	79	310	9
Patrick Doyle	78	80	73	80	311	10

U.S. Open: June 20-23, 1963

Julius Boros	71	74	76	72	293		
					70	1
Jackie Cupit	70	72	76	75	293		
					73	T2
Arnold Palmer	73	69	77	74	293		
					76	T2
Paul Harney	78	70	73	73	294	4
Billy Maxwell	73	73	75	74	295	T5
Bruce Crampton	74	72	75	74	295	T5
Tony Lema	71	74	74	76	295	T5
Gary Player	74	75	75	72	296	T8
Walter Burkemo	72	71	76	77	296	T8
Dan Sikes	77	73	73	74	297	10

U.S. Open: June 16-19, 1988

Curtis Strange	70	67	69	72	278		
					71	1
Nick Faldo	72	67	68	71	278		
					75	2
D.A. Weibring	71	69	68	72	280	T3
Steve Pate	72	69	72	67	280	T3
Mark O'Meara	71	72	66	71	280	T3
Scott Simpson	69	66	72	74	281	T6
Paul Azinger	69	70	76	66	281	T6
Fuzzy Zoeller	73	72	71	66	282	T8
Bob Gilder	68	69	70	75	282	T8
Payne Stewart	73	73	70	67	283	T10
Fred Couples	72	67	71	73	283	T10

Scorecard

HOLE	YARDS	PAR
1	452	4
2	185	3
3	448	4
4	338	4
5	439	4
6	312	4
7	201	3
8	385	4
9	510	5
OUT	3270	35
10	439	4
11	453	4
12	450	4
13	433	4
14	527	5
15	434	4
16	185	3
17	381	4
18	438	4
IN	3740	36
TOTAL	7010	71

GOLF *Magazine* Rankings:
48th in the World
29th in the U.S.A.

HAZELTINE NATIONAL GOLF CLUB

CHASKA, MINNESOTA
U.S. Open: 1970, 1991

Totten P. Heffelfinger had a problem bigger than his name. In Minneapolis during the late 1950s plans were afoot for a major highway that would cut through the heart of his beloved Minikahda, the site of the 1916 U.S. Open. So Heffelfinger led a band of his fellow members in search of a place to establish a second 18 holes. Before long they found a stretch of beautifully rolling farmland, bordered by a mile-long lake and the bluffs of the Minnesota River. But when Heffelfinger presented his plan to the rest of the Minikahda membership, they rejected it.

Undaunted, Heffelfinger formed a syndicate of investors and purchased the property anyway. The most important of those investors turned out to be Robert Trent Jones, who after visiting the property so loved it that he asked to participate financially in the project as well as design the course.

In 1962 Hazeltine National Golf Club was opened for play. At the time, it was intended to be not simply a golf club but the beginning of a grand scheme by Jones, a transcontinental network of Executive Golf Clubs with reciprocal playing privileges. But these

16th hole

were the psychedelic '60s, and the notion of Executive anything was not in sync with the heartbeat of America. The idea flopped, only to reappear in the '80s under the aegis of the PGA Tour's Tournament Players Clubs and of other properties run by the Landmark Land Company.

A mere eight years after its opening, Hazeltine hosted its first U.S. Open. Some say that was too soon. Full of blind shots and sharp doglegs, it lacked definition. "Too often there was no target at all at Hazeltine," wrote Robert Sommers in his definitive history of the U.S. Open. "On the first tee, for example, the players could see neither the green nor the fairway. As targets, they picked a passing cloud or a red Mustang parked in a field off in the pasture." Jack Nicklaus bemoaned the fact that the course, despite its length of 7151 yards, prevented the stronger players from using drivers from the tee because of the acute angles of the doglegs. He and many others were forced to play 1-irons to position A because, in Nicklaus's words, "At Hazeltine, there are no position B's."

But the most vitriolic words came from Dave Hill, the man who would finish second in the Open. Asked what Hazeltine lacked he replied, "About eighty acres of corn and some cows. They ruined a good farm when they built this course." Asked what he would recommend be done with the course, he said, "Plow it under and start over. The man who designed this course had his blueprints upside down." When the Minneapolis morning papers carried all this, the manure hit the fan, and the next day Hill's gallery greeted his appearance on the first tee with a chorus of "moos."

Trent Jones responded in kind. "If you built the kind of holes the pros like you would have dead flat greens and dead flat fairways, very little rough and very few traps. That kind of course wouldn't require an architect. You could order it from a Sears Roebuck catalog."

The confrontation over the course was more spirited than the competition on it. Tony Jacklin won by seven strokes, the largest margin in half a century. Jacklin's score of seven under par 281 was the only total under par as virtually all the rest of the field struggled. Gary Player shot 302, Nicklaus 304, Arnold Palmer 305.

The major reason for the big numbers was the weather in round one, characterized by Herbert Warren Wind as "more suitable to hunting caribou than playing golf." Gale-force winds ripped through the course, tearing down tents, and churning the waters of Lake Hazeltine to a froth that left the entire 10th green covered with foam. On the downwind 3rd hole several drives measured over 340 yards, one of them by 58-year-old Sam Snead. With the wind, greens were nearly impossible to hold; against it they were nearly impossible to reach.

Nicklaus played the front nine in 43 and finished with an 81, his highest score ever in an Open. "Excuse me while I go and throw up," he said, brushing by a reporter on his way to the locker room. Barely half the field broke 80 and only one man broke par—Jacklin. Eleven months earlier the 24-year-old Englishman had served notice that he could beat the world's best when he won the British Open at Royal Lytham. Now, with a round of 71 that incredibly had included six birdies, he had a two-stroke head start on his second major victory.

The next day, after a 70, he increased it to three over Hill, and that is as close as anyone would come during the weekend. Jacklin, a former steelworker, thus became the first Englishman since Ted Ray in 1920 to win the U.S. Open.

Corn field or not, it was a course in need of work, and reconstruction began almost immediately after the tournament, with doglegs being straightened and green contours softened. The alterations were sufficient to earn the course a second Open in 1991, but soon after the announcement another call went out to a Jones. Not Trent Jones but Rees Jones, the younger of his two sons, both of whom have forged impressive design careers of their own.

Jones the younger worked at Hazeltine from 1987-89, further enhancing the visibility and definition of the course, and the result was a more honest layout. Whereas in 1960 eleven greens were invisible from their respective tees, today that is true on only three or four holes. However, from the back tees of 7149 yards Hazeltine remains a stern test of golf, just as Trent Jones intended it to be.

Rees's changes began with the very first hole, where he repositioned the tee both to shorten the hole and reduce the angle of the dogleg, shaved off the left side of a blinding hill, and kept everyone honest by adding a big bunker on the left side of the landing area.

The 2nd hole, on the other hand, was made tougher by bringing a fairway bunker closer to the fairway, adding a grass bunker and some defining mounds to the outside edge of the right-to-left dogleg, and deepening the two greenside bunkers.

Trent Jones is well known for his grand scale—big tees, big greens, big bunkers—but his greenside bunker at the par-five 3rd was uncharacteristically narrow, making for inordinately difficult recoveries. Son Rees widened it, deepened it, and canted it for better playability. He also raised the back tee for better visibility and shortened the hole slightly. In the 1970 Open, it played 585 yards to an elevated green, and only one player got home in 2.

Number 4, the only par three without a water hazard, is nonetheless a testing shot because it is surrounded by trees that filter the wind, making club selection difficult. Hazeltine club lore claims that one member, after making a hole-in-one here, was asked by his playing partners to play a second shot from the tee because he had failed to tee his first ball from within the designated teeing area.

Tony Jacklin's best shot in the 1970 Open may have been the 7-iron he ripped out of the rough to within two feet of the hole at number 5. This is a short but treacherous par four with out of bounds on the left and a green that is not simply bunkered, but forested. Trees—twenty-six species—are abundant at Hazeltine, and among them roam and fly over 100 different species of birds and animals.

OPPOSITE: *17th hole*. INSET: *17th hole*

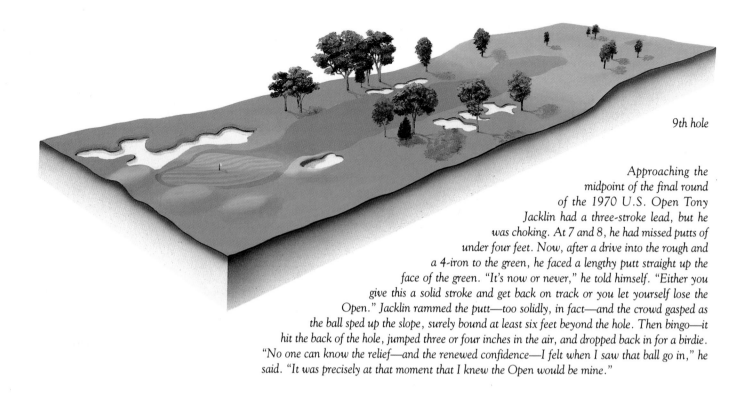

9th hole

Approaching the midpoint of the final round of the 1970 U.S. Open Tony Jacklin had a three-stroke lead, but he was choking. At 7 and 8, he had missed putts of under four feet. Now, after a drive into the rough and a 4-iron to the green, he faced a lengthy putt straight up the face of the green. "It's now or never," he told himself. "Either you give this a solid stroke and get back on track or you let yourself lose the Open." Jacklin rammed the putt—too solidly, in fact—and the crowd gasped as the ball sped up the slope, surely bound at least six feet beyond the hole. Then bingo—it hit the back of the hole, jumped three or four inches in the air, and dropped back in for a birdie. "No one can know the relief—and the renewed confidence—I felt when I saw that ball go in," he said. "It was precisely at that moment that I knew the Open would be mine."

U.S. Open: June 18-21, 1970						
Tony Jacklin	71	70	70	70	281	1
Dave Hill	75	69	71	73	288	2
Bob Lunn	77	72	70	70	289	T3
Bob Charles	76	71	75	67	289	T3
Ken Still	78	71	71	71	291	5
Miller Barber	75	75	72	70	292	6
Gay Brewer	75	71	71	76	293	7
Billy Casper	75	75	71	73	294	T8
Larry Ziegler	75	73	73	73	294	T8
Bruce Devlin	75	75	71	73	294	T8
Lee Trevino	77	73	74	70	294	T8

U.S. Open: June 13-17, 1991						
Payne Stewart	67	70	73	72	282	
				75		1
Scott Simpson	70	68	68	72	282	
				77		2
Larry Nelson	73	72	72	68	285	T3
Fred Couples	70	70	75	70	285	T3
Fuzzy Zoeller	72	73	74	67	286	5
Scott Hoch	69	71	74	73	287	6
Nolan Henke	67	71	77	73	288	7
Raymond Floyd	73	72	76	68	289	T8
J.-M. Olazabal	73	71	75	70	289	T8
Corey Pavin	71	67	79	72	289	T8

Scorecard

HOLE	YARDS	PAR
1	440	4
2	435	4
3	580	5
4	194	3
5	412	4
6	405	4
7	518	4
8	166	3
9	432	4
OUT	3582	35
10	410	4
11	556	5
12	432	4
13	204	3
14	357	4
15	590	5
16	384	4
17	182	3
18	452	4
IN	3567	36
TOTAL	7149	71

During a wild and woolly week in 1970, Britain's Tony Jacklin was untouchable, becoming the first Englishman since 1920 to win the U.S. Open. Photo: Walter Ioos Jr. for Sports Illustrated © Time Inc.

3rd hole

The 6th, a par four dogleg left of 405 yards with a pond protecting the left side of the green, was the toughest hole in the 1970 Open, and with a new back tee it has not become any easier.

Number 7 is a mid-length par five, a dogleg to the right with a pond at greenside. Rees Jones relocated the tee to straighten this hole a bit, added grass mounds and pockets to catch long teeshots that don't have the requisite fade, and rebunkered the green. It is reachable with two solid shots.

Finesse is the key at the 166-yard 8th, where a pond runs the entire right side of the hole and bunkers guard the left. But it's back to full-blooded golf at the 9th, a 430-yard uphill par four where the aesthetic bunkers are nice to look but hellish to play from. In the final round of 1970, Jacklin sank a confidence-building birdie putt here.

Rees Jones took the blindness out of another teeshot at the 10th, where the tee was elevated, improving the view of a pretty hole that tumbles down to the edge of Lake Hazeltine. From there it's uphill on the par-five 11th, a big dogleg right that got lots of remodeling work, including a lowering of the landing area, a cluster of cross bunkers to clear on the second shot, a bold series of mounds along the left rough, and new bunkers and mounding at the green. The hole is shorter than it was in 1970, but anyone who wants to reach it in two had better play a very careful second shot.

Accuracy is paramount at the 12th, where chutes of trees tighten both the teeshot area and the green, and the par-three 13th also requires care, surrounded by bunkers, a pond on the left, and a grassy hollow to the right rear. Birdies come frequently at 14, a straightforward par four of only 340 yards with a level, inviting green, but players had best save their strength for 15, a par five of 590 yards.

There are no bunkers at the 16th hole, but it hardly needs them, with the teeshot having to carry nearly 200 yards over Lake Hazeltine. There is also a stream running down the left side, and the peninsular green juts out into the water. In the 1970 Open, this hole was a par three, and when the pin was on the extreme left of the green, several trees blocked the teeshot and the hole played like a one-shot dogleg.

Putting is often the main challenge at 17, where the 182-yard teeshot must not only avoid a pair of ponds and a trio of bunkers, it must find the correct level of a multitiered green.

The course concludes uncharacteristically with a dead-straight hole where nothing is hidden. Rees Jones moved back the tee and rebunkered both the fairway and the green. Here, as throughout the course, his goal was to ensure that his father's creation remains a stern challenge for the game's best players.

The face-lifted course got rave reviews from the competitors in 1991, but Hazeltine's second Open was marred by tragedy when, in the middle of round one, a thunderstorm blew in and lightning struck down six spectators who had huddled under a tree near the 11th tee, killing one of them. Then, in the second round, a small stairway to one of the grandstands collapsed, injuring more people.

By the weekend, however, the only calamities were those befalling the players, as windy conditions blew most scores well over par. In the end it came down to a battle between 1989 PGA Champion Payne Stewart and 1987 U.S. Open Champion Scott Simpson. Simpson seemed to have it won, holding a two-stroke lead with three holes to play, but he bogeyed both 16 and 18 as Stewart parred in to tie him at 282, six under par. In the 18-hole playoff the next day, it was déjà vu, Simpson two ahead with three holes to play. But this time, Simpson bogeyed all three of the finishing holes as Stewart sank a 20-footer for birdie at 16—the most menacing hole on the course—and then parred in for a two-stroke victory.

THE INVERNESS CLUB

TOLEDO, OHIO
U.S. Open: 1920, 1931, 1957, 1979
PGA Championship: 1986

A tragic collapse, a magic explosion, and everything in between—through nine decades and five major championships, Inverness has seen it all.

And some of it has been downright comical. Inverness, after all, is the only club whose original nine-hole course was designed with eight holes, the only course where one U.S. Open player teed off from his knees, the only site where the Open took 144 holes to complete, and the only place where a twenty-five-foot fir tree grew overnight. For ninety years it has been golf's prime purveyor of the sublime and the ridiculous.

It all began with the handiwork of Bernard Nichols. The annals of golf architecture don't have much to say about Bernard, and that's probably just as well, for it was he who came to the eleventh hour on the original design of Inverness before realizing that his nine-hole course had a missing link. A short par three was hurriedly squeezed in.

That was back in 1903. Nichols's half-course remained in play for another fifteen years before the Inverness members decided it was time to upgrade. They acquired some nearby property, heavily wooded and filled with meandering streams, and they hired Donald Ross. A prolific Scotsman credited with over 600 American courses, Ross reworked Nichols's nine while adding nine of his own. When the Ohio State Open was held on the new course in 1919, it got great reviews, and shortly thereafter the USGA announced that the 1920 U.S. Open would be held at Inverness.

This was a watershed Open, the end of one era and the birth of another. At Inverness Bobby Jones, Gene Sarazen, Tommy Armour, Johnny Farrell, and Leo Diegel all competed in their first Open. Over the next thirteen years that fivesome would win a total of eight U.S. Opens, five British Opens, and six PGA Championships. But it was also the last appearance in a U.S. Open by two of the game's titans from England, Harry Vardon and Ted Ray.

Whoever set the pairings that year had a touch of the prophet, as 18-year-old Jones and 50-year-old Vardon were paired for the two qualifying rounds, the only time they played together in a major championship. Jones had never met the venerable Vardon and was understandably nervous, hoping to impress him. But at the 7th hole of the second round he topped a simple pitch shot into a bunker.

"Mr. Vardon, did you ever see a worse shot than that?", he said, turning to Vardon.

"No," was all the master replied.

Bobby recovered his composure sufficiently to finish tied for 8th, but it was Vardon who took hold of the tournament. With a flawless one-under-par 71 in the third round his 54-hole total was one lower than that of Jock Hutchinson and Leo Diegel, two ahead of Ted Ray. In the afternoon, he went out in 36 and appeared to have the Championship well in hand—a back-nine score of 41 would have won it for him. But a vicious windstorm blew up off Lake Erie and Vardon, never a powerful man, had to lean hard just to stand up to the gale. His shots began to stray, his 50-year-old putting nerves unraveled, and he staggered through the last seven holes in seven over par, one stroke too many.

The next day he told the press, "Even as tired as I was, I can't see yet how I broke so badly. Why, I am sure I could go out now and do better by kicking the ball around with my boot."

The beneficiary of Vardon's collapse was his countryman Ted Ray. A big, burly man with a soup-strainer mustache, a floppy felt fedora, and a briar pipe, Ray was hardly a stylist. When asked by a struggling amateur for advice on the driver, he would say, " 'it 'em 'ard, mate, like I do." If the pupil complained that he did hit hard but failed to obtain the desired result, Ray's reply was, "then 'it 'em a bloody sight 'arder."

In the final round at Inverness Ray began by sinking putts of thirty-five, twenty-five, forty, and fifteen feet on the first four holes, then used his prodigious strength to carry the trees and cut the dogleg on the 334-yard 7th, making his fourth birdie there in as many rounds. Out in 35, he held on through the wind for a 75—295 that edged Vardon, Diegel, and Hutchinson by one. Age 43 at the time,

Ray was the oldest golfer to win the U.S. Open. (Hale Irwin, who won his third Open in 1990 at the age of 45, now holds that distinction.) He also became the last British golfer to win the U.S. Open until Tony Jacklin a half century later. The foreigner's victory also sparked a spirit of retaliation, referred to as the Oath of Inverness, a resolve on the part of the top American players to make their presence felt at ensuing British Opens until someone evened accounts by bringing the old claret jug to the States. It didn't take long: Walter Hagen had the pleasure at Sandwich in 1922.

It was Hagen also who led a movement for better treatment of professionals by host clubs. Before Inverness, the pros were treated little better than their caddies; they were not permitted in the clubhouse, and no courtesies were extended them. But at Inverness that changed; the pros were invited to change in the locker room and dine in the club's restaurants. Rooms were reserved for them at the local hotels and cars were provided to transport them to and from the course. The pros were deeply appreciative, and Hagen took the lead again, this time taking up a collection from his colleagues to buy a handsome cathedral chime clock, eight feet tall, which was presented to the club. It still stands in the main clubhouse, with the inscription:

> God measures men by what they are
> Not what in wealth they possess
> This vibrant message chimes afar
> The voice of Inverness

Ironically, the site of Bobby Jones's first Open also was the site of the first Open thereafter in which he did not compete. In 1931,

a year after Jones completed the Grand Slam and retired, the National Championship returned to Toledo.

The course had changed a bit, to keep pace with the new steel-shafted clubs. A.W. Tillinghast, who lived in Toledo at one time, had designed four new greens, added a few bunkers, and increased the length about 300 yards to 6529 yards while lowering the par from 72 to 71. It was a long course, and this was a long Open—the longest.

The winner was Billy Burke, a cigar-smoking ironworker who had lost part of the fourth finger of his left hand. No one ever worked harder for victory. The Championship was played in heat and humidity that earned it the nickname Inverness Inferno. What's more, it took five days—and 144 holes—to complete.

At the end of regulation play Burke was tied at 292 with George Von Elm, a Californian who had turned pro after a distinguished amateur career that had included a victory over Jones in the 1926 U.S. Amateur. Calling himself a "businessman golfer," Von Elm was now in the game strictly for profit, the forerunner of today's million-dollar earners. On the 72nd hole he had canned a brave ten-footer to tie Burke and force a 36-hole playoff.

The playoff was a contrast of styles, the long-hitting Von Elm against the scrappy Burke, but the match could not have been more even. Once again, Von Elm holed a tieing putt on the final green, this one from twelve feet to equal Burke's 149 total. Thus they went out for another 36 holes the next day, and this time Burke prevailed. His score of 148, 71 in the afternoon, beat Von Elm by a single stroke.

It had been a terrific back-and-forth battle throughout the seventy-two holes. Von Elm, down by four strokes at one point, had

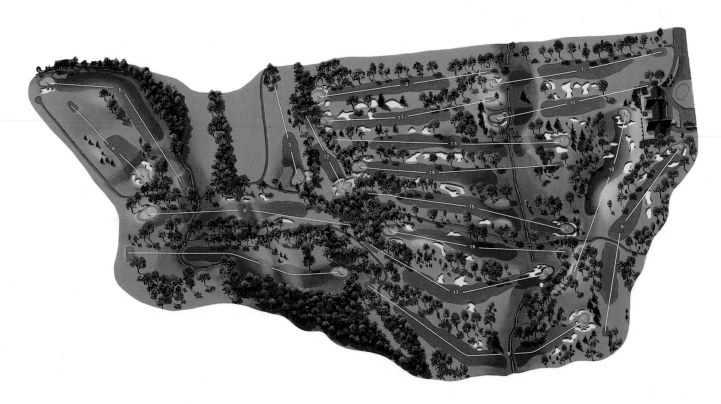

birdied four holes in a row and moved two ahead; then Burke had battled back. When it was over, Burke admitted to having smoked thirty-two cigars—four per round—and claimed to have lost nine pounds during the Championship. This was his only major victory, and history remembers him as the man who had to play two Opens to win one.

The Open didn't return for twenty-six years, but there was plenty of action at Inverness through the popular Inverness Four Ball event that the club hosted from 1935 to 1953. One of the first and most successful invitational events, it involved two-man teams and used the better score of the two balls on each hole. Ben Hogan and Jimmy Demaret paired together and won it four times, as did Sam Snead with four different partners.

During 1940-44 Byron Nelson was the club professional at Inverness. He credits the club for giving him invaluable training. "I used to play against the best ball of four of our best golfers," he said. "There was many a day when I shot 66 and lost." During his tenure at Inverness Nelson played about seventy-five tournaments and won about 45 percent of them. Nelson also set a course record of 62.

But that was a course that bears no resemblance to the current one. In the mid-'50s architect Dick Wilson looked at Inverness and said, "Anyone who changes this Rembrandt is crazy." Then he proceeded to rebuild ten of the tees, recontour several fairways, add bunkers around landing areas and greens, convert the 9th hole from a par five to a par four, and extend the course more than 400 yards.

The Inverness that hosted the 1957 Open was much harder than anything the pros had seen from Toledo—a par 70 of 7013 yards. It was enough to make the game's best player withdraw. During one of the practice days, Ben Hogan over-exerted himself and developed "a cold in the back," later diagnosed as pleurisy. When on opening day Hogan was unable to raise his arms above his chest, the USGA took the unprecedented step of postponing his starting time nearly an hour, but to no avail. He withdrew.

However, his old four-ball partner did well. Jimmy Demaret, a 47-year-old grandfather, took the lead after fifty-four holes, then added a 72 in the final round for a 283 that looked as if it might be good enough for at least a playoff. But then both Dick Mayer and Cary Middlecoff sank difficult ten-foot putts on the 72nd hole to edge him by a stroke.

Mayer had thrown away an Open three years earlier at Baltusrol when he sliced his final teeshot into jail, making a fatal 7 where a 4 would have won it.

For most of 1957 Middlecoff, the defending Champion, had been unable to recapture the winning form he had displayed at Oak Hill. But on the eve of his defense, a three-hour practice session with Byron Nelson had helped. Although eight strokes behind at the halfway point, he stormed home on the last day with a pair of 68s, his last round being the lowest finishing score in an Open in twenty-five years. In the playoff, however, the mental and physical strain was too much for him. "If I could have walked from the 72nd hole

to a playoff, I think I would have beaten Dick," he said later. "But I couldn't relax Saturday night. I didn't sleep and in the process I lost all my momentum." Mayer won easily, 72 to 79.

This Inverness Open was also the first Open for 18-year-old Jack Nicklaus, as the 1920 Open had been for Bobby Jones at the same age. Jack birdied the first hole with a thirty-five-foot putt, parred the next two, and suddenly found himself in the lead. Then he fell apart, shooting a pair of 80s and missing the cut.

Stranger things would happen, if not to Nicklaus, then certainly to Inverness, in 1979. The center-ring competition lacked the drama of previous Opens here, but the sideshow acts alone were worth the price of admission.

They began on Wednesday when the USGA removed a fellow from the course. He had played nine holes of a practice round, had had his picture taken with Jack Nicklaus, and wasn't even entered in the tournament.

Then came Lon Hinkle, a plump, cherub-faced journeyman with a sunny disposition and a left-to-right fade on most of his shots. It was that fade that caused Hinkle to make history.

The 8th hole at Inverness is a 528-yard par five that doglegs left around a line of trees. It is one of four new holes that were designed in 1977 by George and Tom Fazio as part of an updating for the Open. Lon didn't like that right-to-left teeshot much because it didn't fit his fade. Ah, but he saw an alternative. Just to the left of the tee was a large gap between two huge oak trees—if he could thread his teeshot between those trees, and hit a fade down the 17th fairway, which ran parallel to 8, he'd have a shot to the green and would also cut about seventy yards off the hole. (Hinkle had tried a similar strategy in the 1978 New Orleans Open, shortcutting a hole three times and making birdie each time. He won that event by a stroke.) That's exactly what he did, drilling a 1-iron between the trees, then a 2-iron back over some more trees and onto the green. From there he two-putted for a birdie.

Five other players used the shortcut on Thursday—three of them making pars and two making birdies. This left the USGA with a dilemma. They could either move the tee forward, past the space in the trees, or they could somehow block the opening. Chi Chi Rodriguez, one of the shortcutters, predicted that Friday morning would bring the biggest hot dog stand in Open history.

He was wrong. Friday morning brought a twenty-five-foot-high, sixteen-foot-wide Black Hills spruce, festooned with a waggish sign: "Hinkle Tree." It did little to deter Lon or any of the others who favored the shortcut. The next day Hinkle hit a driver through the slightly smaller opening and again made birdie. But neither he nor anyone else used this ploy to great advantage. Hinkle finished twenty strokes off the pace in fifty-third place, and at least one player, Tom Purtzer, blew his chance for victory on number 8. In the final round Purtzer was in second place, three strokes behind the leader,

OPPOSITE: *8th hole.* INSET: *7th hole*

18th hole

Bob Tway and Greg Norman were tied with one hole to go in the 1986 PGA Championship. When Tway's approach shot finished at the base of the deep right-hand bunker while Norman safely found the front fringe of the green, the clear advantage went to the Australian. Then Tway played the bunker shot of the decade, maybe of all time, splashing the ball softly out of the sand, onto the green, and into the hole for an astonishing birdie to win his first major championship.

when he tried the Hinkle route—it put him in a ravine, which led to further trouble and a triple-bogey 8 that took him completely out of contention.

While all this was going on, there was yet another act on display. Bobby Clampett, the talented young amateur from California, had missed the cut and was a spectator for the weekend. But David Edwards was all alone as the first player off the tee, and he needed some company. Clampett was invited to play along. On the 1st tee he stunned the gallery by striking a drive 220 yards down the middle of the fairway—from a kneeling position. Later in the round he putted the ball between his legs, plumb-bobbed shots from bunkers, hit a few more kneelers, and generally entertained the crowd almost as much as he upset the USGA. At the 12th tee a blue-blazer approached him and told him to leave the course. Surely he is the only player eliminated from the same Open two times.

Throughout all this nonsense there was also an Open being played, and won handily, by Hale Irwin. Shortly after Purtzer made his eight on 8, Irwin found himself with a six-stroke lead going into the final nine. Irwin, the 1974 Open Champion and a man with a record of strong performances on the tough courses, had shot a course-record 67 in the third round. One of the game's best shotmakers and a fierce competitor, he had the championship locked, even though he stumbled through the finishing holes. His back nine of 40 included a double bogey at 18, but it was good enough for a two-stroke victory over two other Open Champions, Gary Player and Jerry Pate. Irwin thus became the fourteenth player to win two Opens—and the first winner with braces on his teeth. His 72-hole score of 284 also made him the first man in four Opens to match the Inverness par.

Seven years later par was not only matched, it was bludgeoned. In the 1986 PGA Championship no fewer than ten players bettered

Irwin's score, Irwin's course record was broken and then broken again, and Greg Norman looked for a while as if he'd set a new PGA Championship mark.

But this was the year Greg Norman looked as if he'd do a lot of things. The leading money winner on the Tour, he had won three events, including the British Open, prior to Inverness. However, he had also been the leader after fifty-four holes of the Masters and U.S. Open, and had been unable to win either. At Inverness, his frustration in the majors would continue: he would lead after eighteen, thirty-six, fifty-four and sixty-three holes—but not after seventy-two.

Rain on the Wednesday night before the tournament assured that the scores would be low, and when Norman sank an eleven-foot birdie putt at the 18th, he had the lead on a course-record round of 65. A pair of 68s in the second and third round took him to 202, one shy of the 54-hole PGA record. A third straight 68 would have given him the tournament record. Meanwhile, however, he had relinquished his Inverness record to a third-round 64 by Bob Tway. Tway had been having a pretty good 1986 himself. Second on the money list to Norman, he had won three times prior to Inverness. Now he was four behind Norman, and no one else was within five. It would be a two-man fight.

They had played only the 1st hole—both in par—when a heavy rainstorm forced a postponement until Monday. At the par-three 3rd hole Norman hit his teeshot over the green and bogeyed as Tway sank a twelve-footer for birdie. Just like that, the lead halved to two strokes. But the bogey-birdie tradeoff went back the other way at the 9th, so with nine holes to play Norman led by four. At 11 Norman hit his teeshot into a sand-filled divot, a bad break that resulted in an errant iron into a bunker and ultimately a double bogey. Back to two shots. When Tway birdied 13 it was down to one, and when Norman bogeyed 14 they were even with four to go. They remained even through 15, 16, and 17, thanks to some superb wedge play by Tway.

Then came the fateful final hole. Tway drove into the rough and then missed his approach shot into the deep right-hand bunker, pin-high with the hole. Norman found the fairway with his teeshot, then lofted a wedge that struck the green, took a bounce toward the hole, and then sucked back thirty feet into the collar of tall fringe.

Jack Nicklaus, who had just completed his 100th major championship—at the same site as his first—and had tied for sixteenth, had climbed into the 18th hole commentary position for ABC-TV. When he saw Tway's ball come to rest, he noted that Tway had missed his shot into the best possible place. Playing from sand is easier than trying to escape from heavy greenside rough, and Tway had a clean lie in the base of the bunker. Still, he faced a shot that had to be hit perfectly if he wanted to salvage par. With a high lip and twenty feet of fast green between him and the hole, he couldn't afford to be either too delicate or too forceful.

He was neither; the ball lofted up and over the lip, struck the green, and ran straight into the center of the cup for the most electrifying final-hole shot the game had seen in a long while. Tway jumped up and down a half dozen times as Norman contemplated his fate. The Australian had planned to chip up short of the hole and make a safe par—now he had to hole it for a tie. He tried his best to jam the ball straight at the flag, but went well by. Incredibly, the tournament he had dominated was lost with a closing 76.

Norman took his medicine like a champion, and predicted he'd come back with a victory the very next week and the week after that and the week after that. He did not win the next week. But the next month he did—the European Open—and thus began a run of six straight tournament victories in Europe and Australia, the longest streak since Byron Nelson's eleven in a row in 1945.

Four Opens were held at Inverness, each one on a markedly different course. Even the par changed, from 72 in 1920 to 71 in 1931 to 70 in 1957, then back to 71 for 1979 and the 1986 PGA. Furthermore, for every winner at Inverness there has been at least one architect. From Nichols to Ross to Tillinghast to Wilson to two Fazios, this has been a course in constant flux.

One reason for all this change is the nature of the terrain. Inverness is stretched across rolling land, and ten of the holes run parallel across a series of gulleys and hills. As golf equipment improved, longer hitters were able to reach the downward slopes of the landing areas, thus benefiting from huge forward bounces, and turning 400-yard par fours into drive-and-pitch holes.

Today's 6982-yard course is still not a long one by Open standards, nor is it as tree-tightened as other Open sites such as Medinah and Oak Hill. Its enduring challenge has been the quality of its greens. Tiny, severely canted, and sown with a strain of German bentgrass that is no longer available—the same grass used at Winged Foot and Oakmont—they have a smoothness and at times a speed that is virtually unattainable elsewhere. In 1957 they were so fast that the USGA instructed the course superintendent to slow them down. In 1977, when the Fazios relocated several greens, they actually picked up the precious turf from the old greens and resodded it into the new sites, whose contours were replicas of the originals.

These greens, combined with a strong assortment of long and short par fours, are the key to Inverness. The original Ross features are still in evidence, as at the 385-yard 2nd hole, where the undulating green falls off in several directions, presenting chipping challenges galore. The 3rd hole, one of the Fazio additions, doesn't really fit the Inverness look, with its broad pond, grass bunker, and three-level green, but it did produce the birdie-bogey swing in the Tway/Norman battle. The hole that Ted Ray drove, back in 1920, is now number 4, and more than its number has changed. At 466 yards it is not within reach of any mortal, and is arguably the hardest hole on the course. It is followed by another tough Fazio creation of 401 yards, with a stream running parallel to the right side of the right-to-left dogleg.

The 7th hole plays 452 yards, and its pulpit green is one of the toughest to putt. Tway and Norman both faced downhill fifteen-footers for birdies—but from above the hole—and both hit their putts off the green.

Number 8, the Hinkle Tree hole, is a severe dogleg left whose bunker-flanked two-level green is within reach of two long, well-positioned shots, even when they're played down the proper fairway. In 1986 no one tried the 17th hole shortcut, the Hinkle fir having been joined by a few others that created a forbidding wall.

One of the prettiest greensites in golf is at the 10th, one of the sub-400-yard doglegs for which Inverness is famed. The approach is from a steeply downhill fairway and the green sits just beyond a stream in a natural amphitheater backed by trees. The 11th, another short four of 378 yards, is a birdie hole, but it was here that Greg Norman took the double bogey that led to his demise.

Number 13, like 8, is a par five that is reachable by most of the pros. In 1979 Tom Weiskopf rifled a 4-iron to eight feet here in the third round and made the eagle putt to cut Hale Irwin's lead from four strokes to two. Irwin, standing in the fairway directly behind him, then hit a 2-iron from a sidehill lie and drilled it to two feet to regain the strokes.

The course finishes with a string of five par fours. The 14th and 15th total over 900 yards between them and anyone who pars both for four days will gain ground. The undulating green at 14 may be the hardest to putt on the course, while the teeshot at 15 must be played through a 100-yard-long chute of trees.

OVERLEAF: *18th hole.* INSET: *A jubilant Bob Tway after the greatest stroke of his career, a bunker shot that found the 72nd hole for a birdie that edged Greg Norman for the 1986 PGA Championship. Photo: AP/Wide World Photos*

The 405-yard 16th presents a birdie opportunity, but caution will be required on the last two holes. Number 17 is the hole where the Fazios had to tone down the slope of the green. Yet it remains a difficult target to find—often from a blind second shot—and to negotiate. It was here that Bob Tway played a pitch shot that was arguably better than his hole-out at 18. From a downhill lie in heavy rough—a position from which few observers thought he could hold the green—he lobbed the ball to three feet from the hole to save par.

The 18th, even at its Fazio-stretched length of 354 yards, is one of the shortest finishing holes on any major championship site, but Jack Nicklaus calls it "the hardest easy hole I ever played." From a slightly raised tee the fairway doglegs softly right to a tiny plateau green surrounded by bunkers and heavy rough and nestled at the foot of the clubhouse's back lawn. A well-placed teeshot leaves an intimidating wedge; a teeshot into the rough leaves mission impossible. It's no wonder that, from Vardon and Ray to Norman and Tway, this hole—and for that matter, this course—has been the scene of high drama.

U.S. Open: August 10-13, 1920

Ted Ray	74	73	73	75	295	1
Harry Vardon	74	73	71	78	296	T2
Jack Burke	75	77	72	72	296	T2
Leo Diegel	72	74	73	77	296	T2
Jock Hutchinson	69	76	74	77	296	T2
Charles Evans, Jr.	74	76	73	75	298	T6
Jim Barnes	76	70	76	76	298	T6
Robert T. Jones, Jr.	78	74	70	77	299	T8
Willie MacFarlane	76	75	74	74	299	T8
Bob MacDonald	73	78	71	78	300	10

U.S. Open: July 2-6, 1931

Billy Burke	73	72	74	73	292	
	73	76	77	71	297	1
George Von Elm	75	69	73	75	292	
	75	74	76	73	298	2
Leo Diegel	75	74	73	72	294	3
Wiffy Cox	76	74	74	72	296	T4
Bill Mehlhorn	77	73	75	71	296	T4
Gene Sarazen	74	78	74	70	296	T4
Mortie Dutra	71	77	73	76	297	T7
Walter Hagen	74	74	73	76	297	T7
T. Philip Perkins	78	73	76	70	297	T7
Al Espinosa	72	78	75	74	299	T10
Johnny Farrell	78	70	79	72	299	T10
Macdonald Smith	73	73	75	78	299	T10

U.S. Open: June 13-15, 1957

Dick Mayer	70	68	74	70	282	
					72	1
Cary Middlecoff	71	75	68	68	282	
					79	2
Jimmy Demaret	68	73	70	72	283	3
Julius Boros	69	75	70	70	284	T4
Walter Burkemo	74	73	72	65	284	T4
Ken Venturi	69	71	75	71	286	T6
Fred Hawkins	72	72	71	71	286	T6
Sam Snead	74	74	69	73	290	T8
R. De Vicenzo	72	70	72	76	290	T8
Chick Harbert	68	79	71	72	290	T8
Billy Maxwell	70	76	72	72	290	T8
Billy Joe Patton	70	68	76	76	290	T8

U.S. Open: June 14-17, 1979

Hale Irwin	74	68	67	75	284	1
Gary Player	73	73	72	68	286	T2
Jerry Pate	71	74	69	72	286	T2
Bill Rogers	71	72	73	72	288	T4
Larry Nelson	71	68	76	73	288	T4
Tom Weiskopf	71	74	67	76	288	T4
David Graham	73	73	70	73	289	7
Tom Purtzer	70	69	75	76	290	8
Jack Nicklaus	74	77	72	68	291	T9
Keith Fergus	70	77	72	72	291	T9

PGA Championship: August 7-11, 1986

Bob Tway	72	70	64	70	276	1
Greg Norman	65	68	69	76	278	2
Peter Jacobsen	68	70	70	71	279	3
D.A. Weibring	71	72	68	69	280	4
Bruce Lietzke	69	71	70	71	281	T5
Payne Stewart	70	67	72	72	281	T5
Mike Hulbert	69	68	74	71	282	T7
Jim Thorpe	71	67	73	71	282	T7
David Graham	75	69	71	67	282	T7
Doug Tewell	73	71	68	71	283	10

Scorecard

HOLE	YARDS	PAR
1	398	4
2	385	4
3	185	3
4	466	4
5	401	4
6	220	3
7	452	4
8	528	5
9	420	4
OUT	3455	35
10	363	4
11	378	4
12	167	3
13	523	5
14	448	4
15	458	4
16	405	4
17	431	4
18	354	4
IN	3527	36
TOTAL	6982	71

GOLF *Magazine* Rankings:
53rd in the World
33rd in the U.S.A.

4th hole

MEDINAH COUNTRY CLUB

MEDINAH, ILLINOIS
U.S. Open: 1949, 1975, 1990

Clubhouse

Medinah, the home of the Mohammedan religion, is a city in Saudi Arabia, about 110 miles from the Red Sea. Its distinguishing feature is the fact that its borders are defined by double walls.

Medinah, the site of three U.S. Opens, is a country club in northern Illinois, about twenty miles from Lake Michigan. Its distinguishing feature is the fact that its fairways are defined by double walls—of trees.

A "claustrophobia of trees" is the way Alistair Cooke referred to this big, difficult golf course, a course lined with 4,700 specimens of oaks and other species, a course stretchable to over 7600 yards, a course where only the strong—and straight—survive.

It didn't start that way. Medinah Number 3, as it is known, was originally intended as the third-string course for the Chicago chapter of the Ancient Order of Nobles of the Mystic Shrine. The Shriners, a fun-loving, philanthropic group derived from the Freemasons, were thriving during the Roaring Twenties, and over 50,000 of them lived in and around the Windy City. At Medinah a handful of them decided to form a club. One noble proposed anoth-er who proposed another and so on until, by 1925, the club was full, with 1,500 members (the same size as today, although only about 160 of the current members are Shriners).

Each of Medinah's charter members paid the then-steep initiation fee of $1,000, and with that opening ante they did some serious spending. They acquired 650 acres of property and installed a swimming pool, a polo field, an amphitheater, a boathouse, a gun club, an archery range, a skating rink, an equestrian club, a toboggan run, and a ski jump. This was a country club with the emphasis on country.

The centerpiece of it all was a clubhouse whose opulence never will be equaled. An entire village of artisans and workers labored four years on the 60,000-square-foot mosque. A combination of Byzantine, Italian, Louis XIV, and Oriental styles, its focal point is a sixty-foot-high rotunda inlaid with mosaics. The main ballroom sports a frescoed ceiling worthy of any Florentine cathedral. In the late '20s, the bill for all this was $600,000; the replacement cost today would be over $20 million.

When the club formally opened in 1925, one course was completed, a second was under construction, and the third—the site of the Opens—was still on the drawing board. Squeezed into eighty acres, Number 3 was intended for the wives and daughters of the Shriners, "a sporty little course that will become famous the country over to and for women."

The designer was one of the Shriners, Tom Bendelow, an expatriate Scot who had come to the States to work as a compositor on the *New York Herald*. He later had gone to work for A.G. Spalding as an architectural consultant. The Spalding Company, manufacturing thousands of golf clubs and balls, had an obvious interest in producing places for people to play, so Bendelow's assignment was to design courses and design them fast. This he did, often in as little as a day, for a fee of only $25. His method was denigrated as "18 stakes on a Sunday afternoon," and the courses became known as "Bendelow Specials," but today he is credited with nearly 300 designs.

As a woman's course, Medinah Number 3 was a complete failure. A par 71 of 6215 yards, it was longer than many LPGA Tour courses today, and far too stern a test for the hickory-swinging Chicago matrons. "Only excellent or par golfers would enjoy it," said an early review, and one member complained that the tee on the 17th hole was so far back that the golfer couldn't see the water (perhaps a blessing in disguise). In 1929, a few months after the course had opened, the club scrapped its women's-only plans and decided to re-create Number 3 in the form of a championship test.

They failed again. The new course, a par 70 of 6261 yards, got its first big test when sixty-two pros and five amateurs arrived for the Medinah Open in 1930. Lighthorse Harry Cooper, then the club pro at nearby Glen Oak, won with a 36-hole total of 136, the insulting part being his final round score of 63.

So it was back to the blueprints again. This time Englishman Harry Collis helped to create seven new holes, remodel two others, and add nearly 600 yards that played even longer since they were accompanied by a watering system. When it reopened in 1934, the par-72 course included four par fours of over 440 yards, and its par fives averaged over 550.

"It gives me the shakes," wrote Arthur B. Sweet in *The Camel Trail*, the club's publication. "Let Mr. Harry Cooper try to shoot a 63 over this new course. It will never be done—never."

Mr. Sweet was right. The 1935 Medinah Open was won by Cooper, but with a 72-hole score of 289, one over par. Version 3 of Number 3 remained untouched for fifty-two years, and from the championship tees, no one ever scored lower than 67.

The man to set that course record was Tommy Armour, hired as the club's professional in 1933. He once referred to Number 3 as "an examination in golf, as fine a test of golfing ability as one could ever find." Perhaps the best iron player the game has ever seen, Armour

OPPOSITE: *1st hole*

believed in hitting the ball hard with the hands. For him, that was easy; his paws were immense. A story holds that he once matched strength with Jack Dempsey, each of them holding a billiard cue out from his body by grasping it at the tip. Armour's hand proved twice as strong as Dempsey's.

Armour was an insightful teacher but not a particularly attentive one. Medinah lore claims that he used to amuse himself during dull lessons by shooting a .22 caliber rifle at chipmunks. One day a member, impatient with Armour's neglect, said, "When are you going to stop that and take care of me?" to which the Silver Scot replied, "Don't tempt me, you sonofabitch."

During the 1930s, Medinah grew in reputation to the point that it became ranked in the top 10 of America's golf courses. It also rated well with the game's finest players; Gene Sarazen won the 1937 Chicago Open at Medinah and Byron Nelson won the Western Open in 1939. It was not until ten years after that, however, on the occasion of the club's Silver Anniversary, that Number 3 reached the big time, with the 1949 U.S. Open.

With Ben Hogan out of action recuperating from his near-fatal auto accident, the favorite was Sam Snead, and if the Slammer could have parred the last two holes, he would have won. But at the 17th he faltered, taking three shots from the side of the green. The victory went instead to Cary Middlecoff, a young Memphis dentist who had been named to the 1947 Walker Cup Team but had declined in order to pursue a career in pro golf.

Herbert Warren Wind referred to Middlecoff as "the happy refugee from subgingival curettage." Cary had done a stint in the Army Dental Corps, where he claimed, "I bet I pulled 7,000 teeth before I discovered the Army had another dentist." That wrenching experience was enough to turn him toward golf, despite the efforts of his father, also a dentist, to convince him to remain an amateur. Middlecoff the elder went so far as to ask Bob Jones to prevail upon his son to stay an amateur, and Jones tried, but without success.

Middlecoff opened with a quiet 75 and then followed with rounds of 67-69 to take a one-stroke lead over the relatively obscure Buck White. White never got any closer, but early in the final round Clayton Heafner came from three strokes back to catch Cary, and the two of them battled throughout the back nine. When Heafner bogeyed 15, it was all the edge Middlecoff needed. His 73-287 was good for a one-stroke victory over Heafner and Snead. Middlecoff credited his victory to a swing tip he had received years earlier—coincidentally at Medinah and from the same Buck White—to get his chin off his chest in order to improve his backswing turn.

A comical footnote accompanies this Open. Marvin "Bud" Ward, near the lead after 36 holes, is said to have stopped at the bar for a breakfast bracer prior to the final 36-hole day. A friend stopped by and Ward offered him a drink; the kindness was repaid. Then another friend came by. Ward never made it to the first tee.

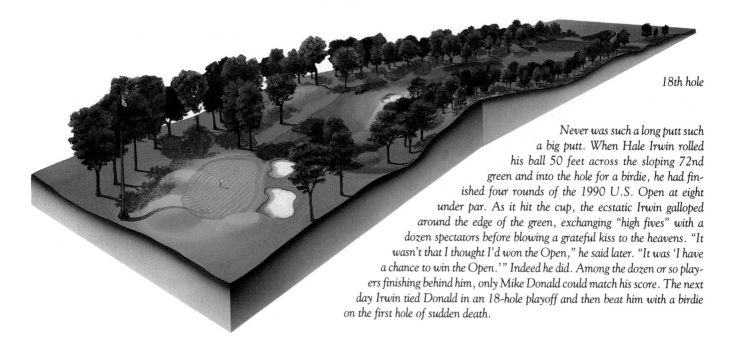

18th hole

Never was such a long putt such a big putt. When Hale Irwin rolled his ball 50 feet across the sloping 72nd green and into the hole for a birdie, he had finished four rounds of the 1990 U.S. Open at eight under par. As it hit the cup, the ecstatic Irwin galloped around the edge of the green, exchanging "high fives" with a dozen spectators before blowing a grateful kiss to the heavens. "It wasn't that I thought I'd won the Open," he said later. "It was 'I have a chance to win the Open.'" Indeed he did. Among the dozen or so players finishing behind him, only Mike Donald could match his score. The next day Irwin tied Donald in an 18-hole playoff and then beat him with a birdie on the first hole of sudden death.

After 1949, no other Open competitor reached the first tee of Medinah again until 1975. This was not a vintage Open. In fact, Mark McCormack characterized it in his annual *World of Professional Golf* as a dull event with dull weather and a dull winner, adding that he thought Medinah—now a par 71 of 7032 yards—was a highly overrated golf course.

The list of strong contenders that year was an impressive one. Nicklaus, Miller, Irwin, Trevino, and Weiskopf were all in their primes. Crenshaw and Watson were coming on strong, and Palmer and Player were still threats every week.

Watson, the reigning British Open Champion, took a share of the lead in round one with a 67, then added a 68 on Friday, tieing the 36-hole Open mark, thanks to a Medinah that had been softened by four straight days of rain. Just prior to teeing off in that second round, in which he was paired with Trevino and Bobby Nichols, Watson sniffed the air, turned on his heel and went back to the clubhouse. A veteran of many a Kansas City thunderstorm, he had sensed that lightning was on the way. Trevino and Nichols remained on the tee as officials pursued Watson. His gesture was delaying play, but Watson refused to return, as is a player's right if he feels he is endangered by the elements. Shortly thereafter a thunderclap rattled the course, and the siren was blown signifying suspension of play. Later the storm cleared and the round was completed. The irony of all this is that a week later at the Western Open another storm struck, and three golfers were felled by lightning. Two of them were Lee Trevino and Bobby Nichols.

Watson had a three-stroke lead on second-place occupant Ben Crenshaw, but the next day they both collapsed. Tom three-putted the first, missed from two feet at the second, and never recovered his confidence, carding a 78 as the errant Crenshaw communed with the Medinah trees en route to a 76. Into the breach jumped

Frank Beard, whose 67 staked him to a three-stroke lead over Watson and Pat Fitzsimons, four over Crenshaw, Lou Graham, and England's Peter Oosterhuis.

The last few holes of the last round, as played by the last few competitors, cause this to be remembered as the Open no one wanted to win.

It had come down to Messrs. Beard, Crenshaw, and Graham plus John Mahaffey, who had climbed into it from six strokes back, and the ominous Jack Nicklaus, seven behind at the start. A 34 on the front nine, combined with some stumbling by the leaders, put Nicklaus back into the fray, and after fifteen holes he had pulled to within a stroke of the leaders. Nicklaus, who built his reputation and record on an ability to grind out pars as others falter in the heat of battle, needed three such pars to win. Instead, he made three bogeys and finished at four over. When Mahaffey parred the last two holes, his 287 beat Jack by two.

That left Beard, Crenshaw, and Graham out on the 16th at two over. Any of them could have parred-in and won; none of them did. Beard bogeyed both 16 and 17 to go four over, and Crenshaw splashed his teeshot into the lake on 17 for a fatal double bogey. Graham was able to stay in the lead until the final hole, where he bunkered his approach shot and made bogey to tie Mahaffey at three over par.

The playoff was a bit dull, too. It was the only one of the ten Open playoffs since 1931 in which neither of the two competitors was a prior winner of a major championship. They began by exchanging bogeys at the first, and neither player excelled during the rest of the day. Graham, however, had the steadier putter all day. He took a three-stroke lead after ten holes, and eventually won by two on a round of even par.

Controversy surrounded the 18th hole. Basically, it was a dogleg that bent too soon, forcing the world's best players to lay up with irons, then face a disproportionately lengthy second shot. It was also lacking from a spectator standpoint, with greenside seating for only about 500 people. These two factors led the USGA to vow never to return to Medinah.

The club didn't like the sound of that. Members conferred with USGA officials, hired architect Roger Packard, and tore up not simply the last hole but most of their back nine. The list of changes reads like a report from a federal government agency: Former holes 12 and 13 became 15 and 16; former holes 16 and 17 became holes 12 and 13; the par-four 14th became a par five; the former 15th, a par four, became the new par-five 14th; the new 17th became a short lake-crossing imitation of old 17; and the finisher became a 440-yard par four with gallery seating for 5,000. The changes, which cost the members $1.2 million, boosted the course from a par of 71 to 72, from a maximum length of 7056 to a maximum of 7667 yards, and to a rating from the Chicago District Golf Association of 77.3, one of the highest in the country.

In 1984 the USGA had a look at the new layout, and later awarded the club the 1988 Senior Open, won by Gary Player. More important, they announced that Medinah would host the 1990 Open.

It was an Open awaited with more than the usual excitement because this was the year Curtis Strange had a chance to become the first three-in-a-row winner since Willie Anderson in 1903-5.

Hale Irwin romps in delight after sinking a mammoth putt to tie for the 1990 Open lead after seventy-two holes. The next day he beat Mike Donald in a playoff for the title. Photo: © Robert Walker

Playing the course for the first time in the summer of '89, Curtis pronounced it to his liking, "a lot like The Country Club and Oak Hill [sites of his '88 and '89 victories] but longer."

When that 1990 Open was over, a man had won his third U.S. Open, but it wasn't Curtis Strange, who tied for 21st, it was Hale Irwin, who at age 45 added to his victories at Winged Foot and Inverness and became history's oldest U.S. Open Champion, triumphing in a playoff over Mike Donald.

The key in regulation play was the seventy-second hole where Irwin rammed home an incredible 50-foot putt for a birdie that gave him the clubhouse lead at eight under par 280, an unusually low score, thanks to a course that had been soft all week due to intermittent rain. Donald, playing several holes behind Irwin, held a one-stroke edge until the 16th hole where he bogeyed. He then made two routine pars to tie Irwin. Moments before Donald, Masters Champion Nick Faldo had lipped out a birdie putt at 18 to finish one out of the playoff. Had Faldo made that putt, he might have duplicated Hogan's Triple Crown, since he went on to win the 1990 British Open at St. Andrews.

The smart Monday money was on the veteran Irwin, renowned for his gritty prowess on difficult courses. But Donald, a winless journeyman in his eleventh year, played courageously during the playoff and when it was over they had again tied, this time at 74. Sudden death ensued, and it was just that for Donald, who yielded to Irwin's ten-foot birdie putt at the first hole.

Irwin, who had not won a tournament in five years, had begun the championship on a special exemption from the USGA, an invitation that freed him from having to qualify. Ninety-one holes later, he proved that the Association's confidence was well-founded as he became the only man to hold exactly three Open titles. (Willie Anderson, Bobby Jones, Ben Hogan, and Jack Nicklaus each have four.) The following week he won the Buick Classic, and he went on to have the finest season in his twenty-two-year career.

This is not a finesse course, it's a place that rewards good ball-strikers, players who can display distance with accuracy. The ground rules become apparent from the very first hole, a par four that demands precision. A pushed or pulled teeshot will be in the trees, a pushed or pulled iron will be in sand or heavy collar grass. The same fates apply on nearly all the ensuing seventeen holes.

One of the criticisms of the current course is that three of its four par threes present the same type of shot, a lengthy carry across Lake Kadijah (named after Mohammed's wife). The first of these is number 2, 167 yards to a green that slopes steeply from back to front. Pat Fitzsimons made an ace here in 1975 to take a share of the first-round lead with Tom Watson.

The next five holes are vintage Medinah—four intimidatingly long and tight par fours mixed in with two not-really-reachable fives. The second shot to number 3 is partially blind, and the green is so narrow that its assailants are frequently surprised to find that their balls have found one of the flanking bunkers. A big drive at the 4th sometimes leaves a downhill lie and a long or middle iron shot to a green perched atop the highest point on the property. Par is a great score here, even for the best pros in the world. The par-five 5th is reachable but only with two powerfully propelled yet carefully placed shots. The drive must avoid a huge bunker in the right side of the landing area, and the uphill second will have to avoid two deep bunkers. At 6, for the first time, the view from the tee is a bit more open, at least on the left, but that's a mixed blessing as out of bounds runs along that side. The green is one of the largest on the course, but it should be—from the back tees this hole measures 445 yards.

Number 7 is loved by some, reviled by others, a sharp dogleg-right par five where a teeshot missed even slightly to the right leaves a difficult-to-decipher second that must either be sliced around the corner or hoisted over the trees to a position from which the plateau green may be safely attacked. The 8th is a straightforward par three except for its subtle tree-filtered winds, and 9 is a birdie hole for those courageous enough to cut its dogleg with a big, high draw over the trees.

The 10th is a patience hole, a three-shot par five where birdies should be accepted, not sought, especially from the severely sloping green. Most of the pros will hit 3-woods and irons from the tee at 11, rather than risk nailing a long, straight drive through the corner of the right-to-left dogleg, where trees and rough await. The green here is long but narrow, cinched by sand.

Number 12 is one of the most difficult par fours in the world. Formerly the 16th hole, it was the beginning of Nicklaus's demise in 1975, when he hooked his drive into tree trouble. The ideal teeshot is a long one that rolls to the bottom of a swale about 270 yards down the right side of the fairway. From there, it's still a middle or long iron uphill to the green precariously perched on the side of a hill.

Number 13 proved unlucky for Crenshaw in '75, but back then this hole was the 17th. Depending on the tee used, it can play from 150 to nearly 240 yards, downhill and across Lake Kadijah, to a green with bunkers at three, six, nine, and twelve o'clock. In 1949, both of Middlecoff's closest pursuers, Clayton Heafner and Sam Snead, bogeyed this hole to fall a crucial stroke behind. Snead, who tried to putt his ball from heavy fringe, was later asked why he didn't chip. "Man, if I had chipped, I might have left the ball at my feet," he said. "Then where would I be? Right back where I started."

The first 200 yards of the 14th come back across the lake to an uphill fairway. From there the fairway becomes a tree-lined corridor to a green surrounded by bunkers. It's reachable, but a front bunker will give pause to all but the brave. The last birdie opportunity on the course comes at the par-four 15th, where the main challenge will be the sloping green.

Number 16 is another controversial hole, a par four that doglegs abruptly left and uphill at about the 200-yard mark. Some have said that it doglegs too soon and too sharply, forcing a layup off the tee

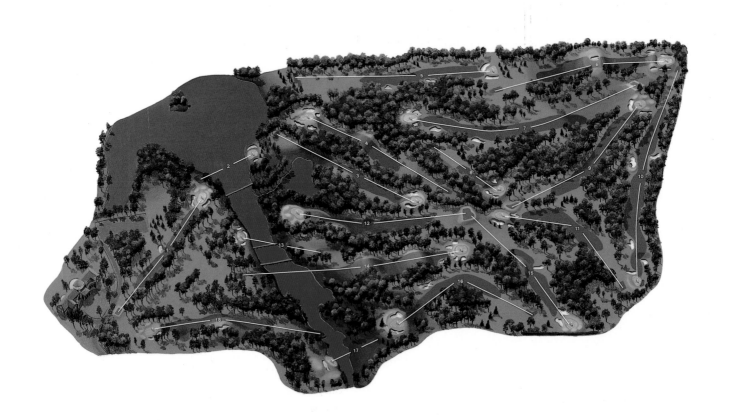

13th hole

and then an overly long approach. The perched green is all carry with a mid to long iron. A shot that does not fly to the green may roll 50 yards back down the fairway. On the other hand, a shot that goes over the green will leave a difficult downhill chip where simply keeping the ball on the surface will be a good shot. This hole, voted by the PGA of America as one of the toughest in the country, was pivotal to Irwin's victory. In the final round, after a poor teeshot, he hooked a 2-iron onto the green and sank an eight-foot putt for a birdie.

Number 17 is the last of the lake-leaping par threes, a 168-yarder to the most severe green on the course, carved out of the slope on the bank of the lake. Bunkers to the left and rear complicate the challenge. Scott Simpson led the 1990 U.S. Open until the third round when he put his teeshot in the back bunker. He left the green with a triple-bogey 6 and was never in serious contention again.

As for the final hole, it has been lengthened and aired-out a bit. Today, it is a 440-yard slight dogleg left. The uphill teeshot, like so many at Medinah, is about half-blind, leaving a middle iron to a wide but shallow green that is full of subtle undulations and has room for several thousand spectators, most of whom had ringside seats on Sunday of the 1990 Open when Hale Irwin rolled in the putt of his life.

17th hole

U.S. Open: June 9-11, 1949

Cary Middlecoff	75	67	69	75	286	1
Clayton Heafner	72	71	71	73	287	T2
Sam Snead	73	73	71	70	287	T2
Jim Turnesa	78	69	70	72	289	T4
Bobby Locke	74	71	73	71	289	T4
Buck White	74	68	70	78	290	T6
Dave Douglas	74	73	70	73	290	T6
Johnny Palmer	71	75	72	73	291	T8
Claude Harmon	71	72	74	74	291	T8
Pete Cooper	71	73	74	73	291	T8

U.S. Open: June 19-22, 1975

Lou Graham	74	72	68	73	287	
					71	1
John Mahaffey	73	72	71	71	287	
					73	2
Bob Murphy	74	73	72	69	288	T3
Hale Irwin	74	71	73	70	288	T3
Ben Crenshaw	70	68	76	74	288	T3
Frank Beard	74	69	67	78	288	T3
Jack Nicklaus	72	70	75	72	289	T7
Peter Oosterhuis	69	73	72	75	289	T7
Arnold Palmer	69	75	73	73	290	T9
Tom Watson	67	68	78	77	290	T9
Pat Fitzsimons	67	73	73	77	290	T9

U.S. Open: June 15-18, 1990

Hale Irwin	69	70	74	67	280	
					74-3	1
Mike Donald	67	70	72	71	280	
					74-4	2
Nick Faldo	72	72	68	69	281	T3
Billy Ray Brown	69	71	69	72	281	T3
Tim Simpson	66	69	75	73	283	T5
Mark Brooks	68	70	72	73	283	T5
Greg Norman	72	73	69	69	283	T5
Scott Hoch	70	73	69	72	284	T8
Tom Sieckmann	70	74	68	72	284	T8
Craig Stadler	71	70	72	71	284	T8
Fuzzy Zoeller	73	70	68	73	284	T8
Steve Jones	67	76	74	67	284	T8
J.-M. Olazabal	73	69	69	73	284	T8

Scorecard

HOLE	YARDS	PAR
1	385	4
2	180	3
3	412	4
4	434	4
5	526	5
6	445	4
7	581	5
8	190	3
9	429	4
OUT	3582	36
10	577	5
11	402	4
12	462	4
13	199	3
14	545	5
15	384	4
16	436	4
17	168	3
18	440	4
IN	3613	36
TOTAL	7195	72

GOLF *Magazine* Rankings:
40th in the World
24th in the U.S.A.

MERION GOLF CLUB

ARDMORE, PENNSYLVANIA
U.S. Open: 1934, 1950, 1971, 1981

She has been called a dowager, a damsel, a siren, a sorceress, and the Princess Grace of fairways and greens. She is the hostess with the mostest, the site of more national championships than any other club—thirteen of them—dating back to the U.S. Women's Amateur in 1904. And in the annals of golf she has produced more magnificent moments than any place this side of St. Andrews. Such is the feminine mystique of Maid Merion, a 120-acre Philadelphia beauty who has teased and tortured the game's finest players for over three quarters of a century.

Not bad for a gal who started out in cricket. In the spring of 1865, fifteen young men from Philadelphia founded the Merion Cricket Club. Its first president, Archibald Montgomery, was unable to sign the club's charter because he had lost his right arm, owing to the premature discharge of a saluting cannon, while he was on duty at the funeral of President Lincoln on April 22, 1865.

Golf was then unheard of in America, but within a few years Andrew Carnegie would become hooked on the game and declare it to be "the necessary adjunct of high civilization," and since no civilization was higher than Philadelphia's, Merion's Main Liners soon began congregating with their clubs on the nearby estate of Clement A. Griscom. (Griscom's daughter Frances, known as Pansy, won the 1900 U.S. Women's Amateur and was the true force behind the Curtis Cup matches—the Curtis sisters merely donated the trophy.)

In 1896 the club bought 100 acres of land about a mile from the

Basketwork pins unique to Merion Golf Club

cricket grounds, and built nine undistinguished holes at a cost of $600. By year's end 152 cricketers had become golfers, and as their numbers grew, so did the need for a bigger playground. In 1900 another nine was added. It was over that course that the 1904 and 1909 Women's Amateur championships were played.

In 1910 the club bought an L-shaped property of 120 acres in Haverford Township, described as "worn-out farmland, none too well adapted in dimension or topography for golf course purposes." On the land was a farmhouse, built in 1824, which still stands today as the core of the Merion clubhouse.

A five-man committee was appointed to oversee design and construction of a new golf course. Its chairman and the man who became the principal course architect was Hugh Wilson, a Princeton graduate and keen golfer. Wilson, an insurance broker, had had no training as an architect, but then, neither had his fellow Philadelphians A.W. Tillinghast (Baltusrol, Winged Foot) and George C. Thomas (Riviera, Los Angeles North).

When the committee sent Wilson to England and Scotland to study the great courses, he took his work seriously, returning with sheaves of drawings and notes. He also sought the advice and assistance of C.B. MacDonald and MacDonald's son-in-law H.J. Whigham, the first two U.S. Amateur Champions. MacDonald, highly praised for his design of the National Golf Links on Long Island, had made the same pilgrimage Wilson had, but had confined his studies to Scotland. As a result, the National, although it fits the bleak, windswept terrain of Eastern Long Island, is full of blind holes and surprises whereas Wilson's Merion has a simple honesty that recalls the English heath and parkland courses as much as the seaside Scottish links.

The course became known as Merion East, because Wilson later designed a West course as well. He did almost no architectural work beyond these two, save for a couple of lesser courses in Philadelphia, although he did put the finishing touches on George Crump's Pine Valley. But with his work at Merion alone, Wilson's place in the pantheon of golf course architects is secure.

The noted golf writer Charles Price captured the fascination of this course when he observed, "Almost anyone can design a course on which par can be broken as easily as crystalware. And almost anyone can design a course on which par can never be broken. Hugh Wilson... paradoxically, accomplished both feats at Merion."

The shortest Open course since World War II, Merion has not changed a great deal since it was unveiled in 1912. In the words of Price, "Merion wouldn't alter the course for the Second Coming, let alone another golf championship." Walter Hagen, who made one of his last appearances here in the 1934 Open and shot a 318 that included the only recorded instance of a competitor *putting* out of bounds, nonetheless had praise for Merion. "This is the type of course where you feel after every round that you can break 70 your next round," he said. "But you don't."

Lean and mean, Merion is designed for control, accuracy, and smarts. She cannot be beaten into submission, only coaxed and coddled. None of her lovely features stands out; they are all in balance. When a hole calls for a long approach shot, its green is generous; when the shot in is a short one, the target area is small. Some fairways bend left, others right, some play downhill, others up, and every hole is shrewdly bunkered. The greens are similarly varied, some of them almost flat, others mildly contoured, and others fiercely sloped and hellish to putt. These were greens designed in the days when mowing equipment was relatively primitive; the surfaces were shaggy, so the ups and downs could be made severe. But combine some of those slopes with today's close-cutting mowers, and the result, under Open conditions, can be terrifying.

Yet Merion demands nothing unfairly; she just demands everything. During the 1971 U.S. Open, which he lost in a playoff, Jack Nicklaus said, "Acre for acre it may be the best test of golf in the world." And perhaps the ultimate accolade comes from Tom Doak, a golf course architect, golf writer, and the administrator of *GOLF Magazine*'s biennial ranking of the 100 Greatest Courses in the World. A harsh critic of many of the top-rated layouts, he says, "I've seen a lot of golf courses that are more difficult and a lot that are more spectacular also, but somehow Merion has an aura of perfection . . . it is about the only course I know where a golf architect would be hard pressed to suggest any improvements."

Clubhouse

11th hole

Bobby Jones hit no heroic shots at Merion's 11th hole, but it was here in September of 1930 that he completed the Grand Slam. Jones was seven holes up on Gene Homans in the 36-hole final match for the U.S. Amateur when both players lofted their approach shots over the Baffling Brook and onto the green. Jones stroked his first putt close to the cup, and then Homans, needing to sink a lengthy putt to stay alive, missed, as Jones capped the greatest season in golf history.

That aura begins right at the first hole. When Dan Jenkins selected *Sports Illustrated*'s Best 18 Holes in America, only one course was represented with two holes—Merion—with holes 1 and 11. From a teesite so close to the clubhouse that, in the words of Arnold Palmer, "a golfer with a long, flat swing is liable to knock a pot of tea off a luncheon table," it winds gently uphill and to the right to a green 365 yards away. A big hitter may try to cut the dogleg, but a series of bunkers will give him pause. There are twelve bunkers on this relatively short hole—twelve White Faces of Merion. Legend holds that architect Wilson dispatched construction foreman Joe Valentine with white sheets which Valentine unfurled at the proposed sites of bunkers as Wilson assured himself, from afar, that the bunkers would be both pleasing and intimidating to the observer.

The 2nd, a shortish par five, is reachable by any player with strength, accuracy, and guts. Normally, 535 yards is simply two strong whacks, but on this hole the right side is lined with out of bounds. However, the player who is brave enough to strike a drive down the right side of the fairway will be rewarded with the most open approach to the green. It is this type of decision-making that is delightfully constant at Merion.

In the playoff for the 1971 Open, Jack Nicklaus took a bogey six at the 2nd and then double bogeyed number 3, a par three whose sloping plateau green is turfed over the site of an old barn.

Perhaps the only element of imbalance at Merion is in the fact that the last par five on the course occurs at the 4th hole. But architect Wilson knew this was the perfect site for a long hole and he had the courage to put it here. The fairway tumbles 600 yards to a pear-shaped green fronted by a creek, meaning that position is important on both the drive and the second shot, which often will be played from some sort of hilly lie.

More strategy comes into play at the 5th, where the aggressive player may try to shorten the hole by playing down the left side of the fairway, but must do so knowing that the terrain slopes to the left and a creek lurks just in the rough.

The next four holes are a slicer's nightmare, with out of bounds down the right side of each of them. Number 6, at 428 yards, is the longest par four on the nine. Lee Trevino won the 1971 Open despite a triple-bogey 7 here in round two. Holes 7 and 8 are drive-and-pitch fours with small greens. Smart players tee off with a club that will leave them about 100 yards to the hole, enabling a full wedge shot with enough backspin to keep the ball on the putting surface.

Number 9 is the most picturesque hole on the course, a downhill par three to a green fronted by Cobbs Creek and surrounded by white faces.

Long hitters may launch into the inward nine by trying to drive the green at the 310-yard 10th. It's reachable, but even more reachable is the enormous bunker smack on the straight-line route from tee to green. Like many of the bunkers at Merion, it is bearded with dune grass and Scotch broom, adding interest to the escape shot.

Ben Crenshaw, co-holder of the competitive record at Merion

OVERLEAF: *9th hole.* INSET: *During the summer of 1971, Lee Trevino's rare form brought him three national championships in a span of twenty-one days. Photo: © Leonard Kamsler*

13th hole

(64) and a golf historian, says he gets goose bumps every time he steps to the tee of number 11. A par four that plays 369 yards downhill and across the Baffling Brook, it is the most storied hole at Merion and arguably in Open history. It was here that Gene Sarazen made a damaging seven and Nicklaus made a damaging 6. It was here also, in the third round of the 1934 Open, that the leader, Bobby Cruickshank, after watching his brook-bound approach bounce off a rock and onto the green, jubilantly tossed his niblick into the air, only to have it come down on his head, knocking him cold. "Aye," he said, after coming to, "that's the first time I've made a par hitting two rocks on the same hole."

And it was of course on this 11th hole that Bobby Jones defeated Eugene Homans 8 and 7 in the final of the 1930 U.S. Amateur to complete the greatest achievement in the history of golf, the Grand Slam. But this is a difficult hole, whether you're playing for the Grand Slam or just a par. As architect Robert Trent Jones sees it, "If you hit this green with your second shot, you heave a sigh of relief so deep that it is usually audible a mashie shot away."

From a tee deep in a chute of trees, the 12th hole climbs back uphill while doglegging sharply right. The second shot can be difficult to judge, and there is not much room for error, since a large bunker fronts the green and Ardmore Avenue is just beyond the back edge. It was from this green in 1934 that Walter Hagen putted a ball out of bounds. Even more agonizing was the fate of his fellow

competitor, Wiffy Cox, whose approach shot lodged in the coat of a spectator. Startled, the spectator leaped to his feet, snatching the coat in an instinctive action. Out popped the ball, and it rolled out of bounds. Today, the Rules would allow the ball to be replaced without penalty, but back then it cost Wiffy two strokes, precisely the margin by which he finished second.

The tiny 13th hole may be viewed as a breather, but don't tell that to Hubert Green. Green served a short time at Merion as assistant professional, but that didn't prepare him for what happened in 1981 when his teeshot to 13 struck the "flag" and bounced into a bunker, resulting in a double-bogey 5.

The "flag" Hubert hit was not a flag at all but a Merion basket. One of the British features that Hugh Wilson adopted was the inverted-pear-shaped wicker basket used atop the flagsticks at Sunningdale Golf Club near London. Sunningdale stopped using them long ago, but they remain a fixture at Merion, where they are woven in the maintenance shop. The front-nine baskets are crimson, the back nine tangerine. The baskets add not only character but difficulty to Merion, where the small greens become even more elusive when one is unable to read the wind by checking a flag.

Number 14, a long dogleg left, starts the difficult road home. Out of bounds looms on the left, but the overly cautious may easily catch a bunker on the right. Three more bunkers grasp the sides and back of the green, but the front is open, allowing for a rolling approach.

Clever bunkering creates interest on the 15th, where the ideal drive is a power fade. A deep bunker to the right of the green makes the approach difficult if the pin is on that side. Olin Dutra, Lee Trevino, and David Graham all sank dramatic birdie putts here en route to their victories.

The 16th is known the world over as the quarry hole. An old limestone quarry stretches from about the 300-yard mark to the green, a wild wasteland from which there is virtually no return. The key is to keep the teeshot in the fairway in order to insure a safe approach over the chasm to a slippery, two-tiered green.

Number 17 comes back across the quarry from an elevated tee. Even strong players use anything from a 4-iron to a fairway wood to cover its 222 yards. The green, a large one for Merion, has a drop of four feet from back to front and is ringed with six bunkers.

Ironically, this shortest of championship courses concludes with one of the longest finishing holes, 463 yards. The teeshot is semi-blind over an arm of the quarry, and a big carry it is. All serious golf fans know the famous photograph of Ben Hogan playing a 1-iron to this green in 1950 to clinch a spot in the playoff.

Merion first drew national attention in the summer of 1916, when the U.S. Amateur Championship arrived, bringing with it a lad whose name would become inextricably linked with the course, Bobby Jones. It was Jones's first national championship. Aged 14, 5 foot 4 and a chunky 165 pounds, he appeared at the course wearing his first pair of long pants and a pair of army shoes into which he had screwed a set of spikes.

Jones had played on Bermuda greens all his life, and had never seen surfaces as smooth and fast as Merion's. In his first practice round he putted one ball off a green and into a water hazard. But this was not a boy without credentials—earlier in the year he had won the Georgia State Amateur. Still, quite a stir arose when Jones led the field of qualifiers with a 74 in the first round. He soared to an 89 in the afternoon, but still qualified easily.

Cocky and temperamental like most 14-year-olds, Jones put on a show for the gallery. Herbert Warren Wind recalled in *The Story of American Golf*:

> After a poor shot the youngster threw clubs and recited some of the most fragrant cursewords he had learned on the back steps of the Jones house on Willow Street from the cook's brother . . . Jones was the sensation of the tournament. Everyone went home raving about the boy from Atlanta who hit the ball so naturally and perfectly that even at 14 he was one of the longest drivers in the field.

Jones won his first two matches before losing to the defending champion, Bob Gardner, as Chick Evans claimed the title, thus becoming the first man to win both the U.S. Amateur and U.S. Open in the same year. (For the record, it was also Evans who coined the term "White Faces of Merion.")

In 1924 an older and wiser Jones returned to Merion, played and putted beautifully all week, and won his first U.S. Amateur, defeating George Von Elm in the final match 9 and 8.

Six years later he returned again to the site of his first national championship and played his last national championship, the 1930 U.S. Amateur. With the British Open and the Amateur championships of the U.S. and Britain already under his belt, this was the most important tournament of his—or any—career.

"Multiply the tension of a no-hitter by fifty," said Wind. "No-hitters are spun in less than three hours. Jones had been working for four months on the Grand Slam, on two continents, in all sorts of weather, in all sorts of form." Added to this was the pressure of being the most popular athlete of an era which included heroes such as Babe Ruth, Bill Tilden, and Jack Dempsey. As his friend and biographer O.B. Keeler reported in the 1931 *Golfer's Yearbook*, "Certainly there was never an intenser, more unanimous or more universal desire for the winning of one particular competitor in any one sporting event."

No one was aware of the pressure more acutely than Jones. Despite it being the era of prohibition, he had arrived at his hotel with a bottle of whiskey in his suitcase. (When the bellman dropped the case roughly, there was a sound of breaking glass, and the telltale amber liquid seeped out.) This was the only championship in which Jones admitted he was unable to sleep at night. Nonetheless, he led the qualifying with a 69-73—142, and would have broken the qualifying record had he not overhit the final green and made bogey.

The first two rounds of the Amateur in those days were 18-hole matches, the remaining three rounds went 36. Jones always felt the earlier matches were more hazardous, mindful that any player can get hot over a short stretch. But this time he had little to fear, winning both matches by the score of 5 and 4. He then beat Fay Coleman 6 and 5 in the third round, and in the semi-final coasted by Jess Sweetser 9 and 8.

Gene Homans had defeated Lawson Little and Charlie Seaver (baseball player Tom's father) en route to the finals. As the one remaining obstacle to the Slam, he was nervous, and he didn't par a hole until the 6th. After the morning eighteen, Bobby was seven up.

Both players reached the twenty-ninth hole in two, and Jones laid his approach putt close to the cup. Thus, to keep the match alive, Homans had to make a long putt. He stroked it carefully, but as soon as he saw it veer off line, he strode over to be the first to congratulate Jones.

The denouement was captured eloquently by Wind:

> Protected by a Marine bodyguard, which had dashed on the green the second the match was over, the authentic hero walked thoughtfully to the clubhouse, acknowledging as best he could the respect his thousands of rejoicing subjects were paying him, unable to digest the fact that the Herculean task

he had set himself was actually accomplished, tired, very tired after pushing himself all week and happy, so very happy, that at last it was all behind him. The walk to the clubhouse seemed to take days, and it seemed weeks before the hordes of friends and admirers were finished shaking his hand and telling him how overjoyed they were, but at length, everyone had the good sense to clear out of the locker room and give Bob a few minutes alone with his dad, the old Colonel. The great friends let themselves go completely, and in the furious outpouring of heart and head, Bobby finally washed himself clear of the strain he had been carrying around for months.

After that, there were no worlds left to conquer for the emperor Jones. In his autobiography, *Golf Is My Game*, he said, "I wasn't quite certain what had happened or what I had done. I only knew that I had completed a period of most strenuous effort, and that at this point nothing more remained to be done, and that on this particular project, at least, there could never be at any time in the future anything else to do." And so at age 28, he retired from competitive golf to pursue other interests, foremost among them the establishment of the Augusta National Golf Club and The Masters.

The next winner at Merion was far from the favorite. A 20-1 shot at the beginning of the week, Olin Dutra triumphed over the course, the field, and a case of amoebic dysentery. After the first 36 holes he was eight strokes behind Bobby Cruickshank and five in back of the man expected to win, Gene Sarazen.

But on the windy morning of the final day, Dutra shot a 71 to pull into the thick of the chase. During the lunch break Sarazen approached him and asked what he'd shot. When Dutra told him, Sarazen simply frowned and walked away. The Squire had posted a 73 to pull ahead of Cruickshank, who had blown to a 77, but now he knew he'd have to keep an eye on Dutra, just three behind.

Dutra, whom *New York Times* reporter William Richardson described as "a massively constructed Californian," was paired with then British Open champion Lawson Little, another big fellow. Herb Graffis said the twosome "ambled around the course looking for all the world like a couple of youths who thump down from trucks, walk up to doors and ask the lady of the house, 'Where d'ya want me to lift the piano into?'"

But Dutra negotiated Merion with delicacy. With nine holes to go, he was still three strokes behind Sarazen, but then Gene suffered disaster at 11. Choosing an iron from the tee in order to stay in play, he nonetheless hooked his ball into the Baffling Brook. He then took a drop and knocked the third shot into a bunker. The result was a seven, which brought him even with Dutra, who was playing three holes behind him.

Sarazen played the next few holes without further trouble, but so did Dutra, and as Gene reached the 18th green, Olin stood ready to putt at 15. Each man faced a lengthy birdie putt, Dutra's a twisting ninety-footer. Sarazen, concerned at the progress of his pursuer,

had dispatched runners all afternoon to keep him abreast of Dutra's round, but this time he decided to see for himself. Climbing atop his caddie's back, he watched in stupefaction as Dutra smacked the putt into the hole to pull even. The shaken Squire then three-putted for a bogey. The third putt was the stroke by which he lost.

Tom Creavy shot 66 in the final round, breaking the Merion record and tieing the finishing-round score of Sarazen in the 1922 Open at Fresh Meadow, an Open record. Creavy's was the only score all week under 70.

In June of 1950 the Open returned to Merion, sixteen years after Olin Dutra's victory and sixteen months after Ben Hogan's near-fatal automobile accident. Wrapped in bandages from his ankles to his knees, Hogan arrived determined to withstand the special rigors of the Open. Earlier in the year he had stunned the golf world not simply by returning to play but by nearly winning his first event, the Los Angeles Open, where he tied Sam Snead after 72 holes before losing in an 18-hole playoff.

After each round at Merion Hogan was forced to put his legs in traction to improve circulation. Each evening he took the bandages off and soaked in a tub.

He shot 72 in the opening round but found himself eight strokes in back of an obscure pro named Lee Mackey who had just set a new Open record on a round of 64 that had included seven 3s and a 2. (Mackey shot 81 the next day and eventually tied for twenty-sixth.)

A 69 in round two left Hogan two behind Dutch Harrison, with the Open's torturous double round to go. On the morning of the final day Hogan posted another 72 to pull within one of Harrison but two behind the new leader, Lloyd Mangrum. Then, despite reaching the turn in 37, he took the 63-hole lead as both Harrison and Mangrum floundered with 41s.

Philadelphia native George Fazio had also shot the front nine in 37, and had come home in three under to post a 70 for a total of 287. Mangrum, playing about an hour ahead of Hogan, finished in 35 for a 76 that put him too at 287 as Harrison failed by a stroke to tie.

Meanwhile, Hogan had a three-stroke lead but was suffering. Throughout the day his caddie had picked his ball out of the holes and Cary Middlecoff, playing with him, had marked the ball to save wear and tear on Hogan's legs. But as he lashed into his teeshot at the 12th hole, his knees locked and he almost fell. He staggered to the side of the tee where a friend of his, Harry Radix, stood.

"Let me hang on to you, Harry," he said. "My God, I don't think I can finish." Hogan managed to hit the 12th in two but three-putted for a bogey. He parred the next two, then struck an iron to eight feet at 15 only to three-putt again, reducing his lead to one. He parred 16 but then bunkered his teeshot at the short 17th, made bogey, and his lead was gone. But with a perfect drive and a stinging 1-iron he reached the final hole in two, then two-putted to join Fazio and Mangrum in the playoff.

Through the first nine holes the next day, Hogan and Mangrum each had 36, Fazio 37. But Fazio would gradually fade away on the

One of the most famous photographs in golf, Ben Hogan playing his 1-iron approach to the 72nd hole in the 1950 U. S. Open. Photo: Hy Peskin for Life Magazine © Time Inc.

back nine and finish with a 75, so it became a Hogan-Mangrum battle. With three holes left, Hogan held a one-stroke lead.

Then Mangrum made a mistake. After missing the 16th green, he chipped to eight feet, from where he needed the par putt to remain one behind. As he stood over the putt, he noticed an insect on his ball, and without thinking he placed the head of his putter next to the ball to mark its position, then picked up the ball and blew the bug away. He then replaced the ball, made the putt, and walked to the 17th tee, thinking he was still one back.

But he was approached by USGA official Isaac Grainger, who informed him that he had violated the Rules of Golf. Lifting a ball in play was then an infraction punishable by a two-stroke penalty in medal play.

"You mean I had a 6 instead of a 4?" Mangrum asked.

"Yes," Grainger replied.

Mangrum glared at Grainger for a moment, then cooled down. "Well," he said, "I guess we'll all eat tomorrow."

But Hogan would eat the best. With the pressure off, he rolled in a 50-foot putt for a deuce on 17, and won handily with a 69 to Mangrum's 73.

In the clubhouse, Hogan is said to have overheard a national sports columnist say, "Well, the little man has done it, and he might as well enjoy it. Now he has proved himself. He has been given a fat settlement by the bus company because of the accident. He's rich and contented. He'll never win another big one."

The enraged Hogan confronted the scribe. "You wouldn't want to bet on that, would you?" he said. Embarrassed, the writer nonetheless agreed to a wager of a dozen $10 ties. Ten months later, Hogan won not only the ties but a green coat at the Masters.

It would be twenty-one years before the Open returned again, but in between Merion hosted the 1960 World Amateur Team competition, won by an American team led by a prodigy named Jack Nicklaus. Under conditions that were admittedly softer than Open standards, Jack played some spectacular golf, shooting rounds of 66-67-68-68—269, eighteen strokes lower than Hogan had.

The Golden Bear also played well in the 1971 Open at Merion—but not quite well enough. When, on the 72nd hole his fourteen-foot birdie putt skimmed past the cup, he tied Lee Trevino at 280.

The next day, the best two players of their time went at it head to head. It began with Trevino playfully throwing a rubber snake at Nicklaus on the first tee, and it ended with Trevino throwing a 68 at Nicklaus and Merion, winning the playoff by three.

Nicklaus struggled most of the day, finding bunkers and bogeys at the 2nd and 3rd to fall two strokes behind. Through fourteen holes it remained that way. Then Nicklaus hit his approach eight feet from the flag at 15, about twenty feet inside Trevino's, and it seemed as if he might close the gap. But Trevino stroked in his own lengthy birdie, and after Jack sank his the margin remained two. When at 17 Jack again failed to get up and down from the sand, Trevino had all the cushion he needed.

"I have no ambition to win all of the four major championships," said the Merry Mex after his victory. "I just want to win tournaments, whether it's the Screen Door Open or the Canadian Bacon Open. My ambition is to win a million dollars, and when I do that I may go south of the border."

His modest goals notwithstanding, Trevino's win at Merion was the beginning of an incredible month in which he won the national championships of America, Great Britain, and Canada. In 1972 he added another British Open, and in 1984 a PGA Championship, and although he never won The Masters, in 1989, at the age of 49, he was one of the co-leaders after 36 holes. In a quarter-century of professional golf Trevino has won not one but several million dollars on the PGA and Senior Tours, while remaining decidedly north of the border.

Par had never been broken over four rounds of an Open at Merion until 1981, when five players did it and one man—David Graham—did it in grand style. Starting the final round three strokes behind George Burns (who had set a new 54-hole Open record on rounds of 69-66-68—203) Graham, a meticulous, feisty Australian, played one of the finer last rounds in Open history. He missed only one fairway—the 1st—and putted for birdie on every hole, usually from inside twenty feet, sinking four of them, the clinchers coming at the 14th and 15th, for a 67 that brought him a three-stroke victory.

Graham's score of 273—one off the 72-hole Open record set a year earlier by Jack Nicklaus at Baltusrol—added fuel to a controversy that had been festering with regard to the ability of little Merion to challenge the game's best players. Today's superbly conditioned professional golfers, armed with technologically advanced clubs and balls and competing over flawlessly manicured courses, are capable of playing more aggressively than their brethren of a half century ago. A 6500-yard course such as Merion, no matter how cleverly designed, inevitably becomes vulnerable, and with it so do the Open records.

The Open probably will not return to Merion. There are reasons other than the course—notably an insufficiency of parking space for the tens of thousands of spectators who are now part of every Open—but while the USGA and the club can keep a cap on attendance, they have little control over scoring, except by "tricking up" the course with unreasonably long rough and obscure pin positions or, as Jack Nicklaus has suggested, by throttling back the velocity of the golf ball by 5 percent, neither of which the USGA seems inclined to do.

So it looks as if Maid Merion has joined Myopia and Minikahda and Midlothian in the ranks of former Open courses. But only for men.

U.S. Open: June 7-9, 1934

Olin Dutra	76	74	71	72	293	1
Gene Sarazen	73	72	73	76	294	2
Wiffy Cox	71	75	73	76	295	T3
B. Cruickshank	71	71	77	76	295	T3
Harry Cooper	76	74	74	71	295	T3
Billy Burke	76	71	77	72	296	T6
Macdonald Smith	75	73	78	70	296	T6
Ralph Guldahl	78	73	70	78	299	T8
Johnny Revolta	76	73	77	73	299	T8
Jimmy Hines	80	70	77	72	299	T8
Tom Creavy	79	76	78	66	299	T8

U.S. Open: June 8-11, 1950

Ben Hogan	72	69	72	74	287		
					69	1
Lloyd Mangrum	72	70	69	76	287		
					73	T2
George Fazio	73	72	72	70	287		
					75	T2
E.J. Harrison	72	67	73	76	288	4
Joe Kirkwood	71	74	74	70	289	T5
Jim Ferrier	71	69	74	75	289	T5
Henry Ransom	72	71	73	73	289	T5
S. William Nary	73	70	74	73	290	8
Julius Boros	68	72	77	74	291	9
Cary Middlecoff	71	71	71	79	292	T10
Johnny Palmer	73	70	70	79	292	T10

U.S. Open: June 17-20, 1971

Lee Trevino	70	72	69	69	280		
					68	1
Jack Nicklaus	69	72	68	71	280		
					71	2
Bob Rosburg	71	72	70	69	282	T3
Jim Colbert	69	69	73	71	282	T3
Jim Simons	71	71	65	76	283	T5
Johnny Miller	70	73	70	70	283	T5
George Archer	71	70	70	72	283	T5
Ray Floyd	71	75	69	69	284	8
Gay Brewer	70	70	73	72	285	T9
Bert Yancey	75	69	69	72	285	T9
Larry Hinson	71	71	70	73	285	T9
Bobby Nichols	69	72	69	75	285	T9

U.S. Open: June 18-21, 1981

David Graham	68	68	70	67	273	1
Bill Rogers	70	68	69	69	276	T2
George Burns	69	66	68	73	276	T2
John Cook	68	70	71	70	279	T4
John Schroeder	71	68	69	71	279	T4
Frank Conner	71	72	69	68	280	T6
Lon Hinkle	69	71	70	70	280	T6
Sammy Rachels	70	71	69	70	280	T6
Jack Nicklaus	69	68	71	72	280	T6
Chi Chi Rodriguez	68	73	67	72	280	T6

Scorecard

HOLE	YARDS	PAR
1	362	4
2	536	5
3	181	3
4	600	5
5	418	4
6	420	4
7	350	4
8	360	4
9	193	3
OUT	3420	36
10	310	4
11	369	4
12	371	4
13	127	3
14	408	4
15	366	4
16	428	4
17	220	3
18	463	4
IN	3062	34
TOTAL	6482	70

GOLF Magazine Rankings:
10th in the World
3rd in the U.S.A.

MUIRFIELD

GULLANE, SCOTLAND
British Open: 1892, 1896, 1901, 1906, 1912,
1929, 1935, 1948, 1959, 1966, 1972, 1980, 1987, 1992

In the United States, in Europe, and throughout the rest of the world as the twenty-first century approaches, scores of venerable golf clubs are celebrating their 100th anniversaries. Meanwhile, in a quiet corner of Scotland, one special club is on the verge of its quarter millenium. The Honourable Company of Edinburgh Golfers—the oldest golf club in the world—will soon turn 250.

It began in 1744 when "several Gentlemen of Honour skilful in the ancient and healthful exercise of Golf" petitioned the city of Edinburgh to provide a silver club for an annual competition on the Links of Leith, a couple of miles west of the city on the Firth of Forth. The competition was open to "as many Noblemen or Gentlemen or other Golfers" as submitted their entries by the deadline, eight days before the competition. Only a dozen men took part, and the winner was John Rattray, an Edinburgh surgeon who

was immediately crowned "Captain of the Golf" and empowered with the authority to arbitrate all disputes on the links.

In the same year these gentlemen of honour wrote the first Rules of Golf, a pithy thirteen in number, the first of which read: "You must tee your ball within one club's length of the hole." It would be ten years before the Royal & Ancient Golf Club of St. Andrews was formed, and when that group came into being, it adopted virtually verbatim the Rules of the Edinburgh golfers. (The broader Rules of Golf as we know them today were not promulgated by the R&A until 1888. And it wasn't until five years after that that prescribed teeing areas replaced club-length measurements for determining the launching point of the drive!)

By 1764 the competition had been restricted to members of the Honourable Company of Edinburgh Golfers, each of whom paid

James Braid won two consecutive Opens at Muirfield back in the days when much of the course was bordered by a stone wall. Photo: © Nick Birch

five shillings per year "for keeping the Links in Good Order." The Leith course had only five holes, but each was about 400 yards. A vivid description, one of the first literate allusions to golf, appeared in Smollett's *Humphry Clinker* in 1771:

> Hard by, in the fields called the Links, the citizens of Edinburgh direct themselves at a game called golf, in which they use a curious kind of bats topt with horn, and small elastic balls of leather, stuffed with feathers, rather less than tennis balls, but of a much harder consistence—these they strike with such force and dexterity from one hole to another that they will fly to an incredible distance. Of this diversion, the Scots are so fond that when the weather will permit, you will see a multitude of all ranks, from the senator of justice to the lowest tradesman, mingled together in their shirt, and following the balls with the utmost eagerness.

The "multitude of ranks" eventually became too much for the little course, and in 1836 the club moved its playing ground up the Firth a couple of miles to Musselburgh, where a part of the seven-hole course ran beside a racetrack and one bunker had the glorious name Pandemonium. But by 1891 the club had again outgrown its facilities, and so it moved a bit farther upriver, to Gullane and its present home, where Old Tom Morris designed the Muirfield course.

By this time the Honourable Company had joined together with the R&A and the Prestwick Golf Club in conducting the British Open. Beginning in 1860, Prestwick had hosted the championship twelve straight years; then the three clubs had rotated it for two decades at Prestwick, the Old Course at St. Andrews, and the Musselburgh Links. When the HCEG left for Muirfield they took the Open with them, much to the resentment of the Musselburghers.

The first British Open at Muirfield, in 1892, was also the first major championship contested over seventy-two holes. It was won by an amateur, Harold Hilton, on a remarkably low score of 305, considering he was using a gutta-percha ball. Hilton would win again in 1897 at his home course, Hoylake. Since that year, the only amateur to win the Open has been Bobby Jones. Hilton is also the only Briton ever to win the U.S. Amateur.

Hilton's score prompted widespread criticism that Muirfield was not long or difficult enough to test the pros. Accordingly, the club sought the services of P.H. Don Wauchope, a former rugby halfback, who added 600 yards to the course, bringing it to 6194 yards. When the Open returned in 1896, the course was said to be at least four strokes tougher.

A then-unknown named Harry Vardon won that Open on a score of 316. Standing 200 yards from the final green, Vardon was faced with a choice of either playing for the pin, tucked behind a bunker, which would give him a possible birdie and victory, or

shooting safely to the middle of the green for a par and a playoff spot. He opted for the latter, then won the first of his record six Open championships in a 36-hole playoff over J.H. Taylor. The playoff, incidentally, was not held the day after the tournament proper. Another tournament had been schedule at North Berwick, a couple of miles away, so both Vardon and Taylor fulfilled their obligations there, then returned to Muirfield the next day. Today, such a scenario would be unimaginable.

In 1901 another one of the game's greats, James Braid, won his first Open, beating Vardon by three strokes on a score of 309. Braid began and ended things inauspiciously; in round one he hooked his opening teeshot out of bounds over the wall that surrounded much of the course, and on his approach to the seventy-second green the shaft of his club splintered and the clubhead flew down the fairway. But Braid got his game and gear in shape in time for a return to Muirfield in 1906, when he won the Open again, this time by four strokes over Taylor, five over Vardon. By then, two English courses, Hoylake and Sandwich, had been added to the rota, and Muirfield, down to 5934 yards, was the shortest of the five Open courses.

Braid won five of the first ten Opens of this century, and obviously had a special fondness for the Honourable Company. When a son was born to him, he named the boy Harry Muirfield Braid.

Any amateur who has won his club championship will appreciate the achievement of Robert Maxwell, a member of the Honourable Company, who in both 1903 and 1909 won not simply his club championship but the British Amateur Championship on his home course.

When the Open returned in 1912, another of Britain's finest players, Ted Ray, rose to the fore, winning his only British Open as Harry Vardon finished second. A few months later, the two of them traveled to America and tied for the lead after seventy-two holes of the U.S. Open before losing the epic playoff to Francis Ouimet.

That 1913 Open is recognized as the coming of age of American golf, the point at which it became clear that the best players in the U.S. were as good as the best of Britain. In 1929 at Muirfield, it became evident that the Americans were not simply equal to the Brits, they were better.

On a new and improved Muirfield, upgraded by H.S. Colt and Tom Simpson, eight of the first ten and ten of the first fourteen places went to Americans as Walter Hagen waltzed to a six-stroke victory, the last of his major championships. Bernard Darwin told the story of Hagen staying up late on the evening before the final day, playing cards at the Marine Hotel with several of his cronies. At 4 or 5 A.M., one of them became a bit concerned, and opined that Hagen's nearest rival, Leo Diegel, had been in bed for several hours. "But," replied the Haig, "he won't be asleep," knowing that Diegel had an extremely nervous temperament.

Hagen was right. The next day, Diegel, displaying the awkward elbows-out putting style which was his trademark, three-putted five times as Hagen played perhaps the best golf of his life, blazing to a final round of 67, the lowest fourth round in the history of the Open to that point. Golf historian Robert Browning recorded the day:

> The people who used to think of Hagen as gaining his championships by incredible recoveries after still more incredible mistakes, were forced to recognize an immense change that "Sir Walter" affected in his play in the four years that intervened between his second and third championships. . . . He was hitting the ball almost along a chalk line from tee to pin all the way. . . . There was never a more convincing round.

By contrast, no one would have predicted that Alfred Perry, an unheralded journeyman with an excessively strong grip, would triumph in 1935. Said Bernard Darwin, "About his game . . . is something which looks a little uncertain until the results are scrutinized." After thirty-six holes Perry was one behind the prohibitive favorite, Henry Cotton, then roared to the front with a 67 in the third round, followed by a closing 72 that was good enough for a four-stroke win.

Cotton, who folded on rounds of 76-75, left Muirfield in defeat, but thirteen years later he returned in triumph. Hitting fifty-three of the fifty-six holes that required a driver, Cotton strode to a five-stroke victory, the last of his three British Open wins. The key was his second round, played in the presence of King George VI, an honorary life member of the HCEG. Cotton shot a regal 66, the lowest round in an Open since his own 65 at Sandwich in 1934.

It was a comparatively weak field that came to Muirfield in 1959, and a comparatively weak start—a 75—that launched young Gary Player to victory. But the tenacious little South African came from eight strokes back on the last thirty-six holes. Still, when he finished the 18th with a double bogey, he was crushed, thinking he had lost it all. To this day, he denies that he actually cried during the moments after posting his score, but according to one British newspaper his level of anguish was "astonishing to behold." In the end, however, his 284 was enough to edge Fred Bullock and Flory Van Donck by a stroke. It was the first of Player's nine major championships and the first of his three British Open victories over three different decades.

In 1959, also, Jack Nicklaus first came to Great Britain, and to Muirfield, as part of the victorious U.S. Walker Cup team, thus marking the start of a love affair that endures to this day. Returning in 1966, Nicklaus found a more demanding course than he had as an amateur, with the fairways narrowed to twenty-five yards and rough grown in some spots to knee height. More golf balls were lost by competitors during that week than in any major championship of modern time. "I wish I had the hay concession," said Doug Sanders.

Walter Hagen was at the peak of his game in 1929, taking a six-stroke victory as eight of the top ten places went to Americans. Photo: Bettmann/Hulton

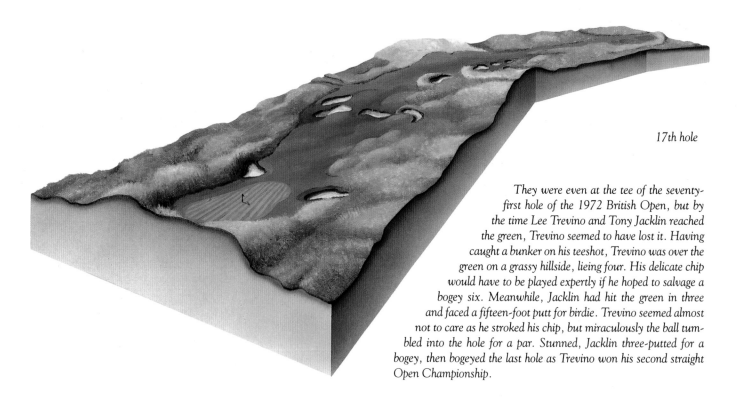

17th hole

They were even at the tee of the seventy-first hole of the 1972 British Open, but by the time Lee Trevino and Tony Jacklin reached the green, Trevino seemed to have lost it. Having caught a bunker on his teeshot, Trevino was over the green on a grassy hillside, lieing four. His delicate chip would have to be played expertly if he hoped to salvage a bogey six. Meanwhile, Jacklin had hit the green in three and faced a fifteen-foot putt for birdie. Trevino seemed almost not to care as he stroked his chip, but miraculously the ball tumbled into the hole for a par. Stunned, Jacklin three-putted for a bogey, then bogeyed the last hole as Trevino won his second straight Open Championship.

Nicklaus picked the course apart with his powerful long-iron game, staking himself to a three-stroke lead after two rounds. Halfway through round three he had increased that margin to seven over his nearest pursuer, Phil Rodgers, and looked to be running away with it. But at the end of the day he was two strokes behind. Nicklaus had shot 36-39—75 as Rodgers had countered with 40-30—70. "Forty-thirty," Rodgers mused. "Anyone for tennis?"

But, perhaps fortunately for Jack, this was the first year in which the Open was played over four separate days. By Sunday the tide had turned again. Rodgers folded as Nicklaus returned to form. On the final hole Nicklaus struck a long drive, a beautifully controlled 3-iron to the heart of the green, and two-putted for par to finish one stroke ahead of Sanders and Dave Thomas. His first victory in the Open (as it had been for Vardon, Braid, and Player), Muirfield was also the place where Nicklaus completed his first circuit of victories in all four major championships, thus joining Messrs. Sarazen, Hogan, and Player. So taken was Jack with this golf course that, in 1974, he named his own course in Ohio Muirfield Village.

But if Muirfield is the place that brought Nicklaus great joy, it is also the place that broke his heart. Ask Jack about the tournament he most regrets, and he'll immediately tell you the 1972 British Open.

It was the championship billed as The Grand Slam Open, because Jack, at the peak of his considerable powers, had earlier won both The Masters and the U.S. Open. Had Nicklaus been able to play the final three holes in the same scores he played them in 1966—par three, birdie four, par four—he would have won leg three of the Slam. Instead, he finished in 4-5-4 and lost by a stroke.

However, Jack Nicklaus was only one character in the drama of

Muirfield '72. The final act turned out to be a duel between Lee Trevino and Tony Jacklin. Trevino, the defending Champion, had taken a one-stroke lead after fifty-four holes on the heels of a third-round 66, which he had capped with a dramatic string of five closing birdies. The run included a hole-out from sand at 16 and a chip-in from the back of the 18th green. Jacklin, paired with Trevino, shot a 67 to go one stroke behind him.

On Sunday they played together and battled tooth and nail. As they came to the 17th hole they were even. Jacklin reached the green of the par five in three with a fifteen-foot birdie putt, but Trevino had trouble. A drive into a fairway bunker, a hack out, then a 3-wood and an errant iron left him over the green and several feet up a grassy bank, lieing four. It looked as if Jacklin would surely gain one shot, possibly two.

Normally, Lee would have stalked the little shot he faced, but he seemed instead to have given up. He simply stepped to the ball and gave it a listless nudge. But a listless nudge was exactly what the shot required. The ball flopped onto the edge of the green, trickled down the slope, and dropped into the center of the hole for a par five.

Jacklin sat stunned on the bank of the green, the roar of the gallery ringing in his ears. He then rammed his birdie attempt three feet past the hole and failed to make the comebacker. Six. Incredibly, he had **lost** a stroke. "By tenfold that was the worst shock I've ever had on a golf course," he said. Trevino, with his back to the ropes, had delivered a knockout punch. Jacklin bogeyed the final hole and finished in third place, two behind Trevino, one back of Nicklaus.

The Englishman was never the same again, and it was more than a decade before he got any measure of revenge, when the European Ryder Cup teams he captained in 1985 beat the American team headed by captain Trevino.

Ironically, the next time the Open came to Muirfield, Trevino stepped one place back, just as Nicklaus had from 1966 to 1972. The 1980 Open belonged to Tom Watson, who set a new four-round record for Muirfield of 271 on rounds of 68-70-64-69, enough for a four-stroke victory over Trevino. This time Nicklaus dropped another notch, finishing tied for fourth with Carl Mason.

There were other low scores in 1980. Isao Aoki tied the one-round British Open record with a 63, and two other players shot 64, Hubert Green and Horacio Carbonetti, a lawyer from Argentina. Carbonetti's other rounds were a pair of 78s, so he missed the cut for the final day.

By contrast, consistency was the key to Nick Faldo's victory at Muirfield in 1987. The only man in the field to shoot par or better in each of the four rounds, Faldo strung together a 68, a 69, and two closing 71s for a one-stroke victory over Paul Azinger and Australia's Roger Davis.

In the final round, played in a shroud of fog, a half dozen players including Ben Crenshaw, Craig Stadler, and Tom Watson had chances to win, but it came down to Faldo and Azinger. Faldo was at his consistent best, making eighteen consecutive pars while the young American, under the heat of major championship pressure for the first time, faltered. Azinger had a one-stroke lead coming to

Nick Faldo sinks a four-footer for his eighteenth consecutive par of the day and his first major championship, the 1987 British Open. Photo: © Phil Sheldon

the 17th, but there he bunkered his drive and bogeyed, then bunkered his approach at 18 and left his putt for par—and playoff— short, as Faldo became the first Englishman to regain the old claret jug since Jacklin in 1969.

In 1985, when *GOLF Magazine* became the first publication actually to rank the world's courses numerically from one to 100, the course that came out on top—Number One—was Muirfield. In a bit more than ninety years, it had come a long way.

When Old Tom Morris's original design was unveiled, it was hardly a world beater. "An auld watter meadie" (water meadow) is the way crusty St. Andrews professional Andra Kirkaldy described it shortly after the 1892 Open. His opinion might have had something to do with the fact that the original course was enclosed almost completely by a stone wall, thus giving the feel of an inland course.

Muirfield was also one of the first "created" links, with its tees, greens, and bunkers placed strategically rather than being concoctions of nature. As such it was open to criticism like that from Horace Hutchison, in *The Badminton Library*:

> It is a links of eighteen holes, but they are less good holes than the old nine at Musselburgh. The first tee is close beside a wall which skirts a wood—the hole is about a full drive, or brassy shot, along the wall; and nothing is more annoying than to pull your first tee-shot over this wall, into the wood— nothing, that is to say, unless it be to see your adversary play the same sort of stroke, and striking a big bough of a tree, jump back on to the green. . . . One plays along inside this wall, skirting it all the time. . . . It suggests a cemetery, rather, and the somber firwoods around it heighten the impression.

Morris's original course saw several improvements, updates, and expansions, most notably in the '20s by Colt and Simpson, who retained the best holes while improving the weak ones. At that time fifty acres were added to the course, and the present design took its shape. The stature of the course grew with each staging of the Open and with the addition of each new champion. Indeed, along with Royal Birkdale, Muirfield boasts the most prestigious list of champions of any venue in the world.

Today, Muirfield remains an unprepossessing course. It lacks the gargantuan sandhills of Birkdale, the heaving greens of St. Andrews, the insidious burn of Carnoustie, the brawling sea of Turnberry. Said Bernard Darwin a century ago, "I admire it very much, but I cannot find in it the charm and supreme thrill that belong to some courses."

Muirfield's holes aren't the prettiest, but they may be the fairest. As Ben Crenshaw has said, "Stand on almost any tee or fairway at Muirfield and you know exactly what is expected. The pitch and

OPPOSITE: *11th hole*

contour of the land, the crisp collar of rough, the shadowy lips of the pot bunkers all tell you where—and where not—to hit the ball. The course talks to you every step of the way."

Where not to hit the ball is the rough, which is the lushest of any major British course. But the perils within the fairways are even more daunting. Each hole at Muirfield is arrayed with numerous bunkers—ten on average—cleverly plotted to catch long downwind drives one day, shorter upwind drives the next, and approach shots every day. In the words of Patric Dickinson, the bunkers "lurk everywhere for the least weakness, fade or draw, swallowing your ball like medicine, as if to say, 'This will do him good.'"

Here it is likely that the verb "revet" entered the golf lexicon. Derived from the French *revetir*, to reclothe, it refers to the method by which the sides of the Muirfield bunkers have been constructed, by reinforcing the natural wall with a layer of grass sod. It is this technique that allows the errant shots to roll into the bunkers from all angles. Jack Nicklaus called them the most fastidiously built bunkers he had ever seen, "the high front walls fitted together so precisely you would have thought a master mason had been called in." Nicklaus was so charmed by this feature that he adopted it in his own designs. Although American turf does not permit the revetting technique, many of Nicklaus's bunkers are so constructed as to create the shadowy look from a distance, and in the early part of his architectural career Jack pointed to this as the one signature of his designs.

The greens are smallish, gently contoured, and despite the profusion of bunkers most of them may be reached with a running approach. They are also said to be the best conditioned of any of the rota courses.

For a course that was one of the first "designs," Muirfield boasts an ingenious layout based on two concentric circles, the first nine heading clockwise and the second, within it, going counterclockwise. Thus, no hole is far from the clubhouse, and in only one case do as many as three consecutive holes play in the same direction. This is doubly important along the Firth of Forth, because of the wind. Indeed, according to Muirfield's historian, George Pottinger, "A true Muirfield man has been known to complain that, on calm days, he finds it difficult to maintain balance, 'for lack of something to lean against.'"

The original 1st hole was a par three of over 200 yards. Now it is a par four of 449 yards, into the prevailing wind, that may be the toughest opener in championship golf. The tee tends to point drives toward the right, where the golfer will get his first taste of Muirfield rough. On the left is a large C-shaped bunker. On a blustery day, even the pros cannot reach this green in two.

The 2nd, the only hole that is unchanged from the 1891 course, when it was hole number 3, is a short downhill par four to a large, open target, the only threat being the nearness of out of bounds just beyond the green. Two huge hillocks add both aesthetic and athletic interest to the 3rd hole. Miss the teeshot right or left and the

approach will be blinded by one of the hills, each of which holds a bunker.

Depending on the wind, the 181-yard 4th can call for anything from a wedge to a driver. Like all the short holes at Muirfield, the target is an elevated green. This one is three clubs deep, and at first glance not tightly guarded, but the putting surface slopes away toward the lapping bunkers.

Brian Barnes once aced number 4, then made a double bogey at the 5th after some bunker trouble. Seven of the sandy menaces await teeshots here—five on the right and two on the left—spaced at intervals that insure they will catch all lengths and varieties of drives. A par five of 558 yards, it's uphill all the way to a two-tiered green that leans toward the bunkers on the left. Downwind, Nicklaus reached it in 1966 with a driver and an 8-iron. Six years later, into the wind, Johnny Miller needed a 3-wood to get home, but he made good use of it, knocking the ball into the hole for a double eagle.

Number 6 is one of those ancient British holes that no designer would get away with today. The teeshot is not exactly blind, but it is at least vision-impaired, to a rising fairway that doglegs sharply left. At a point 116 yards from the green the *mur* of Muirfield, a four-foot-high stone wall, juts out into the fairway. Three bunkers lurk beside the green.

The only par three that plays into the prevailing wind is the 7th, where the large plateau green cants strongly from back to front. With nothing but sky beyond this target, club selection is a real challenge.

Muirfield bunkering is at its intimidating height at the 8th, where in the middle of the fairway nine shadowy faces stare their assailant down. To avoid them, the drive must be played well left, lengthening this rightward dogleg of 444 yards. In 1929, Walter Hagen had other ideas; he banged his teeshots intentionally into the right-hand rough, cutting at least fifty yards off the hole en route to two birdies that helped him to victory on the final day. Shortly thereafter, the club planted a spinney of buckthorns and other trees that now prohibit such brazen tacking.

Number 9 is on everyone's list of classic championship holes. Although under 500 yards, it plays into the west wind and the teeshot must be squeezed into a landing area that at one point narrows to as little as fifteen yards. On the right are bunkers and deep rough, on the left is out of bounds fronting the stately Greywalls Hotel. In 1959, Peter Thomson saw his chances for victory sail over that wall. The out of bounds continues all the way up the left, as does the rough up the right along with a string of bunkers, most notably the mammoth Simpson's Bunker, named after the architect. All in all, it is a difficult five, but it has been conquered. In 1972, in their close head-to-head final-round battle, both Tony Jacklin and Lee Trevino made eagles here.

At 475 yards, the 10th hole is only one yard short of the regulation length for a par five. Instead, it signals the start of a difficult

13th hole

back nine. In 1966, Arnold Palmer had a shot at the Open title until he found rough here and took a seven in the final round. It is followed by the only truly blind teeshot on the course. Number 11 heads up and over a massive ridge directly toward the Firth of Forth to a sloping green ringed by seven bunkers.

From there the course turns for home, through a straightforward par four at 12 to the first of two devilish par threes. The 13th goes uphill to a long, narrow, and fast green cradled in the hillocks and guarded by bunkers where a golfer has as much trouble getting himself out as his ball. The green slopes fiercely from back to front, and in 1929 Hagen is reputed to have hit into a bunker intentionally, accepting an uphill explosion rather than the prospect of a downhill putt.

Number 14 plays 447 yards, usually into the wind, with a trio of gaping bunkers jutting across the left side of the driving area. The green is full of subtle breaks. Not so subtle is the green of the 396-yard 15th, called Camel's Back, which tosses putts in all directions. Number 16, the longest of the short holes at 188 yards, is where Trevino nearly broke the flagstick, one-hopping a ball from a bunker and into the hole during his streak of five straight birdies in 1972. The green is large but heavily defended with seven bunkers.

The par-five 17th, like the other two long holes, can play like a hard five or an easy four, depending on the wind. Nicklaus hit a 3-iron teeshot, then reached the green with a 5-iron to set up the birdie that clinched his 1966 title. But it is also the place where Trevino needed to chip in for par and where both Jacklin and Azinger made disastrous bogeys. After a slightly uphill drive to the corner of the right-to-left dogleg, the second shot must be played across some of the most extraordinary terrain in golf, a 100-yard expanse of humps, hollows, dips, and ridges containing three enormous bunkers. Once this area is hurdled, it's a simple shot to a green nestled among sandhills.

Two bunkers pinch the landing area for the teeshot at 18. If they can be avoided, the second shot will be a middle iron directly at the old sandstone clubhouse to a large green with a deep strip bunker on the left and another large bunker, with an island of turf in its center, on the right.

An additional challenge at Muirfield is the fact that there are no yardage markers along the way. That is in keeping with the minimalism of this place—no pro shop, no snack bar, no tee pegs or pencils, no pars listed on the scorecard. It's all part of the spartan charm that makes this one of the places every serious golfer wants to play. Indeed, the American traffic has increased steadily over the last few decades, but has been carefully controlled. Visitors must have a handicap of eighteen or less, must apply for a tee time well in advance, and must deal with the club secretary. For many years, this meant an audience with Captain P.W.T. "Paddy" Hanmer, who guarded the gates with a gruff voice and a stern hand. Beneath the curmudgeonly exterior, however, was a man of great warmth and humor.

British Open: September 22-23, 1892

Harold Hilton	78	81	72	74	305	1
John Ball	75	80	74	79	308	T2
Hugh Kirkaldy	77	83	77	76	308	T2
Alex Herd	77	78	77	76	308	T2
J. Kay	82	78	74	78	312	T5
Ben Sayers	80	76	81	75	312	T5
Willie Park, Jr.	78	77	80	80	315	7
Willie Fernie	79	83	76	78	316	8
Archie Simpson	81	81	76	79	317	9
H.G. Hutchinson	74	78	86	80	318	10

British Open: June 10-11, 1896

Harry Vardon	83	78	78	77	316		
					157	1	
J.H. Taylor	77	78	81	80	316		
					161	2	
F.G. Tait	83	75	84	77	319	T3	
Willie Fernie	78	79	82	80	319	T3	
Alex Herd	72	84	79	85	320	5	
James Braid	83	81	79	80	323	6	
Ben Sayers	83	76	79	86	324	T7	
D. Brown	80	77	81	86	324	T7	
A.H. Scott	83	84	77	80	324	T7	
Tom Vardon	83	82	77	83	325	10	

British Open: June 5-6, 1901

James Braid	79	76	74	80	309	1
Harry Vardon	77	78	79	78	312	2
J.H. Taylor	79	83	74	77	313	3
Harold Hilton	89	80	75	76	320	4
Alex Herd	87	81	81	76	325	5
J. White	82	82	80	82	326	6
J. Kinnell	79	85	86	78	328	T7
J.E. Laidlay	84	82	82	80	328	T7
P.J. Gaudin	86	81	86	76	329	T9
J. Graham	82	83	81	83	329	T9

British Open: June 13-15, 1906

James Braid	77	76	74	73	300	1
J.H. Taylor	77	72	75	80	304	2
Harry Vardon	77	73	77	78	305	3
John Graham	71	79	78	78	306	4
Rowland Jones	74	78	73	83	308	5
Arnaud Massy	76	80	76	78	310	6
Ted Ray	80	75	79	78	312	T7
G. Duncan	73	78	83	78	312	T7
T.G. Renouf	76	77	76	83	312	T7
D. Kinnell	78	76	80	79	313	10

British Open: June 24-25, 1912

Ted Ray	71	73	76	75	295	1
Harry Vardon	75	72	81	71	299	2
James Braid	77	71	77	78	303	3
G. Duncan	72	77	78	78	305	4
Alex Herd	76	81	76	76	309	T5
L. Ayton	74	80	75	80	309	T5
F. Collins	76	79	81	74	310	T7
J. Gassiat	76	80	78	76	310	T7
R.G. Wilson	82	75	75	78	310	T7
Arnaud Massy	74	77	82	78	311	10

British Open: May 8-10, 1929

Walter Hagen	75	67	75	75	292	1
Johnny Farrell	72	75	76	75	298	2
Leo Diegel	71	69	82	77	299	3
Abe Mitchell	72	72	78	78	300	T4
Percy Alliss	69	76	76	79	300	T4
B. Cruickshank	73	74	78	76	301	6
Jim Barnes	71	80	78	74	303	7
Gene Sarazen	73	74	81	76	304	T8
Al Watrous	73	79	75	77	304	T8
Tommy Armour	75	73	79	78	305	10

British Open: June 26-28, 1935

Alfred Perry	69	75	67	72	283	1
Alfred Padgham	70	72	74	71	287	2
C. Whitcombe	71	68	73	76	288	3
Lawson Little	75	71	74	69	289	T4
B. Gadd	72	75	71	71	289	T4
Henry Picard	72	73	72	75	292	6
S. Easterbrook	75	73	74	71	293	T7
Henry Cotton	68	74	76	75	293	T7
W.J. Branch	72	73	76	74	294	9
L. Ayton	74	73	77	71	295	10

British Open: June 30-July 2, 1948

Henry Cotton	71	66	75	72	284	1
Fred Daly	72	71	73	73	289	2
Norman Von Nida	71	72	73	73	290	T3
J. Hargreaves	76	68	73	73	290	T3
C.H. Ward	69	72	75	74	290	T3
R. De Vicenzo	70	73	72	75	290	T3
Johnny Bulla	74	72	73	72	291	T7
Flory Van Donck	69	73	73	76	291	T7
S.L. King	69	72	74	76	291	T7
Alfred Padgham	73	70	71	77	291	T7

British Open: July 1-3, 1959

Gary Player	75	71	70	68	284	1
Flory Van Donck	70	70	73	73	286	T2
Fred Bullock	68	70	74	74	286	T2
S.S. Scott	73	70	73	71	287	4
Christy O'Connor	73	74	72	69	288	T5
John Panton	72	72	71	73	288	T5
R.R. Jack	71	75	68	74	288	T5
S.L. King	70	74	68	76	288	T5
Dai Rees	73	73	69	74	289	T9
L. Ruiz	72	74	69	74	289	T9

British Open: July 12-15, 1966

Jack Nicklaus	70	67	75	70	282	1
Dave Thomas	72	73	69	68	283	T2
Doug Sanders	71	70	72	70	283	T2
Gary Player	72	74	71	69	286	T4
Bruce Devlin	73	69	74	70	286	T4
Kel Nagle	72	68	76	70	286	T4
Phil Rodgers	74	66	70	76	286	T4
Dave Marr	73	76	69	70	288	T8
Peter Thomson	73	75	69	71	288	T8
S. Miguel	74	72	70	72	288	T8
Arnold Palmer	73	72	69	74	288	T8

British Open: July 12-15, 1972

Lee Trevino	71	70	66	71	278	1
Jack Nicklaus	70	72	71	66	279	2
Tony Jacklin	69	72	67	72	280	3
Doug Sanders	71	71	69	70	281	4
Brian Barnes	71	72	69	71	283	5
Gary Player	71	71	76	67	285	6
D. Vaughan	74	73	70	69	286	T7
Tom Weiskopf	73	74	70	69	286	T7
Arnold Palmer	73	73	69	71	286	T7
G.L. Hunt	75	72	67	72	286	T7

British Open: July 17-20, 1980

Tom Watson	68	70	64	69	271	1
Lee Trevino	68	67	71	69	276	2
Ben Crenshaw	70	70	68	69	277	3
Jack Nicklaus	73	67	71	69	280	T4
Carl Mason	72	69	70	69	280	T4
Craig Stadler	72	70	69	71	282	T6
Andy Bean	71	69	70	72	282	T6
Hubert Green	77	69	64	72	282	T6
Ken Brown	70	68	68	76	282	T6
Jack Newton	69	71	73	70	283	T10
Gil Morgan	70	70	71	72	283	T10

British Open: July 16-19, 1987

Nick Faldo	68	69	71	71	279	1
Paul Azinger	68	68	71	73	280	T2
Roger Davis	64	73	74	69	280	T2
Ben Crenshaw	73	68	72	68	281	T4
Payne Stewart	71	66	72	72	281	T4
David Frost	70	68	70	74	282	6
Tom Watson	69	69	71	74	283	7
Nick Price	68	71	72	73	284	T8
Craig Stadler	69	69	71	75	284	T8
Ian Woosnam	71	69	72	72	284	T8

Scorecard

HOLE	YARDS	PAR
1	449	4
2	349	4
3	379	4
4	181	3
5	558	5
6	471	4
7	185	3
8	444	4
9	495	5
OUT	3511	36
10	475	4
11	386	4
12	381	4
13	153	3
14	447	4
15	396	4
16	188	3
17	542	5
18	447	4
IN	3415	35
TOTAL	6926	71

GOLF *Magazine* Rankings:
5th in the World
1st in the U.K.

OAK HILL COUNTRY CLUB

PITTSFORD, NEW YORK
U.S. Open: 1956, 1968, 1989
PGA Championship: 1980

Deep in the basement of the USGA headquarters in Far Hills, New Jersey, a massive computer keeps track of myriad facts and figures on golf. One of those facts is this: Among the 14,000 or so golf and country clubs in America, no fewer than twenty-two are named Oak Hill. And yet, for anyone with an appreciation of golf history and tradition, there is only one Oak Hill, the one near Rochester, New York.

This is perhaps the ultimate thinking man's course—built by a university, nurtured by a doctor, and subdued by four of the savviest players in history.

When in 1924 the University of Rochester decided to expand its campus, the academics cast an envious eye on the nearby property of the Oak Hill Country Club, and the civic-minded club members granted their wishes. In exchange for the land, the university agreed

13th hole

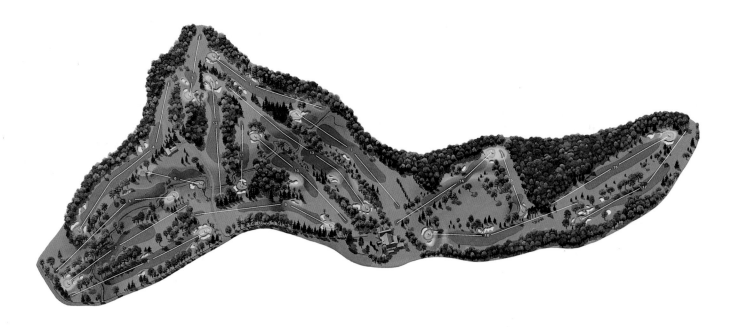

to finance the design and construction of two new courses on 355 acres of land in nearby Pittsford.

The property, originally settled by the League of Iroquois Indians, had been farmed to death, and when the club took it over it was deemed "barren, cheerless, and singularly lacking in beauty." But two men salvaged it.

The first was Donald Ross, who designed two fine courses with wide, rolling fairways, par fours in the 300-400 yard range, and crowned greens fashioned by leveling off the tops of hills. The second was Dr. John R. Williams, an Oak Hill member and botany lover, who made it his personal project to cover the bleak property with trees, especially oak trees. Using his own backyard as an incubator, Williams planted seeds and raised them to saplings, then transplanted them to the club property. As his project became widely known, people began sending him seeds and acorns from all over the country. One came from a tree planted by George Washington on the property of his home at Mount Vernon, another from the Shakespeare Oak in Stratford-on-Avon, England, and another from the Smithsonian Institution belonging to a metasequoia that had been dormant for three million years.

Williams had a vision of Oak Hill as a golf course within a park, and today that vision is reality. The Oak Hill property is clad with over 80,000 trees, 34,000 of them on the championship East course, including thirty varieties of oaks alone as well as twenty types of deciduous species and pines, virtually every sort of tree capable of growing in the northern United States.

As the little trees grew, so did the reputation of the course, and in 1934, Rochester's centennial year, Oak Hill hosted the Hagen Memorial Open. (Walter Hagen was a Rochester native.) It was won by Leo Diegel. In 1941, Sam Snead won the Times-Union Open at Oak Hill, and a year after that Ben Hogan, on his thirtieth birthday, shot a 64 en route to victory in the Rochester Open.

But the course didn't come into the national spotlight until it was visited by USGA Executive Director Joe Dey in 1948. "Where have you been for twenty years?" he said to the club officers. "There's nothing like this in the whole country." A year later the U.S. Amateur was played at Oak Hill with Charles Coe the winner, and in 1956 the club was awarded the U.S. Open.

But prior to that Open, the club brought in Robert Trent Jones, a Rochester native who had revamped Oakland Hills for the 1951 Open and Baltusrol for 1954. Jones changed seventeen of the eighteen holes, added 364 yards, and reduced the par from 72 to 70. He also added twenty-six bunkers and converted twenty-seven others from Ross's grassy-edged style to his own "flashed" look, where the sand laps up the sides.

Prior to that Open, record-holder Hogan deemed the course too easy for championship play. But the Oak Hill he found in 1956 was not the one he had played in '42. Several holes had been lengthened, and those trees had continued to enlarge. In the first round no one broke par, and after seventy-two holes the winning score was 1 over. The victor was Cary Middlecoff, the slow-playing Memphis dentist who dominated the game as much as anyone did in the handful of years between the Hogan and Palmer eras. In 1955 he had won six events, including the Masters, and in '56 he had posted two victories prior to the Open.

Both Bobby Jones and Jack Nicklaus have said that Opens are lost more frequently than they are won, and that was surely the case at Oak Hill. During the last two rounds, only eight birdies were made by the entire field. Even Middlecoff tried to give it away, bogeying 16 and 17, then missing both the fairway and green at the last hole before a fine pitch from the rough allowed him to sink a four-footer for par. He then went into the clubhouse and waited as his pursuers collapsed over the last three holes, the stretch known as Heartbreak Bend.

Ted Kroll, Ben Hogan, and Julius Boros all had chances not only to catch Middlecoff but to win outright, but each stumbled. Kroll found tree trouble at 16 and made a triple-bogey 7. Hogan, who by this point in his career had lost his putting and was wishing golf were a game of hitting fairways and greens, missed a number of short putts on the way in, the killer coming at 17, where his two-footer failed to drop. Boros needed to birdie one of the last three to tie, but made a trio of pars, his fifteen-foot attempt at 18 lipping the hole.

This was known as the Rhubarb Open, and not because of the length of the rough. First there was an argument over the purse, the pros griping that several lesser tournaments offered more than the $24,000 put up by the USGA. (The winner got $6,000 and tenth place was worth only $416.) There were also skirmishes among a few of the pros over who would get which caddies. And on the 17th hole during the first round the British master, Henry Cotton, was accused of cheating. His playing partners, Jimmy Demaret and Middlecoff, claimed that Cotton had clipped the top of his ball before tapping it into the hole and had thus taken one more stroke than he had recorded on his card. Cotton denied it, and the USGA accepted his word.

In contrast to the difficult scoring in 1956, the '68 Open saw a barrage of birdies and a winning score that tied the Open record. That score came from an unlikely source, a Mexican-American born out of wedlock and raised by his grandfather in a shack devoid of plumbing and heating, a guy who quit school in the eighth grade and became a machine-gunner in the Marines, who taught himself golf in a pasture with a found club and later hustled people by breaking par while swinging a Dr. Pepper bottle, who honed his game in the Texas winds, often donning scuba goggles to keep the dust out of his eyes. A man who, after Oak Hill, would go on to become the second best player of his time, win five major championships and several million dollars, go through a half dozen agents and two wives, both named Claudia, write a book on his swing, become a TV commentator, sire his last child at the age of 49, and then tear up the Senior Tour. The last of the old-fashioned success stories began at Oak Hill, when Lee Trevino came to the fore.

Trevino shot 69-68 in the first two rounds, but that was good enough for only second place as Bert Yancey tied the 36-hole Open record with 67-68—135. However, the two of them had nearly lapped the field. Jack Nicklaus was in a three-way tie for third place, and he was seven behind Yancey.

Lee Trevino sinks the pivotal putt of the 1968 Open, a thirty-five-footer for birdie at number 11 that gave him a three-stroke lead. Photo: AP/Wide World Photos

On Saturday, Yancey opened up a five-stroke lead by the 10th hole, but Trevino nearly erased it with three birdies coming in as Yancey played one-over golf. Yancey's 205 again broke an Open record, but it didn't break Trevino, one back. Nicklaus continued to lurk in third, still seven behind.

Trevino appeared at the tee on Sunday wearing the outfit which became his signature during his first few years on Tour. A red shirt, black pants, red socks, and black shoes. On his head he wore a black baseball cap, and under that cap he wore a face of grim determination. When Yancey missed short par putts on three of the first five holes, Trevino took a one-stroke lead. Meanwhile, Nicklaus had begun to make a move, birdieing both 4 and 5 to pull within three strokes.

Yancey missed another short one at 10 to fall two back, and then Trevino sank the killer, a thirty-five-foot birdie putt at the 11th hole. It was an impressive moment because, just before he stroked the putt, a roar had come out of the trees at the 10th hole—Arnold Palmer, well out of contention, had made a birdie, to the delight of his army. Trevino stepped away, rubbed his hands together very deliberately, readdressed the putt, and rammed it into the hole for a deuce.

He followed that, as he had a day earlier, with a second straight birdie at the 12th. Trevino later recalled this moment for Nevin Gibson in *Great Moments in Golf*:

As I left the 12th green, I could hardly wait to get a look at the scoreboard to find out how I stood with the Golden Bear. I looked and saw that I was five strokes in front of him! For a moment my nerve ends stood out so far I was certain I looked like I needed a shave, my stomach had such an empty sensation that I felt my throat had been cut for a week, and my heart had stopped beating! Man, in this one moment I knew that if lightning didn't strike me, I could be the 1968 U.S. Open Champion.

From 13 through 18 he scrambled home in even par, beating Jack by four, the unfortunate Yancey by six, and tieing Nicklaus's championship record with a four-foot par putt on the seventy-second hole. In doing so, Trevino completed a feat that has never been equaled in Open competition: he shot all four of his rounds in the 60s: 69-68-69-69. He also duplicated another Nicklaus feat—the U.S. Open was Lee Trevino's first victory as a professional.

Trevino's low scores caused the USGA to look askance at Oak Hill. Perhaps, they reasoned, Ben Hogan had been right all along—the course was not stern enough to hold an Open. When in the mid-70s a group of influential Oak Hill members approached the USGA for a third Open, they were denied.

That prompted the club to make some changes—controversial changes. Over a five-year period, the architectural team of George and Tom Fazio made the course Tour-ready, lengthening some holes, adjusting others to better accommodate spectator logjams, and eliminating several blind bunkers. The net result was that they created four virtually new holes at the 5th, 6th, 15th, and 18th, while making some major changes in others. In the process, some of the feel of the original Donald Ross course was destroyed.

The early reviews were not good. One forty-year member likened the redesign to "painting a mustache on the Mona Lisa." Tom Fazio defended the changes, saying that they added "something Oak Hill never had, intimidating holes that offer the threat of a double or triple bogey." The PGA of America was sufficiently impressed to accord its 1980 Championship to the new Oak Hill.

When the pros saw it, they were nearly universal in their dislike, temperamental Tom Weiskopf leading the week-long protest by forming a mythical "Society for the Preservation of Donald Ross Courses." Jack Nicklaus, never one to withhold his opinions, had mixed feelings. "I think the new holes are good," he said, "and they're more difficult than the old ones. But why did they do it? It's incongruous."

But Nicklaus warmed to the new territory quickly, making a hole-in-one on the 15th during one of his practice rounds. The ace was an augur of good things to come for Jack, who at age 40 was in the midst of a second spring. Two months earlier he had won his fourth U.S. Open at Baltusrol, breaking his and Trevino's record 275 by three strokes.

In 1968 at Oak Hill, Nicklaus had hit sixty-one of seventy-two greens in regulation, more than Trevino or anyone else, but he had putted uncharacteristically poorly, missing at least a dozen birdie opportunities in the four- to eight-foot range. A dozen years later, everything had turned 180 degrees. His tee-to-green game was weak, but his putting was awesome.

Actually, he had putted well at Baltusrol, and then had lost his touch, but just before Oak Hill a tip from son Jackie, to swing through the ball rather than at it, had helped tremendously. As a result, August 7-10, 1980, in Nicklaus's words, "might just have been my best-ever week of putting in a major."

He was one behind Gil Morgan at the halfway point, but at the first hole on Saturday he rammed in a fifty-footer for a birdie. Then at the 206-yard third, he struck a 1-iron to within six inches of the cup. Meanwhile, Morgan was playing the first trio of holes in two over; suddenly, Jack had a three-stroke lead. It remained that way after fifty-four holes, and on Sunday he made it a rout. He played conservatively, waiting for others to make mistakes, as he had en route to so many championships, and as usual the strategy worked. On rounds of 70-69-66-69—274, Nicklaus was the only man to finish under par. His seven-stroke triumph over Andy Bean was the most decisive win in the stroke-play history of the PGA. The victory—Nicklaus's fifth in the PGA—also had an element of poetic

OPPOSITE: *15th hole*

justice, as he tied local boy Walter Hagen as the only men to win the championship five times.

The cream seems to rise to the top at Oak Hill, and that was true again in 1989, when Curtis Strange successfully defended his 1988 Open title and became the fifth man in history (the first since Hogan in 1950-51) to win two Opens back to back.

It didn't come easily, and Strange later said that "patience was the key." Perhaps his toughest opponent was the weather, "the worst string of days we've ever had," according to P.J. Boatwright, the USGA's director of rules and competitions. Rain hit on Wednesday night and continued through most of the rest of the week, turning Oak Hill into Soak Hill. At one point, Lee Trevino quipped, "It's so wet out here, I can't reach the par threes."

In round one, everyone threw darts at the soft Oak Hill greens, as a record twenty-one players scored in the 60s and Bernhard Langer, Payne Stewart, and little-known Jay Don Blake each shot 66 to share the lead. Jack Nicklaus and Tom Kite were among five others at 67, while Strange, thanks to a double bogey at the 17th, could do no better than a one-over-par 71.

But on day two Curtis served notice that he was up to the challenge, tieing another Hogan mark, the course record of 64. It took him into the lead at 135, one stroke ahead of Kite, two over Blake and 1987 Open Champion Scott Simpson. Strange's round included five birdies and a holed-out ninety-yard wedge shot at the 4th for an eagle. Curtis had also holed out a full-swing shot at The Country Club a year earlier, and two of them at Olympic in 1987. "I don't know," he said, "I guess you aim better at the Open."

Indeed, the big news of Friday was even more strange than Curtis. It was aces. Four of them. On the same hole. With the same club. Within a span of only two hours. Against odds of several million to one, Doug Weaver, Mark Wiebe, Jerry Pate, and Nick Price each scored a one at the 167-yard 6th hole.

On rainy Saturday, Tom Kite took charge. The little pro in wire-rimmed glasses, putting cross-handed for the first time in his life, posted his third sub-70 score to take a one-stroke lead over Simpson, three over Strange as Curtis struggled to a 73. It looked as if Kite, a bridesmaid in several majors, might finally break through for the big one.

With fourteen holes left on the final day, Kite seemed even more certainly the champion. He had played the first four holes in one under, Simpson in one over, and he had a three-stroke lead. But unusual things happen in the last round of the Open. At the 5th, a picturesque par four playing alongside a creek, Kite pushed his teeshot into the water. After a drop-out and a layup short of the water that crossed in front of the green, he flipped a wedge to ten feet. Needing that putt to salvage a bogey, he missed, and then incredibly missed the eighteen-inch comebacker. Triple-bogey 7.

Suddenly the Open was truly open again. A dozen players had good chances to win. But only one played steadily enough to do it. Mr. Patience.

When Curtis Strange teed off on round four, he had not made a birdie since the 16th hole on Thursday. And when late on Sunday afternoon he returned to that 16th green, with three holes remaining in the Open, he still had not made a birdie. But he had made thirty-five consecutive pars, and that was good enough. At two under par, the same score he had held for twenty-two hours, he was now back in the lead. Kite had fallen completely out of the fight, and Curtis's chief rivals were Chip Beck and Ian Woosnam, both of whom had completed play at one under, and Mark McCumber, one under with one hole to play.

Curtis stroked his fifteen-foot putt into the heart of that 16th hole, and suddenly his lead doubled. Up ahead, McCumber missed a twenty-foot attempt to get to two under, so Strange had two strokes in hand with two to go.

Still, one of those holes was the 17th, a long, tight par four that he had not parred all week. But he did par it when it counted—a perfect drive, a perfect approach, and two putts. When he three-putted the final hole for a bogey, it was meaningless. Strange had beaten the field, the course, the weather, and the pressure for a second straight Open championship.

Curtis established his consistent performance on a course that is consistently demanding, from the first hole to the last. Even with

Curtis Strange sinks the fifteen-foot birdie at hole number 16 that secured him his second straight U.S. Open. Photo: © Leonard Kamsler

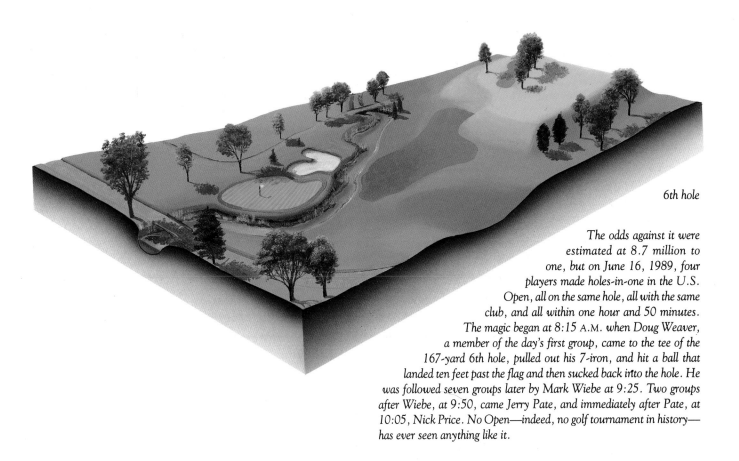

6th hole

The odds against it were estimated at 8.7 million to one, but on June 16, 1989, four players made holes-in-one in the U.S. Open, all on the same hole, all with the same club, and all within one hour and 50 minutes. The magic began at 8:15 A.M. when Doug Weaver, a member of the day's first group, came to the tee of the 167-yard 6th hole, pulled out his 7-iron, and hit a ball that landed ten feet past the flag and then sucked back into the hole. He was followed seven groups later by Mark Wiebe at 9:25. Two groups after Wiebe, at 9:50, came Jerry Pate, and immediately after Pate, at 10:05, Nick Price. No Open—indeed, no golf tournament in history—has ever seen anything like it.

the changes by the Fazios, it remains a classic old-style northeast course, lush, verdant, and tree-lined, with a creek meandering through seven of its holes. Half the greens are like tabletops, uphill at least slightly from the fairway, which puts a premium on the ability to play high, stopping iron shots. Seven pars fours measure 430 yards or more. Furthermore, the two par fives are basically unreachable in two shots. In the 1989 Open the combined scores of the field were over par on the 4th and 13th holes.

Oak Hill is a fader's course—one reason Trevino and Nicklaus have done well there. Five of its long holes, including both 17 and 18, bend from left to right, and no hole turns hard to the left.

Ben Hogan called the 1st hole at Oak Hill "the toughest starting hole in golf," and with good reasons. On three separate occasions he made 6 here in competition, and in the final round of the 1956 Open he made a bogey en route to his loss to Middlecoff by one stroke. A 440-yard par four, it appears to have a generous fairway, but with out of bounds on the right, accuracy off the tee is essential. A creek cuts across the fairway about eighty yards in front of the green—not a problem unless the teeshot has found trees or the rough.

The four par threes are well balanced in terms of length—at 167, 177, 192, and 211 yards—and the longest and toughest of them is number 3. The original Donald Ross green is perched atop a glacial drumlin over 25,000 years old. It is small and hard to hold, particularly with a long-iron shot.

Cary Middlecoff scored his 1956 victory despite two 7s, one of

which came at the 4th hole. Out of bounds again haunts the right side of this par five, which swings hard to the right on its way to a two-tiered green. Most of the pros either can't reach the green or don't even try to thread the opening between two greenside bunkers. It was here that Strange made his wedge-in eagle.

Number 5 is the hole Lee Trevino called the best par four he had ever played. Tom Kite doubtless would not agree, but few holes make better use of a water hazard. It is called double trouble because neither shot is safe. The drive through a corridor of trees must avoid the creek on the right. Then the second must again avoid the creek in front of the green. It ranked as the second most difficult hole in the 1989 Open, as Tom Kite was one among nine competitors who posted 7 or higher.

The name of the 6th hole is Pin Point, and how appropriate that is for the hole on which the four aces were made. One of the Fazio holes, it plays downhill to a green guarded in front by a gargantuan bunker and to the left and rear by Allen's Creek.

The creek again comes into mind if not into play at the 7th, crossing the fairway at the 320-yard mark, thereby assuring that Greg Norman and his like will never be able to hit a half wedge to this 431-yard hole. Nicklaus sank a twenty-foot birdie putt here in the third round of the 1980 PGA. After that he was never out of the lead. Two more tree-lined par fours complete the front nine.

Sadly, many of those trees were struck down in an ice storm that hit Rochester in March of 1991. Notable among the casualties was a 120-foot-high red oak that had stood sentinel at the 9th tee. Over one hundred trees were toppled and more than 10,000 damaged. "The integrity of the course is intact and it is playable," said Joseph Hahn, the club's green superintendent, "but there will be visual differences."

The 10th is similar to the 1st in that the stream that crosses the fairway does not come into play unless one's teeshot catches a tree or heavy grass. Three bunkers protect a classic Donald Ross green. Number 11, a 192-yard par three, was a key to Trevino's Open victory as Supermex posted three 2s and a 3 here. On the other hand, it crushed Arnold Palmer in 1956. In the final round Arnie was still in contention when he hit his ball into the water in front of the green and made a triple-bogey 6.

Twelve is named Leaning Oak, for the huge tree that tilts on a 45-degree angle into the fairway, pinching the teeshot area on the right, turning a straight hole into one that calls for a fade. The 13th is what *GOLF Magazine* calls an "untouchable," one of a select group of holes that no man has reached in two shots. It is 594 yards—more than a third of a mile long—with the last 300 of them uphill and through a valley to a green ringed by six bunkers in a natural amphitheater. Tom Kite frittered away his last chance in the '89 Open when he took a 7 here on Sunday.

After a breather 323-yard par four at 14 the last of the par threes presents itself. Another Fazio creation, it plays downhill to a green hugged by a pond on the right, with the putting surface banked toward that pond. Strange made a gutsy five-footer for par here to keep his lead in the last round.

In 1956 the pros labeled Oak Hill's last three holes Heartbreak Bend. Three bruiser pars fours averaging over 445 yards, they may be the toughest finishing trio on any U.S. Open course. Sixteen, the baby of the three at a mere 439 yards, plays straightaway to a fairway that tosses the ball to the left. Two bunkers flank the entrance to the circular green.

The hardest hole on the course is unquestionably the 17th. It plays 458 yards while twisting from left to right at about the 240-yard mark. A well-placed drive down the right side will leave a long-iron shot to a green that slopes away and is guarded by two bunkers. Middlecoff took a 7 here in 1956, and bogeyed it his final round, but so did one of his closest pursuers, Hogan. In 1989, the world's best players compiled a stroke average of 4.49 on this hole.

At 18, a members' five played as a four by the pros, the Fazios turned a difficult hole into a bear when they lengthened it to 440 yards, leaving a huge ravine in front of the shallow green. The teeshot must avoid trees and rough on the left and a huge many-fingered bunker on the right. Big hitters have downhill lies for the lengthy approach shots. After a mammoth drive, Ian Woosnam, the diminutive Welshman who finished as co-runner-up to Strange, reached this green with an 8-iron on Sunday, but most mortals will require three or four clubs more.

18th hole

Clubhouse

U.S. Open: June 14-16, 1956

Cary Middlecoff	71	70	70	70	281	1
Julius Boros	71	71	71	69	282	T2
Ben Hogan	72	68	72	70	282	T2
Ed Furgol	71	70	73	71	285	T4
Peter Thomson	70	69	75	71	285	T4
Ted Kroll	72	70	70	73	285	T4
Arnold Palmer	72	70	72	73	287	7
Ken Venturi	77	71	68	73	289	8
Doug Ford	71	75	70	74	290	T9
Wes Ellis	71	70	71	78	290	T9
Jerry Barber	72	69	74	75	290	T9

U.S. Open: June 13-16, 1968

Lee Trevino	69	68	69	69	275	1
Jack Nicklaus	72	70	70	67	279	2
Bert Yancey	67	68	70	76	281	3
Bobby Nichols	74	71	68	69	282	4
Don Bies	70	70	75	69	284	T5
Steve Spray	73	75	71	65	284	T5
Bob Charles	73	69	72	71	285	T7
Jerry Pittman	73	67	74	71	285	T7
Gay Brewer	71	71	75	69	286	T9
Bill Casper	75	68	71	72	286	T9
Bruce Devlin	71	69	75	71	286	T9
Sam Snead	73	71	74	68	286	T9
Al Geiberger	72	74	68	72	286	T9
Dave Stockton	72	73	69	72	286	T9

PGA Championship: August 7-10, 1980

Jack Nicklaus	70	69	66	69	274	1
Andy Bean	72	71	68	70	281	2
Lon Hinkle	70	69	69	75	283	T3
Gil Morgan	68	70	73	72	283	T3
Howard Twitty	68	74	71	71	284	T5
Curtis Strange	68	72	72	72	284	T5
Lee Trevino	74	71	71	69	285	T7
Bobby Walzel	68	76	71	71	286	T8
Bill Rogers	71	71	72	72	286	T8
Tom Watson	75	74	72	67	288	T10
Peter Jacobsen	71	73	74	70	288	T10
Tom Weiskopf	71	73	72	72	288	T10
Jerry Pate	72	73	70	73	288	T10
Terry Diehl	72	72	68	76	288	T10

U.S. Open: June 15-18, 1989

Curtis Strange	71	64	73	70	278	1
Ian Woosnam	70	68	73	68	279	T2
Mark McCumber	70	68	72	69	279	T2
Chip Beck	71	69	71	68	279	T2
Brian Claar	71	72	68	69	280	5
Masashi Ozaki	70	71	68	72	281	T6
Scott Simpson	67	70	69	75	281	T6
Peter Jacobsen	71	70	71	70	282	8
J.-M. Olazabal	69	72	70	72	283	T9
Hubert Green	69	72	74	68	283	T9
Tom Kite	67	69	69	78	283	T9
Paul Azinger	71	72	70	70	283	T9

Scorecard

HOLE	YARDS	PAR
1	440	4
2	401	4
3	211	3
4	570	5
5	406	4
6	167	3
7	431	4
8	430	4
9	419	4
OUT	3475	35
10	432	4
11	192	3
12	372	4
13	594	5
14	323	4
15	177	3
16	439	4
17	458	4
18	440	4
IN	3427	35
TOTAL	6902	70

GOLF *Magazine* Rankings:
34th in the World
20th in the U.S.A.

OAK TREE GOLF CLUB

EDMOND, OKLAHOMA
PGA Championship: 1988, 1994

When in the mid 1970s architect Pete Dye got the job of designing Oak Tree Golf Club, he was given only one directive: "Make it the hardest golf course in the world."

He succeeded. At least that's the opinion of the majority of people who have played it. When in 1988 the PGA Championship came to Oak Tree, the pros faced a course with a USGA rating of 76.9 for its par of 71, the highest course rating in the country. Under normal conditions, this may indeed be the hardest course in the world.

One reason for that, aside from Dye's diablerie, is the fact that normal conditions at Oak Tree include a 30 mph breeze. This is Oklahoma, where the wind comes sweeping down the plain. More important, however, is the fact that normal conditions at Oak Tree include management by the folks at Landmark Land.

Those folks are Ernie Vossler and Joe Walser. Twenty years ago they were a couple of club professionals, giving lessons and selling golf balls by the sleeve. Today they are two of the richest men in golf, a pair of real estate magnates whose holdings include a network of golf courses and residential properties stretching from Palm Springs to Palm Beach.

Their success story began in Oklahoma. Vossler was the head pro at Quail Creek Golf Club in Oklahoma City and Walser was his assistant when they noticed that the club's adjacent real estate lots were selling fast. In 1971 they attracted financing and formed a land development company called Unique Golf Concepts. After an initial project in Greensboro, North Carolina, bore fruit, they began to develop their own backyard, a 1,300-acre property in Edmond, a quiet suburb about thirty miles north of Oklahoma City.

The project included fifty-four holes, all designed by Pete Dye; an opulent 70,000-square-foot clubhouse; a $5-million indoor sports complex with an Olympic pool, six tennis courts, two racquetball courts; a fitness center and spa; an indoor track; and facilities for basketball and soccer. Surrounding and financing all of this were 550 lots for single-family homes and condominiums.

To hear Walser, the hardest part about putting all this together was finding a name. "For a while we were going to call it Deer Creek, after a nearby town," he says, noting that the design team even created a logo with a deer in it. Abandoning that, they latched onto Waterloo, reflecting the difficulty of the course, but that gave way to Robin Wood, the robin being native to the area. They also considered Scissortail, the state bird of Oklahoma. "But we kept coming back to words that represented the golf course, especially woods and oaks," says Walser.

There is an actual oak tree after which the club logo was patterned. It stands on the 5th hole of the course, but today it is the symbol for more than one club. Today it stands for all of Landmark Land, the company that absorbed Vossler and Walser's company in 1974, making both of the pros wealthy men in the process. Landmark's other properties include the PGA West, La Quinta Hotel, and Mission Hills resorts in southern California, the Kiawah resort in South Carolina, the Palm Beach Golf & Polo Club near Miami, and two dozen other courses on both coasts and in between. Each resort is distinguished by high quality; each course is distinguished by high difficulty.

"When I was working on Oak Tree," says Dye, "the only comment Ernie and Joe made was, 'Can't you make it any harder?'" Dye calls it the finest inland golf course he has ever built, carefully excluding his seaside gems at Harbour Town, Casa de Campo, TPC Sawgrass, and Long Cove. All of those Dye courses are ranked among GOLF Magazine's 100 Greatest in the World, but so is Oak Tree, number 81.

The course has everything—sand, water, trees, length, thick rough, and fiercely contoured greens. The property is gently rolling, and Dye added a few bumps and hollows of his own along the fairways. The holes meander through oak forests, across streams, and around lakes. Water comes into play on thirteen holes, including each of the par threes, where it is a huge factor in a wind.

Although the championship tees measure 7015 yards, accuracy

1st hole

is more important than distance. This is a modern course where target golf is the key. The fairways look wide enough off the tee, but on most holes there is only one good area to land the teeshot. Why? Because this is Pete Dye unchained. The Oak Tree greens are small, full of severe slopes, and surrounded by trouble. They are hard to hit, hard to hold, hard to hole-out on, the way the greens at the TPC at Sawgrass were before the pros complained. So unless they are approached from the best direction, par becomes a challenge, birdie an accident. At Oak Tree it's often no advantage for a big hitter to boom a teeshot forty yards longer than his opponent's, if it means he'll be left with a sloping lie and a narrow opening to the target.

Since these greens are missed more often than they are hit, nowhere on earth is a well-oiled short game of greater service. The key weapon is a gentle flop shot that will get the ball out of the wiry rough and stop it softly on the green before it boards a roller coaster to jail.

Traditional course architecture calls for a relatively straightforward, even easy, 1st hole, sort of a warm welcome. Not Oak Tree. Here, the welcome mat is a 441-yard par four that most mortals have to attack as a par five. The drive plays downhill to a fairway that kicks everything to the left. If the ball kicks too far left, the second will have to be played from rough, over a lake, over sand, over trees, then more sand, to a green that is only a few steps wide. Imagine that into a wind—or even downwind—and you'll understand why even some of the pros lay up short of the green, then hope for a pitch-and-putt par.

The fairway at number 2 is generous, but the player had best find it. A lake runs down the entire left side, and there is out of bounds to the right. The water curls around the left and back of the two-level green.

Dye's favorite hole is the 582-yard 3rd, an unreachable par five where even the second shot must be played carefully around the right-to-left dogleg, with water again down the left side. The third

shot here is a wedge, but must be a good one since the green is one of the smallest on the course and is guarded in front by a cavernous pot bunker.

The 4th hole, a par three of 200 yards, is one of the most photographed holes in golf, 190 of those 200 yards playing over water to a green bulkheaded with several dozen of Pete Dye's signature railroad ties. (Someone estimated that Dye used 8,000 ties at Oak Tree.) It was here in 1988 that Paul Azinger knocked a 6-iron into the hole to take a four-stroke lead in the third round of the PGA.

The longest hole on the course, the 590-yard 5th, calls for a teeshot straight over the top of "The Oak Tree." Despite its length, long hitters may try for this one in two, since the last half of the hole plays slightly downhill, and roll-on approaches are possible. But so are roll-off approaches, and this small target sits on a peninsula ringed first by sand, then water. It was here that Jeff Sluman struck the shot that spurred him to victory in the PGA, a 115-yard wedge that went into the cup for an eagle.

The best birdie opportunity may be at the 6th, which at 377 yards is the shortest par four on the course and has only one bunker. But trouble returns at the 440-yard 7th, where the only way to shorten the dogleg is to hug the trees, rough, and water on the left.

The 171-yard 8th hole is sort of a shortened version of the 4th, playing over water to a bulkheaded green. Wind—and therefore careful club selection—is a big factor here. In round three of the PGA, Ray Floyd made an ace here only a half hour before Azinger did the deed at the 4th.

Front-nine finishers are greeted by a three-tiered green fronted by a deep "Valley of Sin," placing a high premium on accuracy, both on the teeshot and the approach.

Dye's masterpiece Teeth of the Dog course at Casa de Campo in the Dominican Republic introduced the concept of waste areas, expanses of unraked sand and scrub lining and crossing fairways. They are not fairway, but not hazards either, since the player may ground his club when playing from these areas. At Oak Tree such an area runs down the entire right side of the 10th hole. If that can be avoided, this par four offers a good birdie opportunity.

The next two par fours do not. Number 11 was named by the PGA of America as the toughest 11th hole in the country. Stretching 466 yards, it plays to an elevated green with a nearly ten-foot-deep bunker to the left. The 12th plays 445 yards through an undulating valley to a green framed by bunkers and trees.

Number 13 was unlucky for Seve Ballesteros in 1988. In the second round of the PGA, when his teeshot overflew the green of this little par three, the Spaniard found his ball lying in a creek bed just a few feet from the four-foot-high stone wall that supports this green. Attempting a quick-rising cut shot, he skulled the ball into the wall. It nearly hit him on the rebound, settling in some thick brush. From there he needed three more strokes to reach the green, where he sank a ten-footer for a triple-bogey 6. He shot 75 and missed the cut.

The 14th is named Augusta, and this 453-yard tree-lined dogleg does have the minimal bunkering and undulating green characteristic of the Masters course. The creek which courses along the right of the hole before crossing in front of the green conjures visions of Augusta's famed 13th. The difference is that that hole, just a few yards longer, is a par five while this is a four.

After a relatively straightforward par four at the 15th, Oak Tree finishes with a tantalizing five, a testing three, and a torturous four.

A noose hangs from a tree to the left of the 16th green, presumably for anyone who by this time is ready to commit suicide. Birdies are frequent on this comparatively short par five, but the green is protected on the left by two huge bunkers and a creek, and the fast split-level green presents all sorts of chipping challenges. In the second round of the PGA there were nine eagles here—and one score of 9—by the most unlikely of competitors. Jack Nicklaus blocked his teeshot into the hazard, then lost his 3-wood approach in the trees to the right of the green en route to a quadruple bogey. It was the first time in competition—professional or amateur—that Nicklaus had lost two balls on the same hole, and it led to his missing the PGA cut for only the third time in twenty-seven years.

Like the three other short holes, number 17 plays entirely over water, this time to a very deep and narrow green where club selection can vary three clubs or more, depending on pin placement. A beach bunker, stretching into the water, is on the right side, but the huge grassy mounds on the left are the places to be avoided at all costs.

The 18th hole was actually the 9th on the Oak Tree design, but the two holes switched places for the PGA under the theory that

4th hole

Three behind Paul Azinger with fourteen holes to go, little Jeff Sluman had a tall assignment as he stepped to the 5th tee in the final round of the 1988 PGA. After a solid drive, he pushed his second shot into rough to the right side of the fairway. From there he faced a ticklish approach over a sea of sand to a narrow green with more sand beyond. But he caught the ball perfectly with his sand wedge. It lofted high and landed softly just over the fringe, then rolled across the green and into the cup. Eagle three. When, moments later, Azinger made 6 on the same hole, they were tied. After that, the tournament belonged to Sluman.

this hole made for a more dramatic finish. The teeshot must finish high on a plateau in order to leave a reasonable approach to the green, which is flanked by a huge "graveyard" bunker on the right and grass bunkers to the left.

The course got its first test in 1984 when the U.S. Amateur arrived. Truly, however, it was the amateurs who were tested. In the stroke-play qualifying segment, the best young players in the country were taxed for an average of 79.43 strokes, almost half of them failing to break 80. Scott Verplank, then age 20, won the qualifying medal and went on to win the championship in 106-degree heat. In his final match, against Sam Randolph, Verplank birdied five times in eight holes to go from two down to a four-and-three victory, the winner coming on a double-breaking thirty-footer at the 15th hole.

Verplank later became one of the Oak Tree Boys, a group of nine PGA Tour players who bought homes and settled in Edmond. The others were Andy Dillard, David Edwards, Mark Hayes, Andrew Magee, Gil Morgan, Doug Tewell, Bob Tway, and Willie Wood, together responsible for two dozen victories and nearly $15 million in Tour earnings.

The smart money said that one of this ninesome would be the victor at the 1988 PGA, but the local boys did not make good. Only three of them survived the cut, and the highest finisher was Edwards, who tied for twenty-fifth.

Local knowledge turned out to be less than vital on the first two days, perhaps because there was an absence of the vaunted wind. Scoring over the first thirty-six holes of the championship was as hot as the 100-degree air. Thirty-one players broke par as Bob Gilder led the pack with a course-record 66. His record lasted only one day, however, as Dave Rummels followed an opening 73 with a seven-under-par 64. Rummels made nine birdies, including five in a row on holes 4 through 8, as this time a record forty-four players bet-

tered par, with Paul Azinger taking the 36-hole lead at 133 and club pro Jay Overton a stroke back. The cut came at 144, a record low for the PGA.

Azinger shot a 71 on Saturday to hold his lead as the wind came up and blew several players out of contention. One shot that helped him was his teeshot at number 4, which sailed across the pond, took two bounces, and went into the hole for an ace. Azinger thrust his fist into the air and tossed his visor to the heavens. At that point he had a four-stroke lead. But by day's end, it was down to one as Rummels stayed hot with a 68. Three off the lead was diminutive Jeff Sluman, at 5 foot 7 inches and 135 pounds the smallest player on the Tour. Sluman, playing steadily, had attracted little notice while bettering par in each of his three rounds: 69-70-68.

Azinger found himself in a familiar position. Three weeks earlier he had led the British Open after fifty-four holes only to lose it to Nick Faldo with bogeys at 17 and 18. Now Faldo was in fourth place, four back. As for the two nearer pursuers, neither Rummels nor Sluman had ever won on the Tour.

But on Sunday, Sluman would win in the most decisive way, with a round of 65 that tied David Graham's 1979 mark as the lowest winning final round in PGA history. His score of 272 was only one off the championship record and it made him the first player since Jerry Pate in 1976 to make a major championship his inaugural victory.

The key hole was number 5 where Azinger made a bogey 6 and Sluman stunned the field by holing out a 115-yard wedge shot for eagle 3. "As soon as I hit it I knew it was going to be close," he said. "When it went in, it was the first time in 95-degree heat that I've had chills all up and down my body."

Azinger followed his bogey with another bogey at 6 as Sluman birdied 7 to go two ahead. Three more birdies on the back nine

sealed it for him. Azinger tried to catch him, birdieing 16 and then hitting the stick with his teeshot at 17, his ball stopping only three inches away. But he needed another birdie at 18, and instead he made a bogey.

Prior to Oak Tree, Sluman had had trouble finishing tournaments. Although he ranked fourth in scoring average on the Tour (70.23), his third-round average of 71.5 ranked 112th and his final round average of 71.9 was 106th. He had blown leads at three tournaments earlier in the year. But this time, over the final thirty-six holes, he outplayed the field by five strokes. In the last round he missed only one fairway, only three greens. No one lost this PGA. Jeff Sluman won it.

PGA Championship: August 11-14, 1988

Jeff Sluman	69	70	68	65	272	1
Paul Azinger	67	66	71	71	275	2
Tommy Nakajima	69	68	74	67	278	3
Tom Kite	72	69	71	67	279	T4
Nick Faldo	67	71	70	71	279	T4
Dave Rummels	73	64	68	75	280	T6
Bob Gilder	66	75	71	68	280	T6
Dan Pohl	69	71	70	71	281	8
Mark O'Meara	70	71	70	71	282	T9
Greg Norman	68	71	72	71	282	T9
Payne Stewart	70	69	70	73	282	T9
Ray Floyd	68	68	74	72	282	T9
Kenny Knox	72	69	68	73	282	T9
Steve Jones	69	68	72	73	282	T9

Scorecard

HOLE	YARDS	PAR
1	441	4
2	392	4
3	584	5
4	200	3
5	590	5
6	377	4
7	440	4
8	171	3
9	386	4
OUT	3581	36
10	379	4
11	466	4
12	445	4
13	149	3
14	453	4
15	434	4
16	479	5
17	200	3
18	429	4
IN	3434	35
TOTAL	7015	71

GOLF Magazine Rankings:
81st in the World
49th in the U.S.A.

LEFT, BOTH PICTURES: *Jeff Sluman, the smallest player on the PGA Tour, also had the lowest total in the 1988 PGA. Photos: Jacqueline Duvoisin for Sports Illustrated © Time Inc.*

OAKLAND HILLS COUNTRY CLUB

BIRMINGHAM, MICHIGAN
U.S. Open: 1924, 1937, 1951, 1961, 1985
PGA Championship: 1972, 1979

"The Lord intended this for a golf links," said Donald Ross in 1916 as he surveyed the rolling, tree-clad parcel of land eighteen miles northwest of Detroit. Thirty-five years later, Ben Hogan stood on the same property and pronounced it a monster. Through three-quarters of a century and seven major championships Oakland Hills has inspired both the divine and the demonic.

It started with two men. One of them was Norval Hawkins, head of sales for Ford. Back when the Model-T was the cat's meow and the Ford assembly line was cranking out 900 cars a day, Hawkins was said to be making a dollar for every car. Along with an accountant colleague named Joseph Mack, Hawkins invested his fortune in a real estate venture outside Birmingham, Michigan. But no houses were ever built. Instead, as golf caught fire in the Midwest, the two men declared that their 250 acres of farmland would become a coun-

try club, a place where they and their fellow carmakers could gather together and play in style.

To prove they were serious, they brought in the eminent Ross as architect and invited him to design not one but two courses. The club's first pro shop was an old chicken coop, and the roost was ruled by 1914 U.S. Open Champion Walter Hagen, hired as head professional. Hagen's assignment was to act as sort of a public relations man, to teach the Detroiters how to play the game and simultaneously to romance them into becoming members. But the Haig saw this sinecure as little more than an excuse to practice.

Feisty little Cyril Walker stood up to Bobby Jones and a stiff breeze to take the 1924 Open. This was his winning putt. Photo: United States Golf Association

"I had a queer way of teaching," he admitted in his autobiography, *The Walter Hagen Story*. "I'd have the pupil take a couple of practice swings, then I'd grab the club from his hand and spend the rest of his paid-for time showing how it should be done. The guy was darned lucky who managed to get that club from my hand before his time was up."

Shortly after the Oakland Hills courses were built, Hagen quit. By this time he had sharpened his game sufficiently to have won a second Open, in 1919, and had decided that life on the Tour as a "businessman golfer" could be lucrative. Before leaving he had the cheek to suggest that the club hire Mike Brady, whom Hagen had beaten in the playoff for that 1919 Open. They did, and the consolation prize turned out to be a satisfying one for Brady, who stayed on at Oakland Hills for several years.

Both Hagen and Brady finished in the top ten when Oakland Hills' South Course hosted its first Open in 1924, but this was the beginning of the era when the man to beat was Bobby Jones, and at Oakland Hills, only one man beat him, a feisty little Englishman named Cyril Walker.

Although only 118 pounds, Walker was a fine wind player, having honed his low-hitting style on the Lancashire Coast at Hoylake, where he battled the gales off the Irish Sea. When a breeze blew across Oakland Hills for the final round, he was ready. Coming to the last three holes he had a two-stroke lead over Jones and the knowledge that Bobby had finished with three fours. Walker finished 3-3-5 and won by three. His winning total of 297 was the only one under 300.

Walker was no runner. A notoriously slow player, in fact, at one event he became such an impediment to the pace of play that he was asked to withdraw. When he refused, officials dragged him bodily from the course. He was also a proud little fellow, with something of a Napoleon complex. Six months after Oakland Hills, when he was introduced on the first tee of the Los Angeles Open, the man with the microphone asked whether he was the champion of any state. "State!" he screamed, "I'm the champion of the whole goddam 48!"

Golf lore says that at Oakland Hills Walker gave his entire $500 first prize to his caddie. He might better have salted it away, for years later he lost his shirt in a Florida land deal, became a caddie himself, and died in poverty.

When the Open returned in 1937, the players found an Oakland Hills that had been lengthened more than 100 yards. The stretching had come in response to a decade which had produced three major advancements in the quality of golf equipment: the wound-center ball, the steel shaft, and the sand wedge. Indeed, even the new Oakland Hills at 7037 yards was no match for technology, and this Open produced two scoring records.

In round two long-hitting Jimmy Thomson had a chance to break Gene Sarazen's one-round record of 66, shot at Fresh Meadow in 1932. With two holes to go Thomson was eight under par, on

course for a 64. But at 17 he missed a two-foot par putt and at 18 he missed another short one, so he settled for a 66.

After 54 holes the lead belonged to Ed Dudley at 211. One behind him was lanky Texan Ralph Guldahl, tied with a 25-year-old rookie named Sam Snead. Despite his inexperience, Snead was one of the pre-tournament favorites, and he had opened with a 69 to take a share of the lead. But this week turned out to be the start of the Slammer's frustrated career-long quest for the Open title. In the final round Snead shot 71, and when he walked into the locker room he was greeted by Tommy Armour. "Laddie," said the Silver Scot, "you've just won yourself the Open."

Little did Armour know that Guldahl had eagled the 8th hole and birdied 9 to reach the turn in 33 strokes. Standing on the 10th tee, he realized he needed to finish in 37 to become the winner. He told himself, "If you can't play this last nine in 37 strokes, you're just a bum and don't deserve to win the Open."

Guldahl promptly bogeyed both 10 and 11. Now he needed a birdie and six pars. At the next hole he got his birdie, and then at the par-three 13th he nearly holed his 6-iron teeshot, setting up a two. From there forward he parred in for a 69, a two-stroke victory, and a new 72-hole Open record of 281.

For Guldahl, who a year earlier had almost given up the game in disgust, this was the beginning of a three-year run during which he was the finest player in the game. In 1938 he defended his title successfully, only the third man in history to do so, and between 1937 and 1939 he won eight events, including a Masters and two Western Opens (the Western was then regarded as a major championship). Shortly thereafter he lost his game, never winning again after 1940.

The year 1951 marked the 150th anniversary of Detroit and the beginning of a new breed of U.S. Open course. By this time, with continued advancements in clubs and balls, it had become clear that the grand old courses that had tested Bobby Jones & Co. would not test Ben Hogan & Co. In the face of this, the USGA decided that if they were going to return to their favorite layouts, those layouts would have to be updated.

Enter Robert Trent Jones. The Cornell graduate had spent half a lifetime studying and training for this opportunity, and he made the most of it, not simply redesigning Oakland Hills but ushering in a new era of course architecture in which drives were directed not to fairways but to landing areas, approaches were played not to greens but to targets.

Before he ever unrolled a blueprint or cranked up a bulldozer, Jones did a study of the playing skills of modern professional golfers, and determined that the average pro was able to hit a teeshot that carried 236 yards. That told him that a great many fairway bunkers on Donald Ross's original design were irrelevant. So he began filling-in those obsolete bunkers and replacing them with new ones in the 230-270-yard range.

Jones followed the route of the original course but altered every hole, using his large bunkers to pinch in the waists of the fairways

and tighten the diameters of the greens. *Golfing Magazine* editor Herb Graffis wrote that the bunkers hugged their targets "like sinister Don Juans on the make." In all, he added sixty-six bunkers.

Jones also added mounds and undulations that enhanced the contours of Ross's surfaces, giving them a pitch and roll that has been likened to the North Atlantic during a midwinter storm. He shortened the course 110 yards, but also lowered its par from 72 to 70, converting two short par fives—the 8th and the 18th—to fours that played 458 and 459 yards. His stated objective in all this: "to give the pros the shock treatment."

To complete the challenge, the USGA stepped in and narrowed Oakland Hills's tumbling fairways, creating the slimmest landing strips the Open had ever seen, some of them no more than 25 paces across.

The players were completely daunted, and in the first round not one member of the 162-man field matched par, as Sam Snead led with a 71. Ben Hogan, who was defending the title and had won his first Masters a few weeks earlier, arrived five days before the championship and practiced with typical resolve, mentally photographing every inch of the new course. But when the bell rang, he stumbled to a 76, which he later characterized as "the stupidest round of golf I ever played." In round two, Snead fell to a 78 as Hogan improved to a 73, but both stood five off the pace of the new leader, Bobby Locke. "I'd have to be Houdini to win now," said Hogan. "I'd need 140 and how can anybody shoot 140 on this course?"

Everyone was struggling with Oakland Hills. "The course is playing the players instead of the players playing the course," said Walter Hagen, on hand as an observer. What some players had done, in hopes of avoiding Jones's grasping fairway bunkers, was club down with fairway woods and irons off the tees. It was this cautious tactic, however, that had brought Hogan his opening 76. He,

among others, realized that such clubbing-down only made for longer, more difficult approach shots.

But on Saturday morning Hogan began to correct his errors. Through thirteen holes he worked himself to three under par for the day, only to give one back at the 14th, then slip to a double-bogey six at the 15th and another bogey at 17. In with a 71, he nonetheless gained ground and stood two behind co-leaders Locke and Jimmy Demaret as, through 54 holes, not a soul had managed to shoot a round in the 60s.

In the afternoon Hogan resumed his attack, playing through the first nine in even par. At the 10th, a par four of 448 yards, he hit the shot of the week, a 2-iron that stopped five feet from the pin for a birdie. After pars at 11 and 12 he sank a fifteen-footer for a birdie at 13 to go two under. A bogey five at the 14th cost him, but at 15, his Waterloo in the morning, he got revenge, lofting a 6-iron to four feet and dropping the putt for a three. Two more pars brought him to the final tee.

By this time Demaret had shot himself out of contention, and Locke, playing nine holes behind Hogan, was struggling. Hogan thus sensed that if he could par 18, he would likely win his third Open title in his last three attempts. The Hawk did better than par. After a long, aggressive drive, he struck a 6-iron fourteen feet from the flag and rammed home the putt for a round of 67. It was more than enough for victory as only one other player, Clayton Heafner, bettered 70 with a round of 69 to finish second, two back.

Hogan had improved his score in each round—76-73-71-67—and called his closing 18 "under the circumstances the greatest round I have played." To this day, many agree that it was the single greatest round in Open history, the other candidates being Arnold Palmer's 65 at Cherry Hills (1960), Johnny Miller's 63 at Oakmont (1973), and David Graham's 67 at Merion (1981).

In accepting the trophy he said, "I'm just glad that I brought this course, this monster, to its knees." Moments later he was approached by Ione Jones, the architect's gracious wife, who congratulated him on his superb play. "Mrs. Jones," he said grimly, "if your husband had to play golf on the courses he designs, your family would be on the bread line."

Nonetheless, the 1951 Open was as important to Trent Jones as it was to Hogan. The architect used it as a springboard to a career of designing—and redesigning—hundreds of courses throughout the world, including pre-Open rejuvenations of Baltusrol (1954), Olympic (1955), Oak Hill (1956), Southern Hills (1958), and Congressional (1964).

Immediately after the tournament, the course was softened so that at least a few of the Oakland Hills members could break 90 in their club events. And by 1961 when the Open returned for the fourth time, it was a more mature, mellower place to play. Jones had removed seven of his toughening bunkers, and the USGA had not cinched the fairways with the heavy rough of 1951. Still, the course remained, in Jones's opinion, "the world's most severe test of golf."

On the eve of the 1961 Open, Oakland Hills host professional Al Watrous predicted that the winner would be the man who played the par-three holes best. He was right, as the title went to Gene Littler, who tamed the one-shotters in three-under par.

It was one of those Opens where the first-round lead went to a comparative unknown, Bobby Brue, a bespectacled young pro from Menominee Falls, Wisconsin, who used only twenty-six putts en route to his 69. Ben Hogan looked as if he might recapture the glory of a decade earlier when he wedged his third shot into the cup for an eagle at the 2nd, then birdied the 3rd, but he fell to a 71 as Brue was the only man to better par. In the second round, however, Oakland Hills was battered more severely than in any other Open as ten players shot in the 60s and Bob Rosburg and Doug Sanders posted 67s to share the lead at 139. Sanders took sole possession after 54 holes at even par 210, with Littler tied for fourth place, three behind him.

Littler had been a phenom in his pre-pro years, winning the 1953 U.S. Amateur as well as the 1954 San Diego Open as an amateur. He had also finished second to Ed Furgol in the 1954 Open at Baltusrol, a missed nine-foot putt at the 72nd hole costing him a

10th hole

shot at the title. No less than Bobby Jones had declared the smooth-swinging Californian to be "the coming golfer." But lean years had followed. Throughout the later '50s, Littler had merely lurked, just as he had seemed to do at Oakland Hills.

But in the final round, he struck. Birdieing the 7th, 11th, and 13th holes, he took the lead, then parred the next four and bogeyed 18 to come in with a 69—281. Sanders, two holes behind, needed a birdie to tie, but could muster only a pair of pars. He finished tied for second with Bob Goalby. Tied for fourth were Mike Souchak and a 21-year-old amateur named Nicklaus. Littler was in the press tent when he was officially informed that he had won. "Men," he said, "it's been a long wait."

The 1972 PGA at Oakland Hills was almost the golf tournament of the century. Two weeks earlier, had Lee Trevino not sunk a chip shot on the seventy-first hole at Muirfield, turning a bogey into par and victory, it is very possible that Jack Nicklaus would have come to Detroit with that year's Masters, U.S. Open, *and* British Open all in his pocket, and a unique opportunity to win the only modern Grand Slam.

Neither Nicklaus nor Trevino turned out to be a factor at Oakland Hills, but it was nonetheless a tournament replete with

A look of jut-jawed determination creases the face of Gary Player as he battles to a two-stroke victory in the 1972 PGA. Photo: John D. Hanlon for Sports Illustrated © Time Inc.

interesting characters. The first-round lead went to Stan Thirsk and Buddy Allin at 68. Allin, a wiry Vietnam veteran, looked to be the sole leader until the day's last starting time brought home Thirsk, a club pro from Kansas City who years later would gain a degree of fame for having been the earliest teacher of Tom Watson. (As is so often the case in the majors, neither Allin nor Thirsk maintained the pace, Allin finishing fifty-third, Thirsk seventy-second.) Meanwhile, Arnold Palmer shot 69, and heading a large contingent at even par was the day's biggest surprise, 60-year-old Sam Snead. Thirty-five years after he had led the first round of the 1937 Open, the Slammer was back, and in those three and a half decades he had slipped only one stroke.

At the halfway point the lead belonged to young Jerry Heard at 139. Palmer had faltered with a 75, and Nicklaus was eight behind. But the other member of the trio then known as golf's Big Three, the one whose credentials for membership had recently come under question, was asserting himself. Gary Player had moved within range at 142.

On Saturday—moving day—Player made his move, shooting a 67 that gave him the lead, despite a bogey at 18. (A number of players had complained that the final hole—a 459-yard dogleg with an all-carry approach—was simply too severe, that it should have been returned to its original status as a par five. Through three days, the field had played this hole in 246 over par.) One stroke behind Player was Billy Casper, and just behind him were Heard, Gay Brewer, and Phil Rodgers.

On Sunday seven different players bobbed in and out of the lead, as no one took charge on the front nine, least of all Player. Bogeying three of the first four holes, he was out in 37. But the day before he had said that the tournament would not begin until the final nine holes.

He was right, and the man who began that beginning was unlikely Jim Jamieson, a roly-poly Michigander who had started the day four back of Player. When he birdied 11 and 12, he took the lead at even par. Three more pars kept him there, but then Player birdied 11 to draw even. From there they did an Alphonse and Gaston act, Jamieson bogeying 16 and 17 while Player did the same at 14 and 15. Now they were still even, Jamieson with one difficult hole to play, Player with three of them.

The odds on Player winning lengthened when he sliced his teeshot on 16 into rough. The par-four hole is a sharp dogleg right around a large pond to a rolling green. When Player reached his ball he discovered that his shot to the green was blocked by a huge weeping willow tree. He could hit a wedge over the tree, but that would not be enough to carry the water. He'd need an 8-iron for distance, but that wouldn't get him over the tree. Player settled on a 9-iron and resolved to hit it as hard as he could. Aligning himself with the seat stick of a spectator at the green, he slugged the ball up and over the tree. It barely missed the top branches, flew over the water, and stabbed the green four feet from the hole, one of golf's greatest shots under pressure. Moments after that, Jamieson missed a short par putt at 18. With a pair of closing pars, Player took a two-stroke victory and his sixth major title.

Tommy Aaron finished in a tie for second with Jamieson, and behind them, in a tie for fourth, was the incredible Mr. Snead. At age 60 he had outplayed Nicklaus, Palmer, Trevino, and roughly 100 professionals a quarter century younger than he.

No one bettered par for 72 holes in that 1972 PGA, but seven years later the championship returned, and this time the monster was not simply tamed, it was trampled. There were sixty-six sub-par rounds, and the top fifteen finishers beat or tied Player's 281, with the winning total an Oakland Hills record of 272, eight under par.

Two players shot that score, Ben Crenshaw and David Graham. They had begun the day two strokes and four strokes, respectively, off the 203 pace of Rex Caldwell. But as Caldwell played one-over-par golf on Sunday, Crenshaw and Graham made birdies galore—thirteen between them. Birdies at the first three holes took Crenshaw into a tie for the lead by the 6th tee, but then he cooled a bit as Graham caught fire. As Ben bogeyed 10 and 11, David birdied the same holes and suddenly the three-stroke lead was his. But then Crenshaw, playing behind the Australian, birdied 12 and 13 and the margin was back to one.

Graham, with the wind in his face at the 15th, knifed a 4-iron three inches from the cup for a birdie that took him two ahead. Thereafter Crenshaw would gain no ground on par, so Graham needed to play the final three holes in one over to win. He made a routine par at 16, then sank a gutsy 12-footer at 17 to save his par three. With one hole to go, he seemed to have the championship in the bag.

But there was more than the championship at stake. In that year GOLF Magazine was offering a $50,000 bonus to any player who could break the 18-hole or 72-hole record in any of the four majors. The PGA records were 63 and 271. If Graham could birdie 18 he would shoot 62—269, breaking both records and winning $100,000. A par would give him 63—270, good for $50,000. A bogey would give him no money, but a victory nonetheless.

Graham blew it all, with a double bogey. He pushed his drive into the rough, overclubbed on his second and wound up on a grassy hill in back of the green, then played too delicately from there, leaving his ball in the heavy fringe. From there he chipped to five feet and missed the putt. His 65 put him at 272, in a sudden-death play-off with Crenshaw.

Few players in history have been the equal to Ben Crenshaw as a putter, but in the playoff Graham was more than a match. At the first hole he sank a 25-footer to halve Crenshaw's par, at the second he made a 10-footer to halve Crenshaw's birdie, and at the par-three third, after Crenshaw bunkered his teeshot and could do no better than bogey, Graham settled matters by rapping in a 15-footer for a deuce.

With his superb final round, Graham won that tournament. Six

"Two-Chip" Chen and the shot that made him famous, an agonizing double-hit pitch that led to his demise in the 1985 U.S. Open. Photo: AP/Wide World Photos

years later, when the Open returned to Oakland Hills, the title was just as surely lost, with a disastrous final round precipitated by one nightmarish swing. The victim was T.C. Chen of Taiwan. The T.C. stands for Tze-Chung, but to all golf fans he will be remembered forever as "Two Chip" Chen, thanks to a bizarre occurrence at Oakland Hills' 5th hole.

The former sailor in the Chinese navy led the tournament from round one when his course-record-tieing 65 included a double-eagle at the second hole, the first albatross in Open history. A 69 on Friday kept him one ahead of Jay Haas and 1978 Open Champion Andy North, North shooting a 65 of his own, the only round of the week that did not include a bogey. On rainy Saturday, another 69 for Chen gave him a two-stroke cushion over North. After four holes on Sunday, the lead had grown to four over North and six over Canada's Dave Barr. Chen seemed on the verge of becoming the first Oriental to win a major championship.

But at the 5th hole a disaster hit Chen that brought North, Barr, and a half dozen other players back into contention. Although he hit a perfect teeshot, he pushed his 4-iron approach into rough

OVERLEAF: *11th hole.* INSET: *12th hole*

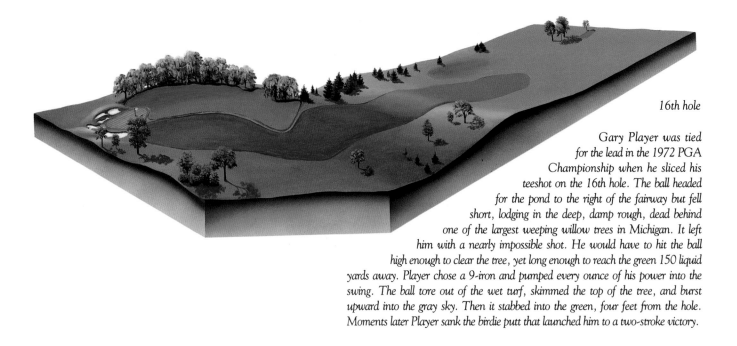

16th hole

*Gary Player was tied
for the lead in the 1972 PGA
Championship when he sliced his
teeshot on the 16th hole. The ball headed
for the pond to the right of the fairway but fell
short, lodging in the deep, damp rough, dead behind
one of the largest weeping willow trees in Michigan. It left
him with a nearly impossible shot. He would have to hit the ball
high enough to clear the tree, yet long enough to reach the green 150 liquid
yards away. Player chose a 9-iron and pumped every ounce of his power into the
swing. The ball tore out of the wet turf, skimmed the top of the tree, and burst
upward into the gray sky. Then it stabbed into the green, four feet from the hole.
Moments later Player sank the birdie putt that launched him to a two-stroke victory.*

thirty yards right of the green. He then left his pitch shot short of the green. From there he played the oddest shot anyone can remember. Using a wedge, he chopped at the ball, and then, as the ball lofted into the air, the blade of his wedge rose up and made contact with it a second time, flipping it high into the air and to the left, onto the collar of the green. By hitting the ball twice in one swing, he was penalized a stroke. Suddenly, Chen lay five, and was still not on the green. Stunned, he took a quadruple-bogey 8. In one hole, his entire lead had evaporated.

It got worse. Chen bogeyed the next three holes and went from four ahead of North to three behind him. Meanwhile, Dave Barr and Payne Stewart had also pulled ahead of him. With nine holes to go, North led Barr by one, Stewart and Chen by two.

The final nine was a melee in which North, Barr, and Chen all held the lead at various points. With two holes to go, North was one ahead, but at the short 17th his teeshot pelted into the deep bunker to the right of the green. From there he played the shot that won the tournament, an exquisitely deft explosion that nearly went into the hole. At 18 he needed only a bogey, and that is what he made.

Just as he had at Cherry Hills seven years earlier, North made that final bogey for a 74 and a one-stroke victory. His round hadn't been pretty. He had hit only four fairways, and in four days he had made only nine birdies. But it was also true that he had made only eight bogeys, far fewer than any other player, and only two of them had come in the last 36 holes. In a week in which the monster had bitten back, Andy North had been merely nipped. He became the fifteenth man in history to win at least two Opens, and the only man on that roster whose list of other accomplishments includes just one other victory.

Today's Oakland Hills is neither as vulnerable as the course Guldahl subdued in 1937 nor as brutal as the one Hogan battled in 1951. Over the years it has earned the three-word characterization sought by every major championship venue: tough but fair.

That character is evident from the very first hole, a par four that plays 436 yards from an elevated tee to a broad, kidney-shaped green. Jones's cinching bunkers, at about the 250-yard range, will catch many drives, but the best of teeshots can clear them, and the green, although large, is complicated by the presence of a swale running through its center.

Chen's double-eagle hole, the 527-yard 2nd, is a vulnerable five if the teeshot can avoid the nest of deep bunkers at the crook of its dogleg. The 1985 Open program speculated that "the longer players will be able to reach this green, probably with a three wood." Fred Couples promptly hit it with a 6-iron.

The first of four lengthy par threes, the 199-yard 3rd plays to a green set on a diagonal to the fairway and surrounded by five grasping bunkers, one of which caught and killed Ben Crenshaw in the playoff for the PGA.

Number 4 is sort of a junior version of the 2nd, doglegging left through a clutch of Jonesian bunkers to a green ringed with more sand.

Bobby Locke hated the 5th hole. On two occasions he hit his ball into the same fairway bunker, which he claimed cost him the '51 Open title. "It was a blind bunker," he complained, in apparent disagreement with Tommy Armour, who once said, "It's only blind the first time you play it." Whether or not the teeshot finds a bunker, this hole is long and hard. Guldahl sank a fifty-footer for a birdie here in the final round of the '37 Open, and the fringe of this green is where Two-Chip Chen got his name.

Most of the pros will go with irons off the tee of number 6, the shortest par four on the course. But the green is set on top of a hill and, as always, encircled by sand. A little pond adds interest to the 7th, a 405-yard dogleg right that also slopes to the right toward the water. The green is long and narrow, and so is the bunker that stretches along its right flank.

Number 8 is one of the two holes that Trent Jones converted from a par five to a four. Today it plays 439 yards to a green set twenty-five feet above the fairway. In 1937, when it was still a five, Guldahl chipped in for an eagle that spurred him to victory. This was also the place where Denis Watson waited too long for his birdie putt to drop. In the first round of the '85 Open the South African stroked his ball to the edge of the cup; then he dawdled a bit instead of tapping it in. Eventually the ball fell, but an official informed Watson that since he had waited more than the "few seconds" the Rules allow, his score was a four plus two penalty strokes for a total of six. The penalty turned out to be costly, as Watson finished the championship in second place, one stroke behind Andy North. The incident later caused the USGA to modify this Rule, and today the maximum penalty is one stroke.

Through four rounds of the 1979 PGA, David Graham played holes 5 through 8 in eight under par, ten strokes better than Ben Crenshaw, who in sixteen tries on that quartet of par fours could do no better than two over. Crenshaw dominated the par threes that year, as well as in 1985, when he scored a hole-in-one at number 9.

It was quite an ace, because this hole plays 217 yards, uphill and all carry. The green is very fast and slopes steeply from back to front, probably the most three-puttable surface on the course.

Bobby Jones might have won the 1924 Open had he not had to play the 10th hole. In four trips through the testing par four, Bobby made one bogey and, incredibly, three double bogeys. In the final round he was tied with Walker when he came to 10, hit a splendid drive of nearly 300 yards, but still managed to make only a six. In those days it took two well-struck woods to reach the elevated green. Today, distance is not as important as accuracy, with huge bunkers in the drive zone, the one on the left hillside being the largest on the course. In 1951 Hogan called the 2-iron he hit to five feet here the finest shot of his finest round.

The 11th parallels 10, threading past a large hill to an elevated

18th hole

green. Next comes the longest hole on the course, the 560-yard 12th. It's reachable to the longest players, but bunkers directly in front of the green caution against aggressiveness. It is followed by the shortest hole. Number 13 plays 172 yards to a green ringed by seven bunkers. The front of the putting surface is three feet lower than the back.

At 14, for the first time, there are no fairway bunkers, but that's only appropriate on a 465-yard par four with woods along both sides. Incredibly, in the 1951 Open it did not yield a single birdie to the entire field. The last good birdie chance comes at 15, a sharp dogleg left with a lone bunker dead-center at the knee of the dogleg. If that bunker can be avoided, the terraced green is not hard to find.

Number 16, where Gary Player struck his dramatic 9-iron, was a straight and simple 350-yard hole before Jones brought the big pond into play. In a sense it's out of character at Oakland Hills, in the same way that the 4th at Baltusrol, another Jonesian pond hole, is a misfit on that course. But it has created plenty of drama for pros and amateurs alike. Each month over 200 golf balls are fished out of the pond.

Deep bunkers flank the target at 17, where the plateau green is thirty feet above the tee, making this 201 yards play like 220 or more. But the hardest hole on the course is the last, a bruising 453-yard dogleg right, its teeshot landing area tightened by bunkers on both sides. Since the hole was originally designed by Donald Ross to be a par five, the humpbacked green is shallow, meaning that the 200-yard approach must be played with the precision of a wedge.

U.S. Open; June 5-6, 1924

Cyril Walker	74	74	74	75	297	1
Bobby Jones	74	73	75	78	300	2
Bill Mehlhorn	72	75	76	78	301	3
B. Cruickshank	77	72	76	78	303	T4
Walter Hagen	75	75	76	76	303	T4
Macdonald Smith	78	72	77	76	303	T4
Abe Espinosa	80	71	77	77	305	T7
Peter O'Hara	76	79	74	76	305	T7
Mike Brady	75	77	77	77	306	9
Chick Evans	77	77	76	77	307	T10
Eddie Loos	73	81	75	78	307	T10
Dave Robertson	73	76	77	81	307	T10

U.S. Open: June 15-17, 1961

Gene Littler	73	68	72	68	281	1
Bob Goalby	70	72	69	71	282	T2
Doug Sanders	72	67	71	72	282	T2
Mike Souchak	73	70	68	73	284	T4
Jack Nicklaus	75	69	70	70	284	T4
Dow Finsterwald	72	71	71	72	286	T6
Eric Monti	74	67	72	73	286	T6
Doug Ford	72	69	71	74	286	T6
Jacky Cupit	72	72	67	76	287	T9
G. Dickinson	72	69	71	75	287	T9
Gary Player	75	72	69	71	287	T9

U.S. Open: June 13-16, 1985

Andy North	70	65	70	74	279	1
Denis Watson	72	65	73	70	280	T2
Dave Barr	70	68	70	72	280	T2
Tze-Chung Chen	65	69	69	77	280	T2
Lanny Wadkins	70	72	69	70	281	T5
Payne Stewart	70	70	71	70	281	T5
Seve Ballesteros	71	70	69	71	281	T5
Johnny Miller	74	71	68	69	282	8
Fuzzy Zoeller	71	69	72	71	283	T9
Corey Pavin	72	68	73	70	283	T9
Jack Renner	72	69	72	70	283	T9
Rick Fehr	69	67	73	74	283	T9

U.S. Open: June 10-12, 1937

Ralph Guldahl	71	69	72	69	281	1
Sam Snead	69	73	70	71	283	2
B. Cruickshank	73	73	67	72	285	3
Harry Cooper	72	70	73	71	286	4
Ed Dudley	70	70	71	76	287	5
Al Brosch	74	73	68	73	288	6
Clarence Clark	72	75	73	69	289	7
Johnny Goodman	70	73	72	75	290	8
Frank Strafaci	70	72	77	72	291	9
Chuck Kocsis	72	73	76	71	292	T10
Henry Picard	71	75	72	74	292	T10
Gene Sarazen	78	69	71	74	292	T10
Denny Shute	69	76	75	72	292	T10

PGA Championship: August 3-6, 1972

Gary Player	71	71	67	72	281	1
Jim Jamieson	69	72	72	70	283	T2
Tommy Aaron	71	71	70	71	283	T2
Sam Snead	70	74	71	69	284	T4
Ray Floyd	69	71	74	70	284	T4
Billy Casper	73	70	67	74	284	T4
Jerry Heard	69	70	72	74	285	T7
Doug Sanders	72	72	68	73	285	T7
Phil Rodgers	71	72	68	74	285	T7
Gay Brewer	71	70	70	74	285	T7

Scorecard

HOLE	YARDS	PAR
1	436	4
2	527	5
3	199	3
4	433	4
5	457	4
6	359	4
7	405	4
8	439	4
9	217	3
OUT	3472	35
10	454	4
11	411	4
12	560	5
13	172	3
14	465	4
15	399	4
16	409	4
17	201	3
18	453	4
IN	3524	35
TOTAL	6996	70

U.S. Open: June 14-16, 1951

Ben Hogan	76	73	71	67	287	1
Clayton Heafner	72	75	73	69	289	2
Bobby Locke	73	71	74	73	291	3
Lloyd Mangrum	75	74	74	70	293	T4
Julius Boros	74	74	71	74	293	T4
Al Besselink	72	77	72	73	294	T6
Paul Runyan	73	74	72	75	294	T6
Fred Hawkins	76	72	75	71	294	T6
Dave Douglas	75	70	75	74	294	T6
Skee Riegel	75	76	71	73	295	T10
Al Brosch	73	74	76	72	295	T10
Smiley Quick	73	76	74	72	295	T10

PGA Championship: August 2-5, 1979

David Graham	69	68	70	65	272		
					4-3-2	1
Ben Crenshaw	69	67	69	67	272		
					4-3-4	2
Rex Caldwell	67	70	66	71	274	3
Ron Streck	68	71	69	69	277	4
Gibby Gilbert	69	72	68	69	278	T5
Jerry Pate	69	69	69	71	278	T5
Howard Twitty	70	73	69	67	279	T7
Jay Haas	68	69	73	69	279	T7
Don January	69	70	71	69	279	T7
Gary Koch	71	71	71	67	280	T10
Lou Graham	69	74	68	69	280	T10

GOLF *Magazine* Rankings:
18th in the World
12th in the U.S.A.

OAKMONT COUNTRY CLUB

OAKMONT, PENNSYLVANIA
U.S. Open: 1927, 1935, 1953, 1962, 1973, 1983, 1994
PGA Championship: 1922, 1951, 1978

Just to be sure his bunkers were a challenge, Henry Fownes had them furrowed with a special triangular-tooth rake weighted down with a 100-pound slab of steel.

Tommy Armour called it "the final degree in the college of golf." Oakmont, the site of more men's major championships than any course in America—nine of them, with a tenth on the way—is more than a golf course. It is an institution.

Its founder, Henry Fownes (pronounced "phones"), was a Pittsburgh steel magnate who knew nothing about golf until his fellow tycoon Andrew Carnegie introduced him to it in 1899. Despite being over 40 years old, Fownes mastered the game quickly and by 1901 competed in the first of his four U.S. Amateur championships.

Fownes, an imperious autocrat, liked to do things his way, and in 1903 he decided to build himself a place to play. Reversing the normal progression, he designed the eighteen holes of Oakmont before ever selecting a property on which to build them. Once he found the site—a plateau high above the Allegheny River—he brought in 150 men and two dozen mule teams to stamp his blueprint upon the land.

And what a blueprint it was. When it opened in 1904 Oakmont had eight par fives, one par *six*, a total par of 80, and a stated purpose of being the hardest course in the world. It was not a pretty site. There was no water, and Fownes made it even less appealing by chopping down most of the few trees on the property. His ambition was to simulate a British moorland course—raw, flat, and barren—and to an extent he succeeded. But Oakmont was unlike any moorland course England or Scotland had ever seen.

For one thing, it had 220 bunkers—and these were not normal bunkers. Since the clay-rich soil of western Pennsylvania prevented Fownes from duplicating the deep and menacing pot bunkers of Britain, he created a unique challenge of his own, devising a special rake with triangular teeth and weighted down by a 100-pound slab of steel. It scratched furrows in the sand, furrows that were three inches deep and ran perpendicular to the play of the hole, making escape next to impossible. Said Jimmy Demaret, "You could have combed North Africa with it and Rommel wouldn't have got-

ten past Casablanca." Ted Ray once approached a bunker, looking for his ball, and was told by a spectator that it was in aisle seven.

For another thing, Oakmont had eighteen greens—and these were not normal greens. They were the fastest in creation, thanks to another Fownsian formula. First they were shaved as close as turn-of-the-century mowing equipment could cut. Then they were packed down by eight men pushing a 1,500-pound roller. Kerr Petrie, writer for the *New York Herald Tribune*, once observed this process and asked greenkeeper Emil Loeffler, "Why don't you just dig them up and pour in concrete?" And his colleague, Jimmy Powers of the *New York News*, wrote that "putting on Oakmont's greens is like putting down a marble staircase and trying to hole out on the third step from the bottom." To this day they remain the fastest, truest greens in the world. According to British golf writer Peter Dobereiner, "They are shaven like a monk's tonsure, and the areas around the cups are polished, or so it seems."

Fownes's chief consultant was his son William C. Fownes, Jr. (named after his uncle but strangely given the "Jr." anyway), who eclipsed his formidable father both in golf skill and audacity. Fownes the younger qualified for the U.S. Amateur twenty-five times and won it in 1910. He was also the self-appointed patroon of Oakmont. Periodically he would wander the course, watching people play it. If he saw someone boom a teeshot over a bunker, he'd put in another bunker. This practice got out of hand to the extent that at one point the course had 350 bunkers, an average of nearly twenty per hole. It was Bill Fownes's conviction that "a shot poorly played should be a shot irrevocably lost."

Young Fownes got a chance to battle his own beast when the Amateur came to Oakmont in 1919. He did well, too, reaching the semifinals before losing to a precocious 17-year-old named Bobby Jones. Local knowledge won out in the end, however, as Jones lost

in the final, 5 and 4, to another Oakmont member, David Herron. It was a week of rugged weather, beginning with a hailstorm in the qualifying round, and the chunky Jones is said to have lost eighteen pounds during the tournament.

Six years later the Amateur returned to Oakmont, and so did Jones, now at the peak of his game. In the most dominating performance in the history of the tournament, he won his series of 36-hole matches 11 and 10, 6 and 5, 7 and 6, and 8 and 7. In the final he beat fellow East Lake member Watts Gunn, the only time in history that two members of the same club have reached the final of a national championship. Gunn had played some impressive golf of his own. In his first-round match he had been three down after eleven holes, before reeling off the longest winning streak in Amateur Championship history, taking the next fifteen holes in succession to gain an 11-and-10 victory.

In between those two Amateurs, Oakmont hosted its first big professional event, the 1922 PGA Championship. Gene Sarazen was on top at the end, after having almost missed the beginning. Sarazen was late for his opening-match tee time. Normally that would have called for disqualification, but since The Squire was the reigning U.S. Open Champion, PGA officials let it slide. He went on to beat Emmett French in the final, 4 and 3, thus becoming the first man in history to win the U.S. Open and the PGA in the same year. When he added the British Open in 1932 and The Masters in 1935, Sarazen also became the first man to win each of the four modern major championships.

Oakmont played to 6965 yards when its first Open arrived in 1927, and the winning totals of 301—thirteen over par—were the highest in modern history. They were recorded by luckless Harry Cooper and feisty Tommy Armour. In *The World of Golf*, Charles Price captured the climax colorfully: "Armour whistled a mid-iron ten feet from the hole on the last green and then, with the calm expected of a man who once climbed out of a tank to throttle a German officer with his bare hands, sank the putt to tie the fast-stepping Harry Cooper, whom he beat by three strokes in a play-off."

Cooper, often described as the finest player never to win a major championship, that year was a victim of misinformation. With two holes to go in the final round, he thought he needed a birdie and a par to win, when in fact he needed only two pars. After hitting his approach twelve feet from the 17th cup, he gunned his putt for the birdie, then missed coming back. A par at the last put him in the playoff.

The next day Cooper was one ahead after fourteen holes, but at 15 Armour ran in a fifty-footer for birdie, then went one ahead when Cooper found sand and bogeyed 16. At the 17th Cooper came back, knocking his approach eighteen inches from the hole, but the scrappy Scotsman knocked it *inside* him. He won 79 to 76.

Gene Sarazen's electrifying double-eagle at The Masters was still topic number one in the game when the Open returned in 1935 with The Squire the prohibitive favorite. Said Herb Graffis in *Golfing,* "It's the general notion that this year Sarazen stands in about the same spot Jones did before he retired. It's the field against Sarazen. Pro authorities now murmur that if Sarazen doesn't win the National Open at Oakmont the question will be 'Why did Gene flop?'"

After it was over, the answer was: "Because the entire field flopped." This was an Open won by the golf course. Despite being armed with the new steel shafts and high-performance balls, despite being the first field able to gouge at Oakmont's bunkers with Sarazen's invention, the sand wedge, not a soul broke 70 all week, and in the final round, not one top player managed to score under 75.

Sarazen was in the hunt, as was virtually every top player of the day—Walter Hagen, Horton Smith, Denny Shute, Paul Runyan, Jimmy Thomson. They all made the top ten, but none of them won. Instead, the title went to an unknown, an Oakmont member and former captain of the University of Pittsburgh golf team named Sam Parks.

Parks wasn't so much the winner as the last man left standing. For the first half of the tournament Jimmy Thomson seemed the man to beat. In round two he had used his prodigious strength to reach a greenside bunker at the 621-yard 12th hole, then had nearly holed the explosion for eagle. After thirty-six holes, he had the lead at 146. The next day he again showed his power, driving the par-four 17th hole, but this time the notorious Oakmont greens got him; he four-putted, and nearly five-putted, sinking a tricky three-footer for his bogey 5. "I could have six-putted," he said grimly, adding the darkly humorous claim that the dime he'd used to mark his ball had slid off the green.

Nonetheless, after three rounds Thomson still had a share of the lead with Parks, who, with scores of 77-73-73, was actually the hottest player in the field. At lunch before the final round, a golf equipment manufacturer offered Parks $1,000 for his name on a set of clubs. That afternoon, the fee rose about $100 per hole. Parks's final round was a 76—hardly heroic, but lower than Thomson's 79 as Jimmy unraveled by three-putting both 16 and 17.

"Sure the kid was lucky," observed Graffis. "So is his neighbor Andy Mellon lucky to have so much currency. So is Lindbergh lucky The Parks young man is also smart, courageous, patient, and studious."

The first college graduate to win the Open, Parks was also the third Oakmont member to take a national title, joining Amateur champions Bill Fownes and David Herron. After his victory, Parks returned to obscurity, never winning another tournament, and in 1937 he left the Tour for a club pro job. Golf history records him as the quintessential dark horse champion.

The winner of the 1951 PGA at Oakmont was far from a dark horse, as Sam Snead took the title for a third time, tieing Gene Sarazen's record. In his final match, against Walter Burkemo, Snead took charge immediately, chipping in on the 1st hole for a birdie and rushing to a five-up lead after the first six holes. Burkemo got back to three down after the morning round, but Snead bolted from the gate after lunch, winning the first three holes en route to a 7-and-6 victory.

Two years later, however, Snead found himself on the other end of just as decisive a defeat in the 1953 Open. Not that Sam played badly, he simply played the foil at a time when Ben Hogan summoned perhaps the finest golf of his career. The Open that year became the centerpiece in Hogan's triple crown. He had won the Masters in April, and would go on to take the British Open in July. The Hawk's repeating swing was at peak efficiency, and through four rounds at Oakmont he drilled teeshot after teeshot, approach after approach, smack on target. Philip Wreen, writing for *The New Yorker,* observed that "Hogan hit only three shots during the seventy-two holes that were open to reasonable question."

He opened the tournament with a 67 and led all the way. Snead crept from five back after round one to two at the halfway point, to one after fifty-four holes, and with seven holes to go he was still within a stroke of Hogan, but there he collapsed, missing a series of short putts that cost him five strokes to par over the finishing stretch as Hogan played the back nine in 33, including a 3-3-3 finish (par-birdie-birdie). The result was a six-stroke victory, Snead coming in second for the fourth time in his Open career, Hogan winning for the fourth time.

Hogan's 283 total was also sixteen strokes lower than any competitor had ever posted in the two previous Opens at Oakmont. It should be noted, however, that this was a gentler Oakmont than had been encountered in any previous championship. By this time the fiendish Fowneses had died, and management of the course had fallen into the hands of an eighteen-man board possessed of more humanity. Still, it was a remarkable exhibition by Hogan.

PALMER +3
NICKLAUS -1

The armed marshalls were there to protect them from the galleries, not each other, but Arnold Palmer and Jack Nicklaus fought fiercely for the 1962 Open. Nicklaus finally won in an eighteen-hole playoff. Photo: UPI/Bettmann

The cream rose to the top again in 1962 when, after seventy-two holes, two men tied Hogan's 283 mark—Arnold Palmer and Jack Nicklaus. In one of the classic confrontations in professional golf history Palmer, the reigning king of the game, squared off against Nicklaus, his heir apparent.

They were paired together in the first two rounds, and the 22-year-old strongboy from Ohio immediately showed he would not be intimidated by Palmer, birdieing the first three holes. But he then cooled as Palmer took command and moved to a share of the 36-hole lead, with Bob Rosburg and Billy Maxwell, at 139. Nicklaus, playing a bit erratically but putting the Oakmont greens with a surgeon's touch, was three strokes behind. Arnie kept a share of the lead after fifty-four holes, tied at 212 with Bobby Nichols. One back was Phil Rodgers, despite a quadruple-bogey 8 on one hole and a four-putt on another. At 214 was Jack.

Arnie had shown signs of cracking toward the end of round three, missing three two-foot putts, one of them at the 18th green. But as the final eighteen began, it was Nicklaus who three-putted the first green. (Incredibly, this was his only three-putt in ninety holes.) Meanwhile, Palmer birdied 2 and 4, and by the 9th tee he had a three-stroke lead. Facing that short par five, he had visions of increasing his margin with a birdie. Instead, he found rough on his approach, needed two more to get out, and two more to get in for a bogey. Up ahead, Nicklaus had picked up a birdie at 11 to move within one. When Arnold bogeyed 13 they were tied, then each of them parred their remaining holes to force an 18-hole playoff.

That night Palmer confessed, "I wish I were playing anybody but that big, strong, happy dude." He was well aware of Nicklaus's talent, of his two U.S. Amateur Championships, and perhaps most of all, he was aware that Jack, at age 20, had finished second to him in the Open two years earlier at Cherry Hills, when Arnold had needed a final-round 65 to beat him.

Arnie's anxieties were well-founded, as Jack took the early lead in the playoff and was never behind. After six holes, Arnold was four behind, partly because of continued putting problems. He rallied with birdies at 9, 11, and 12 to come within one stroke, and one of his patented charging victories seemed imminent. Palmer, whose hometown of Latrobe is only thirty-five miles from Oakmont, had the gallery solidly in his corner. But he bogeyed the 13th as he had a day earlier, and that was it. Nicklaus won the playoff, 71 to 74.

An interesting quirk occurred at the final green. Palmer holed out for a bogey, and when Nicklaus, with three strokes in hand, rolled his birdie putt within a couple of feet of the hole, Arnie, acknowledging defeat, conceded Jack's par putt, picked up the ball, and handed it to Jack as he congratulated him. They were walking off the green when USGA Executive Director Joseph C. Dye stopped them. This was stroke play, not match, he told them, and as such the final putt could not be conceded. Jack was obliged to hole out. Dutifully, Nicklaus replaced the ball and made his tap-in. Rules sticklers, undoubtedly Palmer fans, later claimed that Nicklaus should have incurred a two-stroke penalty for the mental lapse, but it was never assessed.

This was Nicklaus's first victory as a professional. At age 22, he announced a simple goal. "I want to be the best golfer the world has ever seen." Twenty-six years later, he was declared exactly that when *GOLF Magazine* led a celebration of the Centennial of Golf in America, culminating in a black-tie dinner at the Waldorf Hotel in New York City where it was announced that a blue-ribbon panel of the game's leading authorities had named Nicklaus the Player of the Century.

The 1962 Open at Oakmont had signaled the start of the greatest career in the annals of golf, and arguably in sports. Never in the history of athletic competition has a game been dominated as long or as surely as Nicklaus dominated the game of golf. For nearly a quarter century, whenever and wherever the world's best players assembled for a major championship, Jack was the man to beat.

On his next visit to Oakmont, Nicklaus took one stroke off his 283 total, and so did Palmer, but 282 wasn't good enough. The two titans tied for fourth place along with Lee Trevino as a new star outshone them all. The 26-year-old Johnny Miller burst to prominence by winning this Open in style, with a final-round 63 that shattered not only the Open record but the Oakmont members.

Golden Boy Johnny Miller with wife Linda and the Open trophy in 1973, moments after he had stunned Oakmont and the golf world with a closing round of 63. Photo: © Leonard Kamsler

"Lie still, Mr. Fownes, lie still," host professional Lew Worsham was seen muttering as he walked across the grounds on Sunday evening. Miller's spectacular performance ranks with Palmer's 65 at Cherry Hills, Nicklaus's 65 at Baltusrol, Graham's 67 at Merion, and Hogan's 67 at Oakland Hills as one of the greatest finishes in Open history. And by pure numbers, it is indeed the greatest.

There is, however, a slight asterisk. A violent tropical storm on the eve of the Open had taken much of the fire out of the famed greens, and more rain on Saturday had put so much water on the course that the third round had nearly been postponed. As a result, the players were free to fire at the flags.

During the mid-1970s, no one fired at a flag more accurately than Johnny Miller. In three years on the Tour he had shot several low scores, including a 61 in the Phoenix Open. Miller had an almost uncanny ability not only to hit the ball straight but to judge distances. Late in his career, he recalled: "For a while during my prime, I was disappointed every time a short iron shot failed to hit the stick."

A 76 in the third round had left Miller six strokes off the pace set by Palmer, Julius Boros, Jerry Heard, and John Schlee. But on Sunday, Miller moved quickly. At the 1st he hit a 3-iron five feet from the hole and made the putt for birdie. Then he almost holed a 9-iron at 2, leaving himself a foot for a second birdie. At the 3rd he dropped a 5-iron twenty-five feet from the hole, and sank it for three in a row. The 4th is a 549-yard par five, and Miller's big drive allowed him to go for it, but he pushed the shot into a bunker on the right side. However, he exploded the ball to within six inches of the hole. Suddenly, he was four under for four holes, two behind the leaders who were just teeing off. He faltered with a three-putt at the 8th, but came back with a birdie at 9 to make the turn in 32, one under par for the tournament.

In back of him, no one was making much of a move. With nine holes to go, Palmer, Boros, and Tom Weiskopf were in the lead at four under par. But by this time, Miller was at the 15th, and he was also at four under, having birdied 11, 12, and 13 and narrowly missed a twelve-footer for a birdie at 14. At 15 he knocked his 4-iron approach ten feet from the hole and stroked it in for his ninth birdie of the round. He got down in two from fifty feet for a par at the 16th, just missed a ten-footer for a birdie at 17, and then at 18 he crushed a long drive and played a 5-iron eighteen feet above the hole. His putt for a 62 lipped the cup.

Fourteen men were still out on the course, half of them with a chance to catch him. But an hour later, when the last of his challengers failed to equal his 279, Miller was the champion.

Miller had hit each green in regulation or less, had taken twenty-nine putts, and had not made a score higher than 4. Ten of his iron shots finished less than fifteen feet from the cup, five inside six feet. His 63 remains the lowest round in Open history, although it has since been tied by both Nicklaus and Weiskopf, during the first round at Baltusrol in 1980.

The Oakmont elders were shocked and embarrassed that their course had yielded such a score, and they vowed that no one would humble Oakmont again. To sharpen their monster's teeth, they called in the local boy who had twice been bitten, Arnold Palmer. Together with his architectural partner, Ed Seay, Palmer put in several new tees that lengthened the course and brought bunkers into play. They also recontoured the 17th fairway to make the hole a distinct dogleg left, and a far less drivable par four. Not surprisingly, they didn't touch the greens.

The result: Another record was set, but not a low-scoring record. In the 1978 PGA Championship John Mahaffey, a 30-year-old Texan best known for having lost two Opens, set a new mark for the biggest come-from-behind victory. Seven strokes back with one round to go, he tied Tom Watson and Jerry Pate, and then beat them in a sudden-death playoff.

Once again, the course was wet, and Watson took advantage of it early, shooting a 67 to take the lead. Adding a 69 and another 67 in rounds two and three, he was one off the PGA 54-hole record with a five-stroke edge on Pate, six on Tom Watson and Joe Inman. Mahaffey was in fifth place.

With fourteen holes left to play on Sunday, Mahaffey was still seven behind, and Watson had increased his lead to six over Pate. But then Watson bogeyed 6 and 7 and Mahaffey sank a thirty-five-footer at the 6th to pull within four. Then Mahaffey and Pate each birdied the long par-three 8th to cut the margin to three. Moments later Pate birdied 9 to make it two. Mahaffey could muster only a par there, but Watson struck back with a marvelous 4-wood shot that stopped three feet from the hole. In went the putt for an eagle 3 that put him back in the lead by four over Pate, five over Mahaffey.

At the very next hole, Mahaffey erased three of those strokes, sinking a forty-five-foot birdie putt as Watson struggled to a double-bogey six. At that point Watson began to steer the ball while Pate and Mahaffey charged. With five holes to go, they were all tied. At 14, Mahaffey's wedge approach hit the stick, and he made a four-footer to take the lead. Incredibly, in a span of fourteen holes, he had picked up eight strokes. But he bogeyed 16 to go back in a tie with Pate as Watson, also bogeying 16, dropped one behind. Pate drove into a bunker at 17 but blasted out to four feet and sank the birdie putt to go one ahead with one to go. Behind him, Watson also birdied the hole on a fine ten-foot putt as Mahaffey parred. So with one hole left, Pate held a one-stroke lead on Mahaffey and Watson.

For Pate, it came down to a four-foot putt at the final hole—and he missed it, opening the door for the two behind him. Neither Watson nor Pate could make the winning birdie, but both made pars to force the first three-man playoff in PGA history. Each had shot 276, the lowest total ever at Oakmont, but Mahaffey had reached it with a 66, Pate a 68, and Watson a 73.

All three made scrambling pars at the 1st hole, and at number 2

Pate missed the green, Watson left his approach thirty feet from the hole and Mahaffey's finished twelve feet away. Moments later, Mahaffey sank that putt to win the only major championship of his career.

Mahaffey continued his Oakmont mastery for the first two rounds of the 1983 Open, taking a share of the lead at 141, but he collapsed badly over the final thirty-six holes, finishing in a tie for thirty-fourth. Instead, it was Watson who once again came to the fore—and once again suffered a bitter defeat, joining Arnold Palmer in a two-man fraternity of dubious distinction: superstars twice thwarted at Oakmont.

When Watson, the defending Open champion, reached the 54-hole mark at 212, he had a share of the lead with Seve Ballesteros. Sunday shaped up as another classic Oakmont battle of the titans, in the tradition of Hogan/Snead and Nicklaus/Palmer.

Instead, Watson tore through the first nine holes with six birdies en route to a 31 that left the stunned Spaniard five strokes behind. But one other player had entered the fray. On Saturday, Larry Nelson, the quiet Georgian, had birdied seven of his last eleven holes for a 65 that had put him one back of Watson and Ballesteros. On Sunday, he had made the turn in 33 and was three in back of Watson with the last nine to go.

At that point two things happened—a storm began to brew and Watson began to crack. Just as he had in 1978, Watson stumbled at the beginning of the back nine, bogeying the 10th and 12th holes as Nelson caught him with a pitch shot that landed a foot from the 14th hole. They remained tied for one more hole, and then the lightning and thunder struck, suspending play until ten o'clock the next morning, with Watson facing a thirty-five-footer for birdie at the 15th, Nelson at the tee of the par-three 16th. No one else had a chance to win.

On Monday Watson narrowly missed the birdie, and Nelson hit the green but left himself over sixty feet from the hole. But he struck with some lightning of his own—he sank the putt to take the lead. He parred 17 but three-putted 18 to come in at 280, four under par.

Watson got his par at 16 but missed the green with his approach at 17, chipped weakly to five feet, and then missed the putt to fall to three under. He needed a birdie at 18, and didn't get it.

Nelson's last two rounds were 65-67—132, the lowest last thirty-six holes in the history of the Open, eclipsing by four strokes a record Gene Sarazen had established at Fresh Meadow in 1932. Oakmont thus became another incredible chapter in the story of a man who had not taken up golf until 1969, after he had returned from the Vietnam War at age 21 (an age by which Tom Watson and Nelson's other contemporaries had already hit a million balls). But within a year, Nelson broke 70 and within three years he qualified for the PGA Tour. Today his achievements include a dozen victories worldwide, including two PGA Championships as well as his Open at Oakmont.

Oakmont has changed remarkably little since it held its first

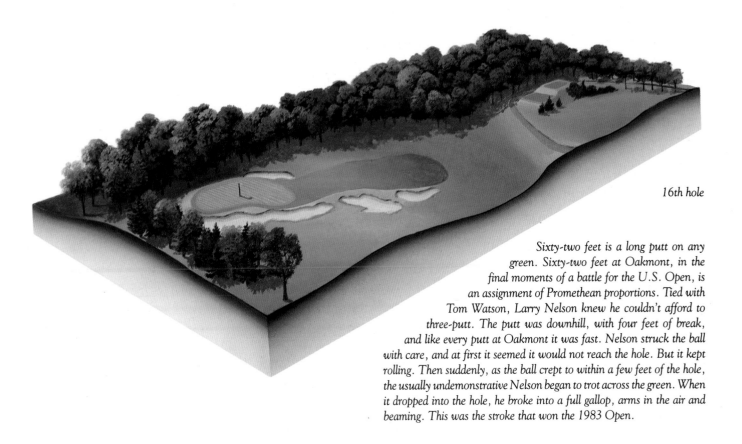

16th hole

Sixty-two feet is a long putt on any green. Sixty-two feet at Oakmont, in the final moments of a battle for the U.S. Open, is an assignment of Promethean proportions. Tied with Tom Watson, Larry Nelson knew he couldn't afford to three-putt. The putt was downhill, with four feet of break, and like every putt at Oakmont it was fast. Nelson struck the ball with care, and at first it seemed it would not reach the hole. But it kept rolling. Then suddenly, as the ball crept to within a few feet of the hole, the usually undemonstrative Nelson began to trot across the green. When it dropped into the hole, he broke into a full gallop, arms in the air and beaming. This was the stroke that won the 1983 Open.

major championship seventy years ago. Oh, the bunkers are no longer furrowed—that practice was phased out, first at greenside for the 1953 Open, then altogether in 1962—and today's course has about 190 bunkers instead of the original 220, but the length of the layout is within 100 yards of what it was for the 1927 Open, and the greens are as treacherous as ever.

The severity of the challenge is evident from the very beginning. Hole number 1 played the toughest of any hole in the '78 PGA and '83 Open. Bunkers, trees, and out of bounds await the teeshot, which had better be long as well as straight, since this converted par five is 469 yards. But the hardest part may be the large green which, like many of Fownes's creations, slopes sharply from front to back and right to left.

After crossing a bridge that traverses the Pennsylvania Turnpike, the player gets a bit of a reprieve. The 2nd plays to the same par of four but is 126 yards shorter than number 1. Most players select irons off the tee, both to avoid the mammoth bunker on the right side of the rolling fairway and to get in position to avoid the eight smaller bunkers that ring the green. This was the site of Mahaffey's winning birdie.

It's at the 425-yard 3rd hole that a player gets his first look at the Church Pews, an enormous expanse of sand with eight symmetrical ridges of turf, each about eighteen inches high, running from side to side at regular intervals. Those who wish to extricate themselves from this temple of doom had best use both a swing and a prayer.

Charles Price once observed that there are two problems the bunkering of a golf course presents—placement and shaping, and that Oakmont solved the first problem by placing them everywhere. At no hole is that more apparent than the par-five 4th. First are the same Church Pews, which haunt the left side of this hole since it runs parallel to the 3rd. But anyone who bails out to the right will find five more bunkers, smack across the fairway from the pews. The long hitter who can thread this needle will find himself in reach of the green, but if he fades or hooks his fairway wood, he'll find himself in one of several greenside bunkers of every shape and size.

Bunkering is again the key at number 5, where the tee is angled directly at the fairway bunkers on the left and the view of the narrow green presents more sand than grass. Snead holed-out a thirty-foot explosion shot here in the 1951 PGA to go four up in the first five holes of his final match against Walter Burkemo.

The Nicklaus/Palmer playoff took a pivotal turn at the 201-yard 6th hole, where Arnie three-putted and Jack sank for a birdie that gave him an insurmountable four-stroke lead. A severe right-to-left tilt to this green makes players worry about their second putt before they've struck their first.

From the back tees, a full-blooded smack is needed to reach the crest of the fairway at number 7. From there it's a mid or short iron to a green that is inordinately tough to putt, even by Oakmont's high standards.

OVERLEAF: *3rd hole*

The flattest green on the course comes at the next hole, but that's only fair because it calls for the longest shot. At 255 yards, this is one of the longest par threes in championship golf. As if sheer length is not a sufficient challenge, the green is protected by a bunker called Sahara—130 yards long, 30 yards wide—a quarter acre of sand. Imagine having to rake that on a hot day.

After 8, it's back across the turnpike for the final ten holes, beginning with a good birdie opportunity at the 9th, a par five that runs 480 yards uphill to the verandah of the clubhouse. Through Oakmont's championships it has produced plenty of drama. It was here in '62 that Palmer, in search of a birdie to extend his final-round lead, made a damaging bogey instead. It was here that Watson made the eagle that made him seem indomitable in the last round of the '78 PGA. And perhaps most notably, it was here in the '73 Open that Tom Weiskopf, in pursuit of Johnny Miller, boomed a second shot that landed in a hot dog stand, right on the counter next to the mustard. He took a free drop, pitched to four feet, and made the birdie. The green on this hole is so deep it's also the practice putting green. With three tiers and a strong pitch, it is about as readable as a physician's signature.

Number 10 runs parallel to the 1st, and is similar in character, tumbling 462 yards to a green that slopes from front to back. Approach shots from the rough must be played to land well short of the green, otherwise they'll never stay on the putting surface. In the Armour/Cooper playoff, Tommy hit his 1-iron well over the green, but a fan kicked it back on. If Phil Rodgers had managed to two-putt instead of four-putt this green in 1962, he would have joined Nicklaus and Palmer in the playoff.

In the third round of the 1953 Open, a bogey at 10 was the last straw for Cary Middlecoff. He walked off the course. Back in the clubhouse Jimmy Demaret asked him what had happened.

"I picked up," said Middlecoff.

"Where?" asked Demaret.

"At the 11th tee," said Middlecoff.

"What happened, did you have a bad lie?" quipped Demaret.

"The ball's not in my pocket," said the doctor. "It's in some truck on the Pennsylvania Turnpike." Middlecoff had shot rounds of 76-73, a 38 on the front nine, a bogey at 10, and had launched his last drive into the traffic.

Tom Watson must have vile memories of the 12th. In the last rounds of both the '78 PGA and the '83 Open he bogeyed this testing par five. Bunkers and trees lurk all along the way to this eminently three-puttable green. And a long way it is, 603 yards in all. Tommy Armour took a 7 here in 1927 and had to play his last six holes in two under to reach the playoff.

Number 13 was the hole that proved unlucky for Palmer. Although only 185 yards—the only par-three under 200—its kidney-shaped green is difficult to putt, and Arnie bogeyed it in both the final round and the playoff of '62.

Chick Evans was so frustrated by the green at the 14th that, after

Clubhouse

three unsuccessful putts, he holed his ball out with his umbrella. That was back in the 1925 Amateur, but the long, deep green remains the main challenge on this shortish par four.

Many consider the 15th to be the finest hole on the course. A backbreaking par four of 453 yards, it plays through sand and trees to an angled green. The approach must avoid a bunker large enough to hold a Greyhound bus. The green was once 100 yards deep but is now a mere 60 yards. Thus, putts of 150 feet or more are not uncommon, and if the putt is from back to front, three-putting is not a possibility, it's an accomplishment. It's no coincidence that many of the winners at Oakmont—Armour, Snead, Hogan, Nicklaus, Miller—are known for their sharp iron play. With greens like 15 that are both vast and fast, the key on the lengthy approach is not simply to find the putting surface but to get the ball close.

Inaccuracy off the tee at the 228-yard 16th cost Harry Cooper the 1927 Open. He found sand, failed to get out on his first try, and made a double bogey that put him two strokes behind Tommy Armour in their playoff. When Hogan won in 1953, he called the brassie he hit twenty-five feet from this hole his best shot of the day. And while the sixty-two-footer that Larry Nelson sank may not be the longest putt of his career, it was certainly the biggest.

Herbert Warren Wind once called the 17th "an ugly mongrel of a par four." Mongrel or not, this has been a best friend to some players while viciously biting others. Until Palmer and Seay rerouted the rough in 1973 the hole was often driven and eagled. Although now 322 yards, it is still drivable to the longest hitters, and Nicklaus reached it in 1973, but the teeshot must avoid a bunker at the front right appropriately named Big Mouth. And there are also a few oak trees to be avoided. In 1962 Phil Rodgers found a particularly tenacious tree. He tried to hit his ball out, and it stayed. Then he tried again, and again, and again. When he finally holed out, his score was 8. It was an expensive tree, since Rodgers ended up just two strokes out of the Palmer/Nicklaus playoff.

The 18th hole has always been a strong finish, but in 1983 a new bunker was built in the driving zone, adding challenge to the teeshot. The approach must be played over a cross bunker to a rising, undulating green where even the pros are happy to take two putts.

When the Open returns in 1994 the pros will be taking their divots out of a monument. In 1987 Oakmont became the first golf course in America to be declared a national historic landmark.

PGA Championship: August 12-18, 1922

Gene Sarazen defeated Emmett French, 4 & 3

U.S. Open: June 14-16, 1927

Tommy Armour	78	71	76	76	301	1
					76	
Harry Cooper	74	76	74	77	301	2
					79	
Gene Sarazen	74	74	80	74	302	3
Emmett French	75	79	77	73	304	4
William Mehlhorn	75	77	80	73	305	5
Walter Hagen	77	73	76	81	307	6
Archie Compston	79	74	76	79	308	T7
Johnny Farrell	81	73	78	76	308	T7
John Golden	83	77	75	73	308	T7
Harry Hampton	73	78	80	77	308	T7

U.S. Open: June 6-8, 1935

Sam Parks, Jr.	77	73	73	76	299	1
Jimmy Thomson	73	73	77	78	301	2
Walter Hagen	77	76	73	76	302	3
Denny Shute	78	73	76	76	303	T4
Ray Mangrum	76	76	72	79	303	T4
Henry Picard	79	78	70	79	306	T6
Gene Sarazen	75	74	78	79	306	T6
Alvin Krueger	71	77	78	80	306	T6
Horton Smith	73	79	79	75	306	T6
Dick Metz	77	76	76	78	307	T10
Paul Runyan	76	77	79	75	307	T10

PGA Championship: June 28-July 3, 1951

Sam Snead defeated Walter Burkemo, 7 & 6

U.S. Open: June 11-13, 1953

Ben Hogan	67	72	73	71	283	1
Sam Snead	72	69	72	76	289	2
Lloyd Mangrum	73	70	74	75	292	3
Pete Cooper	78	75	71	70	294	T4
George Fazio	70	71	77	76	294	T4
Jimmy Demaret	71	76	71	76	294	T4
Ted Kroll	76	71	74	74	295	T7
Dick Metz	75	70	74	76	295	T7
Jay Hebert	72	72	74	78	296	T9
Marty Furgol	73	74	76	73	296	T9
Frank Souchak	70	76	76	74	296	T9

U.S. Open: June 14-17, 1962

Jack Nicklaus	72	70	72	69	283	1
					71	
Arnold Palmer	71	68	73	71	283	2
					74	
Bobby Nichols	70	72	70	73	285	T3
Phil Rodgers	74	70	69	72	285	T3
Gay Brewer	73	72	73	69	287	5
Tommy Jacobs	74	71	73	70	288	T6
Gary Player	71	71	72	74	288	T6
Billy Maxwell	71	70	75	74	290	T8
Gene Littler	69	74	72	75	290	T8
Doug Ford	74	75	71	70	290	T8

U.S. Open: June 14-17, 1973

Johnny Miller	71	69	76	63	279	1
John Schlee	73	70	67	70	280	2
Tom Weiskopf	73	69	69	70	281	3
Arnold Palmer	71	71	68	72	282	T4
Lee Trevino	70	72	70	70	282	T4
Jack Nicklaus	71	69	74	68	282	T4
Lanny Wadkins	74	69	75	65	283	T7
Julius Boros	73	69	68	73	283	T7
Jerry Heard	74	70	66	73	283	T7
Jim Colbert	70	68	74	72	284	10

PGA Championship: August 3-6, 1978

John Mahaffey	75	67	68	66	276	
					4-3	1
Jerry Pate	72	70	66	68	276	
					4-4	T2
Tom Watson	67	69	67	73	276	
					4-4	T2
Gil Morgan	76	71	66	67	280	T4
Tom Weiskopf	73	67	69	71	280	T4
Craig Stadler	70	74	67	71	282	6
Andy Bean	72	72	70	70	284	T7
Graham Marsh	72	74	68	70	284	T7
Lee Trevino	69	73	70	72	284	T7
Fuzzy Zoeller	75	69	73	68	285	10

U.S. Open: June 16-20, 1983

Larry Nelson	75	73	65	67	280	1
Tom Watson	72	70	70	69	281	2
Gil Morgan	73	72	70	68	283	3
Calvin Peete	75	68	70	73	286	T4
Seve Ballesteros	69	74	69	74	286	T4
Hal Sutton	73	70	73	71	287	6
Lanny Wadkins	72	73	74	69	288	7
Ralph Landrum	75	73	69	74	291	T8
David Graham	74	75	73	69	291	T8
Chip Beck	73	74	74	71	292	T10
Andy North	73	71	72	76	292	T10
Craig Stadler	76	74	73	69	292	T10

Scorecard

HOLE	YARDS	PAR
1	469	4
2	343	4
3	425	4
4	561	5
5	379	4
6	201	3
7	434	4
8	255	3
9	480	5
OUT	3547	36
10	462	4
11	371	4
12	603	5
13	185	3
14	360	4
15	453	4
16	228	3
17	322	4
18	456	4
IN	3440	35
TOTAL	6987	71

GOLF Magazine Rankings:
14th in the World
8th in the U.S.A.

THE OLD COURSE

ST. ANDREWS, SCOTLAND
British Open: 1873, 1876, 1879, 1882, 1885, 1888,
1891, 1895, 1900, 1905, 1910, 1921, 1927, 1933, 1939,
1946, 1955, 1957, 1960, 1964, 1970, 1978, 1984, 1990, 1995

Any British golfer will tell you, "There is the Open Championship, there is the Open Championship in Scotland, and there is the Open Championship at St. Andrews." No course is quite like the Old Course.

Maybe it's because St. Andrews got a head start. Golf probably began here about 1100, the best guess being that the Dutch brought a primitive stick-and-ball game called *kolven* across the North Sea on trade visits. The earliest reference to the game was in 1457, when James II decreed that "Futeball and Golfe be utterly cryit doune, and nocht usit." England and Scotland were constantly battling in those days, and the Scottish Parliament did not want its lads neglecting their archery practice.

The first documented reference to golf in St. Andrews came in 1552, when the city council licensed Archbishop John Hamilton to preserve rabbits "within the northern part of the common links adjoining the Water of Eden." It was stipulated that such husbandry should not interfere with "the play at golf, football, archery, all games and pastimes as anyone pleases."

Still, the rabbits deserved certain rights inasmuch as they—as much as anyone else—were the original course architects. There are several descriptions of the formation of original links courses, but none more straightforward than the one by J. B. Salmond in *The Story of the R&A:*

In summary what happened was that the winds of the world blew seeds into the sand, the birds of the air were responsible

The "Custodian of the Links" for forty-four years, Old Tom Morris was also a four-time British Open Champion and St. Andrews' most beloved citizen. On the day he died in 1908, all play on the Old Course was suspended.

for supplying others, while their droppings acted as a fertiliser. Grasses of many kinds took root, and in their strange annual death provided a surface layer for humus. Those grasses made their root-roads underground, and so spread and tightened up the texture. Heather and whins found a home and with their natural determination took Lebensraum whenever it was to be found. Then the ubiquitous rabbit arrived, made its runs through the whins and heather, and cropped the grass. Finally man on his lawful occasions widened the runs into paths. The first golfers took those paths for their fairways, and a course came into being.

As for the famed St. Andrews bunkers, other mammals were responsible, according to Herbert Warren Wind:

Many of the sand bunkers were dug by the sheep that huddled together behind high dunes to shelter themselves from the piercing winds off the sea. Other bunkers had a more banal genesis. On some holes, because of the undulation of the land, a high proportion of the golfers' tee shots ended up in natural gathering spots at the base of a slope or several slopes. As was inevitable with so many players hacking away in these spots on their second shots, the turf there became sparser and sparser. . . .When the people charged with maintaining the links in good condition decided that reseeding such scrapes was not a sensible condition, they generally converted them into permanent hazards—clearly defined sand bunkers.

Swilcan Bridge

As early as 1691 St. Andrews was described as a "Metropolis of Golfing," but in truth it was more than that and remains so today. The appeal of this town is four-fold.

First, it is the ecclesiastical center of Scotland, named for Andrew, the patron Saint of Scotland and son of Christ's first apostle, Simon Peter. Andrew was crucified in the first century and died with his arms and legs bound to an X-shaped cross, the same style that appears in white against a blue background in the Scottish flag and is the symbol of the Royal & Ancient Golf Club of St. Andrews. The St. Andrews cathedral took 159 years to build and was finished in 1160. In the middle ages the town was the Scottish headquarters of the Roman Catholic Church, so when the Reformation broke out it became the eye of the storm and the site of some of the most bloodthirsty episodes in Scottish history. Protestants Patrick Hamilton and George Wishart were burned at the stake as Cardinal Beaton watched; then Beaton was slain as the reformationists, led by John Knox, swept the country. The cardinal's body was spread-eagled from a window of the cathedral for all to see. Shortly afterward the cathedral was looted and destroyed.

Second, St. Andrews is a seaside resort, one of the most popular vacationing places in the British Isles. Each August, when most of Britain's businesses and factories shut down for a summer holiday, hundreds of Scotsmen flock to the beaches and fishing villages of the East Neuk, with St. Andrews their primary mecca.

Third, it is home to the oldest university in Scotland, founded in 1412 and still going strong, just a rung below Oxford and Cambridge scholastically and perhaps even more fashionable among the sons and daughters of the British gentry. During the school year, the streets of the old gray town are awash with scarlet-gowned students.

But finally, fundamentally, St. Andrews is the home of golf. A century ago Horace Hutchinson observed that "the very name St.

Andrews calls to mind not a saint nor a city nor a castle nor a university, but a beautiful stretch of green links with a little burn, which traps golf balls, and bunkers artfully planted to try the golfer's soul." At about the same time James Balfour opined that "no portion of ground of the same size on the whole surface of the globe has afforded so much innocent enjoyment to so many people of all ages from 2 to 89, during so many generations." But perhaps Bernard Darwin best captured the spirit of St. Andrews. "It is delightful to see an entire town given up to golf," he said, "to see the butcher and the baker and the candlestick maker shouldering his clubs as soon as his day's work is done and making a dash for the links."

Beyond being golf's home, it is golf's headquarters. On May 14 in 1754, twenty-two men met at St. Andrews to adopt thirteen rules and establish a competition open "to all in the British Isles" for a silver club, the winner to attach a silver ball with his name engraved on it. Thus was formed "The Society of St. Andrews Golfers," later to be called the Royal & Ancient Golf Club of St. Andrews.

Those original rules bear little resemblance to the complex code under which we play today. One of them reads: "If you draw your club, in order to stroke, and proceed so far in the stroke as to be bringing down your club; if then your club shall break, in any way, it is to be accounted a stroke." But it was the acceptance of those rules by other golfing societies that ordained the St. Andreans as the powers in golf. In 1834 King William IV conferred the title "Royal & Ancient," and the society of golfers proclaimed St. Andrews the home of golf and themselves the ultimate authority. Today, the Royal & Ancient is, along with the USGA, the official administrator of the Rules of Golf, and while the USGA governs only the U.S., Puerto Rico, and Mexico, the R&A is responsible for more than fifty countries.

Apart from being one of the game's administrators, the Royal & Ancient Golf Club remains a private club, numbering 1,800 mem-

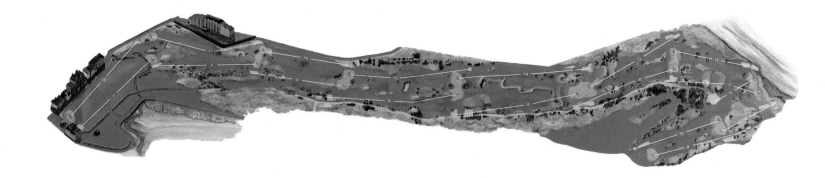

bers worldwide including 275 Americans. One does not apply for membership, one is invited, and the current waiting list is at least fifteen years. The club has had 223 captains (the British equivalent to the club president), including five members of royalty and three Americans: Francis Ouimet, Joseph C. Dey, and Bill Campbell. Each September, at the autumn meeting of the club, tradition calls for the new captain to "drive himself into office" by hitting a ceremonial ball from the first tee of the Old Course.

Not surprisingly, the first golf course produced the first professional golfer, a fellow named Allan Robertson. Born in 1815, he was trained as a golf ballmaker, in the footsteps of his father and grandfather. He was also a fine player, possessed of a neat and efficient swing and an unflappable temperament. Robertson was the first man to break 80 on the Old Course, shooting 79 in 1858, a time when the equivalent of today's scratch players were happy to break 100. Had he not died of jaundice a few months later, the British Open Championship, which began in 1860, almost certainly would have been added to his titles. Robertson may also be said to have been the first golf course architect, as it was he who supervised the most important alteration in the history of the Old Course, the widening of the fairways that allowed for the current out-and-back design. Robertson is buried in the Old Town Churchyard of St. Andrews, where his tombstone includes a banner that attests to his game: "far and sure."

Robertson's epitaph also says that he was never beaten, but there are historians who claim that at least one man did the deed—Old Tom Morris. Morris was 18 when he became Robertson's apprentice in the ballmaking trade. The association worked well until the day Tom played in a match using a gutta-percha ball instead of a Robertson featherie. (Featheries, the first golf balls, were made by boiling as many feathers as would fill a top-hat and stuffing them between pieces of leather that had been partially sewn, then finishing the sewing and hammering the ball into round. The guttie was made of rubber native to India which was heated and then molded into a ball, a much easier process.) When Robertson got wind of Morris's transgression there was a tiff, and Morris left to set up his own shop, where he made both kinds of balls.

Three years later, in 1851, he left St. Andrews to become "keeper of the green" at Prestwick, where he stayed for fourteen years, a span that included the start of the Open Championship which Old Tom won three times at Prestwick (1861, 1862, and 1864). In 1864 he returned to St. Andrews where he was given the official title of "Custodian of the Links." He spent the next forty-four years of his life there, becoming the most beloved citizen the town has ever known. Morris competed in every Open except one from 1860 to 1896 (when he was 75), and won a fourth title at Prestwick in 1867. The day he died in 1908, play on the Old Course was suspended.

In sharp contrast to Old Tom's long and full life was the brief and tragic story of his son, the most brilliant player of the nineteenth century and a young man who could have been one of the all-time greats, had his life not ended prematurely.

Young Tom learned the game quickly at the knee of his dad, and by age 16 he finished fourth in the British Open, the same 1867 Open his father won. Thereafter he went on a tear, winning the title three years in a row in 1868, 1869, and 1870 by margins of 3, 11, and 12 strokes. His third victory came on a 36-hole score of 149, the lowest total ever made with a gutta-percha ball. In those days the winner was given custody of an elaborate belt, festooned with silver medallions. When Young Tom won it for the third time, he was given the belt permanently.

Young Tom had a powerful thrusting swing, was a superb iron player, and was the first to use a lofted niblick, traditionally a bunker weapon, from the fairway, playing it with an open stance in order to put backspin on approach shots. He won his fourth Open in 1872, at the age of 21.

The young genius might have gone on to win a dozen Opens, but three years later his world was turned upside down. While playing with his father in a challenge match at North Berwick against the brothers Willie and Mungo Park, a telegram arrived at the clubhouse. Young Tom's wife, in the throes of childbirth, was dangerously ill. A yacht was arranged and Tom and his father sped across the Firth of Forth to St. Andrews. As they walked from the harbor a second telegram brought the news that Tom's wife and baby had died.

Young Tom never recovered from the shock. Three months later, after having Christmas Eve dinner with a few friends, he retired and died in his sleep on Christmas Day, 1875. Historians differ on the cause of his death; some say it was pleurisy, others emphysema; some point to an uncharacteristic overindulgence in alcohol that caused a burst blood vessel. But no one argues that the root cause was a broken heart.

A record total of twenty-four British Opens have been played at St. Andrews, beginning in 1873 when the winner was a caddie by the name of Tom Kidd. His scores of 91-88—179 were enough for a one-stroke victory. The 1876 Open is distinguished as the only major championship where there has been a winner who did not beat the runner-up. Bob Martin and Davie Strath tied with totals of 176, but Martin won because Strath refused to take part in the playoff. It seems he got involved in a rules imbroglio. At the 17th hole he had played his approach shot before the players in front of him had left the green. They lodged a protest, insisting on disqualification, citing the rule that provided that no one should play to a green with players on it. The R&A decided that the tie would be played off, pending the protest. But when no decision came on the protest, Strath refused to play.

The next three Opens were won by Jamie Anderson, the three after that by Bob Ferguson, each of them taking one of their titles at St. Andrews, as the championship in those days rotated among Prestwick, Musselburgh, and the Old Course. Martin won again in 1885 by a single stroke over the powerful Archie Simpson, who came within a couple of yards of driving the 359-yard 6th hole.

Martin's winning score of 171 was matched by Jack Burns in 1888, but in 1891 Hugh Kirkaldy shot the lowest Championship winning score in the history of the Old Course, 166 on two consecutive 83s, nipping his brother Andra, who shot back-to-back 84s. It was the lowest score because this was the last Open played over thirty-six holes. Beginning in 1892 the Championship went to

For many years a parallel railway was part of the challenge of the finishing stretch. Here, James Braid gets back on track en route to victory in 1905.

two days of thirty-six holes each, with a total purse of 100 pounds, 40 pounds going to the Champion.

At the turn of the century British golf was dominated by three players who came to be known as the Great Triumvirate—Harry Vardon, James Braid, and J.H. Taylor. Between the years 1894 and 1914 these three men won sixteen of the twenty-three Opens— Vardon winning six, Braid and Taylor five each. Surprisingly, none of Vardon's victories came on the Old Course, but Taylor won there twice (1895 and 1900) and so did Braid (1905 and 1910).

Taylor and Braid were a contrast in styles, the former a flatfooted, compact stylist and the latter a tall power player who sometimes strayed off line but was perhaps the game's first great scrambler.

In the first quartet of St. Andrews Championships won by this duo, Taylor's winning score was 322; in the last of them Braid won on a total of 299. The difference can be attributed to the introduction of the wound Haskell ball, a development that ushered in longer drives that bounced and ran up to 20 percent farther than shots played with the gutta-percha ball. Holes that had never been reached in two suddenly became easy fours.

The beginning of American domination of the Open may be traced to the Old Course in 1921, when Jock Hutchison became the first American to take the Championship. It was only small consolation to the Brits that Hutchison was a transplanted Scot, born in St. Andrews.

Hutchison's 72-hole total of 296 was a new mark for the Old Course, and it came with the help of a hole-in-one at the 8th hole in round one, followed by a teeshot at the par-four 9th that might have hit the pin and dropped for a second-straight ace, had a member of the group playing ahead not removed the flagstick. But in any case, Hutchison's 296 was matched by Roger Wethered, an amateur and Oxford undergraduate whose sister Joyce, later known as Lady Heathcoat Amory, had a few months earlier won the English Ladies' Championship. Wethered might have won it outright had he not committed a foolish error in round three. At the 14th hole he walked forward to inspect the green for his approach and then, upon returning, stepped on his ball in the rough, thereby incurring a one-stroke penalty.

The 1921 Open is noteworthy for the presence of another amateur, a young American who became so frustrated with his inability to handle the Old Course that he stomped off in anger after eleven holes of the third round. No one could have envisaged that six years later this same man would be carried off the course on the shoulders of the adoring Scots.

He was, of course, Bobby Jones, and in the next Open at St. Andrews, 1927, he would begin with a 68 and lead all the way to a resounding six-stroke victory, setting a British Open record of 285, thus defending the title he had won for the first time a year earlier at Royal Lytham. Recalling the happy throng who hoisted the victor aloft, British historian Charles Mortimer wrote: "Our warm-hearted people had so taken Bobby Jones into their respectful care and affection that no one gave a thought to the fact that a great American amateur was about to carry off the Cup once more to a land overseas." (Actually, as an honorary member of the R&A, Jones left the Cup in the custody of the club.)

Jones returned to St. Andrews in 1930 and won seven 18-hole matches plus a 36-hole final against Roger Wethered to take the first leg of his Grand Slam. His toughest match was a seesaw thriller won in sudden-death over Cyril Tolley. After his victory at the 19th hole Jones said, "I felt the same exultation and desperate urgency I should expect to feel in a battle with a broadsword or a cudgel."

Such was the affection of the St. Andreans for this soft-spoken young man who had learned his long, smooth swing from their countryman Stewart Maiden, that when Jones returned for a casual match in 1936 shops closed and virtually the entire town turned out to watch their hero. Twenty-two years later, they made him a Freeman of the Burgh of St. Andrews, only the second American in history to be so honored, the other being Ben Franklin in 1759. Toward the end of his acceptance speech Jones said, "I could take out of my life everything except my experiences at St. Andrews, and I would still have a rich, full life."

A couple of weeks before the 1933 Open on the Old Course, America had lost the Ryder Cup to Great Britain when Denny Shute had taken three putts at the final green of the deciding match. But at St. Andrews six of the first nine places went to

Americans, and the winner was Shute in a playoff over countryman Craig Wood. Syd Easterbrook, the man who had beaten Shute in the Ryder Cup, had a chance to do the deed again at St. Andrews, but took a 7 at the 14th in the final round and missed the playoff by a stroke, as did Gene Sarazen, who took an 8 on the same hole. The jittery Leo Diegel also had a chance to make the playoff but three-putted the final hole, actually whiffing his short putt to tie.

Shute's 292 total came on four steady 73s while Wood varied from 77 to 68, and in the playoff the pattern continued as Wood opened with a pair of sixes while Shute made two par fours and went on to an undramatic five-stroke victory.

The last Open before the seven-year break for World War II went to Lancashire-born professional Richard Burton, whose finishing 71 was the low round of the afternoon and took him past five other players to a two-stroke victory on a total of 290.

That was in 1939. It was seven years before Burton defended his title again at the Old Course. Perhaps because the War had ended only a few months earlier, the American contingent was relatively small. Byron Nelson did not go, nor did Ben Hogan, and Sam Snead almost didn't but at the last minute decided to give it a try.

Never have golf fans taken to a champion the way the Scots did to Bobby Jones. Here he tees off for the final round of the 1927 Open. After his six-stroke victory, the gallery carried him off on their shoulders. Photo: Bettmann/Hulton

As his train pulled into St. Andrews Snead looked out the window and said, "Look, there's an old abandoned golf course." Later he said, "Until you play St. Andrews it looks like the type of real estate you couldn't give away." But by the end of the week he was glad he came, having taken a four-stroke victory over Johnny Bulla and Bobby Locke. It was the only major national championship Snead would ever win.

Victors such as Snead, Jones, Taylor, and Braid attest to the ability of the Old Course to identify the game's finest. Two more were victors at St. Andrews during the 1950s. The first was Peter Thomson in 1955, who had presaged both his competitive mettle and his affinity for the Old Course a year earlier when, in the fourth round of the News of the World match-play championship at St. Andrews, he had come to the last two holes two down to John Panton, but finished eagle-birdie to tie the match, then won on the twenty-second hole. Two days later he won the final match, again on the fourth hole of sudden death.

Thomson's opponent in the final was Johnny Fallon, and it was also Fallon who finished runner-up in the '55 Open. In the last round, Fallon rushed to the turn in 31 strokes to make up the four strokes by which he had trailed. But he faltered to a 39 coming in and Thomson defended successfully the title he had won a year earlier at Birkdale.

This was an era when the Open was dominated by Thomson and by South Africa's Bobby Locke. In the ten years between 1949 and 1958 each won the Championship four times. The last of Locke's victories came at St. Andrews in 1957, where the runner-up was, naturally, Thomson.

Accepting the claret jug, Locke called his win on the Old Course the greatest day of his life, but the event was marred by controversy eight days later when a TV tape showed that, when Locke had marked his ball on the final green to allow fellow competitor Bruce Crampton to putt out, he had failed to replace his ball in the same position. He had been just two feet from the hole, with a three-stroke lead, but he had nonetheless broken a Rule. The Championship Committee of the R&A reviewed the situation and decided that "special circumstances" prevailed. In the spirit of equity, they allowed the victory to stand.

The centennial of the Open Championship was marked in 1960 on the Old Course, but the event was something of an anticlimax. Arnold Palmer had won both the Masters and U.S. Open and was in search of a modern Grand Slam, but after 36 holes and nearly as many missed short putts, he found himself seven strokes off Roberto DeVicenzo's 134 pace. The Argentinian collapsed to a 75-73 finish, and Arnold came on with 70 and 68, but it was Australia's Kel Nagle who prevailed, sinking a brave ten-footer at the seventy-first hole, then jabbing a not-so-brave three-footer nine inches short of the final hole. He made the ensuing tiddler for an Old Course record of 278 and a one-stroke victory over Palmer.

"The Old Lady has been swept off her feet only once," wrote Jock McVicar of the Scottish Daily Express after Champagne Tony Lema came to St. Andrews in 1964 and won the British Open in his first try. The devil-may-care Lema came to Scotland just two days before the tournament, and barely got in two practice rounds, but he was nonetheless confident. He had won four of the last five tournaments in which he had played, and his caddie for the week was Tip Anderson, a St. Andrews veteran.

In difficult conditions the opening day Lema shot 73, then added a pair of 68s to take a two-stroke lead into the final round. Jack Nicklaus played the last two rounds in 134 strokes, but he had begun with 76-74, so could climb only to second place as the slim, charismatic Californian covered the final thiry-six in six under par and took away a five-stroke victory, the only major championship in a brief, brilliant career which ended tragically two years later in a fatal plane crash.

Tragedy of a different sort struck Doug Sanders in 1970 when on the seventy-second hole he had a chance to win the Open, but instead stabbed at his three-foot putt, never hitting the hole. It left him in an 18-hole playoff with Jack Nicklaus.

The next day Nicklaus took a four-up lead with five to play, but Sanders bravely came back. With one hole left, he was a stroke behind. It was on the 18th tee, however, that Nicklaus hit one of the most storied shots of Open history. Shedding the sweater he had worn all day, he reared back and slugged a teeshot of over 360 yards, to and through the back of the 18th green. From there he chipped to eight feet and then, knowing that Sanders had a shorter birdie putt to tie, sank the delicate downhill putt for a one-stroke victory. In an uncharacteristic surge of emotion, Nicklaus hurled his putter joyously skyward; on the way down it just missed beaning the disconsolate Sanders.

Ask Nicklaus to name the most memorable moments of his career and he will always mention St. Andrews in 1978, when thousands of adoring Scots leaned from the windows of the old gray buildings lining the final hole and cheered him to his third British Open victory.

Despite excellent weather, it wasn't an easy Open, for Nicklaus or anyone else, as the ageless Old Course frustrated the field. Lanny Wadkins twice made 8 at the 14th hole. Arnold Palmer twice made 7 at the 17th (and he was in contention each time), and Tommy Nakajima, among the leaders after two rounds, saw his hopes go adrift in a storm of sand at the same Road Hole in round three. After putting his third shot into the deep bunker at the front left of the green, he slugged at the sand repeatedly, finally holing out in nine. It took the Japanese permanently out of the running but gave birth to a nickname for the imposing bunker: the Sands of Nakajima.

Ten players were within three strokes of the lead with one round to go, but on Sunday morning when Jack Nicklaus rose from his bed in the nearby Rufflets Hotel and saw the way the wind was blowing, he smiled. A few days earlier, when several of his cohorts had gone off to play a nearby course, Nicklaus had opted for an extra

practice round because he had noticed the unusual wind conditions, with the opening holes playing upwind, the finish downwind. Under identical conditions in the final round, Nicklaus turned in a steady 69 and, despite spirited challenges from Ben Crenshaw, Ray Floyd, Tom Kite, and New Zealand's Simon Owen, he won a two-stroke victory. He thus became the only man to have won each of the four major championships at least three times.

None of the millions who watched the 1984 British Open on television will ever forget the image of the triumphant Seve Ballesteros at the 18th green, repeatedly punching the air in joy after he had holed a twenty-foot birdie putt to clinch the title.

In truth, Ballesteros had won it a hole earlier where, after pushing his teeshot into dense rough on the left, he played a courageous 6-iron approach that bounced and rolled to the top of the shallow green, setting up his first par on the Road Hole all week. Moments later at the same hole, his pursuer, Tom Watson, played an aggressive drive that came to rest on a slight upslope on the right side of the fairway. From there he selected a 2-iron, hoping to hit a high, soft shot that would land on the green. But he hit the shot too solidly, and his ball ran through the green, across the road, and within three feet of the stone wall at the other side. From there he was able

Seldom has utter joy been expressed as vividly as by Seve Ballesteros when he sank the 72nd-hole birdie that won the Open in 1984. Photos: © Phil Sheldon

18th hole

to do no better than a bogey that left him two strokes back with one to go. That is where he finished, tied with Bernhard Langer as Ballesteros lowered the Old Course Open record to 276.

For Watson, who had won five of the previous ten Opens, the loss seemed a knockout punch. He has not won a major championship since St. Andrews and has recorded only two victories, never approaching the dominance he had enjoyed through the late 1970s and early '80s.

The 1990 Open was dominated by the man who has played far better than any other man in the major championships of the past few years, 33-year-old Nick Faldo, who scored a virtually flawless five-stroke victory while breaking the previous St. Andrews 72-hole record by six strokes.

Faldo signaled that it would be his week when on Thursday he hit a prodigious drive down the 18th fairway and then ran his approach through the Valley of Sin, up onto the green and into the hole for an eagle 2 that gave him a round of 67, one behind co-leaders Michael Allen and Greg Norman. The next day it was Norman and Faldo in an intense battle, Norman shooting a 66, Faldo a 65, to share the lead at twelve under, four strokes clear of the rest of the field. Golf fans hoped for a titanic weekend tussle between the two top players in the world, but it was not to be, as on Saturday Norman struggled to a 76 (the third highest score in the field) as Faldo continued his mechanically efficient assault on the Old Course, carding another 67 that put him at 199, seventeen under par, for a new 54-hole Open record.

He began Sunday with a five-stroke lead, and only Payne Stewart got within two before faltering at the finish. The 1990 Masters Champion—and the man who had come within a lipped putt on the seventy-second at Medinah of reaching a playoff for the 1990 U.S. Open title—thus won his second major of the year and his fourth in as many years. In 72 holes he had hit only one bunker, had made only four bogeys (three of them at the 17th), and had not three-putted once.

Faldo played the Old Course more expertly than anyone ever had, but the 1990 Open was played under four days of nearly ideal conditions. This is a course that has been condemned as an anachronism, cursed as unfair, called ridiculously easy on windless days and impossibly difficult in a gale. But no course commands greater affection from those who have come to understand it.

The key is in taking the time to reach that understanding, as Bobby Jones perceived. In his autobiography, *Golf Is My Game*, he wrote: "I began to see her as a wise old lady, whimsically tolerant of my impatience, but all the while ready to reveal to me the secrets of her complex being, if I would only take the trouble to study and learn. . . . The more I studied the Old Course, the more I loved it, and the more I loved it, the more I studied it."

Jones claimed the genius and delight of the course is in the fact that "there is always a way, and in trying to find it, there is more to be learned on this British course than in playing a hundred ordi-

nary American courses." Indeed, there are usually two or three ways. One may play a safe drive, well away from the bunkers and rough, but the result will be a much more difficult second shot. Alternatively, one may take the more daring route, challenging the perils, and, if successful, the reward will. be a much less vexing approach.

The first known version of the Old Course had 22 holes—11 out and 11 in. In those days the course was barely 40 yards wide, the breadth of the greens was less than a third of the present surfaces, and each green had only one cup, homeward players having the right-of-way. (Among the early British clubs there was no standard number of holes; the Links of Leith and Musselburgh had 5 each, North Berwick had 7, Prestwick 12, Gullane 13, and Montrose 13.) Then in 1764 the Society of St. Andrews golfers resolved that the first four double-holes were too short and should be converted into two, a change that reduced the course from 22 holes to 18. Still it was nearly a century before the number 18 became officially accepted, when in 1857 the R&A passed a resolution declaring that, unless otherwise stipulated, 18 holes would be considered a match.

In 1832 several of the double greens were enlarged, and for the first time separate cups were used for the outward and inward holes, a change that speeded up play enormously. Another significant change came in 1848 when Allan Robertson supervised the removal of large tracts of gorse, increasing the width of the playing area to between 90 and 100 yards. This allowed for separate, parallel fairways going out and in. Now, instead of having to play their shots across the tops of the bunkers, golfers could skirt them to one side

Nick Faldo was in flawless form in 1990, adding the British Open to the Masters he had successfully defended earlier in the year. Photo: © Phil Sheldon

or another, and strategy became an important element of the game. The widening came just in time, as the advent of the gutta-percha ball not only made for longer—and wider—drives, but brought many more people onto the links.

At the same time Robertson designed a new 17th green, perhaps the first man-made green in golf. The changes left the Old Course with four single greens—1, 9, 17, and 18—and seven double greens shared by outward and inward holes—2/16, 3/15, 4/14, 5/13, 6/12, 7/11, and 8/10. It has remained that way for nearly a century and a half, the only significant change being the addition of an automatic fairway watering system in 1969. Some claim that that addition has softened the course, made it too easy for the game's best players. In the 1988 Dunhill Cup, an annual event in which several nations send three-man teams to compete in a unique medal-match play format, Curtis Strange humbled the old lady with a 62, playing the 7th through 12th holes with six straight birdies, scores of 3-2-3-3-2-3.

But for most mortals the Old Course remains a challenge. When you play here (and it remains a public course, with current green fees running 25 pounds—about $50) you indulge not only in golf but in elements of chess, billiards, sailing, and lawn bowling as well.

It begins with the widest fairway in the world, an enormous, virtually flat expanse that serves as the landing area for teeshots on both 1 and 18. A century and a half ago a large bunker made the teeshot more demanding, but today the assignment is merely to make solid contact while knowing that one is standing in the shadow of the R&A clubhouse and teeing off on the most famous golf course in the world.

The hole is only 370 yards long, usually a drive and a mid-iron, a wedge when played downwind, but Jerry Pate recalls playing a college event in 60 mph winds and having to hit a driver and a 3-wood to reach the green. The second shot is all carry because the green is guarded by the Swilcan Burn. "It is an inglorious little stream enough," wrote Bernard Darwin. "We could easily jump over it were we not afraid of looking foolish if we fell in, and yet it catches an amazing number of balls." When Leslie Balfour-Melville won the 1895 British Amateur, he defeated three consecutive opponents at the 19th hole, each of them hitting an approach shot into the burn.

It was on the broad, flattish green that Bobby Jones beat Cyril Tolley, his toughest match in the 1930 British Amateur, after laying Tolley an unplayable stymie. (The R&A abolished the stymie in 1952.)

The player with a draw, or even a hook, can get away with murder on the Old Course, particularly from the first few tees, where the right-to-left ball usually finds nothing but an incoming fairway. But the right side is a different story. Beginning at the 411-yard 2nd

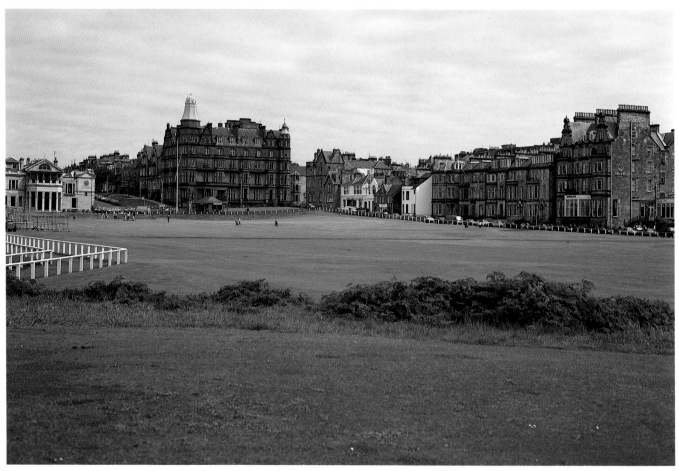

1st and 18th holes

Gorse

hole, a line of gorse and heather hugs the path to the green, as it will each fairway through the 7th. A clutch of bunkers also lurks on the right, the worst of them being Cheape's Bunker, named after the family which to this day owns most of the land on which the course is plotted. A pot bunker eats into the first of the double greens, separating the 2nd-hole sector from the 16th. Although wide, the green is not deep, so accurate club selection is important.

Hole number 3 is similar to 2 except that it is about forty yards shorter. The safe drive is to the left, avoiding the rhubarb and bunkers, but the easier approach is from the peril-strewn right from whence a running pitch may be played to the hole. From the left side, the only alternative is a lofted shot, over the grinning Cartgate Bunker, to this green which slopes fiercely from front to back and left to right. It has been said that the greens of the Old Course guard themselves, and this one is a prime example.

Commenting on holes 2, 3, and 4, Darwin observed, "There is something in these three holes that makes them quite ridiculously difficult for the stranger to disentangle them one from the other." He is correct, the truth being that each is a relatively straight par four in which the cautious drive to the left is presented with a daunting angle to the green.

The most daunting hazard at the 4th is the broad Cottage Bunker, in the middle of the fairway about 275 yards off the tee. But this proved undaunting to the Emperor Jones who, in the first round of the 1930 Amateur, holed his 140-yard approach from the sand for an eagle 2.

The first of the two par fives makes its appearance at number 5. Again there is death on the right, in the form of the Seven Sisters, a swarm of tiny pot bunkers. The best drive is to the left into an area called the Elysian Fields. From there the largest green on the course—about an acre in total area—is reachable, often with an iron.

In the final round of the 1946 Open Sam Snead had a long struggle here. Playing into the wind, he pulled his teeshot into the cavernous Hell Bunker that normally comes into play only at the 14th. From there he sliced a 3-iron into a clump of gorse, where it lodged a foot off the ground and swayed there back and forth in the wind. Snead had to summon all his athletic ability just to make contact with the ball, but he managed to smack a 6-iron into the front of the steep-faced Spectacle Bunker, 140 yards short of the green. From there he picked a 9-iron to the green, twenty feet away. Two putts later he had a hard-earned six.

The teeshot from the 6th hole is blind over a hill of gorse and heather, so the caddies usually tell their charges to aim at the Leuchars Air Station, about three miles in the distance. The green is guarded by a swale, and it slopes away from front to back. The hole is named Heathery because in the early days the green was composed of earth, heather, and shells.

OVERLEAF: *14th hole.* INSET: *14th hole*

11th hole

In the third round of the
1921 British Open, 19-year-old
Bobby Jones had played the first nine
holes of the Old Course in 46, then took a double-bogey 6 at the 10th. But it was the 11th that broke
his back—and his spirit. His teeshot went over the green,
then he misplayed a relatively simple chip that rolled back across the
green and into the Strath Bunker. It was there that Jones committed what
he later referred to as his "one last superbly childish gesture," picking up his ball
and stomping off the course. Six years later an older, wiser Jones returned to St.
Andrews to play the best golf the Old Course had ever seen, opening the 1927 Championship
with a 68 and leading from start to finish for a six-stroke victory and a record total of 285. He was
carried from the links on the shoulders of his adoring British fans.

The 359-yard 7th hole signals the start of The Loop, a sequence of six holes where many golfers have made six consecutive 3s. The only true dogleg on the course, it bends to the right, around a massive sea of gorse, one of the few places on the course where one may lose a ball. The fairway crisscrosses the fairway of the 11th hole on its way to their shared green, which tumbles steeply from the 11th hole on the left down to the 7th, where a spine runs across it. The pros have relatively little trouble here, but a poorly hit approach shot by an amateur will catch the huge Shell Bunker, fifty yards short of the green.

The 8th is a relatively dull par three of 166 yards. The huge, rather flat green is hard to miss, but there is a lone bunker at the left front, and the tendency is to place the flag there. When Jock Hutchison made his ace here in 1921 he amazed the gallery by hitting an iron that hit beyond the hole and sucked back into the cup. The hole is perhaps most noteworthy because it was here, during his casual round in 1936, that Bobby Jones says he was paid the most sincere compliment of his life. Having hit a 4-iron eight feet from the hole, he stepped back for his playing partner to hit, at which point his caddie, a young Scotsman, looked at him and said, "My, but you're a wonder, sir."

The easiest hole on the course is without question number 9, a par four of 318 yards that is drivable by strong players except when played into a strong wind. Two pot bunkers toward the right side of the fairway catch their share of unhappy souls, but the green is unguarded and flat as a board. Indeed, the last fifty yards of the hole

are also flat, and many players choose a putter for their approach shots. The fairway here once consisted entirely of heather but was turfed by Old Tom Morris. Today, patches of heather remain in the left rough.

More heather and gorse—the same tract of gorse that threatened the drive at 7—comes into play on the 10th hole teeshot. But this is another par four that is unguarded and reachable to the pros. The green slopes sharply from front to back. According to Darwin, holes 9 and 10 "constitute a small blot on the fair fame of the course."

At the par-three 11th tee, however, the true challenge of the Old Course begins. It was here that the 19-year-old Jones walked off in a fit of frustration. The broad, elevated green sits in plain view but is banked like an Indianapolis turn from back to front while also falling from left to right. In front is the deep Strath Bunker, where Jones met his angry demise, and to the right is the gaping Hill Bunker. As if those were not enough, just beyond the green is the River Eden. All of this, when considered in the presence of a strong wind, makes this teeshot one of golf's stiffer tests. Darwin called it "the most fiendish short hole in existence."

One of the most controversial holes on the course is the 12th, where the center of the fairway is home to a swarm of deep bunkers, several of which are not even visible from the tee. This invisibility relates to the fact that, for many years, the Old Course was played backwards as well as forwards. Play began at the 1st tee but followed the broad fairway not to the 1st green but to the 17th. From there it proceeded up the 17th fairway to the 16th green, and so on. Up until World War I the "right and left-handed courses" were used alternately a week at a time. The practice was begun by Old Tom Morris, who felt that the course got too much of a beating when played the same way all the time. In any case, bunkers such as those in the 12th fairway, although invisible today, were plainly in sight on the left-handed route to the 11th green.

If one can avoid this minefield, the 2nd is played to a shallow shelf of a green, the tightest target on the course, befitting one of the shortest par fours. In 1970 Jack Nicklaus drove this green and made an eagle en route to victory. No wonder the hole is on his list of the eighteen greatest in golf.

Number 13 begins the sternest stretch of the course. A range of heather and gorse runs along the right side of the fairway, then cuts a ridge across at about the 225-yard mark, creating a blind approach. A drive that is too long will come up against the ridge. The enormous plateau green, shared with number 5, is fronted by a ragged grassy area that tends to kick the ball in all directions, most hurtfully into the Lion's Mouth, a small pot bunker just short and left of the green.

The 14th hole is one of the classic par fives in golf, because there are numerous ways to play it, none of them safe. Says Darwin, "I have frequently seen four individuals playing the long hole, and deliberately attacking it four different ways, and three out of the four were probably right in playing it in the ways they selected." Three features dominate the hole—the stone wall denoting out of bounds which lines the right side, the mammoth Hell Bunker that looms over the second shot, and the billowing green which is fronted on the right by a pronounced knoll.

The most difficult shot is the teeshot, which must find fairway between the OB right and a clutch of bunkers on the left known as the Beardies. British golf writer Pat Ward-Thomas once declared: "For most golfers there is no greater sense of relief on the Old Course than to see the drive finishing safely in the lovely sweep of fairway known as the Elysian Fields." From there the task is to avoid the cavernous Hell at the 410-yard mark. Downwind, the green may be in reach, but into the face of the prevailing breeze, Hell is very much in mind. Gene Sarazen lost the 1933 Open when he took three shots to get out of Hell, made 8, and finished one stroke out of the playoff won by Denny Shute.

Out of bounds continues to haunt the right side at the 15th hole, where the caddies implore their players to drive at a church steeple

11th hole

The Road Hole as it appeared at the turn of the century. A par five until the late 1950s, today it is the world's most brutal four. Photo: © Nick Birch

in the distance. The major hazard is the Sutherland Bunker. In 1885 the green committee in power decided to cover over this bunker, but the change was an unpopular one. Three days later resistance forces had restored the bunker, and it has remained. Up at the green a protective ridge guards the right side, making this one of the few holes that is best approached from the left.

In 1905, when a railway line paralleled the last few holes of the course, James Braid drove over the wall at both 15 and 16, but made six on each hole, playing from the railroad tracks, and saved his victory. Today the bold line at 16 is between the OB fence and the Principal's Nose, a prominent bunker in the center of the fairway. The alternative, as usual, is to play safely to the left, but again, as usual, this leaves a more difficult approach, threatened by the Grant's and Wig Bunkers. The 1978 Open turned here when Jack Nicklaus birdied while his closest pursuer, Simon Owen, made 5.

The 17th at the Old Course—or the Road Hole, as it is more commonly known—may be the most famous hole in the world. A par five until the late 1950s, it is now an awesome four of 461 yards. It calls for a daring drive that must cut across property now owned by a hotel, then a lengthy shot to a green not designed to hold lengthy shots. Originally, this was a straight hole, but when the railroad came in the late nineteenth century, sidings and sheds were built that impinged on the fairway, forcing a blind drive over them. Restored versions of the sheds are still in place.

The green is set on a diagonal to the line of play, with its right side four feet lower than the left and the ledge marked by the presence of the greedy little Road Bunker, a hazard, in the words of Patric Dickinson, "so perfectly placed that it dominates play even from the tee, and by sheer force of its spidery personality drives its victims either to avoid it too carefully and chance the road, or play

too safely, and so come into its parlor." Six feet deep, with a high, steep bank, it is golf's most formidable, intimidating hazard without water.

Just beyond the green, at the foot of a grassy bank, is the road for which the hole is named. Until 1952 it was considered out of bounds, but today it is in play as part of the hole. In the 1984 Open, under four days of assault by 144 of the best players in the world, the hole yielded only eleven birdies.

Countless important shots—both good and bad—have been played on this hole, but perhaps the best came from an amateur, Marvin "Vinny" Giles III, who in his 1971 Walker Cup match against now-secretary of the R&A Michael Bonallack hit his second shot onto the road, leaving a virtually impossible shot back to the pin. But Giles clipped the ball off the road and straight at the hole; it hit the flagstick about a foot high and dropped in the cup for a winning birdie, whereupon the usually unflappable Bonallack thrust his visor to the ground in disgust. Giles won the match but his heroics went for naught as Great Britain and Ireland defeated the U.S., 13 to 11.

After 17, the final hole is unquestionably an anticlimax, 354 straight yards up the broad, bunker-free fairway shared with the 1st hole to a large sweeping green. The only trouble off the tee—and more for amateurs than pros—is the town, just on the other side of Links Road, which runs down the right side of the hole. Having avoided a confrontation with the row of gray stone houses, one must merely clear the Valley of Sin, the deep swale in front of the final green. Otherwise, the third shot will likely be a putt or running chip of 100 feet or more, to be negotiated while under the gaze of the dozen or so tourists and passersby leaning on the white railing that separates the green from the Royal Burgh of St. Andrews.

British Open: October 4, 1873

Tom Kidd	91	88	179	1
Jamie Anderson	91	89	180	2
Tom Morris, Jr.	94	89	183	T3
Bob Kirk	91	92	183	T3
Davie Strath	97	90	187	5
Walter Gourlay	92	96	188	6
Tom Morris, Sr.	93	96	189	7
Henry Lamb	96	96	192	8
Robert Martin	97	97	194	T9
Willie Fernie	101	93	194	T9

British Open: October 7, 1876

Bob Martin	86	90	176	1
Davie Strath	86	90	176	2
Strath did not show up for the playoff				
Willie Park	94	89	183	3
Tom Morris, Sr.	90	95	185	T4
Willie Thompson	90	95	185	T4
Mungo Park	95	90	185	T4
Henry Lamb	94	92	186	7
George Paxton	95	92	187	T8
Walter Gourlay	98	89	187	T8
Bob Kirk	95	92	187	T8

British Open: October 4, 1879

Jamie Anderson	84	85	169	1
James Allan	88	84	172	T2
Andrew Kirkaldy	86	86	172	T2
George Paxton	89	85	174	4
Tom Kidd	87	88	175	5
Bob Ferguson	89	86	176	6
D. Anderson	94	84	178	7
J.O.F. Morris	92	87	179	T8
Tom Dunn	90	89	179	T8
W. Gourlay	92	87	179	T8

British Open: September 30, 1882

Bob Ferguson	83	88	171	1
Willie Fernie	88	86	174	2
Jamie Anderson	87	88	175	T3
Jack Kirkaldy	86	89	175	T3
Bob Martin	89	86	175	T3
Fitz Boothby	86	89	175	T3
Willie Park, Sr.	89	89	178	T7
David Ayton	90	88	178	T7
James Mansfield	91	87	178	T7
James Rennie	90	88	178	T7

British Open: October 3, 1885

Bob Martin	84	87	171	1
Archie Simpson	83	89	172	2
David Ayton	89	84	173	3
Willie Fernie	89	85	174	4*
Willie Park, Jr.	86	88	174	5*
Bob Simpson	85	89	174	6*
Jack Burns	88	87	175	7
Peter Paxton	85	91	176	8
Willie Campbell	86	91	177	T9
J.O.F. Morris	91	86	177	T9
*after a playoff				

British Open: October 6, 1888

Jack Burns	86	85	171	1
Ben Sayers	85	87	172	2*
D. Anderson, Jr.	86	86	172	3*
Willie Campbell	84	90	174	4
Leslie Balfour	86	89	175	5
Andrew Kirkaldy	87	89	176	T6
Davie Grant	88	88	176	T6
Alex Herd	93	84	177	8
David Ayton	87	91	178	9
J.E. Laidlay	93	87	180	10
*after a playoff				

British Open: October 6, 1891

Hugh Kirkaldy	83	83	166	1
Andrew Kirkaldy	84	84	168	2*
Willie Fernie	84	84	168	3*
S. Mure Fergusson	86	84	170	4
W.D. More	84	87	171	5
Willie Park, Jr.	88	85	173	6
David Brown	88	86	174	7
W. Auchterlonie	85	90	175	8
Tom Vardon	89	87	176	T9
Ben Sayers	95	81	176	T9
*after a playoff				

British Open: June 12-13, 1895

J.H. Taylor	86	78	80	78	322	1
Alex Herd	82	77	82	85	326	2
Andrew Kirkaldy	81	83	84	84	332	3
G. Pulford	84	81	83	86	334	4
Archie Simpson	88	85	78	85	336	5
Willie Fernie	86	79	86	86	337	T6
D. Brown	81	89	83	84	337	T6
D. Anderson, Jr.	86	83	84	84	337	T6
Ben Sayers	84	87	85	82	338	T9
A. Toogood	85	84	83	86	338	T9
Harry Vardon	80	85	85	88	338	T9
Tom Vardon	82	83	84	89	338	T9

British Open: June 6-7, 1900

J.H. Taylor	79	77	78	75	309	1
Harry Vardon	79	81	80	77	317	2
James Braid	82	81	80	79	322	3
Jack White	80	81	82	80	323	4
W. Auchterlonie	81	85	80	80	326	5
Willie Park, Jr.	80	83	81	84	328	6
Robert Maxwell	81	81	86	81	329	T7
A. Simpson	82	85	83	79	329	T7
Ben Sayers	81	83	85	81	330	9
Andrew Kirkaldy	87	83	82	79	331	T10
Alex Herd	81	85	81	84	331	T10
Tom Vardon	81	85	84	81	331	T10

British Open: June 9-11, 1905

James Braid	81	78	78	81	318	1
Rowland Jones	81	77	87	78	323	T2
J.H. Taylor	80	85	78	80	323	T2
James Kinnell	82	79	82	81	324	4
Ernest Gray	82	81	84	78	325	T5
Arnaud Massy	81	80	82	82	325	T5
R. Thomson	81	81	82	83	327	7
J. Sherlock	81	84	80	83	328	8
T. Simpson	82	88	78	81	329	T9
Harry Vardon	80	82	84	83	329	T9

British Open: June 22-25, 1910

James Braid	76	73	74	76	299	1
Alex Herd	78	74	75	76	303	2
George Duncan	73	77	71	83	304	3
L. Ayton	78	76	75	77	306	4
Fred Robson	75	80	77	76	308	T5
Willie Smith	77	71	80	80	308	T5
Ted Ray	76	77	74	81	308	T5
J. Kinnell	79	74	77	79	309	T8
D.J. Ross	78	79	75	77	309	T8
T.G. Renouf	77	76	75	81	309	T8
E.P. Gaudin	78	74	76	81	309	T8

British Open: June 22-25, 1921

Jock Hutchison	72	75	79	70	296	
			74	76	150	1
R.H. Wethered	78	75	72	71	296	
			77	82	159	2
Tom Kerrigan	74	80	72	72	298	3
Arthur Havers	76	74	77	72	299	4
George Duncan	74	75	78	74	301	5
F. Leach	78	75	76	73	302	T6
Walter Hagen	74	79	72	77	302	T6
Joe Kirkwood	76	74	73	79	302	T6
Arnaud Massy	74	75	74	79	302	T6
Alex Herd	75	74	73	80	302	T6
Jim Barnes	74	74	74	80	302	T6
Tom Williamson	79	71	74	78	302	T6

British Open: June 12-14, 1927

Bobby Jones	68	72	73	72	285	1
Aubrey Boomer	76	70	73	72	291	T2
Fred Robson	76	72	69	74	291	T2
E.R. Whitcombe	74	73	73	73	293	T4
Joe Kirkwood	72	72	75	74	293	T4
C.A. Whitcombe	74	76	71	75	296	6
Arthur Havers	80	74	73	70	297	T7
B. Hodson	72	70	81	74	297	T7
Henry Cotton	73	72	77	76	298	9
Alex Herd	76	75	78	71	300	T10
Tom Williamson	75	76	78	71	300	T10
R. Vickers	75	75	77	73	300	T10
W.B. Torrance	72	80	74	74	300	T10
T.P. Perkins	76	78	70	76	300	T10
P.H. Rodgers	76	73	74	77	300	T10
Percy Alliss	73	74	73	80	300	T10

British Open: July 6-8, 1933

Denny Shute	73	73	73	73	292	
			75	74	149	1
Craig Wood	77	72	68	75	292	
			78	76	154	2
Gene Sarazen	72	73	73	75	293	T3
Leo Diegel	75	70	71	77	293	T3
Syd Easterbrook	73	72	71	77	293	T3
Olin Dutra	76	76	70	72	294	6
Reg Whitcombe	76	75	72	72	295	T7
Alf Padgham	74	73	74	74	295	T7
Ed Dudley	70	71	76	78	295	T7
Henry Cotton	73	71	72	79	295	T7
Abe Mitchell	74	68	74	79	295	T7

British Open: July 5-7, 1939

Richard Burton	70	72	77	71	290	1
Johnny Bulla	77	71	71	73	292	2
Sam King	74	72	75	73	294	T3
Reg Whitcombe	71	75	74	74	294	T3
Alfred Perry	71	74	73	76	294	T3
Bill Shankland	72	73	72	77	294	T3
John Fallon	71	73	71	79	294	T3
Martin Pose	71	72	76	76	295	8
Percy Alliss	75	73	74	74	296	T9
E.W.H. Kenyon	73	75	74	74	296	T9
Bobby Locke	70	75	76	75	296	T9

British Open: July 3-5, 1946

Sam Snead	71	70	74	75	290	1
Bobby Locke	69	74	75	76	294	T2
Johnny Bulla	71	72	72	79	294	T2
Norman Von Nida	70	76	74	75	295	T4
C.H. Ward	73	73	73	76	295	T4
Henry Cotton	70	70	76	79	295	T4
Dai Rees	75	67	73	80	295	T4
Fred Daly	77	71	76	74	298	T8
Joe Kirkwood	71	75	78	74	298	T8
Lawson Little	78	75	72	74	299	10

British Open: July 6-8, 1955

Peter Thomson	71	68	70	72	281	1
John Fallon	73	67	73	70	283	2
F. Jowle	70	71	69	74	284	3
Bobby Locke	74	69	70	72	285	4
K. Bousfield	71	75	70	70	286	T5
Antonio Cerda	73	71	71	71	286	T5
Bernard Hunt	70	71	74	71	286	T5
Flory Van Donck	71	72	71	72	286	T5
Harry Weetman	71	71	70	74	286	T5
Christy O'Connor	71	75	70	71	287	T10
R. Barbieri	71	71	73	72	287	T10

British Open: July 3-5, 1957

Bobby Locke	69	72	68	70	279	1
Peter Thomson	73	69	70	70	282	2
Eric Brown	67	72	73	71	283	3
A. Miguel	72	72	69	72	285	4
Dave Thomas	72	74	70	70	286	T5
W.D. Smith	71	72	72	71	286	T5
Flory Van Donck	72	68	74	72	286	T5
T.B. Haliburton	72	73	68	73	286	T5
Henry Cotton	74	72	69	72	287	T9
Max Faulkner	74	70	71	72	287	T9
Antonio Cerda	71	71	72	73	287	T9

British Open: July 6-9, 1960

Kel Nagle	69	67	71	71	278	1
Arnold Palmer	70	71	70	68	279	2
Bernard Hunt	72	73	71	66	282	T3
Harold Henning	72	72	69	69	282	T3
R. De Vicenzo	67	67	75	73	282	T3
G. Wolstenholme	74	70	71	68	283	6
Gary Player	72	71	72	69	284	7
Joe Carr	72	73	67	73	285	8
Dai Rees	73	71	73	69	286	T9
Peter Thomson	72	69	75	70	286	T9
Harry Weetman	74	70	71	71	286	T9
Eric Brown	75	68	72	71	286	T9
David Blair	70	73	71	72	286	T9
S.S. Scott	73	71	67	75	286	T9

British Open: July 8-10, 1964

Tony Lema	73	68	68	70	279	1
Jack Nicklaus	76	74	66	68	284	2
R. De Vicenzo	76	72	70	67	285	3
Bernard Hunt	73	74	70	70	287	4
Bruce Devlin	72	72	73	73	290	5
C. O'Connor, Jr.	71	73	74	73	291	T6
Harry Weetman	72	71	75	73	291	T6
Harold Henning	78	73	71	70	292	T8
Gary Player	78	71	73	70	292	T8
A. Miguel	73	76	72	71	292	T8

British Open: July 8-12, 1970

Jack Nicklaus	68	69	73	73	283		
						72	1
Doug Sanders	68	71	71	73	283		
						73	2
Harold Henning	67	72	73	73	285	T3	
Lee Trevino	68	68	72	77	285	T3	
Tony Jacklin	67	70	73	76	286	5	
Peter Oosterhuis	73	69	69	76	287	T6	
Neil Coles	65	74	72	76	287	T6	
H. Jackson	69	72	73	74	288	8	
John Panton	72	73	73	71	289	T9	
Peter Thomson	68	74	73	74	289	T9	
Tommy Horton	66	73	75	75	289	T9	

British Open: July 12-15, 1978

Jack Nicklaus	71	72	69	69	281	1
Simon Owen	70	75	67	71	283	T2
Ray Floyd	69	75	71	68	283	T2
Ben Crenshaw	70	69	73	71	283	T2
Tom Kite	72	69	72	70	283	T2
Peter Oosterhuis	72	70	69	73	284	6
Isao Aoki	68	71	73	73	285	T7
Bob Shearer	71	69	74	71	285	T7
John Schroeder	74	69	70	72	285	T7
Nick Faldo	71	72	70	72	285	T7

British Open: July 19-22, 1984

Seve Ballesteros	69	68	70	69	276	1
Bernhard Langer	71	68	68	71	278	T2
Tom Watson	71	68	66	73	278	T2
Fred Couples	70	69	74	68	281	T4
Lanny Wadkins	70	69	74	68	281	T4
Greg Norman	67	74	74	67	282	T6
Nick Faldo	69	68	76	69	282	T6
Mark McCumber	74	67	72	70	283	8
Graham Marsh	70	74	73	67	284	T9
Sam Torrance	74	74	66	70	284	T9
Ronan Rafferty	74	72	67	71	284	T9
Hugh Baiocchi	72	70	70	72	284	T9
Ian Baker-Finch	68	66	71	79	284	T9

British Open: July 19-22, 1990

Nick Faldo	67	65	67	71	270	1
Mark McNulty	74	68	68	65	275	T2
Payne Stewart	68	68	68	71	275	T2
Jodie Mudd	72	66	72	66	276	T4
Ian Woosnam	68	69	70	69	276	T4
Greg Norman	66	66	76	69	277	T6
Ian Baker-Finch	68	72	64	73	277	T6
David Graham	72	71	70	66	279	T8
Steve Pate	70	68	72	69	279	T8
Donnie Hammond	70	71	68	70	279	T8
Corey Pavin	71	69	68	71	279	T8

Scorecard

HOLE	YARDS	PAR
1	370	4
2	411	4
3	371	4
4	463	4
5	564	5
6	416	4
7	372	4
8	178	3
9	356	4
OUT	3501	36
10	342	4
11	172	3
12	316	4
13	425	4
14	567	5
15	413	4
16	382	4
17	461	4
18	354	4
IN	3432	36
TOTAL	6933	72

GOLF Magazine Rankings:
7th in the World
2nd in Great Britain & Ireland

THE OLYMPIC CLUB

SAN FRANCISCO, CALIFORNIA
U.S. Open: 1955, 1966, 1987

Its name is The Olympic Club. Its nickname is Giant Killer. Three U.S. Opens have been held here, and in each of them, a titan was toppled.

Hogan, Palmer, and Watson. Each had victory in his grasp, and each let his golden opportunity slip through the Golden Gate. Collectively, before arriving at Olympic, this trio had won a total of twenty-four major championships. Collectively, after leaving Olympic, they never won another. Each left his heart in San Francisco.

"This is not a golf course," wrote *GOLF Magazine* columnist Jim Murray, "it's a 6700-yard haunted house. If it were human, it'd be Bela Lugosi. I think it turns into a bat at midnight. It's Public Enemy No. 1. Al Capone. John Wilkes Booth."

Perched on the inland side of a spine of sandhills separating the Pacific Ocean from Lake Merced, Olympic has an undeniably eerie, brooding air, particularly when shrouded in an early-morning fog. But despite its forbidding countenance, this is a place with a wide welcome mat.

8th hole

THE OLYMPIC CLUB ▪ 173

Olympic is a club for Everygolfer. Its membership of 4,700 comes from all walks of life and all ranges in income, from $20,000 to $2 million. It had its beginnings in 1860 when two brothers, Arthur and Charles Nahl, made room for a gym in the basement of their San Francisco home. Later that year they drew up bylaws and adopted the winged O as their symbol. Thus was formed the first athletic club in America.

Golf didn't come into the picture until more than a half century later, when the club purchased 365 acres on the western edge of town, where the floundering Lakeside Club had already built a course. But so many Olympians wanted to play the game that in 1924 two new courses were built, the famed Lake Course on which the three Opens have been held and the less severe Ocean Course, incorporating some holes from the original layout.

However, throughout this expansion and to this day, the Olympic Athletic Club has kept the emphasis on "athletic," fostering individual and team competition in a variety of sports. Between 1904 and 1960, club members won twenty-two gold, ten silver, and ten bronze Olympic medals in track and field, swimming, diving, and rugby. In 1987, the year of its most recent U.S. Open, the club also spent $200,000 to send its athletes to tournaments all over the world—in wrestling, squash, swimming, and basketball. Today, a separate downtown athletic club thrives with a membership of 8,000.

Gentleman Jim Corbett was an Olympic member when he put up his dukes and beat John L. Sullivan for the world heavyweight championship. And years later Ty Cobb became a golf member at Olympic. Cobb quickly displayed his natural talent, breaking 70 shortly after he took up the game, but strangely, he lost his touch just as fast, and spent many a frustrating afternoon chasing his ball up and down Olympic's billowing fairways. Perhaps his blackest day came when he was beaten, 7 and 6, in a match for the club championship, beaten by a pudgy little 12-year-old named Bob Rosburg. The members gave Cobb such a hard time that he cleaned out his locker and never returned.

Rosburg, however, went on to win the PGA Championship and four more events, while two other Olympic prodigies—Ken Venturi and Johnny Miller—grew up to become U.S. Open Champions. Each of those players will attest that this is a superb place to develop as a golfer, not only because of the demanding Lake Course but because the Olympic membership includes a deep pool of feisty, talented players. The club roster shows over 200 members with single-digit handicaps, with more than two dozen at scratch or one.

Perhaps the ultimate Olympic golfer was John Swanson, a fellow they say dressed like Archie Bunker and played like Minnesota Fats. Back in 1959, 19-year-old Jack Nicklaus had traveled west for the U.S. Amateur, and when he reached Olympic he found Swanson on the first tee.

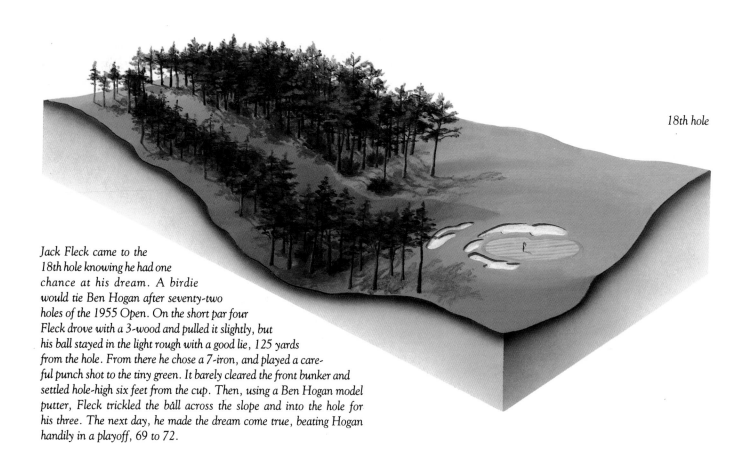

18th hole

Jack Fleck came to the 18th hole knowing he had one chance at his dream. A birdie would tie Ben Hogan after seventy-two holes of the 1955 Open. On the short par four Fleck drove with a 3-wood and pulled it slightly, but his ball stayed in the light rough with a good lie, 125 yards from the hole. From there he chose a 7-iron, and played a careful punch shot to the tiny green. It barely cleared the front bunker and settled hole-high six feet from the cup. Then, using a Ben Hogan model putter, Fleck trickled the ball across the slope and into the hole for his three. The next day, he made the dream come true, beating Hogan handily in a playoff, 69 to 72.

Thousands of spectators witness one of the game's great upsets as Jack Fleck completes his playoff victory over a very tired, very disappointed Ben Hogan, standing at right. Photo: AP/Wide World Photos

"How many strokes do you want?" asked Nicklaus.

"Strokes!" said Swanson. "Listen, fat boy, I don't need anything from you. It's you and me, belly to belly, for all your trophies." After sixteen holes, Swanson was one up. Nicklaus had to finish eagle-birdie to beat him.

Had Swanson won, he would merely have continued a tradition established by Jack Fleck. Son of an Iowa truck farmer, the 32-year-old Fleck was probably not much better a player than Swanson. He had tried the Tour, but without much success, in three years pocketing a total of $7,500, plus one local victory in the 1953 Waterloo Open. Prior to 1955, his best finish in a U.S. Open had been a tie for fifty-second.

Early in the week at Olympic, Fleck looked unlikely to finish as high as fifty-second, let alone first. One of his practice rounds was an 87. In the final round, however, he would lop twenty strokes off that score.

Meanwhile, the center of attention, as always during this era, was Ben Hogan. Ten years older than Fleck, and with four Opens in his pocket, Hogan desperately wanted a record fifth. In the spring he took time off from his budding golf club business and began honing his game for Olympic. In early June he arrived at the course and began schooling himself in its ups and downs, its bumps and bends.

This was a course that required study. The most severe test since Oakland Hills in 1951, it had been stiffened by the same man who had doctored Detroit—Robert Trent Jones. He had reduced the par from 71 to 70 while adding about 2,500 yards to the course and also narrowing the fairways. Furthermore, he had increased the penalty for missing those fairways, by allowing the thick Italian rye grass rough to grow up to eight inches or more, in the words of Jim Murray, "high enough to hide a lion."

In the first round, over half the field failed to break 80 and only one man bettered par. Tommy Bolt used just twenty-five putts in fashioning a 67 as Hogan, with a 72, began the tournament five back. But when Bolt ballooned to a 77 the next day, Hogan's 73 put him one off the lead. Julius Boros was also at 145, as was Jack Fleck, who had followed his opening 76 with a 69.

On the final day Hogan played a steady 72 in the morning as Bolt and Fleck turned in 75s. When The Hawk followed with a masterful 70 in the afternoon, he looked to have Open number five locked up. Hogan was so sufficiently convinced that he handed USGA Director Joe Dey his ball, saying, "Here, this is for Golf House," the USGA Museum. Later he sat in the locker room, sipping a scotch as Gene Sarazen, doing the TV commentary, signed off the telecast with congratulations to Ben Hogan.

The next morning, thousands of people were stunned at the lead story on the sports pages. Fleck had tied Hogan. With five holes to go, he had needed a birdie to force a playoff. Then he had bogeyed 14 to fall two behind Hogan. But when his iron shot stopped five feet from the par-three 15th he got one back. His third shot missed the green at the par-five 16th but he chipped stiff and made par. Two wood shots got him to the back of the 17th hole and he lipped his birdie putt. Thus, he needed a birdie on the final hole.

Fleck pulled the teeshot slightly, but his approach finished six feet from the hole. According to eyewitness Herb Graffis, "Fleck took exactly twenty-four seconds from the time he lined the putt up from the far side of the hole and firmly tapped it in."

Hogan had been hoping Fleck would make either two or four on that hole, because his legs, still aching from his near-fatal auto accident in 1949, had bothered him all week. He still wore a brace, still soaked in Epsom salts each night, and the Open's two-round final day had taken its toll on him. He dreaded the thought of eighteen more holes. The next day, he limped around the course as Fleck attacked it. Down three strokes by the 13th tee, Hogan fought back to within one with the final hole to go. But on his teeshot his foot slipped and he hooked the ball into deep rough on the hill to the left of the fairway. He needed three more strokes to get out of the weeds, and ended up sinking a thirty-two-foot putt for a six as Fleck made four for a 69 and a three-stroke victory.

Hogan, exhausted and bitterly disappointed, announced he was entering semiretirement. "I will never work this hard again to win a tournament," he said. He played a limited schedule for another dozen seasons, but won only one other tournament, the 1959 Colonial National Invitation in his home town of Fort Worth, Texas.

That 1955 Open was the first appearance for a muscular young Pennsylvanian named Arnold Palmer. He survived the cut and shot 303 to tie for twenty-first place, winning $226.15. Back then he was the reigning U.S. Amateur Champion. But when the Open returned to Olympic eleven years later, Palmer was the game's reigning king, winner of four Masters, two British Opens, forty other professional titles, and more money than anyone in history.

Prior to Olympic Palmer had worked on his swing, converting his long, drawing teeshots to long fades to match the predominant left-to-right movement of Olympic's par fours and fives.

But if Palmer had a fatal flaw, it was his boldness. In a preview article in *GOLF Magazine*, Ken Venturi suggested that Arnold and Olympic were not an ideal match. "A man of Palmer's aggressiveness will find it hard to hold himself in check," wrote Venturi. "Without making book, it is the kind of course over which you might keep your eyes on such as Billy Casper." Casper had one advantage—he hadn't needed to change his swing for Olympic—his trademark was a sliding fade. What's more, he was the best putter in the game. And perhaps most of all, Casper, a Mormon with

eleven children, was a man of great patience. He cut a wide figure on the fairways despite adhering to an odd diet to combat allergies. His cuisine included a variety of meats ranging from beef to buffalo, with hippopotamus, elephant, reindeer, bear, and antelope in between. While Palmer had animal magnetism, Billy had animal metabolism.

Meanwhile, Olympic was hardly the beast it had been in 1955. At 6719 yards it was nineteen yards longer, but the rough was not nearly as long—a maximum of five inches. In round two, it yielded a course and U.S. Open record of 64 to an unlikely club pro named Rives McBee, a former schoolteacher whose members at the Midland Club in Texas had raised $500 to send him to the Open. McBee stung the course for nine 3s, finishing with a flourish of birdies at 17 and 18. But since he had shot a 76 in round one, he was three behind the co-leaders, Palmer and Casper.

Palmer had shot a second-round score of 66, Casper 68, to move in front at 137, Arnie playing his aggressive game while Billy scrambled much of the way, including a 62-foot bunker shot that went into the hole at 17 for a birdie. The next day, for the first time, the USGA paired its two leaders together. Palmer took command early, birdieing the 1st and 5th holes. But he bogeyed 8 and then hit "an old-fashioned slice at the 12th hole," where the timing on his fade swing failed and he took a double-bogey. On the back nine he recovered with birdies at 14 and 16, the latter on a sixty-footer. As Casper posted a sluggish 73, Palmer moved into a three-stroke lead on a round of 70. One in back of Casper was Jack Nicklaus. No other player was within five strokes.

On Sunday, Palmer and Casper were paired once again, and once again it was Palmer who charged from the gate. With birdies at the 1st and 2nd, he pulled six in front of Casper, who found sand and bogeyed number 2. Out in 32, Palmer stood at the 10th tee with a seven-stroke lead.

At that point Palmer understandably began to let visions dance in his head. Years later, in his book *Go for Broke* Arnie recalled this pivotal moment:

I felt so confident of victory that I let my attention wander from the realities—winning this tournament—to pursuing another goal: beating the U.S. Open record of 276 shot by Ben Hogan in 1948. I already had set the British Open record several years earlier, and I was beguiled by the thought of holding both the U.S. and British Open records.

I wasn't alone in my expectations of victory. As we stood on the 10th tee, Casper turned to me and said: "I'm really going to have to go to get second, Arnie."

My reply sounded like a pompous gaff. "Don't worry, Bill," I said, "you'll get second."

I was trying to reassure him, not put him down. For I knew he was thinking about the pursuit of Jack Nicklaus, who was just a stroke or two behind him.

15th hole

This was the bizarre "discipline" of that final nine at Olympic. Bill Casper with his mind on the man behind him—not on a win; myself with my mind on a record—not a win.

Thus began the Great Collapse of '66. Palmer lost a stroke when he missed the green at 10. He matched birdies with Casper at 12, then lost another stroke as Billy birdied the 13th. When both men parred 14, Palmer retained a five-stroke lead with four holes to go. The big swing came at the 15th, where Casper knocked his teeshot fifteen feet from the hole as Palmer found a bunker. Birdie-bogey, and the margin was suddenly down to three. At 16, Casper sank another fifteen-footer for a birdie as Palmer struggled the length of the hole, finding first trees, then rough, then sand for a 6. One stroke. Both players missed the green at 17. Palmer pitched to twelve feet, Casper to four; Casper sank, Palmer missed, and they were tied with one to go. A pair of pars at 18 put them in the playoff. Casper had played the last nine holes in 32 strokes, Palmer in 39.

In the playoff the plot moved the same way. Palmer reached the turn in 33 and took a two-stroke lead, but things evened up when Arnie bogeyed 11 as Casper sank a twenty-five-footer for birdie. Then Billy sank a fifty-footer for birdie at 13 to go one up. When

he covered the next three holes in 4-3-6 against Palmer's 5-5-7, the game was over. Casper shot 69, Palmer 73. It was a knockout punch from which Arnie never quite recovered.

Twenty-one years elapsed before the Open came back to Olympic, but the course had changed little—it had merely speeded up. Early in the week, the Stimpmeter clocked the greens at 13, and some of the fairways were nearly as fast. Jack Nicklaus, who had finished seven strokes out of the Palmer/Casper playoff, offered a pre-tournament assessment that sounded similar to Venturi's in '66. He predicted that the Open would be won by "a plodder, someone who just hits the ball in the fairway, hits it on the green, and doesn't try to be a hero."

He was right. The 1987 U.S. Open was won by Scott Simpson, a quiet man with a quiet swing, who in seven previous appearances in the Open had never finished higher than 13th. As with the two other Opens at Olympic, the bigger story was who lost, and this time it was Tom Watson.

The undisputed successor to Nicklaus, Watson had dominated the game for a decade, winning thirty-one U.S. events plus five British Opens. In the eight years between 1977 to 1984 he had been named the PGA Player of the Year six times. But then his putting—always the strength of his game—had gone sour. When he arrived at Olympic he had been winless for almost three years.

Watson's opening round of 72 attracted little attention, but on Friday he drove the ball superbly and suddenly regained the touch that had brought him fame, firing a 65 that he described as "one of the top ten rounds of my life." It gave him a share of the lead with Mark Wiebe at 137. On Saturday, although he shot only a 71, Watson held the lead as Wiebe collapsed with a 77. Meanwhile, Keith Clearwater tied the course record with a 64 and jumped over fifty-four players into second place, a stroke behind. With him was Simpson on steady rounds of 71-68-70. Seven others, including Seve Ballesteros, Ben Crenshaw, and reigning Masters Champion Larry Mize, were within three.

On Sunday, however, no one made a charge. Although Watson fell back, bogeying three of his first five holes, so did his pursuers. When Watson recovered with birdies at 8 and 9, he was back to one under par and in the lead. Only Simpson, one behind, seemed a threat. Watson held his lead until 14, when Simpson hit his best approach shot of the day, a 160-yard 7-iron that stopped five feet from the cup, setting up a birdie that tied it up. Moments later each of them faced a twenty-footer for birdie, Simpson at 15 and Watson at 14. Simpson curled his in, and then Watson, the cheers ringing in his ears, bravely matched it. At 16 Simpson birdied again, from fifteen feet, as Watson watched from the fairway. Then Watson hit his own approach 15 feet from the hole—and missed.

When Simpson put his approach shot to the long, difficult 17th in the left-hand bunker, 70 feet from the hole, he seemed likely to relinquish his one-stroke advantage. But from there he played the shot of the championship, a deft explosion that rolled to a halt six feet from the cup. He sank the gutsy putt, then made a textbook par at 18 to come in at three under par. While several of the game's finest players had folded around him, he had played the last five holes of the U.S. Open in three under par.

Watson, needing to birdie one of the last two holes to tie, played aggressively and knocked his approach 30 feet above the hole at 17, then left his tricky approach putt six feet away. But just as Simpson had moments before, he made a courageous save. Then at 18, after playing a 2-iron to the center of the fairway 112 yards from the hole, he hit a wedge that covered the flag, but had too much spin. It sucked back 35 feet short of the hole, just off the green. From there he rapped a heart-stopping putt that nearly grazed the lip of the cup. But it wasn't enough.

Watson's loss may not have been as agonizing as Hogan's or Palmer's, but it was painful nonetheless, particularly because he had seemed to be emerging from his slump. Instead, the slump continued. Although he beat twenty-nine other players in the Nabisco Championships later that year, Watson has never won another full-field tournament.

On the surface, a strange phenomenon exists at Olympic. At roughly 6715 yards, it is the shortest course among the active U.S. Open sites. And yet, in three U.S. Opens, only four men have managed to better par for 72 holes.

Why is this? Why is Olympic, in the words of Ben Hogan, "the longest short course in the world?" Number one, the San Francisco climate, full of mist and rain, weighs heavily on the golf ball and inhibits full flight. Simultaneously, all that wetness keeps the fairways cool, damp, and green (and the rough dense) all year round, limiting roll as well. Number two, Olympic is full of doglegs that all but eliminate long drives. Number three, it's full of hills, and although a few of them add distance, many of them stop the ball on the fly or soon thereafter. Number four, it's full of trees, and one tends not to let 'er rip when staring at a bowling alley bordered by forests of eucalyptus. Number five, this par-70 has only two par fives, and three of its four par threes average under 160 yards. Its dozen par fours therefore average over 400 yards—while doglegging amid the trees, up and down the hills, through the heavy air, and across the lushly carpeted turf. That's why.

Despite being barely 500 yards from the ocean and even closer to a large lake, Olympic has no water hazards. Nor is the course severely bunkered. There is only one fairway bunker, and all but three greens are accessible with a running approach. The true hazards at Olympic are what Charles Price once called "bunkers in the sky." They are the trees.

This was virtually bare terrain—quasi-linksland—when the club bought it. Originally, the Ocean Course was intended to be the

1st hole

number one layout, "the St. Andrews of America." But in 1925 earth slides decimated that course only a year after it was built, and the focus shifted to the Lake Course. Course architect Sam Whiting, hoping to embellish the layout, planted trees—30,000 trees—and created perhaps the only course in the world that can be described as a links-forest.

Today the Lake Course is nearly choked with these specimens of pine, cypress, eucalyptus, cedar, and redwood, many of them well over 100 feet high. The fairways wind through tunnels and funnels, like eighteen peninsulas in a jungle. Indeed, the argument may be made about Olympic, as it may about Medinah or Winged Foot, that the trees have grown so tall and wide, they have sapped the course of much of its charm and interest. When trees encroach as they do on certain holes at Olympic, strategic options are eliminated. For example, sixty-five years ago, Bobby Jones cut the corner of the dogleg at the 16th hole and got home in two. Today, despite improved equipment, that hole is untouchable because of the trees.

The most open part of the course may be its first 100 yards. Hole number 1 is a reachable 533-yard par five, a slight dogleg right that plays downhill.

After that benign opener it's down to business at the 2nd hole where the "swoop factor" comes sharply into play. Virtually every hole at Olympic owes some aspect of its challenge to the fact that the terrain swoops from the seaside sandhills down toward the west shore of Lake Merced. The 2nd hole plays across the side of that hill, with the terrain pitching the ball from right to left. At the same time, the hole moves slightly against that hill toward a plateau

green offset to the right. The genius of this hole is that visually it does not engender comfort, either from the tee or on the approach.

Holes 3 through 6 are known as Earthquake Corner. Says Johnny Miller: "To get through those four holes you have to make four great drives and approach shots, then hold onto your shorts. You can get four over real fast." Ben Crenshaw likens the stretch to walking through a minefield.

Number 3 is the postcard hole, a par three of 233 yards that plays downhill to a narrow green protected by five bunkers. The strength of this hole may be its scenic value rather than its shot value. On fogless days it offers a spectacular view of the Golden Gate Bridge. This was the scene of a pivotal moment in the Fleck/Hogan playoff. Hogan stung a 2-iron three feet away while Fleck finished twenty feet away after bouncing his ball off the edge of a bunker. When Fleck made his putt and Hogan missed, Fleck gained not only a stroke but the confidence that "Hogan was human after all."

Holes 4 and 5 are two of the toughest back-to-back par fours in championship golf. The teeshot at 4 may be the most demanding on the course, calling for a string-straight shot through the chute of trees to the landing area about 240 yards out. From there the hole angles sharply left and uphill. The tendency on this 438-yard hole is to leave the approach shot short, and two long strip bunkers await anyone who does.

The 5th runs back down the hill, parallel to 4. It is a hole one struggles against, because it doglegs right as its slope pushes everything to the left, with tall pines guarding both sides all the way. As if the accuracy demands of this hole were not enough, at 457 yards it is also the longest par four on the course.

The only fairway bunker at Olympic is on the inside corner of the dogleg at number 6, ready to catch anyone who hopes to cut distance from this par four. Directly across the fairway a huge pine grabs out from the right side. The approach is complicated by a large valley fronting the green.

The shortest par four, and probably the easiest hole on the course, is number 7, 288 yards uphill and over a fronting bunker to a fast three-tiered green. It is followed by the shortest par three, a 137-yarder that plays uphill and semi-blind over a huge bunker. A pair of huge cypress trees overhangs the green set in a natural amphitheater. In the late 1960s, when the two trees were pruned, 105 balls fell out.

Four more mid-length par fours turn the corner into the back nine. The toughest of them is the 11th, which plays 430 yards into the prevailing wind. It was here that the playoff for the 1966 Open took a turn when Casper holed a thirty-footer for birdie as Palmer missed from four feet.

Holes 13 through 15 play along the bottom end of the course, with a deep culvert running along their left side. The par-three 15th, although only 149 yards in length, is severely bunkered on all sides and is one of the tiniest targets on a course where the average green is smaller than most Beverly Hills swimming pools. In 1987 Scott Simpson birdied it four days in a row.

Number 16 plays in an endless right-to-left crescent. Despite its 609-yard length, it's a patience hole, and like Olympic in general,

it can't be bullied. Two well-placed wood shots will leave a short iron or wedge to the green. Palmer made a 6 here in the last round, a 7 in the playoff, yet still ranks the hole as one of his favorite par fives.

The hole that follows it is not a par five, but it used to be, and some claim it still plays that way. Number 17 was originally a 522-yard uphill par five. It was shortened to a 461-yard four for the 1955 Open, to 435 for 1966, and to 428 in 1987, and even then it remained the hardest hole on the course, playing to an average score of 4.56. It plays into the wind, and into a fairway that falls severely—and some say unfairly—from left to right. In 1987, even some perfectly played teeshots rolled off the short grass and into the long. The approach is usually a long iron or fairway wood that must avoid bunkers right and left.

After 17, the last hole is an anticlimax, but a beautiful one. From an elevated tee it plays into a valley, then climbs back up to a tiny green nestled at the foot of a horseshoe-shaped hill beneath the clubhouse. There is thick rough on the left side of the fairway, but once again the terrain slopes so severely to the right that one is tempted to flirt with the high grass rather than risk rolling into the trees below.

In the third round of the 1987 Open, Japan's Tommy Nakajima hit his second shot into the top of a pine tree just short of the right side of the green. It stayed there. Among the half dozen leaders at the time, Nakajima was never in contention again.

U.S. Open: June 16-19, 1955

Jack Fleck	76	69	75	67	287	
					69	1
Ben Hogan	72	73	72	70	287	
					72	2
Sam Snead	79	69	70	74	292	T3
Tommy Bolt	67	77	75	73	292	T3
Julius Boros	76	69	73	77	295	T5
Bob Rosburg	78	74	67	76	295	T5
Bud Holscher	77	75	71	73	296	T7
Doug Ford	74	77	74	71	296	T7
E. Harvie Ward	74	70	76	76	296	T7
Mike Souchak	73	79	72	73	297	T10
Jack Burke	71	77	72	77	297	T10

18th hole

U.S. Open: June 16-20, 1966

Billy Casper	69	68	73	68	278	
					69	1
Arnold Palmer	71	66	70	71	278	
					73	2
Jack Nicklaus	71	71	69	74	285	3
Tony Lema	71	74	70	71	286	T4
Dave Marr	71	74	68	73	286	T4
Phil Rodgers	70	70	73	74	287	6
Bobby Nichols	74	72	71	72	289	7
Wes Ellis	71	75	74	70	290	T8
Doug Sanders	70	75	74	71	290	T8
Mason Rudolph	74	72	71	73	290	T8
Johnny Miller	70	72	74	74	290	T8

U.S. Open: June 18-21, 1987

Scott Simpson	71	68	70	68	277	1
Tom Watson	72	65	71	70	278	2
Seve Ballesteros	68	75	68	71	282	3
Bernhard Langer	69	69	73	72	283	T4
Ben Crenshaw	67	72	72	72	283	T4
Curtis Strange	71	72	69	71	283	T4
Larry Mize	71	68	72	72	283	T4
Bobby Wadkins	71	71	70	71	283	T4
Jim Thorpe	70	68	73	73	284	T9
Dan Pohl	75	71	69	69	284	T9
Tommy Nakajima	68	70	74	72	284	T9
Lennie Clements	70	70	70	74	284	T9
Mac O'Grady	71	69	72	72	284	T9

Scorecard

HOLE	YARDS	PAR
1	533	5
2	394	4
3	223	3
4	438	4
5	457	4
6	437	4
7	288	4
8	137	3
9	433	4
OUT	3340	35
10	422	4
11	430	4
12	390	4
13	186	3
14	417	4
15	149	3
16	609	5
17	428	4
18	343	4
IN	3374	35
TOTAL	6714	70

GOLF *Magazine* Rankings:
22nd in the World
15th in the U.S.A.

PEBBLE BEACH GOLF LINKS

PEBBLE BEACH, CALIFORNIA
U.S. Open: 1972, 1982, 1992
PGA Championship: 1977

It is Jack Nicklaus's favorite course. And why not? It is the place where he won a U.S. Amateur, a U.S. Open, and three Bing Crosby National Pro-Ams. "Pebble Beach stimulates me," he confesses.

But the fact is, from Jack Nicklaus to the lowliest 40-handicapper, this course stimulates every golfer on earth. Pebble Beach is God's gift to golf.

It was bestowed by the grace of one visionary man, Samuel F. B. Morse, the grandnephew of the inventor. Morse, captain of the 1906 Yale football team, was an avid sportsman and one of the first environmentalists. He fell in love with the Monterey Peninsula during a visit in 1908 and seven years later got a job with the Pacific Improvement Company, a consortium of West Coast real estate titans including Leland Stanford and Charles Crocker. In 1915, when he was given the assignment of liquidating some of the company's assets, Morse bought for himself 7,000 acres of the Peninsula, including seven miles of Pacific oceanfront, for $1.3 million, and formed a company called Del Monte Properties.

Golf in America had caught fire, with Francis Ouimet beating Vardon and Ray in the 1913 U.S. Open, and the game had begun to spread west. Morse's dream was to use part of his property to create the ultimate golf resort. When the Lodge at Pebble Beach opened on Washington's Birthday, 1919—thirty-one years to the day after the Apple Tree Gang of Yonkers, New York, introduced golf to the United States—it was everything Morse wanted it to be. Today the Lodge remains one of the finest golf resorts in the world.

It remains that way because Morse did something that virtually no modern developer would dare consider—he set aside his best property for the golf course. Then he took a risk and selected as his course architects Jack Neville and Douglas Grant, two top amateur players—and amateur architects. Neither had designed a course, but each was a dominant player in the Pacific Northwest, and that was good enough for the Duke of Del Monte. Besides, Grant was a serious student of golf architecture; he had visited and studied the great links of Britain and had compiled a sketch book filled with drawings of many of the great holes of the world.

It took the architects only three weeks of walking the dramatic stretch of land along the cliffs of Carmel Bay before they had mentally laid out the course. "It was all there in plain sight," said Neville. "Years before it was built I could see Pebble Beach as a golf links. Nature had intended it to be nothing else."

A little-known fact is that the course opened prematurely in 1918. In the inaugural competition, professional Mike Brady shot scores of 79 and 75 and beat the rest of the field by thirteen strokes; the course was thereby deemed to be too difficult for the average golfer, and was immediately closed for revision.

A decade later, after softening by the original architects and later by H. Chandler Egan, Pebble Beach was chosen to host the 1929 U.S. Amateur, the first national championship staged west of the Mississippi. It is a tournament remembered not for the man who won but for the man who didn't. In the first round, Johnny Goodman of Omaha, an American of Polish ancestry who had traveled to California in a cattle car, stunned the sports world by beating Bobby Jones. It was the only amateur championship in the last seven years of Jones's career in which he failed to reach the final match. On five of the six other occasions, he was the winner.

Jones's friend and biographer, O.B. Keeler, later wrote in *The American Golfer*: "While Omaha doubtless regards Johnny Goodman as a prime hero, California considers him a painful accident that came over 2,000 miles to happen."

Goodman, who was a good enough player to add the 1933 Open to his laurels (the last amateur to win an Open), lost in the second round at Pebble Beach as Harrison R. (Jimmy) Johnston beat Dr. O.F. Willing, an Oregon dentist, in a 36-hole final match that was distinguished by only one birdie.

In 1947 the Amateur Championship returned and Skee Riegel beat a strong field. In the same year Pebble Beach became the

anchor course of the Bing Crosby National Pro-Am, and the final round has been staged there each ensuing winter. It remains so today, although corporate sponsorship has intervened—the tournament is now known as the AT&T Pebble Beach National Pro-Am.

The Amateur Championship returned in 1961 when Jack Nicklaus played some of the best golf of his life in beating Dudley Wysong 8 and 6 in the final match. As a footnote, this is also the week that Nicklaus adopted a practice from his friend Deane Beman, a practice that is now standard procedure for Tour pros—charting exact yardages on every hole.

For more than a half century Pebble Beach was neglected as a potential Open site, because it was not near a major metropolitan city, and therefore couldn't guarantee appreciable attendance. Sam Morse invited the USGA for the 1966 Open, but they opted instead for Olympic, a bit more than two hours north and just a few minutes outside San Francisco. However, the swelling crowds at the Crosby convinced the association that Pebble could draw, and in 1972 the Open came.

Once again, Nicklaus was in rare form. He had already won his second Crosby earlier that year, not to mention his fourth Masters. His opening round of 71, one under par, was good for the lead. But unlike all other Open courses, Pebble was familiar ground to the American pros, and five other players matched Nicklaus's 71, the most ever tied for a first-round lead.

On Friday Nicklaus bogeyed two of his last five holes to come in at 73 for 144, but that was good enough to hold a share of the lead, as a third of the field failed to break 160. Tied with Nicklaus was the less than forbidding foursome of Cesar Sanudo, Kermit Zarley, Bruce Crampton, and Homero Blancas. But Arnold Palmer had made a run with a second-round 68, despite missing nine putts under twenty feet, and he was one back. One more back was defending champion Lee Trevino, who earlier in the week had slept twenty straight hours trying to rid himself of a case of pneumonia.

When Jack shot par on windy Saturday, he had the lead to himself, with Trevino one back, Crampton and Zarley two, and Palmer three.

Sunday dawned as one of the ruggedest days in Open history, as the field got a dose of Crosby weather—January in June. Small-craft warnings were in effect for Carmel Bay, but although the yacht races were canceled, the Open was not. Trevino fell out of the running early when he made a bogey 6 to Jack's birdie at 2, and after nine holes Nicklaus was four strokes clear of the field.

But Jack had some tough holes to go. On the 10th tee the wind caught his drive and he made 6 from the beach. Then he missed the green at the 12th hole and found himself staring at an eight-footer for a bogey. At the same moment Palmer, up ahead, faced a putt of the same length for a birdie at 14. Had Palmer made the putt and Nicklaus missed, Palmer would have pulled ahead of Jack. Instead, it went the other way—Jack saved his bogey and Arnold settled for par—and Jack held onto a one-stroke lead.

Palmer then bogeyed both 15 and 16 and eventually fell four strokes out. Nicklaus iced his victory at the par-three 17th, where he hit perhaps the finest iron shot of his career, a 1-iron into the teeth of the wind. It hit the flagstick, bounced once, and stopped inches away. He bogeyed 18 and finished with a round of 74, but under the circumstances, it was a great 74. In truth, Pebble Beach won this Open; Jack was merely the low survivor. His 290 remains the highest winning total in any major championship in the past quarter-century. The victory made Jack the only man in history to

OVERLEAF: *9th hole*. INSET ABOVE: *The Golden Bear played brilliantly on Sunday in 1972, and won a raw, rugged Open with a score of 290, two over par. Photo: Walter Ioos, Jr. for Sports Illustrated © Time Inc.* INSET BELOW: *Lanny Wadkins jumps for joy over the biggest victory of his career, the 1977 PGA in which he beat Gene Littler in the first sudden-death playoff in major championship history. Photo: © Leonard Kamsler*

win the Amateur and Open on the same American course. (Jones had done it in Britain, at St. Andrews.) The next year Nicklaus again won the Crosby at Pebble, thereby notching three victories on the same course in a span of fifty-three weeks.

He nearly continued his domination of Pebble when the PGA Championship arrived in 1977. California that year was suffering from a drought so severe that tournament officials had had to go to court to get permission to water the greens. The fairways, however, were baked dry, and some of them had actually developed cracks, from which the competitors were permitted to lift their balls. The hardened turf made for some long drives, but it also complicated approach shots and generally made Pebble Beach a totally different course from the one the pros were used to in the Crosby. Still, it was no easier, and after fifty-four holes only one man was under par.

Gene Littler, at 206, had a four-stroke lead at the start of the final round, and when he played the first nine holes in even par, his margin grew to five and the tournament seemed over. But then Gene the Machine suddenly sputtered, bogeying 10, 12, 13, 14, and 15. In jumped two players—Lanny Wadkins and the ever-present Nicklaus. As Littler played the 16th hole, Jack took the tee at 17, and Wadkins completed his round on 18; all three were at two over par for the tournament. But the hole that had been good to Jack in 1972 grabbed him this time. His 3-iron teeshot missed the green and he made a bogey. Littler parred in for a 76 that tied Wadkins, whose 70—the lowest score of the day—had taken him from six strokes behind.

The first sudden-death playoff in PGA history brought together two hard-luck cases. Littler had recovered from lymph cancer a couple of years earlier. At age 47 he was playing with a relearned swing, and this was his last hurrah as a regular Tour player. Wadkins,

a man whose career has been a roller-coaster ride, had been in a prolonged dive, without a victory since 1973.

At the first playoff hole Wadkins missed the green, leaving himself a slick twenty-footer to tie Littler's par. He sank it. "I was stunned when he made that putt," said Littler later. "He couldn't do it again with twenty or thirty balls." Both players birdied the par-five 2nd hole, and both drove well at the 3rd.

Earlier in the day Littler had hit his approach to this hole over the green and out of bounds. Perhaps with that memory in his mind, he this time left his shot well short. The aggressive Wadkins played to the back fringe. Littler pitched to twelve feet, Wadkins chipped to six. Littler missed his putt, and Lanny made his to win the only major championship among his twenty tournament victories.

By 1982, when the Open returned to Pebble Beach, Jack Nicklaus had begun to share his dominance with Tom Watson. Since his first victory, the 1974 Western Open, Watson had notched two dozen more, plus two Masters and three British Opens. For four years in a row (1977-80) he had led the Tour money list and been named the PGA Player of the Year. But he had not won the event he wanted most—the U.S. Open.

On two occasions, Watson had blown opportunities—at Winged Foot in 1974 and Medinah in 1975—and those performances had earned him a reputation as a choker. But in 1977 he had silenced many of his critics, winning two head-to-head battles with Nicklaus in the Masters and the British Open at Turnberry. At Pebble, he would duel Nicklaus once again.

Watson knew the course well. A Stanford graduate, he had often piled into a car with his fellow golf team members and barreled down Highway 101 to Carmel for a couple of quick eighteens. He had also won back-to-back Crosbys in 1977 and 1978.

After two rounds, however, neither Watson nor Nicklaus was at the top. Both had shot 144, even par, and that left them five behind the pace being set by 44-year-old Australian Bruce Devlin. On Saturday, as Devlin faltered with a 75, Watson made his move. His 68 took him into a tie for the lead with Bill Rogers. Nicklaus, on a 71, lurked at 215, three behind.

When Jack began the final round with two 5s, he seemed out of the chase. But then he reeled off five straight birdies and suddenly pulled ahead of Watson into a tie for the lead with Rogers, playing with Watson two holes behind him.

At that point, all three of them faltered. Rogers began a string of mistakes that would take him to a round of 74 and a tie for third. Nicklaus missed the green at the 8th hole and bogeyed, while Watson missed a two-foot par putt at the 7th. With nine holes to go, the two superstars were tied.

The back nine was championship drama at its best. Watson, after hitting his second to the very edge of the precipice at 10, sank a twenty-footer to save par to take a one-stroke lead over Jack who had three-putted 11. He then birdied 11 on a twenty-two-footer to go two ahead. But not for long as a bogey at 12 halved his lead.

The miracle chip at 17 that turned an apparent bogey into a birdie and gave Tom Watson a one-stroke lead over Jack Nicklaus in the 1982 U.S. Open. Photo: © Lawrence N. Levy

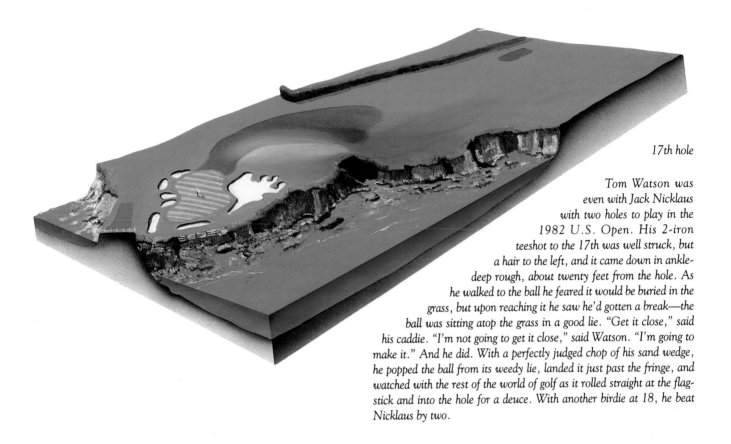

17th hole

Tom Watson was
even with Jack Nicklaus
with two holes to play in the
1982 U.S. Open. His 2-iron
teeshot to the 17th was well struck, but
a hair to the left, and it came down in ankle-
deep rough, about twenty feet from the hole. As
he walked to the ball he feared it would be buried in the
grass, but upon reaching it he saw he'd gotten a break—the
ball was sitting atop the grass in a good lie. "Get it close," said
his caddie. "I'm not going to get it close," said Watson. "I'm going to
make it." And he did. With a perfectly judged chop of his sand wedge,
he popped the ball from its weedy lie, landed it just past the fringe, and
watched with the rest of the world of golf as it rolled straight at the flagstick and into the hole for a deuce. With another birdie at 18, he beat
Nicklaus by two.

Walking to his drive at 13, he heard a roar up ahead—Nicklaus had birdied 15, and they were tied.

Watson made a routine par at 13, then rolled in yet another long birdie putt—this one from forty feet—at 14 to regain the lead. Up ahead, Nicklaus finished with three immaculate pars. If Watson could do the same, he would win.

But at 16 he hit his only poor teeshot of the day, a push into a deep right-hand bunker. With no shot to the green, he pitched out sideways, got on in three, and two-putted for a bogey. Back to even with Nicklaus.

When Watson's teeshot at 17 landed in the heavy rough a few feet off the left side of the green, par seemed a very good score. But it was from there that he played one of the most famous shots in Open history, popping the ball out of the rough and into the hole for a two. Suddenly, he was back to one ahead. At 18, playing for only a par, he lagged a twenty-footer that fell into the hole for birdie and a two-stroke victory. Once again, he had beaten Nicklaus, but this time at Pebble Beach and this time for the U.S. Open. Said Watson, "I couldn't have written the script better."

Robert Trent Jones observed that Pebble Beach is "a complex of ordinary holes and thrilling stretches," and the argument is often made that Pebble's first five holes lack the quality of its last thirteen. From a scenic standpoint, that is undeniable, but as a test of shotmaking, the opening stretch at Pebble is a fitting crescendo to that which follows.

The first hole, like the last hole and several in between, owes its ultimate flavor to H. Chandler Egan, a two-time U.S. Amateur Champion whom Sam Morse called in to strengthen the course for the 1929 Amateur. The original layout had been 6314 yards with a par of 74, and Egan remodeled several greens and bunkers and stretched the length nearly 200 yards. At number 1 Egan converted a nondescript straight hole into an interesting dogleg. In the mold of the openers at Merion and Shinnecock, it is a relatively easy 4 but a relatively difficult 3, particularly because of its narrow, fast green.

"On the face of it, number 2 is a logical birdie hole," says Jack Nicklaus, "except that there's a lot more to the hole than first meets the eye. . . . It can destroy you unless you handle it with care." Nicklaus prefers to keep his teeshot to the right on this 502-yard par five, and claims he never tries to fly his second to the green, fearing that a slightly pulled shot could catch the overhanging branches of a tree, a slightly strong shot could find jail in the bushes beyond. On the other hand, the approach must be hearty enough to clear the broad barranca that crosses the fairway less than a hundred yards in front of the green. Nonetheless, this is the easiest hole on the course. Birdies abound, and in the third round of the PGA, Lanny Wadkins helped his cause by knocking his second shot to four feet for an eagle.

Wadkins won his playoff with Littler at the 388-yard 3rd, a sharp dogleg left to a slightly raised green guarded on both sides by bunkers. Nicklaus also won one of his Crosby's here in a playoff over Johnny Miller. Number 4 is the first of eight holes that snake along the cliffs. Architect Neville favored small greens, and this is the smallest on the course, but he also knew how to balance shotmaking demands—this is also the shortest par four on the course. At 327 yards it calls for a well-judged short iron that must clear a fronting bunker and stop on a surface which slopes fiercely from back to front. And on both the teeshot and the second, the major consideration is the cliff. Says Herbert Warren Wind, "Such features have a powerful subconscious effect on people wearing spiked shoes."

The 5th hole, a par four of 166 yards, seems out of place. Densely tree-lined from tee to green, it looks as if it has been transplanted from Oak Hill or Medinah. It is the only hole between 4 and 10 that is not on the water, and had Sam Morse had his way, it would have completed the stretch. Morse wanted to build a little one-shotter down to the sea, but the landowner refused to sell the needed property. Water or not, this uphill shot to a canted green is plenty of challenge, as Ben Crenshaw will attest. In the opening round of the PGA, Crenshaw notched a 9 here.

Lee Trevino once said, "If you're 5 over when you get to the 6th tee at Pebble Beach, it's the best place in the world to commit sui-

cide." This is where the course begins to show its beautiful teeth, smiling and sneering at its assailants, coaxing and conning them to play their best or suffer the worst.

The 6th is the easiest of the next four holes, and there's nothing easy about it. A par five that reads 516 yards on the card, it can play 615 or more in a wind. From an elevated tee, the teeshot is played to a broad valley of a fairway. On the hillside to the left is a fifty-yard-long bunker, and to the right are the cliffs, dropping fifty feet into Stillwater Cove, a breathtakingly beautiful inlet where yachts float, sea lions bark, and otters (and golf balls) splash in the surf. At about the 350-yard mark the fairway swoops steeply uphill to a headland for the last 100 yards of the hole. A strong drive and a strong second shot are needed to reach that plateau. From there, the highest point on the shoreline, the assignment is to decipher the day's wind and play a confident pitch shot while remembering that the cliff continues to lurk on the right.

The next seven full swings must be made with the sea in sight, in play, and in mind. Number 7 is one of the most famous and photographed holes in the game, a 107-yard par three that plays downhill to a green squeezed onto a tiny spit of land, a green on which

8th hole

16th hole

waves crash, a green which at its narrowest point is only eight steps wide and shrinks with every gust of wind. It's the shortest hole in major championship golf, but yard for yard it is the hardest hole in the world.

Under normal circumstances, it's a three-quarter wedge shot, but circumstances on this tee are never normal. During one Crosby Eddie Merrins, the little pro from Bel-Air, made an ace by slugging a 3-iron into the face of a gale. And one day Sam Snead was so intimidated by the wind that he *putted* the ball down a dirt path to the hole. Downwind it may be even tougher since the assignment is to keep the ball from being launched out to sea, to hit a shot *short* enough to stay on this green.

It's difficult to conceive of a more difficult trio of back-to-back par fours than the 8th, 9th, and 10th holes at Pebble. Continuing the route along the cliffs, 8 calls for a blind drive uphill to the plateau shared with number 6. It then angles dramatically to the right 180 yards across a 100-foot-deep chasm filled with rocks, thick grass, and the encroaching sea. Nicklaus calls the long iron over this chasm the greatest second shot in golf. The small green, redesigned by Alister Mackenzie when he was building nearby Cypress Point, slopes toward the ocean and is the fastest on the course. The only word that accurately describes this hole is "awesome."

The hardest hole on the course—and a strong candidate for hardest in the world—is number 9. Its 464-yard fairway falls sharply from left to right toward the sea. (You can understand why the fade-playing Trevino recommended hara-kari.) But those who seek to avoid the perils on the right risk a brawl with rough and bunkers on the left. The green sits on the brink of the cliff, and people have been known to hit putts off the edge and onto the beach below. In the 1963 Crosby Dale Douglas took a 19 here. Yes, you read that right—19!

Number 10 is nearly forty yards shorter than 9 but it tilts more precipitously toward the cliffs. Hit a teeshot dead down the center of this fairway, and there's a better than even chance it will end up on the rocks. What's more, the green is even more precariously perched than the one at 9. In the final round of the '72 Open Nicklaus almost crashed and burned when he sent his approach down on the beach, but managed to hold the damage to a double-bogey 6.

After 10 the course moves inland and begins the loop home through stretches of oak, cypress, and eucalyptus trees. The 11th may be the most pedestrian hole on the course, a semiblind uphill par four of 384 yards, but Curtis Strange added some excitement to it in 1988. That year the Nabisco Championships, the richest tournament in the game, was played at Pebble, and Strange won the $360,000 first prize thanks in part to a 135-yard 8-iron he hit into the hole for eagle here in the first round.

The 12th is a 202-yard par three that must be attacked in Nicklausian style, with an iron that is hit high as well as long, in order to hold this hard, shallow green. Consider the stretch from the 5th to the 12th holes, and marvel at the accomplishment of Ken Venturi, who in the final of the 1956 California Amateur came to the 5th tee two down, then made eight consecutive threes, eventually winning, 2 and 1.

The green at the par-four 13th is another Mackenzie redesign, and it tilts hard from right to left while a menacing bunker protects the right side. Number 14 is a classic three-shot par five that sweeps from left to right and concludes with an uphill pitch to the most fiercely contoured green on the course. The left side of the green is four feet higher than the right, and is protected by a gaping bunker collared with kikuyu grass. In the PGA Danny Edwards took six putts—yes, six—here. Before 1967 this hole was a bit more difficult due to the presence of a large cypress tree on the right side of the fairway, but in the final round of the Crosby that year Arnold Palmer, one behind Nicklaus and trying for the lead, twice went for the green in two and twice struck that tree. That night, a storm hit the area; lightning struck the tree, uprooted it, and blew it to the ground. What Palmer couldn't accomplish, Mother Nature did.

The next two par fours call for good driving; at the 15th a draw will leave a short iron to the green—a strong, straight shot will go out of bounds—while at 16 the preferred teeshot is a slight fade. Number 16 is another hole that was improved by Chandler Egan. He moved the original green back 100 yards behind a ravine and into an opening amid several pine and cypress trees. In 1972, at age 81, Jack Neville was "rehired" by the USGA to restore parts of his original course. He reworked several bunkers, most notably one to the right of this fairway, which he deepened. It didn't have a pivotal effect that year, but a decade later it snared Tom Watson for a bogey in the final round.

Watson of course got the stroke back with his miracle chip at 17, a par three that can play from 170 to 218 yards, depending on tee and pin position, and can call for anything from a 9-iron to a driver, depending on wind direction. It is usually a mid to long iron, played straight at the ocean. The wide but shallow green is cinched at the waist, creating a two-tiered target with the left side higher than the right. The right-front area is open to the fairway, the rest of the green is surrounded by sand and high grass.

In the 1951 Crosby, singer Phil Harris sank a lengthy putt here to clinch the pro-am title for him and his pro partner, Dutch Harrison.

"Exactly how long was that putt?" someone asked him that evening.

"I don't know," said Harris, "but I'd like to have that much footage on Wilshire Boulevard."

"Was it a hundred feet?" he was asked.

"Hell," said Harris, "it *broke* that much.

The 18th at Pebble Beach is the grand finale of all time, a magnificent beast of a par five that curls 548 yards in a counterclockwise crescent. It was a 379-yard par four until Chandler Egan moved the tee back onto a promontory just behind the 17th green. A good teeshot now finishes near two large pines on the right side of the fairway, well clear of the ocean on the left. Another tall pine, just short of the green on the right, blocks entry to the green from that side and encourages the more daring route along the sea. The hole is reachable in two, but rarely; both the player and the following wind must be strong. In the 1982 Open it was a true "finishing" hole for the five players who made eights, not to mention the two who scored nines.

The only public course on which the Open has ever been played, Pebble Beach was purchased in September of 1990 by Ben Hogan Properties, a division of a Japanese company called Cosmo World. The purchase prompted fears that the resort would be converted into a private club for the Japanese. To date, however, no major changes have been made, except that Jack Nicklaus's architectural firm was hired to prepare the golf course for the 1992 U.S. Open. The layout and scenery remain as spectacular as ever. At $175 for a green fee and cart, the price to play may be steep, but if any course is worth it, Pebble Beach is the one.

U.S. Open: June 15-18, 1972

Jack Nicklaus	71	73	72	74	290	1
Bruce Crampton	74	70	73	75	293	2
Arnold Palmer	77	68	73	76	294	3
Lee Trevino	74	72	71	78	295	T4
Homero Blancas	74	70	76	75	295	T4
Kermit Zarley	71	73	73	79	296	6
Johnny Miller	74	73	71	79	297	7
Tom Weiskopf	73	74	73	78	298	8
Cesar Sanudo	72	72	78	77	299	T9
Chi Chi Rodriguez	71	75	78	75	299	T9

PGA Championship: August 11-14, 1977

Lanny Wadkins	69	71	72	70	282	
					4-4-4	1
*						
Gene Littler	67	69	70	76	282	
					4-4-5	2
Jack Nicklaus	69	71	70	73	283	3
Charles Coody	70	71	70	73	284	4
Jerry Pate	73	70	69	73	285	5
Al Geiberger	71	70	73	72	286	T6
Lou Graham	71	73	71	71	286	T6
Jerry McGee	68	70	77	71	286	T6
Don January	75	69	70	72	286	T6
Tom Watson	68	73	71	74	286	T6

*won on third hole of sudden-death playoff

U.S. Open: June 17-20, 1982

Tom Watson	72	72	68	70	282	1
Jack Nicklaus	74	70	71	69	284	2
Bobby Clampett	71	73	72	70	286	T3
Dan Pohl	72	74	70	70	286	T3
Bill Rogers	70	73	69	74	286	T3
Gary Koch	78	73	69	67	287	T6
Jay Haas	75	74	70	68	287	T6
Lanny Wadkins	73	76	67	71	287	T6
David Graham	73	72	69	73	287	T6
Calvin Peete	71	72	72	73	288	T10
Bruce Devlin	70	69	75	74	288	T10

Scorecard

HOLE	YARDS	PAR
1	373	4
2	502	5
3	388	4
4	327	4
5	166	3
6	516	5
7	107	3
8	431	4
9	464	4
OUT	3274	36
10	426	4
11	384	4
12	202	3
13	392	4
14	565	5
15	397	4
16	402	4
17	209	3
18	548	5
IN	3525	36
TOTAL	6799	72

The Lodge

RIVIERA COUNTRY CLUB

PACIFIC PALISADES, CALIFORNIA
U.S. Open: 1948
PGA Championship: 1983

1st hole

Frank Garbutt stood on the brink of an eighty-foot precipice, looked down upon the bleak, scrub-infested canyon below, and smiled. "This is it," he said, "this is it."

The year was 1922, the place was Pacific Palisades, California, and the "it" was Riviera Country Club. Garbutt, vice president of the Los Angeles Athletic Club, had been told to search out a site for the club to build a golf course. In this 243-acre parcel of the Santa Monica Canyon, he had found it.

Garbutt's next job was to find an architect, and his first choice was George C. Thomas, the Philadelphia aristocrat for whom golf

course architecture was but one of several avocations, the others including the study of Pacific game fish, the breeding of Irish setters, and the horticulture of roses. "He doesn't have to do this [architecture] work as a means of livelihood," a friend of Thomas's once said, "he does it out of sheer love for the game." Thomas is credited with over two dozen courses, and his book, *Golf Architecture in America*, is considered a classic.

Thomas wasn't as wild about Garbutt's site as Garbutt was, nor was he shy about expressing his opinions. After making an initial inspection of the property, Thomas announced that, while a golf course could be built, it wouldn't be much of a layout because of the limitations of the natural terrain. But he allowed as how it would be "good enough for the Los Angeles Athletic Club."

Those words rankled the club leaders, who let Thomas know that the best course in the world would be none too good for the LAAC. They may also have suggested to Thomas that the project was beyond his capabilities, for in the end Thomas not only took the job, he did it for no fee.

But he spared no expense in the construction process. Thomas brought in a team of 200 men who swarmed across the canyon, chopping down brush and planting sycamores and eucalypti. They also installed 100,000 feet of pipe, hauled in 19,000 pounds of grass seed, and sowed it into mountains of topsoil imported from the fertile San Fernando Valley. For the bunkers, 1,350 tons of sand were shoveled off the Pacific beach, two miles to the west. Back in those days, most golf courses were built for less than $100,000. Riviera cost $657,000.

Ah, but the LAAC members got what they paid for. When Riviera opened in 1927 it was hailed as the Pine Valley of the West, and in 1939, when the National Golf Foundation named the ten best courses in America, there was Riviera in third place, just behind Pine Valley and Pinehurst No. 2. Today it remains securely among the elite, ranking thirtieth on *GOLF Magazine's* list of the 100 Greatest Courses in the World.

From the beginning, this was Hollywood's course, with a membership that glittered. Among the early Rivierites were Douglas Fairbanks, Mary Pickford, Basil Rathbone, W.C. Fields, and Johnny Weissmuller. Howard Hughes, the reclusive billionaire, at one time yearned to be national amateur champion, and brought a camera crew to Riviera to film his swing. During the '30s a Mr. and Mrs. Taylor of England joined the club as equestrian members, and their 11-year-old daughter worked out daily on her horse Hal on the Riviera steeplechase course, for she had been selected to play the lead role in an MGM feature film. The title of the film was *National Velvet*, and Miss Taylor's name was Elizabeth. More recently the membership has included Burt Lancaster, Gregory Peck, Sammy

Davis, Jr., James Garner, Robert Wagner, Glen Campbell, Peter Falk, and Dean Martin.

Riviera also has served as the location of several movies, including scenes from *Pat and Mike*, starring Riviera members Spencer Tracy and Katharine Hepburn, and *The Caddy*, with two more members, Dean Martin and Jerry Lewis. And back in the days when on-location sites were sometimes impractical, the fairway substituted for English countryside in *Forever Amber*.

But the highest form of drama at Riviera has come not from film-makers but from professional golfers. In 1929 the Los Angeles Open came to Riviera for the first time, and the course has hosted the tournament on and off for sixty years, including every year but one since 1973. Messrs. Palmer and Nicklaus have never won on Riviera, but virtually every other top player of the past half century has: Hogan, Nelson, Snead, Demaret, Mangrum, Casper, Miller, Watson. In the words of two-time L.A. Open champion Tom Watson, "Things happen on this course."

The man who made many of those things happen was Ben Hogan. In a span of seventeen months he won two L.A. Opens and a U.S. Open, all on Riviera. Prior to the first of those victories Hogan had won a few tournaments, including the 1946 PGA Championship, but it was at Riviera that his greatness as a player first became evident. In the 1947 L.A. Open his winning total was 280; a year later he lowered that to 275, and in May of the same year he won his second PGA title. So when the Open came to town later that year, The Hawk was unquestionably the man to beat.

This was the first Open held on the Pacific Coast, and at 7100 yards Riviera was one of the longest Open courses to that time. But Hogan took charge of it immediately, birdieing four of the first five holes en route to a share of the opening-round lead wih Lew Worsham. On day two, a pair of snarling, yapping canines dogged Hogan's gallery, and he claimed they were part of the reason he could post no better than a 72. As a result, the other heavy favorite, Sam Snead, took the lead at 138, his pair of 69s setting a new half-way record for the Open. Also in the hunt were Jimmy Demaret and South Africa's Bobby Locke, on one of his money-making forays to the U.S. Tour.

Ben Hogan plays from the bunker in the middle of the 6th green. The Hawk mastered Riviera three times in a span of seventeen months. Photo: AP/Wide World Photos

A virtually flawless 68 put Hogan back in the driver's seat after fifty-four holes, two ahead of Demaret and four in front of Snead, whose loose putting had dragged him to a 73. In the final round Hogan birdied the first hole and the last hole in fashioning a 69 that gave him not only victory but a new U.S. Open record, slashing five strokes off a Ralph Guldahl mark that had lasted eleven years. Hogan's 276 set a standard that was not bettered until 1967. In capturing his first of four Open titles Hogan also became only the second man in history (after Gene Sarazen) to win the Open and PGA in the same year. He would go on to win a total of ten events in 1948, sixty-three overall.

Demaret, who finished second by two strokes and himself beat the old Open record by three, conceded that "Riviera is just Hogan's Alley." That has been its nickname ever since.

Riviera was also the site of Hogan's comeback following the accident in which his car collided with a Greyhound bus on a lonely stretch of Texas highway one foggy morning in February of 1949. The bus had attempted to pass a truck and had hit Hogan's car head-on. Hogan had thrown himself across his wife, and in so doing he probably saved not only her life but his own, since he would surely have been impaled on his steering wheel. As it was, he suffered a multiply fractured pelvis, a shattered collarbone, several broken ribs, a broken ankle, and much arterial clotting. Doctors said he would never play competitive golf again.

But they didn't know Hogan. For though his flesh had been torn and his bones shattered, his nerves were intact, and his heart was as big and strong as ever. It was 58 days before he got out of bed, three months before he got outside, but in August, he picked up a golf club, and in December, he played his first round, with his legs covered from ankles to thighs with bandages. A month later, he entered the L.A. Open; he had played only four rounds of golf since the accident.

"Everyone was delighted to see him," wrote Grantland Rice,

"but we thought he'd just be a spectator, not an entrant." Then Hogan reeled off four practice rounds in ten under par. Four days later, he stunned the world by posting a total of 280—a total that looked to have the tournament won, until Sam Snead birdied 17 and 18 to tie him.

Rain delayed the 18-hole playoff for a week, and by that time the golf gods had given the storybook ending a rewrite. Snead won by four. But at Riviera Hogan had served notice that there was a lot of good golf left in him.

Years later, a movie was made of his life. *Follow the Sun* starred Glenn Ford as Hogan, and the golf sequences were all filmed at Riviera. Long after his playing days were over, Hogan retained an affinity for the course, and consistently named it among his favorites in the world. "Even those two dogs that drove me half crazy weren't such bad animals," he recalled. In 1987, when officials from the Ben Hogan Golf Company asked whether he would agree to hit a couple balls for a television commercial, Hogan agreed. He had not left his hometown of Fort Worth in a decade, but at age 75 he boarded a jet and flew to Los Angeles to film the commercial on the 6th fairway of Riviera.

Thirty-five years passed between the 1948 Open and the next and only other major championship at Riviera—the 1983 PGA. It was led from wire to wire by a stocky, blonde 25-year-old named Hal Sutton. The 1980 U.S. Amateur Champion, Sutton had burst onto the Tour with a victory his rookie year in the 1982 Walt Disney Classic and had followed by winning the prestigious Tournament Players Championship, earlier in 1983. Pundits across the country were calling him the heir to Nicklaus, the Bear Apparent. Even Jack predicted that Sutton would be the game's next dominant player.

Those prognostications turned out to be incorrect—but at Riviera Sutton played well enough to beat a strong field of challengers headed by Nicklaus himself. Sutton's opening 65 gave him a two-stroke edge over an obscure 36-year-old club pro named Buddy Whitten and over Scott Simpson, whose day in the California sun would have to wait three years for the Open at Olympic. The next day Prince Hal blitzed the course for eight birdies, adding a 66 for a two-day total of 131 that broke the PGA record.

The 43-year-old Nicklaus, however, had Friday's best round, a 65. But because he had opened with a 73, he stood seven strokes behind. The group between him and Sutton was headed by Ben Crenshaw at 134 and Pat McGowan at 135. Meanwhile, Gibby Gilbert had tied the PGA nine-hole record, opening eagle-birdie-birdie to shoot 29 on the outward side. But he made no birdies after the 7th hole and settled for a 66 that left him at 136, tied for fourth.

In round three Sutton could do no better than a 72, and when Crenshaw chipped in at 18 for a 71, he crept within two. Nicklaus also had a 71 and stood six back. But with one round to go he and a half dozen other players were still in the hunt, and they knew it. So did Sutton. Just two weeks earlier, he had entered the last day of the Anheuser Busch Classic with a six-stroke lead, only to blow it all as Calvin Peete repeated as champion.

Late in the final round at Riviera, it looked like *déjà vu*. As Crenshaw crumbled to a 77, Sutton built his way to a six-stroke margin through eleven holes. But then he bogeyed 12, 13, and 14 while Nicklaus was birdieing 14 and 16. Suddenly the Bear was within a hair of his heir. Meanwhile Peter Jacobsen had come from way behind—eight strokes back—with a superb round. When he birdied 17 to go seven under for the day, he too was within a stroke of Sutton.

At that point Sutton had a chat with himself. "Hey, let's go," he said. "Let's not embarrass yourself like this." Then, as Jacobsen bogeyed 18 and Nicklaus parred the last two holes, Sutton gutted out four solid pars that gave him a one-stroke win.

Sutton's total of 274 was four strokes higher than Gil Morgan's winning total that year in the L.A. Open, and ten higher than Lanny Wadkins's record at Riviera. But Riviera in August is a markedly different course from Riviera in February, and the reason may be summed up in one strange word: kikuyu.

A strong, tough strain of grass—actually a weed—it was imported from Africa over sixty years ago, and planted along the banks of the broad barranca that comes into play on half of Riviera's holes. During heavy rains, the barranca had always flooded, and in 1937 a particularly heavy deluge had washed parts of a half dozen holes out to sea. To prevent such erosion, the kikuyu was introduced; it spread its roots quickly, and today it covers most of the course, giving Riviera a playing characteristic that is unique among the world's championship sites.

Imagine playing golf on a carpet of spongy Velcro, and you'll have some idea of the feel of Riviera in summer, when the kikuyu is thick and lush. The first effect is on distance. When a teeshot comes down on a kikuyu fairway it tends not to bound forward. Instead, it pops almost straight up, then plops down, leaving a better-than-average lie, but a shorter-than-average drive. Long kikuyu rough is more gnarly and grabby than other strains, making for unpredictable impacts, but the grass is most vexing around the green where the collar of kikuyu is almost like a hazard. A pitch

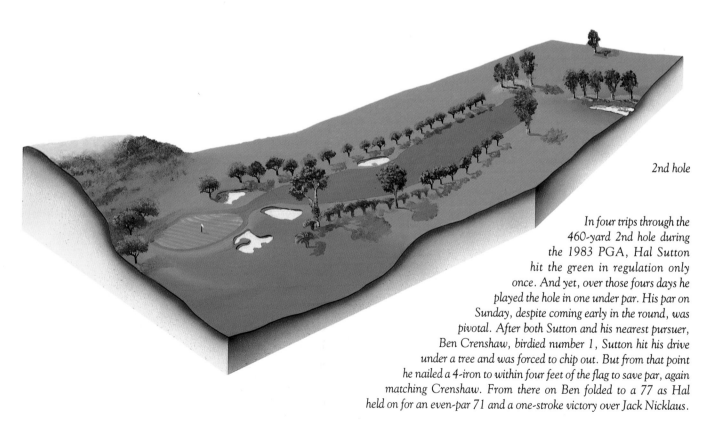

2nd hole

In four trips through the 460-yard 2nd hole during the 1983 PGA, Hal Sutton hit the green in regulation only once. And yet, over those fours days he played the hole in one under par. His par on Sunday, despite coming early in the round, was pivotal. After both Sutton and his nearest pursuer, Ben Crenshaw, birdied number 1, Sutton hit his drive under a tree and was forced to chip out. But from that point he nailed a 4-iron to within four feet of the flag to save par, again matching Crenshaw. From there on Ben folded to a 77 as Hal held on for an even-par 71 and a one-stroke victory over Jack Nicklaus.

5th hole

shot that lands in kikuyu fringe simply pops up and stops instead of hopping forward onto the green. This makes the standard pitch-and-run shot virtually unplayable.

The kikuyu has enhanced and protected George Thomas's lay-out against the advancements in golf equipment, and today Riviera remains the strong test it was in the '20s with virtually no major changes in its design. Balance is the key to this course—balance and proportion. Some holes are long—very long—and others are short—very short. But when a hole calls for a lengthy approach the green is generous and easily hittable; when the shot in is a wedge, the target is tiny and elusive.

There is a fairness about Riviera. It offers no blind shots, no hid-den tricks. On the other hand, the golfer does not always draw con-fidence from what he beholds. At the opening hole, much of the course is visible from the tee perched eighty feet above the canyon floor. But what the golfer sees when he looks at the first fairway is a strip of turf that seems no wider than a bowling alley, with thick trees to the right and out of bounds left. And even a strong, straight teeshot is in jeopardy when the wind is following, since the bar-ranca makes its first pass at about the 280-yard mark. This 501-yard

par five is the easiest hole on the course, a great place to start with an eagle—or a 7.

It is followed by the toughest hole on the course. The Riviera members play number 2 as a par five, but for the pros the hole is shortened to one of the best tests in the West. Tree-lined most of the way, it plays to a green that slopes hard from right to left and is protected by deep bunkers. Says Lee Trevino, "I have to play two woods, and the second of them has to be a great one to hold that green." In the last round of the PGA, Hal Sutton found tree trou-ble and was 205 yards from the green lieing two, but played a 4-iron to four feet and saved his par.

Ben Hogan, seldom effusive in his praise of anything, calls Riviera's 4th "the greatest par three in America." At 238 yards it is unquestionably one of the longest. Generally the pros try to reach it with a high 4-wood shot that will clear the mammoth front bunker and land gently on the sloping green.

George Thomas was an innovator, and at the 5th and 6th holes he let his imagination run. The right side of the green at the 422-yard 5th is barricaded by a grass mound the size of a schoolbus, and at the 6th a pot bunker sits in the middle of the green, converting

it into a doughnut. Two more bunkers—one in front of the green and one in back—complicate this 170-yard assignment. However, in the 1985 L.A. Open none of this sand play deterred Mike Reid, who aced the hole on Thursday and then followed with three straight birdies. His total of seven strokes on the hole for four days is an all-time PGA Tour record.

Thomas's original design of the 8th hole included another gambit—the divided fairway—a device that Jack Nicklaus adopted on several of his courses. But one of those fairways is now gone, and the landing strip that remains at 8 is a narrow one.

Ben Crenshaw, a serious student of golf architecture, calls the 10th at Riviera the finest short par four he has ever played. At 311 yards, it is within reach of the longest hitters, but only at great risk, for its slender, shallow green is guarded by a broad bunker, falls hard from right to left, and is virtually unholdable except with a well-judged, crisply played short iron from the fairway.

If a birdie doesn't come at 10, 11 may be the last chance on the back nine. It is a straight par five of 561 yards, and is reachable to a pro who can put together two solid shots. Dozens of eucalyptus trees add difficulty to the teeshot at 12, but the real demon is a sycamore just to the left of the green, said to have caught more stray rubber than any guardrail on the L.A. Freeway.

Out of bounds hugs the entire left side of the 13th hole, which runs along the south wall of the canyon with a half dozen multi-million-dollar homes hovering above. The green on this lengthy par four is relatively small, and becomes even smaller when one realizes that OB lurks only five paces off its left edge.

Two shortish but bunker-choked par threes at 14 and 16 sandwich a monster par four. Number 15 plays 447 yards in a left-to-right dogleg. The challenge is to keep the teeshot away from the eucalypti that cordon the right side of the hole, then find the correct level of the two-tier green.

Only a handful of men have reached the 17th hole in two, a 575-yard par five that plays to another bi-level green. Lanny Wadkins claims that the third shot here is the key. "It's vital to keep the ball below the hole," he says. "If you're long, especially when the pin is cut on the second tier, you have no chance of getting it close."

The fairway at 18 swoops majestically uphill while banking from left to right like a speedway turn. On the card it reads 447 yards, but it plays longer. A drive to the left will leave a "shank" lie with the ball below the feet. The terrain on the right side is level but the approach may be blocked by the last of the ubiquitous eucalypti. The green sits in a natural amphitheater just beneath Riviera's opulent Spanish-style clubhouse. The toughest chip shot in golf may be the one played from the kikuyu grass on the hill to the left of the green when the pin is also on the left side. In such a situation, the only way to get up and down is to sink a forty-foot putt.

18th hole

16th hole

U.S. Open: June 10-12, 1948

Ben Hogan	67	72	68	69	276	1
Jimmy Demaret	71	70	68	69	278	2
Jim Turnesa	71	69	70	70	280	3
Bobby Locke	70	69	73	70	282	4
Sam Snead	69	69	73	72	283	5
Lew Worsham	67	74	71	73	285	6
Herman Barron	73	70	71	72	286	7
Johnny Bulla	73	72	75	67	287	T8
Toney Penna	70	72	73	72	287	T8
Smiley Quick	73	71	69	74	287	T8

PGA Championship: August 4-7, 1983

Hal Sutton	65	66	72	71	274	1
Jack Nicklaus	73	65	71	66	275	2
Peter Jacobsen	73	70	68	65	276	3
Pat McGowan	68	67	73	69	277	4
John Fought	67	69	71	71	278	5
Bruce Lietzke	67	71	70	71	279	T6
Fuzzy Zoeller	72	71	67	69	279	T6
Dan Pohl	72	70	69	69	280	8
Mike Reid	69	71	72	70	282	T9
Doug Tewell	74	72	69	67	282	T9
Scott Simpson	66	73	70	73	282	T9
Ben Crenshaw	68	66	71	77	282	T9
Jay Haas	68	72	69	73	282	T9

In 1983, Hal Sutton overcame the kikuyu grass, the field, and his own history of failure to take the PGA title. Photo: Peter Read Miller for Sports Illustrated © Time Inc.

Scorecard

HOLE	YARDS	PAR
1	501	5
2	460	4
3	434	4
4	238	3
5	426	4
6	170	3
7	406	4
8	368	4
9	418	4
OUT	3421	35
10	311	4
11	561	5
12	413	4
13	420	4
14	180	3
15	447	4
16	168	3
17	578	5
18	447	4
IN	3525	36
TOTAL	6946	71

GOLF *Magazine* Rankings:
30th in the World
19th in the U.S.A.

British Open
ROYAL BIRKDALE
SOUTHPORT, ENGLAND
British Open: 1954, 1961, 1965, 1971, 1976, 1983, 1991

Royal Birkdale didn't join the rotation of British Open venues until 1954, but in the almost four decades and six championships since then it has made up for lost time. No course in Britain—or America for that matter—has produced grander champions or higher drama.

The club was founded quietly in 1889, a year after the birth of golf in America, when nine residents of Birkdale, on England's Lancashire Coast, anted up one pound five pence each and drew up a set of bylaws. Within a few weeks, they had themselves a nine-hole course "of a thoroughly sporting character," designed at a cost of about $10. Five years later, with a swelling membership, the club moved to its current site, leasing land from a skeptical laird who insisted that the game of golf would be nothing more than a passing fancy "like ping pong."

It was a marvelous place for a golf course, a sweep of massive sandhills about two miles from the Irish Sea. Bernard Darwin, after visiting the course for the first time in 1922, wrote:

> There is nothing like a range of noble sandhills to set the heart of the average golfer leaping with excitement. . . . Nowhere else . . . are there hills so tall and numerous. . . . I can quite believe one enthusiastic gentleman who declared that in winter, when the hills were snowcapped, one could believe oneself among the Alps. "Hills" is an inadequate word at Birkdale: there are mountains and whole ranges of them.

In and among those hills the Birkdale golfers happily pursued their balls along the eighteen holes designed by George Lowe, the architect of nearby Royal Lytham & St. Annes. But it was not until 1932 that the club got a true championship layout, when architect Frederick Hawtree teamed with five-time Open Champion J.H. Taylor on a major redesign.

Their philosophy was to snake the holes through the flat-bottomed valleys among the dunes, thus creating a series of wind-guarded, self-enclosed tests, and a course unlike any other links in the British Isles. As a result, there are few blind shots, few uneven lies, except for the player who strays into the hills. Birkdale therefore has the reputation of being the fairest test of shotmaking on the current British Open rota. It rewards straight hitting and penalizes inaccuracy, in much the manner of America's modern target courses but with twice the charm. Another unwittingly modern aspect of Birkdale is the fact that it is a splendid spectator course; on several holes the looming sandhills serve as tee-to-green grandstands. As such, it was an unintentional prototype of the stadium courses now in vogue on the U.S. PGA Tour.

The galleries got their first look at Birkdale in the 1954 British Open, the tournament that saw the emergence of Peter Thomson, the quiet, businesslike Australian who would dominate the championship for the remainder of the decade.

Thomson is rarely given the credit he deserves for his achievements in the Open, partly because he scored his victories over fields that often lacked the top American stars of the day, partly because he never did very well on his playing visits to America (he won only one tournament, and never finished higher than fourth in a Masters or U.S. Open) and partly because of his straightforward manner on the course and occasional abrasiveness with the press.

But no one can deny the fact that he won three straight Opens from 1954 through 1956, then finished second to Bobby Locke in 1957 at St. Andrews before winning again in 1958 and returning to Birkdale for his swan song in 1965. Thomson's "three-peat" in 1954-56 marks the last time any major championship has been won three years in succession.

When Thomson came to the first tee of the final round, tied for the lead with Dai Rees and Syd Scott, he had no thoughts of three straight victories, but he may very well have feared the prospect of three straight near-misses. In both 1952 and 1953 he had finished as runner-up.

Thomson played the front nine in 35, then bogeyed the 12th but

17th hole

In the final round of the 1954 British Open, when Peter Thomson's second shot found a bunker twenty-five yards short of the green at Birkdale's 16th (now 17th), it looked as if he might finish second for the third straight year. "My heart was in my mouth when I saw the lie," Thomson recalled. "The ball was lying relatively cleanly, but it was on such a steep slope that, when I addressed it, my left foot was nearly a foot higher than my right. To make matters worse, there was another huge bunker directly between me and the green, so that if I caught the shot a bit too heavily I was dead. This was normally a birdie hole, but now I was just hoping to get my third shot into a position from which I could get down in two for a par five." He did better than that—he splashed the ball onto the green, three inches from the cup. With pars at the last two holes he took a one-stroke victory over Dai Rees, Bobby Locke, and Syd Scott.

birdied 14. After a par at 15, he found himself with a one-stroke lead over Rees and Tony Cerda of Spain with Bobby Locke a shot further back. When his second shot pelted in the face of a greenside bunker at the par-five 16th (now 17th), he seemed to be in trouble, but instead he played what he later called the finest pressure shot of his life, a perfectly judged splash that stopped inches from the hole for a birdie. Two routine pars later the title was his.

British golf writer Pat Ward-Thomas later observed that "for all the closeness of the scoring in perfect conditions, there was a sense of the inevitable about Thomson's victory. His poise and assurance were remarkable in a young man of 24. As he casually tapped in his final tiny putt with the back of the club, the winning of this Open seemed the easiest thing in the world."

The winning of the 1961 Open at Birkdale seemed one of the hardest things in the world. Winds blew throughout the tournament, and in round two they were at gale force, knocking down tents, sending milk crates through the air like kites, and dashing the chances of most of the field. But on that day, Arnold Palmer took charge, lashing his low teeshots into the hearts of the fairways and punching his irons smack at the flags. Playing while the gale was at its peak, he birdied five of the first six holes. Despite faltering at 7 and 9, he posted a 34 for the front side on a day when only three other players bettered 40. He eventually shot 73, but it could easily have been a 72. While standing over a bunker shot at the 16th hole, Palmer saw his ball move. Only he saw it, but he never hesi-

Arnold Palmer impressed the Birkdale galleries with his low, punched iron shots en route to victory in 1961. Photo: AP/Wide World Photos

OPPOSITE: *7th hole*

tated in calling the one-stroke penalty on himself, taking a double-bogey 7 for the hole. His two-round total of 143 left him tied with defending champion Kel Nagle, one stroke behind Dai Rees, who had been the only other player to handle the wind, with a 74.

The weather was so bad the next day that the third round was called off. When Rees began on Saturday he immediately relinquished his lead, with a triple-bogey 7 on the first hole, and at the turn Palmer found himself with a four-stroke lead. But the Welshman, who had come so close so often to winning the championship, played on heroically and finished with a 71 to Palmer's 69. Nagle meanwhile faded with a 75, so with the afternoon round to go, it was Palmer one up on Rees.

The front nine again belonged to Arnold, who built his lead to four. But Dai Rees finished strongly, playing the last four holes with three birdies and a par to come in at 285. But once again, that was good for second, as Palmer matched his 72 and posted a 284. The key shot, and one of the most famous in British Open history, occurred at the 15th hole, number 16 on the current course. Trying to shave the corner on the left-to-right dogleg, Palmer put his ball in terrible jail near a blackberry bush in the right-hand rough. It

was a lie from which most mortals would use a wedge and a prayer. But Palmer took a 6-iron, closed down the face of the club, and gouged at the ball with all his might. He not only got it out, he got it to the green, where it settled fifteen feet from the hole, virtually guaranteeing his par.

With three more pars coming in, he had his victory. Today, a plaque marks the point of origin of this shot, which was pivotal not simply because it carried Arnie to the first of two straight British Open titles but because his victory ignited a renewed interest in the championship among American players, an interest which has grown to such an extent that many players—and even a few Americans—consider the British Open the ultimate championship.

Astonishingly, despite the harsh weather Palmer's winning score was only one stroke higher than Thomson's had been in 1954. In some quarters, this was seen as a further reflection of the superior quality of American players and another slap in the face of Thomson and the rest as second-class players. After all, Thomson, despite his domination of the Open, had never beaten a field that included Palmer or Player or Nicklaus.

11th hole

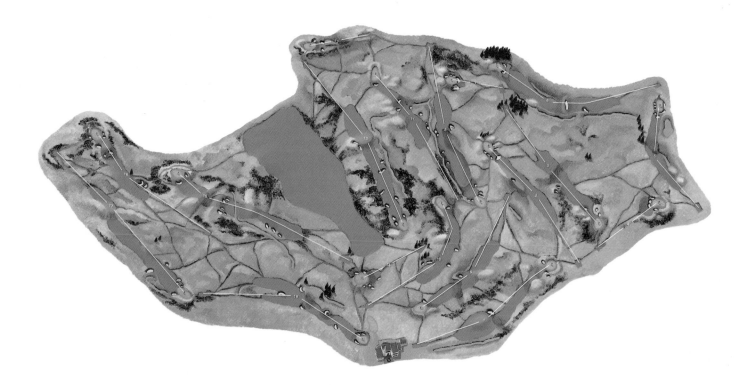

Until 1965, when he came back to Birkdale and beat all three. Thomson did not make an auspicious start, his 74 leaving him six strokes behind the pacesetter and defending Champion, Tony Lema, but his second round of 68 moved him within two of Lema and Bruce Devlin.

A strong wind blew up for the final day, the last year in which the Open finished with two rounds on the same day, and Thomson's 72 in the morning gave him a one-stroke edge over Lema and Devlin, with Christy O'Connor, Roberto DeVicenzo, and Arnold Palmer a stroke further back. When Thomson made the turn in even par his lead grew to three, but it soon fell to one as he missed a series of short putts.

By this time the course had gone through a bit of updating and lengthening at the hands of Frank Hawtree, the original architect's son, with the result that Birkdale had the longest finish in golf—its final four holes included three par fives and measured 536, 401, 510, and 512 yards. Coming to the 17th tee, Thomson knew he needed a par and birdie to guarantee his victory. He went one better and made two flawless birdies, for a two-stroke victory. His final score was 285—two higher than in 1954 and one above Palmer's wind-battered performance in 1961—but it was Thomson's proudest moment, because this time he had beaten the best in the world.

In an article for *GOLF Magazine*, CBS-TV commentator Ben Wright recalled the victor on the evening of his win, walking into the lounge of the hotel where all the players were staying. Said Wright, "I have never seen a more seraphic smile than that which creased Thomson's feaures as he peeked into the cocktail bar and watched Nicklaus and Palmer [who had finished 12th and 13th]

'drowning their sorrows.' Thomson's triumph was truly complete at that moment."

In 1971 Birkdale served as the site for the 100th Open Championship as Lee Trevino wrote his name into the record books by becoming only the fourth man in history to win the U.S. and British Opens in the same year. Fresh from a playoff victory over Nicklaus at Merion, as well as a win in the Canadian Open two weeks later, Trevino was at the peak of his form. At Birkdale he chose to play the smaller British ball, claiming that it gave him more distance.

When he concluded his second round by playing holes 15 through 18 in birdie-birdie-par-eagle Trevino joined Tony Jacklin in the lead at 139. One behind them was Liang Huan Lu of Formosa, henceforth known as Mr. Lu, who had the endearing habit of tipping his porkpie hat after each applause from the gallery. Lu did not hit a long ball but he did hit a straight one, and thereby dogged the heels of the leaders.

A 69 in the third round put Trevino in front alone at 208, a stroke ahead of Jacklin and Lu. And as had Thomson and Palmer in Opens past at Birkdale, he surged even further ahead on the front nine of the final round, one-putting seven of the first eight greens en route to a 31 that staked him to a four-stroke margin over Lu.

At the 17th tee, Trevino's lead was still three, with Lu the only man with a chance to catch him. No one could have guessed at the drama that would ensue from that point. On his penultimate drive Trevino's trademark fade failed to materialize and instead he watched his ball sail into a hillside of willow scrub on the left. Taking a wedge, he chopped at it but moved it only a few feet. His third shot flew across the fairway into rough on the right. Still short of the green in four, he pitched on and two-putted for a double-bogey 7. Lu meanwhile had an opportunity to birdie the hole and tie things up, but failed to reach the green in two, pitched rather indifferently, and settled for a par, leaving Trevino with the one-stroke lead.

At 18 Lu's second shot darted well left of the green and struck a woman spectator, bringing her to the ground. She was not seriously injured, but Lu was unnerved, and he could not get his pitch closer than eight feet. Trevino's approach landed just beyond the green, and he putted up to within twenty inches. Lu then courageously sank his eight-footer, forcing Trevino to hole his for the victory. Lee did so, taking almost no time before dropping the putt for his third national championship in a month.

With the exception of one player, every champion at Birkdale has been a multiple winner of the British Open. Peter Thomson and Tom Watson each have five victories, Arnold Palmer and Lee Trevino each have two. Furthermore, in each case the victory was part of a streak of consecutive Open triumphs, three by Thomson, two by each of the others. But the exception is no slouch, he's Johnny Miller, the 1973 U.S. Open Champion and, except for Nicklaus and Trevino, the winningest player of the 1970s.

When Miller played his best, no one—not even Nicklaus or Trevino—could touch him, and at Birkdale in 1976 he played his best. Nicklaus finished in a tie for second that year, and he was six strokes behind.

The British weather in the summer of 1976 was almost as hot as Johnny, and the Birkdale fairways were dry and hard. As a result, distance wasn't important but accuracy was, since drives that were not straight (and even those that were straight but were too long for the doglegging fairways) invariably bounded and rolled into trouble. Playing a two-piece Slazenger ball under a British contract, Miller chose a 1-iron off most of the tees, still got 250 yards of carry and roll, and missed only two fairways all week.

Nonetheless, Miller did not lead this tournament until the final round. The big story was a 19-year-old Spaniard named Severiano Ballesteros, who led or shared the lead on each of the first three days, catapulting to the top after day three on the heels of an eagle at the 526-yard 17th. With 18 to go, Ballesteros was at 211, Miller at 213. Nicklaus was in a group tied for fourth at 216.

But the final day belonged to Miller. Although Ballesteros birdied the 1st hole to take a three-stroke lead, Miller was in command thereafter, as the young Spaniard's errant teeshots hurt him. Two-stroke swings occurred at the 2nd, 6th, and 8th holes, and suddenly it was Miller with the three-stroke advantage. When Johnny birdied the short 12th and then eagled 13, the outcome was a foregone conclusion. Miller's closing 66 tied the Birkdale record.

However, the 1976 British Open will always be remembered not only as Miller's victory but as Seve's coming out party. He closed the tournament in style, eagling 17 and birdieing 18 to share sec-

ond place with Nicklaus. Over the next dozen years he would win three British Opens, two of them at nearby Lytham and one at St. Andrews. In that span only one player would compile a better record—Tom Watson.

Watson had scored his first Open victory on his first try, at Carnoustie in 1975, and would notch his last in 1983, at Birkdale. In weather more typical of the U.S. Open than the British—four windless days with temperatures in the 90s—Watson posted rounds of 67-68-70-70 to defend successfully the title he had taken at Troon a year earlier. His 275 is a Birkdale record, and the third and fourth round cut scores of 146 and 217 set new records for the championship, remarkable in view of the fact that the fairways were narrow and the rough was more lush than in any past Open.

It was a strong cast in contention, and after three rounds Watson, at 205, led Craig Stadler by one, Nick Faldo, Ray Floyd, and David Graham by two, Lee Trevino by three, and Hale Irwin by four. Irwin should have been a stroke closer. One of his seventy-two strokes came when he missed a putt that was only two inches long. It turned out to be a major mistake, as on Sunday Irwin shot 67 to finish tied for second with Andy Bean—one stroke behind.

Watson struggled a bit on the front nine of the final day but took charge with birdies at 11, 13, and 16. Standing on the 17th tee, he needed two pars to win. He got his five at 17, then played a long straight drive from the 18th tee, leaving an approach of 213 yards on this hole which had been converted for the Open from a short five to a long and difficult four. From there he struck what he later characterized as the finest 2-iron of his life. It never left the flag, and settled fifteen feet from the hole, guaranteeing him his fifth British Open in nine years. No player has hoisted the old claret jug so many times in so short a period.

At one point, four of Birkdale's last six holes were par fives, and its back nine had a par of 38, with par for the front at 34. Today, for championship play, the nines are a bit more balanced at 35 and 37. Hole number 6 is now a par five.

But at least two other holes on the outward half can play like fives, and one of those is the 1st, a wake-up call of 448 yards. Most of the long holes at Birkdale favor a fade, but not number 1 whose broad, flat fairway bends from right to left. For shorter hitters, the hole is almost a double dogleg, a sand dune just short of the green on the right inhibiting a running approach from that side so that the entry to the green actually angles a bit from left to right. Before the '83 Open that dune was lowered a bit so that players with teeshots on the right side would not have to walk to the left side of the fairway in order to get a clear view of the flagstick. The change was made in the interest of eliminating delays in play.

Number 2, one of the few holes that has seen little change from the original George Lowe design, is another lengthy right-to-left par four, threaded through a natural valley in the sandhills. A half dozen bunkers dot the path to the green. The 3rd then runs back parallel past more dunes to a green nestled snugly among hillocks.

Hail to the conqueror. After striking the spectacular 2-iron to the final hole in 1983, Tom Watson strides toward the completion of an extraordinary record: five British Open titles in nine years. Photo: © Phil Sheldon

The longest of the short holes occurs at the 4th where, from a slightly elevated tee, the assignment is to find a target 203 yards away that is fronted by bunkers and backed by gnarly scrub. For many years a massive dune ran across this fairway, obscuring the pin from the view of anyone playing from the forward tee. The Birkdale club history notes: "A number of members went to their graves firmly convinced that they had achieved that elusive prize, a hole in one, whereas the sad truth of the matter was that a shot hit adjacent to the pin was occasionally 'helped' into the hole by a caddie, who was fully aware of the reward he could expect if his jubilant employer believed he had holed in one."

In 1967, the club decided to eliminate the blindness (and thus the chicanery) by reducing the height of the dune. Unfortunately, the contractor in charge of the work misunderstood his assignment and eliminated the dune entirely, thus robbing the hole of its most distinguishing characteristic. But it remains a challenge, particularly when played into the wind.

Also in 1967, number 5 underwent a change. Originally a dead-straight hole, it was susceptible to flooding, and in order to alleviate the problem the fairway was rerouted to the left of its former path. A ridge was created on the right side of the new fairway, thus creating a sharp left-to-right dogleg.

Today the 6th hole is a relatively easy par five. For most of its life, however, it was a virtually impossible par four. In 1971, the British Open field played it in an average of 4.63 strokes. The main feature is a low line of dunes that crosses the fairway just beyond the 250-yard mark, one of the only such instances at Birkdale where the dunes cross rather than parallel the play of the hole. Since these dunes can't be carried, the teeshot distance is limited and the length of the approach on this 498-yard hole is maximized. After that it's the little 7th, a charming but frightening shot of 154 yards played from a high tee to another green cradled in the hills and hugged by five bunkers.

Another quintet of bunkers greets teeshots at the 8th, and the distant green is guarded by five more, making this lengthy 458-yard par four an examination in accuracy as well as strength. The only truly blind teeshot on the course is at 9, where on busy days the members climb a watchtower to the left of the tee and check that the coast is clear before hitting their drives. The narrow, hogbacked fairway has been criticized as too small a target, but a well-played fade will hold it and leave a shortish iron to a plateau green that falls off toward the back.

The back nine begins with a pair of par fours that require accurate hitting from the tee. Number 10 moves from right to left, but if the teeshot is a hook rather than a draw, trees and rough await. In the 1983 British Open, South Africa's Denis Watson had his problems here, reaching the green in four and then taking **six** more strokes for an even 10, two of those strokes coming on a penalty for hitting a moving ball. The elevated tee at number 11 makes judgment of the teeshot a challenge, particularly in a wind, and the narrow hillside green is set at a diagonal to the path of the fairway.

The 12th hole, a 184-yard par three set in the dunes, is the youngest on the course, a 1963 addition by Frank Hawtree which involved the removal of 6,000 tons of sand. The hole had actually been a part of the original plan submitted by Hawtree's father in 1932, but it had been omitted because of a lack of funds. When the 12th hole was added to the course, the former 17th was omitted, and former holes 12 through 16 became 13 through 17.

Number 13 was lucky for Johnny Miller in 1976. It was on this 508-yard par five in the final round that he chipped in for an eagle that all but guaranteed him victory. Today, however, an eagle will be very unlikely on this hole. It is now a par four of 472 yards from the championship tee.

The 14th hole, a 199-yard par three, will haunt Hale Irwin until his dying day. This was where he missed the two-inch putt which, as it turned out, was the stroke by which he failed to gain a playoff with Watson for the 1983 Open.

ABOVE: *15th hole*. BELOW: *18th hole*

Number 15 may be the finest hole on the course. Two strong, straight shots are needed to carry the echelon of bunkers at about the 475-yard mark, and if either swing is a bit loose, the ball will find dense rough on both sides. One of the distinguishing features of Birkdale is the variety of shrubs and flora that clings to its hills— creeping willow, sea buckthorn, creeping blackberry, yellow wort, marsh orchids, and, of course, the tenacious willow scrub whose pretty primrose blossoms belie its dangerous grasp.

Number 16, the hole where Palmer had his heroics, calls for a careful teeshot with a long iron or a driver played with the confident fade of Trevino. It must clear a tangle of rough and scrub and find a fairway that angles rightward toward an elevated green. In a wind, the approach to this green may be the hardest shot on the course.

Two huge dunes, nicknamed Scylla and Charybdis, loom on either side of the entrance to the fairway at 17. If the teeshot can be threaded into the thirty-yard gap between them, the hole can be

had. In a practice round for the 1965 Open, Jack Nicklaus once got home with a drive and a wedge. But it was one of those dunes that led to Trevino's near-fatal seven in the closing round of 1971.

The finishing hole is a long, testing four in the tradition of those at Troon, Royal St. George's, and nearby Lytham. From its tee up in the dunes, it calls for a powerful drive that also avoids three well-positioned bunkers. From there the assignment is a straight and strong shot such as the one played by Tom Watson to win in 1983.

Many dramatic victories have been consummated on this green, but surely the most stirring moment came on a tie. In the 1969 Ryder Cup matches Great Britain and America were tied as the final pairing—Tony Jacklin vs. Jack Nicklaus—came to 18. Jacklin had just sunk a fifty-five-foot eagle putt on 17 to square their match. At 18 both men hit the green, and it came down to two putts, one of four feet for Nicklaus, one of just over two feet for Jacklin. Nicklaus sank his, then in a gesture of supreme sportsmanship, conceded Jacklin's putt for the halve.

British Open: July 7-9, 1954

Peter Thomson	72	71	69	71	283	1
Bobby Locke	74	71	69	70	284	T2
Syd Scott	76	67	69	72	284	T2
Dai Rees	72	71	69	72	284	T2
J. Adams	73	75	69	69	286	T5
Joe Turnesa	72	72	71	71	286	T5
Antonio Cerda	71	71	73	71	286	T5
Peter Alliss	72	74	71	70	287	T8
S.L. King	69	74	74	70	287	T8
Flory Van Donck	77	71	70	71	289	T10
Jimmy Demaret	73	71	74	71	289	T10

British Open: July 7-10, 1971

Lee Trevino	69	70	69	70	278	1
Liang Huan Lu	70	70	69	70	279	2
Tony Jacklin	69	70	70	71	280	3
C. Defoy	72	72	68	69	281	4
Charles Coody	74	71	70	68	283	T5
Jack Nicklaus	71	71	72	69	283	T5
Billy Casper	70	72	75	67	284	T7
Gary Player	71	70	71	72	284	T7
Doug Sanders	73	71	74	67	285	T9
Peter Thomson	70	73	73	69	285	T9

British Open: July 14-17, 1983

Tom Watson	67	68	70	70	275	1
Hale Irwin	69	68	72	67	276	T2
Andy Bean	70	69	70	67	276	T2
Graham Marsh	69	70	74	64	277	4
Lee Trevino	69	66	73	70	278	5
Seve Ballesteros	71	71	69	68	279	T6
Harold Henning	71	69	70	69	279	T6
Denis Durnian	73	66	74	67	280	T8
C. O'Connor, Jr.	72	69	71	68	280	T8
Bill Rogers	67	71	73	69	280	T8
Nick Faldo	68	68	71	73	280	T8

British Open: July 11-14, 1961

Arnold Palmer	70	73	69	72	284	1
Dai Rees	68	74	71	72	285	2
Neil Coles	70	77	69	72	288	T3
C. O'Connor, Jr.	71	77	67	73	288	T3
Eric Brown	73	76	70	70	289	T5
Kel Nagle	68	75	75	71	289	T5
Peter Thomson	75	72	70	73	290	7
K. Bousfield	71	77	75	68	291	T8
Peter Alliss	73	75	72	71	291	T8
Syd Scott	76	75	71	71	293	T10
Harold Henning	68	74	75	76	293	T10

British Open: July 7-10, 1976

Johnny Miller	72	68	73	66	279	1
Jack Nicklaus	74	70	72	69	285	T2
Seve Ballesteros	69	69	73	74	285	T2
Raymond Floyd	76	67	73	70	286	4
Mark James	76	72	74	66	288	T5
Hubert Green	72	70	78	68	288	T5
Tom Kite	70	74	73	71	288	T5
C. O'Connor, Jr.	69	73	75	71	288	T5
Tommy Horton	74	69	72	73	288	T5
V. Fernandez	79	71	69	70	289	T10
Peter Butler	74	72	73	70	289	T10
Norio Suzuki	69	75	75	70	289	T10
George Burns	75	69	75	70	289	T10

Scorecard

HOLE	YARDS	PAR
1	448	4
2	417	4
3	409	4
4	203	3
5	346	4
6	490	5
7	154	3
8	458	4
9	414	4
OUT	3339	35
10	395	4
11	409	4
12	184	4
13	472	4
14	199	3
15	543	5
16	414	4
17	525	5
18	472	4
IN	3613	36
TOTAL	6952	71

British Open: July 7-9, 1965

Peter Thomson	74	68	72	72	285	1
Brian Huggett	73	68	76	70	287	T2
C. O'Connor, Jr.	69	73	74	71	287	T2
R. De Vicenzo	74	69	73	72	288	4
Bernard Hunt	74	74	70	71	289	T5
Kel Nagle	74	70	73	72	289	T5
Tony Lema	68	72	75	74	289	T5
Sebastian Miguel	73	73	72	73	290	T8
Bruce Devlin	71	69	75	75	290	T8
John Panton	74	74	75	70	293	T10
Max Faulkner	74	72	74	73	293	T10

GOLF Magazine Rankings:
24th in the World
8th in Great Britain & Ireland

ROYAL LYTHAM
& ST. ANNES

LYTHAM ST. ANNES, ENGLAND
British Open: 1926, 1952, 1958, 1963, 1969, 1974, 1979, 1988

In 1926 Bobby Jones mastered Royal Lytham & St. Annes, but in the seven British Opens since then no American has followed him. For more than sixty years, Lytham has remained the only active Open course where a U.S. professional has never won.

The fact is, Jones almost didn't win here, because Jones almost didn't play. When he left America in early June of that year he had no intentions of competing in the British Open. He was going over for the Walker Cup matches and then the British Amateur at Muirfield. But a couple of days before he was due to board the steamship *Aquitania* for the return trip, he decided to stay and play. Jones felt a debt to the Open, having walked off the course in anger at St. Andrews in 1921.

This was the first year in which qualifying rounds were held, and Jones joined the group at Sunningdale where he stunned everyone with a score of 66—33 swings and 33 putts. In those days, it was near perfection. His mastery may have been a good omen, because Lytham had been added to the Open rotation (replacing Prestwick) after a facelift by Sunningdale's designer, H.S. Colt.

Jones greeted the course with an erratic tee-to-green game, but one-putted each of the last four greens to post a 72, then added another 72 the next day to take a share of the lead with Bill Mehlhorn, one ahead of Walter Hagen and two up on Al Watrous.

But by the final afternoon it was Watrous who had taken command. In those days, pairings were done at random, but luck had brought together Jones and Watrous for the last round. With five holes to go, Watrous had a two-stroke lead over Jones when he began to show the strain of the competition, three-putting both 14 and 15 to fall back into a tie.

They were still even after their teeshots at 17, but the edge was decidedly with Watrous, who had found the fairway whereas Jones had pulled his ball into trouble. There is some debate as to whether the ball settled in a bunker or in a sandy area in the rough. What is beyond debate is that Jones struck a masterful shot, lofting the ball over the dunes and onto the green, inside Watrous's ball.

Unnerved, Watrous again three-putted and Jones went on to victory. Today, a plaque marks the spot from which the shot was played. With typical British understatement it reads simply "R.T. Jones, Jnr., The Open Championship, 25th June 1926."

The first four finishers were Americans—Jones, Watrous, Hagen, and George Von Elm—and Americans took eight of the top thirteen places. Flamboyant Hagen, two strokes behind with one hole to play, had a long-shot chance of tieing Jones, and he made the most of it theatrically if not practically. After a strong drive, he walked up to inspect the green, then asked his caddie to tend the flagstick so that his iron shot might have a better chance of going into the hole. Then he marched back to his ball, 150 yards down the fairway, and played a valiant shot that jumped over the hole. Ironically, had the pin been in, the ball might have hit the stick and dropped. Instead, it bounded into a bunker in back of the green, and Hagen double-bogeyed the hole, finishing four behind Jones.

Two interesting incidents bracketed Jones's final eighteen. After his morning round, he had gone back to the Majestic Hotel for lunch and had left his player's badge there by mistake. When he returned to the Lytham gate, the guard on duty didn't recognize him and would not grant him admission. Unfazed, Bobby went to the turnstiles, paid a half crown, and bought himself a ticket to his own victory.

The other incident relates to the fact that there is no photo of the winning putt. Jones's final stroke was from a distance of two feet or so, and as he prepared to hit it, a newsreel cameraman began to crank into action. Distracted, Jones straightened up and pointed an imperious finger at the offender. The man put down his camera, and apparently so did every other photojournalist in the area.

It was the first of two straight British Opens and three in five years by Jones, who returned to the States and at Inwood won his first U.S. Open as well, thus becoming the first man to win both national championships in the same year.

Over a quarter-century passed before the Open came back, and

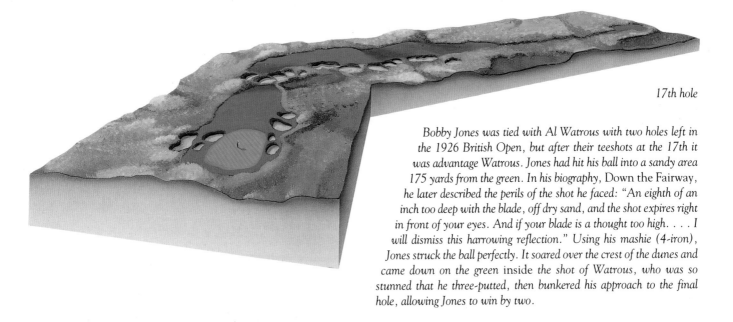

17th hole

Bobby Jones was tied with Al Watrous with two holes left in the 1926 British Open, but after their teeshots at the 17th it was advantage Watrous. Jones had hit his ball into a sandy area 175 yards from the green. In his biography, Down the Fairway, he later described the perils of the shot he faced: "An eighth of an inch too deep with the blade, off dry sand, and the shot expires right in front of your eyes. And if your blade is a thought too high. . . . I will dismiss this harrowing reflection." Using his mashie (4-iron), Jones struck the ball perfectly. It soared over the crest of the dunes and came down on the green inside the shot of Watrous, who was so stunned that he three-putted, then bunkered his approach to the final hole, allowing Jones to win by two.

its return marked the beginning of a parade of international champions at Lytham, the most diverse ethnic variety of any major championship course. In the past forty years Opens at Lytham have been won by a Briton, an Australian, a Spaniard, a New Zealander, and two South Africans, all of them the finest players their countries have produced.

South African struck first in the portly form of another Bobby, Arthur D'Arcy Locke. During the late '40s and early '50s, Locke was arguably the best player in the world. He had won the British Open in both 1949 and 1950 before finishing joint runner-up to Max Faulkner in 1951.

Locke was not a stylist, but he knew his game. He played every shot with a wide, sweeping hook; in a right-to-left wind, he would sometimes aim fifty yards or more to the right of the target, then draw the ball back, to the amazement of the gallery. He was also the finest putter of his era, and a fierce competitor. When he came to America for the first time, he played a series of exhibition matches against Sam Snead, winning twelve out of sixteen. Then he took the Tour by storm, winning six of the fourteen events he entered. In one of them, he beat Ben Hogan by ten strokes; in another he beat him by fifteen.

At Lytham, with virtually no prominent Americans in the field, Locke was touted as a 4-1 pick to win. He came through, but hardly with flying colors. His last two rounds were 74-73, and at the penultimate hole he missed a par putt of just eighteen inches. But this was an Open where no one sparkled, so "Old Muffin Face," as he was known, squeaked out a one-stroke victory, his third title in four years.

The man who finished second to Locke was a 22-year-old Australian named Peter Thomson. Five years later, at St. Andrews, Thomson would again finish second to Locke. But in three of those five intervening years—three in a row from 1954 to 1956—he won. So when Locke and Thomson returned to Royal Lytham in 1958 the score was four Opens for Locke, three for Thomson. When they left,

it was four apiece. The old claret jug that Bobby Locke brought to Lytham went home with Peter Thomson.

Locke was never a factor in this championship, or any subsequent Open for that matter, his first round of 76 leaving him an even ten strokes off Thomson's pace. After a 72 in the second round, the Australian found himself in third place, behind Christy O'Connor at 135 and Leopoldo Ruiz at 136. Thomson was tied with Dave Thomas, the Welshman he would ultimately have to beat.

Scoring in round three was torrid by the standards of those days. Thomson took the lead with a 67, but Belgium's Flory Van Donck matched him, and Eric Brown posted a 65. Brown remained a factor until the final moments of the afternoon when he, O'Connor, and Ruiz each came to the last hole needing a par to tie for the championship, but none of them could do it. It was an extremely international group that came down the stretch that afternoon, and when it was all over the first seven places belonged to men from seven different countries: Australia, Wales, Scotland, Ireland, Belgium, Argentina, and South Africa. Ironically, at this championship played in England no home-bred man finished higher than a tie for eighth. The low American was the old American, Gene Sarazen, who at the age of 56 posted a 288 to tie for sixteenth, ten strokes back.

But in the end it was a struggle between Thomson and Thomas. The Australian had relinquished his lead early but fought back to tie Thomas at the 17th. Both men reached the last hole in two and two-putted for pars. The playoff was something of an anti-climax, with Thomson winning 139 to 143.

Another playoff marked the next Open at Lytham when in 1963 Bob Charles prevailed over Phil Rodgers, thus becoming the only left-handed player and the only New Zealander ever to win a major championship.

It was Rodgers who took command of the early going, his rounds of 67-68 giving him a one-stroke edge on the ever-present Thomson, three over Jack Nicklaus, four over 1960 champion Kel

Nagle, and five over Charles. But in round three Charles demonstrated why he is thought to be one of the greatest putters in the history of the game, sinking several impressive putts for birdies and pars en route to a 66 as Rodgers fell to a 73. With eighteen holes left he was one ahead of Thomson, two up on Nicklaus and Rodgers.

Thomson surprised all by playing his worst round ever while in contention for an Open—a disastrous 78 that took him to fifth place. Meanwhile Nicklaus was able to make up only one of the two strokes he needed. At the final hole a par would have put him in the playoff, but he found sand on his drive and bogeyed, carding a 70 to Charles's 71. Rodgers, however, scrambled to a 69 that secured the tie. Once again, the playoff was anticlimactic as Charles continued his brilliant putting and shot 140 while Rodgers struggled to 148. Not surprisingly, this was the last of the 36-hole playoffs. The R&A went to eighteen holes in 1970, and by 1985 a new system was in place involving an immediate playoff on either four or five holes, depending on the configuration of the hosting course.

Charles never won another major championship, but he did come close in 1969 when the Open returned to Lytham. He took the first-round lead with a 66, then added a 69 to go one up on Christy O'Connor at the halfway mark. But when his putting failed in round three he fell to a 75 and a new name rose to the top of the leaderboard: Tony Jacklin.

Here, for the first time in nearly two decades, was an Englishman, the 27-year-old son of a truck driver from Scunthorpe, with a chance to win the national championship. For three years Jacklin had risen through the ranks, first winning local assistant pro championships, then adding victories in Africa and New Zealand, then the Dunlop Masters, and finally a U.S. event, the 1968 Jacksonville Open.

He had started the tournament with a birdie 2 that had spurred him toward a 70. He had followed with a 68 and then another 70. At 208, he held a two-stroke lead over Charles, five over Jack Nicklaus, Brian Huggett, Roberto DeVicenzo, and Peter Thomson, who at age 39 was once again playing well at Lytham.

Jacklin and Charles were paired together in the final round. After Charles bogeyed the 1st and Jacklin birdied both 3 and 4, his lead grew. Through nine holes he was four strokes clear of the field.

Charles then began to come back, gaining strokes at the 10th and 13th. But that was as close as he came. On the 18th tee, Jacklin retained a two-stroke edge. Still, on this testing par four dotted with bunkers, many others had lost opportunities in Opens past. Not Jacklin. He played a magnificent drive and a green-splitting iron to within 12 feet of the pin. The jubilant cheers of the crowd rang out after he tapped in for his final four and the first British Open victory by a British golfer in eighteen years. The following June he traveled to Hazeltine and won the U.S. Open, becoming the first Briton ever to hold both titles at the same time.

Jacklin's win at Lytham not only launched his own career, it spurred a steady revival of European professional golf. During the 1960s only two major championships had been won by players from Britain and Europe—the British Open victories by Jacklin and Thomson. By the 1980s the tables had turned, with the Europeans winning five British Opens and four Masters. In addition they won the Ryder Cup twice and tied it once, one of those victories coming for the first time ever on American soil.

Gary Player had to hit his final stroke left-handed from the side of the clubhouse, but he had room to spare on the leaderboard and won the 1974 British Open by four strokes. Photo: Bettmann/Hulton

Prior to that renaissance, the "foreign threat" in most major championships consisted of one man. Prior to 1980 only one non-American player had won the Masters—but he had won it three times. He had also won a U.S. Open, two PGA's, and three British Opens. Today he remains the most prolific international champion the game has ever known, with well over 100 victories worldwide. Small in stature, but possessed of massive determination and indomitable spirit, he is South Africa's Gary Player.

The last of his three British Open victories—over three different decades—came at Lytham in 1974. Although 37 years old, Player was in superb condition as he has remained throughout his career. What's more, he had revamped his swing at the start of the year, had won the Masters, and had made a strong bid for victory in the U.S. Open. With typical effusiveness, he was predicting he'd climb to new heights.

At Lytham he was in his element, a course that required accuracy more than length and a course whose more than 200 bunkers might impede others but would merely enable him to show that he was the best sand player in the world. In addition, there was a strong wind most of the week, and in two decades of playing all over the globe, Gary Player had learned how to stand up to a wind. When in the second round the gusts blew at 30 miles per hour, Player turned in the day's low score, a 68 that put him at 137 for thirty-six holes and gave him a five-stroke lead, the largest halfway lead in forty years. He slipped to a 75 in round three, but under the windy conditions it cost him only two strokes. With 18 to go he was three ahead of Peter Oosterhuis and four clear of the man who at Lytham seemed always to lurk but never lead, Jack Nicklaus.

The last day belonged to Player. He birdied the 1st and 2nd holes and reached the turn in 32. Then, when it looked as if Oosterhuis might gain a little ground, Player chipped in from the back of the green for a birdie at 13. With two holes left, his lead was six. It was at 17 that he got a bit of a scare when his second shot thumped into heavy rough to the left of the green. At first, the ball could not be found. With Oosterhuis facing a makable birdie putt, and the specter of having to go back down the fairway and play a fourth shot, with the likely result a 6 or 7, things were not as rosy as they had seemed.

Thousands of spectators had seen the ball bury in the grass, but they could not help search for it, except to shout directions to the players and caddies who were on their knees sifting through the grass. But just before the expiration of the five-minute search time allowed by the Rules, Player's caddie, Rabbit Dyer, unearthed the ball. Gary played without delay and made a 5, salvaging five/sixths of his lead. At 18 he made another five after having to play his third shot left-handed from the side of the clubhouse behind the final green. Still, the victory was his, by a comfortable four strokes.

Player's victory was his eighth major championship, surpassing Palmer. When in 1978 he won the Masters, he tied Hogan's nine majors. Only Walter Hagen (eleven), Bobby Jones (thirteen), and

Jack Nicklaus (eighteen) have more. Among active players, Tom Watson has eight victories, and few other players have a chance of breaking into this elite group. One is Seve Ballesteros. Now in his mid-30s, Ballesteros has five majors. Three of those are British Opens, and two of those British Opens were won at Lytham.

Ballesteros came to Lytham on the Friday before the 1979 Championship and spent the next seven days learning as much as he could about the course. By the time the bell rang he had played 126 practice holes. He was ready.

But having spent a week learning how to find Lytham's narrow fairways, he spent much of the next four days missing them. To give him his due, the fairways were hard as rock, and the tournament was played in four days of strong wind, as it had been five years earlier. The last five holes, heading straight into the breeze, played so long that two of the par fours—the 15th and 17th—were virtually unreachable.

The Spaniard's opening 73 was good enough under the conditions, but it left him eight behind the surprise leader, Bill Longmuir, a little-known British professional who had gone out early in the day, before the wind had geared up. Longmuir, playing the front nine mostly downwind, turned in a record 29, then came back in 36 for a 65. His closest pursuer was the reigning U.S. Open Champion, Hale Irwin, at 68.

The next day, as everyone expected, Longmuir toppled with a 74 as Ballesteros made his move on a 65 that was capped by a brilliant finish. On this day many reckoned the last five holes to be playing to pars of 4-5-4-5-4. Seve played them in 3-3-4-3-3. When Irwin, who teed off two hours later than Ballesteros, was told of this feat, he was incredulous. "He did what?" said Irwin. "He must have cut out some holes!"

Irwin posted a second straight 68 to take the lead, but now Ballesteros was only two behind. On Saturday, as the wind died down a bit, the rain came. It was a difficult day for scoring, and Irwin and Ballesteros, paired together, each shot 75 but maintained their positions at the top of the pack. Although the scores were identical, the way they achieved them couldn't have been in greater contrast. Irwin, the steady stylist, kept the ball in play but failed to ignite a charge of any kind. Meanwhile, the powerful Ballesteros hit his teeshots in all directions but rescued himself with magical trouble shots and superb putting.

The next day Ballesteros played one of the more dramatic rounds in Open history, beginning with a birdie two at the 1st and highlighted by another succession of brilliant recoveries from all points on the compass. His Houdini act took the air out of Irwin's sails, and at the turn the lead had switched. Seve, with a 34, was

OVERLEAF: *9th hole*. INSET LEFT: *9th hole*. INSET RIGHT: *In 1979, a youthful Seve Ballesteros won his first major championship, driving the ball in all directions but escaping like Houdini and putting like an angel. Photo: © Phil Sheldon*

one ahead of Irwin, on 37. When Irwin three-putted 11, he lost another stroke.

Two stretch holes were emblematic of their battle. The first was 13, where Ballesteros nearly drove the green but caught a bunker, then exploded to the fringe before holing a chip shot for a birdie. Irwin meanwhile hit a shorter, straighter drive, a pitch shot to twenty feet, and two-putted for par to go three down. He remained that way until the next pivotal hole, number 16. Playing downwind, this was another nearly drivable par four for Seve, and he gave it all he had, almost decapitating himself on his follow-through. It was a big hit, but also a wide one—nearly forty yards right of the fairway—and it finished near a hospitality tent, underneath an illegally parked car. He was lucky. Since the car was locked, it was an immovable obstruction and Seve was allowed a free drop. He played a fine pitch over a nest of bunkers to within twenty feet of the hole, then rammed home the putt for a birdie. Irwin, who made another conventional par, could only shake his head.

Ballesteros hit two more errant drives at 17 and 18, but made two more deft recoveries and two more pars to come in with a round of 70, the lowest score among the top ten players. He had hit only one fairway with his driver, and had missed each of the last six. In the process, he had absolutely demoralized Irwin, who crumbled to a 78. As the twosome approached the last green Irwin pulled a handkerchief from his pocket and waved it in surrender. "I cannot believe anyone can drive as badly as that and still win an Open," he said later.

But win Ballesteros did, and by three strokes over Ben Crenshaw and the ever-present Jack Nicklaus. (In four Open appearances at Lytham, Jack had finished third, sixth, third, and second.) At age 22, the dashing Spaniard became the youngest British Open victor since Willie Auchterlonie in 1893, and only the second European to win the title, the other being Frenchman Arnaud Massy in 1907. Five years later he became the first European to win two Opens, with a dramatic triumph at St. Andrews. Four years after that he returned to Lytham for victory number three.

Ironically, his 1979 win at Lytham had not only launched him into the international spotlight, it had saddled him with a reputation as a wild and woolly player who got lucky, the "parking lot" champion whose undeniable talent was not tempered by sensible course management. Ballesteros strongly resented these views, and although his subsequent victories in the British Open and two Masters helped to dispel them, his lack of success in both the U.S. Open and PGA have added fuel to the fire.

It was appropriate, therefore, that in the final round of the 1988 Open at Lytham, the career of Ballesteros came full circle. He came to the tee, as he had ten years earlier, wearing a navy sweater, navy trousers, white shoes and a white shirt with the collar tucked neatly under the sweater. As in 1979, he came to that tee two strokes behind, but this time he came with a more controlled swing, a more controlled game.

He was trailing Nick Price of Zimbabwe, and once again it became a battle of talent and nerves, as it had with Irwin. But Price did not crack; on this pressure-filled afternoon he stared Ballesteros in the eye and shot a 69. In response, Ballesteros shot the round of his life—a near-flawless 65.

Parring the first six holes, he drew within one of Price, who had bogeyed the 2nd. They both birdied 6, and then at 7 Price struck his second shot three feet from the flag, virtually assuring him of an eagle. But Seve answered. After a huge drive he hit a 5-iron to the green, then holed a putt of twelve feet for a 3 of his own. He followed that with a birdie at 8 to pull even.

Both men parred 9, then both birdied 10, Ballesteros sinking from twenty feet, Price from four. It was at 11 that Ballesteros turned the tide, with another twenty-footer into the heart for birdie as Price missed from twelve feet. The Spaniard thus regained for the first time a lead he had not held since his opening round of 67.

But at the next hole he lost it again. With his first loose swing of the day, he missed the green at the par-three 12th, taking his first bogey in twenty-four holes. At 13 Price played the shot of the day to that point, a wedge approach that stopped two inches from the hole. But Ballesteros calmly rammed home an eighteen-footer to stay even.

They halved with bogeys at 14, with pars at 15. Then, on the hole where in 1979 he had driven his ball under a parked car, Ballesteros took not a driver but a 1-iron and expelled the final ghosts of his errant past by drilling his ball into the heart of the fairway, then caressing a 135-yard 9-iron to within three inches of the cup. He had reversed the tables on Price, who faced a birdie putt to tie, and when the Zimbabwean's attempt slid away, Seve had the lead. Matching pars at 17 kept him one ahead with one to go.

At 18 Price's second shot found the green about forty feet from the hole as Ballesteros's approach came to rest just off the back edge in an awkward lie sixty feet away. It was a difficult chip under normal circumstances, let alone with the Open on the line. Ballesteros chose a sand wedge, and with a deftness that perhaps only he could summon under such pressure, coaxed the ball to within inches of the hole, nearly sinking it. Price, knowing he had to hole his lengthy birdie to force a playoff, hit the putt boldly and it finished eight feet past the hole. He missed the return putt also, and so the margin of victory was two. It was four more strokes to third place Nick Faldo, the defending champion, and no American player finished within seven of Seve.

Two years prior to the 1988 Open, Lytham had celebrated its centennial. Its first clubhouse back in 1886 was a room in the old St. Anne Hotel. It was another eleven years before they made a move to the current site, then described as an open and level field, on which George Lowe plotted the course.

Squeezed onto a narrow finger of land about a half mile from the Irish Sea, Lytham is the farthest from the ocean of all the British Open courses, but it is still undeniably a links, blessed with fine

11th hole

sandy soil and ideal land for golf. At the turn of the century Bernard Darwin observed that the course "has beautiful turf, but not much else of beauty; no one could fall in love with it at first sight, and no one could fail to be impressed by its difficulties."

Nicklaus, perhaps in frustration, calls it "merely a very good course and not a great one." However, it does share the same out-and-back routing of the Old Course and Royal Troon, with the front nine playing with the prevailing west wind, the back coming into the teeth of it.

The key to the course is its bunkers. There are 192—more than on any major championship course (Oakmont is second with a current count of 187), and at one point there were a hundred more. In the words of Horace Hutchinson, Lytham presents "a profusion of natural hazard which needs the wisdom of a serpent to avoid." The bunkers come in all shapes and sizes, further tightening the already slender fairways and fast greens. The first rule here is "keep the ball out of the sand."

This is the only championship course to begin with a par three. A 206-yard shot to a green well guarded with bunkers and out of bounds to the right, it signals the start of a course that calls for relentless precision. The out of bounds, defined by a railway line,

continues to haunt the right of holes 2 and 3, a pair of stern par fours that fortunately play with a helping wind. For those who want to give the tracks a wide berth, a profusion of bunkers lurks on the left side of both holes.

The course takes a brief about-face with number 4, heading back to the clubhouse and therefore into the prevailing wind. A slight dogleg right, with a gaggle of bunkers at its elbow, this 393-yarder, like several of Lytham's fours, is best attacked with a long iron from the tee.

In 1979 Jack Nicklaus made an ace at the 212-yard 5th. It plays longer than it looks, and the five bunkers crowding the front part of the green argue for plenty of club. At holes 6 and 7 we see another Lytham quirk, back-to-back par fives. Downwind and of only moderate length at 486 and 551 yards, these are the places to make some hay, as Fred Couples did in the final round of the 1988 Open. Although well out of the running at the start of the day, he pulled into contention with two consecutive eagle threes, only to fall away again on the back nine. As always there are bunkers to be avoided—ten of them at number 6, and a whopping seventeen at 7.

Holes 8, 9, and 10 are at the far end of the course, nearest the sea, and here the terrain is contoured with the humps, hillocks, and dunes of traditional links courses. Some of these features were created by man, but they have been in place so long that they have a completely natural look.

Ballesteros says that the wind can be felt more acutely on the 394-yard 8th than anywhere else on the course, adding difficulty to the second shot, which must be played to a plateau green with a large swale in front.

One of the less attractive aspects of Lytham is the fact that it is penned in by dozens of old red brick houses that are characteristic of northern England. At the tee of the 164-yard 9th there is the sense of hitting the ball straight into town. But this is pure target golf, with the green surrounded by no fewer than ten bunkers.

The 10th hole, at 334 yards, is the shortest four on the course, but since it signals the turn back into the wind, it can come as a rude awakening. Back in 1926 the 12th hole was 600 yards. Said Bobby Jones, "It was a new experience for me to bang three woods as hard as I could and then have a pitch left to the green." Today it is fifty-eight yards shorter, but into a wind, no one gets home in two. Indeed, into a wind, no one even gets aggressive, because a mini-forest comes into play for the first time, along the left side of the fairway and through to the back of the green.

The 12th is one of the most deceptively difficult par threes in the world. The forest shelters the tee so the player cannot feel either the direction or the severity of the wind. But once the ball is in the air, it is buffeted. Many a player is stunned to watch what he had thought to be a perfect shot blown back into one of the six bunkers surrounding the green. Out of bounds on the right adds to the challenge.

The last good birdie chance comes at 13, a downwind par four that is drivable if the ball can somehow avoid all sixteen bunkers. Ballesteros hit into one of them in the final round of 1979, but still made three.

Number 14, at 445 yards, is the start of Lytham's awesomely difficult finish, perhaps the toughest in championship golf, with the exception of Carnoustie. Into a stiff wind, this par four is unreachable in two. With thick rough on the right, the best way to approach the small green is from the left side of the fairway. Ballesteros calls number 15 the hardest hole on the course, a 463-yard par four down a humpy, bunker-crowded fairway to a severely sloping green, another untouchable on windy days.

Number 16, the pivotal hole in the final round of each of Ballesteros's victories, begins with a semiblind teeshot, and that may be just as well, for this is one of those holes, as described by Bernard Darwin, where the ground seems to be sown with bunkers like a mine field. For the 1988 Open, the right side of the hole was lined by out of bounds. Prior to the championship, in an article for *The Times of London*, Seve said he'd probably attack the hole with a 1-iron and a 9-iron, and that is exactly how he fashioned his winning birdie.

Number 17, the site of Jones's stroke of genius, is as tough a test as it was in his day, 462 yards with eighteen bunkers, about half of them down the shorter left-hand side of the right-to-left dogleg. And then there is 18, a classic finisher that was lengthened twenty-five yards for the most recent Open, now playing 411 yards to a long, narrow green set beneath the red brick clubhouse.

That green has seen its share of dramatic moments, from Jones to Ballesteros, but it has also been the stage for a chap of lesser skill named Donald Beaver. Tony Nickson, in his comprehensive history, *The Lytham Century*, recalls that his friend Beaver's bunker shot "became lodged in the ivy on the clubroom windowsill. Obeying the 'no spikes in the clubhouse' rule he removed his shoes, went upstairs to the window in question and, from a precarious perch, chipped his ball back to the green."

Beaver was later disqualified for leaving the course.

Clubhouse

British Open: June 23-25, 1926

Bobby Jones	72	72	73	74	291	1
Al Watrous	71	75	69	78	293	2
George Von Elm	75	72	76	72	295	T3
Walter Hagen	68	77	74	76	295	T3
Abe Mitchell	78	78	72	71	299	T5
T. Barber	77	73	78	71	299	T5
Fred McLeod	71	75	76	79	301	7
Jose Jurado	77	76	74	76	303	T8
Emmett French	76	75	74	78	303	T8
Bill Mehlhorn	70	74	79	80	303	T8

British Open: July 9-11, 1952

Bobby Locke	69	71	74	73	287	1
Peter Thomson	68	73	77	70	288	2
Fred Daly	67	69	77	76	289	3
Henry Cotton	75	74	74	71	294	4
Tony Cerda	73	73	76	73	295	T5
Sam King	71	74	74	76	295	T5
Flory Van Donck	74	75	71	76	296	7
Fred Bullock	76	72	72	77	297	8
A. Lees	76	72	76	74	298	T9
Norman Von Nida	77	70	74	77	298	T9
Eric Brown	71	72	78	77	298	T9
Willie Goggin	71	74	75	78	298	T9
Syd Scott	75	69	76	78	298	T9
Harry Bradshaw	70	74	75	79	298	T9

British Open: July 2-4, 1958

Peter Thomson	66	72	67	73	278	
			68	71	139	1
Dave Thomas	70	68	69	71	278	
			69	74	143	2
Eric Brown	73	70	65	71	279	T3
C. O'Connor, Jr.	67	68	73	71	279	T3
Leopoldo Ruiz	71	65	72	73	281	T5
Flory Van Donck	70	70	67	74	281	T5
Gary Player	68	74	70	71	283	7
Harry Weetman	73	67	73	71	284	T8
Henry Cotton	68	75	69	72	284	T8
E. Lester	73	66	71	74	284	T8

British Open: July 10-12, 1963

Bob Charles	68	72	66	71	277	
			69	71	140	1
Phil Rodgers	67	68	73	69	277	
			72	76	148	2
Jack Nicklaus	71	67	70	70	278	3
Kel Nagle	69	70	73	71	283	4
Peter Thomson	67	69	71	78	285	5
C. O'Connor, Jr.	74	68	76	68	286	6
Gary Player	75	70	72	70	287	T7
Ramon Sota	69	73	73	72	287	T7
Sebastian Miguel	73	69	73	73	288	T9
Jean Garailde	72	69	72	75	288	T9

British Open: July 9-12, 1969

Tony Jacklin	70	68	70	70	280	1
Bob Charles	66	69	75	72	282	2
R. De Vicenzo	72	73	66	72	283	T3
Peter Thomson	71	70	70	72	283	T3
Christy O'Connor	71	65	74	74	284	5
Davis Love, Jr.	70	73	71	71	285	T6
Jack Nicklaus	75	70	68	72	285	T6
Peter Alliss	73	74	73	66	286	8
Kel Nagle	74	71	72	70	287	9
Miller Barber	69	75	75	69	288	10

British Open: July 10-13, 1974

Gary Player	69	68	75	70	282	1
Peter Oosterhuis	71	71	73	71	286	2
Jack Nicklaus	74	72	70	71	287	3
Hubert Green	71	74	72	71	288	4
Danny Edwards	70	73	76	73	292	T5
Liang Huan Lu	72	72	75	73	292	T5
D. Swaelens	77	73	74	69	293	T7
Tom Weiskopf	72	72	74	75	293	T7
Bobby Cole	70	72	76	75	293	T7
Johnny Miller	72	75	73	74	294	10

British Open: July 18-21, 1979

Seve Ballesteros	73	65	75	70	283	1
Ben Crenshaw	72	71	72	71	286	T2
Jack Nicklaus	72	69	73	72	286	T2
Mark James	76	69	69	73	287	4
Rodger Davies	75	70	70	73	288	5
Hale Irwin	68	68	75	78	289	6
Graham Marsh	74	68	75	74	291	T7
Isao Aoki	70	74	72	75	291	T7
Bob Byman	73	70	72	76	291	T7
Bob Charles	78	72	70	72	292	T10
Masashi Ozaki	75	69	75	73	292	T10
Greg Norman	73	71	72	76	292	T10

British Open: July 14-18, 1988

Seve Ballesteros	67	71	70	65	273	1
Nick Price	70	67	69	69	275	2
Nick Faldo	71	69	68	71	279	3
Fred Couples	73	69	71	68	281	T4
Gary Koch	71	72	70	68	281	T4
Peter Senior	70	73	70	69	282	6
David Frost	71	75	69	68	283	T7
Payne Stewart	73	75	68	67	283	T7
Isao Aoki	72	71	73	67	283	T7
Sandy Lyle	73	69	67	74	283	T7

Scorecard

HOLE	YARDS	PAR
1	206	3
2	437	4
3	457	4
4	393	4
5	212	3
6	490	5
7	549	5
8	394	4
9	164	3
OUT	3302	35
10	334	4
11	542	5
12	198	3
13	342	4
14	445	4
15	463	4
16	357	4
17	462	4
18	412	4
IN	3555	36
TOTAL	6857	71

GOLF Magazine Rankings
67th in the World
17th in Great Britain & Ireland

ROYAL ST. GEORGE'S

SANDWICH, ENGLAND
British Open: 1894, 1899, 1904, 1911,
1922, 1928, 1934, 1938, 1949, 1981, 1985, 1993

Given the fact that golf's Scottish roots go back more than a half century, it is astonishing that the game did not spread southward into England until late in the 1800s. Royal St. George's or Sandwich, the town name by which it is more familiarly known, was the first English course to join the British Open rota, and is one of the oldest clubs in England. Yet it is no older than the first golf clubs in America.

St. George's was founded in 1887 when Dr. William Laidlaw Purves, a Scottish-born golf fanatic, traveled to England's Kentish coast and discovered it. Purves was a member of Royal Wimbledon near London, but that club prohibited golf on Sundays, a rule that didn't sit well with the doctor. In retaliation, he decided to found his own course. For days Purves tramped across the dune-lined shores of southeast England to no avail. Then one day he climbed to the top of the Norman tower of St. Clement's Church in Sandwich, looked out over the rolling terrain that stretched between the town and the river Stour, and proclaimed, "There I will build my golf course!"

On May 23, 1887, Purves and his friends formed the Sandwich Golfing Association, purchasing the land and the old farmhouse which still stands as the Royal St. George's clubhouse. The original 18 holes, designed by Purves, measured 6012 yards and were hailed as a course for heroes. "The first five holes at Sandwich are so good that, in our opinion, they are nowhere excelled," wrote Horace Hutchinson in *Golf: The Badminton Library*, and Bernard Darwin, for whom the

In 1934, Henry Cotton played the first 36 holes in a record 132 strokes, the last 36 in 151, but still won the Open by five. Photo: AP/Wide World Photos

course was a personal favorite, considered it "as nearly my idea of heaven as is to be attained on any earthly links."

Royal St. George's has been lengthened over 800 yards since then, but its routing is relatively unchanged, and it remains a stern test of shotmaking. In the course of eleven British Open Championships spanning almost a century and involving nearly 1,000 players, par of 280 has been bettered by only one player.

Indeed, when the first Open was played here, in 1894, it produced the highest winning total in the history of the Championship—326 by J.H. Taylor. Taylor never once broke 80 but nevertheless annexed the title by five strokes. However, if his scoring was less than noteworthy, his victory was significant. He was the first English-born professional to win the Open, appropriate since this was the first year the Open was played in England. Together with James Braid and Harry Vardon, Taylor formed the Great Triumvirate, a threesome that would dominate the Open for the next two decades, winning all but five of the twenty Opens between 1894 and 1914, with at least one of them finishing in the top three every year.

Two of Vardon's six victories came at Sandwich, the first in 1899 by a convincing five strokes over Jack White of Seaford and later Sunningdale. White reversed the tables the next time the Open came to St. George's, in 1904, beating Vardon by six and Taylor and Braid by one on a score of 296, an even thirty strokes lower than Taylor's score a decade earlier. White was not a long hitter, and he had an unusual putting stance in which he stooped severely and gripped way down on the shaft of his putter. But it worked. His last round of 69 made him the first winner to post a score under 70, a feat not matched until Bobby Jones in 1927.

By contrast, Vardon struggled home in 80 in the final round of the next Open at Sandwich, in 1911, and as a result he found himself in a 36-hole playoff with Arnaud Massy. Vardon hadn't won an Open in seven years, the course now played to a length of 6728 yards, and given his faltering finish the younger Massy seemed the stronger bet. But the two remained even through fourteen holes and at the 15th it was the Frenchman who blinked with a double bogey. By the lunch break Vardon was five up, and by the time the pair returned to 15 in the afternoon, Vardon's lead was seven. Massy "retired" at the 17th green.

In 1922 Sandwich saw Walter Hagen win the first of his four British Opens in a span of eight years and also become the first American-born player to take home the claret jug. It wasn't easy. After a 79 in the third round Hagen found himself two strokes behind Jock Hutchison. In typically flamboyant style, Hagen hired a half dozen runners to bring him reports of Hutchison's final round. But in the end it was not Hutchison but George Duncan who made the boldest bid. Four behind Hagen at the start of the round, Duncan put together a 69. He had needed a birdie four on the final hole to catch The Haig and force a playoff, and after a fine drive and a strong approach he was in good shape, in a small hollow at the left side of the green, facing a chip to the pin. Hagen, who had finished earlier, was among those in the gallery who watched as Duncan failed to give the chip enough steam to climb the hill. It stopped fifteen feet short, and Duncan left his birdie putt on the lip. Ever since, that greenside area has been known as Duncan's Hollow.

Hagen gave the fifty-pound first prize to his caddie, later declaring, "I never wanted to be a millionaire, just live like one."

Over the next six seasons Hagen added a second British Open and, incredibly, four consecutive PGA Championships, a record that will surely never be equaled in any event. But despite these successes The Haig admitted that he had never approached a big event with less confidence than he did the 1928 Open at Sandwich. The reason had a lot to do with an exhibition match he had played a few weeks prior to the Championship, a 72-hole match against one of the top British players, Archie Compston, in which Compston had defeated Hagen by 18 up with 17 to play, the longest margin of victory ever recorded in such an event.

But somehow, before the bell rang, Hagen got his game face on and played four strong rounds in a total of 292, giving him a two-stroke victory over Gene Sarazen and a three-stroke revenge over Compston. It was the first time a champion had gotten through four rounds of the Open at St. George's without a score of 79 or more. Hagen did not record a number higher than five all week, and saved himself time after time with deft recovery shots, most notably in the final round on a chip shot from the cross bunker at the difficult 15th, where he laid the ball stone dead for a saving par.

The Haig was presented the trophy by the Prince of Wales, a golf fanatic and captain of the Royal & Ancient, who later developed a friendship with Hagen. Although he would win his fourth Open the following year, Hagen looked back on Sandwich in '28 as his most treasured triumph.

Hagen's breakthrough victory at St. George's in 1922 had signaled the beginning of a period of American domination of the British Open. Between 1922 and 1933, American players won the Championship ten out of twelve years, with Hagen taking four of

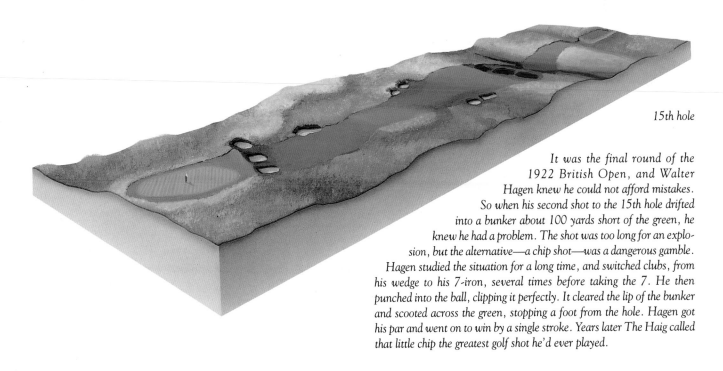

15th hole

It was the final round of the 1922 British Open, and Walter Hagen knew he could not afford mistakes. So when his second shot to the 15th hole drifted into a bunker about 100 yards short of the green, he knew he had a problem. The shot was too long for an explosion, but the alternative—a chip shot—was a dangerous gamble. Hagen studied the situation for a long time, and switched clubs, from his wedge to his 7-iron, several times before taking the 7. He then punched into the ball, clipping it perfectly. It cleared the lip of the bunker and scooted across the green, stopping a foot from the hole. Hagen got his par and went on to win by a single stroke. Years later The Haig called that little chip the greatest golf shot he'd ever played.

them, Bobby Jones three. But when the Open returned to Sandwich in 1934 it again marked a turning of the tide, this time back toward the Brits. In the twenty-six years between 1934 and 1960, the Open would be won by Americans only twice, once by Snead and once by Hogan.

The new era was ushered in by a methodical 27-year-old Englishman named Thomas Henry Cotton, who unleashed an extraordinary stretch of controlled, low-scoring golf. He began in the qualifying round with a 66 that broke the course record for Sandwich, then opened the tournament with a 67, tieing the lowest round ever in the Open, on a day when no one else bettered 70. But even that did not prepare the world of golf for what would follow—a round of 65 (on a course only 150 yards shorter than the current layout) that continues to be hailed as the finest eighteen holes in the history of the Championship. It was later honored by the Dunlop Company with a new golf ball—the Dunlop 65—that remained the best-selling ball in Britain for decades. Setting a 36-hole record of 132 that still stands today, Cotton took an insurmountable nine-stroke lead. Despite a nervous 79 in the last round, he won a comfortable five-stroke victory over Sid Brews and tied Gene Sarazen's 283 at Prince's in 1932 for the lowest winning score to that date.

Harry Vardon, the inspiration to all the players of Cotton's generation, was by then in his mid-60s and in failing health. Although he had been present for Cotton's stunning early rounds, he had not had the strength for the final day. But Cotton, after receiving the jug, took it up to Vardon's bedroom in the nearby Guilford Hotel, where the two of them shared tears of joy.

Said Cotton, "I feel very much like a medical student or other person who has passed an exam. That person is just as clever some months before that exam as he is immediately afterward. But once he has passed that exam, he is qualified. I don't think I am a better player today than I was a week before the championship, but I am qualified."

Cotton added his second Open Championship in 1937, over Reg Whitcombe at Carnoustie, and a year later Whitcombe himself passed the championship exam by battling some of the worst weather in the history of the Championship, at Sandwich.

Final days at Sandwich have been tough on the winners, but this one was tough on everyone. "The wind was the strongest I have personally ever known in the Open Championship," wrote Henry Longhurst. "On the way out against the full force of the wind it was like playing in the days of the guttie ball." Several scores were in the 80s, and there were also a few in the 90s. Cyril Tolley, who had shot a 68 the day before, posted a pair of 86s, and at the Suez Canal hole, number 14, played his second shot into the face of the gale, a 1-iron that cleared the Canal only to be blown back into it.

Under these circumstances, Whitcombe's scores of 75 and 78 were remarkable—and he could have been at least four strokes better—for Whitcombe is surely the only winner of a major champi-

onship who, on the final day, four-putted not one but two greens.

Following in the paths of the English and the Americans, the South Africans scored their first Open victory in 1949 at Sandwich, when portly Bobby Locke took the title in a playoff over equally portly Harry Bradshaw, a snakebit Irishman who is remembered for having lost this Open over a broken beer bottle. On the fifth hole of his second round Bradshaw discovered that his wayward teeshot had come to rest in the bottle. (Sam Snead is said to have encountered a similar problem when his ball rolled into a paper bag. The cunning Snead simply put a match to the bag, but Bradshaw had no such option.) Without waiting to see whether he could get relief (which he could not then, but could now), Bradshaw closed his eyes and smacked the bottle with his wedge. The ball moved about thirty yards, and Bradshaw ended up with a 6 on the hole. He shot 77 that day, which together with his other rounds of 68, 68, and 70 put him in a 36-hole playoff with Locke, which Locke won by a whopping twelve strokes, the first of his four Open victories.

Soon after that Championship the R&A took St. George's off the Open rotation, citing insufficient housing and poor access to the golf course, with only one main road into town and many narrow, winding streets to be negotiated. But by 1981 those problems were addressed and the Open returned.

This was the Open that produced the only man ever to break par at St. George's. He was Bill Rogers, a relatively unknown American whose 276 was seven better than any other champion's total at Sandwich. Granted, in the thirty-two intervening years golf equipment and learning had advanced, but the course had been strengthened as well, and Rogers's mark is not viewed as a reflection of a weakened St. George's. For one thing, no other player bettered 280. For another, the average score for the four days of the championship, under assault by the world's best players, was 74.7. Indeed, this was the year that Jack Nicklaus opened the tournament with an 83, his highest score ever in a major championship, inspiring one British columnist to write, "I've always wanted to play like Jack Nicklaus, and now I do." (To Nicklaus's credit, he came back with a 66 and made the cut.)

The fact is that 1981 was simply Bill Rogers's year, a year when he notched seven victories worldwide, including the Australian Open and the World Series of Golf. At Sandwich Rogers opened with a 72, then made his move on Friday and Saturday with rounds of 66 and 67 and took a five-stroke lead into the final round.

Rogers seemed to throw it away when, at the 7th hole, a short par five that may be the easiest hole on the course, he took a double-bogey 7 and his lead dwindled to one, but he got himself together and outplayed his challengers from there forward. His victory came by four strokes over Germany's Bernhard Langer.

Rogers was the 1981 Player of the Year, but almost immediately thereafter he lost the magic, dropping to twenty-seventh on the U.S. money list in 1982, forty-second in 1983, and into obscurity thereafter.

But Bernhard Langer continued to play well, winning the Masters in 1985 and challenging that year in the Open, which had returned quickly to Sandwich. Through three rounds Langer shared a three-stroke lead at 219 with David Graham, but in the end neither prevailed. Instead, the man Greg Norman named "Sleepy Sandy," Scotland's Sandy Lyle, plugged to the fore.

As Langer and Graham were folding with 75s, Lyle birdied the 14th and 15th holes to go on top. Pars at the 16th and 17th left him with one par to go for victory. But at 18, which had been converted into a long and difficult par four, he pulled his 6-iron approach into rough about forty feet from the hole. It left him with a difficult pitch over Duncan's Hollow to the top of a knoll, then a downhill slope to the hole. Lyle underplayed the shot, and his ball rolled back down the hill, leaving him twenty-five feet from the flag. He dropped to his knees in anguish when he saw the result, but then gathered himself and two-putted for a bogey.

Langer and Graham, playing behind him, each needed a birdie to force a playoff, and although both tried gamely, Graham found greenside sand and took 5 and Langer also missed the green and bogeyed, joining Graham in a five-way tie for third. In the end, Payne Stewart, on a closing round of 68, finished second one stroke behind Lyle, whose victory marked the end of sixteen years without a British Champion. .

If a poll were taken of the current generation of Open competitors, Royal St. George's would doubtless be voted the least popular of today's venues. The reason is that it has the same topographical features as Old Prestwick—lots of humps, hollows, and surprises, even in the middle of the fairway, or, as one stylist described it, "a wilderness of bent and broken hillocks throughout which bunkers of portentous size and shape gape with hungry maws for errant balls."

PGA Tour Commissioner Deane Beman, who won the 1959 British Amateur here, claims he didn't have one flat lie during the entire championship. "I'd hit a shot perfectly but moments later I'd be standing on my ear trying to play my second."

But Beman won that championship because in the final match he didn't miss a putt under ten feet, a statistic that says volumes not only about the Commissioner's touch but about the greens of Sandwich. They are big and beautifully smooth, many of them the work of Alister Mackenzie, who came in during the 1920s and moved several targets from hollows to plateaus.

Some of Sandwich's early blind holes, notably the Maiden (a huge hill of sand that had a forced carry of nearly 200 yards) and the Sahara, have been leveled, so the course is a more straightforward test. None of its holes run parallel, and with the vast sandhills everywhere, each hole has a feeling of splendid isolation. Architect/golf writer Tom Doak, who administers GOLF Magazine's rankings of the 100 Greatest Courses in the World, calls St. George's "the best links course in England."

As is the case with most of the courses on the British Open rotation, the first nine holes at Sandwich are less daunting than the return. However, the 1st hole is a tough one, a 445-yard par four where the ideal teeshot must find what Bernard Darwin termed "an insidious and fatal little hollow" known as the kitchen. The lengthy second must avoid a trio of deep bunkers about twenty yards short of the green.

1st hole

More cross bunkers confront the drive at the 2nd, but they are easily carryable today, and if the approach shot to this short par four can avoid the hollow to the right of the green, this hole is not difficult.

Bernard Darwin once wrote, "There are few more absolute joys than a perfectly hit shot that carries the heaving wave of sand which confronts us at the 3rd tee." But that was over a half century ago, when this hole was called the Sahara. Today, the 214-yard teeshot is no longer blind and is played from a perch in the sandhills. The green, originally a punchbowl, is now two-tiered. This hole is easier than the one Darwin loved, but also more fair.

At the 4th tee a towering mound of sand stares players in the face, but except in the strongest headwinds, this drive is not as tough a shot as it looks. However, in the 1979 English Amateur, 54-year-old Reg Glading found trouble here. After taking his younger opponent into extra holes, Glading pelted his drive into the bunker. In attempting to play the ball out, he lost his balance and did a double backward somersault, tumbling twenty-five feet into the bottom of the bunker—whereupon he was struck by his own ball. Glading conceded the match. His experience notwithstanding, the key on this 470-yard par four is the second shot. Leave it short and the result will be a long putt up a giant slope. Hit it too long, and it will likely finish out of bounds.

The distinctive flagstick

4th hole

8th hole

Another blind teeshot occurs at the 5th, a slight dogleg left through a valley between the dunes. From the tee there seems to be no fairway at all. This is where Bradshaw had his encounter with the beer bottle.

Number 6, known as the Maiden, is the sibling of the third hole, and like the Sahara was a blind par three over a massive sandhill. But it too has been reworked, so that the forty-foot-high hill serves largely as a place for spectators to sit and watch the play. On a clear day, it affords good views of the 3rd, 5th, and 7th holes, not to mention the gleaming white cliffs of Pegwell Bay. Today, the green is in full view, as are the four deep bunkers that surround it.

The first of the two par fives at Sandwich comes at number 7. At only 529 yards, it is one of the easier fives on the rota, but it gave Bill Rogers a jolt in the final round of the '81 Open. Without visiting any of the hole's nine bunkers Rodgers made 7.

Architect Frank Pennink made several changes to the course in the 1970s, in preparation for the return of Sandwich to the Open rotation. One of the biggest alterations came at the 8th, which he converted from a par three to a par four. It is only 415 yards, but against the wind the drive will have to be hit squarely in order to carry a ridge and reach the desired landing area, and the approach will have to be both far and sure to find the narrow green.

The nine concludes with a hole called Corsets after a pair of daunting bunkers that cinched the fairway in the original design.

The current hole is a relatively easy par four, a good place to make par or birdie and gird oneself for the rigors of the incoming nine.

The challenge at the 399-yard 10th is the second shot, which must be played to one of Mackenzie's elevated greens. Shots that miss the target will probably end up in one of four hungry bunkers. It was here that Tom Kite blew his chances on Sunday of the 1985 Open, taking a 6 that sent him out of the lead for good.

Number 11 was originally a par four of 384 yards, a hole which, in the final round of the 1938 Open, Alf Padgham drove and then one-putted for an eagle. But today it is a 216-yard par three, played from a tee atop a ridge which the old drive had to carry.

The last reasonable birdie opportunity is at the 362-yard 12th, where the long hitter can cut the left-to-right dogleg, leaving a half wedge to the relatively unprotected green. At 13 the teeshot is blind once again, and should be aimed at the remote white clubhouse of the adjoining Prince's Golf Club. The ball will then sail over a diagonal line of dunes and rough, leaving an approach over a skein of bunkers to a green with a spine running through its middle.

Number 14, the Suez Canal hole, is where Gene Sarazen came to grief in the 1928 Open. After hitting into the rough off the tee he went against his caddie's advice and tried to carry the canal with a wood. He failed, and the result was a 7. The canal cuts across the fairway at the 328-yard mark, and beyond it the path to the green narrows markedly. Still, if the teeshot stays out of the rough, this is

OPPOSITE: *14th hole*

a very vulnerable par five. In the 1975 British PGA Arnold Palmer charged to victory on an eagle here, reaching the green with a 3-iron and then sinking an eight-foot putt. In 1985, Sandy Lyle was forced to lay up short of the canal on his second but still made birdie after stinging a 2-iron 220 yards into the wind.

Number 15 is one of the all-time classic par fours, a long straight hole that weaves through a quartet of fairway bunkers en route to a narrow, humpy green that is all carry, being guarded by three more bunkers.

The last of the par threes, number 16, is only 165 yards but can be as much as a 3-iron when into the wind. Eight bunkers surround the target. In the 1981 Championship it yielded three aces.

The fickle wind can be a huge factor at the 425-yard 17th, where in one round of the 1985 Open Seve Ballesteros failed to reach the raised green with two wood shots in the morning and then Sandy Lyle got home with a driver and 9-iron in the afternoon.

Par is a superb score at the final hole, a 458-yard par four in the tradition of the stern finishes at Lytham, Troon, and Birkdale. Often played into the wind, the approach is one of the most intimidating in golf, with Duncan's Hollow on the left, a grasping bunker on the right, and out of bounds beyond.

In 1985, Scotland's Sandy Lyle emerged from a final-round stampede to win his first major championship. Photo: © Phil Sheldon

British Open: June 11-12, 1894

J.H. Taylor	84	80	81	81	326	1
D. Rolland	86	79	84	82	331	2
Andrew Kirkaldy	86	79	83	84	332	3
A. Toogood	84	85	82	82	333	4
Willie Fernie	84	84	86	80	334	T5
Ben Sayers	85	81	84	84	334	T5
Harry Vardon	86	86	82	80	334	T5
Alex Herd	83	85	82	88	338	8
Freddie Tait	90	83	83	84	340	9
James Braid	91	84	82	84	341	T10
A.D. Blyth	91	84	84	82	341	T10

British Open: June 7-8, 1899

Harry Vardon	76	76	81	77	310	1
Jack White	79	79	82	75	315	2
Andrew Kirkaldy	81	79	82	77	319	3
J.H. Taylor	77	76	83	84	320	4
James Braid	78	78	85	81	322	T5
Willie Fernie	79	83	82	78	322	T5
Freddie Tait	81	82	79	82	324	T7
J. Kinnell	76	84	80	84	324	T7
A. Tingey	81	81	79	85	326	T9
T. Williamson	76	84	80	86	326	T9

British Open: June 8-10, 1904

Jack White	80	75	72	69	296	1
J.H. Taylor	77	78	74	68	297	T2
James Braid	77	80	69	71	297	T2
T. Vardon	77	77	75	72	301	4
Harry Vardon	76	73	79	74	302	5
J. Sherlock	83	71	78	77	309	6
Andrew Kirkaldy	78	79	74	79	310	T7
J. Graham	76	76	78	80	310	T7
Alex Herd	84	76	76	75	311	9
Robert Maxwell	80	80	76	77	313	T10
Ben Sayers	80	80	76	77	313	T10

British Open: June 28-29, 1911

Harry Vardon	74	74	75	80	303	
					143	1
Arnaud Massy	75	78	74	76	303	
					148	2
Harold Hilton	76	74	78	76	304	T3
Alex Herd	77	73	76	78	304	T3
James Braid	78	75	74	78	305	T5
Ted Ray	76	72	79	78	305	T5
J.H. Taylor	72	76	78	79	305	T5
George Duncan	73	71	83	79	306	8
L. Ayton	75	77	77	78	307	9
J. Hepburn	74	77	83	75	309	T10
F. Robson	78	74	79	78	309	T10

British Open: June 22-23, 1922

Walter Hagen	76	73	79	72	300	1
George Duncan	76	75	81	69	301	T2
Jim Barnes	75	76	77	73	301	T2
Jock Hutchison	79	74	73	76	302	4
C.A. Whitcombe	77	79	72	75	303	5
J.H. Taylor	73	78	76	77	304	6
J. Gassiat	75	78	74	79	306	7
Harry Vardon	79	79	74	75	307	T8
T. Walton	75	78	77	77	307	T8
Percy Alliss	75	78	78	77	308	10

British Open: June 9-11, 1928

Walter Hagen	75	73	72	72	292	1
Gene Sarazen	72	76	73	73	294	2
Archie Compston	75	74	73	73	295	3
Percy Alliss	75	76	75	72	298	T4
Fred Robson	79	73	73	73	298	T4
Jim Barnes	81	73	76	71	301	T6
Aubrey Boomer	79	73	77	72	301	T6
Jose Jurado	74	71	76	80	301	T6
Bill Mehlhorn	71	78	76	77	302	9
W.H. Davies	78	74	79	73	304	10

Clubhouse

British Open: June 27-29, 1934

Henry Cotton	67	65	72	79	283	1
Sid Brews	76	71	70	71	288	2
Alf Padgham	71	70	75	74	290	3
Macdonald Smith	77	71	72	72	292	T4
M. Dallemagne	71	73	71	77	292	T4
Joe Kirkwood	74	69	71	78	292	T4
Bert Hodson	71	74	74	76	295	T7
C.A. Whitcombe	71	72	74	78	295	T7
E.R. Whitcombe	72	77	73	74	296	T9
Percy Alliss	73	75	71	77	296	T9

British Open: July 6-8, 1938

R.A. Whitcombe	71	71	75	78	295	1
James Adams	70	71	78	78	297	2
Henry Cotton	74	73	77	74	298	3
A. Dailey	73	72	80	78	303	T4
J.J. Busson	71	69	83	80	303	T4
Alf Padgham	74	72	75	82	303	T4
Richard Burton	71	69	78	85	303	T4
Fred Bullock	73	74	77	80	304	T8
Wiffy Cox	70	70	84	80	304	T8
Bobby Locke	73	72	81	79	305	T10
C.A. Whitcombe	71	75	79	80	305	T10
B. Gadd	71	70	84	80	305	T10

British Open: July 6-8, 1949

Bobby Locke	69	76	68	70	283	
			67	68	135	1
Harry Bradshaw	68	77	68	70	283	
			74	73	147	2
Roberto DeVicenzo	68	75	73	69	285	3
C.H. Ward	73	71	70	72	286	T4
S.L. King	71	69	74	72	286	T4
A. Lees	74	70	72	71	287	T6
Max Faulkner	71	71	71	74	287	T6
W. Smithers	72	75	70	71	288	T8
J. Fallon	69	75	72	72	288	T8
J. Adams	67	77	72	72	288	T8

Scorecard

HOLE	YARDS	PAR
1	445	4
2	376	4
3	214	3
4	470	4
5	422	4
6	156	3
7	529	5
8	415	4
9	387	4
OUT	3414	35
10	399	4
11	216	3
12	362	4
13	443	4
14	508	5
15	467	4
16	165	3
17	425	4
18	458	4
IN	3443	35
TOTAL	6857	70

GOLF *Magazine* Rankings:
36th in the World
12th in Great Britain & Ireland

British Open: July 16-19, 1981

Bill Rogers	72	66	67	71	276	1
Bernhard Langer	73	67	70	70	280	2
Mark James	72	70	68	73	283	T3
Raymond Floyd	74	70	69	70	283	T3
Sam Torrance	72	69	73	70	284	5
Manuel Pinero	73	74	68	70	285	T6
Bruce Lietzke	76	69	71	69	285	T6
Howard Clark	72	76	70	78	286	T8
Ben Crenshaw	72	67	76	71	286	T8
Brian Jones	73	76	66	71	286	T8

British Open: July 18-21, 1985

Sandy Lyle	68	71	73	70	282	1
Payne Stewart	70	75	70	68	283	2
Mark O'Meara	70	72	70	72	284	T3
Bernhard Langer	72	69	68	75	284	T3
Jose Rivero	74	72	70	68	284	T3
David Graham	68	71	70	75	284	T3
C. O'Connor, Jr.	64	76	72	72	284	T3
Tom Kite	73	73	67	72	285	T8
D.A. Weibring	69	71	74	71	285	T8
Anders Forsbrand	70	76	69	70	285	T8

Starter's Shack

Shelter

British Open

ROYAL TROON

TROON, SCOTLAND
British Open: 1923, 1950, 1962, 1973, 1982, 1989

On the official seal of the Royal Troon Golf Club the club's motto reads: "Tam Art Quam Marte." Translated into English, it means "as much by skill as by strength." Translated into action, it explains how six men have won the British Open here by displaying equal parts power and finesse.

Founded as a five-hole course in 1878, Troon took form on a stretch of genuine linksland a few yards from the Firth of Clyde on Scotland's western coast. Before it became a golf course, it was the home of several dozen cattle and sheep. Indeed, during the club's first few years, the sheep served as greenkeepers.

Within its first decade the course grew to six holes, then twelve, then eighteen. The modern layout follows the St. Andrews format—the front nine heads basically one way, the back nine more or less parallels it. Since the outward nine plays with the prevailing wind, the inward nine against it, on a gusty day the element of skill is needed early while strength may be saved for the finish.

The British Open was not held at Troon until 1923, when the club filled in for Muirfield, which was undergoing reconstruction. This was also Gene Sarazen's first appearance in the Championship, and it was hardly auspicious. Although the reigning U.S. Open Champion did well enough in his first round of qualifying— a 75—he caught some vile weather the next day and never recovered from an 8 on the second hole of the Troon municipal course. With an 85 his total was 160, one stroke too high to get him into the Championship. Sarazen later described it as "the most crushing blow to my self-esteem I have ever received." Exactly fifty years later he would return to Troon as a special invitee to the 1973 Open, and at the age of 71 he would shoot the same score—160—for the first two rounds of the Championship, including a hole-in-one at the 8th hole.

But in 1923 the victor was Arthur Havers, hailed by Bernard Darwin as having "a fine physique and a great power, a well-controlled style and a firm and steadfast way of striking with his irons." In the end it was finesse that won it for Havers. After plunking his final approach in a bunker to the right of the 18th green, he exploded the ball into the hole for a birdie 3. Moments later Walter Hagen hit into the same bunker and needed to execute the same shot to tie Havers, but narrowly missed.

This Open was also marked by an equipment debacle. When several of the American competitors were seen putting lots of backspin on their approaches to the Troon greens, concern was expressed with regard to the punched faces of their irons. On the day before the qualifying rounds the R&A posted the following notice:

> The Rules-of-Golf Committee has decided that irons with corrugated, grooved, or slotted patterns constitute a substantial departure from the traditional and accepted form and make of golf clubs—and accordingly [are] not permissible; also, clubs with faces so marked by punches so as to produce an effect similar to those described.

That evening Duncan McCulloch, the Troon professional, sent out to local carpenters and shipbuilders for rasps and files, then worked through the night filing down the offending weapons.

The week was also marked by one of the more bizarre shots in golf history, when Aubrey Boomer, in exploding from a bunker during one of the qualifying rounds, hit his ball into the pocket of his own jacket.

The Open did not return until 1950, when Bobby Locke shot rounds of 69-72-70-68—279, defending the title he had won a year earlier at Sandwich and also becoming the first man to break 280 in the British Open. This was a year in which the entire field scored well. Over four rounds, not a soul posted a score over 79, and there were only two totals higher than 77.

One reason for the low scoring was the perfectly manicured Troon greens, which the R&A kept soft through watering. The story goes that, early in the week, Australia's Norman Von Nida asked the Championship Committee whether they planned to continue watering the greens throughout the tournament, and when they said yes, Von Nida declared that Locke (the finest putter of his era) would win the tournament, and backed him with the bookies. Later that week, both the Australian and the South African were big winners.

Another reason for the low scoring was the fact that Troon was playing to only 6600 yards. Not once in seventy-two holes did Locke use a driver from the tee as he lowered by four strokes a record that had stood for eighteen years. His victory came by two over Roberto DeVicenzo, three over Dai Rees and Fred Daly. In the same tournament, Frank Stranahan set an amateur record for the Open, shooting a 66 in the final round.

After the lushness of 1950, the conditions at the next Troon Open, in 1962, were in stark contrast. A prolonged drought in Britain had left the course baked dry, and the greens were uneven and below the high Troon standard. By this time the course measured nearly 7000 yards, but as hard and fast as it was, length was not a prime requirement.

Arnold Palmer, who a year earlier had finished as runner-up to Kel Nagle at St. Andrews, this time turned the tables and beat Nagle by six strokes, the rest of the field by thirteen, setting another new British Open record of 276. At one point in the final round he had a colossal ten-stroke lead. The key to his week was pinpoint play from the tee, as he 1-ironed the course into submission. Only six scores in the tournament were under 70 and Palmer posted three of them, the most noteworthy being his third round. After four holes he was one stroke behind Nagle, but he birdied 5 and 6, and then caught fire on the back nine with birdies at 13, 14, 16, and 17 en route to what he called "my best round ever," a 67 that set a record for the newly stretched Troon course. "I don't think I have ever hit the ball more accurately in my life," said Palmer.

If one hole can be said to have been crucial, it was the Railway hole, number 11. Railroad tracks mark the out of bounds that runs all the way up the right side of this par five. Palmer played the hole with a par, two birdies, and an eagle, using a 1-iron for both drive and second shot in each of the four rounds. In the same tournament two scores of 11 were made on this hole, one by Max Faulkner, who hit his own foot; and there was also a 10 by Jack Nicklaus, one of whose strokes was what the Brits call an "air shot"—a whiff.

This year was Nicklaus's debut in the British Open. As was the case with Sarazen in 1923, Nicklaus was the holder of the U.S. Open title. And also as with Sarazen, Nicklaus played poorly. He opened with an 80, closed with a 79, and finished tied for thirty-second, twenty-nine strokes behind Palmer.

It was also the year that the Women's Lib movement hit the Open, when Mrs. E. Beck of Wentworth became the first female to file an entry for the Championship. The R&A refused her application.

In 1973 Tom Weiskopf matched Palmer's 276 total and took his only major title, a three-stroke victory over Neil Coles and Johnny Miller. Playing on a rain-soaked Troon that measured 7064 yards, Weiskopf, who then reckoned himself to be the best driver in the world, proved that his entire game was solid. He played the seventy-two holes without a three-putt green, and led after each round.

He began the last eighteen with a one-stroke lead on Miller and moved to three up by the turn. Coming in, Miller had chances to put pressure on Weiskopf, but missed short birdie putts at 15 and 16. Coles came from well back with a 66, and Nicklaus set a new course record with a closing 65 to take fourth place. Later that evening, in

Arnold Palmer runs home the final putt of the 1962 British Open for a record total of 276 and his second consecutive title. Photo: AP/Wide World Photos

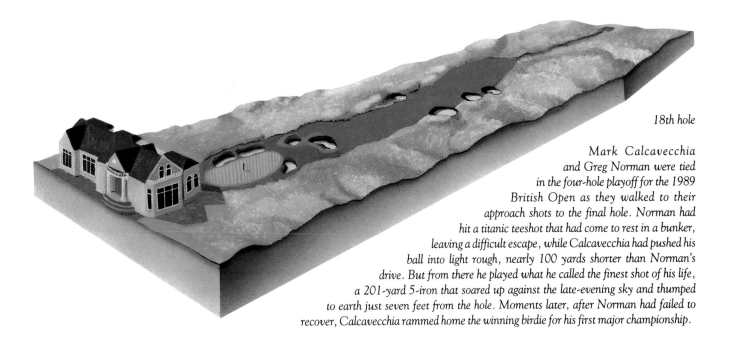

18th hole

Mark Calcavecchia
and Greg Norman were tied
in the four-hole playoff for the 1989
British Open as they walked to their
approach shots to the final hole. Norman had
hit a titanic teeshot that had come to rest in a bunker,
leaving a difficult escape, while Calcavecchia had pushed his
ball into light rough, nearly 100 yards shorter than Norman's
drive. But from there he played what he called the finest shot of his life,
a 201-yard 5-iron that soared up against the late-evening sky and thumped
to earth just seven feet from the hole. Moments later, after Norman had failed to
recover, Calcavecchia rammed home the winning birdie for his first major championship.

the Marine Hotel just off the 18th fairway, the Golden Bear salut-ed his fellow Ohioan, joining him in a raucous singing of "Amazing Grace."

For Weiskopf it was without question the biggest victory in a career characterized more often by frustration and unrealized potential. It's likely that he has found greater fulfillment in his sec-ond career, as a golf course architect in partnership with Jay Morrish, his most highly rated course being a private layout in Arizona—named Troon.

The story of the 1982 Championship is a tale of two Opens. The first thirty-six holes were dominated by a young, goldilocked Californian named Bobby Clampett. Using an ultra-mechanical swing based on Homer Kelley's physics text/ golf book, *The Golfing Machine*, Clampett fashioned rounds of 67-66 to take a five-stroke lead at the halfway mark. But he would play the last two rounds in 78-77 to finish tied for tenth. The tournament thereby turned into a free-for-all until the final stages, when it became clear that South Africa's Nick Price would win it.

Except he didn't. With nine holes left, Price was one ahead of Des Smyth and Tom Watson. Then he reeled off three straight birdies at 10, 11, and 12, pulling away from Smyth as Watson stayed within two, thanks to an eagle three at the 11th.

But it was at this point that Price faltered, with a bogey at 13, a disastrous double bogey at 15, and another bogey at 17, losing four strokes to par in five holes. Meanwhile, Watson played the last five holes in one under, and quietly backed into the fourth of his five British Opens. Since he had won the U.S. Open a few weeks earli-er at Pebble Beach, Watson became the fifth man in golf history to win both national championships in the same year.

When the Open returned to Troon in 1989, Great Britain was in the throes of the hottest, driest summer in decades; rain had fallen

only three and a half days in two and a half months. Temperatures during the tournament were consistently in the 80s, and the course was hard, dry, and fast. At each of the two front-nine par fives Greg Norman recorded drives in excess of 400 yards. But on the final hole of the final day the prodigious power that had helped him all week buried him.

Norman had begun the last round seven strokes off the lead held by his countryman, Wayne Grady, with a dozen players—including Watson, Payne Stewart, Mark Calcavecchia, and Fred Couples—ahead of him. But he burst from the gate and birdied each of the first six holes, so that by the time Grady began his round, Norman was only one behind. He played the next four holes in one over, but then reached both back-nine par fives in two for birdies while also rolling in a thirty-five-footer for a birdie at 13. Out in 31, in in 33, he set a course record and final-round British Open record of 64, and a Troon Open record total of 275. Then he waited.

When Grady birdied the 12th and went to fifteen under, he was two ahead of Norman's pace, one up on Watson, and in the driver's seat. At this point, no one was giving much thought to Mark Calcavecchia. He had begun the day three behind, and had lost another stroke to par on the front nine. But he picked up two birdies on the back nine and came to the final hole needing a three to tie Norman's total. After a superb drive he struck an 8-iron to three feet, and suddenly there were two players at 275.

It was about then that Grady began to fold, just as Price had seven years earlier, bogeying both of the finishing par-three holes, 14 and 17. When he could do no better than par at 18, the seven-ty-two holes of regulation ended in a triple tie.

The stage thus was set for the British Open's first three-man playoff, and the first playoff under the multi-hole system, a method the R&A had had in place for several years but had not had occasion to use. A compromise between sudden death and a full 18-hole playoff, it calls for four or five holes, depending on the configuration of the course, with the low total for the holes determining the winner. If, after the holes are completed, a tie persists, sudden-death goes into effect.

At Troon the playoff holes were the 1st, 2nd, 17th and 18th, pars of 4-4-3-4. Norman birdied each of the first two holes (at this point he had played twenty holes, birdieing eleven of them) as Calcavecchia parred 1 and birdied 2 and Grady parred both holes. It was at the 3rd playoff hole, number 17, that Norman made a questionable club selection that cost him a bogey. After hitting a splendid 3-iron that went straight at the flag but rolled just off the back of the green, about forty-five feet from the hole, he chipped the ball rather than putting it. The ball spurted off his clubface, and rolled about ten feet past the hole. From there he two-putted for a bogey as Calcavecchia parred to pull even. Grady, with a bogey, took himself out of serious contention.

The pivotal moment came at the 18th tee. After Calcavecchia struck his drive into light rough on the right, Norman pummelled a tremendous teeshot down the right side of the fairway. It bounced and rolled a total of 325 yards, into a bunker. Norman had used a driver all week and had not come close to the bunker, but now he was up against the face of it.

His assignment became all the more dire after Calcavecchia

struck what he called "the best shot I've ever hit," a majestic 201-yard 5-iron that came to rest seven feet from the pin. Norman tried to power-lift his ball from its sandy grave but succeeded only in finding another bunker. From there he half-skulled a shot over the green and out of bounds. It was over. Calcavecchia didn't need to make his final putt for birdie, but displaying the stuff of a champion, he rammed it home.

For Norman, who had played brilliantly all day, it was another bitterly disappointing defeat in a major championship, added to Bob Tway's blast-in at the seventy-second hole of the 1986 PGA at Inverness and Larry Mize's chip-in at Augusta in 1987. The defeat at Troon made him the only player to have lost major championship playoffs in the Masters, U.S. Open, and British Open, and in three different formats. No player in golf history has suffered more frustration, but perhaps no player has been better equipped to handle it. "Destiny has a funny way of saying, 'Hey this is the way it's got to be'" said Norman. "But we all accept fate. It's what keeps us coming back, hoping. You've got to think positively. I have to believe my time will come soon."

The holes used for the 1989 playoff played over the same turf as

In 1989, Australians Greg Norman and Wayne Grady took home silver bowls, but it was the applauding Mark Calcavecchia (right) who got the claret jug. Incredibly, this was the first three-man playoff in the 117-year history of the British Open. Photo: © Phil Sheldon

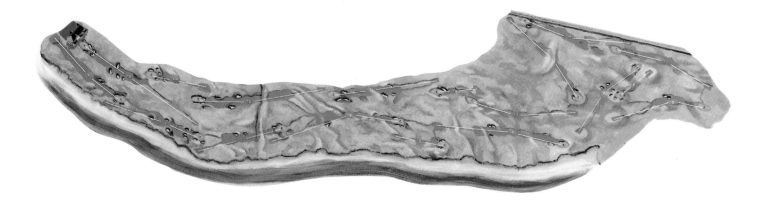

the original five-hole course designed in 1878 by Charles Hunter, the successor to Old Tom Morris as greenkeeper and pro at nearby Prestwick. It was George Strath, brother of 1865 Open Champion Andrew Strath, who became the club's first professional in 1881, and supervised the building of several new holes. Strath was paid one pound per week, and it is he who is credited with nurturing Troon's splendid greens. By the time he left for America in 1887, at least fourteen holes were in play. His successor, Willie Fernie, fashioned the 18-hole championship layout that is used today.

Fernie, who also designed both of the original courses at Turnberry, brought Troon to a length of 5656 yards, long for the days of hickories and gutties. He also designed the adjacent Portland Course to ease overcrowding. In the last century the main course has undergone constant updating and lengthening, but has seen comparatively little change in its fundamental design. Probably the biggest alterations were made by James Braid prior to the 1923 Open. He changed the 5th hole from a par four to a three, repositioned the 8th, and added forty bunkers. Modern changes have been responses not only to increased distance among the game's top players but to encroachment by Mother Nature. In recent years the coastline has receded, to the point that the tee on the 2nd hole had to be rebuilt before the 1989 Open.

Although its out-and-in routing is patterned after the Old Course, there is more sternness and less strategy here than at St. Andrews. Troon's fairways are narrow, so there is no choice of line to the green. One must simply keep the ball in play. And since the fairways are fraught with humps and hollows, as well as bunkers, one must take one's lumps. A good drive may dart sideways into the rough or settle on a hump with the ball well below or above the feet.

Also, as at the Old Course and at Royal Lytham, under prevailing conditions the front nine is a good deal easier than the back, so the key is to make one's move early and then hold on.

It begins with perhaps the easiest hole in championship golf, the one Calcavecchia calls "the worst hole on the course," a straightforward drive-and-pitch par four which, when played downwind, is merely a drive for the stronger pros. But the wind can also play havoc; in 1923 a fellow named Frank Clark reached the green in two but when he went to mark his ball saw that the wind had blown it into a bunker.

Number 2 is named Black Rock, as is the house beside its green, after the large black reef just off the coast between the 2nd and 3rd holes. During World War II a Flying Fortress aircraft from the Prestwick air station crashed on those rocks. But despite the recent addition of a trio of cross bunkers just short of the green, few players have real trouble on this hole. In the 1989 playoff, Calcavecchia sank a thirty-five-footer for a birdie, and then Norman matched him from ten feet.

The 3rd hole is named "Gyaws," an old Scottish word for the ditch that crosses this fairway at about the 300-yard mark. When played downwind, teeshots will have to be laid up short of this hazard. Bunkers await a miss to the left of the fairway on this, the toughest of the three all-too-similar opening par fours.

A good birdie opportunity awaits at the first of Troon's par fives, the 556-yard 4th. Two fairway bunkers are the only major problems, one awaiting slightly pushed or faded teeshots at 245 yards, another ready to grab pulled or hooked seconds about 90 yards short of the green. More bunkers flank the green, but the entrance is generous, and good players will get home in two here with a long iron.

Bobby Locke's 1950 victory came despite a triple-bogey six at number 5. Locke missed the green and then duffed his chip into a bunker, reinforcing the notion that success here demands a strong, straight long iron shot to the heart of the green. Hit it right, and the ball may find the seaside dunes, the beach, or perhaps even the Firth; miss to the left, and the result almost certainly will be sand.

Number 6, at 577 yards, is the longest hole in British Open competition. It was here that Bobby Clampett came to grief, carding an 8 in his third round of the 1982 Open. Twenty years earlier Arnold Palmer managed to reach the green in two en route to his magnificent 67. The teeshot landing area falls from right to left toward a pair of large bunkers, one of which snared Clampett. If they can be avoided, the second shot is played up an ever-tightening fairway to a long but narrow green nestled in the first of the sandhills that roam through the south end of the course.

The charming 7th hole has the very un-British name Tel-el-kebir. It seems that in 1882, when this hole was under construction, British forces were at war with Muslims in Egypt. Tel-el-kebir was the site of a battle which lasted only forty minutes but resulted in the death of 10,000 Egyptians, while the British lost only fifty-seven men. The namesake hole packs peril for all nationalities. From an elevated tee, the hole plays across 200 yards of heavy rough to a fairway threaded between hills. The green is tucked amid steep sandhills and deep bunkers. The most famous shot here was played nearly a century ago, by Willie Park. On the sixty-first hole of a challenge match against Willie Fernie in 1898, Park holed a full brassie shot to take the prize of 200 pounds.

Troon's most famous hole is unquestionably number 8, the Postage Stamp. Playing straight toward the firth, it is 126 yards of compressed architectural chutzpah. Originally, it was a blind hole of about 175 yards, the green hidden by the sandhill that now stands to its left side. Then it was reshaped into its present form, to mixed reviews. The hole got its name in 1923 when Willie Park referred to its tiny green as "a pitching surface skimmed down to the size of a postage stamp." Prior to that year, members caromed their teeshots off the prominent hillock to the left of the green, but with the club's first Open on the way James Braid put a stop to that by cutting two bunkers into the hillside. The ploy caught Walter Hagen, who double-bogeyed the hole in the final round, eventually losing by one.

To the right, the green drops off nearly ten feet to another bunker, while still another gapes in the front. Downwind, it's the softest of sand wedges; into a gale, it's the purest of long irons. But no matter what the conditions, this is a green that must be hit and held.

In 1950 Roberto DeVicenzo hit his ball into one of the bunkers, took a look at the lie, and immediately declared the ball unplayable. Under a Rule then in force, he headed back to the tee and then struck a second teeshot (under a penalty of distance, no stroke). It hit the flagstick and stopped an inch from the hole. DeVicenzo tapped in for a par. In the same Open, Germany's Herman Tissies recorded the second highest score in British Open history. Tissies visited three bunkers, took five swings in each of two of them, and finally one-putted for a 15 en route to a 92.

7th hole

15th hole

When Sarazen returned here in 1973 and punched his 5-iron shot into the cup, television cameras recorded the feat and the next day's papers carried the headline, "Sarazen Licks Postage Stamp." The next day, his teeshot found one of the bunkers, but the plucky Squire blasted it out and into the cup for a deuce.

During the mid-1980s word circulated through the golf fraternity that Britain's Princess Diana had played Troon and scored a hole in one on the Postage Stamp. Several American golf publications printed the news before the story was revealed to be a hoax. Diana does not even play the game.

The front nine finishes with a 419-yard par four whose humpy fairway doglegs right, leaving a blind second to a plateau that holds the unbunkered green. In the 1920s, this green was only a short distance from the 10th tee of the Prestwick Golf Club, and members of both clubs would play from Troon to Prestwick in the morning and then, having had lunch at Prestwick, would play nine more holes on each course in the afternoon.

From the 10th tee at the southernmost edge of the course the route begins its return to the clubhouse over the longest back nine in the British Open. The semi-blind teeshot is to a narrow fairway that heads uphill, leaving a long-iron shot to the hogback green set among sandhills. At one point in the 1973 Open the prevailing wind meant that this hole was directly in the flight path of the nearby Prestwick Airport. Pilots were warned to be watchful for flying golf balls.

The back tee of the 11th hole sits right up against the railway line, as does the green, and the tracks are out of bounds all the way. This was the hole Palmer subdued in 1962, and that Watson eagled in the last round of 1982, but it has turned the tables on hundreds of lesser mortals. This par five measures just 481 yards, and there is only one bunker, at the left-front of the green, but with gorse on the left, OB on the right, and a stiff wind in the face, caution is the byword here.

At 12 is Troon's least problematic teeshot, a 432-yard par four down a broad fairway. This is perhaps the last respite on the inward half. It was here in the final round of the 1989 Open that Mark Calcavecchia saved himself at least a stroke and perhaps two or three. On a grassy hillside sixty feet from the pin, Calcavecchia faced a difficult up and down for par. Bogey seemed likely, but instead he wedged the ball up in the air and into the cup on the fly for a birdie three.

The stretch run to the clubhouse begins with one of the most difficult holes on the course. Number 13 is a hefty par four of 468 yards. On opening day in 1973 Tom Weiskopf got the only birdie in the entire field. It is a dogleg right where one may bite off as much rough as one dares, but the fairway is invisible from the tee.

The first of two testing inward par threes is at 14, where the key is to avoid three front bunkers. The green is lightbulb-shaped and widens at the back, so there is little penalty for a strong teeshot. Australian trick shot artist Joe Kirkwood had a sizable lead in the last round of the 1923 Open until he double-bogeyed here, leading to a crash which saw him finish 6-7-3-5—six over par—losing the title by three strokes.

The hardest hole on the course is probably the 15th which in the most recent Open taxed the world's best players for an average of 4.61 strokes. As at the par-five 6th hole, bunkers frame the driv-

OVERLEAF: *8th hole.* INSET: *8th hole*

ing area and the approach to the green. This hole will demand a long, straight drive followed by an equally long, equally straight second shot.

Number 16 is a par five that has maintained its challenge to today's long-hitting pros through the presence of the Gyaws Burn, which crosses the fairway at 270 yards. Long hitters must therefore lay up short of the water, leaving second shots of 275 yards or more to the green. This did not stop Greg Norman in 1989, as he hit a driver off the deck and got home in two en route to his record 64. Most other players will be left with a pitch to this large green guarded by three bunkers on the right, two on the left.

The last of the short holes, named Rabbit, is actually a tiger. Unquestionably the most difficult par three on the course, it calls for an all-carry teeshot of 223 yards which, into the wind, can be as much as a driver. And the only safe place to land the ball is the center of the green, with bunkers front right and front left and steep

slopes to all sides. Several players have lost the Open with bogeys and worse on this hole, whereas almost none have birdied en route to victory. It is one of those holes where one makes par and goes quietly to the next tee.

For a number of years 18 was a less than stirring finish, even into the wind, but for the 1989 Open the tee was moved back twenty-five yards and a bit to the left, with a bunker being added in the left driving area. Three bunkers line that side, with one, the one that caught Greg Norman, on the right. The long green is guarded at the front left and right by more sand, but this is one hole where it is not wise to take plenty of club, for just two or three steps beyond the putting surface is the concrete stoop of the clubhouse, out of bounds. When Walter Hagen nearly holed his greenside bunker shot to tie Arthur Havers for the 1923 Open, *Golf Monthly* columnist Sir Guy Campbell called it "the bravest and most determined individual shot I have seen in golf."

British Open: June 13-15, 1923

Arthur Havers	73	73	73	76	295	1
Walter Hagen	76	71	74	75	296	2
Macdonald Smith	80	73	69	75	297	3
Joe Kirkwood	72	79	69	78	298	4
T.R. Fernie	73	78	74	75	300	5
George Duncan	79	75	74	74	302	T6
C.A. Whitcombe	70	76	74	82	302	T6
H.C. Jolly	79	75	75	74	303	T8
J. Mackenzie	76	78	74	75	303	T8
Abe Mitchell	77	77	72	77	303	T8
W.M. Watt	76	77	72	78	303	T8

British Open: July 11-14, 1973

Tom Weiskopf	68	67	71	70	276	1
Neil Coles	71	72	70	66	279	T2
Johnny Miller	70	68	69	72	279	T2
Jack Nicklaus	69	70	76	65	280	4
Bert Yancey	69	69	73	70	281	5
Peter Butler	71	72	74	69	286	6
Bob Charles	73	71	73	71	288	T7
C. O'Connor, Jr.	73	68	74	73	288	T7
Lanny Wadkins	71	73	70	74	288	T7
Lee Trevino	75	73	73	68	289	T10
Gay Brewer	76	71	72	70	289	T10
Harold Henning	73	73	73	70	289	T10
Brian Barnes	76	67	70	76	289	T10

British Open: July 20-23, 1989

Mark Calcavecchia	71	68	68	68	275		
			4-3-3-3	13	1		
Wayne Grady	68	67	69	71	275		
			4-4-4-4	16	T2		
Greg Norman	69	70	72	64	275		
			3-3-4-X	XX	T2		
Tom Watson	69	68	68	72	277	4	
Jodie Mudd	73	67	68	70	278	5	
Fred Couples	68	71	68	72	279	T6	
David Feherty	71	67	69	72	279	T6	
Eduardo Romero	68	70	75	67	280	T8	
Paul Azinger	68	73	67	72	280	T8	
Payne Stewart	72	65	69	74	280	T8	

British Open: July 5-7, 1950

Bobby Locke	69	72	70	68	279	1
R. De Vicenzo	72	71	68	70	281	2
Fred Daly	75	72	69	66	282	T3
Dai Rees	71	68	72	71	282	T3
E. Moore	74	68	73	68	283	T5
Max Faulkner	72	70	70	71	283	T5
Fred Bullock	71	71	71	71	284	T7
A. Lees	68	76	68	72	284	T7
Frank Stranahan	77	70	73	66	286	T9
Flory Van Donck	73	71	72	70	286	T9
S.L. King	70	75	68	73	286	T9

British Open: July 15-18, 1982

Tom Watson	69	71	74	70	284	1
Peter Oosterhuis	74	67	74	70	285	T2
Nick Price	69	69	74	73	285	T2
Nick Faldo	73	73	71	69	286	T4
Des Smyth	70	69	74	73	286	T4
Tom Purtzer	76	66	75	69	286	T4
Massy Kuramoto	71	73	71	71	286	T4
Fuzzy Zoeller	73	71	73	70	287	T8
Sandy Lyle	74	66	74	73	287	T8
Jack Nicklaus	77	70	72	69	288	T10
Bobby Clampett	67	66	78	77	288	T10

Scorecard

HOLE	YARDS	PAR
1	362	4
2	391	4
3	381	4
4	556	5
5	210	3
6	577	5
7	400	4
8	126	3
9	419	4
OUT	3422	36
10	437	4
11	481	5
12	432	4
13	468	4
14	180	3
15	457	4
16	542	5
17	223	3
18	425	4
IN	3645	36
TOTAL	7067	72

GOLF *Magazine* Rankings:
41st in the World
13th in Great Britain & Ireland

British Open: July 11-13, 1962

Arnold Palmer	71	69	67	69	276	1
Kel Nagle	71	71	70	70	282	2
Brian Huggett	75	71	74	69	289	T3
Phil Rodgers	75	70	72	72	289	T3
Bob Charles	75	70	70	75	290	5
Peter Thomson	70	77	75	70	292	T6
Sam Snead	76	73	72	71	292	T6
Peter Alliss	77	69	74	73	293	T8
Dave Thomas	77	70	71	75	293	T8
Syd Scott	77	74	75	68	294	10

SHINNECOCK HILLS GOLF CLUB

SOUTHAMPTON, NEW YORK
U.S. Open: 1896, 1986, 1995

Shinnecock Hills is the finest British Open course in America.

And it began in France. In Biarritz during the winter of 1890-91 William K. Vanderbilt, son of dynasty maker Cornelius Vanderbilt, was on vacation with friends Duncan Cryder and Edward S. Mead when they encountered Willie Dunn, a scion of another sort of dynasty—Scottish golf professionals. Dunn had been summoned to the European spa to design an 18-hole course, and the three

Americans asked him to give a demonstration of this strange new stick-and-ball game.

Dunn chose a hole 125 yards over a deep chasm, teed up several balls, and hit all of them onto the green, some of them close to the flag. "Gentlemen," said Vanderbilt to his friends, "this beats rifle shooting for distance and accuracy. It is a game I think would go in our country." Shortly thereafter Cryder wrote to a man named

18th hole

Samuel Parrish, a friend of his who was traveling in Italy. Cryder told Parrish of his golf epiphany and suggested that the two of them try to introduce the game at their shared American playground in Southampton, Long Island.

In 1891 a twelve-hole course was created. For nearly a century, the designer of that course was assumed to have been Willie Dunn. But recent evidence has shown that Dunn did not arrive at Shinnecock until 1895, and that he merly took credit for the work of another Scotsman, Willie Davis, who come down on loan from his position as professional at Royal Montreal.

Regardless of who designed the course, it was constructed over a period of three months with the help of 150 Shinnecock Indians, a tribe from the Algonquian nation who had lived at the Eastern end of Long Island since the fifteenth century. (The current course superintendent at Shinnecock, Peter Smith, is one of the last of the Shinnecock Indians.)

The construction of the course posed some unique challenges, if we can believe the recollections of the self-promoting Mr. Dunn:

> Except for several horse-drawn roadscrapers, all the work was done by hand. The fairways were cleaned off and the natural grass left in. The rough was very rough, with clothes-ripping blueberry bushes, large boulders, and many small gullies. The place was dotted with Indian burial mounds and we left some of these intact as bunkers in front of the greens. We scraped out some of the mounds and made sand traps. It was here that the Indians buried their empty whiskey bottles, but we did not find this out until later when playing the course. One never knew when an explosion shot in a trap would bring out a couple of firewater flasks, or perhaps a bone or two.

Other challenges for the early Shinnecock golfers included a family of skunks that roamed the fairways and a group of bald eagles with a propensity to swoop down and appropriate golf balls.

The club was incorporated on September 21, 1891, making it, officially, the first golf club in America. (History shows that golf had been played at the St. Andrew's Golf Club in Hastings, New York, and history hints that the game was afoot in areas of West Virginia and Kentucky, but none of these clubs was incorporated.) At the time, however, the Southamptonites assumed they were America's only golfers. About a month after the founding of the Shinnecock club Samuel Parrish was visited in his Manhattan office by John C. Ten Eyck, one of the St. Andrew's founders, who told Parrish he'd heard that golf was being played on Long Island. "Why, yes," said Parrish. "Does anyone else play golf in this country?" Ten Eyck invited Parrish up for a game, marking the first time that members of different American clubs played together. Ten Eyck won the match, played over St. Andrews's six-hole course.

For about two years Shinnecock and St. Andrew's were the only places in America to play golf, and they presented distinctly differ-ent challenges, one bleak and windblown, the other lush and crowded with apple trees. In his book, *Scotland's Gift—Golf*, Charles Blair Macdonald includes a story from a Judge O'Brien, who, having niblicked his way through St. Andrew's, traveled to Shinnecock for the first time and declared with full confidence that it "was not a golf course at all . . . because it had no apple trees over which to loft and play."

By June of 1892 Shinnecock had America's first clubhouse, a white-shingled country house designed by Stanford White, whose previous credits included Madison Square Garden, where he lived in a "tower studio," and Pennsylvania Station. It has been enlarged several times, and was renovated just prior to the club's centennial in 1991, but the core structure still stands proudly atop Shinnecock's highest hill.

By the time the clubhouse was finished, Shinnecock boasted seventy members—men and women—and social activities, teas, and dances were just as important as golf. Shinnecock had become a hub of Southampton society. Even on the golf course, members dressed the part, resplendent in red coats with brass buttons and white knickers or flannels. The women's membership was both proficient and militant. Among the early members were Mrs. Charles Brown, winner of the first women's U.S. Amateur Championship in 1895; teenage phenomenon Miss Beatrix Hoyt, the Amateur Champion in 1896, 1897, and 1898 (at ages 17 to 19); and Mrs. Arthur B. Turnure, runner-up in 1896. Such was the intensity of interest among the distaff set that they were quickly accorded their own nine-hole layout, known as the Red Course (perhaps the origin of red tees for women). But since not all of the ladies had games equal to Misses Brown, Hoyt, and Turnure, the Red Course served as a sort of training ground. No woman could set foot on the long course until she had qualified by playing the Red Course three separate times in a certain number of strokes.

Shinnecock went along with twenty-one holes for four years before the two courses were combined into one 18-hole layout totaling 4423 yards. The consolidating architect is generally agreed to have been Willie Dunn, who had been hired on as the club's professional and had set the twelve-hole course record of 47.

In 1894 Shinnecock joined the St. Andrew's Golf Club, the Chicago Golf Club, the Country Club in Brookline, Massachusetts, and the Newport (R.I.) Country Club as the five charter members of the United States Golf Association (USGA). Officers were elected, and Samuel Parrish became the Association's first treasurer. A year later, Shinnecock played host to the second U.S. Open.

More important back then was the fact that Shinnecock hosted the second U.S. Amateur. Until well into the twentieth century, the pros took a deep back seat. The defending champion from the first U.S. Amateur was C.B. Macdonald but this time he was not a factor, reportedly suffering the effects of ptomaine poisoning. Instead, the Championship was won by his son-in-law, H.J. Whigham, a newspaper foreign correspondent who had attended

Oxford and learned his golf in England. Eighty players entered the qualifying rounds, and Whigham won the medal with 86-77 as the top sixteen players went into match play. In the final Whigham defeated J.G. Thorp, 8 and 7. The next year, at the Chicago Golf Club (designed by Macdonald), Whigham prevailed again, defeating W. Rossiter Betts, a Yale undergrad representing Shinnecock, in the final match.

The prohibitive favorite for the Open at Shinnecock was Willie Park, Jr., a two-time British Open champion from Scotland, who had agreed to come over for the Championship. But he never played, his boat docking a day after the tournament was over. The title was won by James Foulis, the professional from the Chicago Golf Club, whose 78-74-152 beat defending champion Horace Rawlins by three strokes. But four strokes behind Rawlins was the story of this Open, John Shippen, a former caddie of half Black/half Shinnecock Indian descent. Shippen had helped to build the course, and Willie Dunn had taken a liking to him and taught him the game. Within a short time, Shippen was good enough to beat any Shinnecock member, and so the club entered him in the Open. Just prior to the start of play a number of professionals held a meeting and told the USGA that they would not compete if the field included Shippen and another Shinnecock caddie, Oscar Bunn, who was a full-blooded Shinnecock Indian. Theodore Havemeyer, the USGA's first president, responded that Shippen and Bunn would play in the Open, even if no one else did.

Shippen's opening round tied him for the lead, and he was still tied after twelve holes of the final round. But at the 13th hole he took a disastrous 11. His 81 left him tied for fifth at 159, tied with Whigham who had won the Amateur the day before. Only twenty-eight players had competed, but this was a considerable improvement over the 1895 field of eleven.

By the time the Open returned to Shinnecock, both the Championship and the golf course had undergone major changes. The U.S. Open had become the most coveted title in golf, and Shinnecock had lengthened nearly 2500 yards into a raw test of golf skill, both mental and physical.

The naming of Shinnecock for the 1986 Open was a surprise, for although the course had been revered by all who played it, its remote location and small seasonal membership were points strongly in its disfavor. The modern Open attracts thousands of spectators, and with only one main road leading to Shinnecock, traffic jams loomed likely. Furthermore, today's Open is a two-year exercise in planning and manpower tantamount to the invasion of Normandy. It calls for an army of volunteers doing everything from keeping score to serving hot dogs, and the traditional nucleus of that army is the membership of the host club. Shinnecock offered no such nucleus.

But it did offer a truly spectacular site, and in the words of Frank Hannigan, then the USGA's Executive Director, there was "a general, pervasive wistfulness" among the USGA people to return to Shinnecock on the ninetieth anniversary of the club's only other Open. When the Suffolk County government agreed to spend $80,000 on a footbridge that would enable spectators to cross the busy main highway to the course, the USGA decided to take a gamble and go to Shinnecock, running the Open with USGA staff and committeemen instead of the club members.

The result was not the financial success that most Opens are, but artistically it was an unqualified blockbuster. There were virtually no traffic problems, and the players raved over the course, some saying it was the best Open course they had ever played. In 1995, on the occasion of the Open's 100th anniversary, it will return to Shinnecock.

Only Mother Nature failed to cooperate completely, assailing round one with 30 mile-per-hour winds. Over half the field failed

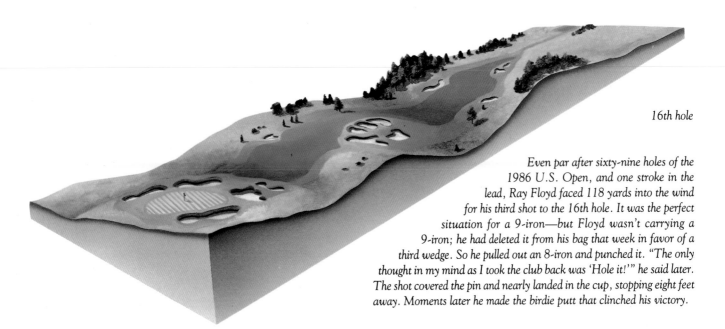

16th hole

Even par after sixty-nine holes of the 1986 U.S. Open, and one stroke in the lead, Ray Floyd faced 118 yards into the wind for his third shot to the 16th hole. It was the perfect situation for a 9-iron—but Floyd wasn't carrying a 9-iron; he had deleted it from his bag that week in favor of a third wedge. So he pulled out an 8-iron and punched it. "The only thought in my mind as I took the club back was 'Hole it!'" he said later. The shot covered the pin and nearly landed in the cup, stopping eight feet away. Moments later he made the birdie putt that clinched his victory.

to break 75 as Bob Tway took the lead with a round of even par 70. This was the day that Jack Nicklaus lost his first golf ball ever in an Open, shot 77, and pronounced it "the most difficult day I have ever seen in American championship golf."

In round two the winds subsided and Joey Sindelar set a course record of 66. His 31 on the back nine was also a record for a few moments, until Danny Edwards posted a 30, matching the nine-hole U.S. Open mark. Unfortunately, Edwards missed the cut, since he had shot 83 on Thursday. The lead went to Greg Norman on 139, with Lee Trevino and Denis Watson three behind. Norman, who had won two tournaments and finished a stroke behind Nicklaus at the Masters, was playing well. In the words of Nicklaus, Greg was playing as well as he had ever seen anyone play the game. After three rounds, it was still Norman in the lead, but now by only one over Trevino and Hal Sutton, with thirteen players within four strokes of him.

Sunday was like a cavalry stampede as various players held or shared the lead. First Norman, then Norman and Trevino, then Norman, Sutton, and Trevino, then—after a string of three birdies—it was Ben Crenshaw, followed by Mark McCumber on a streak of his own. During the back nine Bob Tway took the lead for a moment or two, and then it was Lanny Wadkins and Chip Beck, coming from six strokes behind.

An hour and a half after the leaders had teed off, the scoreboard showed that eight men were tied for the lead at one over par: Norman, Sutton, Trevino, Tway, McCumber, Wadkins, Beck, and Payne Stewart. Norman and Sutton had completed seven holes, Wadkins had gone through sixteen, and the rest were in between.

None of them would win. For at about this point the leaders began to falter, and one man began to rise—Raymond Floyd. No one had touted him. For one thing, despite his superb overall record that included two victories in the PGA plus a Masters, Floyd had never been a strong contender in the Open, his best finish in twenty-one tries being a tie for sixth. For another thing, just a week earlier at the Westchester Classic, he had blown a lead in the final round, ballooning to a 77.

But during the three-hour drive from Westchester to Southampton, Maria Floyd had given her husband a pep talk, and it worked. When Floyd's 6-iron approach to the 13th stopped four feet from the hole he had a birdie, and when his playing companion, Payne Stewart, bogeyed the hole they were tied for the lead. Then Stewart bogeyed 16 and it was Floyd's Open for the taking. At the par-five 16th he took it, with an aggressive punched 8-iron that stopped eight feet away. In went the putt for a birdie. With two closing pars he had a 66 and a two-stroke victory.

At age 43 Floyd became the oldest man to win an Open, a dis-

15th hole. INSET: *The shot that won the 1986 Open was this 8-iron that Ray Floyd punched to the 16th hole. Floyd later said he was trying to hole it; he missed, but the birdie gave him a lead of two strokes, his margin of victory. Photo: © Leonard Kamsler*

tinction he held until Medinah in 1990 when 45-year-old Hale Irwin took it from him. Impressively, Floyd won his Open with nerveless putting. Although records of this sort are unofficial, it's unlikely that anyone had ever completed four rounds of a U.S. Open with fewer than the 111 putts used by Ray Floyd at Shinnecock.

An article in *Scribner's Magazine* in 1895 described the Shinnecock Hills course as a golfing Eden:

The great rolling sand-hills, covered with short, stiff grass, lying between Peconic Bay on the north and Shinnecock Bay on the south, with the ocean beyond, are picturesque in their beauty, and since the resolution of matter from chaos have been waiting for the spiked shoe of the golfer . . . the breezy freshness of the air, the glory of the boundless expanse of downs and water, and the splendor of the sunsets, make a perfect setting for the beauty of good golfing.

In the first golf book published in the United States, appropriately entitled *Golf in America*, James P. Lee observed that "for natural fitness and suitability, no links in the country can be said to excel those of the Shinnecock Hills Golf Club."

Nearly a century has passed since those assessments were made, and in that century more than 15,000 golf courses have been stamped upon the American landscape, but today Shinnecock retains its lofty position, standing sixth in the U.S.A. and twelfth in the world on *GOLF Magazine*'s biennial list.

Why? Partly because it remains a rare patch of Scotland in America. There are very few courses in America that resemble the Scottish links, but Shinnecock Hills, with its windswept sandhills, tall rough, and rolling treeless fairways, is one of them. In the fall the terrain takes on a gorgeous purplish hue, and there are even specimens of authentic Scottish thistle. As one early writer speculated: "They were not planted by the hand of man, but may have been by his feet; for golfers in Scotland, as elsewhere, often wear hobnailed soles to their shoes and the soil in the interstices between the nails may well have brought over the seed embedded in the hard mud, and when the wearers were playing out at Shinnecock, small fragments would here and there work out and plant the handsome emblem of the old Scots."

But just as important as the Scottish-style charm is the American-style challenge. The scores of the 1896 Open—several in the 70s—led to an immediate strengthening and lengthening of the course to 5369 yards, and in 1901 a new championship course was designed. It measured 6249 yards, and lasted until the late 1920s when Suffolk County decided to extend a major highway into Southampton, with the route cutting straight through the Shinnecock course. This prompted Lucien Tyng, then the president of the club, to purchase some land to the north of the old course, which he eventually sold to the club for $20,000. They then hired the architectural firm of Toomey and Flynn to design a completely new course on this rolling property just to the bay side of the clubhouse. Dick Wilson supervised the construction of Bill Flynn's design, and the result was a masterpiece. The sternest of critics, Ben Hogan, traveled to Southampton to play it, and later offered this observation:

To me Shinnecock affords any golfer a most pleasant 18 holes of golf. By this I mean each hole is different and requires a great amount of skill to play it properly. As I think back, each hole has complete definition. You know exactly where to shoot, and the distance is easy to read. All in all, I think it is one of the finest courses I have ever played.

There are no let-up holes, no blind holes on this course. And although it is usually played in a buffeting southwest wind off the Atlantic, the architects have made wise adjustments; most of the long par fours (over 450 yards) play with the prevailing breeze and most of the short ones (under 400 yards) play against it.

Fundamentally, it is a test of driving. Bunkers—over 150 of them—are well placed and intimidating. The heaviest rough is not four inches tall as at most Open courses; it is four feet. And the fairways, which roll up and down, also veer subtly right and left. Often, what appears to be a straight hole is a quasi dogleg, or needs to be attacked that way in order to give a properly wide berth to the deep bunkers and high grass. The greens are small, and they fall off to all sides, but most of them may be reached with roll-on approaches. It is the fairways at Shinnecock, not the greens, that are the island targets. The championship course is a par 70 of 6912 yards, but it plays much longer, much tighter.

Hogan undoubtedly liked the course because strategy is involved on every shot, nowhere more pointedly than at the elevated tee of number 1, a 394-yard dogleg right which invites players to bite off as much as they dare. The fairway is normally 46 yards wide, but for the Open the USGA narrows it to 28 yards. Deep rough and five bunkers line the right side of the fairway, but the opening to the green is wide.

The longest of the short holes is number 2, playing 226 yards uphill, but usually downwind, to a large green protected by three bunkers. Back in 1973, a young amateur named Ben Crenshaw played a casual round of 65 at Shinnecock, setting a course record. His only bogey came at this hole.

The 3rd hole plays along the same downwind line, 453 yards to an elevated green that has more undulations than most of the surfaces at Shinnecock. Just through the trees on the left of the hole is the 10th hole of the National Golf Links, designed by C.B. Macdonald in 1911. Number 4 is nearly 50 yards shorter, but it turns back against the wind along a fairway tightened by four bunkers on the right. Four more bunkers guard the small green.

Number 5 is a superb and unusual par five calling for a long and

10th hole

straight drive over no fewer than seven fairway bunkers, spreading out in a Y-shape from 200-250 yards. The hole is a reachable 535 yards, but two bunkers narrow the opening, and beyond the perched green is dense shrubbery from which there is no return.

The only water on the golf course appears at number 6, a daunting dogleg par four of 471 yards. From the back tees, the drive here must carry nearly 250 yards over a tract of rough, mounds, and bunkers. During a practice round for the 1986 Open, the straight but short-hitting Calvin Peete hit two teeshots, failed to reach the fairway with both of them, and walked off in disgust. But even a strong drive here leaves a long approach over a pond and up a hill to the green, avoiding a large bunker on the left. The pond is 50 yards short of the green and doesn't pose much of a problem for the pros. Nonetheless, this is the hardest hole on the golf course.

The 7th is a copy of the famed Redan Hole originated at North Berwick, Scotland, its large, high-walled green canting steeply from front-right to left-rear. Since this hole plays into a crosswind from the right, the ideal shot is a mid-iron that fades into the slope of the putting surface. Four bunkers surround this green, and when a

teeshot plugs in any of them the result will almost certainly be a bogey or worse.

The shortest par four on the course is number 8, but its 367 yards play into the wind. Position A off the tee is in the left center, but that calls for a drive over a nest of six bunkers. The green is set on a diagonal to the fairway and falls off to the left rear.

Number 9 was lengthened 35 yards for the 1986 Open, bringing it to 447 yards, the first 337 winding through a humpy valley and the last 100 or so straight up a steep hill covered with thick rough. In the first round of the Open it played dead into the wind and was all but unreachable. Since the green is at the highest point on the course, it is hard and fast, and its steep back-to-front slope can leave some terrifying putts.

One of the few blind shots on the course is the teeshot at 10. The pros often lay up with a long iron or fairway wood to avoid a downhill lie on this fairway that moves like a roller coaster, steeply down and then steeply up to the green. Accurate club selection on the approach is absolutely vital—too little and the ball may tumble fifty yards back down the fairway; too much and it may bounce into brush beyond. This is the hole where Nicklaus suffered the only lost ball he could remember in major championship competition.

When the wind blows, no matter in what direction, the 158-yard 11th hole is the most vexing on the course. Fifty feet above the tee, the small, fiercely canted green sneers at its assailants from its perch among a quartet of deep bunkers. "You better use a small ball there," says Lee Trevino, "because you can't keep a big one on the green." It was here that Ray Floyd started his final-round charge by coaxing in a slippery eighteen-footer for a two.

The scorecard reads 472 yards/par four for number 12, but playing downwind from an elevated tee to the broadest fairway on the course, it's not as tough as it seems. The flat green is relatively unprotected, and this is the least interesting hole on the course. It is followed by one of the most devilish, a narrow, angular dogleg of 377 yards where placement off the tee means everything. The pros normally select irons to find this surging fairway, leaving a short but demanding approach to the angled green which falls off on the left and is guarded by a deep bunker at the right. It was here on Sunday in 1986 that Floyd struck his 6-iron to four feet and made the birdie that gave him a share of the lead.

Number 14 is named Thom's Elbow after Charlie Thom, the beloved Scottish professional who served at Shinnecock for over sixty years, and lived in a cottage a few feet from this hole's tee. A beautifully natural hole, it plays from an elevated tee through a narrow funnel-like valley, doglegging right and slightly uphill to a green nestled among four bunkers. In 1986 it was named one of the 100 Best Holes in America by *Golf Magazine*.

From the 14th green the route to the 15th tee is a steep uphill climb, leaving a broad view of the rolling dogleg right. Three bunkers at the corner tighten the drive zone, and four bunkers at the front of this green make it the only one on the course where a bounce-on approach is out of the question. Floyd holed a sand shot for a birdie here in the third round of the Open.

As the crow flies, the par-five 16th is straight, but ingenious bunkering forces the fairway to snake its 544 yards to the green. Dead into the wind, that 544 can feel like 644, and the third shot must be played to the most fiendishly sloped, tightly bunkered green on the course. With his final birdie here, Floyd dipped under par for the first time in the tournament, and that was all he needed.

Crosswinds are the unseen demon at the 17th, a par three of 172 yards. The green is set on a diagonal to the tee, amid a trio of bunkers.

The home hole calls for everything, a long, drawing drive to an undulating fairway, then a carefully gauged long iron over an area of bunkers and rough to the climbing amphitheater green. A misplay from the tee will find reedlike rough or one of two deep bunkers, and an incorrectly judged approach will leave a delicate shot either from sand or from a steep grassy slope.

Clubhouse

U.S. Open: July 18, 1896

James Foulis	78	74	152	1
Horace Rawlins	79	76	155	2
G. Douglas	79	79	158	T3
A.W. Smith	78	80	158	T3
John Shippen	78	81	159	T5
H.J. Whigham	82	77	159	T5
Joe Lloyd	78	82	160	T7
Willie Tucker	78	82	160	T7
R.B. Wilson	82	80	162	9
A. Ricketts	80	83	163	10

U.S. Open: June 12-15, 1986

Raymond Floyd	75	68	70	66	279	1
Lanny Wadkins	74	70	72	65	281	T2
Chip Beck	75	73	68	65	281	T2
Lee Trevino	74	68	69	71	282	T4
Hal Sutton	75	70	66	71	282	T4
Ben Crenshaw	76	69	69	69	283	T6
Payne Stewart	76	68	69	70	283	T6
Jack Nicklaus	77	72	67	68	284	T8
Bernhard Langer	74	70	70	70	284	T8
Mark McCumber	74	71	68	71	284	T8
Bob Tway	70	73	69	72	284	T8

Scorecard

HOLE	YARDS	PAR
1	394	4
2	226	3
3	453	4
4	408	4
5	535	5
6	471	4
7	188	3
8	367	4
9	447	4
OUT	3489	35
10	409	4
11	158	3
12	472	4
13	377	4
14	444	4
15	397	4
16	544	5
17	172	3
18	450	4
IN	3423	35
TOTAL	6912	70

GOLF *Magazine* Rankings:
12th in the World
6th in the U.S.A.

SHOAL CREEK GOLF CLUB

BIRMINGHAM, ALABAMA
PGA Championship: 1984, 1990

The 17th hole at the Shoal Creek Golf Club is a 532-yard par five. But it can also be a 450-yard par four. This is a course with plenty of options.

Shoal Creek has been that way ever since founder Hall Thompson invited Jack Nicklaus to do the design. On the day after Christmas, 1974, Nicklaus flew over the site, a valley nestled between Oak and Double Oak mountains twenty-five miles south of Birmingham, Alabama. Later he and Thompson, a millionaire who made his fortune in the heavy-equipment business, walked across the property. "I'm not sure we have a course here," he told Thompson. "We'll have to study it."

Two weeks later, at 11 o'clock one evening, Thompson's phone rang. "Hall," Nicklaus said, "you don't have one golf course. You have two." Thompson opted to build one, but it is one course where most holes offer at least two paths of attack.

"My design ideas change with every course I do, but I believe all my thinking came together at Shoal Creek," said Nicklaus after he completed the course in 1977. "It's better balanced than Muirfield Village [Nicklaus's signature course in Ohio]. There are more options on approach shots and less penal results on missed shots."

From the day it opened in 1977, Shoal Creek was a strong members' course with a championship test lurking at its back tees. The

5th hole

USGA was the first to notice. In 1980 they booked the course for the 1986 U.S. Amateur Championship. Only days later, after some prodding from two of the club's equity members, U.S. Open Champions Hubert Green and Jerry Pate, the PGA of America reserved Shoal Creek for their 1984 Championship, making it (with the lone exception of the Augusta National) the youngest course ever to hold a major championship.

As the tournament approached, Nicklaus said the pros would score well on his 7145-yard, par-72 creation, predicting a winning total of 276 or less. Less it was—273—but that score came from a player of major proportions, Lee Trevino.

Trevino, age 44, had not won a major since the PGA at Tanglewood a decade earlier, and the most recent of his twenty-six tournament victories had come in 1981. But from the moment he saw Shoal Creek, he knew he was at home. The course was not long, but it was plenty tight, and under championship conditions the penalty for errant shots was severe, exactly the way the straight-hitting Trevino liked it.

The rough in particular was difficult—deep, lush, and thick. During one practice round Greg Norman lost his ball in it, not a remarkable occurrence except that Norman's shot had plunked down just two feet off the green. But the grass was long partly because the Birmingham area had received several inches of rain just prior to the championship, slowing down the fairways and greens so that errant drives did not stray into trouble while approach shots could be fired at the flags like darts at a bull's-eye.

All this led to some spectacularly low scores, the first shocker being a practice round by Lanny Wadkins in which he birdied ten of his first thirteen holes and shot 61. Then in the second round of the tournament, a rejuvenated 48-year-old Gary Player tied the PGA Championship record with a round of 63 that included deuces at each of the four par-three holes.

As it turned out, Player and Wadkins were the two other main contenders for the title, but the consistent Trevino would not be denied. Playing seventy-two holes with only two bogeys and one double-bogey, he repeated his U.S. Open feat of sixteen years earlier and became the first man in history to break 70 in all four rounds while winning the championship. Trevino's 69-68-67-69—273 gave him his sixth and final major championship by four strokes.

But it wasn't easy. The Merry Mex began the final round just one stroke ahead of Wadkins and two in front of Player, with the three of them paired together. Trevino took first blood by sinking a 45-foot birdie putt on the opening hole as Player also birdied, but then Wadkins came back with a birdie at the 2nd. Trevino birdied the 3rd, but Wadkins got it back again with a birdie at 6 where Trevino bogeyed, putting them in a tie three ahead of Player. When Wadkins hit his 4-iron second shot twelve feet from the 9th pin and rolled it in, he took a one-stroke lead into the back nine.

But after he found rough and sand at 11, Wadkins posted a bogey, then three-putted the 12th to go from one ahead to one behind Trevino. It was a lead Lee would never relinquish. At 14 he stung a 7-iron to the green and sank the eight-foot putt to double his margin. A birdie by Wadkins at 15 put the lead back at one, but it was the 16th hole that was decisive.

After Wadkins struck his teeshot within twelve feet of the hole on this 197-yard par three, Trevino knocked his ball well over the green and then chipped poorly, eighteen feet from the hole. At that point, a miss by Trevino and a make by Wadkins would have put Wadkins in the lead. But instead Trevino ran in his eighteen-footer and Wadkins missed—a pair of pars, and the lead stayed with Lee. At both 17 and 18 aggressiveness got the better of Wadkins and he picked up a pair of bogeys. Meanwhile, Trevino made a routine par at 17 and then birdied the home hole, capping an extremely popular victory, his last as a PGA Tour player.

Although he struck the ball with characteristic control all week, the key to Trevino's mastery was his putting, or more precisely his putter, an old Ping model he had bought a few weeks earlier in a pro shop at the Dutch Open. He had been putting poorly all year, his frustrations capped by the seventy-one strokes he had taken over the last two rounds of the British Open at St. Andrews.

"I wanted a Ping because everyone was using them," he said. "But this was an upright putter, so I took it back to my hotel room and banged it on the floor as hard as I could, to flatten it. Then I stomped it with my heel to take some loft off it."

In the eight rounds after buying the magic wand and prior to the PGA, Trevino was forty-six under par. "It's ugly," he said, "but I feel like every putt is going into the hole—and it is." Certainly he made his share at Shoal Creek, where he saved himself time after time with brilliant putts of every distance and seized his chances with nineteen birdies over the four days.

Controversy preceded the return to Shoal Creek for the 1990 PGA. A month prior to the championship Hall Thompson stated in an interview that black members would never be admitted to his club, saying "That's not done in Birmingham." His remarks spurred an immediate reaction from civil rights leaders who threatened to picket the championship. The major advertisers involved with the telecast pulled millions of dollars of sponsorship.

The issue quickly spread from Shoal Creek to involve other clubs holding major championships, as well as PGA Tour sites and private country clubs across the nation. In the wake of the controversy the PGA of America, the USGA, and the PGA Tour all announced that no future tournaments would be held at clubs that discriminate in policy or practice on the basis of race, creed, national origin, or gender. Even the Augusta National Golf Club agreed to admit at least one black member before the 1991 Masters. Under all this pressure, Shoal Creek, too, backed down and announced that it had extended honorary membership to a black man, Louis Willie, a 65-year-old insurance executive who had not played the game in twenty years. The club also said that it had initiated plans to invite another black member.

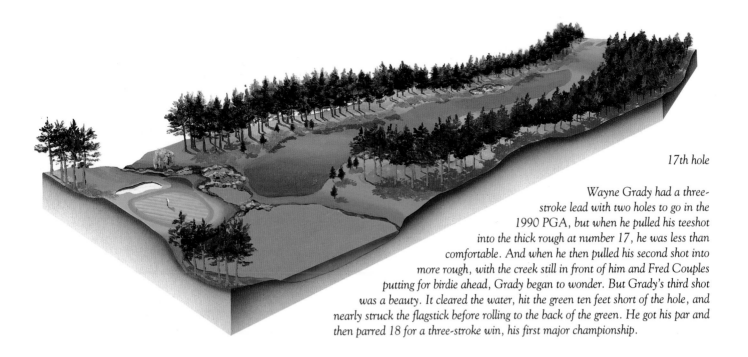

17th hole

Wayne Grady had a three-stroke lead with two holes to go in the 1990 PGA, but when he pulled his teeshot into the thick rough at number 17, he was less than comfortable. And when he then pulled his second shot into more rough, with the creek still in front of him and Fred Couples putting for birdie ahead, Grady began to wonder. But Grady's third shot was a beauty. It cleared the water, hit the green ten feet short of the hole, and nearly struck the flagstick before rolling to the back of the green. He got his par and then parred 18 for a three-stroke win, his first major championship.

Whether the Shoal Creek incident has spawned a true revolution in the membership practices of golf clubs across America, or merely a period of tokenism, only time will tell.

As for the 1990 PGA at Shoal Creek, the course discriminated against everyone. The rough was just as thick and gnarly as in 1984—up to six inches deep in spots—but the fairways were a bit narrower. Shots that failed to land in the short grass simply disappeared into the cloying vegetation. Tournament marshals used wooden tongue depressors to mark the positions of the balls.

There was no such thing as a long shot from the rough. Players routinely raked the ball back to the fairway with their wedges. Shots around the green became a guessing game. Any contact that was solid enough to raise the ball from its grassy grave invariably produced a shot that was too hot to stay near the hole.

On top of this, the greens had aged six years and had become much firmer. "You couldn't dent some of these greens with a shot-put," said Tim Simpson after round one.

And he had shot a 71 to be among the leaders. At the top was Bobby Wadkins with a 68, followed by Fred Couples at 69 and Mark O'Meara at 71. Meanwhile the game's titans had been toppled. Greg Norman, Hale Irwin, Seve Ballesteros and Trevino all shot 77s, Jack Nicklaus had a 78, and Curtis Strange and Tom Kite took 79s.

Day two brought more of the same. "This is the hardest course I've ever played in my life," said Fuzzy Zoeller, at 143 one of only nine players under par. But Australia's Wayne Grady found it to his liking, posting a 67 to take the lead at 139. Couples shared second with Larry Mize, a stroke behind as Messrs. Nicklaus, Strange, and Ballesteros all missed the cut, Seve after a second round of 83. The average score for the field was 76.

An efficient 72 kept Grady in the lead after fifty-four holes, now by two strokes over Couples (who had hit the ball all over the place but used just twenty-one putts) and the defending Champion, Payne Stewart. Meanwhile, 43-year-old Gil Morgan played the round of the week, a seven-under-par 65 that jumped him over fifty-one players into fourth place.

Among the top four players only Stewart had won a major championship. The phlegmatic Couples had frittered away chances at several events, major and otherwise, and Grady had registered only four victories worldwide against two dozen runner-up finishes, the most agonizing of them at Troon in the 1989 British Open where he had led until a bogey at the seventy-first hole thrust him into a playoff with Norman and the eventual winner, Mark Calcavecchia.

On Sunday it came down to a battle between Couples and Grady. When he rolled in a lengthy putt for a birdie at the 12th hole, he tied Grady at seven under par, and when Grady, playing directly behind him, bogeyed the hole, the lead belonged to Fred.

But he immediately bogeyed four straight holes, his putter suddenly unable to save him as it had for three and a half days. Grady continued to make pars, and his victory came by three strokes on a score of 282.

Jack Nicklaus got the design job at Shoal Creek through a reference from Clifford Roberts, co-founder with Bobby Jones of the Augusta National Golf Club. Thompson, an Augusta National member, asked Roberts, "If you were going to redesign the Augusta National, who would you have do it?" His unhesitating answer was

OVERLEAF: *18th hole.* INSET ABOVE: *18th hole.* INSET BELOW: *Lee Trevino kisses the magical putter that brought him his first major championship in a decade, the 1984 PGA. Photo: Michael O'Bryon for Sports Illustrated © Time Inc.*

11th hole

Nicklaus, who has in fact instituted several changes in the Masters course during the last decade or so.

It was a propitious marriage, Shoal Creek and Nicklaus, for the site fit his vision. "Watching the flight of the ball is at the heart of golf's appeal," he says, "and I don't like blind shots. When a player can see all the challenges confronting him, the demands of the course can be raised." The ideal Jack Nicklaus course would play downhill from the 1st tee to the 18th green. That's never possible, but with each property that is his ideal. At Shoal Creek, he didn't have to try hard. Cut from a rich forest on the slope of a mountain grown with pines, dogwoods, and azaleas, with a creek meandering at its base, this property resembles the Augusta National, full of ups, downs, and gentle rolls. Several tees are elevated, and throughout the course there is a sense of playing downward from tee to green.

The greens are neither large nor terrifyingly contoured, but every green except the 4th is guarded by sand; several are also surrounded by grass-covered humps and hollows from which no appreciable backspin may be applied. Imagine a chip from a steep downhill lie in Brillo rough to a sloping surface of linoleum and you have an idea of Shoal Creek's greenside challenge.

The course opens tamely enough, with a straight 410-yard par four marked by two large bunkers, one to the left of the driving zone, another at the left of the green. Originally the green was one of the smallest targets on the course, but criticism during the 1984 PGA led to several refinements, one of which was a 1,500-square-foot addition to its right side. Wayne Grady barely reached this green on Sunday in 1990, but then sank a putt of over sixty feet for a birdie that launched him to victory. In 1984, Trevino sank a birdie putt of almost that length in the final round of the PGA.

Number 2 is a lengthy dogleg right, one of only three holes where the green is not visible from the tee. The bunkerless fairway allows a bit of freedom, but a large bunker to the left of the green adds strategy, beckoning aggressive teeshots that stay close to the inside of the dogleg to allow an open approach.

The 3rd hole is the first of four marvelous par fives. Reflecting another Nicklaus philosophy, one he shares with Bobby Jones, each of them is reachable in two shots, but the two shots had better be well planned and superbly executed. Although this hole appears straight to the eye, clever bunkering forces most golfers to do some tacking, hitting the teeshot to the right, then the second to the left, before coming back to the right on the third. No hole saw more changing and rechanging than this one, as Thompson and Nicklaus argued endlessly about the shape, placement, and bunkering of the green. During the construction process there was one earthmover operator who, when asked what he did for a living, replied, "The 3rd green at Shoal Creek." Still, it is probably the best birdie opportunity on the course.

There are no tricks or traps at number 4, just 456 yards of unbunkered fairway to a 10,000 square-foot plateau green. When this hole plays into a stiff prevailing wind, only the strong survive with par.

One of the charms of Shoal Creek is its constantly varying pace; never do we encounter more than two consecutive holes of the same par, and from the 2nd through the 9th each hole signals a change: 4-5-4-3-5-4-3-4. Thus the raw, brutish 4th is followed by the sylvan, picturesque 5th, a par three of 190 yards over a small pond. At this hole, which plays downhill with a majestic mountain as a backdrop, even a poor teeshot can be a pleasure to watch.

Nicklaus's favorite hole is the par-five 6th, which calls for not one but two carries over the creek. After a good drive the player may opt either to gun for the green or lay-up to the left side of this rightward dogleg. The creek winds around the left side of the green, and three bunkers guard the other flanks. For the members this is the number-one handicap hole.

The teeshot is the key at number 7, a 448-yard par four played slightly sidehill to a green that is nearly fifty yards long but not very wide. Fortunately, the prevailing wind follows the path of this fairway. Then it's back to finesse again at the 8th, another downhill par three with water front and left and bunkers front and rear. After the 1984 PGA the green was extended on the left, bringing it to the edge of the water. At 173 yards, it is the shortest hole on the course, but not short on severity.

The outward nine finishes with a 437-yard par four that bends slightly left to a green set on a spit of land. The water that guards three sides does not seem in play until one finds the rough with his teeshot; then the green begins to look like a floating cupcake. There's a bailout area on the right, if two large bunkers may be deemed a bailout area. The square green is one of the most undulating on the course.

Options are again available at number 10, a 421-yard par four where the key is the second shot, since the green is tri-level and each tier has several pin placements. Shots that miss to the left will flirt with the creek for which the course is named. Nick Faldo was in contention to win his third major championship of 1990 until in the third round he took a 7 here.

The 11th is another gambler's-delight par five, 516 yards with the second shot all carry over the creek which meanders across the fairway not once but twice in the last 150 yards. Small pot bunkers guard the front of the green, with a large bunker on the left. Beyond the green is more water.

Although the 12th hole plays from an elevated tee, this is also the only hole on the course where the second shot plays uphill. A par four of 451 yards, it calls for a mid- to long iron to a medium-sized green. When Lanny Wadkins three-putted here in the final round, Trevino took hold of the '84 PGA for good.

The main criticism from the players during that championship centered on the sameness of the par threes. Although each played in a different direction, each of the first three played over water and each of them was about the same length. "You use the same club, a 6-iron, on all of them," said Tom Watson. Nicklaus rectified that by lengthening the 13th hole to 195 yards. It plays from a tee on the hillside across a valley to a green on another hillside, with a stream at the extreme front and bunkers front, right, and left. A miss here is costly. The shortest par four on the course is number 14, a dogleg right of 379 yards to a small sand-flanked green. It is followed by another short four, 405 yards, this one curving slightly left around a mammoth fairway bunker to a green which seems to have an elephant buried in its center.

Grady got a great break here in 1990 when his rightward veering teeshot hit a tree and bounced back into the fairway, enabling him to reach the green and make his par.

The 16th is another par three that has been lengthened since the 1984 PGA, although it plays shorter than its 215 since it's downhill. A lone dogwood tree, encroaching on the left of the green, complicates this teeshot. Here it was that Trevino sank an eighteen-footer for par to retain his lead with two holes to go, as Wadkins, fifteen feet away, failed to convert his birdie opportunity.

For a while, before the '84 PGA, there was talk that the 17th hole would play as a par four on two days and a par five the other two days, but the PGA people decided to play it straight as only a par five. A slight dogleg right, with a large bunker marking the pivot point of the inside corner, it calls for a long, downhill approach to a wide, flat, shallow green that is guarded in front by water—in fact, by a waterfall. When Nicklaus said he wanted more than a simple lake in front of this green, Thompson summoned a few of his bulldozers to plop down several huge boulders to the right front of the green, creating a waterfall that has made this the most photographed hole on the course.

After that hole the 18th is aesthetically an anticlimax, but it is a stern place to have to make par. The hardest hole of the 1990 PGA, it plays 446 yards straight at the clubhouse to a green surrounded by sand, the sand surrounded by grassy swales, and the swales surrounded by water. A big basin in the green provides for three separate target areas, any of which can be elusive when a championship—or even a $2 nassau—is on the line.

PGA Championship: August 16-19, 1984

Lee Trevino	69	68	67	69	273	1
Lanny Wadkins	68	69	68	72	277	T2
Gary Player	74	63	69	71	277	T2
Calvin Peete	71	70	69	68	278	4
Seve Ballesteros	70	69	70	70	279	5
Scott Simpson	69	69	72	70	280	T6
Gary Hallberg	69	71	68	72	280	T6
Hal Sutton	74	73	64	69	280	T6
Larry Mize	71	68	67	63	280	T6
Russ Cochran	73	68	73	67	281	T10
Tommy Nakajima	72	68	67	74	281	T10
Victor Regalado	69	69	73	70	281	T10

PGA Championship: August 9-12, 1990

Wayne Grady	72	67	72	71	282	1
Fred Couples	69	71	73	72	285	2
Gil Morgan	77	72	65	72	286	3
Bill Britton	72	74	72	71	289	4
Chip Beck	71	70	78	71	290	T5
Billy Mayfair	70	71	75	74	290	T5
Loren Roberts	73	71	70	76	290	T5
Mark McNulty	74	72	75	71	292	T8
Don Pooley	75	74	71	72	292	T8
Tim Simpson	71	73	75	73	292	T8
Payne Stewart	71	72	70	79	292	T8

Scorecard

HOLE	YARDS	PAR
1	410	4
2	417	4
3	516	5
4	456	4
5	190	3
6	540	5
7	448	4
8	173	3
9	437	4
OUT	3587	36
10	421	4
11	516	5
12	451	4
13	195	3
14	379	4
15	405	4
16	215	3
17	530	5
18	446	4
IN	3558	36
TOTAL	7145	72

GOLF *Magazine* Rankings:
49th in the World
30th in the U.S.A.

SOUTHERN HILLS
COUNTRY CLUB

TULSA, OKLAHOMA
U.S. Open: 1958, 1977
PGA Championship: 1970, 1982

In the depths of the Depression era, a time when golf clubs across America were closing by the hundreds, Southern Hills Country Club opened. It opened in the arid plains of Oklahoma, a place that John Steinbeck's Joad family and thousands of real families, destitute families, were fleeing, hauling their few earthly possessions down a long dusty road to the greener pastures of the West.

Southern Hills opened both because and in spite of this most distressing period in America's economic history. When a rumor circulated among Tulsa's elite that the Tulsa Country Club was about to succumb and convert to a public facility, a group of alarmed members approached wealthy oilman Waite Phillips (of the Phillips Petroleum family), who owned several hundred acres of land, and asked for his help. Phillips told them he would give them the land if they could raise $150,000 within two weeks and agree to spend it over a two-year period on a true country club, a place that would include not simply a golf course but tennis courts, a swimming pool, and other recreational facilities.

Since most of these members were oilmen themselves, and hardly impoverished, pledges for the $150,000 were easily secured, and Perry Maxwell was hired as the designer. He built them a course that would not only survive the Depression but thrive for generations to come.

Although it was completed in 1936, Southern Hills didn't host a major championship until the USGA arrived in 1958 for what history records as the Blast Furnace Open. The temperatures hovered close to 100 all week, and Maxwell's steeply banked greens putted like greased linoleum. In round one, Gene Sarazen shot an 84 and pronounced the course "ridiculous." Sam Snead opened with a 75, followed that with an 80, and missed the Open cut for the first time in eighteen years.

Amid all this, one man kept his cool. He was the least likely of men to do so, the terrible-tempered Tommy Bolt, who played the best golf of his career en route to a four-stroke victory. Bolt, a native Oklahoman, seemed impervious to the heat that dogged the rest of the field, but he also claimed to have found a new sense of inner cool. "I was at peace with the world," he recalled years later. "I even had a double bogey on 18 in the third round to finish at 69, and it never fazed me." In his pocket that week he carried a card that read "God give me the serenity to accept the things I cannot change, the courage to change the things I can, and the wisdom to know the difference."

Bolt never shot higher than 72 whereas every other competitor posted at least one round of 75 or higher. Second place went to a 22-year-old Open rookie named Gary Player, who announced with determination, "I have set four goals for myself. I want to win the U.S. Open, the Masters, and the American PGA Championship, and I want to be the leading money winner on the Tour." He would do all those things, and many more.

Bolt was calm, Player was resolute, and in 1970 when the PGA came to Southern Hills, the winner, Dave Stockton, was a bit of both. Prior to the tournament Stockton had read a book on psychocybernetics, and he was feeling the power of positive thinking. "I just thought of myself as the PGA Champion all week," he said.

Stockton had been comparatively unknown before August 13 to 16, but this was his week in the sun—the hot sun. Temperatures ranged between 105 and 112, but Stockton shot two rounds of par to take a share of the halfway lead with Larry Hinson, two ahead of Arnold Palmer, Dick Lotz, and Billy Casper. In the third round, Stockton got a hot putter and posted a 66 that took him to a three-stroke lead.

On the final day Bob Murphy and Jack Nicklaus shot 66s, but both of them had been too far back to threaten Stockton, who could afford to bogey 17 and 18 for a round of 73 yet still take a two-stroke victory. Before he stepped up to his winning putt Stockton scanned the large gallery and saw his wife, Cathie, standing next to the 1966 PGA Champion, Al Geiberger. Tears welled up in his eyes, and he

OPPOSITE: *12th hole*

had to ask his caddie for a towel. "I realized the championship was mine to take, and all that it meant," he said. His reign was the shortest of any champion, as the 1971 PGA was played in February and won by Jack Nicklaus.

A special kind of mental fortitude was again needed by the winner of the next major championship at Southern Hills. Hubert Green led or shared the lead in the 1977 U.S. Open for each of the first three rounds, and was still in front as he made the turn into the back nine on Sunday. But after he putted out on the 14th green a phalanx of Tulsa police walked out of the trees and USGA Vice President Sandy Tatum approached Green. He told Hubert that a threat had been made on his life. A frantic woman had phoned the FBI and said that three men were on their way to Tulsa to assassinate Green. "I know they're serious," she had said. "They showed me their guns."

Tatum gave Green a choice. He could withdraw, he could ask for play to be suspended, or he could continue to play. Green chose to play, and even joked that the threat had probably come from an old girlfriend. He played the last few holes flanked by armed guards.

As it turned out, the main danger came from the 1975 Open Champion, Lou Graham, who made four birdies in five holes, the last of them at the 16th, where he drew even with Green, then playing the 13th hole. Graham nearly birdied the 17th hole despite a poor drive, because he escaped from trees with one of the most masterful recovery shots in Open history, a low hook under the branches that rolled to within eight feet of the hole. But then he missed

Hubert Green battled not only the course and the world's best players but a death threat to prevail in the 1977 U.S. Open. Photo: AP/Wide World Photos

When Hubert Green reached the 18th tee, he knew he needed a bogey five to beat Lou Graham by one and win the 1977 U.S. Open. With self-deprecating humor, he later recalled his thoughts while playing that hole. "I told myself not to hit the drive into the rough—then I did. I told myself to keep the second shot out of the bunker—then I hit it into the bunker. I told myself not to chunk the bunker shot—then I chunked it well short of the hole. And I told myself not to leave more than a tap-in for my second putt—then I left it four feet short." But Green sank that four-footer for a truly courageous victory.

18th hole

1st hole

the birdie putt. Graham finished the tournament at one under par, 279, one stroke shy of Green.

No player of the modern era is a better front-runner than Raymond Floyd. In the 1969 PGA he led from wire to wire and in the process set an 18-hole PGA record of 65. In the 1976 Masters he again led from start to finish and again went into the record books, tieing Jack Nicklaus's 72-hole mark of 271. And when the PGA came to Southern Hills in 1982, Floyd did it again, opening the championship by tieing another record—a 63 that he called "the best round of golf I've played anywhere." From the 6th through the 14th holes, Floyd scored nine straight threes, five of them birdies. He thereby lowered the course record of 65 that, coincidentally, he himself had set (along with Lee Trevino) in the 1970 Open, and tied the PGA mark set by Bruce Crampton at Firestone in 1975.

At that point it was Floyd's championship to win or lose, and few doubted that he would win it. He followed with rounds of 69 and 68 to set 36-hole and 54-hole PGA lows, and would have broken the 72-hole mark had he not double-bogeyed the final hole. Still, it was good enough for a three-stroke victory over Lanny Wadkins.

But this was the year that everyone beat up on Southern Hills. Despite the usual 100-degree heat, an unprecedented number of players bettered par in each round, and Fred Couples equaled the nine-hole PGA record with a 29. The course was virtually the same as the one played in the 1958 Open, except for one important difference—the greens were syringed with water, keeping them soft and susceptible to dartlike approach shots. Meanwhile, the fairways were dry and hard and the ball rolled forever. On one hole in the second round Bob Gilder, in second place after a 66, laid up with a 5-iron from 283 yards and watched as his ball bounced and rolled to within ten yards of the green.

The ball rolls at Southern Hills because, despite its name, the course is basically flat. The only major elevation changes occur at the 1st and 10th holes, which play from an elevated tee beside the clubhouse, and the 9th and 18th, which head back up the same hill.

"It doesn't look as tough as it is," says Byron Nelson, perhaps because Southern Hills has no one outstanding aspect of difficulty. It is simply tough all over. It is long—nearly 7000 yards at a par of 70. It is tight, with corridors of tall trees lining the fairways, most of which curve or bend around corners. It is penal, with Bermuda rough so thick that Ben Hogan injured his wrist while playing from it and was forced to withdraw from the 1958 Open. Its greens are tightly guarded with bunkers filled with sand from the nearby Arkansas River, a mixture called Number Six Wash that has the

4th hole

consistency of talcum powder. And its greens are steeply banked from back to front and, during major championships, excruciatingly fast. In '58, Bolt hit fifty-nine out of seventy-two greens in regulation yet finished three over par. Architect Maxwell is famed for his greenmanship, and did redesign work on stiff putting tests, Augusta National and Pine Valley. The game's finest putter, Ben Crenshaw, maintains that when playing a Maxwell course it's important to put your approach on the correct side of the green because putting up or down one of Perry's surfaces is "an invitation to three-putt."

Added to all this are the whims of Mother Nature. The standard weather forecast for major championships at Southern Hills includes heat intense enough to cause a sane man to aim his teeshots for the trees, plus high winds, dust storms, "gully-washer" thunderstorms, tornadoes, and now and then a plague of locusts. And sometimes all of this occurs in the same day. Native son Will Rogers said of the Oklahoma weather, "If you don't like it, stick around a minute; it'll change."

The same might be said of Southern Hills. Dave Stockton claims, "It's a course that turns you around every other hole. You can make eagle, which I did, then double bogey." Stockton's victory total in 1970 also included twenty-one birdies—and nineteen bogeys.

It begins with an excellent bogey opportunity. Although number 1 plays downhill, it measures 459 yards into the prevailing south wind, and doglegs left toward a green guarded by two deep bunkers. Contrary to most openers, it is a stiff assignment in both distance and accuracy.

Things don't get much easier at the 450-yard 2nd, where the teeshot must carry 230 yards over a stream while avoiding two bunkers across the landing area. From there a mid to long iron remains to a plateau green surrounded by four bunkers. Both the drive and the second must cross water at number 3, but these creeks will not come into play except in a very stiff breeze, or if the second must be played from the thick rough. This trio of fours may constitute the strongest start in championship golf.

The best chance for birdie comes at the straightforward 360-yard 4th, assuming the prevailing headwind is not too strong. Then an all-out effort will be needed at 5, a leftward-turning par five that can be stretched to 630 yards, with water skirting the right of the green. The hardest par three on the course comes at number 8 in the form of a 218-yard shot that must avoid bunkers right and left. The 9th doglegs right and moves slightly uphill and into the wind to a green whose entrance is narrowed by two bunkers.

Southern Hills's back nine begins and ends at the clubhouse as the front does, but the rest of the time the twain never meet, the outward holes meandering off to one side of the property, the inward holes on the other.

The challenge is built around two pairs of back-to-back par fours, 12/13 and 17/18. Ben Hogan called the 12th hole "the greatest par-four 12th in the United States," undoubtedly using the qualifying "par-four" in deference to the par-three 12th hole at the Augusta National. It is a hole perhaps only Hogan could love, a 456-yard dogleg left requiring a great drive followed by an equally great second shot. The fairway is lined with trees and rough, and at the crook of the dogleg is a large bunker. The lengthy approach must be played to a green guarded by water to the front and right with bunkers and trees to the back and left. Robert Trent Jones calls the view of this green "spectacular and frightening at the same time." Arnold Palmer made a double bogey here in the 1970 PGA, when he lost to Dave Stockton by two strokes, yet Arnie included this hole in a book of his fifty-four favorite holes in golf.

The Southern Hills members play number 13 as a 551-yard par five, but for the pros it becomes a nasty 470-yard four. The short hitter will be left with a blind second shot, but that may be a blessing, because the ball will have to carry not one but two ponds and find a smallish green amid five bunkers. When the wind turns around and comes from the north, this hole is virtually unreachable.

On paper the 355-yard 17th doesn't seem like much of a challenge, but bold play here could produce a 6 as easily as a 3. Those who try to cut the corner of the left-to-right dogleg with a big drive may find rough or trees, and from there they will be all but unable to find and hold the shallow, well-guarded, two-tiered plateau green, the smallest target on the course.

Number 18 is the most difficult hole on the course, and for the same reason it is also the most controversial. A good teeshot will come to rest in an area about 200 yards short of the green, leaving a downhill lie and a long-iron all-carry approach to the elevated green set in front of the clubhouse. Longer-hitting players are unable to gain much advantage off the tee because beyond the landing area lurk two streams and three cross bunkers. The second shot must land on the green, which is appropriately large but fiercely sloped from back to front. In the first round of the 1977 Open this hole played to a stroke average of 4.8, so hard that it was shortened twenty yards for the rest of the tournament. Not even the winners at Southern Hills have conquered it. Bolt and Floyd each made a double bogey here, Stockton bogeyed it three days out of four, and Green struggled all the way to the bogey that won him the Open.

U.S. Open: June 12-14, 1958

Tommy Bolt	71	71	69	72	283	1
Gary Player	75	68	73	71	287	2
Julius Boros	71	75	72	71	289	3
Gene Littler	74	73	67	76	290	4
Walter Burkemo	75	74	70	72	291	T5
Bob Rosburg	75	74	72	70	291	T5
Jay Hebert	77	76	71	69	293	T7
Dick Metz	71	78	73	71	293	T7
Don January	79	73	68	73	293	T7
Ben Hogan	75	73	75	71	294	T10
Frank Stranahan	72	72	75	75	294	T10
Tommy Jacobs	76	75	71	72	294	T10

U.S. Open: June 16-19, 1977

Hubert Green	69	67	72	70	278	1
Lou Graham	72	71	68	68	279	2
Tom Weiskopf	71	71	68	71	281	3
Tom Purtzer	69	69	72	72	282	4
Jay Haas	72	68	71	72	283	T5
Gary Jacobsen	73	70	67	73	283	T5
Tom Watson	74	72	71	67	284	T7
Lyn Lott	73	73	68	70	284	T7
Terry Diehl	69	68	73	74	284	T7
Gary Player	72	67	71	75	285	T10
Jack Nicklaus	74	68	71	72	285	T10
Rod Funseth	69	70	72	74	285	T10
Mike McCullough	73	73	69	70	285	T10
Al Geiberger	70	71	75	69	285	T10
Peter Oosterhuis	71	70	74	70	285	T10

Scorecard

HOLE	YARDS	PAR
1	459	4
2	450	4
3	410	4
4	360	4
5	630	5
6	188	3
7	385	4
8	218	3
9	378	4
OUT	3478	35
10	401	4
11	167	3
12	456	4
13	470	4
14	215	3
15	410	4
16	552	5
17	355	4
18	458	4
IN	3484	35
TOTAL	6962	70

PGA Championship: August 13-16, 1970

Dave Stockton	70	70	66	73	279	1
Bob Murphy	71	73	71	66	281	T2
Arnold Palmer	70	72	69	70	281	T2
Larry Hinson	69	71	74	68	282	T4
Gene Littler	72	71	69	70	282	T4
Jack Nicklaus	68	76	73	66	283	T6
Bruce Crampton	73	75	68	67	283	T6
Dick Lotz	72	70	75	67	284	T8
Raymond Floyd	71	73	65	75	284	T8
Billy Maxwell	72	71	73	69	285	T10
Mason Rudolph	71	70	73	71	285	T10

PGA Championship: August 5-8, 1982

Raymond Floyd	63	69	68	72	272	1
Lanny Wadkins	71	68	69	67	275	2
Fred Couples	67	71	72	66	276	T3
Calvin Peete	69	70	68	69	276	T3
Jim Simons	68	67	73	69	277	T5
Jay Haas	71	66	68	72	277	T5
Greg Norman	66	69	70	72	277	T5
Bob Gilder	66	68	72	72	278	8
Tom Kite	73	70	70	67	280	T9
Tom Watson	72	69	71	68	280	T9
Jerry Pate	72	69	70	69	280	T9
Lon Hinkle	70	68	71	71	280	T9

GOLF *Magazine* Rankings:
28th in the World
17th in the U.S.A.

British Open

TURNBERRY

TURNBERRY, SCOTLAND
British Open: 1977, 1986, 1994

Turnberry served in World War I as a training station for Royal Flying Corps pilots. It served in World War II as a landing strip for Spitfires guarding the Atlantic convoys. And in 1977 it served up World War III, as the two reigning superpowers, Jack Nicklaus and Tom Watson, battled stroke for stroke over seventy-two holes, head to head over the final thirty-six, in what is generally agreed to have been the most stirring display of championship golf the game has ever seen.

The first planned golf resort in Great Britain, and the most scenically impressive of the British Open courses, Turnberry invariably captures the hearts of American golfers. With several holes running along the rock-bound cliffs of the Firth of Clyde, it has the raw, brawling charm of Pebble Beach, and like Pebble Beach it is the only resort course on which an Open is currently held.

The resort was the creation of the Marquis of Ailsa, who had a private course at the Culzean estate a few miles to the north. At the turn of the century he agreed to take over development of this barren and beautiful stretch of land. Working with the Glasgow and South Western Railway, the Marquis commissioned Willie Fernie,

professional and greenkeeper at nearby Troon, to design not one but two courses. In 1907 they were joined by a majestic hotel, high on a hill overlooking the links and sea, and Turnberry had become a tourist mecca with daily train service from Glasgow and an overnight sleeper from London. To this day, it has remained one of the finest golf resorts in the world, rating one of only twenty-one Gold Medals awarded by *GOLF Magazine*.

But periods of strife have punctuated the leisure and recreation at Turnberry. The two wars took their toll, particularly World War II, when Turnberry's fairways were flattened, its bunkers were filled in, and its greens were graded to make room for the landing strips. After the war, however, the courses were resuscitated by Frank Hole, the managing director of British Transport Hotels, together with architect Mackenzie Ross. Hole raised the money to rebuild the courses and Ross, using plastic hole models to show exactly the pitch and roll he wanted, created a masterpiece of modern seaside golf. When the new Turnberry officially opened in 1951, it met with rave reviews.

A bit over a decade later Turnberry hosted the British Amateur

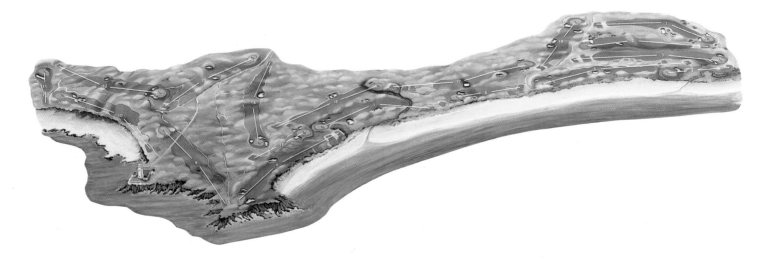

as Michael Bonallack (now secretary of the R&A) won the first of five titles over ten years. And a decade after that it became the venue for the Walker Cup matches, won by America, 12 to 8. These matches, and all major competitions, were played on the longer, seaside Ailsa Course, while the more sheltered Arran remains almost exclusively a resort layout. The Arran was named after a nearby island and Ailsa refers to Ailsa Craig, the massive granite rock that rises from the sea like a prehistoric beast, a few miles off the Turnberry shore. A local saying goes, "If you can see Ailsa Craig, it's about to rain; if you can't see Ailsa Craig, it *is* raining."

Indeed, although Turnberry can be an utterly tranquil place, the site of the most breathtakingly beautiful summer sunsets in Britain, it can also be the site of some of the most demonic weather in Britain, especially in the fall. During the late '60s and early '70s, the John Player Classic was held here, and the 1972 staging of that event is recalled by many players as Mother Nature at her meanest. The first day's conditions were perfect, but things deteriorated rapidly after that. By the final day the temperatures were in the 40s and the wind was at gale force. The goal of most players was not to play good golf, it was to stay warm, dry, and alive while attempting to salvage par as often as possible. Gary Player, the man who tries hard on every shot, posted an 85 as Bob Charles won with a closing 76. The scores of Ryder Cupper and British PGA Champion Peter Townsend reflected the week's worsening conditions: 65-70-75-80.

Turnberry was expected to be a stern test of the world's best players when it joined the British Open rotation in 1977, but an extended drought had left Ailsa's fairways dry and hard, and four days of warm, nearly windless weather made this an Open of record scores. In the second round, Mark Hayes turned in a 63 that set a new British Open mark. And the winning total, posted by Tom Watson, lowered the previous best by a whopping eight strokes.

One behind Watson was Nicklaus, after a battle to end all battles. Earlier in the year they had gone up against each other at the Augusta National, with Watson prevailing despite a closing 66 by the Golden Bear. But the quality and drama of their confrontation at Turnberry eclipsed that Masters and every other major championship that anyone could remember.

Each of them opened with a 68, each followed with a 70, to move one behind leader Roger Maltbie. Then in the third round the two giants began to separate themselves from the pack, with a pair of 65s, Nicklaus's on nines of 31-34, Watson's 33-32. With eighteen holes left to play, they were three strokes clear of the field. Twenty-four hours later, the man in third place, Hubert Green, was ten strokes behind. Green, the only other player to finish the tournament under par, later joked, "I won the Open—those two guys played another game."

Indeed they did. Nicklaus began Sunday by birdieing two of the first four holes, as Watson bogeyed one of them to open up a three-stroke edge. But Watson came back with birdies at the 5th, 7th, and 8th to draw even. Then a bogey at 9, for an outward 34, left him one

The battle of the century took place when Tom Watson and Jack Nicklaus dueled head to head over the final 36 holes in 1977. Watson won by a single stroke on a British Open record of 268 after both players birdied the 72nd hole. Photo: © Phil Sheldon

behind Nicklaus. When Jack holed from twenty-five feet for a birdie at 12, his margin was two strokes.

Never had Jack Nicklaus held a two-stroke lead with six holes to play in a major championship and failed to win, but this time he did. More accurately, Watson took it away from him with a combination of superb shotmaking, guts, and luck that produced four birdies on the homeward holes. At the 13th, he pitched his second to twelve feet and sank it. At the short 15th, he played the shot of the day. After hitting his teeshot into fluffy rough sixty feet from the flag, Watson holed the ball with his putter for an incredible deuce, to pull even. Both players parred the 16th and then Nicklaus sealed his own fate at the par-five 17th. After Watson had reached the green in two, Nicklaus, with a shorter shot, left the ball well shy of the green. He pitched to five feet and after Watson missed his eagle putt, he looked to be safe, but Jack left his birdie putt on the high side. With one hole to play, Watson had drawn one stroke ahead.

But Jack, being Jack, never gave up. Not after he push-sliced his final drive into deep rough, just inches from a gorse bush, as Watson drove perfectly. Not even after Watson hit a magnificent 7-iron to within less than two feet of the pin. No, Nicklaus somehow mus-

16th hole

Greg Norman had a five-stroke lead with three holes to play in the 1986 British Open, but when he pushed his teeshot way right at the 16th hole, he knew he had plenty of work to do. The wind was blowing, and Wilson's Burn loomed just in front of the green. When Norman reached his ball, however, he realized he'd gotten a great break. It had come to rest in a relatively clean lie, on grass that had been trampled down by the galleries. "Perfect, perfect, perfect," he said to his caddie. Norman then played a high fade at the center of the green. Its left-to-right drift was cancelled by the right-to-left wind and the ball came down ten feet from the hole. Victory was sealed.

cled his ball from the deep grass and onto that green, then sank a birdie putt of thirty feet, forcing Watson to hole that little tiddler to win.

The pair of titans left that final green, both smiling broadly, Nicklaus with his arm around Watson's shoulders. For four days they had played their hearts out, and everyone who had watched

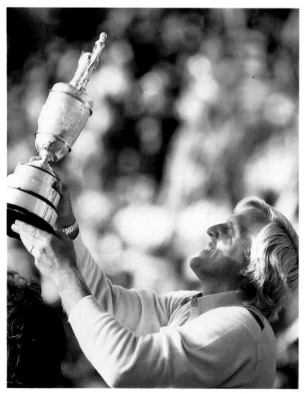

For once Greg Norman displayed the full spectrum of his awesome skills in 1986. His five-stroke victory included a round of 63 that might easily have been a 60. Photo: © Phil Sheldon

it—either at home or on television—knew they had seen something special.

When the Open returned to Turnberry nine years later Watson began with a 77, Nicklaus with a 78. The scores were less a reflection of the players' decreased skill than of the heightened difficulty of Turnberry. This time Great Britain had had a rainy spring and summer. The rough was long and thick, and the fairways were narrow—by the later admission of the R&A, too narrow. When 40 mph winds greeted the competitors on day one, only Ian Woosnam succeeded in matching par of 70. On Friday, conditions were only slightly improved, but Greg Norman nonetheless played one of the rounds of his life.

He began with three straight birdies, and although he dropped shots at the 5th and 8th, he eagled the 7th, reaching the turn in 32. On the way in he birdied 10 and 11, hit the flagstick with his approach at 14 for another birdie, and then added a fourth at the 16th. With two holes to go—one of them a very short par five—Norman was seven under par. An eagle at the short par-five 17th and a birdie at 18 would have given the Australian an inward half of 28 and a 60, three strokes better than the lowest 18-hole score in any major championship. But despite hitting his second shot to 17 within fifteen feet of the flag, Norman settled for birdie there, then three-putted 18 for 31-63. He nonetheless tied the one-round record for the British Open, and staked himself to a four-stroke lead.

The weather turned vile again on Saturday, and a 74 by Norman was enough to give him a one-stroke lead with eighteen holes to go. However, this was a season in which Norman had led both the Masters and the U.S. Open after fifty-four holes, and he had won neither. There were those who speculated that, despite his enormous talent, he lacked what it takes to win the big ones. But the next day Norman proved them wrong. Using advice given to him

5th hole

the night before by Jack Nicklaus, to lighten his grip pressure a bit, he posted a final round of 69 to win the Championship by a comfortable five strokes. In with a score of 280, he was the only man to match par for the seventy-two holes. Norman's victory became the cornerstone of a glittering season in which he won eight times and solidified his position as the number-one ranked player in the world.

The Ailsa course starts quietly enough, with a 350-yard par four that doglegs left. But when played into the teeth of a wind, this hole's narrow fairway can be difficult to find. The wind also becomes a factor on the approach, where out of bounds hugs the back and left of the green. In 1986 Tommy Nakajima began the final round of the Open one stroke behind Norman, but then three-putted this green from five feet for a double bogey that enlarged Norman's lead to three.

That 1st hole is the last par four on Turnberry measuring under 400 yards. Number 2, which runs back parallel to the 1st and slightly uphill, plays a lengthy 428 yards to a green flanked by bunkers. When the European Open was held here in 1979, Sandy Lyle charged to victory by birdieing six of the first seven holes of his final round—this is the one he parred.

Into the wind, number 3 can be one of the hardest holes on the course, a 462-yard par four that plays down a narrow valley of a fairway to an equally narrow green. There are no bunkers along this fairway, but the rough is thick and treacherous, and at the green there is plenty of perdition in the form of two bunkers on the right, one on the left. Norman holed a seventy-five-foot explosion from that left-hand bunker for birdie here in the final round of his victory in 1986.

The 167-yard 4th signals the start of a string of eight holes along Turnberry Bay, the most dramatic and beautiful stretch of golf in the British Open rotation. The tiny green is cut into the side of a mound and any shot that lands on the left side of that mound will bound downward toward the ocean. A miss on the right side may find a steep grassy upslope, and a ball that falls short will land in a huge, deep bunker hollowed from the face of the hill. Combine these perils with a strong wind, and this short hole becomes a tall challenge.

One of the most wonderfully natural golf holes in the world is the 5th, a 441-yard par four (formerly a five) whose broad fairway winds right to left through a corridor formed by two lines of tall sandhills, ending at a natural amphitheater green.

The typical reaction from the first-time player as he steps to the tee of number 6 is, "Is this a par three or a par four?" His elderly Scottish caddie will then answer "Yes." With the possible exceptions of the 16th at Carnoustie and the 8th at Oakmont, this is the longest, strongest "short" hole in championship golf. The scorecard says 222 yards, but into a wind that means unreachable. It plays across a valley to an elevated green set in a nest of sand dunes. Forty yards short of the hole is a "fairway" bunker (par-threes usually don't have fairways, per se, but this one does). Just short and right is another bunker from which the escape will be downhill and toward the sea, and two more bunkers cuddle the left side of the green. In the 1986 Open this was the third most difficult hole on the course, playing to an average of 3.55 strokes.

The view from the 7th tee is a bit more inviting, with the generous dune-enclosed fairway bending gracefully left and uphill 528 yards to a broad green. The prevailing left-to-right wind can be a help here, keeping teeshots away from the knee-high rough that

OVERLEAF: *12th hole*. INSET LEFT: *10th hole*. INSET RIGHT: *16th hole*

lines the left-hand side of the fairway, but if the breeze is against, this green will be reachable only with three strong shots. The 8th is similar in feel, an upward-climbing, leftward bending hole, but this one is a stout par four. The lone fairway bunker is cunningly placed, 250 yards from the tee in the right center of the landing area, and it dominates the drive. Once the sand is avoided, the second shot becomes relatively straightforward, up to another amphitheater green, this one bilevel.

Each of the holes at Turnberry has a name—many of them being quaint Scottish expressions such as "Tappie Toorie" and "Fin' Me Oot," but number 9 is called "Bruce," after Robert the Bruce, the Scottish king from 1306-29, the remains of whose castle lie near the tee of the hole. But this hole, with a championship tee perched on a promontory that drops off fifty feet to the sea below, has a regal bearing all its own. The teeshot calls for a carry of 200 yards to a hogback fairway. It also calls for concentration, since a picture-postcard white lighthouse, set on a rocky point well to the left, competes for one's attention. Few first-time players leave this tee without first taking a photograph or two. This bunkerless hole allows for a long, rolling approach, but the green is full of tricky undulations.

The back nine gets off to a strong start with the 452-yard 10th, a par four that, like so many at Turnberry, bends from right to left, challenging its assailants to play safely to the right or take the more aggressive, shorter route down the left. This time the penalty for mismanaged boldness is a saltwater marsh from which few teeshots are excavated. Smack in the center of the tumbling fairway is a 25-yard-long circular bunker with an island of grass at its center. Since it lies 50 yards short of the green, it doesn't come into play except when the wind is straight against, but it always comes into mind.

Number 11, a par three of 177 yards, can be a test of wind-play shotmaking, particularly when the teeshot is played downwind to a pin tucked behind the front bunker. From there the course heads inland and becomes far less scenic though no less daunting. The wind remains a strong factor at the 441-yard 12th. Although in 1977 Jack Nicklaus reached it one day with a driver and a wedge, when a strong breeze comes from green to tee, this hole is unreachable, even with back-to-back drivers. If the drive strays well left here, the second shot may be played from macadam, a vestige of the old airstrip days. On a hill to the right of the green is a monument to those who died in World War I.

"Tickly Tap" is the name given to number 13, a drive-and-pitch hole and the first one to move left to right since number 1. The key here is the second shot, since it plays to a green set on a diagonal that runs from ten o'clock to four o'clock, opposite to the path of the hole, and is elevated on a three-foot-high plateau in the manner of Donald Ross's greens at Pinehurst Number 2, creating interesting chipping assignments.

The hardest hole in the 1986 Open was number 14, which plays 440 yards uphill and into the prevailing west wind. There were 210 bogeys and 174 pars that year, against only a dozen birdies, two of them by Greg Norman. Greens at Turnberry tend to look a mile away from the tee, and this is one that also plays that way. To make things even tougher, this target is protected by deep bunkers right and left. The hole is aptly named "Risk an' Hope."

The rhythm of the course continues with a punishing little par three, where wind again is a big factor. One bunker is to the right and three are to the left of this hillside green, but a miss badly to the right will drop 40 feet onto the 8th fairway.

The only time that water crosses a Turnberry fairway is at number 16, where Wilson's Burn snakes just in front of the green, creating a deep ravine that sucks in shots that are either short or beyond it. The approach thus calls for more careful club selection than on any other hole. This hole brought about the demise of the British Walker Cup Team when several of their members found water during the final day's matches.

Under normal conditions the 17th may be the easiest par five in the British Open rotation. When played downwind, it is reachable after a drive to its broad valley fairway and a semi-blind middle iron uphill to its inviting green. Of course, into a wind that uphill road can be a long one indeed. Still, birdies here are common and eagles, even from amateurs, are not rare. The 18th is also something of an anticlimax, a dead flat, wide-open, downwind par four of 431 yards whose most distinguishing feature is the imposing orange-roofed Turnberry Hotel, perched on a hill beyond the green. There are bunkers and out of bounds to the left, but even an average teeshot will avoid them. This is a gentle send-off, and on most days, most golfers will be grateful for the reprieve.

British Open: July 6-9, 1977

Tom Watson	68	70	65	65	268	1
Jack Nicklaus	68	70	65	66	269	2
Hubert Green	72	66	74	67	279	3
Lee Trevino	68	70	72	70	280	4
George Burns	70	70	72	69	281	T5
Ben Crenshaw	71	69	66	75	281	T5
Arnold Palmer	73	73	67	69	282	7
Raymond Floyd	70	73	68	72	283	8
Tommy Horton	70	74	65	75	284	T9
Mark Hayes	76	63	72	73	284	T9
Johnny Miller	69	74	67	74	284	T9
John Schroeder	66	74	73	71	284	T9

British Open: July 17-20, 1986

Greg Norman	74	63	74	69	280	1
Gordon J. Brand	71	68	75	71	285	2
Bernhard Langer	72	70	76	68	286	T3
Ian Woosnam	70	74	70	72	286	T3
Nick Faldo	71	70	76	70	287	5
Seve Ballesteros	76	75	73	64	288	T6
Gary Koch	73	72	72	71	288	T6
Brian Marchbank	78	70	72	69	289	T8
Tommy Nakajima	74	67	71	77	289	T8
Fuzzy Zoeller	75	73	72	69	289	T8

Scorecard

HOLE	YARDS	PAR
1	350	4
2	428	4
3	462	4
4	167	3
5	441	4
6	222	3
7	528	5
8	427	4
9	455	4
OUT	3480	35
10	452	4
11	177	3
12	441	4
13	411	4
14	440	4
15	209	3
16	409	4
17	500	5
18	431	4
IN	3470	35
TOTAL	6950	70

GOLF Magazine Rankings:
19th in the World
6th in Great Britain & Ireland

WINGED FOOT GOLF CLUB

MAMARONECK, NEW YORK

U.S. Open: 1929, 1959, 1974, 1984

Golf's first and perhaps only impressario, Fred Corcoran, was fond of observing that never in the history of the U.S. Open has a player come to the seventy-second hole knowing he needed to make a birdie putt to win and then made that putt.

Corcoran, who died in 1977, lived in a white clapboard colonial next to the 15th hole of the West Course at Winged Foot. To date, no one has made that Open-winning birdie putt, but Corcoran's backyard has twice produced spectacular par putts to tie. They struck the final cup 55 years apart, one stroked by an amateur, one by a pro, one an American, one a foreigner. The first man, Bobby Jones, won his ensuing playoff; the second, Greg Norman, lost. But both players, both putts contributed mightily to the lore and luster of the Open and of Winged Foot.

This is a place where pars don't come easily. It was designed in

18th hole

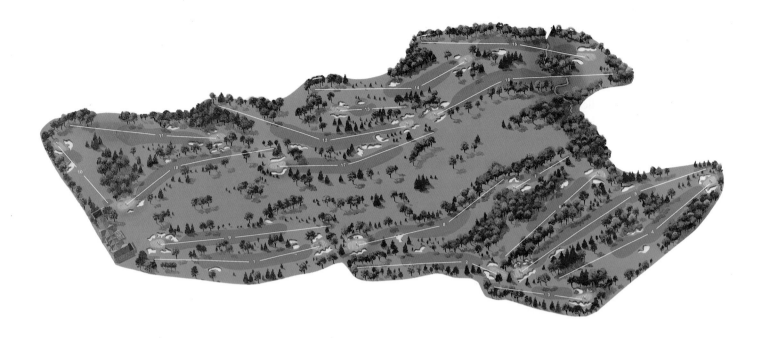

1923 after several members of the New York Athletic Club approached A.W. Tillinghast and told him, "Give us a man-sized course." Tillinghast, a Philadelphia dandy whose waxed mustache had ends so sharp you could spike incoming and outgoing mail on them, had already demonstrated his demonic designs at Baltusrol and Quaker Ridge. But at Winged Foot he topped himself, creating not one but two 18-hole courses, both distinguished by lengthy carries to fiercely sloped greens ringed by massive, deep bunkers. Late in life, Tillinghast declared Winged Foot West and East to be the finest work of his career.

On 280 acres of rolling farmland in Mamaroneck, New York—land where the Mohegan Indians had lived, where armies of the Revolutionary War had camped, and where the Quakers had once settled—Tillinghast brought to bear 220 men, 60 teams of horses, and 19 tractors—and these men, beasts, and machines chopped down 7,800 trees, moved 24,000 cubic yards of turf, installed 46,000 feet of pipe, and wrenched 7,200 tons of rock from the ground, reusing much of it to construct a grand clubhouse.

The cost of the land was $525,000. Today, that kind of acreage in fashionable Westchester County would command a pricetag with at least two more zeros on the end.

Six years after Winged Foot opened, its West Course hosted the U.S. Open. The favorite, as usual in the Roaring Twenties, was Bobby Jones. In every year from 1923 to 1928 Jones had won either a U.S. Amateur or a U.S. Open, and at Winged Foot he kept the streak alive—but just barely.

Although he took the first-round lead with a 69—the only sub-70 score of the championship—a 75 on day two left him two strokes behind Gene Sarazen and Al Espinosa at the halfway point. But Jones turned the tables again with a 71 in round three that put him three strokes ahead of Sarazen, four up on Espinosa.

He began the last round solidly enough until the 8th hole where his approach shot kicked into a bunker. What ensued was a calamity that every Winged Foot regular has suffered, a succession of unsuccessful sand shots. Jones caught the ball too thinly and his third shot sailed into a bunker on the other side of the green. Then he made the same mistake a second time and returned to his original bunker. He finally reached the green in five and two-putted for a triple-bogey seven.

Still, no one else had made a charge, and Jones's closest pursuer, Espinosa, had had a disaster of his own at the par-five 12th, where an 8 had gone on his card. In his epic history, *The Story of American Golf*, Herbert Warren Wind wrote: "On the 13th tee of the last round, no one would have given an enchilada for the chances of the slow-moving Spaniard from Monterey, California." Least of all Espinosa, who played his last six holes in a matter-of-fact twenty-two strokes for a 75—294 that left him the clubhouse leader by default.

Jones had a six-stroke lead with six holes to go, and he lost all of it, first with a bogey at the 13th and then with another triple-bogey seven at 15, where he hooked his teeshot into trees and needed five strokes to reach the green.

Ultimately, he needed to par the final hole to gain a playoff with Espinosa. His approach shot missed the green to the left, leaving a tricky chip from the long grass collar of one of the bunkers. Jones got the ball to twelve feet, leaving himself a devilish putt with a foot of break in it.

"I couldn't look," said O.B. Keeler, Jones's constant companion and biographer. "I was afraid if I watched he would miss the putt." Using his beloved Calamity Jane, Jones made the stroke of his career, coaxing the ball across the slope and to the lip of the cup, where it stopped for an instant and then fell. His playing partner,

Al Watrous, later claimed that the putt was so nicely gauged that if the hole had been a 4 1/4-inch circle on the green, the ball would have stopped in the middle of it. Today, nearly 250 major championships later, it is hard to think of a greater pressure putt. Said Keeler, "I will always believe that the remainder of Bobby's career hung on that putt and that from this stemmed the Grand Slam of 1930."

The next day, in golf's greatest anticlimax, Jones met Espinosa in a 36-hole playoff and beat him by 23 strokes, 141 to 164.

Thirty years passed before the Open returned, but despite the advent of the steel shaft the original Winged Foot West had changed little when the pros arrived in 1959. New tees at three holes had stretched the course from 6781 to 6873 yards, and two members' par fives had been converted to fours for the pros, lowering the par from 72 to 70, but Tillinghast's tiger had basically the same set of teeth it had bared to Jones & Co.

This time, however, there was no dominant player, no Jones, to tame the course. Sam Snead and Ben Hogan were still playing, but at age 47 both were clearly past their primes. Arnold Palmer had won the 1958 Masters, but he was still something of a newcomer, and Jack Nicklaus was still a teenager.

Nicklaus did qualify, but a pair of 77s took him home for the weekend. It was the first of a trio of unsuccessful outings for the Golden Bear on the West Course. (Thirty years later, when asked to rate the difficulty of Winged Foot on a scale of one to ten, Nicklaus gave his reply without hesitation: "Eleven, maybe twelve.")

Messrs. Snead, Hogan, and Palmer fared a bit better. At the halfway point of the Open Ben and Arnie stood at even par with Gary Player, one off the lead; after fifty-four holes, Hogan remained in second while Snead, after a 67, climbed into a tie with Palmer and Bob Rosburg for third. But they all trailed a full-figured Californian named Billy Casper.

Casper had won seven events since joining the Tour in 1955, but this would be his coming of age. He was hardly an impressive-looking player—his teeshots at Winged Foot measured only 251 yards, ranking him 65th in the field—but Casper knew how to play percentage golf, and he was the personification of the adage, "Drive for show, putt for dough."

No one in history has tamed the treacherous Winged Foot greens as certainly as Casper did that week, and it's unlikely that anyone ever will. Using a mallet-headed putter made by an obscure company named Golfcraft Glasshaft Casper took only 114 putts for seventy-two holes, one-putting thirty-one times and three-putting only once. Beginning at the 15th hole in round three, he one-putted nine straight holes, using twenty-seven putts in the third round, twenty-eight in the last. Hogan, who began the final day three strokes behind but finished sixth, is reputed to have told Casper, "If you couldn't putt, you'd be selling hot dogs at the turn."

Still, this Open was hardly stolen by Casper. Billy closed with a 74 over a course still wet from a thunderstorm that had postponed the final round for the first time in history. Palmer also shot 74, Snead shot 75, and Hogan shot 76. A 69 by any of them would have won it.

Among the players in contention, only Mike Souchak and Bob Rosburg made moves. Souchak needed to birdie the last hole to tie and instead bogeyed, dropping into a tie for third with Claude Harmon, who had sunk a long birdie putt to finish at 284, two behind Casper. Rosburg, whose final nine had included a holed-out bunker shot and a fifty-foot putt for birdies, needed one more miracle at 18. But his 6-iron approach stopped thirty feet below the

Bobby Jones sinks the final putt on his 36-hole playoff with Al Espinosa to take the 1929 Open. Jones won, 141 to 164. Photo: UPI/Bettmann

hole, and then he stroked his last chance an inexcusable five feet short.

Casper went on from Winged Foot to win three more events in 1959. He would also win another Open in 1966, the 1970 Masters, fifty-one tournaments in all, and five Vardon Trophies. Despite his extraordinary success he remained the most underrated player of the modern era. When people visit the World Golf Hall of Fame at Pinehurst, they don't dwell at the Casper exhibit, but in a display of golf clubs at the USGA Museum in Far Hills, New Jersey, Billy's old mallet putter gets plenty of attention.

The 1974 Open was dubbed *The Massacre at Winged Foot* by sports journalist Dick Schaap, whose book of that title chronicled the week, hour by hour. This was the year after Johnny Miller had embarrassed Oakmont and the USGA, winning the Open with a final round of 63. Granted he had played darts that day, hitting to greens softened by rain. But there are no pictures in the statistics book, and the Winged Footers were determined to stay out of it. So, with the collusion of the USGA, the fairways of the West Course were tightened, the rough was grown, and the greens were shaved to near-preposterous proportions.

On the first hole of the first round, Jack Nicklaus faced a twenty-five-foot birdie putt, and knocked it clear off the green. He needed eleven putts to cover the first four holes, and shot 75. Reigning Masters Champion Gary Player led the opening day with an even-par 70 as only twenty-three of the 144 players beat Nicklaus's score, and several shot over 85.

Bespectacled Hale Irwin won the first of three Opens at Winged Foot in 1974, and threatened for three rounds in 1984. Photo: © Leonard Kamsler

Sandy Tatum, the chairman of the USGA Championship Committee, was asked, "Is the USGA trying to embarrass the best players in the world?" to which he delivered one of golf's classic replies: "No, we're trying to identify them." In the end, they succeeded in doing just that, as the top ten finishers on Sunday included Nicklaus, Player, Tom Watson, Tom Kite, and at the very top a man who would become a three-time Open Champion—Hale Irwin.

Arnold Palmer and Ray Floyd were also factors in this Open, sharing the halfway lead with Irwin and Player at 143 as Player stumbled with a triple-bogey 7 at the 4th hole. Then it was the young Watson who came to the fore after fifty-four holes with a 69 that gave him a one-stroke edge on Irwin, two on Palmer.

But Watson, age 25, had never won a pro tournament, and had had his problems leading them. The next day he ballooned to a 79, tumbling into a tie for fifth. As he sat by his locker following the play, totally distraught, he was approached by an elderly man who said: "I know how you feel, son. I've thrown away tournaments, too, but all you need is experience. If you ever want to talk about your game, call me." Byron Nelson had watched Watson closely, and had liked his aggressiveness and fire. This was the beginning of a long and close relationship that helped Tom Watson become the dominant player of the next ten years, a decade in which he would win two Masters, five British Opens, and the 1982 U.S. Open. Three times during those eight major championships he would battle down the closing stretches against Jack Nicklaus, and three times Watson would beat him.

On Sunday, June 16, 1974, however, Hale Irwin beat both of them, fighting the oppressive course with the intelligent and gritty style of golf that would become his trademark. At the 9th hole, one of the members' par fives that had become a par four for the championship, Irwin sank a slope-climbing, double-breaking thirty-five-footer for a birdie that gave him the lead at five over par, one ahead of Watson, who would drop into oblivion with bogeys on six of his last nine holes. But meanwhile, another 25-year-old, Forrest Fezler, had climbed into the battle. With one hole to play, he was eight over par and in second place.

Irwin remained five over after fourteen holes, but then bogeyed both 15 and 16. With two difficult par fours to go, and with Fezler playing the final hole just one stroke back, Irwin was far from a lock. And after he pulled his teeshot at the 17th into deep rough and his attempt at escape with a 4-wood moved the ball barely 100 yards, a playoff seemed probable. But from there he lofted a pitch to the green that stopped less than ten feet from the hole, and then slipped in the putt to save par.

As he walked to the final tee, he learned that Fezler had bogeyed the last hole, finishing at nine over. "Right then," said the relieved Irwin, "I was ready to fly home to St. Louis without an airplane." He played 18 perfectly, with a big drive down the middle of the fairway and a masterful 2-iron that covered the flag all the way, stopping twenty feet above the hole. Two putts gave him victory by two strokes. His winning total of 287 was the highest since the weather-beaten Open of 1963 at The Country Club, and the most over par under normal conditions since Olympic in 1955.

Five years later Irwin would grind out a second Open victory, at Inverness, and eleven years after that, at Medinah, he won again at age 45, becoming the oldest U.S. Open Champion in history.

When the Open returned to Winged Foot in 1984, the players faced a more benign golf course. It had been shortened from 6961 to 6930 yards, the greens were about 9 1/2 on the Stimpmeter instead of the 11 they had measured in 1974, and with the course softened from intermittent rain, it yielded more rounds of 70 or better than in the previous three Opens combined. But although the top ten players all bettered Irwin's winning total of 287, only two men bettered par—Fuzzy Zoeller and Greg Norman—and they bracketed the field by five strokes.

Halfway through the tournament, however, it looked like *déjà vu*. Hale Irwin, with a pair of 68s, had taken the lead, with Zoeller one behind, Norman two. Curtis Strange was in fourth at 139, having holed a 100-yard pitch shot for an eagle at the 2nd as well as a 5-iron for an eagle at the 11th.

A 74 in round three took Strange out of contention, to join virtually everyone else, as the top three players all posted 69s. Irwin and Zoeller were paired together on Sunday, and they quickly went in different directions, Irwin stumbling to the turn in 40 strokes, Zoeller in 32. Norman managed a 34 and with nine holes to go was three behind. It remained that way after thirteen holes, and Zoeller, who had played marvelously all week, seemed to be cruising home. But championships have a way of changing quickly, and this one did, at the par-four 14th hole, where Norman holed a twenty-footer for birdie and then Zoeller, just behind him, found deep rough with his teeshot and made 5. Suddenly the margin was only one stroke.

A pair of pars at 15 kept it that way with three to go. From there, Zoeller made par at 16, bogey at 17, and par at 18, while Norman made three of the most heroic scrambling pars in succession the game has ever seen. After missing the 16th green to the left, the Australian faced an impossibly delicate pitch from a downhill lie in the rough. But he played it with impossible delicacy, lofting the ball softly onto the green where it rolled six feet past the hole, from whence he saved par. At 17 he knocked his drive well right, into the trees, and after pitching out he still had a mid-iron to the green. But he hit it to six feet and saved par once again. And at 18, after a perfect drive, he hit his worst shot of the week, a pushed 6-iron that flew so far right it landed in the grandstand. After a free drop, he pitched poorly to the collar of the back-left portion of the green, just beyond the bunker Jones had escaped fifty-five years earlier.

The pin on that 18th hole was also set in the same position it had been in when Jones sank his titanic twelve-footer in 1929, and Norman was on a similar angle—but three times as far away. With

When Greg Norman snaked in this forty-five-footer on the final green, he seemed destined for victory, but a day later Fuzzy Zoeller beat him in a playoff. Photo: © Leonard Kamsler

Zoeller standing in perfect position in the center of the final fairway, Norman knew he needed to make that putt. And somehow, he did, trickling it across a spot he had judged to be on the perfect line. "I had the feeling in my hands," Norman said later. "I just felt it was going to go in."

Never in championship golf had a player sunk a putt that long that meant that much. As Norman galloped across the green in joy, back in the fairway Zoeller, who had assumed the putt was for a birdie, pulled a white towel from his bag and waved it in mock surrender. But then he calmly proceeded to play to the green and made the tieing par.

The playoff was as much an anticlimax as the one between Jones and Espinosa. When Zoeller rolled in a mammoth birdie putt at the 2nd hole, he took a three-stroke lead on Norman, who double-bogeyed it. That set the tone for the day. By the 16th hole, Zoeller's lead had grown to nine strokes. This time it was Norman who pulled out the towel as the pair came up 18. The final score was Zoeller 67, Norman 75.

The popular Zoeller, a carefree character who joked with the fans and whistled his way down many of the ninety holes, was ebullient in victory. "I whipped the great course for five days," he said. "It got Hale yesterday and it got Greg today, and it might have gotten me tomorrow, but I whipped it." Indeed he did. Through four Opens, 600 men have tackled Winged Foot, and Zoeller is the only one to have finished the assignment under par.

The challenge of Winged Foot is remarkable for the fact that this is a course with virtually no out of bounds, a course whose fairways roll but pose no steeply uphill or downhill assignments, a course where water appears only twice (and does not come into play), and where not even a 36-handicapper is likely to lose his ball. Winged Foot is not particularly intimidating from the tees, but from the fairway to the green it can be terrifying.

Tillinghast believed that "holes are like men, all rather similar from foot to neck, but with the greens showing the same varying characters as human faces." He also claimed that "a controlled shot to a closely guarded green is the surest test of any man's golf," and on the West Course those words echo constantly. Ten of the twelve par fours are over 400 yards, and most of them play to smallish greens that are steeply banked, tightly guarded, and manicured to a glass-like smoothness.

The Winged Foot greens average barely 5000 square feet, about three-fourths the size of most greens, whereas the seventy or so bunkers that surround them may average 1,000 square feet, so most Winged Foot members know how to do two things—putt and blast.

Tillinghast took advantage of the rocky Westchester County terrain and built his greens on ledges, many of them elevated above the fairways. Greens such as the par-three 10th can fall as much as seven feet from back to front. "Putting at Winged Foot is like playing miniature golf without the sideboards," says Hale Irwin, and the always colorful Snead calls the West Course greens "harder than a whore's heart." Says the Slammer, "To match par on this course you have to be luckier than a dog with two tails."

Nicklaus, when asked to comment on the course's finishing holes, said, "The last eighteen are pretty tough." Number 1, a 446-yard dogleg left, is one of the hardest starts in championship golf. Even long hitters will have a middle iron left to this green, which slopes severely from left to right and back to front. When Nicklaus knocked his first putt clear off this green in 1974, he was merely mimicking Bobby Jones, who began his 1929 Open victory with a double bogey here.

The 2nd beckons big hitters to try to cut its left-to-right dogleg, but they do so at their own peril. Dense trees line the right side of this hole, and the angled green is virtually unholdable from that side. It was here that Zoeller rolled in a birdie putt measured at sixty-eight feet to take command of his playoff with Norman.

The toughest hole in the 1959 Open was number 3, a par three that plays to a long green whose narrow throat is choked by two bunkers. A swale in front of the green tends to make the shot seem shorter than its 216 yards, and most amateurs fail to take enough club on this tee. But even the pros have their problems here. In 1974 Gary Player's errant teeshot landed in a trash barrel marked "America the Beautiful." Billy Casper may have had the best strategy here. In each of his four rounds in the 1959 Open, he intentionally played short of the green, then wedged on and one-putted for par.

Number 4 is another classic Winged Foot hole, playing 466 yards to a green whose stingy opening is narrowed by bunkers. (Flanking bunkers tighten the entrance of every green except 18.) Gary Player blew his lead in 1974 when he hit his 7-iron approach shot out of bounds here, then dropped a second ball and nearly hit that OB as well. Originally the hole was named Soundview, because the Long Island Sound was visible from its tee. But today, Winged Foot's 20,000 trees have matured, tightening the course as their branches encroach on the fairways and greens.

If Winged Foot can be said to have an Achilles heel, it is its two par fives, both of which are reachable to today's long hitters. The

2nd hole

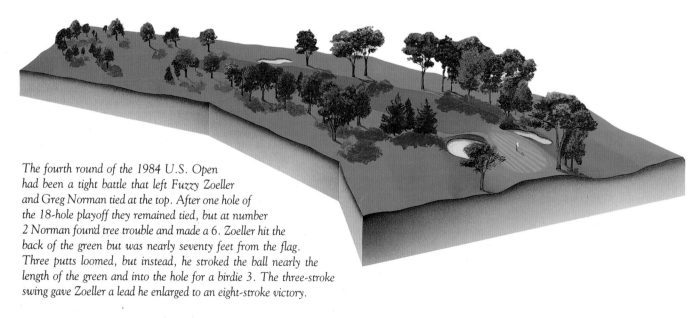

The fourth round of the 1984 U.S. Open had been a tight battle that left Fuzzy Zoeller and Greg Norman tied at the top. After one hole of the 18-hole playoff they remained tied, but at number 2 Norman found tree trouble and made a 6. Zoeller hit the back of the green but was nearly seventy feet from the flag. Three putts loomed, but instead, he stroked the ball nearly the length of the green and into the hole for a birdie 3. The three-stroke swing gave Zoeller a lead he enlarged to an eight-stroke victory.

1st hole

more difficult of the two is unquestionably number 5, which doglegs right to left and uphill to a plateau green described by Tillinghast as a "dog's back," throwing balls left and right into the inevitable bunkers.

It is followed by the shortest par four on the course, playing 324 downhill yards to, appropriately, the most elusive target on the course. Now and then a pro will try to drive this green, but most of them lay up with irons. It's important to put some spin on the approach shot, as a bunker guards the front, a stream and out of bounds lurk behind, and at its shallowest point the green is only a few paces deep. Bill Mehlhorn was going along nicely in the first round of the 1929 Open until he took a ten on this hole.

Johnny Miller, a man who in his heyday hit irons as accurately as anyone in history, once opined that at Winged Foot, "it doesn't do any good to hit it close." In the second round of the 1974 Open Miller hit a near-perfect teeshot to the little par-three 7th called Babe in the Woods. But the pin on this crowned green was cut just ten feet from the deep right-hand bunker and Miller's ball caught the collar of the bunker and rolled back into the sand. Four explosion shots ensued before he reached the green and two-putted for a 7, thus ending any chance of successfully defending his Open title.

The hardest holes on the front nine are the last two, a pair of par fours averaging 450 yards. Number 8 calls for a long and careful drive around its rightward-bending fairway. From there another long and careful shot must thread between the two bookend bunkers where Bobby Jones crisscrossed. The 9th is an easy par five for the members but a bear of a four for the pros. It plays from an elevated tee down a broad fairway toward the clubhouse and a perched green that may be the most severely bunkered of any on the course, five gaping white mouths surrounding its slippery surface.

The 10th is on many lists of the great holes in golf, a par three of 190 yards over a deep swale to a severely tilted green set on a hill. Miss the shot short and it will roll down into the swale, miss it even slightly right or left and it will bound twenty feet down into sand, miss long and the result will be either out of bounds or the most frightening downhill chip on the course. Tillinghast considered this the finest par three he ever built.

Number 11 is a wonderfully subtle par four, playing over a series of humps and ridges with the fairway kicking left toward a bunker at the 260-yard mark. Broad-limbed trees on the right side of this green complicate the approach from that side of the fairway.

The other par five, number 12, doglegs left while climbing to a

second tier of fairway. A slight draw is a good shot from the championship tee, but a big hook is not, as a row of pine trees lines the left side of the hole. The green is very reachable, but if the pin is in front and the ball runs to the back, a two-putt birdie will be well earned.

Number 13 demands a long iron to its slim, pear-shaped green on the side of a hill. A bunker looms on the high left side and two more await on the right below.

Five dogleg par fours form the finish. Both the 14th and 15th call for right-to-left shots from the tee, then proceed to elevated greens that are hard to find, hard to hold, and hard to putt. The 16th is another members' five converted to a four. It winds first from right to left and then calls for a slightly faded shot around the broad trees that hover over the right side of the green.

Number 17 may be the hardest hole on the course, a par four of 444 yards that bends to the right around a nest of fairway bunkers and a stand of tall pines, leaving a lengthy shot to another narrow sausage of a green. Nicklaus calls it "a textbook test of golf, a hole that really pits the player against the designer." Tillinghast usually wins.

A twisting, turning, heaving fairway presents itself at the 18th tee. Jones and Norman saved par dramatically here, but most mortals who fail to find the fairway and green will have their work cut out for them. At 448 yards it is the type of hole that perhaps only a pro can play properly, first with a quiet draw that rolls around its corner, then with a high long iron that lands softly on one of the most severely contoured greens in golf.

Four other National Championships have been played at Winged Foot, the most dramatic of them the 1957 Women's Open on the East Course. It was won by Betsy Rawls, but would have been won by Jackie Pung had she not signed an incorrect scorecard in the final round. Tears streamed down her face as she realized the magnitude of her mistake. After the tournament, the Winged Foot members took up a collection and presented Ms. Pung with a gift larger than the first prize.

The West Course was also the site of the first U.S. Senior Open in 1980, won by Roberto DeVicenzo, as well as the 1949 Walker Cup matches, won by America 10 to 2 over Great Britain and Ireland. That result must have elicited mixed reactions from some of the Winged Foot members, many of whom are of Irish descent. One of them was David Mulligan, who had come to the club in 1937 when he came down from Canada to become manager of New York's Biltmore Hotel. A notoriously slow starter who always welcomed a second chance at the first tee, he is the man for whom the Mulligan was named.

U.S. Open: June 27-30, 1929

Bobby Jones	69	75	71	79	294	
			72	69	141	1
Al Espinosa	70	72	77	75	294	
			84	80	164	2
Gene Sarazen	71	71	76	78	296	T3
Denny Shute	73	71	76	76	296	T3
Tommy Armour	74	71	76	76	297	T5
George Von Elm	79	70	74	74	297	T5
Henri Ciuci	78	74	72	75	299	7
Leo Diegel	74	74	76	77	301	T8
Pat O'Hara	74	76	73	78	301	T8
Horton Smith	76	77	74	75	302	10

U.S. Open: June 11-13, 1959

Billy Casper	71	68	69	74	282	1
Bob Rosburg	75	70	67	71	283	2
Claude Harmon	72	71	70	71	284	T3
Mike Souchak	71	70	72	71	284	T3
Doug Ford	72	69	72	73	286	T5
Ernie Vossler	72	70	72	72	286	T5
Arnold Palmer	71	69	72	74	286	T5
Ben Hogan	69	71	71	76	287	T8
Sam Snead	73	72	67	75	287	T8
Dick Knight	69	75	73	73	290	10

U.S. Open: June 13-16, 1974

Hale Irwin	73	70	71	73	287	1
Forrest Fezler	75	70	74	70	289	2
Lou Graham	71	75	74	70	290	T3
Bert Yancey	76	69	73	72	290	T3
Arnold Palmer	73	70	73	76	292	T5
Jim Colbert	72	77	69	74	292	T5
Tom Watson	73	71	69	79	292	T5
Tom Kite	74	70	77	72	293	T8
Gary Player	70	73	77	73	293	T8
Jack Nicklaus	75	74	76	69	294	T10
Brian Allin	76	71	74	73	294	T10

U.S. Open: June 14-17, 1984

Fuzzy Zoeller	71	66	69	70	276	
				67		1
Greg Norman	70	68	69	69	276	
				75		2
Curtis Strange	69	70	74	68	281	3
Johnny Miller	74	68	70	70	282	T4
Jim Thorpe	68	71	70	73	282	T4
Hale Irwin	68	68	69	79	284	6
Peter Jacobsen	72	73	73	67	285	T7
Mark O'Meara	71	74	71	69	285	T7
Lee Trevino	71	72	69	74	286	T9
Fred Couples	69	71	74	72	286	T9

Scorecard

HOLE	YARDS	PAR
1	446	4
2	411	4
3	216	3
4	460	4
5	515	5
6	324	4
7	161	3
8	442	4
9	456	4
OUT	3431	35
10	190	3
11	383	4
12	535	5
13	212	3
14	418	4
15	417	4
16	452	4
17	444	4
18	448	4
IN	3499	35
TOTAL	6930	70

GOLF *Magazine* Rankings:
17th in the World
11th in the U.S.A.

RECORDS & STATISTICS

THE MASTERS, THE U.S. OPEN, THE BRITISH OPEN,
THE PGA CHAMPIONSHIP

The Masters Tournament
AUGUSTA NATIONAL GOLF CLUB, AUGUSTA, GEORGIA

WINNERS

YEAR	WINNER	SCORE	RUNNER-UP	YEAR	WINNER	SCORE	RUNNER-UP
1934	Horton Smith	284	Craig Wood	1969	George Archer	281	Billy Casper, George Knudson, Tom Weiskopf
1935	*Gene Sarazen	282	Craig Wood				
1936	Horton Smith	285	Harry Cooper				
1937	Byron Nelson	283	Ralph Guldahl	1970	*Billy Casper	279	Gene Littler
1938	Henry Picard	285	Ralph Guldahl, Harry Cooper	1971	Charles Coody	279	Jack Nicklaus, Johnny Miller
1939	Ralph Guldahl	279	Sam Snead	1972	Jack Nicklaus	286	Bruce Crampton, Bobby Mitchell, Tom Weiskopf
1940	Jimmy Demaret	280	Lloyd Mangrum				
1941	Craig Wood	280	Byron Nelson				
1942	*Byron Nelson	280	Ben Hogan	1973	Tommy Aaron	283	J.C. Snead
1943–45	No tournament			1974	Gary Player	278	Dave Stockton, Tom Weiskopf
1946	Herman Keiser	282	Ben Hogan				
1947	Jimmy Demaret	281	Byron Nelson, Frank Stranahan	1975	Jack Nicklaus	276	Johnny Miller, Tom Weiskopf
1948	Claude Harmon	279	Cary Middlecoff	1976	Ray Floyd	271	Ben Crenshaw
1949	Sam Snead	282	Johnny Bulla, Lloyd Mangrum	1977	Tom Watson	276	Jack Nicklaus
				1978	Gary Player	277	Rod Funseth, Hubert Green, Tom Watson
1950	Jimmy Demaret	283	Jim Ferrier				
1951	Ben Hogan	280	Skee Riegel				
1952	Sam Snead	286	Jack Burke, Jr.	1979	*Fuzzy Zoeller	280	Ed Sneed, Tom Watson
1953	Ben Hogan	274	Ed Oliver	1980	Seve Ballesteros	275	Gibby Gilbert, Jack Newton
1954	*Sam Snead	289	Ben Hogan	1981	Tom Watson	280	Johnny Miller, Jack Nicklaus
1955	Cary Middlecoff	279	Ben Hogan				
1956	Jack Burke, Jr.	289	Ken Venturi	1982	*Craig Stadler	284	Dan Pohl
1957	Doug Ford	283	Sam Snead	1983	Seve Ballesteros	280	Ben Crenshaw, Tom Kite
1958	Arnold Palmer	284	Doug Ford, Fred Hawkins	1984	Ben Crenshaw	277	Tom Watson
1959	Art Wall	284	Cary Middlecoff	1985	Bernhard Langer	282	Seve Ballesteros, Ray Floyd, Curtis Strange
1960	Arnold Palmer	282	Ken Venturi				
1961	Gary Player	280	Charles Coe, Arnold Palmer	1986	Jack Nicklaus	279	Tom Kite, Greg Norman
1962	*Arnold Palmer	280	Gary Player, Dow Finsterwald	1987	*Larry Mize	285	Greg Norman, Seve Ballesteros
1963	Jack Nicklaus	286	Tony Lema	1988	Sandy Lyle	281	Mark Calcavecchia
1964	Arnold Palmer	276	Dave Marr, Jack Nicklaus	1989	*Nick Faldo	283	Scott Hoch
1965	Jack Nicklaus	271	Arnold Palmer, Gary Player	1990	*Nick Faldo	278	Ray Floyd
1966	*Jack Nicklaus	288	Tommy Jacobs, Gay Brewer	1991	Ian Woosnam	277	José-Maria Olazabal
1967	Gay Brewer	280	Bobby Nichols				
1968	Bob Goalby	277	Roberto De Vicenzo		*Won playoff		

RECORDS

SCORING

LOWEST SCORE, 72 HOLES
271 — Jack Nicklaus (67–71–64–69), 1965
271 — Ray Floyd (65–66–70–70), 1976
274 — Ben Hogan (70–69–66–69), 1953
275 — Seve Ballesteros (66–69–68–72), 1980

LOWEST SCORE, 72 HOLES, BY NON-WINNER
277 — Johnny Miller (75–71–65–66), 1975
277 — Tom Weiskopf (69–72–66–70), 1975

LOWEST SCORE, FIRST 54 HOLES
201 — Ray Floyd (65–66–70), 1976
202 — Jack Nicklaus (67–71–64), 1965

LOWEST SCORE, LAST 54 HOLES
202 — Johnny Miller (71–65–66), 1975
203 — Nick Price (69–63–71), 1986

LOWEST SCORE, FIRST 36 HOLES
131 — Ray Floyd (65–66), 1975
135 — By nine players

LOWEST SCORE, MIDDLE 36 HOLES
132 — Nick Price (69–63), 1986
133 — Dow Finsterwald (68–65), 1962
133 — Curtis Strange (65–68), 1985

LOWEST SCORE, LAST 36 HOLES
131 — Johnny Miller (65–66), 1975
133 — Gary Player (69–64), 1978
133 — Jack Nicklaus (64–69), 1965

LOWEST SCORE, FIRST ROUND
64 — Lloyd Mangrum, 1940
64 — Mike Donald, 1990

LOWEST SCORE, SECOND ROUND
64 — Miller Barber, 1979

LOWEST SCORE, THIRD ROUND
63 — Nick Price, 1986
64 — Jack Nicklaus, 1965

LOWEST SCORE, FOURTH ROUND
64 — Maurice Bembridge, 1974
64 — Hale Irwin, 1975
64 — Gary Player, 1978
64 — Greg Norman, 1988

LOWEST SCORE, NINE HOLES
30 (front nine) — Johnny Miller, third round, 1975; Greg Norman,
        fourth round, 1988
30 (back nine) — Jimmy Demaret, first round, 1940; Gene Littler, third round, 1966;
        Ben Hogan, third round, 1967; Miller Barber, fourth round, 1970;
        Maurice Bembridge, fourth round, 1974; Gary Player, fourth round,
        1978; Nick Price, third round, 1986; Jack Nicklaus,
        fourth round, 1986

LARGEST WINNING MARGIN
9 — Jack Nicklaus, 1965
8 — Ray Floyd, 1976
7 — Cary Middlecoff, 1955

LARGEST LEAD AFTER 54 HOLES
8 — Ray Floyd, 1976
7 — Seve Ballesteros, 1980

LARGEST LEAD AFTER 36 HOLES
5 — Harry Cooper, 1936; Herman Keiser, 1946; Jack Nicklaus, 1975; Ray Floyd, 1976

LARGEST LEAD AFTER 18 HOLES
5 — Craig Wood, 1941

LARGEST LEAD AFTER 54 HOLES, NON-WINNER
5 — Ed Sneed, 1979

LARGEST LEAD AFTER 36 HOLES, NON-WINNER
5 — Harry Cooper, 1936

LARGEST LEAD AFTER 18 HOLES, NON-WINNER
4 — Jack Burke, Jr., 1955

BEST COMEBACK BY WINNER, FINAL ROUND
8 — Jack Burke, Jr., 1956
7 — Gary Player, 1978
6 — Art Wall, 1959; Fuzzy Zoeller, 1979

BEST COMEBACK BY WINNER, FINAL 36 HOLES
8 — Jack Burke, Jr., 1956

BEST COMEBACK BY WINNER, FINAL 54 HOLES
6 — Jack Burke, Jr., 1956; Gay Brewer, 1967; Craig Stadler, 1982; Jack Nicklaus, 1986

LOWEST SCORE BY WINNER, FIRST ROUND
65 — Ray Floyd, 1976

LOWEST SCORE BY WINNER, SECOND ROUND
65 — Cary Middlecoff, 1955

LOWEST SCORE BY WINNER, THIRD ROUND
64 — Jack Nicklaus, 1965

LOWEST SCORE BY WINNER, FOURTH ROUND
64 — Gary Player, 1978

HIGHEST SCORE BY WINNER, FIRST ROUND
75 — Craig Stadler, 1982

HIGHEST SCORE BY WINNER, SECOND ROUND
76 — Jack Nicklaus, 1966

HIGHEST SCORE BY WINNER, THIRD ROUND
77 — Sam Snead, 1952; Nick Faldo, 1989

HIGHEST SCORE BY WINNER, FOURTH ROUND
75 — Arnold Palmer, 1962

HIGHEST SCORE BY WINNER, 72 HOLES
289 — Sam Snead, 1954; Jack Burke, Jr., 1956

HIGHEST SCORE TO LEAD FIELD, 18 HOLES
71 — Jack Burke, Jr., 1957

HIGHEST SCORE TO LEAD FIELD, 36 HOLES
144 — Billy Joe Patton, 1954; Craig Stadler and Curtis Strange, 1982

HIGHEST SCORE TO LEAD FIELD, 54 HOLES
216 — Jack Nicklaus and Tommy Jacobs, 1966

MOST SUBPAR ROUNDS BY FIELD, TOURNAMENT
100 — 1980

MOST SUBPAR ROUNDS BY FIELD, FIRST ROUND
33 — 1965

MOST SUBPAR ROUNDS BY FIELD, SECOND ROUND
40 — 1980

MOST SUBPAR ROUNDS BY FIELD, THIRD ROUND
27 — 1986

MOST SUBPAR ROUNDS BY FIELD, FOURTH ROUND
30 — 1968

FEWEST SUBPAR ROUNDS BY FIELD, TOURNAMENT
16 — 1956

FEWEST SUBPAR ROUNDS BY FIELD, FIRST ROUND
1 — 1936, 1957, 1982

FEWEST SUBPAR ROUNDS BY FIELD, SECOND ROUND
0 — 1954

FEWEST SUBPAR ROUNDS BY FIELD, THIRD ROUND
0 — 1956

FEWEST SUBPAR ROUNDS BY FIELD, FOURTH ROUND
1 — 1937

MOST SUBPAR TOTALS BY FIELD, TOURNAMENT
25 — 1974

LOWEST 36-HOLE CUT
145 — 1979

HIGHEST 36-HOLE CUT
154 — 1982

LOWEST SCORING AVERAGE OF FIELD, TOURNAMENT
72.77 — 1968

HIGHEST SCORING AVERAGE OF FIELD, TOURNAMENT
77.18 — 1956

LOWEST SCORING AVERAGE OF FIELD, SINGLE ROUND
70.98 — 1986, third round

HIGHEST SCORING AVERAGE OF FIELD, SINGLE ROUND
78.56 — 1956, third round

INDIVIDUAL, CAREER

VICTORIES
6 — Jack Nicklaus (1963, 65, 66, 72, 75, 86)
4 — Arnold Palmer (1958, 60, 62, 64)
3 — Jimmy Demaret (1940, 47, 50)
3 — Sam Snead (1949, 52, 54)
3 — Gary Player (1961, 74, 78)
2 — Horton Smith (1934, 36), Byron Nelson (1937, 42), Ben Hogan (1951, 53), Tom Watson (1977, 81), Seve Ballesteros (1980, 83), Nick Faldo (1989, 90)

CONSECUTIVE VICTORIES
2 — Jack Nicklaus (1965, 66); Nick Faldo (1989, 90)

RUNNER-UP FINISHES
4 — Ben Hogan (1942, 46, 54, 55)
4 — Tom Weiskopf (1969, 72, 74, 75)
4 — Jack Nicklaus (1964, 71, 77, 81)
3 — Johnny Miller (1971, 75, 81)
3 — Tom Watson (1978, 79, 84)
2 — Craig Wood (1934, 35), Harry Cooper (1936, 38), Ralph Guldahl (1937, 38), Byron Nelson (1941, 47), Lloyd Mangrum (1940, 49), Sam Snead (1939, 57), Cary Middlecoff (1948, 59), Ken Venturi (1956, 60), Arnold Palmer (1961, 65), Gary Player (1962, 65), Ben Crenshaw (1976, 83), Tom Kite (1983, 86), Greg Norman (1986, 87), Ray Floyd (1985, 90)

TOP-FIVE FINISHES
15 — Jack Nicklaus
9 — Ben Hogan
9 — Sam Snead
9 — Arnold Palmer
8 — Gary Player
7 — Byron Nelson
7 — Lloyd Mangrum
7 — Tom Watson
7 — Seve Ballesteros
6 — Ben Crenshaw
6 — Tom Kite

TOP-TEN FINISHES
21 — Jack Nicklaus
17 — Ben Hogan
15 — Sam Snead
15 — Gary Player
14 — Byron Nelson
13 — Tom Watson
12 — Arnold Palmer
10 — Tom Kite
9 — Lloyd Mangrum
9 — Ray Floyd
9 — Ben Crenshaw

TOP-TWENTY-FOUR FINISHES
28 — Jack Nicklaus
26 — Sam Snead
22 — Gary Player
20 — Byron Nelson
20 — Ben Hogan
19 — Arnold Palmer
18 — Billy Casper
17 — Gene Littler
16 — Ray Floyd
15 — Ben Crenshaw
15 — Tom Watson

COMPLETED 72 HOLES
31 — Sam Snead
29 — Jack Nicklaus
28 — Gary Player
25 — Arnold Palmer
24 — Byron Nelson
24 — Gene Littler
24 — Ben Hogan

APPEARANCES
44 — Sam Snead
38 — Doug Ford
36 — Arnold Palmer
34 — Gene Sarazen
34 — Billy Casper

CONSECUTIVE TOP-FIVE FINISHES
7 — Jack Nicklaus (1971–77)

CONSECUTIVE TOP-TEN FINISHES
12 — Byron Nelson (1937–42, 46–51)

CONSECUTIVE TOP-TWENTY-FOUR FINISHES
22 — Sam Snead (1939–42, 46–63)

CONSECUTIVE TIMES COMPLETED 72 HOLES
24 — Sam Snead (1937–42, 46–63)

CONSECUTIVE APPEARANCES
44 — Sam Snead (1937–42, 46–83)

LONGEST SPAN, FIRST TO LAST VICTORY
23 years — Jack Nicklaus (1963–86)

LONGEST SPAN BETWEEN VICTORIES
13 years — Gary Player (1961–74)

SCORING AVERAGE (AT LEAST TWENTY-FIVE ROUNDS)
71.29 — Tom Watson
71.34 — Jack Nicklaus
71.44 — Seve Ballesteros
71.96 — Jerry Pate
72.08 — Ben Crenshaw

SUBPAR ROUNDS
59 — Jack Nicklaus

CONSECUTIVE SUBPAR ROUNDS
7 — Arnold Palmer (1963–64–65), Jack Nicklaus (1964–65–66), Tom Weiskopf (1968–69), Tom Watson (1978–81)

ROUNDS IN THE 60S
33 — Jack Nicklaus

CONSECUTIVE ROUNDS IN THE 60S
4 — Tom Watson (1978–79), (1984–85)

SUBPAR 72-HOLE TOTALS
20 — Jack Nicklaus

CONSECUTIVE SUBPAR 72-HOLE TOTALS
10 — Jack Nicklaus (1970–79), Tom Kite (1975–84), Tom Watson (1977–86)

MOST TIMES LED AFTER 54 HOLES
5 — Arnold Palmer
5 — Jack Nicklaus

MOST TIMES LED AFTER 18, 36, OR 54 HOLES
14 — Arnold Palmer
12 — Jack Nicklaus

MOST TIMES LED AFTER 18, 36, OR 54 HOLES, BUT NEVER WON
5 — Lloyd Mangrum, Ken Venturi

PLAYOFF RECORDS (PLAYERS IN MORE THAN ONE PLAYOFF)
Nick Faldo (2–0)
Ben Hogan (0–2)

MISCELLANEOUS

PROGRESSIVE 72-HOLE SCORING RECORD
284, Horton Smith, 1934
282, Gene Sarazen, 1935
279, Ralph Guldahl, 1939; Claude Harmon, 1948
274, Ben Hogan, 1953
271, Jack Nicklaus, 1965; Ray Floyd, 1976

PROGRESSIVE 18-HOLE SCORING RECORD
69, Ed Dudley, Craig Wood, Harold McSpaden, 1934
67, Henry Picard, 1935; Gene Sarazen, Craig Wood, 1936
66, Byron Nelson, 1937; Gene Sarazen, 1939
64, Lloyd Mangrum, 1940; Jack Nicklaus, 1965; Maurice Bembridge, 1974; Hale Irwin, 1975; Gary Player, 1978; Miller Barber, 1979
63, Nick Price, 1986

FOUR SUBPAR ROUNDS, SAME MASTERS
Jimmy Demaret, 1947; Claude Harmon, 1948; Ben Hogan, 1953; Gary Player, 1962–74–80; Arnold Palmer, 1964; Jack Nicklaus, 1965; Ray Floyd, 1968–76; Bob Goalby, 1968; Tom Weiskopf, 1969–74; Gene Littler, 1970; Tom Watson, 1977–79–81; Fuzzy Zoeller, 1979

WIRE-TO-WIRE WINNERS (NO TIES)
Craig Wood, 1941; Arnold Palmer, 1960; Jack Nicklaus, 1972; Ray Floyd, 1976

WIRE-TO-WIRE WINNERS (INCLUDING TIES)
Horton Smith, 1934; Herman Keiser, 1946; Jimmy Demaret, 1947; Arnold Palmer, 1964; Seve Ballesteros, 1980

PLAYERS WHO LED FIRST THREE ROUNDS, DIDN'T WIN
Harry Cooper, 1936; Ken Venturi, 1956; Bert Yancey, 1967; Billy Casper, 1969

NUMBER OF TIMES A LEADER WENT ON TO WIN
18 holes — 14 in 54 tournaments
36 holes — 24 of 54
54 holes — 29 of 54

OLDEST WINNER
46 years, 2 months, 23 days — Jack Nicklaus, 1986

YOUNGEST WINNER
23 years, 4 days — Seve Ballesteros, 1980
23 years, 2 months, 16 days — Jack Nicklaus, 1963

NUMBER OF PLAYOFFS
11 in 54 tournaments

MOST PLAYERS TIED FOR LEAD, 18 HOLES
5 — 1964 (Bob Goalby, Davis Love, Jr., Kel Nagle, Arnold Palmer, Gary Player, 69)

MOST PLAYERS TIED FOR LEAD, 36 HOLES
4 — 1973 (Tommy Aaron, Gay Brewer, Bob Dickson, J.C. Snead, 141)

MOST PLAYERS TIED FOR LEAD, 54 HOLES
3 — 1967 (Julius Boros, Bobby Nichols, Bert Yancey, 211)

WON FIRST TIME PLAYED IN MASTERS
Horton Smith, 1934
Gene Sarazen, 1935
Fuzzy Zoeller, 1979

CONSECUTIVE BIRDIES
6 — Johnny Miller, 2nd through 7th holes, third round, 1975

CONSECUTIVE 3S
7 — Jodie Mudd, holes 16–18 (third round) and 1–4 (fourth round), 1987

MOST SUBPAR HOLES, TOURNAMENT
24 — Seve Ballesteros, 23 birdies and one eagle, 1980

MOST EAGLES, TOURNAMENT
4 — Bruce Crampton, 1974

HIGHEST SCORE, ONE HOLE
13 — Tommy Nakajima, 13th hole, 1978; Tom Weiskopf, 12th hole, 1980

NUMBER OF CHAMPIONS, BY NATIVE COUNTRY
United States, 45
South Africa, 3
Great Britain, 3
Spain, 2
West Germany, 1

AMATEURS

BEST FINISH
Second — Frank Stranahan, 1947; Ken Venturi, 1956; Charles Coe, 1961

LOWEST SCORE, 72 HOLES
281 — Charles Coe, 1961

LOWEST SCORE, 18 HOLES
66 — Ken Venturi, 1956

TOP-TEN FINISHES
3 — Billy Joe Patton, Charles Coe

MOST TIMES, LOW AMATEUR
6 — Charles Coe

Augusta, 17th hole

The U.S. Open

WINNERS

YEAR	WINNER, RUNNER-UP	SCORE	PLAYED AT
1895	Horace Rawlins / Willie Dunn	173	Newport GC / Newport, R.I.
1896	James Foulis / Horace Rawlins	152	Shinnecock Hills GC / Southhampton, N.Y.
1897	Joe Lloyd / Willie Anderson	162	Chicago GC / Wheaton, Ill.
1898	Fred Herd / Alex Smith	328	Myopia Hunt Club / S. Hamilton, Mass.
1899	Willie Smith / George Low / Val Fitzjohn / W.H. Way	315	Baltimore CC / Baltimore, Md.
1900	Harry Vardon / J.H. Taylor	313	Chicago GC / Wheaton, Ill.
1901	*Willie Anderson / Alex Smith	331	Myopia Hunt Club / S. Hamilton, Mass.
1902	Laurie Auchterlonie / Stewart Gardner / Walter Travis	307	Garden City GC / Garden City, N.Y.
1903	*Willie Anderson / David Brown	307	Baltusrol GC / Springfield, N.J.
1904	Willie Anderson / Gilbert Nicholls	303	Glen View Club / Golf, Ill.
1905	Willie Anderson / Alex Smith	314	Myopia Hunt Club / S. Hamilton, Mass.
1906	Alex Smith / Willie Smith	295	Onwentsia Club / Lake Forest, Ill.
1907	Alex Ross / Gilbert Nicholls	302	Philadelphia Cricket C. / Philadelphia, Pa.
1908	*Fred McLeod / Willie Smith	322	Myopia Hunt Club / S. Hamilton, Mass.
1909	George Sargent / Tom McNamara	290	Englewood GC / Englewood, N.J.
1910	*Alex Smith / John McDermott / Macdonald Smith	298	Philadelphia Cricket C. / Philadelphia, Pa.
1911	*John McDermott / Mike Brady / George Simpson	307	Chicago GC / Wheaton, Ill.
1912	John McDermott / Tom McNamara	294	CC of Buffalo / Buffalo, N.Y.
1913	*Francis Ouimet / Harry Vardon / Edward Ray	304	The Country Club / Brookline, Mass.
1914	Walter Hagen / Chick Evans	290	Midlothian CC / Blue Island, Ill.
1915	Jerry Travers / Tom McNamara	297	Baltusrol GC / Springfield, N.J.
1916	Chick Evans / Jock Hutchison	286	Minikahda Club / Minneapolis, Minn.
1917–18	No tournament		
1919	*Walter Hagen / Mike Brady	301	Brae Burn CC / W. Newton, Mass.
1920	Edward Ray / Harry Vardon / Jack Burke / Leo Diegel / Jock Hutchison	295	Inverness Club / Toledo, Ohio
1921	Jim Barnes / Walter Hagen / Fred McLeod	289	Columbia CC / Chevy Chase, Md.
1922	Gene Sarazen / Bobby Jones / John Black	288	Skokie CC / Glencoe, Ill.
1923	*Bobby Jones / Bobby Cruickshank	296	Inwood CC / Inwood, N.Y.
1924	Cyril Walker / Bobby Jones	297	Oakland Hills CC / Birmingham, Mich.
1925	Willie Macfarlane / Bobby Jones	291	Worcester CC / Worcester, Mass.
1926	Bobby Jones / Joe Turnesa	293	Scioto CC / Columbus, Ohio
1927	*Tommy Armour / Harry Cooper	301	Oakmont CC / Oakmont, Pa.
1928	*Johnny Farrell / Bobby Jones	294	Olympia Fields CC / Mateson, Ill.
1929	*Bobby Jones / Al Espinosa	294	Winged Foot GC / Mamaroneck, N.Y.
1930	Bobby Jones / Macdonald Smith	287	Interlachen CC / Minneapolis, Minn.
1931	*Billy Burke / George Von Elm	292	Inverness Club / Toledo, Ohio
1932	Gene Sarazen / Bobby Cruickshank / Philip Perkins	286	Fresh Meadow CC / Flushing, N.Y.
1933	John Goodman / Ralph Guldahl	287	North Shore CC / Glenview, Ill.
1934	Olin Dutra / Gene Sarazen	293	Merion Cricket C. / Ardmore, Pa.
1935	Sam Parks / Jimmy Thomson	299	Oakmont CC / Oakmont, Pa.
1936	Tony Manero / Harry Cooper	282	Baltusrol CC / Springfield, N.J.
1937	Ralph Guldahl / Sam Snead	281	Oakland Hills CC / Birmingham, Mich.
1938	Ralph Guldahl / Dick Metz	284	Cherry Hills Club / Englewood, Colo.
1939	*Byron Nelson / Craig Wood / Denny Shute	284	Philadelphia CC / W. Conshohocken, Pa.
1940	*Lawson Little / Gene Sarazen	287	Canterbury CC / Cleveland, Ohio
1941	Craig Wood / Denny Shute	284	Colonial CC / Fort Worth, Tex.
1942–45	No tournament		
1946	*Lloyd Mangrum / Byron Nelson / Vic Ghezzi	284	Canterbury CC / Cleveland, Ohio
1947	*Lew Worsham / Sam Snead	282	St. Louis CC / Clayton, Mo.
1948	Ben Hogan / Jimmy Demaret	276	Riviera CC / Pacific Palisades, Ca.
1949	Cary Middlecoff / Sam Snead / Clayton Heafner	286	Medinah CC / Medinah, Ill.
1950	*Ben Hogan / Lloyd Mangrum / George Fazio	287	Merion GC / Ardmore, Pa.
1951	Ben Hogan / Clayton Heafner	287	Oakland Hills CC / Birmingham, Mich.

*Won Playoff

YEAR	WINNER, RUNNER-UP	SCORE	PLAYED AT
1952	Julius Boros	281	Northwood Club
	Ed Oliver		Dallas, Tex.
1953	Ben Hogan	283	Oakmont CC
	Sam Snead		Oakmont, Pa.
1954	Ed Furgol	284	Baltusrol GC
	Gene Littler		Springfield, N.J.
1955	*Jack Fleck	287	Olympic Club
	Ben Hogan		San Francisco, Cal.
1956	Cary Middlecoff	281	Oak Hill CC
	Julius Boros		Rochester, N.Y.
	Ben Hogan		
1957	*Dick Mayer	282	Inverness Club
	Cary Middlecoff		Toledo, Ohio
1958	Tommy Bolt	283	Southern Hills CC
	Gary Player		Tulsa, Okla.
1959	Billy Casper	282	Winged Foot GC
	Bob Rosburg		Mamaroneck, N.Y.
1960	Arnold Palmer	280	Cherry Hills CC
	Jack Nicklaus		Englewood, Colo.
1961	Gene Littler	281	Oakland Hills CC
	Doug Sanders		Birmingham, Mich.
	Bob Goalby		
1962	*Jack Nicklaus	283	Oakmont CC
	Arnold Palmer		Oakmont, Pa.
1963	*Julius Boros	293	The Country Club
	Jacky Cupit		Brookline, Mass.
	Arnold Palmer		
1964	Ken Venturi	278	Congressional CC
	Tommy Jacobs		Washington, D.C.
1965	*Gary Player	282	Bellerive CC
	Kel Nagle		St. Louis, Mo.
1966	*Billy Casper	278	Olympic Club
	Arnold Palmer		San Francisco, Ca.
1967	Jack Nicklaus	275	Baltusrol GC
	Arnold Palmer		Springfield, N.J.
1968	Lee Trevino	275	Oak Hill CC
	Jack Nicklaus		Rochester, N.Y.
1969	Orville Moody	281	Champions GC
	Deane Beman		Houston, Tex.
	Al Geiberger		
	Bob Rosburg		
1970	Tony Jacklin	281	Hazeltine National GC
	Dave Hill		Chaska, Minn.
1971	*Lee Trevino	280	Merion GC
	Jack Nicklaus		Ardmore, Pa.
1972	Jack Nicklaus	290	Pebble Beach GL
	Bruce Crampton		Pebble Beach, Ca.
1973	Johnny Miller	279	Oakmont CC
	John Schlee		Oakmont, Pa.
1974	Hale Irwin	287	Winged Foot GC
	Forrest Fezler		Mamaroneck, N.Y.
1975	*Lou Graham	287	Medinah CC
	John Mahaffey		Medinah, Ill.
1976	Jerry Pate	277	Atlanta AC
	Tom Weiskopf		Duluth, Ga.
	Al Geiberger		
1977	Hubert Green	278	Southern Hills CC
	Lou Graham		Tulsa, Okla.
1978	Andy North	285	Cherry Hills CC
	J.C. Snead		Englewood, Colo.
	Dave Stockton		
1979	Hale Irwin	284	Inverness Club
	Gary Player		Toledo, Ohio
	Jerry Pate		
1980	Jack Nicklaus	272	Baltusrol GC
	Isao Aoki		Springfield, N.J.

YEAR	WINNER, RUNNER-UP	SCORE	PLAYED AT
1981	David Graham	273	Merion GC
	Bill Rogers		Ardmore, Pa.
	George Burns		
1982	Tom Watson	282	Pebble Beach GL
	Jack Nicklaus		Pebble Beach, Ca.
1983	Larry Nelson	280	Oakmont CC
	Tom Watson		Oakmont, Pa.
1984	*Fuzzy Zoeller	276	Winged Foot GC
	Greg Norman		Mamaroneck, N.Y.
1985	Andy North	279	Oakland Hills CC
	Denis Watson		Birmingham, Mich.
	Dave Barr		
	T.C. Chen		
1986	Ray Floyd	279	Shinnecock Hills GC
	Lanny Wadkins		Southampton, N.Y.
	Chip Beck		
1987	Scott Simpson	277	Olympic Club
	Tom Watson		San Francisco, Ca.
1988	*Curtis Strange	278	The Country Club
	Nick Faldo		Brookline, Mass.
1989	Curtis Strange	278	Oak Hill CC
	Ian Woosnam		Rochester, N.Y.
	Chip Beck		
	Mark McCumber		
1990	*Hale Irwin	280	Medinah CC
	Mike Donald		Medinah, Ill.
1991	Payne Stewart	282	Hazeltine National GC
	Scott Simpson		Chaska, Minn.

*Won Playoff

RECORDS

SCORING

LOWEST SCORE, 72 HOLES
272 (8 under) — Jack Nicklaus (63–71–70–68), Baltusrol GC, 1980
273 (7 under) — David Graham (68–68–70–67), Merion GC, 1981
274 (6 under) — Isao Aoki (68–68–68–70), Baltusrol GC, 1980
280 (8 under) — Hale Irwin (69–70–74–67), Medinah CC, 1990
280 (8 under) — Mike Donald (67–70–72–71), Medinah CC, 1990

LOWEST SCORE, FIRST 54 HOLES
203 (7 under) — George Burns (69–66–68), Merion GC, 1981
203 (7 under) — T.C. Chen (65–69–69), Oakland Hills CC, 1985
206 (7 under) — Curtis Strange (70–67–69), The Country Club, 1988
209 (7 under) — Mike Donald (67–70–72), Medinah CC, 1990
209 (7 under) — Billy Ray Brown (69–71–69), Medinah CC, 1990

LOWEST SCORE, LAST 54 HOLES
204 (6 under) — Jack Nicklaus (67–72–65), Baltusrol GC, 1967
204 (6 under) — Ray Floyd (68–70–66), Shinnecock Hills GC, 1986
205 (8 under) — Larry Nelson (73–65–67), Oakmont CC, 1983
206 (7 under) — Nick Faldo (67–68–71), The Country Club, 1988

LOWEST SCORE, FIRST 36 HOLES
134 (6 under) — Jack Nicklaus (63–71), Baltusrol GC, 1980
134 (6 under) — T.C. Chen (65–69), Oakland Hills CC, 1985
135 (9 under) — Tim Simpson (66–69), Medinah CC, 1990
136 (8 under) — Jeff Sluman (66–70), Medinah CC, 1990

LOWEST SCORE, MIDDLE 36 HOLES
134 (6 under) — Tommy Jacobs (64–70), Congressional CC, 1964
134 (6 under) — George Burns (66–68), Merion GC, 1981
136 (8 under) — Larry Nelson (67–69), Medinah CC, 1990
136 (8 under) — John Goodman (66–70), North Shore GC, 1933

LOWEST SCORE, LAST 36 HOLES
132 (10 under) — Larry Nelson (65–67), Oakmont CC, 1983
133 (7 under) — Chip Beck (68–65), Shinnecock Hills GC, 1986
136 (8 under) — Gary Koch (69–67), Pebble Beach GL, 1982

LOWEST SCORE, FIRST ROUND
63 (7 under) — Jack Nicklaus, Baltusrol GC, 1980
63 (7 under) — Tom Weiskopf, Baltusrol GC, 1980
64 (6 under) — Lee Mackey, Merion GC, 1950
66 (6 under) — Tim Simpson, Medinah CC, 1990
66 (6 under) — Scott Simpson, Medinah CC, 1990
66 (6 under) — Jeff Sluman, Medinah CC, 1990

LOWEST SCORE, SECOND ROUND
64 (6 under) — Curtis Strange, Oak Hill CC, 1989
64 (6 under) — Rives McBee, Olympic Club, 1966
64 (6 under) — Tommy Jacobs, Congressional CC, 1964
66 (6 under) — Mike Hulbert, Medinah CC, 1990
66 (6 under) — John Goodman, North Shore CC, 1933
66 (6 under) — Jimmy Thomson, Oakland Hills CC, 1937

LOWEST SCORE, THIRD ROUND
64 (6 under) — Ben Crenshaw, Merion GC, 1981
65 (6 under) — Larry Nelson, Oakmont CC, 1983

LOWEST SCORE, FOURTH ROUND
63 (8 under) — Johnny Miller, Oakmont CC, 1973
64 (7 under) — Peter Jacobsen, The Country Club, 1988
65 (6 under) — Arnold Palmer, Cherry Hills CC, 1960
65 (6 under) — Lanny Wadkins, Oakmont CC, 1973
66 (6 under) — Walter Hagen, North Shore CC, 1933

LOWEST SCORE, NINE HOLES
30 — Jim McHale, St. Louis CC, 1947; Arnold Palmer, Cherry Hills CC, 1960; Ken Venturi, Congressional CC, 1964; Steve Spray, Oak Hill CC, 1968; Tom Shaw, Bob Charles, Merion GC, 1971; Ray Floyd, Baltusrol GC, 1980; George Burns, Pebble Beach GL, 1982; Danny Edwards, Lennie Clements, Chip Beck, Shinnecock Hills GC, 1986; Paul Azinger, Scott Simpson, Peter Jacobsen, The Country Club, 1988

LARGEST WINNING MARGIN
11 — Willie Smith, Baltimore CC, 1899
9 — Jim Barnes, Columbia CC, 1921
7 — Fred Herd, Myopia Hunt Club, 1898
7 — Alex Smith, Onwentsia Club, 1906
7 — Tony Jacklin, Hazeltine National GC, 1970

LARGEST LEAD AFTER 54 HOLES
7 — Jim Barnes, Columbia CC, 1921

LARGEST LEAD AFTER 36 HOLES
5 — Willie Anderson, Baltusrol GC, 1903
5 — Mike Souchak, Cherry Hills CC, 1960

LARGEST LEAD AFTER 18 HOLES
5 — Tommy Armour, North Shore CC, 1933

Guard at Entrance, Oakland Hills

LARGEST LEAD AFTER 54 HOLES, NON-WINNER
5 — Mike Brady, Brae Burn CC, 1919

LARGEST LEAD AFTER 36 HOLES, NON-WINNER
5 — Mike Souchak, Cherry Hills CC, 1960

LARGEST LEAD AFTER 18 HOLES, NON-WINNER
5 — Tommy Armour, North Shore CC, 1933

BEST COMEBACK BY WINNER, FINAL ROUND
7 — Arnold Palmer, Cherry Hills CC, 1960
6 — Johnny Miller, Oakmont CC, 1973

BEST COMEBACK BY WINNER, FINAL 36 HOLES
11 — Lou Graham, Medinah CC, 1975

BEST COMEBACK BY WINNER, FINAL 54 HOLES
9 — Jack Fleck, Olympic Club, 1955

LOWEST SCORE BY WINNER, FIRST ROUND
63 (7 under) — Jack Nicklaus, Baltusrol GC, 1980

LOWEST SCORE BY WINNER, SECOND ROUND
64 (6 under) — Curtis Strange, Oak Hill CC, 1989
66 (6 under) — John Goodman, North Shore CC, 1933

LOWEST SCORE BY WINNER, THIRD ROUND
65 (6 under) — Larry Nelson, Oakmont CC, 1983

LOWEST SCORE BY WINNER, FOURTH ROUND
63 (8 under) — Johnny Miller, Oakmont CC, 1973

HIGHEST SCORE BY WINNER, FIRST ROUND
91 — Horace Rawlins, Newport GC, 1895
SINCE WORLD WAR II
76 (6 over) — Ben Hogan, Oakland Hills CC, 1951
76 (6 over) — Jack Fleck, Olympic Club, 1955

HIGHEST SCORE BY WINNER, SECOND ROUND
85 — Fred Herd, Myopia Hunt Club, 1898
SINCE WORLD WAR II
74 (3 over) — Julius Boros, The Country Club, 1963

HIGHEST SCORE BY WINNER, THIRD ROUND
83 — Willie Anderson, Myopia Hunt Club, 1901
SINCE WORLD WAR II
76 (5 over) — Julius Boros, The Country Club, 1963
76 (5 over) — Johnny Miller, Oakmont CC, 1973
75 (5 over) — Jack Fleck, Olympic Club, 1955

HIGHEST SCORE BY WINNER, FOURTH ROUND
84 — Fred Herd, Myopia Hunt Club, 1898
SINCE WORLD WAR II
75 (4 over) — Cary Middlecoff, Medinah CC, 1949
75 (4 over) — Hale Irwin, Inverness Club, 1979
74 (4 over) — Ben Hogan, Merion GC, 1950
74 (4 over) — Billy Casper, Winged Foot GC, 1959
74 (4 over) — Andy North, Oakland Hills CC, 1985

HIGHEST SCORE BY WINNER, 72 HOLES
331 — Willie Anderson, Myopia Hunt Club, 1901
SINCE WORLD WAR II
293 — Julius Boros, The Country Club, 1963

HIGHEST SCORE TO LEAD FIELD, 18 HOLES
89 — Willie Dunn, James Foulis and W. Campbell, Newport GC, 1895
SINCE WORLD WAR II
71 (1 over) — Sam Snead, Oakland Hills CC, 1951
71 (1 over) — Tommy Bolt, Julius Boros and Dick Metz, Southern Hills CC, 1958
71 (1 under) — Tony Jacklin, Hazeltine National GC, 1970
71 (1 under) — Orville Moody, Jack Nicklaus, Chi Chi Rodriguez, Mason Rudolph, Tom Shaw and Kermit Zarley, Pebble Beach GL, 1972

HIGHEST SCORE TO LEAD FIELD, 36 HOLES
173 — Horace Rawlins, Newport GC, 1895
SINCE WORLD WAR II
144 (4 over) — Bobby Locke, Oakland Hills CC, 1951
144 (4 over) — Tommy Bolt and E. Harvie Ward, Olympic Club, 1955
144 (even) — Homero Blancas, Bruce Crampton, Jack Nicklaus, Cesar Sanudo, Lanny Wadkins and Kermit Zarley, Pebble Beach GL, 1972

HIGHEST SCORE TO LEAD FIELD, 54 HOLES
249 — Stewart Gardner, Myopia Hunt Club, 1901
SINCE WORLD WAR II
218 (8 over) — Bobby Locke, Oakland Hills CC, 1951
218 (5 over) — Jacky Cupit, The Country Club, 1963

MOST SUBPAR ROUNDS BY FIELD, TOURNAMENT
124 — Medinah CC, 1990

MOST SUBPAR ROUNDS BY FIELD, FIRST ROUND
39 — Medinah CC, 1990

MOST SUBPAR ROUNDS BY FIELD, SECOND ROUND
47 — Medinah CC, 1990

MOST SUBPAR ROUNDS BY FIELD, THIRD ROUND
24 — Medinah CC, 1990

MOST SUBPAR ROUNDS BY FIELD, FOURTH ROUND
17 — Pebble Beach GL, 1982; The Country Club, 1988

FEWEST SUBPAR ROUNDS BY FIELD, TOURNAMENT
SINCE WORLD WAR II
2 — Oakland Hills CC, 1951

FEWEST SUBPAR ROUNDS BY FIELD, FIRST ROUND
SINCE WORLD WAR II
0 — Oakland Hills CC, 1951; Southern Hills CC, 1958; Winged Foot GC, 1974; Shinnecock Hills GC, 1986

FEWEST SUBPAR ROUNDS BY FIELD, SECOND ROUND
SINCE WORLD WAR II
0 — Oakland Hills CC, 1951

FEWEST SUBPAR ROUNDS BY FIELD, THIRD ROUND
SINCE WORLD WAR II
0 — Oakland Hills CC, 1951; The Country Club, 1963

FEWEST SUBPAR ROUNDS BY FIELD, FOURTH ROUND
SINCE WORLD WAR II
0 — Merion GC, 1950; Northwood CC, 1952; Winged Foot GC, 1959; The Country Club, 1963; Pebble Beach GL, 1972

MOST SUBPAR TOTALS BY FIELD, TOURNAMENT
28 — Medinah CC, 1990

LOWEST 36-HOLE CUT
145 (1 over) — Medinah CC, 1990
145 (5 over) — Oak Hill CC, 1989

HIGHEST 36-HOLE CUT
SINCE WORLD WAR II
155 (15 over) — Olympic Club, 1955

INDIVIDUAL, CAREER

VICTORIES
4 — Willie Anderson (1901, 03, 04, 05)
4 — Bobby Jones (1923, 26, 29, 30)
4 — Ben Hogan (1948, 50, 51, 53)
4 — Jack Nicklaus (1962, 67, 72, 80)
3 — Hale Irwin (1974, 79, 90)
2 — Alex Smith (1906, 10), John McDermott (1911, 12), Walter Hagen (1914, 19), Gene Sarazen (1922, 32), Ralph Guldahl (1937, 38), Cary Middlecoff (1949, 56), Julius Boros (1952, 63), Billy Casper (1959, 66), Lee Trevino (1968, 71), Andy North (1978, 85), Curtis Strange (1988, 89)

CONSECUTIVE VICTORIES
3 — Willie Anderson (1903, 04, 05)
2 — John McDermott (1911, 12); Bobby Jones (1929, 30); Ralph Guldahl (1937, 38); Ben Hogan (1950, 51); Curtis Strange (1988, 89)

RUNNER-UP FINISHES
4 — Bobby Jones (1922, 24, 25, 28)
4 — Sam Snead (1937, 47, 49, 53)
4 — Arnold Palmer (1962, 63, 66, 67)
4 — Jack Nicklaus (1960, 68, 71, 82)
3 — Alex Smith (1898, 1901, 05)
3 — Tom McNamara (1909, 12, 15)
2 — Gilbert Nicholls (1904, 07), Willie Smith (1906, 08), Mike Brady (1911, 19), Harry Vardon (1913, 20), Jock Hutchison (1916, 20), Macdonald Smith (1910, 30), Bobby Cruickshank (1923, 32), Harry Cooper (1927, 36), Gene Sarazen (1934, 40), Denny Shute (1939, 41), Clayton Heafner (1949, 51), Ben Hogan (1955, 56), Bob Rosburg (1959, 69), Al Geiberger (1969, 76), Gary Player (1958, 79), Tom Watson (1983, 87), Chip Beck (1986, 89)

TOP-FIVE FINISHES
11 — Willie Anderson
11 — Jack Nicklaus
10 — Alex Smith
10 — Walter Hagen
10 — Ben Hogan
10 — Arnold Palmer
9 — Bobby Jones
9 — Gene Sarazen
9 — Julius Boros
7 — Sam Snead

TOP-TEN FINISHES
18 — Jack Nicklaus
16 — Walter Hagen
15 — Ben Hogan
14 — Gene Sarazen
13 — Arnold Palmer
12 — Sam Snead
11 — Willie Anderson
11 — Alex Smith
11 — Julius Boros
10 — Bobby Jones

TOP-TWENTY-FIVE FINISHES
22 — Jack Nicklaus
21 — Sam Snead
20 — Walter Hagen
19 — Gary Player
18 — Arnold Palmer
17 — Alex Smith
17 — Gene Sarazen
17 — Ben Hogan
16 — Macdonald Smith
15 — Julius Boros

COMPLETED 72 HOLES
29 — Jack Nicklaus
27 — Sam Snead
26 — Gene Sarazen
25 — Gary Player
23 — Arnold Palmer

CONSECUTIVE TOP-FIVE FINISHES
6 — Bobby Jones (1921–26)

CONSECUTIVE TOP-TEN FINISHES
7 — Bobby Jones (1920–26), Ben Hogan (1950–56)

CONSECUTIVE TOP-TWENTY-FIVE FINISHES
19 — Walter Hagen (1913–16, 19–33)

CONSECUTIVE TIMES COMPLETED 72 HOLES
22 — Walter Hagen (1913–16, 19–36), Gene Sarazen (1920–41), Gary Player (1958–79)

LONGEST SPAN, FIRST TO LAST VICTORY
19 years — Jack Nicklaus (1962–80)

LONGEST SPAN BETWEEN VICTORIES
12 years — Julius Boros (1952–63), Hale Irwin (1979–90)

SUBPAR ROUNDS
32 — Jack Nicklaus

CONSECUTIVE SUBPAR ROUNDS
6 — Sam Snead (1947–48, includes 18-hole playoff)
5 — Brian Claar (1989–90)

ROUNDS IN THE 60S
27 — Jack Nicklaus

CONSECUTIVE ROUNDS IN THE 60S
4 — Lee Trevino (1968), Ben Crenshaw (1986–87)

SUBPAR 72-HOLE TOTALS
7 — Jack Nicklaus

CONSECUTIVE SUBPAR 72-HOLE TOTALS
3 — Curtis Strange (1988–90)

MOST TIMES LED AFTER 54 HOLES
6 — Bobby Jones
4 — Tom Watson

MOST TIMES LED AFTER 18, 36, OR 54 HOLES
10 — Alex Smith
9 — Bobby Jones
9 — Sam Snead
9 — Arnold Palmer

MOST TIMES LED AFTER 18, 36, OR 54 HOLES, BUT NEVER WON
9 — Sam Snead
5 — Mike Brady
5 — Bill Mehlhorn

PLAYOFF RECORDS (PLAYERS IN MORE THAN ONE PLAYOFF)
Willie Anderson (2–0)
Bobby Jones (2–2)
Alex Smith (1–1)
John McDermott (1–1)
Byron Nelson (1–1)
Lloyd Mangrum (1–1)
Ben Hogan (1–1)
Jack Nicklaus (1–1)
Mike Brady (0–2)
Arnold Palmer (0–3)

MISCELLANEOUS

PROGRESSIVE 72-HOLE SCORING RECORD
328, Fred Herd, 1898
315, Willie Smith, 1899
313, Harry Vardon, 1900
307, Laurie Auchterlonie, 1902; Willie Anderson, David Brown, 1903
303, Willie Anderson, 1904
295, Alex Smith, 1906
290, George Sargent, 1909; Walter Hagen, 1914
289, Jim Barnes, 1921
288, Gene Sarazen, 1922
287, Bobby Jones, 1930
286, Gene Sarazen, 1932
282, Tony Manero, 1936
281, Ralph Guldahl, 1937
276, Ben Hogan, 1948
275, Jack Nicklaus, 1967; Lee Trevino, 1968
272, Jack Nicklaus, 1980

PROGRESSIVE 18-HOLE SCORING RECORD

82, Horace Rawlins, 1895

74, James Foulis, 1896; Laurie Auchterlonie, 1902

73, Willie Anderson, 1903

72, Willie Anderson, 1904; Gilbert Nicholls, 1907

68, David Hunter, 1909; Walter Hagen, 1914, 1922; Gene Sarazen, 1922

67, Willie Macfarlane, 1925

66, Gene Sarazen, 1932; John Goodman, Walter Hagen, 1933; Tom Creavy, 1934; Clayton Heafner, 1939

64, Lee Mackey, 1950; Tommy Jacobs, 1964; Rives McBee, 1966

63, Johnny Miller, 1973; Jack Nicklaus, Tom Weiskopf, 1980

FOUR SUBPAR ROUNDS, SAME U.S. OPEN

Lee Trevino, 1968; Tony Jacklin, 1970

WIRE-TO-WIRE WINNERS (NO TIES)

Walter Hagen, 1914; Jim Barnes, 1921; Ben Hogan, 1953; Tony Jacklin, 1970

WIRE-TO-WIRE WINNERS (INCLUDING TIES)

Willie Anderson, 1903; Alex Smith, 1906; Chick Evans, 1916; Tommy Bolt, 1958; Jack Nicklaus, 1972, 1980; Hubert Green, 1977

PLAYERS WHO LED FIRST THREE ROUNDS, DIDN'T WIN

Alex Smith, 1905; Willie Smith, 1908; Mike Brady, 1912; Mike Souchak, 1960; Bert Yancey, 1968; Hale Irwin, 1984; T.C. Chen, 1985

NUMBER OF TIMES A LEADER WENT ON TO WIN

18 holes — 14 in 88 tournaments

36 holes — 24 in 85 tournaments at 72 holes

54 holes — 36 of 85

OLDEST WINNER

45 years, 14 days — Hale Irwin, 1990

YOUNGEST WINNER

19 years, 10 months, 14 days — John McDermott, 1911

NUMBER OF PLAYOFFS

29 in 88 tournaments

MOST PLAYERS TIED FOR LEAD, 18 HOLES

7 — 1977, Southern Hills CC (Hubert Green, Tom Purtzer, Terry Diehl, Rod Funseth, Grier Jones, Florentino Molina, Larry Nelson, 69)

MOST PLAYERS TIED FOR LEAD, 36 HOLES

6 — 1972, Pebble Beach GL (Jack Nicklaus, Bruce Crampton, Homero Blancas, Kermit Zarley, Cesar Sanudo, Lanny Wadkins, 144)

MOST PLAYERS TIED FOR LEAD, 54 HOLES

4 — 1973, Oakmont CC (John Schlee, Arnold Palmer, Julius Boros, Jerry Heard, 210)

Medinah, 1st hole

WON FIRST TIME PLAYED IN OPEN
Horace Rawlins, 1895
Fred Herd, 1898
Harry Vardon, 1900
George Sargent, 1909
Francis Ouimet, 1913

CONSECUTIVE BIRDIES
6 — George Burns, holes 2–7, Pebble Beach GL, 1972

CONSECUTIVE 3S
7 — Hubert Green, holes 10–16, Southern Hills CC, 1977
7 — Peter Jacobsen, holes 1–7, The Country Club, 1988

HIGHEST SCORE, ONE HOLE
19 — Ray Ainsley, 16th hole, Cherry Hills CC, 1938

NUMBER OF CHAMPIONS, BY NATIVE COUNTRY
United States, 66
Great Britain, 20
South Africa, 1
Australia, 1

AMATEURS

CHAMPIONS
Francis Ouimet, 1913; Jerome Travers, 1915; Chick Evans, 1916; Bobby Jones, 1923, 1926, 1929, 1930; John Goodman, 1933

LOWEST SCORE, 72 HOLES
282 — Jack Nicklaus, Cherry Hills CC, 1960

LOWEST SCORE, 18 HOLES
65 — Jim McHale, St. Louis CC, 1947
65 — Jim Simons, Merion CC, 1971

TOP-TEN FINISHES
10 — Bobby Jones

MOST TIMES, LOW AMATEUR
9 — Bobby Jones

COURSE RECORDS (on courses where the U.S. Open has been played more than once)

SHINNECOCK HILLS GC (1896, 1986)
18 holes — 65, Lanny Wadkins, Chip Beck, Mark Calcavecchia, 1986
72 holes — 279, Ray Floyd, 1986

CHICAGO GC (1897, 1900, 1911)
18 holes — 72, John McDermott, Fred McLeod, 1911
72 holes — 307, John McDermott, Mike Brady, George Simpson, 1911

MYOPIA HUNT CLUB (1898, 1901, 1905, 1908)
18 holes — 75, Fred Herd, 1898
72 holes — 314, Willie Anderson, 1905

BALTUSROL GC
(Original Course) (1903, 1915)

18 holes — 72, Jerome Travers, 1915
72 holes — 297, Jerome Travers, 1915
(Upper Course) (1936)
18 holes — 67, Tony Manero
72 holes — 282, Tony Manero
(Lower Course) (1954, 1967, 1980)
18 holes — 63, Jack Nicklaus, Tom Weiskopf, 1980
72 holes — 272, Jack Nicklaus, 1980

PHILADELPHIA CRICKET CLUB (ST. MARTINS COURSE) (1907, 1910)
18 holes — 70, Macdonald Smith, 1910
72 holes — 298, Alex Smith, John McDermott, Macdonald Smith, 1910

THE COUNTRY CLUB (1913, 1963, 1988)
18 holes — 64, Peter Jacobsen, 1988
72 holes — 278, Curtis Strange, Nick Faldo, 1988

INVERNESS CLUB (1920, 1931, 1957, 1979)
18 holes — 67, Hale Irwin, Tom Weiskopf, 1979
72 holes — 282, Dick Mayer, Cary Middlecoff, 1957

OAKLAND HILLS CC (SOUTH COURSE) (1924, 1937, 1951, 1961, 1985)
18 holes — 65, T.C. Chen, Andy North, Denis Watson, 1985
72 holes — 279, Andy North, 1985

OAKMONT CC (1927, 1935, 1953, 1962, 1973, 1983)
18 holes — 63, Johnny Miller, 1973
72 holes — 279, Johnny Miller, 1973

WINGED FOOT GC (WEST COURSE) (1929, 1959, 1974, 1984)
18 holes — 66, Fuzzy Zoeller, 1984
72 holes — 276, Fuzzy Zoeller, Greg Norman, 1984

MERION GC (EAST COURSE) (1934, 1950, 1971, 1981)
18 holes — 64, Lee Mackey, 1950; Ben Crenshaw, 1981
72 holes — 273, David Graham, 1981

CHERRY HILLS CC (1938, 1960, 1978)
18 holes — 65, Arnold Palmer, 1960
72 holes — 280, Arnold Palmer, 1960

CANTERBURY CC (1940, 1946)
18 holes — 67, Chick Harbert, Chandler Harper, 1946
72 holes — 284, Lloyd Mangrum, Byron Nelson, Vic Ghezzi, 1946

MEDINAH CC (NO. 3 COURSE) (1949, 1975, 1990)
18 holes — 66, Tim Simpson, Jeff Sluman, Mike Hulbert, 1990
72 holes — 280, Hale Irwin, Mike Donald, 1990

OLYMPIC CLUB (LAKE COURSE) (1955, 1966, 1987)
18 holes — 64, Rives McBee, 1966
72 holes — 277, Scott Simpson, 1987

OAK HILL CC (1956, 1968, 1989)
18 holes — 64, Curtis Strange, 1989
72 holes — 275, Lee Trevino, 1968

SOUTHERN HILLS CC (1958, 1977)
18 holes — 66, Don Padgett, Jerry McGee, 1977
72 holes — 278, Hubert Green, 1977

PEBBLE BEACH GL (1972, 1982)
18 holes — 67, Larry Rinker, Lanny Wadkins, Peter Oosterhuis, Gary Koch, 1982
72 holes — 282, Tom Watson, 1982

The British Open

WINNERS

YEAR	WINNER, RUNNER-UP	SCORE	PLAYED AT	YEAR	WINNER, RUNNER-UP	SCORE	PLAYED AT
1860	Willie Park Tom Morris, Sr.	174	Prestwick, Scotland	1889	* Willie Park, Jr. Andrew Kirkaldy	155	Musselburgh, Scotland
1861	Tom Morris, Sr. Willie Park	163	Prestwick, Scotland	1890	John Ball Willie Fernie	164	Prestwick, Scotland
1862	Tom Morris, Sr. Willie Park	163	Prestwick, Scotland	1891	Hugh Kirkaldy Andrew Kirkaldy Willie Fernie	166	St. Andrews, Scotland
1863	Willie Park Tom Morris, Sr.	168	Prestwick, Scotland	1892	Harold Hilton John Ball Hugh Kirkaldy	305	Muirfield, Scotland
1864	Tom Morris, Sr. Andrew Strath	160	Prestwick, Scotland	1893	Willie Auchterlonie John Laidlay	322	Prestwick, Scotland
1865	Andrew Strath Willie Park	162	Prestwick, Scotland	1894	J.H. Taylor Douglas Rolland	326	St. George's, England
1866	Willie Park David Park	169	Prestwick, Scotland	1895	J.H. Taylor Alex Herd	322	St. Andrews, Scotland
1867	Tom Morris, Sr. Willie Park	170	Prestwick, Scotland	1896	* Harry Vardon J.H. Taylor	316	Muirfield, Scotland
1868	Tom Morris, Jr. Tom Morris, Sr.	154	Prestwick, Scotland	1897	Harold Hilton James Braid	314	Hoylake, England
1869	Tom Morris, Jr. Tom Morris, Sr.	157	Prestwick, Scotland	1898	Harry Vardon Willie Park, Jr.	307	Prestwick, Scotland
1870	Tom Morris, Jr. David Strath Bob Kirk	149	Prestwick, Scotland	1899	Harry Vardon Jack White	310	St. George's, England
1871	No tournament			1900	J.H. Taylor Harry Vardon	309	St. Andrews, Scotland
1872	Tom Morris, Jr. David Strath	166	Prestwick, Scotland	1901	James Braid Harry Vardon	308	Muirfield, Scotland
1873	Tom Kidd Jamie Anderson	179	St. Andrews, Scotland	1902	Alex Herd Harry Vardon	307	Hoylake, England
1874	Mungo Park Tom Morris, Jr.	159	Musselburgh, Scotland	1903	Harry Vardon Tom Vardon	300	Prestwick, Scotland
1875	Willie Park Bob Martin	166	Prestwick, Scotland	1904	Jack White J.H. Taylor	296	St. George's, England
1876	Bob Martin David Strath	176	St. Andrews, Scotland	1905	James Braid J.H. Taylor Rolland Jones	318	St. Andrews, Scotland
1877	Jamie Anderson Bob Pringle	160	Musselburgh, Scotland	1906	James Braid J.H. Taylor	300	Muirfield, Scotland
1878	Jamie Anderson Bob Kirk	157	Prestwick, Scotland	1907	Arnaud Massy J.H. Taylor	312	Hoylake, England
1879	Jamie Anderson Andrew Kirkaldy James Allan	169	St. Andrews, Scotland	1908	James Braid Tom Ball	291	Prestwick, Scotland
1880	Robert Ferguson Peter Paxton	162	Musselburgh, Scotland	1909	J.H. Taylor James Braid Tom Ball	295	Deal, England
1881	Robert Ferguson Jamie Anderson	170	Prestwick, Scotland	1910	James Braid Alex Herd	299	St. Andrews, Scotland
1882	Robert Ferguson Willie Fernie	171	St. Andrews, Scotland	1911	Harry Vardon Arnaud Massy	303	St. George's, England
1883	* Willie Fernie Robert Ferguson	159	Musselburgh, Scotland	1912	Edward Ray Harry Vardon	295	Muirfield, Scotland
1884	Jack Simpson Douglas Rolland Willie Fernie	160	Prestwick, Scotland	1913	J.H. Taylor Edward Ray	304	Hoylake, England
1885	Bob Martin Archie Simpson	171	St. Andrews, Scotland	1914	Harry Vardon J.H. Taylor	306	Prestwick, Scotland
1886	David Brown Willie Campbell	157	Musselburgh, Scotland	1915–19	No tournament		
1887	Willie Park, Jr. Bob Martin	161	Prestwick, Scotland	1920	George Duncan Alex Herd	303	Deal, England
1888	Jack Burns Ben Sayers D. Anderson	171	St. Andrews, Scotland	1921	* Jock Hutchison Roger Wethered	296	St. Andrews, Scotland

YEAR	WINNER, RUNNER-UP	SCORE	PLAYED AT
1922	Walter Hagen George Duncan Jim Barnes	300	St. George's, England
1923	Arthur Havers Walter Hagen	295	Troon, Scotland
1924	Walter Hagen Ernest Whitcombe	301	Hoylake, England
1925	Jim Barnes Archie Compston Edward Ray	300	Prestwick, Scotland
1926	Robert T. Jones, Jr. Al Watrous	291	Lytham, England
1927	Robert T. Jones, Jr. Aubrey Boomer	285	St. Andrews, Scotland
1928	Walter Hagen Gene Sarazen	292	St. George's, England
1929	Walter Hagen Johnny Farrell	292	Muirfield, Scotland
1930	Robert T. Jones, Jr. Macdonald Smith Leo Diegel	291	Hoylake, England
1931	Tommy Armour Jose Jurado	296	Carnoustie, Scotland
1932	Gene Sarazen Macdonald Smith	283	Prince's, England
1933	*Denny Shute Craig Wood	292	St. Andrews, Scotland
1934	Henry Cotton Sidney Brews	283	St. George's, England
1935	Alfred Perry Alfred Padgham	283	Muirfield, Scotland
1936	Alfred Padgham James Adams	287	Hoylake, England
1937	Henry Cotton Reg Whitcombe	290	Carnoustie, Scotland
1938	Reg Whitcombe James Adams	295	St. George's, England
1939	Richard Burton Johnny Bulla	290	St. Andrews, Scotland
1940–45	No tournament		
1946	Sam Snead Bobby Locke Johnny Bulla	290	St. Andrews, Scotland
1947	Fred Daly Reg Horne Frank Stranahan	293	Hoylake, England
1948	Henry Cotton Fred Daly	294	Muirfield, Scotland
1949	*Bobby Locke Harry Bradshaw	283	St. George's, England
1950	Bobby Locke Roberto De Vicenzo	279	Troon, Scotland
1951	Max Faulkner Antonio Cerda	285	Portrush, Ireland
1952	Bobby Locke Peter Thomson	287	Lytham, England
1953	Ben Hogan Frank Stranahan Dai Rees Peter Thomson Antonio Cerda	282	Carnoustie, Scotland
1954	Peter Thomson Syd Scott Dai Rees Bobby Locke	283	Birkdale, England
1955	Peter Thomson John Fallon	281	St. Andrews, Scotland
1956	Peter Thomson Flory Van Donck	286	Hoylake, England
1957	Bobby Locke Peter Thomson	279	St. Andrews, Scotland
1958	*Peter Thomson Dave Thomas	278	Lytham, England
1959	Gary Player Fred Bullock Flory Van Donck	284	Muirfield, Scotland
1960	Kel Nagle Arnold Palmer	278	St. Andrews, Scotland
1961	Arnold Palmer Dai Rees	284	Birkdale, England
1962	Arnold Palmer Kel Nagle	276	Troon, Scotland
1963	*Bob Charles Phil Rodgers	277	Lytham, England
1964	Tony Lema Jack Nicklaus	279	St. Andrews, Scotland
1965	Peter Thomson Brian Huggett Christy O'Connor	285	Birkdale, England
1966	Jack Nicklaus Doug Sanders Dave Thomas	282	Muirfield, Scotland
1967	Roberto De Vicenzo Jack Nicklaus	278	Hoylake, England
1968	Gary Player Jack Nicklaus Bob Charles	289	Carnoustie, Scotland
1969	Tony Jacklin Bob Charles	280	Lytham, England
1970	*Jack Nicklaus Doug Sanders	283	St. Andrews, Scotland
1971	Lee Trevino Lu Liang Huan	278	Birkdale, England
1972	Lee Trevino Jack Nicklaus	278	Muirfield, Scotland
1973	Tom Weiskopf Johnny Miller	276	Troon, Scotland
1974	Gary Player Peter Oosterhuis	282	Lytham, England
1975	*Tom Watson Jack Newton	279	Carnoustie, Scotland
1976	Johnny Miller Jack Nicklaus Seve Ballesteros	279	Birkdale, England
1977	Tom Watson Jack Nicklaus	268	Turnberry, Scotland
1978	Jack Nicklaus Ben Crenshaw Tom Kite Ray Floyd Simon Owen	281	St. Andrews, Scotland
1979	Seve Ballesteros Ben Crenshaw Jack Nicklaus	283	Lytham, England
1980	Tom Watson Lee Trevino	271	Muirfield, Scotland
1981	Bill Rogers Bernhard Langer	276	St. George's, England
1982	Tom Watson Nick Price Peter Oosterhuis	284	Troon, Scotland
1983	Tom Watson Andy Bean	275	Birkdale, England
1984	Seve Ballesteros Tom Watson	276	St. Andrews, Scotland

YEAR	WINNER, RUNNER-UP	SCORE	PLAYED AT
1985	Sandy Lyle Payne Stewart	282	St. George's, England
1986	Greg Norman Gordon J. Brand	280	Turnberry, Scotland
1987	Nick Faldo Paul Azinger	279	Muirfield, Scotland
1988	Seve Ballesteros Nick Price	273	Lytham, England
1989	*Mark Calcavecchia Wayne Grady Greg Norman	275	Troon, Scotland
1990	Nick Faldo Mark McNulty Payne Stewart	270	St. Andrews, Scotland

*Won playoff

RECORDS

SCORING

LOWEST SCORE, 72 HOLES
268 — Tom Watson (68–70–65–65), Turnberry, 1977
269 — Jack Nicklaus (68–70–65–66), Turnberry, 1977
270 — Nick Faldo (67–65–67–71), St. Andrews, 1990
271 — Tom Watson (68–70–64–69), Muirfield, 1980

LOWEST SCORE, FIRST 54 HOLES
199 — Nick Faldo (67–65–67), St. Andrews, 1990
202 — Tom Watson (68–70–64), Muirfield, 1980

LOWEST SCORE, LAST 54 HOLES
200 — Tom Watson (70–65–65), Turnberry, 1977
201 — Jack Nicklaus (70–65–66), Turnberry, 1977
201 — Mark McNulty (68–68–65), St. Andrews, 1990

LOWEST SCORE, FIRST 36 HOLES
132 — Henry Cotton (67–65), St. George's, 1934
132 — Nick Faldo (67–65), St. Andrews, 1990
132 — Greg Norman (66–66), St. Andrews, 1990

LOWEST SCORE, MIDDLE 36 HOLES
132 — Nick Faldo (65–67), St. Andrews, 1990
132 — Bobby Cole (66–66), Carnoustie, 1975

LOWEST SCORE, LAST 36 HOLES
130 — Tom Watson (65–65), Turnberry, 1977
131 — Jack Nicklaus (65–66), Turnberry, 1977

LOWEST SCORE, FIRST ROUND
64 — Craig Stadler, Birkdale, 1983
64 — Christy O'Connor, Jr., St. George's, 1985
64 — Rodger Davis, Muirfield, 1987

LOWEST SCORE, SECOND ROUND
63 — Mark Hayes, Turnberry, 1977
63 — Greg Norman, Turnberry, 1986
64 — Horacio Carbonetti, Muirfield, 1980

LOWEST SCORE, THIRD ROUND
63 — Isao Aoki, Muirfield, 1980
64 — Tom Watson, Muirfield, 1980
64 — Hubert Green, Muirfield, 1980
64 — Ian Baker-Finch, St. Andrews, 1990

LOWEST SCORE, FOURTH ROUND
64 — Graham Marsh, Birkdale, 1983
64 — Seve Ballesteros, Turnberry, 1986
64 — Greg Norman, Troon, 1989

LOWEST SCORE, NINE HOLES
28 — Denis Durnian, Birkdale, 1983
29 — Tom Haliburton, Peter Thomson, Lytham, 1963; Tony Jacklin, St. Andrews, 1970; Bill Longmuir, Lytham, 1979; David J. Russell, Lytham, 1988

LARGEST WINNING MARGIN
13 — Tom Morris, Sr., Prestwick, 1862
12 — Tom Morris, Jr., Prestwick, 1870
8 — J.H. Taylor, St. Andrews, 1900
8 — James Braid, Prestwick, 1908
8 — J.H. Taylor, Hoylake, 1913

LARGEST LEAD AFTER 54 HOLES
10 — Henry Cotton, St. George's, 1934
7 — Harry Vardon, Prestwick, 1903
7 — Tony Lema, St. Andrews, 1964

LARGEST LEAD AFTER 36 HOLES
9 — Henry Cotton, St. George's, 1934
6 — Abe Mitchell, Deal, 1920

LARGEST LEAD AFTER 18 HOLES
5 — Alex Herd, Muirfield, 1896
5 — Harry Vardon, Hoylake, 1902

LARGEST LEAD AFTER 54 HOLES, NON-WINNER
5 — Macdonald Smith, Prestwick, 1925

LARGEST LEAD AFTER 36 HOLES, NON-WINNER
6 — Abe Mitchell, Deal, 1920

LARGEST LEAD AFTER 18 HOLES, NON-WINNER
5 — Alex Herd, Muirfield, 1896
5 — Harry Vardon, Hoylake, 1902

BEST COMEBACK BY WINNER, FINAL ROUND
5 — Jim Barnes, Prestwick, 1925
5 — Tommy Armour, Carnoustie, 1931

BEST COMEBACK BY WINNER, FINAL 36 HOLES
13 — George Duncan, Deal, 1920

BEST COMEBACK BY WINNER, FINAL 54 HOLES
11 — Harry Vardon, Muirfield, 1896

LOWEST SCORE BY WINNER, FIRST ROUND
67 — Henry Cotton, St. George's, 1934; Tom Watson, Birkdale, 1983; Seve Ballesteros, Lytham, 1988; Nick Faldo, St. Andrews, 1990

LOWEST SCORE BY WINNER, SECOND ROUND
63 — Greg Norman, Turnberry, 1986

LOWEST SCORE BY WINNER, THIRD ROUND
64 — Tom Watson, Muirfield, 1980

LOWEST SCORE BY WINNER, FOURTH ROUND
65 — Tom Watson, Turnberry, 1977; Seve Ballesteros, Lytham, 1988

HIGHEST SCORE BY WINNER, FIRST ROUND
91 — Tom Kidd, St. Andrews, 1873
SINCE 1892 (FIRST 72-HOLE TOURNAMENT)
86 — J.H. Taylor, St. Andrews, 1895
SINCE WORLD WAR II
75 — Gary Player, Muirfield, 1959

HIGHEST SCORE BY WINNER, SECOND ROUND
90 — Bob Martin, St. Andrews, 1876
SINCE 1892 (FIRST 72-HOLE TOURNAMENT)
81 — Harold Hilton, Muirfield, 1892; Willie Auchterlonie, Prestwick, 1893; Arnaud
    Massy, Hoylake, 1907
SINCE WORLD WAR II
76 — Bobby Locke, St. George's, 1949

HIGHEST SCORE BY WINNER, THIRD ROUND
84 — Harold Hilton, Hoylake, 1897
SINCE WORLD WAR II
78 — Fred Daly, Hoylake, 1947

HIGHEST SCORE BY WINNER, FOURTH ROUND
82 — Willie Auchterlonie, Prestwick, 1893
SINCE WORLD WAR II
75 — Sam Snead, St. Andrews, 1946

HIGHEST SCORE BY WINNER, 72 HOLES
326 — J.H. Taylor, St. George's, 1894
SINCE WORLD WAR II
294 — Henry Cotton, Muirfield, 1948

HIGHEST SCORE TO LEAD FIELD, 18 HOLES
91 — Tom Kidd, Jamie Anderson, and Bob Kirk, St. Andrews, 1873
SINCE 1892 (FIRST 72-HOLE TOURNAMENT)
83 — Alex Herd, St. George's, 1894
SINCE WORLD WAR II
71 — Christy O'Connor and J. Garaialde, St. Andrews, 1964

HIGHEST SCORE TO LEAD FIELD, 36 HOLES
179 — Tom Kidd, St. Andrews, 1873
SINCE 1892 (FIRST 72-HOLE TOURNAMENT)
164 — J.H. Taylor, St. George's, 1894
SINCE WORLD WAR II
143 — Fred Daly, Hoylake, 1947

Clubhouse, The Old Course, St. Andrews

HIGHEST SCORE TO LEAD FIELD, 54 HOLES
245 — J.H. Taylor, St. George's, 1894
SINCE WORLD WAR II
215 — Sam Snead, Johnny Bulla, and Dai Rees, St. Andrews, 1946

INDIVIDUAL, CAREER

VICTORIES
6 — Harry Vardon (1896, 98, 99, 1903, 11, 14)
5 — J.H. Taylor (1894, 95, 1900, 09, 13)
5 — James Braid (1901, 05, 06, 08, 10)
5 — Peter Thomson (1954, 55, 56, 58, 65)
5 — Tom Watson (1975, 77, 80, 82, 83)
4 — Willie Park, Sr. (1860, 63, 66, 75)
4 — Tom Morris, Jr. (1868, 69, 70, 72)
4 — Walter Hagen (1922, 24, 28, 29)
4 — Bobby Locke (1949, 50, 52, 57)
3 — Tom Morris, Sr. (1861, 62, 64); Jamie Anderson (1877, 78, 79); Robert Ferguson
    (1880, 81, 82); Bobby Jones (1926, 27, 30); Henry Cotton (1934, 37, 48); Gary
    Player (1959, 68, 74); Jack Nicklaus (1966, 70, 78); Seve Ballesteros (1979, 84, 88)
2 — Bob Martin (1876, 85); Willie Park, Jr. (1887, 89); Harold Hilton (1892, 97);
    Arnold Palmer (1961, 62); Lee Trevino (1971, 72); Nick Faldo (1987, 90)

CONSECUTIVE VICTORIES
4 — Tom Morris, Jr. (1868, 69, 70, 72 — no tournament in 1871)
3 — Jamie Anderson (1877, 78, 79); Robert Ferguson (1880, 81, 82); Peter Thomson
    (1954, 55, 56)
2 — Tom Morris, Sr. (1861, 62); J.H. Taylor (1894, 95); Harry Vardon (1898, 99); James
    Braid (1905, 06); Bobby Jones (1926, 27); Walter Hagen (1928, 29); Bobby Locke
    (1949, 50); Arnold Palmer (1961, 62); Lee Trevino (1971, 72); Tom Watson (1982,
    83)

RUNNER-UP FINISHES
7 — Jack Nicklaus (1964, 67, 68, 72, 76, 77, 79)
6 — J.H. Taylor (1896, 1904, 05, 06, 07, 14)
4 — Tom Morris, Sr. (1860, 63, 68, 69)
4 — Willie Park, Sr. (1861, 62, 65, 67)
4 — Willie Fernie (1882, 84, 90, 91)
4 — Harry Vardon (1900, 01, 02, 12)
3 — David Strath (1870, 72, 76); Andrew Kirkaldy (1879, 89, 91); Alex Herd (1895,
    1910, 20); Peter Thomson (1952, 53, 57); Dai Rees (1953, 54, 61)
2 — Bob Kirk (1870, 78); Jamie Anderson (1873, 81); Bob Martin (1875, 87); Douglas
    Rolland (1884, 94); James Braid (1897, 09); Tom Ball (1908, 09); Edward Ray
    (1913, 25); Macdonald Smith (1930, 32); James Adams (1936, 38); Johnny Bulla
    (1939, 46); Frank Stranahan (1947, 53); Antonio Cerda (1951, 53); Bobby Locke
    (1946, 54); Flory Van Donck (1956, 59); Dave Thomas (1958, 66); Bob Charles
    (1968, 69); Doug Sanders (1966, 70); Ben Crenshaw (1978, 79); Peter Oosterhuis
    (1974, 82); Bernhard Langer (1981, 84); Nick Price (1982, 88); Payne Stewart
    (1985, 90)

TOP-FIVE FINISHES
16 — J.H. Taylor
16 — Jack Nicklaus
15 — Harry Vardon
15 — James Braid
13 — Tom Morris, Sr.
13 — Alex Herd
11 — Willie Park, Sr.
10 — Peter Thomson
9 — Willie Park, Jr.
9 — Roberto De Vicenzo

TOP-TEN FINISHES
23 — J.H. Taylor
20 — Harry Vardon
20 — Alex Herd
19 — James Braid
18 — Peter Thomson
18 — Jack Nicklaus
17 — Henry Cotton
16 — Tom Morris, Sr.
15 — Willie Fernie
14 — Willie Park, Sr.
14 — Andrew Kirkaldy

TOP-TWENTY-FIVE FINISHES
31 — Alex Herd
27 — J.H. Taylor
25 — Willie Park, Jr.
25 — Harry Vardon
23 — James Braid
23 — Peter Thomson
21 — Willie Fernie
21 — Edward Ray
21 — Jack Nicklaus
20 — Tom Morris, Sr.
20 — Andrew Kirkaldy

COMPLETED 72 HOLES
31 — Alex Herd
30 — J.H. Taylor
28 — Edward Ray
28 — Jack Nicklaus
27 — Harry Vardon

CONSECUTIVE TOP-FIVE FINISHES
14 — James Braid (1899–1912)
11 — Jack Nicklaus (1970–80)

CONSECUTIVE TOP-TEN FINISHES
17 — James Braid (1896–1912)
16 — J.H. Taylor (1893–1908)
15 — Jack Nicklaus (1966–80)

CONSECUTIVE TOP-TWENTY-FIVE FINISHES
23 — Alex Herd (1891–1913)
23 — J.H. Taylor (1893–1914, 1920)
21 — James Braid (1896–1914, 1920–21)
21 — Peter Thomson (1951–71)

CONSECUTIVE TIMES COMPLETED 72 HOLES
31 — Alex Herd (1892–1914, 1920–27)
30 — J.H. Taylor (1893–1914, 1920–27)

LONGEST SPAN, FIRST TO LAST VICTORY
20 years — J.H. Taylor (1894–1913)

LONGEST SPAN BETWEEN VICTORIES
12 years — Henry Cotton (1937–48)

ROUNDS IN THE 60S
28 — Jack Nicklaus

CONSECUTIVE ROUNDS IN THE 60S
4 — Seve Ballesteros (1983–84), Nick Faldo (1989–90)

MOST TIMES LED AFTER 54 HOLES
7 — J.H. Taylor
5 — James Braid, Henry Cotton, Peter Thomson, Tom Watson

MOST TIMES LED AFTER 18, 36, OR 54 HOLES
17 — J.H. Taylor, Harry Vardon
14 — Henry Cotton

MOST TIMES LED AFTER 18, 36, OR 54 HOLES, BUT NEVER WON
8 — Dai Rees
5 — James Adams, Eric Brown

PLAYOFF RECORDS (MORE THAN ONE PLAYOFF)
No player has been in more than one playoff

MISCELLANEOUS

PROGRESSIVE 72-HOLE SCORING RECORD
305, Harold Hilton, 1892
300, Harry Vardon, 1903
296, Jack White, 1904
291, James Braid, 1908; Bobby Jones, 1926
285, Bobby Jones, 1927
283, Gene Sarazen, 1932; Henry Cotton, 1934; Alfred Perry, 1935; Bobby Locke, 1949
279, Bobby Locke, 1950; 1957
278, Peter Thomson, 1958; Kel Nagle, 1960
276, Arnold Palmer, 1962; Tom Weiskopf, 1973
268, Tom Watson, 1977

PROGRESSIVE 18-HOLE SCORING RECORD
88, Tom Kidd, 1873 (does not include early British Opens at Prestwick, which was a 12-hole course until 1884)
75, Mungo Park, 1874; Willie Fernie, 1883
74, H.G. Hutchinson, 1892
72, Harold Hilton, 1893; Alex Herd, 1896; Harry Vardon, 1902
69, James Braid, 1904
68, J.H. Taylor, 1904; Bobby Jones, 1927
67, Walter Hagen, 1929; Henry Cotton, 1934
65, Henry Cotton, 1934; Eric Brown, Leopoldo Ruiz, 1958; Peter Butler, 1966; Christy O'Connor, 1969; Neil Coles, 1970; Jack Nicklaus, 1973; Jack Newton, 1975
63, Mark Hayes, 1977; Isao Aoki, 1980; Greg Norman, 1986

WIRE-TO-WIRE WINNERS (NO TIES)
Edward Ray (1912), Bobby Jones (1927), Gene Sarazen (1932), Henry Cotton (1934), Tom Weiskopf (1973)

WIRE-TO-WIRE WINNERS (INCLUDING TIES)
Harry Vardon (1899), J.H. Taylor (1900), Harry Vardon (1903), Lee Trevino (1971), Gary Player (1974)

PLAYERS WHO LED FIRST THREE ROUNDS, DIDN'T WIN
Willie Park, Jr. (1898), Fred Daly (1952), F. Bullock (1959), Seve Ballesteros (1976), Bobby Clampett (1982)

NUMBER OF TIMES A LEADER WENT ON TO WIN
18 holes — 19 times in 88 tournaments at 72 holes
36 holes — 35 of 88
54 holes — 51 of 88

OLDEST WINNER
46 — Tom Morris, Sr., 1867
44 — Roberto De Vicenzo, 1967; Harry Vardon, 1914

YOUNGEST WINNER
17 — Tom Morris, Jr., 1868
SINCE 1900
22 — Seve Ballesteros, 1979

NUMBER OF PLAYOFFS
11 in 119 tournaments

MOST PLAYERS TIED FOR LEAD, 18 HOLES
5 — 1938 (James Adams, Bill Cox, Ernest Whitcombe, M. Dallemagne, J. Fallon, 70)

MOST PLAYERS TIED FOR LEAD, 36 HOLES
3 — 1938 (Jack Busson, Richard Burton, Bill Cox, 140)
3 — 1978 (Ben Crenshaw, Isao Aoki, Seve Ballesteros, 139)

MOST PLAYERS TIED FOR LEAD, 54 HOLES
5 — 1933 (Leo Diegel, Syd Easterbrook, Henry Cotton, Abe Mitchell, Joe Kirkwood, 216)

WON FIRST TIME PLAYED IN BRITISH OPEN
Willie Park, 1860
Tom Kidd, 1873
Mungo Park, 1874
Jack Burns, 1888
Harold Hilton, 1892
Jock Hutchison, 1921
Denny Shute, 1933
Ben Hogan, 1953
Tony Lema, 1964
Tom Watson, 1975

NUMBER OF CHAMPIONS, BY NATIVE COUNTRY
Great Britain, 72 (Scotland, 42; England, 29, N. Ireland 1)
United States, 28
South Africa, 7
Australia, 7
Spain, 3
France, 1
New Zealand, 1
Argentina, 1

SINCE 1892 (FIRST 72-HOLE EVENT)
Great Britain, 41 (England, 28; Scotland, 12; N. Ireland, 1)
United States, 28
South Africa, 7
Australia, 7
Spain, 3
France, 1
New Zealand, 1
Argentina, 1

AMATEURS

CHAMPIONS
John Ball, 1890; Harold Hilton, 1892; Bobby Jones, 1926, 27, 30

LOWEST SCORE, 72 HOLES
285 — Bobby Jones, St. Andrews, 1927; Joe Carr, St. Andrews, 1960

LOWEST SCORE, 18 HOLES
66 — Frank Stranahan, Troon, 1950

MOST TOP-TEN FINISHES
7 — Harold Hilton

COURSE RECORDS (on courses where the British Open has been played more than once)

PRESTWICK (1860–70*, 1872*, 75*, 78*, 81*, 84, 87, 90, 93, 98, 1903, 08, 14, 25)
18 holes — 70, James Braid, 1908; Jim Barnes, 1925
72 holes — 291, James Braid, 1908
*12-hole course

ST. ANDREWS (OLD COURSE) (1873, 76, 79, 82, 85, 88, 91, 95, 1900, 05, 10, 21, 27, 33, 39, 46, 55, 57, 60, 64, 70, 78, 84, 90)
18 holes — 64, Ian Baker–Finch, 1990
72 holes — 270, Nick Faldo, 1990

MUSSELBURGH (1874, 77, 80, 83, 86, 89)
18 holes — 75, Mungo Park, 1874; Willie Fernie, 1883
36 holes — 155, Willie Park, Jr., Andrew Kirkaldy, 1889

MUIRFIELD (1892, 96, 1901, 06, 12, 29, 35, 48, 59, 66, 72, 80, 87)
18 holes — 63, Isao Aoki, 1980
72 holes — 271, Tom Watson, 1980

ROYAL ST. GEORGE'S (1894, 99, 1904, 11, 22, 28, 34, 38, 49, 81, 85)
18 holes — 64, Christy O'Connor, Jr., 1985
72 holes — 276, Bill Rogers, 1981

HOYLAKE (ROYAL LIVERPOOL) (1897, 1902, 07, 13, 24, 30, 36, 47, 56, 67)
18 holes — 67, Roberto De Vicenzo, Gary Player, 1967
72 holes — 278, Roberto De Vicenzo, 1967

DEAL (ROYAL CINQUE PORTS) (1909, 20)
18 holes — 71, George Duncan, L. Holland, 1920
72 holes — 295, J.H. Taylor, 1909

ROYAL TROON (1923, 50, 62, 73, 82, 89)
18 holes — 64, Greg Norman, 1989
72 holes — 275, Mark Calcavecchia, Wayne Grady, Greg Norman, 1989

ROYAL LYTHAM & ST. ANNES (1926, 52, 58, 63, 69, 74, 79, 88)
18 holes — 65, Eric Brown, Leopoldo Ruiz, 1958; Christy O'Connor, Jr., 1969; Bill Longmuir, Seve Ballesteros, 1979; Seve Ballesteros, 1988
72 holes — 273, Seve Ballesteros, 1988

CARNOUSTIE (1931, 37, 53, 68, 75)
18 holes — 65, Jack Newton, 1975
72 holes — 279, Tom Watson, Jack Newton, 1975

ROYAL BIRKDALE (1954, 61, 65, 71, 76, 83)
18 holes — 64, Craig Stadler, Graham Marsh, 1983
72 holes — 275, Tom Watson, 1983

TURNBERRY (1977, 86)
18 holes — 63, Mark Hayes, 1977; Greg Norman, 1986
72 holes — 268, Tom Watson, 1977

The PGA Championship

WINNERS

YEAR	WINNER, RUNNER-UP	SCORE	PLAYED AT	YEAR	WINNER, RUNNER-UP	SCORE	PLAYED AT
1916	Jim Barnes	1 up	Siwanoy CC	1948	Ben Hogan	7 & 6	Norwood Hills CC
	Jock Hutchison		Bronxville, N.Y.		Mike Turnesa		St. Louis, Mo.
1917–18	No tournament			1949	Sam Snead	3 & 2	Hermitage CC
1919	Jim Barnes	6 & 5	Engineers CC		Johnny Palmer		Richmond, Va.
	Fred McLeod		Roslyn, N.Y.	1950	Chandler Harper	4 & 3	Scioto CC
1920	Jock Hutchison	1 up	Flossmoor CC		Henry Williams		Columbus, Ohio
	J. Douglas Edgar		Flossmoor, Ill.	1951	Sam Snead	7 & 6	Oakmont CC
1921	Walter Hagen	3 & 2	Inwood CC		Walter Burkemo		Oakmont, Pa.
	Jim Barnes		Inwood, N.Y.	1952	Jim Turnesa	1 up	Big Spring CC
1922	Gene Sarazen	4 & 3	Oakmont CC		Chick Harbert		Louisville, Ky.
	Emmett French		Oakmont, Pa.	1953	Walter Burkemo	2 & 1	Birmingham CC
1923	Gene Sarazen	1 up (38)	Pelham CC		Felice Torza		Birmingham, Mich.
	Walter Hagen		Pelham, N.Y.	1954	Chick Harbert	4 & 3	Keller GC
1924	Walter Hagen	2 up	French Lick CC		Walter Burkemo		St. Paul, Minn.
	Jim Barnes		French Lick, Ind.	1955	Doug Ford	4 & 3	Meadowbrook CC
1925	Walter Hagen	6 & 5	Olympia Fields CC		Cary Middlecoff		Detroit, Mich.
	Bill Mehlhorn		Olympia Fields, Ill.	1956	Jack Burke, Jr.	3 & 2	Blue Hill CC
1926	Walter Hagen	5 & 3	Salisbury CC		Ted Kroll		Boston, Mass.
	Leo Diegel		Westbury, N.Y.	1957	Lionel Hebert	2 & 1	Miami Valley CC
1927	Walter Hagen	1 up	Cedar Crest CC		Dow Finsterwald		Dayton, Ohio
	Joe Turnesa		Dallas, Tex.	1958	Dow Finsterwald	276	Llanerch CC
1928	Leo Diegel	6 & 5	Baltimore CC		Billy Casper		Havertown, Pa.
	Al Espinosa		Baltimore, Md.	1959	Bob Rosburg	277	Minneapolis GC
1929	Leo Diegel	6 & 4	Hillcrest CC		Jerry Barber		St. Louis Park, Minn.
	Johnny Farrell		Los Angeles, Cal.		Doug Sanders		
1930	Tommy Armour	1 up	Fresh Meadow CC	1960	Jay Hebert	281	Firestone CC
	Gene Sarazen		Flushing, N.Y.		Jim Ferrier		Akron, Ohio
1931	Tom Creavy	2 & 1	Wannamoisett CC	1961	*Jerry Barber	277	Olympia Fields CC
	Denny Shute		Rumford, R.I.		Don January		Olympia Fields, Ill.
1932	Olin Dutra	4 & 3	Keller GC	1962	Gary Player	278	Aronomink CC
	Frank Walsh		St. Paul, Minn.		Bob Goalby		Newtown Square, Pa.
1933	Gene Sarazen	5 & 4	Blue Mound CC	1963	Jack Nicklaus	279	Dallas AC
	Willie Goggin		Milwaukee, Wis.		Dave Ragan		Dallas, Tex.
1934	Paul Runyan	1 up (38)	Park CC	1964	Bobby Nichols	271	Columbus CC
	Craig Wood		Williamsville, N.Y.		Jack Nicklaus		Columbus, Ohio
1935	Johnny Revolta	5 & 4	Twin Hills CC		Arnold Palmer		
	Tommy Armour		Oklahoma City, Okla.	1965	Dave Marr	280	Laurel Valley CC
1936	Denny Shute	3 & 2	Pinehurst CC		Billy Casper		Ligonier, Pa.
	Jimmy Thomson		Pinehurst, N.C.		Jack Nicklaus		
1937	Denny Shute	1 up (37)	Pittsburgh FC	1966	Al Geiberger	280	Firestone CC
	Harold McSpaden		Aspinwall, Pa.		Dudley Wysong		Akron, Ohio
1938	Paul Runyan	8 & 7	Shawnee CC	1967	*Don January	281	Columbine CC
	Sam Snead		Shawnee, Pa.		Don Massengale		Littleton, Colo.
1939	Henry Picard	1 up (37)	Pomonok CC	1968	Julius Boros	281	Pecan Valley CC
	Byron Nelson		Flushing, N.Y.		Bob Charles		San Antonio, Tex.
1940	Byron Nelson	1 up	Hershey CC		Arnold Palmer		
	Sam Snead		Hershey, Pa.	1969	Ray Floyd	276	NCR CC
1941	Vic Ghezzi	1 up (38)	Cherry Hills CC		Gary Player		Dayton, Ohio
	Byron Nelson		Englewood, Colo.	1970	Dave Stockton	279	Southern Hills CC
1942	Sam Snead	2 & 1	Seaview CC		Arnold Palmer		Tulsa, Okla.
	Jim Turnesa		Atlantic City, N.J.		Bob Murphy		
1943	No tournament			1971	Jack Nicklaus	281	PGA National GC
1944	Bob Hamilton	1 up	Manito G&CC		Billy Casper		Palm Beach, Fla.
	Byron Nelson		Spokane, Wash.	1972	Gary Player	281	Oakland Hills CC
1945	Byron Nelson	4 & 3	Morraine CC		Tommy Aaron		Birmingham, Mich.
	Sam Byrd		Dayton, Ohio		Jim Jamieson		
1946	Ben Hogan	6 & 4	Portland GC	1973	Jack Nicklaus	277	Canterbury GC
	Ed Oliver		Portland, Ore.		Bruce Crampton		Cleveland, Ohio
1947	Jim Ferrier	2 & 1	Plum Hollow CC				
	Chick Harbert		Detroit, Mich.				

*Won Playoff

YEAR	WINNER, RUNNER-UP	SCORE	PLAYED AT
1974	Lee Trevino	276	Tanglewood GC
	Jack Nicklaus		Clemmons, N.C.
1975	Jack Nicklaus	276	Firestone CC
	Bruce Crampton		Akron, Ohio
1976	Dave Stockton	281	Congressional CC
	Ray Floyd		Bethesda, Md.
	Don January		
1977	*Lanny Wadkins	282	Pebble Beach GL
	Gene Littler		Pebble Beach, Ca.
1978	*John Mahaffey	276	Oakmont CC
	Jerry Pate		Oakmont, Pa.
	Tom Watson		
1979	*David Graham	272	Oakland Hills CC
	Ben Crenshaw		Birmingham, Mich.
1980	Jack Nicklaus	274	Oak Hill CC
	Andy Bean		Rochester, N.Y.
1981	Larry Nelson	273	Atlanta AC
	Fuzzy Zoeller		Duluth, Ga.
1982	Ray Floyd	272	Southern Hills CC
	Lanny Wadkins		Tulsa, Okla.
1983	Hal Sutton	274	Riviera CC
	Jack Nicklaus		Pacific Palisades, Ca.
1984	Lee Trevino	273	Shoal Creek GC
	Gary Player		Birmingham, Ala.
	Lanny Wadkins		
1985	Hubert Green	278	Cherry Hills CC
	Lee Trevino		Englewood, Colo.
1986	Bob Tway	276	Inverness Club
	Greg Norman		Toledo, Ohio
1987	*Larry Nelson	287	PGA National GC
	Lanny Wadkins		Palm Beach, Fla.
1988	Jeff Sluman	272	Oak Tree GC
	Paul Azinger		Edmond, Okla.
1989	Payne Stewart	276	Kemper Lakes GC
	Mike Reid		Hawthorn Woods, Ill.
1990	Wayne Grady	282	Shoal Creek GC
	Fred Couples		Birmingham, Ala.

*Won playoff

RECORDS

SCORING

(Since beginning of stroke play, 1958)

LOWEST SCORE, 72 HOLES

271 (9 under) — Bobby Nichols (64–71–69–67), Columbus CC, 1964
272 (8 under) — David Graham (69–68–70–65), Oakland Hills CC, 1979
272 (8 under) — Ben Crenshaw (69–67–69–67), Oakland Hills CC, 1979
272 (8 under) — Ray Floyd (63–69–68–72), Southern Hills CC, 1982
272 (12 under) — Jeff Sluman (69–70–68–65), Oak Tree GC, 1988
273 (15 under) — Lee Trevino (69–68–67–69), Shoal Creek GC, 1984
276 (12 under) — Payne Stewart (74–66–69–67), Kemper Lakes GC, 1989

LOWEST SCORE BY NON-WINNER, 72 HOLES

272 (8 under) — Ben Crenshaw (69–67–69–67), Oakland Hills CC, 1979
277 (11 under) — Lanny Wadkins (68–69–68–72), Shoal Creek GC, 1984
277 (11 under) — Gary Player (74–63–69–71), Shoal Creek GC, 1984
277 (11 under) — Mike Reid (66–67–70–74), Kemper Lakes GC, 1989
277 (11 under) — Curtis Strange (70–68–70–69), Kemper Lakes GC, 1989
277 (11 under) — Andy Bean (70–67–74–66), Kemper Lakes GC, 1989

LOWEST SCORE, FIRST 54 HOLES

200 (10 under) — Ray Floyd (63–69–68), Southern Hills CC, 1982
202 (11 under) — Ray Floyd (69–66–67), NCR CC, 1969
202 (11 under) — Greg Norman (65–68–69), Inverness Club, 1986
202 (8 under) — Larry Nelson (70–66–66), Atlanta AC, 1981
204 (12 under) — Lee Trevino (69–68–67), Shoal Creek GC, 1984

LOWEST SCORE, LAST 54 HOLES

201 (12 under) — John Mahaffey (67–68–66), Oakmont CC, 1978
202 (14 under) — Payne Stewart (66–69–67), Kemper Lakes GC, 1989
202 (11 under) — Jack Nicklaus (65–71–66), Riviera CC, 1983
203 (13 under) — Gary Player (63–69–71), Shoal Creek GC, 1984

LOWEST SCORE, FIRST 36 HOLES

131 (11 under) — Hal Sutton (65–66), Riviera CC, 1983
132 (8 under) — Ray Floyd (63–69), Southern Hills CC, 1982
133 (11 under) — Mike Reid (67–66), Kemper Lakes GC, 1989

LOWEST SCORE, MIDDLE 36 HOLES

132 (12 under) — Gary Player (63–69), Shoal Creek GC, 1984
132 (10 under) — Dave Rummells (64–68), Oak Tree GC, 1988
132 (8 under) — Larry Nelson (66–66), Atlanta AC, 1981
133 (11 under) — Mike Sullivan (66–67), Kemper Lakes GC, 1989

LOWEST SCORE, LAST 36 HOLES

132 (10 under) — Miller Barber (64–68), NCR CC, 1969
133 (11 under) — Hal Sutton (64–69), Shoal Creek GC, 1984
133 (9 under) — Gil Morgan (66–67), Oakmont CC, 1978
133 (9 under) — Peter Jacobsen (68–65), Riviera CC, 1983
133 (9 under) — Jeff Sluman (68–65), Oak Tree GC, 1988

LOWEST SCORE, FIRST ROUND

63 (7 under) — Ray Floyd, Southern Hills CC, 1982
64 (7 under) — Doug Tewell, Cherry Hills CC, 1985
64 (6 under) — Bobby Nichols, Columbus CC, 1964

LOWEST SCORE, SECOND ROUND

63 (9 under) — Gary Player, Shoal Creek GC, 1984
63 (7 under) — Bruce Crampton, Firestone CC, 1975
64 (8 under) — Craig Stadler, Kemper Lakes GC, 1989
64 (7 under) — Don Bies, NCR CC, 1969
64 (7 under) — Dave Rummells, Oak Tree GC, 1988
64 (6 under) — Gary Player, Tanglewood GC, 1974
65 (7 under) — Tommy Aaron, Columbine CC, 1967

LOWEST SCORE, THIRD ROUND

64 (8 under) — Hal Sutton, Shoal Creek CC, 1984
64 (7 under) — Miller Barber, NCR CC, 1969
64 (7 under) — Bob Tway, Inverness Club, 1986
65 (7 under) — Isao Aoki, Kemper Lakes GC, 1989

LOWEST SCORE, FOURTH ROUND

64 (6 under) — Jack Nicklaus, Columbus CC, 1964
65 (6 under) — Peter Jacobsen, Riviera CC, 1983
65 (6 under) — T.M. Chen, Cherry Hills CC, 1985
65 (6 under) — Jeff Sluman, Oak Tree GC, 1988
65 (5 under) — Lee Trevino, Southern Hills CC, 1970
65 (5 under) — Andy North, Firestone CC, 1975
65 (5 under) — David Graham, Oakland Hills CC, 1979
66 (6 under) — Don Massengale, Columbine CC, 1967

LOWEST SCORE, NINE HOLES

29 — Fred Couples, Southern Hills CC, 1982
29 — Gibby Gilbert, Riviera CC, 1983

LARGEST WINNING MARGIN
7 — Jack Nicklaus, Oak Hill CC, 1980
4 — Shared by four players

LARGEST LEAD AFTER 54 HOLES
5 — Ray Floyd, NCR CC, 1969
5 — Tom Watson, Oakmont CC, 1978
5 — Ray Floyd, Southern Hills CC, 1982

LARGEST LEAD AFTER 36 HOLES
4 — Tommy Aaron, Columbine CC, 1967
4 — Gil Morgan, Congressional CC, 1976
4 — Tom Watson, Oakmont CC, 1978
4 — Greg Norman, Inverness Club, 1986

LARGEST LEAD AFTER 18 HOLES
3 — Dick Hart, Dallas AC, 1963
3 — Bobby Nichols, Columbus CC, 1964
3 — Ray Floyd, Southern Hills CC, 1982

LARGEST LEAD AFTER 54 HOLES, NON-WINNER
5 — Tom Watson, Oakmont CC, 1978

LARGEST LEAD AFTER 36 HOLES, NON-WINNER
4 — Tommy Aaron, Columbine CC, 1967
4 — Gil Morgan, Congressional CC, 1976
4 — Tom Watson, Oakmont CC, 1978
4 — Greg Norman, Inverness Club, 1986

LARGEST LEAD AFTER 18 HOLES, NON-WINNER
3 — Dick Hart, Dallas AC, 1963

BEST COMEBACK BY WINNER, FINAL ROUND
7 — John Mahaffey, Oakmont CC, 1978
6 — Bob Rosburg, Minneapolis GC, 1959
6 — Lanny Wadkins, Pebble Beach GL, 1977
6 — Payne Stewart, Kemper Lakes GC, 1989

BEST COMEBACK BY WINNER, FINAL 36 HOLES
9 — Bob Rosburg, Minneapolis GC, 1959
9 — Bob Tway, Inverness Club, 1986

BEST COMEBACK BY WINNER, FINAL 54 HOLES
8 — John Mahaffey, Oakmont CC, 1978
8 — Payne Stewart, Kemper Lakes GC, 1989

LOWEST SCORE BY WINNER, FIRST ROUND
63 (7 under) — Ray Floyd, Southern Hills CC, 1982

LOWEST SCORE BY WINNER, SECOND ROUND
66 (6 under) — Payne Stewart, Kemper Lakes GC, 1989
66 (5 under) — Ray Floyd, NCR CC, 1969
66 (5 under) — Hal Sutton, Riviera CC, 1983
66 (4 under) — Lee Trevino, Tanglewood GC, 1974
66 (4 under) — Larry Nelson, Atlanta AC, 1981

LOWEST SCORE BY WINNER, THIRD ROUND
64 (7 under) — Bob Tway, Inverness Club, 1986

LOWEST SCORE BY WINNER, FOURTH ROUND
65 (6 under) — Jeff Sluman, Oak Tree GC, 1988
65 (5 under) — David Graham, Oakland Hills CC, 1979

HIGHEST SCORE BY WINNER, FIRST ROUND
75 (4 over) — John Mahaffey, Oakmont CC, 1978

HIGHEST SCORE BY WINNER, SECOND ROUND
73 (2 over) — Jack Nicklaus, Dallas AC, 1963
72 (2 over) — Dow Finsterwald, Llanerch CC, 1958
72 (2 over) — Bob Rosburg, Minneapolis GC, 1959
72 (2 over) — Al Geiberger, Firestone CC, 1975
72 (2 over) — Dave Stockton, Congressional CC, 1976

HIGHEST SCORE BY WINNER, THIRD ROUND
73 (1 over) — Larry Nelson, PGA National GC, 1987
72 (2 over) — Jay Hebert, Firestone CC, 1960

HIGHEST SCORE BY WINNER, FOURTH ROUND
74 (3 over) — Ray Floyd, NCR CC, 1969
73 (3 over) — Dave Stockton, Southern Hills CC, 1970

HIGHEST SCORE BY WINNER, 72 HOLES
287 (1 under) — Larry Nelson, PGA National GC, 1987
281 (1 over) — Jay Hebert, Firestone CC, 1960
281 (1 over) — Julius Boros, Pecan Valley CC, 1968
281 (1 over) — Gary Player, Oakland Hills CC, 1972
281 (1 over) — Dave Stockton, Congressional CC, 1976

HIGHEST SCORE TO LEAD FIELD, 18 HOLES
69 (1 under) — Jerry Barber, Jackson Bradley, Walter Burkemo, Billy Casper, Dick
             Hart, Chuck Klein, Mike Krak, Gene Littler and Mike Souchak,
             Minneapolis GC, 1959
69 (2 under) — Ray Floyd, Larry Ziegler, Charles Coody, Bunky Henry, Larry Mowry,
             Johnny Pott, Tom Shaw, Bob Lunn, Al Geiberger, NCR CC, 1969
69 (3 under) — Jack Nicklaus, PGA National GC, 1971

HIGHEST SCORE TO LEAD FIELD, 36 HOLES
140 (even) — Larry Hinson, Southern Hills CC, 1970
140 (4 under) — Ray Floyd and Lanny Wadkins, PGA National GC, 1987

HIGHEST SCORE TO LEAD FIELD, 54 HOLES
212 (4 under) — Mark McCumber and D.A. Weibring, PGA National GC, 1987
210 (even) — Doug Sanders, Firestone CC, 1960
210 (even) — Marty Fleckman and Frank Beard, Pecan Valley CC, 1968

MOST SUBPAR ROUNDS BY FIELD, TOURNAMENT
153 — Kemper Lakes GC, 1989

MOST SUBPAR ROUNDS BY FIELD, FIRST ROUND
49 — Kemper Lakes GC, 1989

MOST SUBPAR ROUNDS BY FIELD, SECOND ROUND
54 — Kemper Lakes GC, 1989

MOST SUBPAR ROUNDS BY FIELD, THIRD ROUND
29 — Kemper Lakes GC, 1989

MOST SUBPAR ROUNDS BY FIELD, FOURTH ROUND
31 — Shoal Creek GC, 1984

FEWEST SUBPAR ROUNDS BY FIELD, TOURNAMENT
13 — Firestone CC, 1960

FEWEST SUBPAR ROUNDS BY FIELD, FIRST ROUND
4 — Firestone CC, 1960
4 — Southern Hills CC, 1970

FEWEST SUBPAR ROUNDS BY FIELD, SECOND ROUND
0 — Firestone CC, 1966

FEWEST SUBPAR ROUNDS BY FIELD, THIRD ROUND
3 — Firestone CC, 1975

FEWEST SUBPAR ROUNDS BY FIELD, FOURTH ROUND
1 — Firestone CC, 1960
1 — Congressional CC, 1976

MOST SUBPAR TOTALS BY FIELD, TOURNAMENT
45 — Kemper Lakes GC, 1989

LOWEST 36-HOLE CUT
144 (2 over) — Oak Tree GC, 1988
145 (1 over) — Kemper Lakes GC, 1989

HIGHEST 36-HOLE CUT
154 (14 over) — Llanerch CC, 1958

INDIVIDUAL, CAREER

VICTORIES
5 — Walter Hagen (1921, 24, 25, 26, 27)
5 — Jack Nicklaus (1963, 71, 73, 75, 80)
3 — Gene Sarazen (1922, 23, 33)
3 — Sam Snead (1942, 49, 51)
2 — Jim Barnes (1916, 19), Leo Diegel (1928, 29), Paul Runyan (1934, 38), Denny Shute (1936, 37), Byron Nelson (1940, 45), Ben Hogan (1946, 48), Gary Player (1962, 72), Dave Stockton (1970, 76), Ray Floyd (1969, 82), Lee Trevino (1974, 84), Larry Nelson (1981, 87)

CONSECUTIVE VICTORIES
4 — Walter Hagen (1924, 25, 26, 27)
2 — Gene Sarazen (1922, 23); Leo Diegel (1928, 29); Denny Shute (1936, 37)

RUNNER-UP FINISHES
4 — Jack Nicklaus (1964, 65, 74, 83)
3 — Byron Nelson (1939, 41, 44)
3 — Arnold Palmer (1964, 68, 70)
3 — Billy Casper (1958, 65, 71)
3 — Lanny Wadkins (1982, 84, 87)
2 — Jim Barnes (1921, 24), Sam Snead (1938, 40), Walter Burkemo (1951, 54), Bruce Crampton (1973, 75), Don January (1961, 76), Gary Player (1969, 84)

TOP-FIVE FINISHES
14 — Jack Nicklaus
6 — Billy Casper
6 — Gary Player
5 — Lanny Wadkins

TOP-TEN FINISHES
16 — Jack Nicklaus
8 — Billy Casper
8 — Sam Snead
8 — Gary Player
7 — Gene Littler
7 — Ray Floyd
7 — Tom Watson

TOP-TWENTY-FIVE FINISHES
22 — Jack Nicklaus
16 — Ray Floyd
14 — Tom Watson
13 — Billy Casper
13 — Arnold Palmer

COMPLETED 72 HOLES
25 — Jack Nicklaus
24 — Arnold Palmer
24 — Ray Floyd
21 — Gary Player
19 — Billy Casper

CONSECUTIVE TOP-FIVE FINISHES
5 — Jack Nicklaus (1973–77)
4 — Jerry Pate (1976–79)
4 — Jack Nicklaus (1962–65)

CONSECUTIVE TOP-TEN FINISHES
5 — Jack Nicklaus (1973–77)
5 — Jerry Pate (1976–80)

CONSECUTIVE TOP-TWENTY-FIVE FINISHES
9 — Jack Nicklaus (1969–77)
8 — Tom Watson (1973–80)
8 — Jerry Pate (1976–83)

CONSECUTIVE TIMES COMPLETED 72 HOLES
13 — Ray Floyd (1972–84)
13 — Gary Player (1969–81)

LONGEST SPAN, FIRST TO LAST VICTORY
18 years — Jack Nicklaus (1963–1980)

LONGEST SPAN BETWEEN VICTORIES
13 years — Ray Floyd (1969–1982)

SUBPAR ROUNDS
48 — Jack Nicklaus

CONSECUTIVE SUBPAR ROUNDS
6 — Jerry Pate, 1978–79; Lee Trevino, 1984–85

ROUNDS IN THE 60S
39 — Jack Nicklaus

CONSECUTIVE ROUNDS IN THE 60S
6 — Lee Trevino, 1984–85
5 — Jack Nicklaus, 1973–74; Jerry Pate, 1978–79; Ben Crenshaw, 1979–80

SUBPAR 72-HOLE TOTALS
15 — Jack Nicklaus

CONSECUTIVE SUBPAR 72-HOLE TOTALS
3 — Jack Nicklaus (1963–65, 1973–75); Lee Trevino (1983–85)

MOST TIMES LED AFTER 54 HOLES
4 — Jack Nicklaus

MOST TIMES LED AFTER 18, 36, OR 54 HOLES
9 — Ray Floyd
7 — Jack Nicklaus

MOST TIMES LED AFTER 18, 36, OR 54 HOLES, BUT NEVER WON
4 — Gene Littler, Tommy Aaron, Tom Watson, Mike Reid

PLAYOFF RECORDS (PLAYERS IN MORE THAN ONE PLAYOFF)
Don January (1–1)
Lanny Wadkins (1–1)

MISCELLANEOUS

PROGRESSIVE 72-HOLE SCORING RECORD
276, Dow Finsterwald, 1958
271, Bobby Nichols, 1964

PROGRESSIVE 18-HOLE SCORING RECORD
66, Walter Burkemo, 1958
65, Jerry Barber, 1959; Bruce Crampton, 1963
64, Bobby Nichols, 1964; Jack Nicklaus, 1964; Don Bies, 1969; Miller Barber, 1969;
    Gary Player, 1974
63, Bruce Crampton, 1975; Ray Floyd, 1982; Gary Player, 1984

FOUR SUBPAR ROUNDS, SAME PGA CHAMPIONSHIP
Arnold Palmer, 1964; Ben Crenshaw, 1979; Lee Trevino, Calvin Peete, Seve
Ballesteros, 1984; Jeff Sluman, 1988; Curtis Strange, Ian Woosnam, 1989

FOUR ROUNDS IN THE 60S, SAME PGA CHAMPIONSHIP
Arnold Palmer, 1964; Ben Crenshaw, 1979; Lee Trevino, 1984

WIRE-TO-WIRE WINNERS (NO TIES)
Bobby Nichols, 1964; Jack Nicklaus, 1971; Ray Floyd, 1982; Hal Sutton, 1983

WIRE-TO-WIRE WINNERS (INCLUDING TIES)
Ray Floyd, 1969

PLAYERS WHO LED FIRST THREE ROUNDS, DIDN'T WIN
Jerry Barber, 1959; Tommy Aaron, 1965; Marty Fleckman, 1968; Gene Littler, 1977;
Tom Watson, 1978; Greg Norman, 1986; Mike Reid, 1989

NUMBER OF TIMES A LEADER WENT ON TO WIN
18 holes — 7 in 33 tournaments
36 holes — 10 in 33 tournaments
54 holes — 18 in 33 tournaments

OLDEST WINNER
48 — Julius Boros, 1968

YOUNGEST WINNER
20 — Gene Sarazen, 1922; Tom Creavy, 1931

NUMBER OF PLAYOFFS
6 in 33 tournaments at medal play
(Match play — 5 finals went extra holes in 39 tournaments)

MOST PLAYERS TIED FOR LEAD, 18 HOLES
9 — 1959 (Jerry Barber, Jackson Bradley, Walter Burkemo, Billy Casper, Dick Hart,
    Chuck Klein, Mike Krak, Gene Littler, Mike Souchak, 69)
9 — 1969 (Ray Floyd, Larry Ziegler, Charles Coody, Bunky Henry, Larry Mowry,
    Johnny Pott, Tom Shaw, Bob Lunn, Al Geiberger, 69)

MOST PLAYERS TIED FOR LEAD, 36 HOLES
3 — 1984 (Gary Player, Lanny Wadkins, Lee Trevino, 137)

MOST PLAYERS TIED FOR LEAD, 54 HOLES
2 — 1965 (Tommy Aaron, Dave Marr, 209)
2 — 1968 (Marty Fleckman, Frank Beard, 210)

WON FIRST TIME PLAYED IN PGA CHAMPIONSHIP
Jim Barnes, 1916
Walter Hagen, 1921
Tom Creavy, 1931
Bob Hamilton, 1944
Doug Ford, 1955
Bob Tway, 1986

CHAMPION BREAKDOWN, BY NATIVE COUNTRY
United States, 64
Great Britain, 4
Australia, 2
South Africa, 2

MATCH-PLAY RECORDS (1916–1957)

TIMES IN FINALS
6 — Walter Hagen (winner 1921, 24, 25, 26, 27; runner-up 1923)
5 — Sam Snead (winner 1942, 49, 51; runner-up 1938, 40)
5 — Byron Nelson (winner 1940, 45; runner-up 1939, 41, 44)
4 — Jim Barnes (winner 1916, 19; runner-up 1921, 24)
4 — Gene Sarazen (winner 1922, 23, 33; runner-up 1930)

CONSECUTIVE TIMES IN FINALS
5 — Walter Hagen (runner-up 1923; winner 1924, 25, 26, 27)
3 — Byron Nelson (runner-up 1939, 41; winner 1940)

MATCHES WON
51 — Gene Sarazen
42 — Walter Hagen

CONSECUTIVE MATCHES WON
22 — Walter Hagen (1924–28)
14 — Denny Shute (1936–38)

LARGEST WINNING MARGIN IN FINALS
8 & 7 — Paul Runyan over Sam Snead, 1938

LONGEST MATCH
43 holes — Johnny Golden over Walter Hagen, first round, 1932

COURSE RECORDS (on courses where the PGA Championship has been played more than once)

FIRESTONE CC (1960, 66, 75)
18 holes — 63, Bruce Crampton, 1975
72 holes — 276, Jack Nicklaus, 1975

SOUTHERN HILLS CC (1970, 82)
18 holes — 63, Ray Floyd, 1982
72 holes — 272, Ray Floyd, 1982

OAKLAND HILLS CC (1972, 79)
18 holes — 65, Alan Tapie, David Graham, 1979
72 holes — 272, David Graham, Ben Crenshaw, 1979

SHOAL CREEK GC (1984, 89)
18 holes — 63, Gary Player, 1984
72 holes — 273, Lee Trevino, 1984

BIBLIOGRAPHY

Allen, Peter. *Famous Fairways*. Stanley Paul & Co., Ltd., London, 1968.

_____. *Play the Best Courses*. Stanley Paul & Co. Ltd., London, 1973.

Brown, Gene (editor). *The Complete Book of Golf*. Arno Press, New York, 1980.

Browning, Robert. *A History of Golf: The Royal & Ancient Game*. J.M. Dent & Sons, London, 1955.

Cornish, Geoffrey S., and Ronald E. Whitten. *The Golf Course*. The Rutledge Press, New York, 1981.

Cousins, Geoffrey. *Golf in Britain*. Routledge and Kegan Paul, London, 1975.

Cousins, Geoffrey, and Don Pottinger. *An Atlas of Golf*. Thomas Nelson & Sons Ltd., Nairobi, Kenya, 1974.

Cousins, Geoffrey, and Tom Scott. *A Century of Opens*. Frederick Muller Ltd., London, 1971.

Darwin, Bernard. *The Golf Courses of the British Isles*. Duckworth & Co., London, 1910.

Dickinson, Patric. *A Round of Golf Courses*. Evans Brothers Ltd., London, 1951.

Doak, Tom. *The Confidential Guide to Golf Courses*. Doak Press, New Canaan, Conn., 1988.

Dobereiner, Peter. *The Book of Golf Disasters*. Stanley Paul & Co. Ltd., London, 1983.

Evans, Webster. *Rubs of the Green*. Pelham Books, London, 1969.

Flaherty, Tom. *The Masters*. Holt, Rinehart & Winston, New York, 1961.

_____. *The U.S. Open*. E.P. Dutton & Co., Inc., New York, 1966.

Goodner, Ross. *Shinnecock Hills Golf Club, 1891-1966*. Shinnecock Hills Golf Club, Southampton, N.Y., 1966.

Hagen, Walter. *The Walter Hagen Story*. Simon & Schuster, New York, 1956.

Heilman, H. Richard. *Golf at Merion 1896-1976*. Merion Golf Club, Ardmore, Pa., 1977.

Hobbs, Michael. *Great Opens*. David & Charles, London, 1976.

Hosmer, Howard C. *From Little Acorns, Volume II: The Story of Oak Hill, 1901-1986*. Oak Hill Country Club, Rochester, N.Y., 1986.

Hutchinson, Horace G. *Golf: The Badminton Library of Sports*. Longmans, Green, London, 1890.

Johnson, A.J.D. *The History of the Royal Birkdale Golf Club*. Springwood Books, Ascot, Berkshire, 1988.

Jones, Bobby. *Bobby Jones on Golf*. Doubleday, Garden City, N.Y., 1966.

_____ (and O.B. Keeler). *Down the Fairway*. Blue Ribbon Books, New York, 1927.

_____. *Golf Is My Game*. Chatto & Windus, London, 1959.

Jones, Robert Trent, with Larry Dennis. *Golf's Magnificent Challenge*. Sammis Publishing Corp., New York, 1988.

Lawless, Peter. *The Golfer's Companion*. J.M. Dent & Sons, London, 1937.

Lee, James P. *Golf in America*. New York, Dodd Mead, 1895.

The Lonsdale Library, Volume IX: The Game of Golf. Seeley, Service & Co. Ltd., London, 1931.

Lyle, Sandy, with Bob Ferrier. *The Championship Courses of Scotland*. World's Work, Ltd., The Windmill Press, Kingswood, Tadworth, Surrey, 1982.

McCormack, Mark H. *The Wonderful World of Professional Golf*. Atheneum, New York, 1973.

_____. *The World of Professional Golf* (annual editions for 1966-90). Various publishers.

Macdonald, Charles Blair. *Scotland's Gift—Golf*. Charles Scribner's Sons, New York, 1928.

Mackintosh, I.M. *Troon Golf Club: Its History from 1878*. Troon Golf Club, Ayrshire, Scotland, 1974.

Mahon, James J. *Baltusrol: 90 Years in the Mainstream of American Golf*. Rutledge Books, New York, 1985.

Martin, H.B. *Fifty Years of American Golf*. Dodd, Mead, New York, 1936.

McDonnell, Michael. *Golf: The Great Ones*. Drake Publishers Inc., New York, 1973.

_____. *Great Moments in Golf*. Pagurian Press, Toronto, 1974.

Mortimer, Charles G., and Fred Pignon. *The Story of the Open Golf Championship (1860-1950)*. Jarrolds, London, 1952.

Nicklaus, Jack, with Herbert Warren Wind. *The Greatest Game of All*. Simon & Schuster, New York, 1969.

Nickson, E.A. *The Lytham Century, A History of Royal Lytham and St. Annes Golf Club, 1886-1986*. St. Annes-on-the-Sea, England, 1985.

Palmer, Arnold, with Bob Drum. *Arnold Palmer's Best 54 Golf Holes*. Doubleday, Garden City, N.Y., 1977.

_____, with William Barry Furlong. *Go for Broke*. William Kimber, London, 1974.

Peper, George. *Golf Courses of the PGA Tour*. Harry N. Abrams, Inc., New York, 1986.

_____ (editor). *Golf in America*. Harry N. Abrams, Inc., New York, 1988.

_____. *Golf's Supershots*. Atheneum, New York, 1982.

_____ (editor). *The PGA Championship 1916-1984*. Kingsport Press, Kingsport, Tenn., 1985.

PGA Tour. *PGA Tour Media Guide* (annual editions for 1975-90). PGA Tour, Jacksonville, Fla.

Pottinger, George. *Muirfield and the Honourable Company*. Scottish Academic Press, Edinburgh and London, 1972.

Price, Charles. *A Golf Story*. Atheneum, New York, 1986.

_____ (editor). *The American Golfer*. Random House, New York, 1964.

_____. *The World of Golf*. Random House, New York, 1962.

Roberts, Clifford. *The Story of the Augusta National Golf Club*. Doubleday, Garden City, N.Y., 1976.

Shapiro, Mel, Warren Dohn, and Leonard Berger (editors). *Golf: A Turn-of-the-Century Treasury*. Castle, Secaucus, N.J., 1986.

Smith, Douglas LaRue. *Winged Foot Story*. Western Publishing Co. Inc., Racine, Wis., 1984.

Smith, Garden C. *The World of Golf*. A.D. Innes & Company, London, 1891.

Sommers, Robert. *The U.S. Open: Golf's Ultimate Challenge*. Atheneum, New York, 1987.

Stanley, Louis T. *St. Andrews*. Salem House Publishers, Topsfield, Mass., 1987.

Steel, Donald, and Peter Ryde (editors). *The Encyclopedia of Golf*. Harper & Row, New York, 1978.

Ward-Thomas, Pat, Herbert Warren Wind, Charles Price, and Peter Thomson. *The World Atlas of Golf*. Mitchell Beazley Ltd., London, 1976.

Wind, Herbert Warren, *The Complete Golfer*. Simon & Schuster, New York, 1954.

_____. *The Story of American Golf*. Alfred A. Knopf, New York, 1975.

Magazines:
Golfing
GOLF Magazine
The American Golfer
USGA Golf Journal

Tournament Annuals:
The Masters (1979-90)
The U.S. Open (1985-90)
The British Open (1984-90)
The PGA Championship (1985)

Tournament Programs:
The U.S. Open (1961-90)
The PGA Championship (1960-90)

INDEX

Pages on which pictures appear are in italics.

ACKNOWLEDGMENTS

I am indebted to several people, in several ways. The superb golf course photographs throughout these pages are the work of Mike Klemme. Mike spent the better part of two years traversing the United States and Great Britain on assignment for this book, visiting some of the thirty championship courses more than once. He did most of his work at dawn and dusk, when golf courses are most photogenic, and the results are ample proof that he's the best in the business.

The last few pages of the book comprise the most comprehensive collection of statistics and records ever assembled on the four major championships. They were assembled by *GOLF Magazine* Senior Editor David Barrett, who consulted various books and pored through the final standings of nearly 300 championships in order to verify the accuracy of every name, number, and fact. His accomplishment was formidable, and I am deeply grateful.

The historical photos that accompany each chapter came from a multitude of sources. Many of the black-and-white shots of the British courses came through the help of R.A.L. "Bobby" Burnet, the gracious and tireless historian of the Royal & Ancient Golf Club of St. Andrews. Bobby was also of great help in verifying myriad facts related to the British Open, and for checking the accuracy of the lengthy chapter on the Old Course. Sarah Baddiel has one of the largest collections of golfiana in Great Britain, and she was most generous to loan me several of her rare photographs for reproduction. More recent images were supplied by Frank Christian, Leonard Kamsler, Bill Knight, Phil Sheldon, and other fine photographers.

Thanks are also due Dick Donovan for helping to track down several club histories and championship programs; Rand Jerris of the USGA for answering numerous U.S. Open queries; Rees Jones, for detailing the design changes he has made to the courses at Congressional and Hazeltine; Buzzy Johnson and Kathryn Murphy at the Augusta National, for their help on the Masters chapter; and the dozens of club members and staff people at the various clubs in the U.S. and Britain who generously provided fact verification and encouragement.

This is the third book I've been fortunate to write for Harry N. Abrams, Inc., and with each one I've grown more appreciative of the talents of the Abrams people, notably photo editor John Crowley, designer Bob McKee, production director Shun Yamamoto, and especially executive editor Margaret Kaplan. Margaret is not a golfer, but after having edited *Golf Courses of the Grand Slam*, *Golf in America*, and *Golf Courses of the PGA Tour*, she can match golf knowledge with anyone in the world. More important, she is a superb editor, an invaluable source of advice and encouragement, and the best friend an author could have.

Finally, my biggest thanks go to the artist for this book, my wife Libby, not simply for the sixteen course maps and thirty individual holes she painted so magnificently, but for being my best friend, my inspiration, my patient partner, the mother to our two fine sons, and my one true love.

George Peper
Grandview, New York
September 30, 1990